Seventh Edition

LABOR RELATIONS LAW

Fred Witney
INDIANA UNIVERSITY

Benjamin J. Taylor

Prentice Hall, Englewood Cliffs, New Jersey 07632

Library of Congress Cataloging-in-Publication Data
TAYLOR, BENJAMIN, J.
 Labor relations law / BENJAMIN J. TAYLOR, FRED WITNEY.—7th ed.
 p. cm.
 Includes bibliographical references and index.
 ISBN 0-13-209900-4
 1. Collective labor agreements—United States. 2. Labor laws and
legislation—United States. I. Witney, Fred. [date]. II. Title.
KF3408.T35 1996
344.73'0189 dc20
[347.304189] 94-48750

Acquisitions editor: *Natalie Anderson*
Project management: *Edie Riker*
Buyer: *Vincent Scelta*
Editorial assistant: *Nancy Proyect*

This Book is Dedicated to the Memory of
BEN TAYLOR
My Co-Author, Colleague, Friend

© 1996, 1992, by Prentice-Hall, Inc.
A Simon & Schuster Company
Englewood Cliffs, New Jersey 07632

Printed in the United States of America

10 9 8 7 6 5 4 3 2 1

ISBN 0-13-209900-4

Prentice-Hall International (UK) Limited, *London*
Prentice-Hall of Australia Pty. Limited, *Sydney*
Prentice-Hall Canada Inc., *Toronto*
Prentice-Hall Hispanoamericana, S.A., *Mexico*
Prentice-Hall of India Private Limited, *New Delhi*
Prentice-Hall of Japan, Inc., *Tokyo*
Simon & Schuster Asia Pte. Ltd., *Singapore*
Editora Prentice-Hall do Brasil, Ltda., *Rio de Janeiro*

Contents

PART III   ESTABLISHMENT OF COLLECTIVE BARGAINING

4   CONTROL OF THE BARGAINING UNIT   105

5   ELECTION POLICIES OF NATIONAL LABOR RELATIONS BOARD 129

PART IV   CONTROL OF COLLECTIVE BARGAINING

6   COLLECTIVE BARGAINING UNDER TAFT-HARTLEY   170

7   ENFORCEMENT OF THE COLLECTIVE BARGAINING AGREEMENT 231

PART V INDUSTRIAL CONFLICT

8   STRIKES, LOCKOUTS, AND PICKETING   280

Preface

This book is intended primarily for undergraduate and graduate liberal arts and business school curriculums. However, members of the legal profession and law school students, as well as practicing management-labor relations executives and labor union representatives will find it useful. We deal with the major trends in the law of labor relations, the reasons for the trends, and their impact on the overall operation of collective bargaining.

The law of labor relations has little meaning in the absence of an understanding of the dynamics of labor relations. Consequently, attention has been devoted to the labor relations environment in which the legal structure operates. Moreover, where appropriate, there is economic analysis of the problems resulting from the efforts of government to define the rights, duties, and obligations of labor unions and employers in the area of labor relations and collective bargaining. It is hoped, as a result, that the reader will be in a better position to evaluate public policy in labor relations.

Unlike some previous editions, the focus of this volume is on contemporary labor relations law. However, this is preceded by a background chapter in Part I that deals with the application of the conspiracy doctrine to labor unions through the Wagner Act. Part II contains chapters designed to promote general understanding of Taft-Hartley operations and the jurisdiction of the National Labor Relations Board. Part III establishes the legal basis of collective bargaining in chapters concerning the appropriate bargaining unit and the election policies of the NLRB. How government controls collective bargaining is the subject of the chapters in Part IV. They demonstrate the impact of the NLRB and the federal courts on the collective bargaining process and the enforcement of labor agreements. Part V contains chapters dealing with the area of industrial conflict. Included are the law of strikes, lockouts, picketing, and secondary boycotts. Other areas of government control, including the operation of the Landrum-Griffin Act, public sector collective labor relations, and discrimination in employment are treated in chapters in Part VI. A summary and discussion questions appear at the end of each chapter.

The difficulty of labor relations law, but also its challenge and attraction, is that the law is ever changing and developing. This, of course, is the justification for the new edition. In keeping with the goal of previous editions, I have concentrated on major developments of outstanding significance since the previous edition. Attention, for example, is devoted to permanent replacement of strikers; access of union organizers to employer property; whether employers must hire known and recognized union organizers; sympathy strikes; the Civil Rights Act of 1991; and the attempts of the American labor movement to solicit the help of foreign unions to carry out secondary boycotts. Recent critical decisions of the NLRB and federal courts are highlighted, including *Electromation, American Hospital Association, Dubuque Packing, Lechmere, Health Care & Retirement Corporation*, and *Litton Financial Printing*.

The authors have always been grateful for the reception of the past editions by faculty and students. We have tried to be worthy of the trust of those who use the volume. No text, regardless of its merits, can be successful without quality teaching.

This is particularly true in labor relations law, what with its swift and continuously changing character. Indeed, the teacher has the challenging task of keeping students aware of developments since the publication of the volume. Even before this book reaches the students, the NLRB and the courts will inevitably have changed former policies and added new dimensions to the law of labor relations. Only the teacher can handle these developments in the classroom.

As always, I am indebted to more people than I can thank. An everlasting debt is owed to the late Dr. E. B. McNatt, who provided indispensable assistance in the preparation of the original volume.

Fred Witney

1

Development of Labor Relations Law

If one element of labor relations is a certainty, it is the changing legal climate defining the rights and obligations of workers, unions, and employers. Equally certain is that the swings in the legal climate are directly related to the extent of unionism and the viability of collective bargaining.

For many years, the judicial system was by far the predominant force regulating the relationship between employers and unions. Starting with the dawn of unionism in the early nineteenth century until the 1930s, federal and state courts made it difficult, if not impossible, for workers to form unions and bargain collectively. Indeed, this was the period of hostility and suppression regarding the growth of the labor movement. No question that federal and state courts favored the employers' side of the equation. No question that the judiciary was a willing ally of employers in opposition to unionization. First caught in the web of the conspiracy doctrine, then crippled by the labor injunction and application of antitrust legislation, unions were burdened by the court system.

A dramatic change developed in the 1930s with the passage of federal legislation designed to promote unionism and collective bargaining. Under the Norris–La Guardia and Wagner acts, the climate of law became favorable to unions. The former curbed the courts, and the latter made employer antiunion practices unlawful. Responding to the favorable legal climate, unions successfully organized the mass-production industries shaping the modern character of the labor movement.

With the passage of the Taft-Hartley Act in 1947, the climate again changed, establishing its current character. How the 1947 law impacts on labor relations, collec-

1

tive bargaining, and the vitality of the labor movement is the major concern of this volume. In 1980, total union membership reached its peak of about 22 million but dropped to its current 17 million. Important factors explain this decline, including a remarkable change in the structure of the labor force from industrial to service, blue collar to white collar, the phenomenal growth of working women, the export of millions of manufacturing jobs to low-wage foreign nations, the unfavorable balance of trade changing the United States from the world's greatest creditor nation to the world's greatest debtor nation, the movement of industry to the comparative nonunion Sunbelt, and increased employer resistance. These conditions have made it more difficult for unions to maintain their status within the economy. Given these factors, one cannot contend successfully that the current legal environment solely accounts for the decline in union membership. Nonetheless, as will be demonstrated later, elements of current law play a significant role in the current condition of the labor movement.

This chapter highlights major developments of labor relations law. Only by knowing the past can we understand the contemporary period. Profound changes in any area of society do not arise from a vacuum. Thus, not only are we concerned with the substance of the changing legal climate, but we must also establish the fundamental reasons accounting for its changing character.

ERA OF HOSTILITY:
APPLICATION OF CONSPIRACY DOCTRINE

Philadelphia Cordwainers: The Case against Unions

Unionism is a product of industrialism. Employees began to organize as soon as industry became a reality within the economy. In the early 1800s, permanent unions, consisting of skilled workers rather than unskilled, were formed in the shoemaking, hatmaking, and printing industries. As employers acquired sufficient capital to maintain thriving enterprises, workers responded with collective action. For a time, employers resisted unionization by employing replacements willing to work for wages below the scale demanded by the organized workers.

In 1806, however, some employers struck upon a new method to deal with the shoemakers' unions. They sought the aid of the courts. This procedure—the solicitation of government aid in labor disputes—remains to this day a persistent element in the industrial relations pattern. It is noteworthy that the precedent was established as early as 1806.

Philadelphia shoemaker employers charged that unions were conspiracies. As conspiracies, they contended, labor unions were unlawful combinations. A *conspiracy*, generally defined, is the combination of two or more persons who band together to harm the rights of others or of society. Under the doctrine of conspiracy would fall, for example, the plot of a group of people to bring about conviction of an innocent person. Imprisonment and fines, or both, are penalties inflicted on persons guilty of a conspiracy. Likewise, the conspiracy doctrine would apply to the action of a group that plotted to overthrow an established government. Before conspiracy can be charged, it must be shown that the group has caused or will cause harm to other people or to society. An interesting characteristic about the conspiracy doctrine is that conspirators can be indicted and found guilty before they commit any overt act. For example, it is a crime to plot the murder of a person even if the evil plan is not executed. Another important feature is that an action by one person, though legal, becomes illegal when carried out by a group. This characteristic has particular significance in the labor union conspiracy cases. It was lawful for a single worker to try to increase wages, but unlawful when employees combined to do so.

To prove unions were conspiracies, employers contended that they raised wages, causing harm to the general public. Control of wages by unions, it was argued,

> is an unnatural, artificial means of raising the price of work beyond its standard, and taking an undue advantage of the public.[1]

It was contended that the increase of wages by union pressure led to higher prices of commodities. This in turn was supposed to result in the reduction of demand for products, causing unemployment in the community. The net effect of the union, therefore, was to cause injury to the community, to damage commerce and trade, and to prejudice the rights of all workers. So ran the general argument of the prosecution.

In addition, it was argued that nonunion workers were injured by the refusal of unionists to work beside them. It was contended that

> a master who employs fifteen or twenty hands is called upon to discharge that journeyman who is not a member of the body; if he refuses they all leave him whatever may be the situation of his business.[2]

Unpersuaded by competent counsel who vigorously argued that unions do not produce such evils, courts applied the conspiracy doctrine to labor unions. In the first of these cases, popularly called *Philadelphia Cordwainers*, 1806, the jury, composed solely of business people and property holders, held the unionists guilty of a conspiracy. They were undoubtedly influenced by the judge, who left no mystery as to where he stood on the matter when he charged them:

> A combination of workmen to raise their wages may be considered in a twofold point of view. One is to benefit themselves. The other is to injure those who do not join their society. The rule of law condemns both.[3]

Between 1806 and 1842, seventeen conspiracy trials occurred in which labor unions and their members were convicted of conspiracies. In that era, not only was the legal climate hostile, but it was also downright prohibitive for union operation. Interestingly enough, however, some unions existed, thus showing the determination of workers for collective bargaining despite the negative character of the law.[4] In any event, in those days unions were per se unlawful regardless of what they did or did not do.

Unions Declared Lawful Organizations

With the continued growth of industry, application of the conspiracy doctrine did not fit the times. As business enterprises became larger, the power of individual employees to stand up for their employment rights decreased proportionately. In addition, significant changes were taking place in political philosophy. The more liberal philosophy of Andrew Jackson and Thomas Jefferson was displacing the basically conservative doctrines of Alexander Hamilton. More attention was being given to the rights and liberties of individuals. Some writers in this period stressed that liberty and freedom in economic affairs were not the monopoly of any group, but rather the common heritage of all citizens regardless of occupational status. The poor as well as the wealthy could take action to implement their right "to life, liberty, and the pursuit of happiness." Many workers interpreted the emphasis on liberty "and the rights of man" as a philosophical justification for organization and collective bargaining.

In such a context, the application of the conspiracy doctrine to labor unions appeared incongruous. So incensed were the workers against the courts that in 1836 mass protest demonstrations were held in New York and Washington. During these demonstrations, two judges, who had previously convicted unionists as criminal conspirators, were burned in effigy.[5] Such were the prevailing circumstances when Chief Justice Shaw of the Supreme Judicial Court of Massachusetts handed down his decision in the celebrated case, *Commonwealth* v. *Hunt*.[6] Before the case received Justice Shaw's attention, a lower court had found a group of shoemaker unionists guilty of conspiracy. The workers were convicted in the lower court because they refused to work for an employer who hired a shoemaker not a member of their union. The indictment was that the action of the unionists interfered with the right of the nonunion shoemaker to practice his trade. Shaw struck sharply and repeatedly at the conception that labor unions are evil organizations. He did state that, like any other organization, a labor union may exist for a "pernicious" and "dangerous" purpose. But he emphatically affirmed that labor unions may also exist for a "laudable" and "public-spirited" purpose. Rather than inflicting injury on society, he contended, a union may advance the general welfare of the community by raising the standard of life of the union members. In this connection, Shaw pointed out that labor organizations

> might be used [by workers] to afford each other assistance in times of poverty, sickness, or distress; or to raise their intellectual, moral, and social conditions; or to make improvements in their art.

For a union to be indicted and convicted under the conspiracy doctrine, Shaw contended, it must be shown that the objectives of the union were unlawful, or that the means employed to gain a lawful end were unlawful. Unless this could be proved, a labor organization had to be considered a lawful association. In the case at hand, Shaw held that the prosecution did not prove that the conspiracy doctrine should have been applied to the labor union.

Thus, under *Commonwealth* v. *Hunt*, unions were no longer per se illegal organizations. Indeed, lacking any guarantee in the United States Constitution, or state constitutions for that matter, indicating that employees have the right to form labor organizations and bargain collectively, unions as lawful organizations date from 1842. Since that time, of course, federal and state statutes have established labor unions as lawful organizations. Nonetheless, *Commonwealth* v. *Hunt* stands as the first government action in the United States establishing that workers may lawfully organize and bargain collectively.

From the Conspiracy Doctrine to the Injunction

Despite the unquestioned significance of this decision, one would be dead wrong to conclude it meant that the conspiracy doctrine would no longer be applied to unions. As Chief Justice Shaw held, the conspiracy doctrine could still be applied should the courts hold that the objectives or methods of unions were unlawful. Now it became a question of what unions intended or did to apply the conspiracy doctrine. As a matter of fact, Professor E. E. Witte reported there were actually more labor conspiracy cases in the second half of the nineteenth century than in the first half.[7]

Toward the end of the century, however, the conspiracy doctrine did disappear from the scene. This development, however, did not result from a shift in the basic attitude of the courts toward collective bargaining. Subsequent events underscored the antipathy of the judiciary to the efforts of workers to better their economic position through collective action. Nor did this change in court policy result from a shift in employers' attitudes. They still sought the aid of the judiciary in their conflicts with organized labor. Finally, the conspiracy doctrine did not fade away because of the slackening of the organizational efforts of workers. Organized labor in the second half of the nineteenth century made progress. For example, the Knights of Labor, established in 1869, claimed a membership of 700,000 in 1886, the high-water mark of union membership in the nation up to that time. The conspiracy doctrine faded out of the picture because *it no longer fit the needs of* antiunion employers. They wanted a more effective legal weapon to combat workers in their collective efforts for bargaining.

Prosecution of workers in conspiracy trials was a rather cumbersome affair. Some of the trials lasted several days, and during this time unionists could continue to damage the employers' position. It was becoming increasingly difficult to procure witnesses who would testify against worker defendants. Of even greater importance was the trend toward jury sympathy to worker organizations seeking to raise their economic standards through collective bargaining. Jury requirements were becoming liberalized, with the result that workers might be called upon to help decide labor conspiracy cases. Some jurors, aware of the spread of industrialization and the growth of large corporations, were prone to side with unionists. It was necessary to seek a new legal weapon to discourage unionism. The technique had to meet the requirements of speed, simplicity, and definiteness. Above all, if employers were to resist organization of their firms, it was mandatory to remove the labor dispute from the jurisdiction of a potentially sympathetic jury. All these requirements were met by the labor injunction.

The Labor Injunction

Character of Injunctions

Injunctions are used in labor and nonlabor cases. They are issued by judges (without juries) sitting in courts of equity to enjoin the conduct of an individual or group. Injunctions must be obeyed immediately, and the offenders held in "contempt of court," subject to imprisonment or fines or both. Normally, the same judge issuing an injunction enforces it against violators. Injunctions are frequently issued to protect property from irreparable damage, though they are also used for other purposes. Upon the application of the plaintiff, private parties, or government, injunctions can be of three types: temporary restraining orders, temporary injunctions, and permanent injunctions. Upon issuance, each type must be obeyed immediately even if further proceedings demonstrate the defendant should not have been enjoined in the first place.

Temporary restraining orders are issued under emergency conditions so that property will be protected against irreparable damage when time does not permit the presentation of witnesses or documents. Defendants are seldom in court when such orders are issued. Evidence submitted usually consists of affidavits. The idea behind this order (commonly called *ex parte* injunctions, issued on the application of the charging party in the absence of the defendant) is to preserve the status quo between the litigants. Suppose your neighbor is ready to cut down a row of trees located near the property line. If it is cut down, no matter what damages you collect, assuming in fact the trees belong to you, the trees will not be restored. You will suffer irreparable damage to property. Thus, your attorney rushes to court to secure the *ex parte* injunction to forbid your neighbor's action. No time exists to present witnesses or complicated documents and other matters to prove the exact location of the property line. Later on, in a more complete hearing, the judge will make a decision based on the evidence. If you are proved right, the trees will still be there. If the judge holds against you, your neighbor may lawfully cut down the trees. In the meantime, while the judicial process unwinds, the status quo between you and your neighbor is preserved.

When the temporary restraining order or *ex parte* injunction is issued, the judge will set a prompt date, usually about five days, for a hearing where at least the defendant appears with an attorney. At this stage, *temporary injunction*, the judge will have a better opportunity to get to the truth of the matter. Even here, however, the hearing is not complete—all the evidence is not necessarily available, every witness has not been called, nor have all the material documents been presented. In other words, the full judicial process has not been exhausted.

At the *permanent injunction* level, the full merits of the dispute are explored. All the witnesses are called, questioned, and cross-examined, and all the pertinent documents are submitted. The judge now has full opportunity to examine all the testimony and documents submitted as evidence. At this stage, the judge may terminate the temporary injunction or make it permanent. At this level, the defendant may permanently be forbidden to engage in the conduct in question. True, the defendant may appeal the decision if a higher court is available. The defendant, however, must obey the judge's decision during the appeal proceedings.

Constitutionality and Concept of Property

Injunctions, of course, were not created to deal with labor disputes. They have always been a part of the judicial system. In contrast to nonlabor cases, however, their application to labor disputes resulted in egregious abuses so serious that it took the passage of the 1932 Norris–La Guardia Act to correct them. Until that time, federal and state judges issued injunctions frustrating the attempt of workers to use collective bargaining as a method for achieving a better life. In hundreds of cases, judges—upon the application of employers—seriously interfered with traditional union activities. Prior to 1931, federal and state courts issued a total of 1,845 labor injunctions.[8]

Two major factors resulted in the widespread use of the injunction in labor disputes. In 1895, the U.S. Supreme Court held the injunction could constitutionally be used to forbid union activities.[9] This was in the famous *Debs* case, which arose out of the Pullman strike. When Eugene Debs, president of the American Railway Union, struck the railroads in the effort to aid the workers in the dispute at Pullman, the federal government obtained an injunction against Debs and the union. Federal troops were also used to break the strike. One may speculate on the course of industrial relations had the high court held the injunction could not be issued in labor disputes.

The second factor involved the concept of property used by the courts in labor disputes. As noted earlier, injunctions are used to protect property against irreparable damage. For purposes of labor cases, the term includes much more than tangible items such as machinery, land, buildings, and physical goods. Courts consistently held that the concept included intangible items as well. The right to do business falls squarely within the meaning of the property concept. Likewise, the liberty to hire workers and sell goods to customers is included within the definition. In short, the freedom to run a business in a profitable manner falls within the boundaries of the concept. It is not difficult to see how the broad definition of the property concept would affect labor disputes. If a labor union interfered with the free access of an employer to labor and commodity markets, it was considered that there was damage to property. Should a strike, picketing, or a boycott decrease the opportunities for profitable operation of the business, an injury to property occurred. "Irreparable damage" to property can be inflicted not only by violent destruction of physical items but also by union activities calculated to interfere with the carrying out of business. Judges apparently were not aware that such a broad meaning of property interfered with worker rights for fair treatment, better wages, job security, and the like. Injunctions were to be used to protect employer interests and not worker interests.

Judges as Legislators

By far the most serious abuse of the labor injunction was the legislative character of court action. Through its power to issue injunctions, the judiciary literally enacted legislation. Before a law is passed by Congress or a state legislature, there is ordinarily much debate on the measure. Public hearings are held wherein any citizen has the right to be heard. Some citizens may object to a particular law enacted by a legislative body, but one can be assured that the legislation was passed by the collective judgment of the people elected to represent their interests.

When judges issued labor injunctions, their only standard of reference was their own social and economic predilections. No jury acted in injunction proceedings. In labor disputes, *the judge alone decided whether an objective or activity of a labor union was lawful or unlawful.* Judges outlawed many union activities. Strikes engaged in for certain purposes were stamped out by the labor injunction. Judges forbade the calling of strikes when they deemed their purposes unlawful. The "fairness" or "justice" of the strike's purpose is not the issue here. The important point is that the injunction procedure provided the courts with the power to determine the legal and illegal boundaries of union activities. In the absence of legislation, the courts acted in labor disputes as the legislative branch of government. Clearly, the judges' economic and social attitudes influenced their decisions. Every labor dispute had its social and economic ramifications. The manner in which judges interpreted their environment had an important bearing on whether an injunction would be issued. Judges alone, motivated by their own beliefs, attitudes, and prejudices, decided the issues. The decisions did not indicate dishonesty of the judiciary but rather reflected their legal training, social environment, and lack of knowledge of industrial relations. Whatever the reason, the result was to favor the interests of the property-owning group at the expense of labor groups.

Judges issued so-called "blanket" injunctions that applied to persons not directly involved in a strike, and made illegal acts that in themselves were lawful. This was accomplished when courts enjoined "all other persons whomsoever from doing anything whatsoever" to further a strike that the judge declared unlawful. In 1911, the Supreme Court upheld an injunction that forbade anyone from speaking or writing to further labor union activities.[10] The constitutional guarantee of freedom of speech became a casualty in the Court determination to stamp out union activities undertaken to make strikes, picketing, or boycotts effective.

Additional Abuses

As noted earlier, injunctions are supposed to maintain the status quo between litigants until the entire process is completed. This did not apply in labor cases. Temporary injunction proceedings, regardless of the outcome of subsequent court action, had the effect of discriminating against the labor union. Events in labor disputes move swiftly. The ultimate outcome of strikes, then as now, could be determined in a few days. Interference with strike activities through the injunction process made it difficult for the union to carry the strike to a successful termination.

Contrary to nonlabor cases, judges did not hold a prompt hearing upon the issuance of a temporary restraining order or *ex parte* injunction. Studies indicate that a long time intervened while unions were restrained.[11] By the time the courts held a hearing to determine whether to issue a temporary injunction, the issue had frequently been resolved—strikes had been broken and the union was gone from the scene.

Yellow-Dog Contract and the Injunction

Organized labor in 1917 felt the full impact of the labor injunction on the right to self-organization and collective bargaining. In that year, the Supreme Court handed down the celebrated *Hitchman* decision.[12] The Court held that the labor injunction could be employed to enforce the *yellow-dog contract*. The yellow-dog contract was a device utilized by antiunion employers to stop the progress of the union movement. Its chief characteristic was the promise of a worker not to join a labor union while in the hire of an employer. Originally used extensively in the bituminous coal mines of West Virginia, it spread to many other industries after the *Hitchman* decision.[13]

Obviously, workers did not agree to the yellow-dog contract on a voluntary basis, as when signing a contract to purchase a home, an automobile, and the like. They agreed because of the need for a job to support themselves and their families. It was a question of "sign or starve." Nonetheless, the high court held that workers by their own free will had agreed to the contract. Ironically, the high court said it was protecting not only the employers' right to contract *but also that of the workers*. Three members of the Court, including the legendary Justices Brandeis and Holmes, disagreed, saying it was a fiction to believe workers had voluntarily consented, since it was obvious that they had been coerced to do so out of economic necessity.

In short, *Hitchman* provided employers with a powerful antiunion weapon. Should anyone attempt to organize workers covered by yellow-dog contracts, such person could be imprisoned or fined or both for violation of injunctions issued to enforce the device.

UNIONS AND ANTITRUST STATUTES

Danbury Hatters

Responding to the development of monopolies in many of the nation's basic industries, including steel, shoemaking, machinery, oil, and tobacco, Congress passed the Sherman Antitrust Act in 1890. It represented the nation's dedication to competition as the regulator of economic activity. It provided:

> Sec. 1. That every contract, combination in the form of trust or otherwise, or conspiracy, in restraint of trade or commerce among the several States, or with foreign nations, is hereby declared to be illegal.
>
> Sec. 2. Every person who shall monopolize or attempt to monopolize, or combine or conspire with any other person or persons, to monopolize any part of the trade or commerce among the several States, or with foreign nations, shall be deemed guilty of a misdemeanor, and, on conviction thereof, shall be punished by fine not exceeding five thousand dollars, or by imprisonment not exceeding one year, or by both said punishments, in the discretion of the court.

Ironically, however, rather than business, the labor movement felt the full impact of the Sherman Act. In several landmark cases, the U.S. Supreme Court held that under certain circumstances, unions were combinations in restraint of trade. The precedent was set in *Danbury Hatters*, a case that resulted from the effort of the United Hatters of North America to organize the felt hat industry.[14] Successful in organizing most of the industry, the union status was threatened by the existence of a number of nonunion firms. It recognized that the unionized firms could not compete in national markets with nonunion products. What with lower labor standards, the nonunion firms sold hats at lower prices and gained an advantage in the market.

A major nonunion firm, Loewe & Company, located in Danbury, Connecticut (hence the popular name of the case), resisted organization, breaking a strike undertaken to force the company to recognize the union. Unlike the modern era, laws were not in place to protect employees in their right to strike. With its very existence at stake, the union implemented a secondary boycott to compel recognition. In a secondary boycott, a union exerts pressure on firms not directly involved in a dispute to stop doing business with the company directly involved in the controversy. Using the facilities of the American Federation of Labor, the union induced the public to cease patronizing retail stores selling the Danbury hats.

The boycott was very successful, causing Loewe to lose considerable business. Under the Sherman Act, it sued the union for damages. In 1908, the Supreme Court held the union and its members violated the statute by interfering with interstate commerce. It was a combination in restraint of trade. Later the high court sustained a judgment of $252,000 against the union and its members. Loewe actually lost $85,000, but the figure was tripled as authorized by the Sherman Act. Composed of only 9,000 members, the union, of course, did not have the funds to pay the fine. As a result, the Supreme Court held the members liable, and they lost their savings, homes, and other property to pay off the judgment. It is noteworthy that although Taft-Hartley, enacted in 1947, provides for a number of ways in which labor organizations may be sued by employers, it states that damages can be recovered only from the assets of the unions and not from union members.

Additional Antitrust Prosecution

Following *Danbury Hatters*, other antitrust prosecutions occurred, including the Supreme Court's decision in *Bucks Stove and Range Company*.[15] Economic conditions were the same as in the previous case. Operating without a union, Bucks Stove undersold the unionized firms, a condition the Molders & Foundry Workers Union attempted to remedy. Ultimately, the union and the AFL implemented a boycott against the firm, persuading the public and retail stores not to buy the nonunion stoves. Also, the AFL listed the company's name on the "We Don't Patronize" list in its publication, *American Federationist*. Defying an injunction, Samuel Gompers, founder and first president of the AFL, refused to delete the company from the boycott list. He and two other AFL officers were sentenced to prison for contempt of court. Purely on technical grounds, the Supreme Court dismissed the contempt charges but held the boycott activities illegal under the Sherman Act. Thus, it ruled that the right to engage in business free from union restraint is superior to the right of workers to use free speech and press to advance their cause in a labor dispute.

The Clayton Act and Its Aftermath

Recognizing the impact of the Supreme Court policy in injunction and antitrust cases, the AFL for the first time in its history engaged in national politics. In the election of 1912, it supported Woodrow Wilson for President. With his election and Democratic control of Congress, the labor movement hoped legislation would be enacted to check the courts in labor cases. Specifically, the AFL wanted freedom from prosecution under the Sherman Act and relief from the labor injunction.

Passed in 1914, the Clayton Act contained a provision that dealt with the application of the antitrust statutes to organized labor. Section 6 provided:

> That the labor of a human being is not a commodity or article of commerce. Nothing contained in the antitrust laws shall be construed to forbid the existence and operation of labor, agricultural, or horticultural organizations, instituted for the purposes of mutual help, and not having capital stock or conducted for profit, or to forbid or restrain individual members of such organizations, from lawfully carrying out the legitimate objects thereof; nor shall such organizations, or the members thereof, be held or construed to be illegal combinations or conspiracies in restraint of trade, under the antitrust laws.

Though hailed by Gompers as labor's "Magna Carta," the Clayton Act did not provide protection to the labor movement. Given the language of Section 6 and the antiunion character of the Supreme Court, one wonders why Gompers hailed the law, saying, "Upon it [the working people will] rear their construction of industrial freedom." Who but the federal courts would determine whether unions were "lawfully carrying out [their] legitimate objects . . ." What labor wanted was complete exemption from the antitrust laws. This could have been accomplished by a very simple provision: "Nothing contained in the antitrust laws shall apply to labor organizations." As it turned out, Wilson did not intend to exempt unions from antitrust prosecution despite whatever promises he had made to labor during the campaign of 1912. As one writer put it: "To him [Wilson] must go much of the responsibility for the failure of the Clayton Act to satisfy labor demands"[16]

Bedford Cut Stone: **Failure Clayton Act**

While federal courts were applying antitrust statutes in labor cases, they permitted business to monopolize many of the nation's critical industries. They were able to do this because the Supreme Court had held that "reasonable" restraint of trade by business did not violate the Sherman Act. In labor cases, however, the high court did not apply the rule of reason to union activities.

Despite tolerance for business, the high court in *Bedford Cut Stone* again ruled union activities subject to prosecution under the Sherman Act.[17] If any doubt existed about the Clayton Act's being the protector of labor, it was swept away by this 1927 decision. It was the apex of the long line of cases finding unions guilty under the antitrust statutes. It demonstrated that Section 6 of the Clayton Act failed to do what Gompers believed it might do.

Like the unions in *Danbury Halters* and *Bucks Stove and Range*, the Journeymen Stone Cutters Association implemented the secondary boycott to maintain its existence. In 1921, owners of limestone quarries and mills in the Bloomington-Bedford (Indiana) area ceased recognizing the union as the bargaining representative of the employees and operated on a nonunion basis. This is the most extensive limestone stone area in the nation. The union had contracts with employers in other parts of the country. Recognizing that its very existence depended on its status in Indiana quarries and mills, the Stone Cutters enacted an amendment to its constitution forbidding its members to handle stone "cut by men working in opposition" to the labor organization. This meant Indiana stone would not be installed at building sites by the union members. It invited building contractors to use stone produced by union members in other areas of the nation.

Finding the union guilty under the antitrust statutes, the high court held its action constituted an "unreasonable restraint . . . of commerce within the meaning of the Antitrust Act . . ." Stressing that the rule of reason applied to business, Justice Brandeis vigorously dissented, asserting the majority established a double standard for purposes of the law—one standard for business and a totally different one for unions. He said:

> If, on the undisputed facts of this case, refusal to work can be enjoined, Congress created by the Sherman Law and the Clayton Act an instrument for imposing restraints upon labor which reminds of involuntary servitude. The Sherman Law was held in *United States* v. *United States Steel Corporation . . .* to permit capitalists to combine in a single corporation 50 percent of the steel industry of the United States dominating the trade through its vast resources. The Sherman Law was held in *United States* v. *United Shoe Machinery Co. . . .* to permit capitalists to combine in another corporation practically the whole shoe-machinery industry of the country, necessarily giving it a position of dominance over shoe manufacturing in America. It would, indeed, be strange if Congress had by the same Act willed to deny to members of a small craft of workingmen the right to co-operate in simply refraining from work, when that course was the only means of self-protection against a combination of militant and powerful employers. I cannot believe that Congress did so.

Climate of the Law

Such was the climate of labor relations law prior to the 1930s. When the conspiracy doctrine did not completely fill the needs of antiunion employers, federal or state courts issued injunctions outlawing many vital union activities. The courts provided employers with a powerful weapon when they enforced yellow-dog contracts by the injunction. When unions sought to maintain their status, courts applied the antitrust statutes forbidding boycotts.

Indeed, the courts were a willing ally of employers who refused to recognize and bargain with unions. At the same time, employers were free to use the full spectrum of antiunion activities, such as discharging workers who joined unions, placing industrial spies in plants to report union people to management, creating fake company-dominated unions, and refusing to recognize unions despite their majority status. All these practices were subsequently outlawed in the Wagner Act.

When Congress and state legislatures enacted laws designed to help workers, the U.S. Supreme Court either declared them unconstitutional or interpreted them in a way to make them meaningless. Section 20 of the Clayton Act was designed to protect unions against the labor injunction. Unlike Section 6, the antitrust provision, Section 20 was clearly written, instructing the federal courts to cease interfering with union activities. After the Supreme Court applied Section 20 to a picketing case, it did not offer protection to unions.[18] In a labor dispute with a major steel producer, the union was permitted to station one "missionary" per entrance. The Court did not even use the word "picket," as if to say the term covered an evil practice. At the hands of the courts, the Clayton Act was worthless as a protector of worker rights against court intervention. Congress passed the Erdman Act in 1898, forbidding railroad operators to discharge unionized workers, and made yellow-dog contracts illegal. Such an effort, said the high court, was unconstitutional.[19]

In the 1890s, fifteen states passed similar legislation applying to all workers and employers within their respective jurisdictions. These laws suffered the same fate as the Erdman Act.[20] It was unconstitutional for the legislative branch of government to outlaw discriminatory discharge and yellow-dog contracts. Some states passed laws restricting the power of state courts to issue injunctions in labor disputes. Despite the approval of the Arizona state supreme court, the U.S. Supreme Court held the anti-injunction statute unconstitutional.[21]

Given the climate of labor relations law prior to the 1930s, it is no wonder the American labor movement did not amount to much as far as membership was concerned. Unions may have been able to overcome employer hostility. But when that hostility was reinforced by the courts, unions were powerless to overcome such a formidable obstacle.

ERA OF ENCOURAGEMENT

Norris–La Guardia: Control of Labor Injunction

To this very day, the Great Depression of the 1930s profoundly changed the economic and political life of the nation. Most of all, it defined the role of government in the affairs of society. For our purposes, during the depression years a dramatic change occurred in the climate of labor relations law. In 1932 and 1935, Congress enacted the Norris–La Guardia and the Wagner Acts. Effective implementation of these laws resulted in an explosion of union membership resulting mainly from successful organization of the mass-production industries. In 1933, total union membership amounted to less than 3 million. By the time of the entry of the United States into World War II, it had soared to almost 10 million. Although the revived business conditions were an impetus to union growth, such success would not have occurred without the dramatic change in the law of labor relations.

Both statutes declared unionization and collective bargaining to be matters of U.S. public policy. Given that business developed by the aid of government to organize in the corporate form of ownership, "the individual unorganized worker is commonly helpless to exercise actual liberty of contract . . . to obtain acceptance terms and conditions of employment." Therefore, it was necessary for workers to have full freedom of self-organization and designation of representatives of their own choosing to negotiate the terms and conditions of employment.

Though the laws are bonded by a common purpose, the method for implementation of the public policy is different. As demonstrated by the previous discussion, the judicial system seriously retarded the growth of unions and collective bargaining. And by engaging in serious antiunion practices, employers intervened, coerced, and discriminated against workers who desired to engage in collective bargaining.

Thus, whereas Norris–La Guardia checks the courts, the Wagner Act curbs employers. Both methods were required to achieve the public policy expressed in the statutes. In March 1932, Norris–La Guardia was enacted by overwhelming majorities in both Houses of Congress, and it was promptly signed by President Hoover.

Over the years, Congress has not changed even one word in Norris–La Guardia. It remains exactly the same as on the day of its enactment. The statute is not "history," but it is current policy regulating the courts in the issuance of injunctions in labor disputes.

With the passage of Taft-Hartley in 1947, the courts have regained some power to issue labor injunctions. However, those *injunctions are based on statute*, and not on the basis of the social and economic views of judges. To the extent Congress felt it necessary to provide the federal courts with labor injunction authority, it said so in specific legislation. In other words, except as modified by Taft-Hartley, Norris–La Guardia continues to apply to the federal courts in the same way as before the 1947 statute.

Area of Industrial Freedom

The fundamental purpose of Norris–La Guardia is to keep the courts out of the area of industrial relations. This is the heart and soul of the legislation. As we have learned, judges outlawed union activities when their objectives and methods did not square with the social and economic predilections of federal judges. If the objective of a strike did not square with the subjective judgment of judges, injunctions were issued to break the strike. Injunctions outlawed strikes, for example, that would force employers to recognize unions, would require the reinstatement of workers discharged because they had joined unions, would control the pace of technological change, and would require only union members to work in the shop. When unions used methods such as boycotts, which judges felt were wrong, injunctions made them illegal.

To remove the courts from the area of industrial relations, the law specified that certain union activities were protected from the injunctions. Unions are free to strike regardless of the purpose and objectives. Every strike, of course, may not be justified in terms of equity and social purpose. The point is that Norris–La Guardia has deprived the judges of the power to use their own standards of reference to determine the lawfulness or unlawfulness of strikes. If strike control is deemed necessary, curtailment is the function of the legislative branch of government and not the subjective views of judges.

With regard to union picketing or otherwise giving publicity to a labor dispute, the law forbids the federal courts to outlaw the method unless union activity is associated with violence. To this day, federal courts may regulate picketing by outlawing violence undertaken to prevent access to a struck facility. For example, unions may not prevent persons from working during a strike by using violence or threat of violence. Except for that, however, federal courts may not enjoin picketing by unions.

Injunctions may not be issued forbidding the payment of strike-relief funds to strikers. In the past, when judges outlawed a strike, injunctions were issued to block payment of funds or money to workers on strike. Free from the injunction, unions may persuade workers to participate in a strike provided, of course, the union refrains from violence or threats.

In other words, Congress carved out an area of industrial freedom in which unions and workers may participate free of the injunction. Norris–La Guardia, however, does not provide unions and workers with any new rights. Rather it is a question of what unions can do for themselves not burdened with court intervention. Prior to Norris–La Guardia, the courts were in the employers' corner in labor disputes. In no way does Norris–La Guardia shift the courts to the unions' corner. For example, unions cannot obtain an injunction to force employers to agree to union demands in collective bargaining. Norris–La Guardia simply makes the courts neutral in the matter of labor disputes. Neither party in labor disputes may rely on the courts for help.

The Passing of the Yellow-Dog Contract

The Norris–La Guardia Act effected still another important change in the law of industrial relations. It declared that yellow-dog contracts were not enforceable in any court of the United States. In this manner, it nullified the effect of the *Hitchman* decision, the case in which the Supreme Court upheld the validity and enforceability of the yellow-dog contract. Thus, fifteen years elapsed before organized labor was released from the yellow-dog contract. Just as important is the observation that such relief came not from a change of attitude of the judiciary but from action of the legislative branch of government.

If one is aware of the effects of the yellow-dog contract on the collective bargaining process, it should be easy to understand why the instrument was declared unenforceable by Norris–La Guardia. No other single measure could exceed the effectiveness of a yellow-dog contract when enforced by an injunction. Norris–La Guardia identified public policy as support and endorsement of the collective bargaining process. Since the yellow-dog contract conflicts with such public policy, Congress denied federal courts the authority to enforce such promises.

It is noteworthy that the Norris–La Guardia Act did not outlaw the yellow-dog contract. It made the federal courts unavailable for the enforcement of the instrument. In later years, however, the National Labor Relations Board held that an employer engages in an unfair labor practice if it demands that employees execute such agreements. Thus, the yellow-dog contract, the most powerful of all antiunion measures, was laid to rest by an action of Congress. No federal court is available for the enforcement of a contract, the terms of which require that a worker give up employment on joining a union, nor can an employer require such agreements of employees.

Procedural Limitations

Aside from regulating the substance of injunctions, Norris–La Guardia eliminates procedural abuses that developed before the passage of the statute. Federal courts may still issue injunctions to curb union violence. As a matter of fact, courts may still issue temporary restraining orders or *ex parte* injunctions when employer property is damaged or damage appears imminent. However, Norris–La Guardia automatically vacates this form of injunction after five days, eliminating the previous abuse when the temporary restraining orders remained in effect indefinitely, denying unions their day in court. In other words, when a federal court issues an *ex parte* injunction, it must direct a temporary injunction hearing within five days.

In addition, courts may not issue temporary or permanent injunctions unless witnesses appear to back up the employer's complaint that its property will suffer irreparable damage. No longer may affidavits be used to secure these forms of injunctions. The employer must also prove it does not have an adequate remedy at law. This means no injunction may be issued unless the employer demonstrates it could not recover damages resulting from unlawful activity in a regular trial court proceeding.

To eliminate the abuse of the blanket injunction, the court must exactly name persons and organizations covered by the injunction. Also, it must specifically identify the unlawful acts enjoined. No longer may the courts use ambiguous or catchall phrases such as "whomsoever" or "whatsoever," as was done in the past. No longer may injunctions restrain persons or organizations not directly involved in the dispute. Equally, no longer may lawful conduct be restrained. The requirement for specific terminology applies to all forms of injunctive relief—temporary restraining orders, temporary injunctions, or permanent injunctions.

Constitutionality of Norris–La Guardia

Given the track record of the U.S. Supreme Court in labor cases, it would not have been surprising if the law had been held unconstitutional. Indeed, as noted, the high court declared the Arizona anti-injunction law unconstitutional. It contained language similar to that found in the federal statute. Membership on the high court remained essentially the same as when Norris–La Guardia was reviewed.

Actually, the matter was resolved when the Supreme Court held the Wisconsin anti-injunction law constitutional in *Senn* v. *Tile Layers* in 1937.[22] The margin was by only a single vote, the Court splitting on the issue 5–4. The next year, 1938, the high court upheld the constitutionality of Norris–La Guardia in *Lauf* v. *Shinner*, reversing lower federal courts that had ruled the federal statute unconstitutional.[23] In fact, unions gained a major advantage in the federal case. Unlike the state case, picketing of the business was conducted by persons not employed by the employer. Ruling that so-called "stranger picketing" was lawful, *Lauf* v. *Shinner* broadened the scope of the application of Norris–La Guardia.

To understand why the Supreme Court held the Norris–La Guardia Act constitutional—and the Wagner Act in 1937 for that matter, dramatically reversing its position in labor cases—consider the presidential election of 1936. Franklin D. Roosevelt was overwhelmingly reelected, losing in only two states, a record up to that time. Though widely predicted to lose, the nation endorsed Roosevelt and the New Deal. Before the 1936 election, the Supreme Court held that New Deal legislation was unconstitutional. After his overwhelming victory, Roosevelt chastised the Court, calling it a "horse and buggy" court. To change the composition of the Supreme Court, Roosevelt sponsored his "court-packing" plan providing him with the authority to appoint a new member for each one over seventy years of age who did not retire. Although Congress did not accept the plan, Roosevelt focused public awareness on the Court. Though we will never know for sure, it is not unreasonable to speculate that it was Roosevelt's pressure on the Supreme Court that changed its attitude.

With the declaration of Norris–La Guardia as constitutional, the federal courts' previous intervention in labor disputes was reduced to neutrality. No longer were the federal courts available as a friendly ally to employers. Taking their lead from the federal level, many states enacted laws restricting the power of state courts to issue labor injunctions.

Antitrust under Norris–La Guardia

Congressional Intent

Not only did Norris–La Guardia curb the labor injunction, it also protected unions against prosecution under the antitrust statutes. Although the terms "Sherman Act" or "antitrust laws" are not contained in it, the background of the statute demonstrates that it was the unmistakable intention of Congress to provide unions with the protection they expected but did not obtain from the Clayton Act. On this score, the authors of Norris–La Guardia declared: "The purpose of the bill is to protect the right of labor in the same manner the Congress intended when it enacted the Clayton Act, which act, by reason of its construction by the Federal Courts, is ineffectual to accomplish the congressional intent."[24] Along the same lines, the Supreme Court subsequently said: "The Norris–La Guardia Act was a disapproval of . . . *Bedford Cut Stone* v. *Journeymen Stone Cutters Association* as the authoritative interpretation of Section 20 of the Clayton Act."

The issue was raised in *United States* v. *Hutcheson*, decided by the Supreme Court in 1941.[25] Involved was a jurisdictional dispute between the Carpenters and Machinists unions at Anheuser-Busch, the brewery located in St. Louis. It awarded the job of installing and dismantling machines to the machinists. In retaliation, the carpenters struck the plant and forbade its members to work on new construction taking place on the employer's property. Along with other action, the carpenters instituted a boycott against Anheuser-Busch, persuading persons to refrain from purchasing or selling the employer's beer. Essentially, it was the same kind of conduct unions had displayed in *Danbury Hatters* and *Bucks Stove and Range*, held by the U.S. Supreme Court to be a violation of the Sherman Act.

Reasoning of Supreme Court

In *Hutcheson*, by a 6–3 margin, the Supreme Court held that the Carpenters Union was protected by Norris–La Guardia and that the Sherman Act did not apply to its activities. Despite the fact that the secondary boycott grew out of a jurisdictional dispute between the two unions, the high court held that the terms of Norris–La Guardia were applicable. The reasoning of the Court was that under Norris–La Guardia, the federal court did not have the authority to issue an injunction to restrain the union. Since the activities were lawful under the 1932 anti-injunction statute, they were lawful *under any federal statute*, including the antitrust statutes. How could conduct protected from the injunction under Norris–La Guardia, and hence lawful, be held to violate a sister federal law, and particularly since Section 20 of the Clayton Act, realistically amended by Norris–La Guardia, unambiguously stated that action protected against the injunction should not be "held to be in violation of *any law of the United States*"?

Though the minority agreed an injunction could not be used to restrain its activities, it believed the Carpenters Union could still be subject to damage suits and criminal prosecution under the Sherman Act. Brushing aside that position, Felix Frankfurter, who wrote the majority opinion, stated:

> It would be strange indeed that although neither the Government nor Anheuser-Busch could have sought an injunction against the act here challenged, the elaborate efforts to permit such conduct failed to prevent criminal liability punishable with imprisonment and heavy fines.

Current Status Under Antitrust Statutes

With one major exception, *Hutcheson* and its progeny virtually removed unions from prosecution under the antitrust statutes. The major exception involves circumstances where employers and unions conspire to restrain trade. In the lead case on this issue, *Allen Bradley*,[26] Local No. 3 of the International Brotherhood of Electrical Workers had jurisdiction in New York City covering workers engaged in the manufacture and installation of electrical equipment at building sites. Building contractors in the city agreed not to purchase electrical products from suppliers not under contract with Local No. 3. This meant producers of electrical equipment outside New York were excluded from a very profitable market. On their part, New York manufacturers agreed not to sell electrical equipment to any building contractor unless the firm employed members of Local No. 3.

Save for the public, all parties to this cozy arrangement—manufacturers, contractors, and the local—profited. Ruling it a violation of the Sherman Act, the high court held the agreement an exception to *Hutcheson*. A few other exceptions developed in subsequent litigation, but those need not concern us in a chapter limited to highlighting the major developments in labor relations law prior to 1947.

In short, as long as unions pursue objectives by themselves and do not conspire with employers to restrain trade, they are free from prosecution under antitrust statutes. This does not mean unions are not subject to legal restraint. As will be established in later chapters, Taft-Hartley outlaws and restricts many union activities. As a matter of fact, Taft-Hartley, with a few exceptions, once again outlaws union secondary boycott activity.

The Wagner Act: The La Follette Committee

Officially named the National Labor Relations Act and popularly called the Wagner Act, it was approved by President Roosevelt on July 5, 1935. It was the culmination of past legislative efforts of federal and state governments to protect worker rights to form unions and bargain collectively free from employer interference and coercion. Those attempts either were not effective or were declared unconstitutional by the U.S. Supreme Court. For example, in 1935, the high court held unconstitutional the National Industrial Recovery Act, the New Deal program to deal with the depression.[27] Contained in the NIRA was a provision guaranteeing employee organizational rights.

The catalyst for the Wagner Act was massive employer conduct undertaken to crush unionism and collective bargaining. These antiunion activities were documented by a special committee authorized by Congress and chaired by Senator La Follette of Wisconsin. The La Follette Committee, as it was called, published fourteen thick volumes of testimony based on fifty-eight days of hearings at which 245 witnesses testified. It published a series of summary reports to clarify the mass of evidence collected at the hearings.[28]

The findings revealed a pattern of massive employer antiunion actions calculated to destroy the labor movement. One tactic was the use of industrial spies installed in the workplace to root out union members. The supplying of spies was a lucrative business for private detective agencies, such as Pinkerton, Burns, and the National Corporation Service. On this matter, the La Follette Committee reported:

> From motion-picture producers to steel makers, from hookless fasteners to automobiles, from small units to giant enterprises—scarcely an industry that is not fully represented in the list of clients of the detective agencies. Large corporations rely on spies. No firm is too small to employ them.

In the period 1933–1937, a total of $9,440,132.12 was expended by American firms to combat unions by means of industrial espionage and strikebreaking.

Union leaders were also intimidated and physically assaulted by employer hirelings. One labor leader testified:

> As I was walking toward my car, approaching my car I was about five feet from it there. I turned off the sidewalk to go to my car which was facing north on West Tenth. The man that was on my right side, the man that was walking toward me hit me with a blackjack on the back of my head and the fellow that was coming toward me from the back end of my car hit me on the face with a gun, and I felt the man in back of me grapple me by the neck and put his knee on my back, and immediately then something come into my mouth like a gag, we can call it a gag because it was a rag, and I couldn't say a peep; and I was held on both arms by these two men that evidently wanted to knock me out, and didn't do it, and we struggled there. I happened to get loose some way and I get this man here that was in back of me and I throws him over me, but he went right on top of me, and I happened to hit the ground, and him on top of me, and I held him there.
>
> I was afraid that if I would get kicked in the head that it would be the end of me. I held onto him, and while I was holding onto him these other blokes or thugs were hitting me, kicking me, and swearing. While this was going on they also kicked the fellow that was

up on top of me and he happened to let go and I hollered. As I hollered my brother-in-law and my sister heard me and come to my rescue.

When workers struck for recognition of their unions, employers used every possible method to break the strikes, including fortifying the plant with munitions, hiring professional strikebreakers, and instituting "back-to-work" movements to undermine worker morale. Given special attention was the so-called "Mohawk Valley Formula," a plan used by Remington Rand to break strikes in six of its plants. During many strikes, employers hired *agents provocateurs* to provoke violence to turn public opinion against unions. Particularly illustrative of strikebreaking was the tragic Memorial Day Massacre at a large steel corporation located in Chicago on Memorial Day 1937. Growing out of the recognition strike, the La Follette Committee reported that police killed ten workers and that ninety other unionists were injured, thirty by gunfire.[29] Organizational strikes were frequently bitter because all concerned were aware that the breaking of such strikes would eliminate workers' efforts to form unions.

These and other tactics were used by antiunion employers in their war against unions. For the complete story, read the La Follette Committee Summary Reports. Not only are they informative, gripping, and provocative, but, like no other source, they also paint a picture of a very ugly era of American labor relations. In short, if the public policy encouraging unions and collective bargaining was to be realized, such employer tactics had to be stopped. This was the fundamental purpose of the Wagner Act.

Wagner Act Constitutional

Like the Norris–La Guardia Act, the constitutionality of the Wagner Act was far from assured. Nonetheless, the Supreme Court by a 5–4 vote upheld the constitutionality of the statute. April 12, 1937, the actual date of the decision, stands as a red-letter day in U.S. labor relations law, for on that day, in *Jones & Laughlin*, the high court held that Congress could constitutionally protect the unionization and collective bargaining rights of the nation's workers.[30]

Two critical issues confronted the high court at that time: whether the Wagner Act denied employers constitutional rights by forbidding them to engage in antiunion conduct and whether the law could be applied to manufacturing. As to the former issue, the Court held Congress has the right to free interstate commerce from recognition strikes that burden trade among the states. As experience under the Railway Labor Act demonstrated, lawful recognition of the right of employees to self-organization and collective bargaining is an essential condition for industrial peace.[31] Forbidding employers to interfere with such rights, therefore, is not arbitrary and capricious.

In addition, the high court ruled that employer due-process rights under the Constitution are not violated because the law required a fair procedure to determine whether a violation of the law occurred. At every procedural level, decisions must be supported by evidence, and all decisions are subject to judicial review.

Finally, the Supreme Court held employer constitutional rights are not violated because, under the Wagner Act, employers retain critical management prerogatives. Agreement between the employer and union in collective bargaining is not compelled. Employers have the right to implement major management decisions unilaterally. Despite the Wagner Act, employers may discharge employees for proper cause, limiting that right only to the extent workers may not be dismissed for union activities.

As for the second critical issue, consider that in 1935 approximately 10 million workers were employed in manufacturing. This was a highly organizable group, and long before the statute, unions had unsuccessfully attempted to organize the mass-production industries. We have stressed the bitterness of organizational strikes resulting from the employers' refusal to recognize unions. Under the Wagner Act, employers are legally required to recognize majority-designated unions, making organizational recognition strikes unnecessary.

Even if the Supreme Court upheld the constitutionality of the Wagner Act but denied its application to manufacturing, it would not expand unionization and collective bargaining to any appreciable degree. It would not establish a procedure to make organizational strikes unnecessary. Under those circumstances, the law would be limited to the instrumentalities of commerce, such as interstate bus and water lines, interstate trucking, and telephone and telegraph systems. These industries contain a mere fraction of the nation's organizable workers. Whether manufacturing constituted interstate commerce was a critical issue because the constitutional basis for the Wagner Act is the power of Congress to regulate interstate commerce. The federal government is forbidden to deal with matters occurring solely within a state—that is, intrastate commerce.

In fact, only a year earlier, 1936, the high court had invalidated coal-mining legislation on the grounds that regulation of labor relations in that industry fell primarily on production and not on interstate commerce.[32] That decision cast a dark shadow on Wagner Act coverage of the mass-production industries.

In any event, the majority rejected the proposition that manufacturing is not directly related to interstate commerce. How could there be interstate commerce of steel if steel production is shut down because of an organizational strike? To have interstate commerce, production and transportation are vital links. Remove either of these twin elements and the result is a diminution of interstate commerce. In masterful language, Chief Justice Hughes, writing the majority opinion, observed:

> We are asked to shut our eyes at the plainest facts of our national life and to deal with the question of direct and indirect effects in an intellectual vacuum. Because there may be but indirect and remote effects upon interstate commerce in connection with a host of local enterprises throughout the country, it does not follow that other industrial activities do not have such a close and intimate relation to interstate commerce as to make the presence of industrial strife a matter of the most urgent national concern. When industries organize themselves on a national scale, making their relation to interstate commerce the dominant factor in their activities, how can it be maintained that their

industrial labor relations constitute a forbidden field into which Congress may not enter when it is necessary to protect interstate commerce from the paralyzing consequences of industrial war?

It was by the use of such language that the Supreme Court upheld the Wagner Act's application to manufacturing. The entire theory of the authors of the law was given judicial approval. It was accepted by the Court that not only did organizational strikes involving the railroads or other instruments of commerce burden trade between the states, but also that work stoppages in manufacturing resulting from employer antiunion activities, likewise burdened interstate commerce. It was therefore deemed proper for Congress to eliminate the causes of such strikes, because such action protected and promoted interstate commerce.

With the constitutional issue settled, the National Labor Relations Board, created by the Wagner Act, was prepared to administer and enforce its provisions. It would conduct secret elections to determine whether the majority of employees within a company desired a union. If so, the employer would be required to recognize and bargain with the workers' designated legal representative. It would also be authorized to enforce employer unfair labor practices forbidden by the statute. In the next chapter, we discuss the procedure the Board adopted to conduct elections and enforce unfair labor practices. Here we are concerned with the policies the agency developed to protect worker rights to self-organization and collective bargaining against employer interference and coercion.

Understand that Taft-Hartley *does not repeal worker rights that were established in the Wagner Act*. The purpose of the 1947 law was to place restrictions on labor union activities and not to repeal the 1935 statute. In other words, the Wagner Act is not history but continues currently as a vital element of the nation's labor relations law. Indeed, the policies developed by the Board as indicated directly below remain essentially the same as when they were originally established under the Wagner Act. To round out the picture, some NLRB policies adopted after passage of Taft-Hartley are indicated to the extent they deal with protected worker rights.

Employer Unfair Labor Practices

The Wagner Act made collective bargaining a matter of public policy. Section 7 of the statute declared: "Employees shall have the right to self-organization, to form, join or assist labor organizations, to bargain collectively through representatives of their own choosing, and to engage in concerted activities, for the purpose of collective bargaining or other mutual aid or protection." To make this right effective, Congress outlawed employer practices that operated to deny workers the freedom to carry out the collective bargaining function. In short, Congress was not content merely to state that workers have the right to self-organization and collective bargaining. It was determined to prohibit interference with the exercise of that right.

To accomplish the Section 7 objective, Section 8 of the Wagner Act set forth *five employer unfair labor practices*. These practices were declared unlawful. How has the NLRB interpreted and applied Section 8?

Section 8(a)(1): Interference, Coercion, Restraint

Section 8(a)(1) makes it an unfair labor practice for an employer to "interfere with, restrain, or coerce employees in the exercise of their rights under Section 7." The NLRB has held that violations of this section exist when employees are (1) threatened with the loss of their jobs or other reprisals; (2) granted wage increases and other benefits timed to discourage union membership; and (3) questioned by employers about union sympathy and activities under such circumstances as will tend to coerce them in the exercise of their rights under Section 7.[33] Violations have also been declared when the work place or homes of employees were placed under surveillance by employers to the extent that reasonable communication regarding organization was restricted. In this regard, the utilization of industrial spies constitutes a violation.

Although the Wagner Act did not prevent an employer from utilizing economic power to defeat a strike by peaceful means, the NLRB has ruled that a firm interfered with the right to self-organization by hiring strikebreakers for the purpose of provoking violence or creating fear in the minds of employees. When the NLRB held that the Mohawk Valley Formula, a systematic procedure for breaking strikes, violated the Wagner Act, it stated: "Those activities were employed to defeat the strike, end the strike, rather than settling it through collective bargaining."[34] Inciting to violence against union organizers and members of labor organizations was also deemed an unfair labor practice. In one case, a company was found to have violated this area of the law when a woman supervisor incited violence against a union organizer by suggesting to the employees in her section, "What do you say, girls, we give her a beating?"[35]

Some of the unfair labor practices during World War II had a distinct wartime flavor. A number of employers utilized the wartime environment to interfere, restrain, or coerce workers from exercising their right to self-organization and collective bargaining. A violation of the National Labor Relations Act was found when an employer posted notices throughout the plant suggesting that union organizers were a group of "intimidators" and threatened the "substitution of Naziism for Americanism."[36] Nor was an employer permitted to assert that a union was "backed by Germans" when the intent was to unlawfully discourage membership in the organization. A supervisor implicated his employer in an unfair labor practice by intimating that the company would not ask for occupational army service deferment for an employee if the worker persisted in union activities. Employers were not permitted to distribute "I am an American" buttons to their employees not wearing union buttons. The obvious inference that union members were not loyal Americans evidently prompted the Board's decision. Effecting the arrest of persons distributing union literature in a plant was deemed unlawful, even though the employer argued that the plant was engaged in secret war work and that the persons jailed might have been spies and saboteurs. It was noted that a labor union was organizing the plant's workers when the employer procured the arrest. Nor did the Board sustain the argument that employers could engage in unfair labor practices with impunity because the company was producing materials for the exclusive use of the government. The NLRB further ruled that an employer engaged in an unfair labor practice when it appealed to its workers' patriotism to defeat a union in a bargaining election by drawing a contrast between the hardships endured by men in the armed forces and the attempts of the employees to better their economic position through organization. On the other hand, the Board found no violation of the Wagner Act when union members were discharged because they had violated a Federal Bureau of Investigation domestic security measure. These employees were not permitted to utilize their union status to block dismissal.[37]

In a 1990 case, however, an employer attempted to curb employee falsification of insurance claims, reasons for absence, timecards, funeral leave claims, and related matters. To implement the objective, the employer adopted a rule calling for discipline, including discharge, should an employee "misrepresent any material fact in connection with any claim concerning his employment or his pay. . . ."

While holding the rule interfered with employee rights, the NLRB held the rule was excessively broad because it could be understood to include conduct protected by the law.[38] For example, employees may in good faith misinterpret provisions of the labor agreement and present grievances on the basis of facts which turn out to be wrong. Recognizing an employer has a legitimate interest in curbing falsification, the Board pointed out "it must do so directly, not through an impermissibly broad rule." That is, the employer must establish a policy that specifically says, for example, an employee is subject to discipline should the employee falsify a timecard.

Other forms of employer interference, restraint, or coercion include making employment conditional on the yellow-dog contract;[39] total banning of all union solicitation of new members on employer property;[40] threatening employees with subpoenas as witnesses in federal government proceedings should they sign up with the union;[41] and forbidding the circulation of a cartoon on employer property ridiculing management personnel policies.[42]

This is not to say that all employer conduct within a union context constitutes interference, restraint, or coercion. In a consumer-oriented business (fast foods), an employer was lawfully permitted to enforce a rule forbidding the wearing of all unauthorized buttons, including union buttons, on employee uniforms on the grounds that such a display is not appealing to all customers.[43] An employer may lawfully forbid union solicitation on company property during work time.[44] No violation was held when an employer addressed a "captive audience" (employees forced to attend) without giving the union an equal opportunity to speak to the group.[45] In *Gino Morena Enterprises* (287 NLRB No. 145 [1988]), the NLRB held an employer may truthfully inform its employees they are subject to permanent replacement in the event of an economic strike provided the employer does not make such an announcement within the context of threats and reprisals.

Section 8(a)(2): Domination of a Union

Employer "domination or interference with the formation or administration of a labor organization or contribution of financial or other support to it" is a violation of Section 8(a)(2). It has already been pointed out that a union that is the creature of an employer does not constitute a proper vehicle for the carrying out of the collective bargaining process. Congress was well aware of this fact and consequently outlawed employer domination of labor unions. The NLRB, however, was required to spell out the circumstances under which an employer dominates a labor organization. Specifically, what are the characteristics of an employer-controlled union?

The Board has found a union to be company-dominated in a case where the employer told its employees that they should establish a union and indicated the form that the labor organization should take. If an employer or its representatives actively solicit members on behalf of a labor organization, such a union is illegal. A union may be company-dominated when the employer provides the union with bulletin boards, a company automobile, and stenographic service or office space.

The Board has held that, by advancing money to employees who were unable to pay membership dues, a company contributed support to a union and the organization was ordered dissolved. Another union was held company-dominated because the employer permitted members of the organization to solicit members for the union on the employer's property during working hours and, most important, with the consent of the employer. Employees were fired and threatened with discharge because of their refusal to join the organization for which the employer had expressed its preference, and consequently the NLRB ordered the organization dissolved.[46]

Other employer practices that indicate that a labor organization is the creature of the company include those instances in which the employer has suggested the form of the constitution; in which a few handpicked employees have been urged to create the organization; and in which management has been willing and eager to sign agreements with the organization it helped to create.

An important criterion in determining whether a labor organization is company-dominated may be the extent of collective bargaining between the union and management. The NLRB said:

> If the organization did not make any effort to meet with the employer concerned, and other features of the labor organization are indicative of company-domination, the Board may conclude, on the basis of the laxity in petitioning for a meeting on the part of the labor organization, that the employee's organization is the creature of the employer.[47]

Not only is neglecting to meet with management material evidence that the labor organization is company-dominated, but when conferences do occur, the labor organization in question may be unlawful if the negotiations "be such as to reveal the employer's domination of the organization."[48]

In a 1983 case, beyond the normal remedy directing the employer to cease and desist recognizing a company-dominated union, the NLRB also ordered the employer and union to rebate to employees all dues and initiation fees collected, plus interest.[49] What generated this unusual order was evidence demonstrating that over a three-year period, the employer had kicked back $68,000 to union officials who referred business to the employer from other contacts the union had with businesses.

To clarify this section, the Board adopted a number of principles to determine whether an organization is independent of employer domination. Thus, if members of the organization hold regular meetings on property other than the company's; if members of the union pay dues; if the union has written agreements with the company; if the organization has contacts with other workers' organizations; if the union has the right to demand arbitration of differences whereby management abandons absolute veto power, then, the NLRB found, the organization is clearly its own master and is free to submit the real wishes of its members to management.

On the other hand, a union not affiliated with a national organization is lawful provided it is not employer-dominated. Many unions operate in this fashion, including those at Armco Steel in Middleton, Ohio, and Cummins Engine in Columbus, Indiana. The former is not affiliated with the United Steelworkers of America, and the latter is not affiliated with the United Automobile Workers or with any other national organization. Such unions are perfectly lawful and may represent workers under national labor policy.

Employee Participation and *Electromation*

The American labor relations landscape has always contained programs through which employees have helped employers improve quality, production, and efficiency. They have been called a variety of names, including quality of work circles, employee involvement, labor management cooperation, and employee participation. Whatever they are called, the programs have a common denominator: active employee participation in day-to-day plant operation.

In the face of more intense global competition, those programs started becoming more extensive in the 1980s within unionized and non-unionized companies. By 1993, it was estimated 30,000 employee participation plans were in operation covering 80 percent of the 1,000 largest companies in the United States.[50] Some of the largest corporations in the nation have had such programs in operation, including General Motors, Ford Motor Company, Westinghouse, Boeing, and Caterpillar prior to its labor troubles in the early 1990s.[51]

Given the increasing use of employee participation programs and their success, the NLRB decision in *Electromation*, which found a plan in violation of national labor policy, attracted an unusual amount of interest and controversy.[52]

The locale of the case was the Electromation Company, a small firm producing electronic parts in Elkhart, Indiana. When the case surfaced, the firm was nonunion although the Teamsters were trying to organize the plant. Sixty-eight employees had signed a petition requesting the employer to reconsider its unilateral decision to forego a wage increase in 1989 and to eliminate an attendance bonus program. At this point, Electromation established five so-called "action committees" composed of employees and supervisors.

By a unanimous 4–0 vote, the NLRB held those committees were labor organizations or employee representation committees within the meaning of Section 2(5) of Taft-Hartley that defines a labor organization as follows:

> . . . any organization of any kind, or any agency or employee representation committee or plan, in which employees participate and which exists for the purpose, in whole or in part, of dealing with employers concerning grievances, labor disputes, wages, rates of pay, hours of employment, or conditions of work.

Not only did the Board rule the action committees were labor organizations for purposes of the statute, but the Board also ruled they were illegally dominated and supported by the company in violation of Section 8(a)(2) of the law. Section 8(a)(2) states that it is an unfair labor practice for an employer

> to dominate or interfere with the formation or administration of any labor organization or contribute financial or other support to it: provided that subject to rules and regulations made and published by the Board pursuant to section 6, an employer shall not be prohibited from permitting employees to confer with him during working hours without loss of time or pay.

Under the scheme of the statute, the NLRB must first determine whether a labor organization exists. If the group is not a labor organization, the case is dismissed at this point, and no determination is made whether the employer violated Section 8(a)(2) of the statute. For example, in one case the employer established a committee composed of employees and managers. Its sole function was to determine whether employees' grievances had merit. The committee performed no other function. It was strictly adjudicatory in nature. Under these circumstances, the Board dismissed a complaint claiming the employer in question dominated or supported the committee.[53]

In *Electromation* the Board ruled the action committees were labor organizations or employee representation plans which existed for the purpose of *"dealing with"* the company concerning *"conditions of work."* The action committees were formed to address working conditions, including discipline, plant rules, pay practices and bonuses. Employee members of the committees were expected to discuss the designated matters with other employees and to communicate concerns and ideas to management. True, the employee members did not have the authority to bargain with the management representatives concerning working conditions. In *NLRB* v. *Cabot Carbon*,[54] however, the U.S. Supreme Court held the concept *"dealing with"* as contained in Section 2(5) is not synonymous to *"bargaining with"* as found in Section 8(a)(5). This provision states an employer violates the law when it refuses "to bargain collectively with the representatives of his employees. . . ."

In short, since the action committees addressed employees' concerns through a bilateral process involving employees and management and the employee members of the committees acted in a representation capacity, the NLRB ruled the action committees were labor organizations or employee representation plans within the meaning of Section 2(5) of the national law.

To support its decision that Electromation illegally dominated and supported the action committees, the Board pointed out that the employer initiated the committees, drafted their written purposes and goals, determined and selected the members to serve on each committee, appointed management representatives to facilitate discussions, and permitted the employees to meet on company time in facilities created and supported by management.

Having reached the conclusion that the action committees were creatures of the employer and were dominated by them, the Board directed they be disestablished. This is the traditional remedy when an employer dominates a labor organization.

Predictably, the business community and organized labor differed on the significance of *Electromation*. A spokesperson for the U.S. Chamber of Commerce stated:

> On December 16, 1992, some 15 months following oral argument, the Board issued its long awaited decision, finding that Electromation's five employee involvement committees violated the NLRA. As a result of the Board's much publicized decision, the legality of contemporary employee participation programs under the NLRA is no longer merely an academic issue. Clearly, the genie is now out of the bottle: Section 8(a)(2) of the NLRA can and will be used to strike down employee participation programs in operation today.[55]

AFL-CIO President Lane Kirkland stated:

> . . . the NLRB has not ruled on real workplace committees—where workers choose their own representatives, set their own agenda and have real input in the workplace.
> That kind of committee is not illegal and can in fact benefit employers, employees and the nation. No one in the labor movement and, as I see it, no one at the NLRB is standing in the way of real worker committees in either the union or the non-union workplace.[56]

DuPont: Employee Participation in Union Setting

About six months after *Electromation*, the NLRB ruled on a similar situation but this time within a union setting. Involved were the DuPont Company and Chemical Workers Association, an independent union not affiliated with a national union or the AFL-CIO.[57] DuPont established seven committees, one of which covered employee physical fitness while the other six dealt with occupational safety and health.

Aside from employee members, each group had a management representative. Proposals were discussed between employee members and management members of the committees; however, management representatives had the power to reject any proposal. The Board ruled those discussions constituted "dealings" within the meaning of Section 2(5) as explained earlier. As a matter of fact, the committees dealt with issues identical to those dealt with by the union, and at times with greater success. For example, one committee obtained a new welding shop for a worker who complained of poor ventilation. The union's previous attempt to resolve the same problem had failed. In addition, the committees determined incentive awards for safe work practices.

On the basis of the evidence, the NLRB held DuPont dominated the committees. Any determinations by them were subject to the approval of management members. It set the size of the panels and selected employee members if less than the required number volunteered to serve. The company also had the right to set up or disband any of the committees. In each group, the management member served as the leader and had a key role in establishing the agenda of the group. Given those factors, the NLRB held DuPont illegally dominated the committees in violation of the law. In a concurring opinion, Board member Dennis M. Devaney said the employer's conduct "comes close to a textbook example of an employer's manipulation of employee committees to weaken and undermine the employees' freely chosen exclusive bargaining representative." Needless to say, the NLRB abolished the DuPont committees.

At this writing, it is not safe to predict where the NLRB, courts, and even Congress will go with the principles established in *Electromation* and *DuPont*. Even the NLRB's General Counsel, who has the responsibility to apply the decisions to cases of the same kind, was not certain about the ultimate result of the decisions. In April 1993, he issued a memorandum to all regional offices in which he said:

> Since the Board's decision in *Electromation*, much discussion has been generated as to the impact of *Electromation* on various types of employee involvement programs, such as "quality circles," including those that deal with efficiency and productivity, or that are designed to be a "communication device" to promote the interests of quality or efficiency. In this regard, the Board in *Electromation* stated that its decision did "not reach the question of whether any employer initiated programs that may exist for such purposes . . . may constitute labor organizations under Section 2(5)." The purpose of this Guideline Memorandum is to provide a general overview of the General Counsel's position on various issues that may be affected by *Electromation*, with guidance from prior Board cases, and with an emphasis on both what *Electromation* actually holds, and on the issues that remain open for the Board to decide.[58]

No question exists that employee participation plans serve the national interest. The issue, however, is to develop plans that conform to the law. Even a worthy purpose should not be a facade for law breaking. Either the law should be changed or existing law obeyed. In *DuPont*, the Board suggested some guidelines that would place plans within the scope of the law. Such committees must avoid "dealing" with management as a union might. Committees should exist for "the purpose of imparting information . . . or planning educational programs." To pass legal muster, the Board stresses the employer must not dominate the groups but rather be a participant with a commensurate number of votes.

Section 8(a)(3): Discrimination against Union Members

This section makes it an unfair labor practice for employers to discriminate "in regard to hire or tenure of employment on any term or condition of employment to encourage or discourage membership in a labor organization." This clause was directed against the most common and highly effective antiunion weapon—the discharge of workers who are union members or those who would promote the formation of a labor union. By adopting this provision, Congress endeavored to erase fear from the minds of union-conscious workers. Again, the Wagner Act charged the NLRB with the duty of interpreting and carrying out the terms of the provision. What constitutes discrimination? Is transferring an employee to an inferior job because of union activity discrimination within the meaning of the Act? Can union workers ever be discharged? What evidence will the Board consider material in determining whether an employer truly discriminated against workers for union activity?

The most common form of discrimination that the Board declared an unfair labor practice was discharge of an employee for union activity. When the evidence in a case proved that an employee was discharged because of union activity, the Board ordered reinstatement. In most instances, the employer denied that it had discharged an employee or otherwise discriminated for union activity, and consequently the NLRB would investigate to determine whether there had really been the discrimination prohibited by the Wagner Act. When an employer denied that discharges or other forms of claimed discrimination were within the meaning of the Act, the Board took into account the entire background of the case, reviewing the totality of circumstances to determine the nature of employer action against employees.

Not only will employers usually maintain that they did not discriminate against an employee on the grounds of union activity, but in nearly all cases they will also tender some reasons to the Board for discharging an employee. The most common alleged reason given for the discharge is the employer's claim that the worker was inefficient. In determining whether the employee was inefficient or whether this was a subterfuge for dismissal for union activities, the NLRB considers the following facts: (1) length of total employment; (2) experience in the particular position from which the employee was discharged; (3) efficiency ratings by qualified persons; (4) specific acts showing efficiency or inefficiency; and (5) comparison with other employees. Other reasons advanced for discharge include decrease in productivity, insubordination, infraction of company rules, fighting, and swearing. In all instances, the NLRB will determine if the reasons have "color and substance," or whether they are only a convenient pretext designed to defeat the law.

Employers discriminate against employees and thereby engage in an unfair labor practice if they refuse employment to persons because of their former or current membership in a labor organization. Moreover, discrimination can also occur in respect to other conditions of work. In one case, the Board found that a company had discriminated against employees, transferring some workers to a very difficult section of the firm as punishment for their union activities, or with the intention of making them quit. One union man would have had to move twenty to twenty-five cars of rock and dirt, and in so doing would have been forced to work for a month without pay. Another instance of discrimination occurred when an employer transferred a worker to another position in which he had no experience, with the motive of firing him for the inefficient work that would result.

The Board has also construed discrimination to include those instances in which an employer has temporarily laid off employees for union activity. Refusal to reinstate employees because of union activity also is discrimination within the meaning of the Wagner Act. Other forms of discrimination include those cases in which an employer forces an employee engaged in union activities to work the worst shifts; pays more wages to a nonunion employee than to a union employee doing equal work; violates seniority rules; and discharges a man's wife because he is a union member.

A case before the U.S. Supreme Court involved the issue of whether an employer owning several plants, Deering Milliken, had violated the discrimination provisions of the Act when it permanently closed down one of its plants for antiunion reasons.[59] The plant that was shut down was located in Darlington, South Carolina. The *Darlington* case was first taken before the NLRB as a result of unfair labor practices growing out of a plant shutdown after a vigorous company campaign to resist union organizational efforts. In March 1956, when the organizational campaign was initiated, the company interrogated employees and threatened to close the Darlington plant if the Textile Workers Union won the election. On September 6, 1956, the union prevailed in the Board-held election by a narrow margin. The decision was made to liquidate the plant. Employees were informed by the company that the reason for such a decision was the election result and encouragement was extended for employees to sign a petition disavowing the union. The Board found Darlington in violation of the discrimination provision of the Act. The Board ordered back pay for all employees until they obtained substantially equivalent work or were put on preferential hiring lists at the other Deering Milliken mills. Upon review, a court of appeals denied enforcement and argued that a company had an absolute right to close out a part or all of its business, regardless of antiunion motives.

The U.S. Supreme Court reviewed the case in 1965 and agreed partially with the court of appeals. It held that a single employer could go out of business completely for whatever reason it chose. But "a discriminatory partial closing may have repercussions on what remains of the business, affording employer leverage for discouraging the free exercise of Section 7 rights among remaining employees of much the same kind as that found to exist in the 'runaway shop' and 'temporary closing' cases." The Court held that "a partial closing is an unfair labor practice under Section 8(a)(3) if motivated by a purpose to chill unionism in any of the remaining plants of the single employer and if the employer may reasonably have foreseen . . . that effect."

The Board had ruled only on the basis of the effect the plant closing had had on Darlington employees. The Court test required that a determination be made regarding the effect the closing had had on the employees in other plants owned and operated by the Deering Milliken group. In June 1967, the NLRB held that there was sufficient evidence to support the charge that the shutdown of the Darlington plant was for the purpose, at least in part, of discouraging union membership in other plants owned by Deering Milliken. It also found that the closing had a "chilling" effect on the other plant employees as far as union activity was concerned.

Discrimination with regard to hire or tenure will be found only if employees in other plants are affected by the antiunion behavior of an employer. A decision will have to be made in each case, since a partial closing will not constitute a per se violation of the Act. However, it seems clear that multiplant firms cannot make antiunion decisions in one plant without intending the same result to spill over onto all the others.

Strangely enough, it was not until 1983 that the issue of burden of proof was settled in discrimination cases. In 1980, the NLRB established the *Wright Line* doctrine,[60] in which it held that the General Counsel (whose role will be discussed in the next chapter) need only show by the preponderance of evidence that union activities contributed to a discharge, while the employer had the burden to prove that the discharge would have taken place even if the employee had not engaged in union activities. In the 1983 case, an employee was terminated after he attempted to organize a union. To justify discharge, the employer asserted that the employee was terminated because he had left keys in the bus to which he was assigned and had taken unauthorized coffee breaks. When a supervisor became aware of the employee's union activities, he had threatened to discharge the employee. Sustaining both the Board's reinstatement of the employee and the *Wright Line* doctrine, the U.S. Supreme Court held that the employer had not proven that the employee would have been discharged in the absence of his union activities.[61] The Court found that the employee's infraction of the plant rules was too minimal to warrant discharge.

Before concluding this section on discrimination, understand that an employer has the opportunity to discharge or otherwise discipline its employees for any reason except upon the grounds of union activity. It must not be forgotten that the employer retains the right to discharge an employee for other causes: disobedience, bad work, carelessness, drinking on duty, and so on. The law only forbids an employer from discriminating against a worker solely for membership or activity in a union.

Section 8(a)(4): Use of Board Processes

This section prohibits employers from discharging or otherwise discriminating against an employee because he or she has filed charges or given testimony under the Wagner Act. Thus, Congress provided protection for workers who might bring a charge against an employer alleging violation of the terms of the law. Moreover, since the procedures of the Wagner Act require hearings and court proceedings, it was reasonable to forbid discrimination against workers who would participate in such proceedings.

Over the years, the number of cases under this provision has been miniscule compared with other employer unfair labor practices. Nonetheless, where the employer violates this area of the statute, the NLRB will direct an appropriate remedy, including reinstatement with back pay when the employee is unlawfully discharged. Even when an employee is not discharged, the agency will direct the employer to cease threatening a worker with retaliation should he or she use the Board process.[62] In *Cox Fire Protection*, 1992, for example, the company president believed an employee filed an unfair labor charge against his business. He said to the employee: "This isn't a threat, but I want to kick your ass." Rejecting the company's claim that its president merely used a colorful figure of speech to express his feelings, the NLRB, noting the statement was made in the presence of other employees, held the clear import of the statement was that the company president wanted to retaliate against the employee and was capable of carrying out the threat.

Section 8(a)(5): Bargaining in Good Faith

Finally, Section 8(a)(5) of the Wagner Act makes it an unfair labor practice for an employer to refuse to bargain collectively with the representatives of the employees. By this provision, Congress intended to eliminate the need for the recognition strike. Since employers would be required to bargain collectively, workers would not find it necessary to strike for the recognition of the union. Moreover, this portion of Section 8 constitutes the heart of the Wagner Act, for it was enacted to promote the collective bargaining process once a bargaining unit was established. Once more, the NLRB was required to implement public policy. Specifically, what must an employer do in order to fulfill the legal obligation to bargain collectively? The answer to this problem is embedded in scores of NLRB decisions and orders. A brief analysis of them will reveal the character of employer behavior that satisfies the requirement of the law.

In the first place, if an employer refuses to meet with representatives of the employees, the employer has failed to bargain collectively and so has engaged in an unfair labor practice. Of course, the labor organization must make a proper demand to the employer requesting collective bargaining. A demand to bargain must come from the proper source of the union and must be clearly presented to the representatives of the company who usually deal with matters concerning labor relations. A casual remark is not a sufficient demand, but a request for collective bargaining by registered letter is sufficient.

In practice, employers have advanced various excuses for their refusal to meet or to bargain collectively with representatives of their employees. In various decisions, the Board has held in this respect that an employer is not relieved of the duty to bargain collectively by the outbreak of a strike or lockout.

A more definite action of some employers to avoid collective bargaining is evidenced in their attempts to undermine unions by engaging in other unfair labor practices. There is, of course, no duty to bargain if the union does not represent a majority of employees in the appropriate unit. Thus, on occasion employers have attempted to evade their duty to bargain collectively by attempting to destroy the majority status of the union. The Board has ruled, however, that an employer who engages in unfair labor practices resulting in the destruction of the majority status of the labor organization is not relieved of the duty to bargain collectively with the representatives of that union.

Employers must do more than just meet with the representatives and merely go through the motions of bargaining. To satisfy the requirement of collective bargaining, an employer must bargain in "good faith." In defining that term, the Board held that to bargain in good faith, an employer "must work toward a solution, satisfactory to both sides, of the various problems under discussion by presentation of counterproposals and other affirmative conduct." In another case, the Board declared that "the obligation of the Act is to produce more than a series of empty discussions, [and so] bargaining must mean more than mere negotiations. It must mean negotiations with a bona fide intent to reach an agreement if agreement is possible."[63]

A conference completely dominated by the employer, with the representatives of the union mere auditors to the proceedings, has been held to constitute evidence that the employer does not desire to bargain collectively. If an employer makes no attempt to offer counterproposals during the meeting, the Board has ruled that such action indicates that the employer refuses to bargain in good faith. "The Board has considered counterproposals so important an element of collective bargaining that it has found the failure to offer counterproposals to be persuasive of the fact that the employer has not bargained in good faith."[64]

In a series of decisions, the NLRB has maintained that the nature of the employer's conduct after having been requested to bargain collectively is indicative of whether the employer really desired to negotiate in good faith. An employer does not intend to bargain in good faith when, after being asked to bargain collectively, it restrains and interferes with the employees' right to self-organization; when it attempts to bargain with individual employees; and when it calls a general meeting of its employees, dominates such meetings, and therein attacks the union.

The Board established a rule that if an agreement between a company and a labor organization has been reached through discussion, such an agreement must be embodied in a written contract. In other words, an employer does not fulfill the obligation to bargain collectively—and thereby engages in an unfair labor practice—by refusing to render an agreement reached orally into a written agreement. In dealing with the matter, the NLRB declared in one case that "an assertion that collective bargaining connotes no more than discussions designed to clarify employer policy and does not include negotiations looking toward a binding agreement is contrary to any realistic view of labor relations. The protection to organization of employees afforded by the first four subdivisions of Section 8 can have meaning only when the ultimate goal is viewed as the stabilization of working conditions through genuine bargaining and [written] agreement between equals."[65] Eventually, the Supreme Court of the United States upheld this policy of the NLRB.[66]

Although the NLRB imposed upon employers the duty to bargain collectively, *the law does not require that the parties must reach an agreement.* Consequently, when an impasse in the negotiations between an employer and the representatives of the employees occurs, the employer is not required to continue to bargain collectively. When differences develop between parties over substantive issues and the employer has bargained in good faith, the NLRB has declared that an employer has fulfilled the collective bargaining obligations.

The Principle of Majority Rule

It was necessary that Congress spell out the conditions under which employers are considered to have refused to bargain collectively with the representatives of their employees. Collective bargaining implies negotiations between representatives of management and representatives of employees. Consequently, it was indispensable for the Wagner Act to state the circumstances under which an employer was considered to have refused to bargain collectively. To resolve this problem, Congress adopted the principle of majority rule. For purposes of the Wagner Act, an employer engaged in an unfair labor practice only when it refused to bargain with a union selected by a majority of the employees for purposes of collective bargaining. If a labor organization did not possess the support of the majority, an employer was under no legal compulsion to bargain.

Still another principle of industrial democracy was embodied in the Wagner Act. Under its terms, a union selected by a majority of workers had to represent all workers in the bargaining unit, regardless of their membership status. A majority labor organization must bargain equally for members and nonmembers in respect to rates of pay, hours of work, or other conditions of employment. Moreover, if a majority of the workers in a unit vote for a union, it must represent all workers in the unit regardless of whether they voted for the union, voted against it, or failed to vote.

Some have opposed the majority-rule principle on the ground that it violates the rights of minority groups. Suppose 75 percent of the workers in a plant select a labor organization as their bargaining representative. Under the Wagner Act, the union was not only to represent this 75 percent but also had to bargain for the remaining 25 percent. However, the fact that the labor organization chosen by the majority of workers must represent all workers does not transgress the tenets of democracy.

Nothing is further from the truth. In fact, the principle of majority rule implements the democratic way of life. In political life, a Republican elected to the House of Representatives represents the Democratic members of the district as well as the Republicans. In addition, each Democratic member in the district is bound by decisions that the Republican representative might make.

Not only is the principle of majority rule consistent with democracy, but it is also justified on the basis of effective collective bargaining. If nonunion workers could make their own employment agreements with their employers, the labor union would soon collapse. It would be easy for employers to favor the nonunion workers. These workers could be paid higher wages, helping to lure other workers out of the organization. If a large number of workers withdrew from the union, the labor organization would soon cease to exist. With the disintegration of a union, an employer would not need to be so considerate of the nonunion worker.

There is still another value attached to the principle of majority rule from the viewpoint of effective collective bargaining. Suppose the workers of a factory choose among five labor organizations. Assume that one union received the support of the majority of employees while the others received a scattering of the workers' support. If the minority unions were given the right to bargain for the workers who voted for them, collective bargaining could hardly be conducted successfully. Such "balkanization" of the bargaining unit would defeat the purpose of a law calculated to make collective bargaining effective. Thus, in this example, there would be five contract negotiation sessions, five grievance committees, and five different chances for the plant to shut down because of disagreement over working conditions. Management as well as workers would suffer under such a system. Membership raiding among the unions would be incessant. Production could hardly be carried out effectively in such an environment. What worth would it be to management or to workers if the company negotiated contracts successfully with four of the unions, only to have the plant shut down because the fifth union called a strike over contract terms?

Thus, it can readily be seen that the principle of majority rule satisfies the requirements of democracy and industrial harmony. Majority rule means the promotion of industrial democracy and orderly collective bargaining. Any other principle of representation would mean ineffective collective bargaining, retardation of the rate of production, and general industrial chaos.

The Wagner Act Record

How the Board discharged its responsibility is a matter of public record.[67] In the Wagner Act years of 1936–1947, the NLRB reinstated 76,268 workers who had been discharged because of union activities. Moreover, the Board awarded workers $12,418,000 in back pay. Congress recognized that reinstatement of workers discharged because of union activity without awarding them pay for time lost during their period of discharge would be an empty gesture. Accordingly, the Wagner Act provided that workers discharged because of union activities would be reinstated with back pay. In addition, the NLRB disestablished 1,709 company-dominated unions;

ordered employers to post 8,156 notices stating that the company would henceforth comply with the Wagner Act; and on 5,070 occasions ordered employers to bargain collectively. Finally, the Board ordered 226,488 strikers reinstated on their jobs. Many of these workers had struck because of employer unfair labor practices; still others had suffered discrimination at the termination of a strike. It has been a favorite union-busting technique for employers to refuse to reinstate strike leaders in their jobs after a strike ends. These figures stand as a testimonial to a law and an agency dedicated to the promotion of collective bargaining and the union movement. This record under-scores the proposition that a main source of criticism of the NLRB during its Wagner Act period resulted from the zeal of the agency to perform its duties in a positive and vigorous manner.

Industrial Democracy

During the Wagner Act years, 1936–1947, the NLRB was called upon to determine representatives for collective bargaining in 36,969 cases.[68] Labor unions won lawful bargaining rights in 30,110 instances, and workers voted for "no union" in 6,859 cases. Slightly more than 9 million workers were eligible to vote in representation elections. Of this total, 7,677,135 workers, 84.1 percent, actually cast ballots. Votes cast for labor unions amounted to 6,145,834, and votes against unions numbered 1,531,301. These figures testify to the success of the Wagner Act in establishing an orderly manner for the selection of bargaining representatives. The law substituted the ballot box for industrial warfare. Workers in free secret-ballot elections had the opportunity to select or reject the process of collective bargaining. The Wagner Act established the principle of representative democracy in the nation's industrial life.

Indeed, in December 1976, in an election held in Millers Falls, Massachusetts, some unknown employee cast the *30 millionth* vote in the forty-two-year operation of the NLRB. Speaking of this milestone, Betty Southhard Murphy, then the chair of the Board, stated:

> The statute has stood the test of time. During these four decades, the United States in large measure has achieved industrial democracy under law. The statute has been a key factor in our country's immense economic growth; it has brought an evolution of labor relations from sitdown strikes and violence to a thoughtful bargaining and productive compromise.[69]

To the union movement, however, the significance of the milestone was some-what diminished because of the decline of union success in NLRB elections. Whereas unions had been selected as bargaining agents in about 80 percent of the polls between 1936 and 1947, their success in elections had declined to less than 50 percent in the 1980s. Earlier we indicated the difficulty unions have encountered in organizing in recent years.

On July 5, 1985, the NLRB celebrated its fiftieth anniversary. During that time, it conducted 345,000 elections involving over 32 million employees.[70] Clearly, national labor policy has established the principle of industrial democracy.

SUMMARY

Dramatic and profound changes have occurred in public policy concerning worker rights to organize and bargain collectively. In the era of hostility, unions and their members were regarded as conspiracies. When that method did not fully meet the needs of antiunion employers, the courts obliged by stamping out vital union activities with the labor injunction. Judges made labor law based on their economic and social beliefs coming down hard on the labor movement, supporting employer desire to operate in a union-free environment. Prosecution of unions under the antitrust statutes constituted another formidable legal obstacle to union growth and viability.

While the courts suppressed unionization, employers were free to engage in a wide variety of antiunion tactics. The use of the injunction was a one-way street, available to employers but not to unions. Judges did not regard the workers' quest for collective bargaining and fair treatment on the job as worker property rights.

Whereas the courts accommodated employers who claimed that their property suffered irreparable damage from union activity, they did not enjoin employer antiunion conduct. This made it difficult, if not impossible, for workers to form unions and bargain collectively. Dominating labor relations, courts did not permit government, state or federal, to protect worker rights for effective unionization. The courts either declared protective legislation unconstitutional or interpreted the statutes in a way that made them meaningless.

As a product of the Great Depression, Congress passed the Norris–La Guardia Act and the Wagner Act, establishing a favorable legal climate for union growth and collective bargaining. The former removed the courts from center stage in labor relations. The latter curbed employer antiunion practices. No longer could the courts issue injunctions when judges subjectively believed union objectives and methods unlawful. No longer could employers lawfully engage in conduct calculated to deprive workers of their unionization and collective bargaining rights. With one major exception, the Supreme Court held Norris–La Guardia as a protective shield against union prosecution under antitrust statutes.

By curbing the courts and employers, the public policy to promote unionization and collective bargaining was realized. Between 1936 and 1947, union membership increased from about 4 million to 16 million. Although revived business conditions, particularly during World War II, were a positive factor, union growth was primarily attributable to the favorable legal environment established by the Norris–La Guardia and Wagner acts.

DISCUSSION QUESTIONS

1. The conspiracy doctrine era centered on the *Philadelphia Cordwainers* case of 1806 and the *Massachusetts* v. *Hunt* case of 1842. Discuss how the doctrine differed under the authority of each case.

2. Compare the use of the conspiracy doctrine after 1842 with the use of the labor injunction after 1888 with respect to the impact on employees, employers, and unions.

3. How did the definition of property held by U.S. courts influence the use of the labor injunction? Did this definition differ from that of England, and if so, what difference did it make?

4. How do the decisions made in the *In re Debs* case (1895) and the *Danbury Hatters* case (1908) differ?

5. Five major abuses of labor injunctions by the courts have been identified. Identify each and discuss its effect on unions and labor relations.

6. The *Hitchman* decision of 1917 dealing with yellow-dog contracts reveals a great deal about how labor markets work. Can you identify and describe one or two effects explained by *Hitchman*?

7. Discuss the significant economic issues of the *Danbury Hatters* case.

8. Regarding the Clayton Act, carefully answer the following: Did Section 6 provide exemption from antitrust prosecution?

9. In your opinion, what did the Norris–La Guardia Act of 1932 do that was not done by the Clayton Act of 1914?

10. Discuss the effectiveness of each of the following aspects of Norris–La Guardia:

    a. Effect on the courts in their construction of labor relations rights and responsibilities

    b. Union right to strike and picket

    c. Yellow-dog contract

11. Discuss the importance of the *Hutcheson* and *Allen Bradley* cases to labor union prosecution under the antitrust statutes.

12. What do you consider to be the most significant features and effects of the Supreme Court's 1937 *Jones & Laughlin Steel* case?

13. How fair or unfair do you believe the NLRB has been in the interpretation of the five employer unfair labor practices passed in the Wagner Act?

14. In your opinion, was the Wagner Act effective over the 1935–1947 period?

NOTES

1   John R. Commons and Eugene A. Gilmore, *A Documentary History of American Industrial Society*, III (Cleveland: The Arthur H. Clark Company, 1910), p. 228.

2   *Ibid.*, p. 70.

3   *Ibid.*, p. 233.

4   Selig Perlman, *A History of Trade Unionism in the United States* (New York: The Macmillan Company, 1929), p. 7.

5   Edwin E. Witte, "Early American Labor Cases," *Yale Law Journal*, XXXV (1926), p. 827.

6   *Commonwealth of Massachusetts* v. *Hunt*, Massachusetts, 4 Metcalf 3 (1842).

7   Edwin E. Witte, *The Government in Labor Disputes* (New York: McGraw-Hill Book Company, 1932), p. 234.

8   Witte, "Early American Labor Cases," *op. cit.*, p. 827.

9   *In re Debs*, Petitioner, 158 U.S. 564 (1895).

10   *Gompers* v. *Bucks Stove and Range Company*, 221 U.S. 418 (1911).

11   Witte, *The Government in Labor Disputes, op. cit.*, p. 90.

12   *Hitchman Coal Company* v. *Mitchell*, 245 U.S. 229 (1917).

13   Joel Seidman, *The Yellow-Dog Contract* (Baltimore, Md.: Johns Hopkins Press, 1932). This is the seminal work on the yellow-dog contract.

14   The official name is *Loewe* v. *Lawlor*, 208 U.S. 274 (1908). However, this landmark case is commonly referred to as the *Danbury Hatters* case, for the factory in question was located in Danbury, Connecticut. In 1915, the dispute was tried once more in the Supreme Court. The second case is officially cited as *Lawlor* v. *Loewe*, 235 U.S. 522 (1915).

15   *Gompers* v. *Bucks Stove and Range Company, supra.*

16   Dallas L. Jones, "The Enigma of the Clayton Act," *Industrial and Labor Relations Review*, X, No. 2, January 1957, p. 221.

17   *Bedford Cut Stone Company* v. *Journeymen Stone Cutters Association*, 274 U.S. 37 (1927).

18   *American Steel Foundries* v. *Tri-City Central Trades Council*, 257 U.S. 184 (1921).

19   *Adair* v. *U.S.*, 208 U.S. 161 (1908).

20   *Coppage* v. *Kansas*, 236 U.S. 1 (1915).

21   *Truax* v. *Corrigan*, 257 U.S. 312 (1921).

22   301 U.S. 468 (1937).

23   303 U.S. 323 (1938).

24   House of Representatives, *Document No. 669*, 72d Congress, 1st sess., p. 3.

25   *United States* v. *Hutcheson*, 312 U.S. 219 (1941).

26   *Allen Bradley Company* v. *Local Union No. 3, IBEW*, 325 U.S. 797 (1945).

27   *Schecter Poultry Corporation* v. *United States*, 295 U.S. 495 (1935).

28   *Violations of Free Speech and Rights of Labor, Report of the Committee on Education and Labor*, pursuant to S. Res. 266, 74th Congress.

29   For an account of the Memorial Day tragedy, see La Follette Committee, *The Chicago Memorial Day Incident*, Report No. 46, Part II.

30   *NLRB* v. *Jones & Laughlin Steel Corporation*, 301 U.S. 1 (1937).

31   The Railway Labor Act was passed by Congress in 1926 and has been amended several times since then. It establishes an overall program to promote peaceful labor relations in the nation's railroads and airlines. Aside from protecting railroad and airline workers' unionized collective bargaining rights, it creates the National Mediation Service and emergency boards to encourage settlement of labor disputes.

32   *Carter* v. *Carter Coal Co.*, 298 U.S. 238 (1936).

33   Benjamin J. Taylor, *The Operation of the Taft-Hartley Act in Indiana* (Bloomington: Bureau of Business Research, Indiana University, 1967), p. 3.

34   National Labor Relations Board, *First Annual Report*, 1936, p. 86.

35   National Labor Relations Board, *Decisions and Orders of the National Labor Relations Board*, VII, 1936, p. 54.

36   *Riecke Metal Products Company*, 40 NLRB 867 (1942).

37   Fred Witney, *Wartime Experiences of the National Labor Relations Board, 1941—1945* (Urbana: University of Illinois Press, 1949), p. 21.

38   *Universal Fuels*, 298 NLRB No. 31 (1990).

39   National Labor Relations Board, *Third Annual Report*, 1938, p. 57.

40   *Republic Aviation Corp.* v. *NLRB*, 324 U.S. 793 (1945).

41   *ADCO Metals*, 281 NLRB 1300 (1986).

42   *Trover Clinic*, 280 NLRB 6 (1986).

43   *Burger King* v. *NLRB*, 725 F.2d 1053 (6th Cir. 1984). Actually in this case, the federal appeals court reversed the NLRB decision finding an unfair labor practice.

44   *Republic Aviation Corp., supra.*

45   *Livingston Shirt Corp. et al*, 107 NLRB 400 (1953).

46   *Highway Trailer Company*, 3 NLRB 591 (1937).

47   National Labor Relations Board, *Third Annual Report*, 1938, p. 115.

48   *Seas Shipping Co.*, 7 NLRB 873 (1938).

49   *Jackson Engineering Co.*, 265 NLRB 1688 (1983).

50   Arnold Perl, "Employment Involvement Groups: The Outcry Over NLRB's *Electromation* Decision," *Labor Law Journal*, v. 44, April 1993, p. 196.

51   Arthur A. Sloane and Fred Witney, *Labor Relations* (Englewood Cliffs, N.J.: Prentice Hall, 1994), p. 449.

52   *Electromation, Inc.*, 309 NLRB No. 163 (1992).

53   *John Ascuaga's Nugget*, 230 NLRB 275 (1977).

54   *National Labor Relations Board* v. *Cabot Carbon Company and Cabot Shops, Inc.*, 360 U.S. 203 (1959).

55   Perl, *op. cit.*, p. 195.

56   *AFL-CIO News*, June 14, 1993.

57   *E. I. DuPont De Nemours & Company*, 311 NLRB No. 88 (1993).

58   Office of General Counsel, *Memorandum GC 93-4, Guideline Memorandum Concerning Electromation, Inc.*, 309 NLRB No. 163 (1992).

59   *Textile Workers Union v. Darlington Mfg. Co.*, 380 U.S. 263 (1965).

60   251 NLRB 1083 (1980).

61   *NLRB* v. *Transportation Management Corp.*, 426 U.S. 393 (1983).

62   *Cox Fire Protection, Inc.*, 309 NLRB No. 108 (1992).

63   3 NLRB 10 (1937).

64   National Labor Relations Board, *Third Annual Report*, 1938, p. 97.

65   2 NLRB 39 (1936).

66   *H. J. Heinz Company* v. *NLRB*, 311 U.S. 514 (1941).

67   National Labor Relations Board, *Twelfth Annual Report*, 1947, p. 86.

68   *Ibid.*, pp. 83–90.

69   National Labor Relations Board, *Forty-first Annual Report*, 1976, p. 2.

70   National Labor Relations Board, *The First 50 Years. The Story of the National Labor Relations Board, 1935–1985*, p. 65.

2 ❧

The Taft-Hartley Act: An Overview

The Shift in Government Policy

On June 23, 1947, Congress overrode President Truman's veto and enacted the Taft-Hartley Act.[1] Officially styled the Labor-Management Relations Act, 1947, we shall call it by its popular name, Taft-Hartley. The law was far more controversial than both the Norris–La Guardia Act and the Wagner Act. This time, however, the positions of management and organized labor were reversed. Management defended the congressional action while organized labor denounced it. The controversy began while Congress was debating the law, and it intensified after the law's enactment. With the law's passage, management and labor joined in the battle with renewed vigor. Radio commentators, newspaper journalists, politicians, and students of industrial relations contributed their share to the controversy. The Taft-Hartley Act substantially changed the direction of industrial relations, and its effect was to produce a controversy never before known to follow the passage of a single labor law.

Literally hundreds of articles and tracts have been written on the law. By December 1, 1949, the National Labor Relations Board reported a bibliography on the legislation that included about 300 items. By no means did the list include all the material written or presented in speeches on the legislation. In scholarly publications, popular magazines, newspaper editorials, company and union tracts, public lectures, and radio debates, the people concerned with labor relations law analyzed the Taft-Hartley Act. If the legislation did nothing else, it underlined the importance of industrial relations law to the functioning of trade unions and the collective bargaining process.

Defenders of the legislation generally directed their arguments along the following lines: The law frees workers from the tyrannical hold of "union bosses"; it reduces the monopolistic position of labor unions; it protects the public from catastrophic strikes; it protects management from union abuses; it makes unions legally and financially responsible for their actions; it reduces communism within the union movement; it diminishes the power of "labor dictators"; and it promotes greater equality of bargaining power between management and labor. Additionally, defenders of the law, answering critics, vigorously argued that Taft-Hartley does not "enslave labor"; deprive workers of the legal protection of their right to self-organization and collective bargaining; destroy labor unions; reduce the bargaining power of labor unions; or interfere with the ability of labor to strike for better working conditions. Finally, the supporters of the law claimed that it "equalized" the legal position of employers and unions. The Wagner Act was appraised as one-sided, providing restrictions against unfair labor practices by management but imposing no restraints on labor unions. Taft-Hartley provided measures against union as well as employer unfair labor practices.

Shortly after the passage of Taft-Hartley, a major steel corporation supplied each of its employees with a letter defending the law. In part, it declared:

> The Taft-Hartley Act is designed to protect the rights of the *individual* worker. During the past few years the abuses of individual workers by some union bosses and some unions have become as great as those by the unscrupulous employers of the past era. The Taft-Hartley Act does *not* weaken the power of the Unions. It is aimed at assuring control of the Unions by the *individual* worker and protecting him [*sic*] from *abuse*—abuse in case he disagrees with his Union leaders.[2]

Organized labor regarded the Taft-Hartley Act in a much different light. Union representatives charged that it curtailed the opportunities for the effective operation of the collective bargaining process. They claimed that the law gave aid and comfort to the employer who showed little or no inclination to bargain collectively. It was charged that the law seriously interfered with the right of labor to strike. On the basis of this assertion, labor leaders denounced the statute as a "slave labor law," a claim that was vigorously denied by the law's supporters. New organizational drives, unions claimed, were made difficult or impossible by features of the statute. In general, labor leaders charged that the statute reduced the opportunities for effective collective bargaining, impaired free collective bargaining, promoted industrial strife, forestalled the expansion of unionism into new areas, and threatened the existence of the American labor union movement.

The executive board of the CIO declared, "The sponsors of this legislation have attempted to commit the perfect crime. They seek to destroy labor unions, to degrade living standards, to extinguish and to cripple the exercise of basic rights and forever to prevent the great mass of those whose needs are thus to be sacrificed to reaction and privilege from shaking off this yoke of want and depression."[3]

Not to be outdone by the CIO, the AFL condemned the Taft-Hartley Act in an equally vigorous manner. During the AFL convention of 1947, the Executive

Council of the Federation contended that the statute "seeks to weaken, render impotent, and destroy labor unions. It does so by striking a vital blow at free collective bargaining and substituting a process of government domination over employer-employee relationships."[4]

Factors in Passage

Though a variety of factors resulted in the adoption of the 1947 law, three were crucial. Some employers and their associations and other special-interest groups never accepted the philosophy of the Wagner Act. They were not inclined to feel favorable toward a law that gave effective legal support to the collective bargaining process. The success of the Wagner Act in promoting a strong and expanding union movement served to intensify efforts to destroy the legislation. From the year in which the statute was enacted until the passage of Taft-Hartley, each session of Congress was marked by organized efforts to repeal the Wagner Act.

With the growing strength of organized labor, the public became more aware of the abuses of the labor movement. Aspects of the closed shop, the boycott, strikes of questionable moral justification, discrimination of unions against minority groups, restrictions on output, and laxity in the administration of members' dues served to focus critical attention on the union movement. Actually, these features had been part of the union movement long before the passage of the Wagner Act. With the growing power of labor unions, however, these abuses took on greater proportions in the public mind. People who were basically antiunion made the most of union shortcomings to point to the general undesirability of unions and collective bargaining.

The critical observer of organized labor is well aware of this area of union conduct. As a matter of fact, this aspect of organized labor was recognized by many union leaders. A labor union publication had this to say about antisocial practices of labor organizations:

> Every national union official, as well as the intelligent membership of organized labor, knows there are some things wrong in the trade union movement. In this respect trade unions differ, and they differ in accordance with their age and history, with the attitude of the industry with which they deal, with the type of their membership, and with respect to other factors.[5]

After the end of World War II, a major strike wave hit the nation. In 1946, almost every major industry was shut down. It was by far the worst strike experience before 1946, and it still holds this dubious distinction. In that year, 4,985 strikes occurred, resulting in a record-making 116 million worker-days of lost production.

Actually, the strike wave was rooted in fundamental economic factors. With the end of the war, work-hours declined from a wartime average of 45 per week to a 1946 average of 40.4. At the same time, inflation occurred, particularly after Congress eliminated the wartime program of price and wage controls before industry had the opportunity to convert to peacetime production. In a period of six months, after June 1946, prices shot up by 15.04 percent. Caught between a reduction of take-home pay (shorter hours and rising prices), workers and their unions struck for higher rates of pay.

Another important factor resulted in the 1946 strike experience. During the war, the National War Labor Board in effect wrote the collective bargaining contracts, determining the conditions of employment. In any industry related to the war effort (which just about covered every industry), labor-management contract disputes were settled by the War Labor Board. During the war, it settled approximately 18,000 disputes covering about 12 million workers. Although many of the decisions were not popular with unions or employers, they accepted them to honor the no-strike pledge given by organized labor and the employers' pledge not to lock out. After the war, released from their pledge and from the constraints of compulsory arbitration, both sides engaged in industrial warfare to change conditions of employment imposed by the wartime agency.

In any event, the public, inconvenienced by the postwar strikes, was in a mood to change the direction of labor policy. As far as the public was concerned, unions and the Wagner Act were to blame for the strikes. It did not know or care why they occurred. Clearly, public attitude provided the environment for the passage of Taft-Hartley.

OPERATION OF TAFT-HARTLEY

Agency Reorganization: The General Counsel

Under the Wagner Act, the General Counsel was used by the Board as its legal advisor for directing litigation and supervising Board attorneys, except for the law judges. However, under Taft-Hartley, Congress placed sole responsibility to investigate and prosecute cases with an independent General Counsel, who is appointed by the President with Senate approval for a four-year term. The General Counsel plays a critical and powerful role in the operation of Taft-Hartley. *The Board can only decide cases that are generated by the General Counsel.* Thus, when the General Counsel refuses to issue an unfair labor practice complaint, the NLRB may not reverse the decision. As a matter of fact, if a charge filed by an employer, employee, or union is dismissed by the General Counsel, the charging party may not have the decision reversed by either the NLRB or the courts. *It has been held that the federal courts have no authority to review the day-to-day exercise of the discretion given to the General Counsel in the issuance of unfair labor practice complaints.*[6] In other words, should the General Counsel dismiss a charge, the party has no legal forum to appeal to for the reversal of the decision. Indeed, as recently as 1988, the U.S. Supreme Court again affirmed this policy.[7]

It declined to review a decision by a federal court of appeals that held that a decision of the General Counsel dismissing unfair labor practice charges was not subject to judicial review. The petitioner, an official of the National Right to Work Legal Defense Foundation, had argued that in dismissing the unfair labor practice charges, the General Counsel violated his due process and equal protection rights under the Fifth Amendment.

Of course, this does not mean that in practice the General Counsel will arbitrarily dismiss complaints. When conduct is arguably in violation of the statute as applied and interpreted by the NLRB and the courts, it is expected that a complaint will be issued.

In any event, the role of the General Counsel in the operation of Taft-Hartley cannot be overlooked. Some people may argue that a charging party should have the right to appeal to some legal forum when a General Counsel refuses to issue a complaint. As matters stand now, complaints can be generated only by the General Counsel, and the decision may not be upset by either the NLRB or the courts.

In determining the fundamental reason for the "split personality" in the enforcement of Taft-Hartley, one should recall the bitter criticism leveled against the NLRB during the Wagner Act years. In response to this criticism, Congress reduced the power of the Board by eliminating its investigation and prosecution functions. In any event, unique in federal law, Taft-Hartley is enforced by two separate and independent agencies. At this late date, after about five decades, it is not likely that Congress will bring Taft-Hartley into harmony with the way other federal laws are enforced. Nonetheless, serious doubt exists as to why Taft-Hartley should be singled out for special treatment in the matter of enforcement.

Union Unfair Labor Practices

The congressional attitude toward unions was expressed in important provisions of the Taft-Hartley Act that dealt with the following concerns: (1) union unfair labor practices, (2) the rights of employees as individuals, (3) the rights of employers, and (4) national emergency strikes. Other provisions dealt with internal union affairs, the termination or modification of existing labor contracts, and suits involving unions.

Six union unfair labor practices were identified by the Taft-Hartley Act. Labor organizations operating in interstate commerce were to refrain from the following practices: (1) restraining or coercing employees in the exercise of their guaranteed collective bargaining rights; (2) causing an employer to discriminate in any way against an employee in order to encourage or discourage union membership; (3) refusing to bargain in good faith with an employer regarding wages, hours, and other conditions of employment; (4) certain types of strikes and boycotts; (5) requiring employees covered by union-shop contracts to pay initiation fees or dues "in an amount which the Board finds excessive or discriminatory under all the circumstances"; and (6) "featherbedding," the requirement of payment by an employer for services not performed.

Two of the six provisions have perhaps had the greatest influence on collective bargaining—and undoubtedly a salutary one—since the enactment of Taft-Hartley. The first is the ban on union restraint or coercion of employees in the exercise of their guaranteed bargaining rights, which also entails a union obligation to avoid coercion of employees who choose to refrain from collective bargaining altogether. What constitutes such restraint or coercion? The myriad of rulings rendered by the NLRB and the courts since 1947 has at least indicated that such union actions as the following will always run the risk of being found "unfair": communicating to an antiunion employee that the employee will lose her or his job should the union gain recognition; the signing of an agreement with an employer that recognizes the union as exclusive bargaining representative when in fact it lacks majority employee support; picket-line violence; and threats of reprisal against employees subpoenaed to testify against the union at NLRB hearings.

The second Taft-Hartley provision makes it an unfair practice for a union to cause an employer to discriminate against an employee in order to influence union membership. There is a single exception to this prohibition. Under a valid union-shop agreement, the union may lawfully demand the discharge of an employee who fails to pay the initiation fee and periodic dues. Otherwise, however, unions must exercise complete self-control in this area. They cannot try to force employers to fire or otherwise penalize workers for any other reason, whether these reasons involve worker opposition to union policies, failure to attend union meetings, or refusal to join the union at all. Nor can a union lawfully seek to persuade an employer to grant hiring preference to employees who are "satisfactory" to the union. Subject only to the union-shop proviso, Taft-Hartley sought to place nonunion workers on a footing equal to that of union employees.

Another restriction on union practices pertains to union refusal to bargain. This third Taft-Hartley restriction extended to labor organizations the same obligation that the Wagner Act had already imposed on employers. Prior to 1947, it was widely publicized that some unions merely presented employers with a list of demands on a take-it-or-leave-it basis. To many observers, however, the law's inclusion of this union bargaining provision has meant very little. Unions can normally be expected to pursue bargaining rather than attempt to avoid it. Nevertheless, the NLRB has used this provision to some extent in the years since Taft-Hartley to narrow the scope of permissible union action. The Board has, for example, found it unlawful under this section for a union to strike against an employer who continues to negotiate on a multiemployer basis with the goal of forcing it to bargain independently. It has also found that a union's refusal to bargain on an employer proposal for a written contract violates this part of the law. In short, some inequities seem to have been corrected by this good-faith bargaining provision.

The fourth unfair union practice has given rise to considerable litigation. Indeed, of all six Taft-Hartley union prohibitions, the ban on certain types of strikes and boycotts has proven the most difficult to interpret. Even as "clarified" by Congress in 1959, this area remains a particularly difficult one for labor lawyers.

Briefly, Section 8(b)(4) of the 1947 act prohibited unions from striking or boycotting if such actions have any of the following three objectives: (1) forcing an employer or self-employed person to join any labor or employer organization or to cease dealing with another employer (secondary boycott); (2) compelling recognition as employee bargaining agent from another employer without NLRB certification; (3) forcing an employer to assign particular work to a particular craft.

Particularly in regard to the secondary boycott provision, it does not take much imagination to predict where heated controversy could arise. To constitute a secondary boycott, the union's action must be waged against "another" employer, one who is entirely a neutral in the battle and is merely caught as a pawn in the union's battle with the real object of its concern. But when is the secondary employer really neutral and when is it in fact an ally of the primary employer? The Board has sometimes ruled against employers alleging themselves to be "secondary" on the grounds of common ownership with the "primary" employer and, again, when "struck work" has been turned over by primary employers to secondary ones. But Board and court rulings here have not been entirely consistent.

In its other clauses, too, the Taft-Hartley strike and boycott provisions have led to intense legal battles. When is a union, for example, unlawfully seeking recognition without NLRB certification, and when is it merely picketing to protest undesirable working conditions, a normally legal action? Is a union ever entitled to try to keep within its bargaining unit work that has traditionally been performed by the unit employees? On some occasions, but not all, the Board has ruled that there is nothing wrong with this.

Last—and least in the magnitude of their effect—stand the relatively unenforceable provisions relating to union fees and dues and featherbedding.

The fifth union unfair practice prohibits charging workers covered by union-shop agreements excessive or discriminatory dues or initiation fees. The provision includes a stipulation that the NLRB should consider "all the circumstances" in determining discrimination or excess. Such circumstances, the wording of the Taft-Hartley Act continues, include "the practices and customs of labor organizations in the particular industry and the wages currently paid to the employees affected." Without further yardsticks and depending almost exclusively on the sentiments of individual employees rather than on irate employers for enforcement, this part of the Act has had little practical value. In one of the relatively few such cases to come before it thus far, the Board ruled that increasing an initiation fee from $75 to $250, and thus charging new members the equivalent of about four weeks' wages when other unions in the area charged only about one-eighth of this amount, was unlawful. In another case, it was held that the union's uniform requirement of a reinstatement fee for ex-members that was higher than the initiation fee for new members was *not* discriminatory under the Act.

The sixth and final unfair labor practice for unions has proved even less influential in governing collective bargaining. Taft-Hartley prohibits unions from engaging in featherbedding. The Board has ruled that this provision does *not* prevent labor organizations from seeking *actual* employment for their members, "even in situations where the employer does not want, does not need, and is not willing to accept such services." The NLRB was upheld by the U.S. Supreme Court in 1952 when it ruled that the antifeatherbedding provision applied only if there was payment for services not performed or not to be performed. The high court said that the law leaves to collective bargaining the determination of what work shall be included as compensable services. Mainly because of this interpretation, the antifeatherbedding provision has had little effect. A union would be quite willing to have work performed with the question of need irrelevant. Employer representatives of some industries—entertainment and the railroads, in particular—have succeeded in convincing the public that their unwanted—but performing—workers are featherbedding, but under the current interpretation of the law, such practices are not illegal.

The Rights of Employees

In other areas, the Act attempted to even the scales of collective bargaining and the alleged injustices of the 1935–1947 period. Taft-Hartley, unlike the Wagner Act, recognized a need to protect the rights of individual employees against labor organizations. It explicitly amended the 1935 legislation to give employees the right to *refrain from*, as well as engage in, collective bargaining activities. It also dealt more directly with the question of individual freedoms—even beyond outlawing of the closed shop, union coercion, union-caused employer discrimination against employees, and excessive union fees.

Taft-Hartley provided that should any state wish to pass legislation more restrictive of union security than the closed shop (or, in other words, to outlaw labor contracts that make union membership a condition of retaining employment), the state was free to do so. Some states have enacted legislation to restrict the range of permissible union security. Many states—mainly in the South and Southwest—now have so-called "right-to-work laws." Advocates of such laws have claimed that compulsory unionism violates the basic American right of freedom of association. Opponents of right-to-work laws have pointed out that among other arguments, majority rule is inherent in our democratic procedure. Thus far, however, there has been an impressive correlation between stands on this particular question and attitudes about the values of unionism in general. Individuals opposed to collective bargaining have favored right-to-work laws with amazing regularity. Pro-unionists seem to have been equally consistent in their attacks on such legislation.

Also designed to strengthen workers' rights as individuals was a Taft-Hartley provision allowing any employee the right to present grievances directly to the employer without union intervention. The union's representative was to have a chance to be present at such employer-employee meetings, but the normal grievance procedure, in which the union actively participated, would be suspended. Few employees have thus far availed themselves of this opportunity. Clearly, the action can antagonize the union and, since the employer's action is normally being challenged by the grievance itself, the employee usually prefers to work with the union.

Finally, the Act placed a major restriction on the dues checkoff arrangement. Many employers had been deducting union dues from their employees' paychecks and remitting them to the union. Companies were thus spared the constant visits of dues-collecting union representatives at the workplace; unions had also found the checkoff an efficient means of collection. Under Taft-Hartley, the checkoff was to remain legal, but only if the individual employee had given authorization in writing. Moreover, such an authorization could not be irrevocable for a period of more than one year. This restriction has hardly hampered the growth of the checkoff. Currently, the arrangement is provided for in approximately 80 percent of all labor contracts, compared to an estimated 40 percent at the time of Taft-Hartley passage.

The Rights of Employers

In a third area, Taft-Hartley circumscribed freedom of action of unions in the quest for industrial relations equity. It explicitly gave employers certain collective bargaining rights. For example, although employers were still required to recognize and bargain with properly certified unions, they had more freedom of expression to their views concerning union organization, so long as there was "no threat of reprisal or force or promise of benefit."

Thus, an employer may now, when faced with a representation election, tell employees that unions are worthless, dangerous to the economy, and immoral. Employers may even, generally speaking, hint that the permanent closing of the plant would be the possible aftermath of a union election victory and subsequent high union wage demands. Nor will an election be set aside if employers play upon the racial prejudices of their workers (should these exist) by describing the union's philosophy toward integration, or if they set forth the union's record in regard to violence and corruption (should this record be vulnerable) and suggest that these characteristics would be logical consequences of the union's victory in its plant—although in recent years the Board has attempted to draw the line between dispassionate statements on the employer's part and inflammatory or emotional appeals. An imaginative employer can in fact now engage in almost any amount of creative speaking or writing for employees' consumption. The only major restraint on employers' conduct is that they must avoid threats, promises, coercion, and direct interference with worker-voters in the reaching of their decisions.

Under this section of Taft-Hartley, employers can also (1) call for elections to decide questions of representation; (2) refuse to bargain with supervisors' unions (the Wagner Act protection was withdrawn for these employees, although they are not prohibited from forming or joining unions *without* the NLRB machinery and other safeguards of public policy); and (3) file their unfair labor practice charges against unions.

National Emergency Strikes

Of most direct interest to the general public, but of practical meaning only to those employers whose labor relations can be interpreted as affecting the national health or safety, are the national emergency strike provisions that were enacted in 1947. As in the case of most Taft-Hartley provisions, these remain unchanged to this day.

Sections 206 through 210 of the Act provide for government intervention in the case of such emergencies. If the President of the United States believes that a threatened or actual strike affects "an entire industry or a substantial part thereof" in such a way as to "imperil the national health or safety," he or she is empowered to take certain carefully delineated action. The President may appoint a Board of Inquiry to find out and report the facts regarding the dispute. The Board is allowed subpoena authority and can thus compel the appearance of witnesses. It cannot, however, make recommendations for a settlement. On receiving the Board's preliminary report, the President may apply through the Attorney General for a court injunction restraining the strike for sixty days. If no settlement is reached during this time, the injunction can be extended for another twenty days, during which period employees are to be polled in a secret-ballot election on their willingness to accept the employer's last offer. The Board then submits its final report to the President. The injunction expires on the eightieth day, and a strike may lawfully take place. Should the strike threat still exist after all these procedures, the President is authorized to submit a full report to Congress, "with such recommendations as he may see fit to make for consideration and appropriate action."

By 1995, the national emergency provisions of the law had been invoked thirty-four times, and twenty-seven injunctions had been issued. On five occasions, the Presidents did not elect to seek injunctions and were turned down twice by the federal district courts on the grounds that the strikes did not imperil the national health or safety. Much of the earlier excitement and controversy about this feature of Taft-Hartley has subsided. The last attempt to use it was in 1977 when a federal court refused President Carter's request for an injunction in a coal strike. An injunction was issued for the last time in 1972. The major explanation is attributable to the lessening power of labor organizations within industries in which injunctions were previously issued. For example, in 1993 only about 30 percent of the coal industry was organized, whereas in John L. Lewis's time it was about 95 percent. Given these circumstances, the national emergency dispute provisions of Taft-Hartley are more or less a relic of labor relations law, making unnecessary an extensive analysis of the experience of former years. Except for a monumental increase in union membership within industries in which injunctions were issued, they will probably not be used in the future.

UNFAIR LABOR PRACTICE PROCEDURE

Informal Proceedings

Day-to-day operations under Taft-Hartley take place in the NLRB regional offices located in most large cities. In each region are the regional director, attorneys, field examiners, and supporting staff. When an employee, union, or employer believes a violation of the law has occurred, the complainant files a *charge* in the region in which the alleged unfair labor practice occurred. Unlike some other federal agencies, the NLRB does not search for business. It neither solicits unfair labor practice charges nor seeks petitions for elections. Taft-Hartley operates only when charges or election petitions are filed.

With the charge filed, normally a field examiner investigates the case. (Field examiners need not be attorneys, which provides employment opportunities for college graduates who are interested in labor relations but are not lawyers.) Witnesses are interviewed in person or by telephone depending on the circumstances, and material documents are examined. Board agents may subpoena documents or witnesses should that be necessary.

After the investigation, the regional director may dismiss the charge as being without merit or urge the complainant to withdraw it. In a typical year, most of the charges are either dismissed or withdrawn, making further action under the law unnecessary. In 1990, 34.8 percent were dismissed and 30.3 percent were withdrawn.[8] At this writing, the most recent *Annual Report* of the NLRB is 1990.

To avoid further proceedings, the regional director may effect an informal settlement of the dispute. All settlements, however, must be approved by the regional office. Assume an employee is unlawfully discharged for union activities, and the employer and employee agree to back pay, but not reinstatement. Assuming the regional director approves their agreement, the case is dismissed on that basis. In 1990, 30.1 percent of all charges were settled by the parties.[9] In other words, only about 5 percent of unfair labor practice cases require subsequent formal proceedings.

Formal Proceedings: Complaint and Hearing

Should the parties refuse to settle, or should the regional director rule that a settlement would not be proper, a *complaint* is issued, assuming, of course, that the regional office is satisfied a violation of the law has occurred. It is issued by the regional director on behalf of the General Counsel, specifying the alleged violation, provision(s) of the law involved and notifying all concerned of the time and place of the hearing.

The *hearing* is a formal trial and is presided over by an administrative law judge, an agent of the five-member Board in Washington, not of the General Counsel. It is conducted in accordance with the rules of evidence and procedure that apply in the U.S. district courts. After the hearing, the law judge issues a decision. If a violation is found, the decision includes an appropriate remedy. Any party that disagrees with the law judge's decision may appeal to the Board in Washington within twenty days. The NLRB has full power over the decisions issued by the law judges. It may adopt the decision in whole or in part, or reverse it in whole or in part. In rare cases, the Board may direct the law judge to conduct a new hearing. As required by law, the NLRB must review each administrative law judge's decision appealed to it.

In the majority of cases, a respondent complies with the Board's decision and order. If the respondent does not comply, the Board may seek enforcement of its order through a U.S. court of appeals. Similarly, the party charged with a violation of the unfair labor practice provisions may also appeal the Board's decision to a U.S. court of appeals. Likewise, appeals by the General Counsel may be made if the Board reverses a law judge's decision. If there is dissatisfaction with the circuit court decision, requests may be made to the U.S. Supreme Court for review. Once a circuit court order is finalized (by failure to seek review or denial thereof by the Supreme Court), the party charged must obey the Board order or face contempt-of-court proceedings.

Quality of Service: Unfair Labor Practice Cases

The issue here is whether the NLRB provides prompt and effective enforcement of the unfair labor practice provisions of Taft-Hartley. In this regard, a central proposition is of material importance. Until 1982, the growth in the case load under the law was spectacular. Possibly no other federal law has produced such a massive increase in the number of cases handled by the NLRB.

Consider, for example, the ten-year period between 1970 and 1980. In 1970, the total case load under Taft-Hartley (unfair labor practice charges and election cases) amounted to 33,581.[10] By 1980, the NLRB case load had increased to 57,381.[11] In 1970, 21,038 unfair labor practice charges were filed and 12,543 election petitions submitted. In 1980, employers, unions, and employees filed 44,063 unfair labor practice charges, and 12,701 election cases were submitted. It is evident that the major source of the increased case load was generated by the filing of unfair labor practice charges.

In assessing the reasons for the tremendous growth in the case load, it would not be accurate to conclude that the increase occurred because the law had been broadened to include union activity. Such a reason would explain why the case load increased immediately after Taft-Hartley was enacted, but note that the increase in the number of cases occurred *during* the operation of Taft-Hartley. Undoubtedly, one reason for the increase was intensified union activity and growing employer resistance to organization. As union membership in the United States declined as a percentage of the organizable labor force, the unions, to maintain their position, engaged in more vigorous organizational activity. In many instances, however, employers have resisted organization. When these two factors are meshed, the dramatic increase in Taft-Hartley activity is understandable. Other reasons have been advanced for the phenomenon, including greater public awareness of the operation of the law; more labor lawyers who stimulate usage of the law; some new NLRB jurisdiction policies that have served to expand the coverage of the law; the addition of the health-care industry to NLRB jurisdiction in July 1974; and inadequate penalties that encourage additional violations.[12]

Starting in 1982, however, the NLRB case load began to decline, and by 1990 it had decreased to a total of 41,507 cases.[13] Unfair labor practice cases dropped to 33,833 and election cases to 7,674. The case load in 1990 was the lowest since the early 1970s. In accounting for the decline, the major factor was the decreased union organizational activity. Earlier we indicated the difficulty unions have encountered in organizing new members in the modern era. When organizational effort slackens, or proves unsuccessful, less need exists for NLRB services. Another factor involves the so-called General Counsel's Information Officer program instituted in the 1980s. Under this program, regional offices advise unions, employers, and employees of potential violations of the law. Rosemary Collyer, former General Counsel, attributed some of the decline to this effort, saying that "the continued success of the General Counsel's Information Officer program [where] regional personnel assist members of the public to ascertain whether their concerns come within the jurisdiction of the NLRB . . ." explains part of the decline.[14]

Another factor involves boycott of the NLRB by unions during the Reagan years because they felt the Board was unfair to them. On this issue, the *Wall Street Journal* reported that "some unions are boycotting the conservative Board due to rulings they view unfair."[15] Some of those Reagan Board decisions will be discussed later in this volume. Only time will tell whether the decline in the NLRB case load in the 1980s represents a permanent condition or a temporary aberration.

Time Delay

Whatever the future may bring in terms of case load, the NLRB quality of service will still be of paramount importance. The procedure under the law is too slow and reflects the maxim "Justice delayed is justice undone." Consider the following chart demonstrating the time involved at each stage of the unfair labor practice procedures for 1990.[16]

Stage	Median Days
1. Filing of charge to issuance of complaint	48
2. Complaint to close of hearing	154
3. Close of hearing to issuance of administrative law judge's decision	155
4. Administrative law judge's decision to issuance of Board decision	318
5. Filing of charge to issuance of Board decision	688

Not all cases, of course, are appealed to the NLRB. They may be disposed of at earlier levels in the procedure. Nonetheless, should a case reach the Board, it took 688 *median days* from the filing of the charge to the NLRB decision.

With such a long delay, it is easy to understand why the interests of employers, employees, and unions are adversely affected. For example, an employer may be required to pay a huge amount in back pay awards, a penalty particularly harmful to a small employer. Employees discharged in violation of the law must wait an unreasonable length of time before they receive a remedy, and a union's organizational campaign may collapse while waiting for a decision from the NLRB. Commenting on this problem, a House of Representatives Committee stated:

> The National Labor Relations Board is in a crisis. Delays in decision-making at the Board level and a staggering and debilitating case backlog have [resulted] in workers being forced to wait years before cases affecting their livelihood and the economic well-being of their families are decided. We have reached a point where legal rights given to employees under the National Labor Relations Act are in jeopardy because of the Board's failure to issue timely decisions. Delays by the Board in deciding cases also impact adversely on employers since a company's potential monetary liability rises while the case is pending before the Board.[17]

At a House subcommittee session held in 1990, Chairperson Tom Lantos, California, compared the NLRB to the Bermuda Triangle, where people and things mysteriously disappear. "If there were a board game," said Lantos, "about collective bargaining, union organizing and workers' rights, one of the cards should read 'your case has been appealed [to] the NLRB in Washington—lose five turns.' "[18]

To be fair about it, however, the current NLRB has improved in one part of its work. In 1987, the backlog of cases pending before the NLRB for two or more years was 300. By 1991, the number dropped to only 10 cases.[19] Obviously, this was a spectacular improvement and hopefully a harbinger of similar improvement for other areas of case processing.

Dealing with the Problem

To reduce delay at the NLRB level, Presidents should not allow vacancies on the Board to remain unfilled for a long period of time. For example, Board Member Howard Jenkins left the agency on August 27, 1983, but Reagan did not replace him until March 1985. In January 1990, there were only *two* active members serving on the Board.[20] Indeed, a reason for the agency's slowness was that the NLRB was operating short-handed. Increasing the number of members to seven or nine would expedite the Board's decisions. To speed up its work, the agency should also establish reasonable timetables for deciding cases. In addition, the Board should take action to curb attorneys who file excessive and frivolous exceptions for the sole purpose of causing delay. As a congressional committee put it: The Board should consider disciplinary action against repeat offenders who seek to abuse the Board's processes.[21]

Though these recommendations and the improvement of other internal procedures would reduce delay, a major change in method is not within the power of the NLRB but requires the approval of Congress. Under Taft-Hartley, *the NLRB must review each unfair labor practice administrative law judge decision appealed to it*. In 1990, the Board issued a total of 1,352 decisions: 794 unfair labor practice cases, and 558 election cases.[22]

For many years, it has been proposed that the NLRB should have the authority to refuse to review cases appealed from the administrative law judge; that is, the decision of the law judge would be final unless the NLRB at its discretion elected to review it. Should Congress approve this change in procedure, it would reduce by about a year the processing of those unfair labor practice cases that the NLRB does not elect to review. Under this kind of authority, the NLRB would review only those cases that would be precedent-making, or those cases decided in a manner inconsistent with the policies established by the Board or the courts. These kinds of cases would represent only a small portion of the cases that the Board must now review. This proposal would also serve to reduce substantially the NLRB backlog of cases pending before it.

As many NLRB officials had previously recommended, former Chair Betty S. Murphy advocated that Congress provide the Board with the authority to refuse to review all unfair labor practice cases appealed to the agency. She said that the present system of automatic review was not "a good use of the taxpayers' money."[23]

At this writing, Congress has still refused to enact the necessary legislation. Congress's refusal seems strange, because since 1959 the NLRB has had the power to refuse to review election cases referred to it from decisions of regional directors. Whatever the reason for the refusal of Congress to treat all kinds of cases in the same way, it is not in the public interest to force the NLRB to review every unfair labor practice case appealed to it.

The time delay becomes even more serious when Board decisions are appealed to the courts. After the NLRB issues a decision, a dissatisfied party may appeal to a federal court of appeals and may then elect to have the U.S. Supreme Court review the case. When this occurs, the delay between the filing of the unfair labor practice charge and the ultimate decision of the federal courts is increased significantly. It is not unusual for the courts to take several years before they dispose of a case.

Compounding this problem is that many NLRB decisions are appealed to the courts. As the Board stated:

> The National Labor Relations Board is involved in more litigation in the United States Courts of Appeals than in any other federal administrative agency. In 1990, 161 cases involving the NLRB were decided by federal appeals courts compared with 180 in 1989.[24]

In a typical year, about 50 percent of all NLRB unfair labor practice decisions are appealed to the courts.[25]

Normally, NLRB decisions are sustained by the federal courts. On the average, they have been sustained in whole or in part in about 85 percent of the cases. One explanation for this excellent batting average, however, is that the NLRB is selective in the cases that it allows to be appealed to the courts. In other words, the agency generally will select only cases that have a reasonable opportunity for success.

REPRESENTATION ELECTION PROCEDURE

The Investigation

Representation cases must also follow a prescribed procedure before the Board is empowered to intervene and conduct elections. Representation elections are initiated by the filing of a petition. The petition may be for the purpose of obtaining initial recognition of a union or to decertify the existing bargaining agent. The regional office is authorized to make an investigation of the petition.

An investigation is conducted in order to obtain information about the following: (1) whether the employer's operations meet the Board's jurisdictional standards; (2) the appropriateness of the unit of employees for purposes of collective bargaining (employees are grouped into units where similar interests exist); (3) the sufficiency of employee interest in representation by a labor organization (an election will usually be conducted by the Board if at least 30 percent of the employees indicate an interest in representation); and (4) whether the petition was filed at the proper time. An election may not be conducted if a valid election has been held during the preceding twelve-month period.

Representation petitions may be disposed of before a hearing by the same methods used in closing unfair labor practice cases—by withdrawal, dismissal, or settlement. If the petition has merit and no arrangements for a consent or stipulated election have been made, the parties are entitled to a hearing, normally conducted by a field examiner. The law entitles the parties to a representation hearing, which is a formal proceeding designed to obtain information to aid the regional director in deciding the adequacy of the petition. The regional director must make a decision on the appropriateness of the bargaining unit, the timeliness of the petition, the sufficiency of employee interest, and other pertinent matters. The hearing is not held if the parties enter into a *consent election* agreement, since the matters that must be resolved in the hearing are voluntarily resolved by the parties.

Consent elections have the advantage of being conducted much faster than those that require formal hearings. Also, when the parties consent to an election, the work load of the regional office is reduced. In 1962, 46 percent of all NLRB elections were of the consent variety. By 1993, the percentage dropped to only about 1 percent.[26]

The decline was largely attributable to employers who did not want to relinquish the right to object to elections won by unions. Understand that when the parties consent to an election, neither the union nor employer may object to the election results. Under these circumstances, the parties waive the right to appeal.

Instead of consenting to elections, the parties frequently agree to a *stipulated* election. Under this practice, no hearing is held, but the parties may exercise the right to object to a stipulated election after an election is held. For example, suppose the election were held permitting a certain classification to vote, say supervisors who perform some bargaining-unit work. The union wins the election. Now the employer objects to the result on the grounds that the working supervisors' votes should not have been counted. Of course, should the employees reject the union, the employer would not object.

When the parties neither consent to an election nor agree to a stipulated election, the regional director must determine the controversial issues involved in an election case.

In hearing cases, the regional director reviews the record of the hearing and resolves eligibility, appropriateness of unit, and other requirements and then either directs an election or dismisses the petition. The decision may be appealed to the Board in Washington. In 1959, Congress authorized the NLRB to refuse to review decisions of the regional directors, and in 1961, the Board implemented this new power. Thus, the NLRB has the discretion to review or not to review appeals from the regional directors. In practice, the Board does not accept many cases for review. Those would be cases that present precedent-making issues; those in which the regional directors made grievous errors in applying NLRB or court policies (not a likely event, given the expertise of regional directors); or those in which a party charges that the hearing was not conducted in a fair manner.

Election Supervision

Field examiners supervise the secret-ballot elections after elections are ordered by the regional director or consented to by the parties. Representatives of both employers and unions are entitled to observe the procedure and to challenge any employee who applies for a ballot. Challenges must be based on "reasonable cause." When the election results depend on the challenged ballots, the regional director must conduct an investigation and make a decision on the challenged votes.

Employer or union conduct affecting an election may be subject to objections within ten days after the ballots are counted. Such objections must be investigated by the regional director, and if they are found to be justified, an election may be set aside and a new one ordered. This depends on the nature of the issues and the type of consent agreement executed by the parties. Challenges and objections might or might not be resolved on the basis of the investigation without a hearing. Depending on the circumstances, the ultimate decision on challenges or objections will be made by the regional director or the Board.

A representation petition may be withdrawn at any time—before the hearing, after the hearing, or after an election has been ordered by the regional director or the Board. Once the election has been conducted and all the problems associated with it have been settled, its outcome must be certified. A certification of representatives occurs when a labor organization wins an election. Following certification of representatives, in the absence of an appeal, an employer is obligated to enter collective bargaining negotiations with the appropriate union. Should the labor organization lose, however, there is no certification of results and the employer is not required to bargain.

Quality of Service: Election Cases

The promptness of the election following the filing of the petition depends upon the kind of poll involved. A consent election could be held in a short time, say ten to fifteen days, following the petition. As noted, however, consent elections are rarely held; the parties usually select the stipulated election which in 1993 accounted for about 80 percent of all NLRB elections.[27] When a party exercises its right to object to the results of a poll based upon stipulation, the regional director will review the case and make a recommendation to the NLRB. The NLRB ultimately resolves the controversy involved in the election. This, of course, takes time; in 1990, it took on the average 314 days from the filing of the petition until such time as the Board's decision was issued.[28] Should the regional director order an election, in 1990 it consumed on the average 44 days from the petition until the decision was made. Should an election be directed by the Board or regional director, the actual poll normally is held in a short time. The delay is not in the mechanics of the election; it is waiting for the NLRB's or the regional director's decision.

No question exists that the election process is taking more time. In 1962, 60 percent of all NLRB elections were held within a month or two following the filing of the election petition.[29] By 1993, the percentage had dropped to 34 percent. Delay in the election could favor either the employer or union depending upon the circumstances of a particular case. If the union needs more time to convince employees to vote for it, delay would favor the union. On the other hand, if the employer needs more time to undermine the majority status of the union, delay would obviously favor the employer.

In general, the greater the delay the more likely the union will lose the election. When the poll is conducted within a month or two following the filing of the election petition, unions win about 57 percent of the elections. When elections are held within five or six months, union victories drop to about 46 percent.[30]

Fairness to all concerned would demonstrate that elections be held as quickly as possible after a petition is filed, while recognizing the rights of employers and unions to raise legitimate issues. As noted earlier, Congress took a big step in this direction when in 1959 it authorized the NLRB to refuse to review the decisions of regional directors in election cases. Starting in 1961, the Board took advantage of this authority and delegated to the regional directors the power to make the final decisions in all matters in controversy. For example, regional directors have the final authority to decide which employees would be eligible to vote when this issue is in conflict between the parties. When the Board was required to review all decisions of the regional directors before an election could take place, it is easy to understand why there was often an interminable delay before the poll was conducted. In some cases, a year or more would elapse between the filing of the election petition and the holding of the election. Of course, even under the present situation, there could be long delays when the NLRB elects to review a decision of a regional director. During 1990, as noted, these elections were held in approximately 314 days.[31] However, as stated, the NLRB agrees to review only a small portion of the cases appealed to it by a party dissatisfied with a regional director's decision.

It would be in the interest of all concerned to hold *directed elections* as quickly as possible. This objective could be accomplished by proceeding to an election promptly after the filing of a petition and before a hearing takes place. Then, after the election, a dissatisfied party could raise issues that might result in a decision by a regional director or the NLRB to set aside the results of an election and order a new one, or even to rule that another election not take place. By cutting out the hearing that must now automatically take place, a new procedure would allow the election to be held promptly after the filing of a petition. Under such circumstances, the regional director could establish the ground rules of the election. Should a party be dissatisfied with the determinations, a protest could be made after the election.

Not only would the elimination of automatic hearings before elections improve the speed with which polls are conducted, but it would prevent a party from demanding a hearing just to delay an election. At times employers or unions invoke the hearing for that purpose and raise frivolous issues in the hearing. As matters stand now, it would require approval from Congress to eliminate the compulsory preelection hearing. On this issue, a blue-ribbon Task Force, appointed by former Chair Betty Murphy to improve the quality of service of the agency, said:

> The Task Force is informed that recommendations have been made to Congress that the statute be amended to permit elections without hearings in certain situations. The Task Force sees no way that such elections can be directed under the present statute, and therefore any recommendations by the Task Force would be beyond its jurisdiction.[32]

ENFORCEMENT PROCEDURES

Penalties under Law

When the NLRB determines that the law has been violated, it orders the offender to cease and desist engaging in the conduct. For example, it may order an employer to stop interfering with the right of employees to engage in union activities. When the union is held in violation, the Board may, for example, order the union to cease and desist engaging in an illegal secondary boycott. However, understand that *Taft-Hartley does not provide for criminal penalties or fines when the law is violated.*

Unions in particular claim that the remedies and penalties of Taft-Hartley are inadequate. They say employer violations of the law are encouraged because of knowledge of weak penalties. One union officer put it this way:

> The flagrant union-busting actions by southern textile manufacturers demonstrated that the intent of the law could be frustrated at relatively little cost by employers who refused to accept collective bargaining.
>
> Nowhere is the evidence of cold-blooded and illegal anti-union activity by an employer more shocking, more preponderant, more repeatedly proven before the NLRB and the courts than in the case of J. P. Stevens.[33]

Proposed Changes

During the Carter years, Congress came very close to enacting amendments to Taft-Hartley that would have made enforcement of the law more effective. Under this Carter-supported Labor Law Reform Act of 1977, the NLRB would have been required to seek a court order to reinstate immediately an employee when there existed reasonable grounds to believe he or she was discharged for union activities during an organizational campaign. Thus, the employee would not have to wait until the entire procedure of the law was exhausted. In addition, to make it more expensive for employers to violate the law and deter discharges during organizational campaigns, the employee so discharged would have received double back pay when the NLRB directed reinstatement.

Speedy reinstatement of employees discharged for union activities during an organizing campaign by a court order would eliminate the long delays that have taken place in some cases. The classic example of this situation was involved in the illegal closing of the Darlington, South Carolina, mill of the Deering Milliken textile chain. In the previous chapter, we learned that the mill was shut down illegally after the Textile Workers Union won an election. The shutdown occurred in 1956, which resulted in 556 employees losing their jobs. Though the NLRB and the U.S. Supreme Court ordered back pay for these employees, they did not receive any compensation until August 1981, *twenty-five years* after the illegal closing of the plant. At that time, the former employees or their heirs (about one hundred had died in the interim) received $5 million to distribute among them.[34]

Under the Carter-supported Labor Law Reform Act of 1977, an employer found to have willfully violated a final order of the NLRB or a federal court might have been barred from obtaining contracts from the U.S. government for up to three years. An exception could have been made for national defense reasons. With respect to J. P. Stevens, Textile Workers' President Stetin noted that although this company had violated the law on repeated occasions, it had received contracts from the federal government for more than $100 million.[35]

In October 1977, the House of Representatives enacted the measure, but in the summer of 1978, the Senate failed to pass it because of a filibuster carried on by the law's opponents. Only two votes in the Senate were lacking to end the filibuster.

In November 1983, a congressional committee reported favorably on a bill that would have denied for three years federal government contracts to employers who willfully violated orders of the National Labor Relations Board.[36] However, the bill received no further consideration and was not enacted.

"Make-Whole" Remedy Controversy

Unions also charge that Taft-Hartley remedies are inadequate when an employer violates its obligation to bargain in good faith. When this occurs, the normal NLRB remedy is to direct the employer to comply with the law and bargain with the union. However, this kind of remedy might be of no practical value, since an employer may continue the illegal conduct. In addition, such a Board order does not remedy the losses to employees who were placed at a disadvantage because of the employer's illegal conduct. These considerations prompted a union to request from the NLRB a more meaningful remedy to enforce the national policy.

In *Ex-Cell-O*,[37] an employer refused to bargain collectively for a long period of time after the union was victorious in a representation election. The union requested that the NLRB order the employer to pay to the employees the wages and fringe benefits that they would arguably have obtained through collective bargaining had the employer bargained in good faith. An administrative law judge agreed with the union. In March 1967, two years after the union had been certified as the legal bargaining agent, he stated:

> Employers who promptly comply with their obligations are placed at an economic disadvantage and flouters of the national policy are financially rewarded. These results are completely antithetical to the purposes of the law and call for a remedy which will help restore the situation to that which would have existed but for the unfair labor practices.

Accordingly, the judge not only ruled that the firm must bargain with the union but also directed that it compensate the employees for the money value of the improved wages and benefits that it would be reasonable to conclude that the union would have been able to secure through collective bargaining except for the firm's refusal to bargain. To compute the amount due the employees, the law judge was prepared to compare the wages and benefits received in the plant in question with those prevailing in other plants owned by the company in the area, whose employees were covered by labor agreements negotiated by the same national union. To implement such a "make-whole" remedy, other formulas for computation could be devised.

In other words, the objective of the law judge's decision was to take the profit out of stalling in collective bargaining, making it expensive for a firm to refuse to bargain in good faith. Whatever delight the employees and union received from this decision was short-lived, however, because three years later, the NLRB, by a 3–2 vote, held that it did not have the statutory power to grant such relief. Though the Board unanimously found that the employer had violated the law by its refusal to bargain collectively, the majority (which by this time included two Nixon appointees) held that it could not compel the "make-whole" remedy. What makes the majority decision somewhat questionable is that all five Board members stated that they were in "complete agreement that the customary remedies the NLRB imposes are inadequate." Also, as the minority members stressed, the NLRB under Taft-Hartley in Section 10(c) has the power "to take such affirmative action . . . as will effectuate the policies of this Act." It would seem that under proper circumstances a "make-whole" remedy would be proper to effectuate the law's policy for the promotion of collective bargaining.

Though the NLRB refused to order a "make-whole" remedy in *Ex-Cell-O*, some courts apparently believe that the Board has the legal power to do so. In *Tiidee Products*, a federal appeals court remanded a case to the Board and instructed the agency that it had ample power to issue a "make-whole" remedy to "provide meaningful relief for employees unlawfully denied the fruits of collective bargaining."[38] Also, another federal court held in *J. P. Stevens*[39] that the Board has the power to direct the remedy. In remanding the case to the NLRB to determine whether its narrow remedy was proper in light of the illegal conduct of the company, the court stated that

> although the courts will not lightly interfere with Board orders, the Board is under a complimentary obligation to set forth in valid fashion the relationship between the case and the remedy it orders.

Perhaps one reason for the remand was that J. P. Stevens was notorious for its illegal conduct in combating unions. Thus:

> J. P. Stevens is now in its 12th step in a long chain of litigation, each marked by a separate NLRB order to the company and each involving new problems arising against the background of the preceding step, but all of them relating to the basic controversy over unionization of the Company's numerous plants throughout the South.[40]

However, in October 1980, J. P. Stevens and the Clothing and Textile Workers negotiated a labor agreement covering ten of the corporation's eighty plants and 3,500 of its 30,000 production employees. This constituted the first realistic victory in the union's seventeen-year struggle against the corporation.[41]

In any event, despite the judgment of the courts that the Board has the authority under Taft-Hartley to direct a "make-whole" remedy, the NLRB at this writing still refuses to do so. In January 1972, the Board again refused to direct the remedy in the *Tiidee* case remanded to it by the federal court.[42] To support its position, the NLRB relied heavily upon the United States Supreme Court decision in *H. K. Porter*.[43] In that case, the court ruled that the NLRB did not have the power to compel parties to adopt any contractual provision. Thus, the Board believed that by directing a "make-whole" remedy, it would in effect be writing contractual language. However, as the appeals court stated in *Tiidee*, the remedy does not require the inclusion of contract terms in a labor agreement but does serve to compensate employees for past illegal conduct of the employer. When a labor agreement is actually negotiated, the parties would be free to adopt whatever wage structure results from the collective bargaining process. The idea of the "make-whole" remedy is to award damages to employees to compensate them for previous illegal employer conduct.

In the Labor Law Reform Act of 1977, mentioned earlier, the NLRB would have been authorized to implement the "make-whole" remedy. Under this proposed legislation, should the Board find that an employer illegally refused to bargain collectively for a first contract, it would have been empowered to compensate employees by the following formula: an amount equal to the average wage negotiated at similar plants where collective bargaining proceeded lawfully. The data needed to determine the amount are regularly compiled and published by the Bureau of Labor Statistics.

CHANGING NLRB PERSONNEL AND POLICIES

Criticisms of NLRB

The National Labor Relations Board has been subject to criticism because of changing interpretations placed on the broad legal principles contained in the national labor laws. Charges cast at the Board for preferential treatment of some groups have been an occupational hazard in its fifty-eight years of existence.

Sources of criticism against the Board have not been limited to any single group. Academicians as well as labor, management, and the general public have all expressed opinions regarding the changing character of federal labor policy. Neil Chamberlain, for example, wrote that

> one cannot speak of federal labor policy with definiteness since a policy which is enunciated today may be modified a year from today.[44]

The reasons given for changes in policies are (1) changing Board membership, (2) a realization that some policies are ineffective in practice, and (3) changing social norms. Each of the reasons enumerated, however, may be considered as reflecting the philosophies of Board members, with policy changes coinciding with changing membership.

As we deal with the NLRB in succeeding chapters, there will be numerous examples of how the Board has changed its policies. At this time, we merely mention that policies have changed, sometimes by full circle, and explain that the reason for the change in policy results from the changes in the composition of Board membership.

Contrary to popular conception, there is no statutory political test for Board membership. Naturally, however, Presidents tend to appoint persons who share their general economic and labor relations philosophies. As one study stated:

> . . . no adequate empirical evidence has previously been reported that shows that once appointed, Board members acted in a biased manner. The results of our study strongly suggest that the presidential appointment process has a substantial influence on the adjudication of ULP [unfair labor practice] complaints. Interpretation of the facts and law governing union-management relations is therefore dependent in part on the make-up of the Board.[45]

In the Eisenhower era, the Board was described as quite reluctant to restrict employers in their free-speech policies during election campaigns as well as in other unfair labor practices. On the other hand, the Kennedy and Johnson boards were more restrictive of employer activities.

Labor organizations were highly critical of Board policies during the Eisenhower and Nixon years. In 1955, the CIO said:

> Americans have long been accustomed to believe that under our form of government the law is supreme. The record of the Labor Board under Republican auspices now strikingly reveals how often those who "interpret"—and not the Congress—actually make the law.[46]

Employers have also taken exception to various policies. Both employers and unions approach labor relations from ideological standpoints. Due to the changing character of the five-person Board in Washington, it has long been recognized that both groups are politically oriented toward a policy of generating pressures to attempt to influence decisions. Thus, even if one group had favorable experiences during one political administration, it may have unfavorable ones during the next. So long as Board decisions are partially political, one must expect a political evaluation of the effectiveness of agency administration from the parties who have a continuous relationship with it.[47]

The Ervin Committee

Criticisms by some employer groups have gone far beyond the usual attitude of "keeping the pressure on" in order to influence policies. The Chamber of Commerce and the National Association of Manufacturers (NAM) led a campaign to rewrite the nation's basic labor laws and to abolish the National Labor Relations Board. It was proposed that the functions now performed by the Board be transferred to either a labor court or to federal district courts. The campaign was so intense that the Chamber of Commerce and the NAM appointed a committee of 150 lawyers to draft changes in the National Labor Relations Act. The finished product was a 167-page report circulated under the title "Labor Management Relations Act."[48]

The general charge made against the Board by the pressuring employer groups was that policy is made by the five members, who are allegedly not responsive to Congress or the people, but to labor unions. In this regard, employers charged, the interests of the American worker are not served, but only the interests of labor union leaders are promoted.

In 1968, the anti-Board point of view was vigorously presented in hearings headed by Senator Sam Ervin of North Carolina.[49] By this time, of course, the NLRB was dominated by Kennedy-Johnson appointees. Although some witnesses defended the NLRB (Derek Box, Dean of Harvard Law School, for example), the Ervin Committee was more impressed by those who vilified the agency. Illustrative of the view that the NLRB exceeded its legitimate scope of authority and was making policy based upon subjective judgment and not law was the statement made by Senator Robert Griffin:

> If the Constitution made anything clear, surely it is that policymaking is primarily a function of the Congress . . . The pattern of recent decisions by the NLRB gives rise to a serious concern that policies laid down by Congress, in the Taft-Hartley and Landrum-

Griffin Acts, are being distorted and frustrated, to say the very least. The decisions themselves are startling enough. However, when viewed in the light of some recent extrajudicial pronouncements by Board members, there is reason to wonder whether the NLRB—which was created by Congress—even concedes the constitutional authority of Congress to formulate and establish policy in the labor-management field.

In regard to the Ervin Committee, Daniel Yager stated:

Recognizing this inherent statutory characteristic, the subcommittee still found that, in viewing the Board's positions over time, clear patterns had emerged to indicate that the Board was not fairly balancing the various interests affected by the Act and was, in fact, giving excessive weight to one over all others. While the concerns expressed by the Subcommittee went to the broad issue of NLRB allegiance to statutory intent, the criticism that this had been abandoned was illustrated by a number of specific areas of obvious pro-union bias.[50]

The Reagan Board

With the election of Reagan in 1980 and his reelection in 1984, the NLRB was again criticized, but this time by organized labor. Almost unique in the history of the Board, Reagan was able to appoint all five members, including Chair Donald Dotson, a former management attorney. Stung by what it believed to be many unfair decisions, the labor movement pulled out all stops in its attack against the agency. Speaking at a labor law session, a union attorney described the Reagan-appointed members as "pirates" who had taken over the National Labor Relations Board and "are steering it on an antiworker course."[51] Another veteran labor attorney, for thirty-one years the general counsel of the International Ladies Garment Workers Union, said:

. . . we are dealing with a board whose tilt to Management is the most pronounced in my experience.[52]

Lane Kirkland, president of the AFL-CIO, suggested the repeal of the Taft-Hartley Act and abolishment of the NLRB on the grounds that unions would be better off without them.[53]

That the Reagan Board had reversed former policies is, of course, nothing new. Perhaps what was new involved the comparative rapidity and the large number of reversals. As former Board Member Zimmerman said:

. . . never in the history of the Labor Board have so many major established principles been overruled as in 1984 when a new majority began its revision course.[54]

At the appropriate place in this volume, we shall highlight some of the more controversial policies adopted by the Reagan Board. Though the federal courts, including the U.S. Supreme Court, generally sustained Reagan Board policies, it did not always prevail. In a 1986 case, *NLRB* v. *Food and Commercial Workers*, the high court unanimously held nonunion employees do not have the right to vote in union affiliation elections. Union members voted to affiliate with a national union, excluding nonunion employees from the election. Since they were excluded, the Reagan Board refused to compel the employer to bargain with the union. Pointing out that the policy meddled with the union's internal affairs, the Court said:

> We hold that the Board exceeded its authority under the Act in requiring that nonunion employees be allowed to vote for affiliation before it would order the employer to bargain with the affiliated union.[55]

Some of the actions of the Reagan NLRB, however, did not necessarily deal with major policy reversals but only with the routine handling of cases. In 1975–1976, a Board appointed entirely by Nixon and Ford found for the employer in 29 percent of all contested unfair labor practice and election cases. In the Carter years, the figure dropped to 27 percent. In 1983 and 1984, the Reagan Board found for the employer in 60 percent of all cases.[56] Of course, despite this apparent management tilt, the Reagan Board would assert that its administration of the law was correct, and that in fact its predecessors did not enforce the law in a proper manner.

After the initial Reagan appointees left the NLRB as their five-year terms expired, the agency started to become more evenhanded. The major event was the resignation of Donald Dotson, the management attorney, who served as chair between 1983 and the expiration of his term in December 1987. James M. Stephens was designated as chair in January 1988. He immediately promised

> a commitment to fairness and a belief in our system of peaceful industrial relations through law.[57]

In March 1988, Congresswoman Marge Roukema of New Jersey stated:

> . . . there has been a complete turnover of the membership on the National Labor Relations Board, with little or no controversy associated with the current membership. And although there may be disagreements over particular rulings, I do not believe that anyone would allege that current members have a hidden agenda to undermine the goals of the act.[58]

Even though the Stephens' Board appeared to be more fair to employees, unions, and employers, with one notable exception it did not set aside any of the controversial decisions of the initial Reagan appointees. The exception dealt with the establishment of bargaining units in hospitals to be discussed in the following chapter.

With the election of Bill Clinton as President in 1992, the expected changes in the NLRB were made. Most prominent was the appointment of William Gould IV as chair of the agency. Shortly after his appointment, he said the Board had lost much of its credibility with organized labor and the public because most of its significant decisions in the last decade had favored the employer. His goal, said Gould, was to restore the agency's credibility by a more "balanced approach," and "return the Board to center," making it once again a truly impartial forum in which all parties have confidence.[59]

In a step to implement impartiality, Gould in April 1994 established a National Labor Relations Board Advisory Panel to be composed of fifty attorneys representing management and unions. Appointed to the panel, whose members agreed to serve pro bono, were women, racial minorities, and representatives of established legal organizations.

Needless to say, employers view the Gould Board with trepidation. The president of the Labor Policy Association, a management-oriented group, stated:

> He [Gould] made it very clear in his book that came out during his nomination that he has an agenda for reform. Now he appears to be taking steps to implement that agenda.[60]

And, so it goes—expected change of policy with new faces on the NLRB. If Clinton loses in 1996, it will give the new President a chance to appoint a Board with a different philosophy. All of this is unsettling to the nation's labor relations program. It is additional evidence that labor, employers, and the national interest would be best served by appointing Board members for life just like the federal judiciary.

LANDRUM-GRIFFIN AMENDMENTS

The Taft-Hartley Act remained in force for twelve years before controversy over its provisions resulted in congressional amendments in 1959. The amendments were contained in Title VII of a broader piece of legislation known officially as the Labor-Management Reporting and Disclosure Act of 1959, or more popularly the Landrum-Griffin Act. The first six titles of Landrum-Griffin deal with control of union affairs. They will be treated in a later chapter. Our first concern is with the controversial provisions of Taft-Hartley that led to the Title VII amendments. At appropriate places in later chapters, we shall indicate policies adopted in Landrum-Griffin to change Taft-Hartley.

SUMMARY

Taft-Hartley shifted public policy in labor relations by including union unfair labor practices and individual employee rights, and by providing employers with the opportunity to restrict union activity. In later chapters, how the 1947 law provided employers with this opportunity will become apparent.

Under the 1947 law, Congress restricted the power of the NLRB by providing the General Counsel with exclusive authority to investigate and prosecute unfair labor practice charges. Neither the NLRB nor the courts have the authority to upset General Counsel decisions. Under this system, the NLRB may decide cases only when the General Counsel refers them to it.

Resulting from delays in processing cases, the NLRB has not been able to effectuate fully the purposes and policies incorporated in Taft-Hartley. Congress could significantly alleviate this problem by providing the NLRB with the right not to review every unfair labor practice decision issued by administrative law judges, as it has the authority to use discretion in the review of representation and election decisions made by regional directors.

Enforcement procedures under Taft-Hartley are not fully effective, particularly when workers are discharged in union organizing campaigns, and when employers violate their lawful obligation to bargain in good faith. When Congress attempted to remedy this situation, it failed because of a Senate filibuster.

Uncertainty in the administration of the statute exists because policies change with the changing personnel of the National Labor Relations Board.

DISCUSSION QUESTIONS

1. How significant do you consider the three important factors provided by the authors as explanations for passage of the Taft-Hartley Act?

2. In what important ways did the Office of General Counsel change from the Wagner Act to Taft-Hartley?

3. Evaluate the union unfair labor practices contained in Taft-Hartley from the standpoint of need arising out of abuses, clarity as to congressional purpose, and effectiveness in interpretation and enforcement.

4. Trace the procedure of processing unfair labor practices from the initial charge to their final conclusion.

5. What is your opinion of the quality of the Board's processing of unfair labor practice cases?

6. Describe the NLRB's representation or election case procedures and evaluate the quality of its methods.

7. How effective has the NLRB been in enforcing the Taft-Hartley Act? Can you identify weaknesses or strengths of the process?

8. How serious is political bias in NLRB policies as it is related to changing Board personnel?

NOTES

1   Act of June 23, 1947, 61 Stat. 136.

2   From the authors' personal files.

3   Congress of Industrial Organizations, *Taft-Hartley and You.*

4   *Monthly Labor Review*, v. XLV (1947), p. 529.

5   International Association of Machinists, *The Truth About the Taft-Hartley Law and Its Consequences to the Labor Movement*, Washington, D.C. (April 1948), p. 29.

6   *United Electrical Contractors Association v. Ordman*, 366 F. 2d 776 (2d Cir. 1966); cert. denied 385 U.S. 1026 (1967).

7   *Reed* v. *Collyer*, 108 S. Ct. 2885 (1988).

8   National Labor Relations Board, *Fifty-fifth Annual Report* (1990), p. 5.

9   *Ibid.*

10   National Labor Relations Board, *Thirty-fifth Annual Report* (1970), p. 7.

11   National Labor Relations Board, *Forty-fifth Annual Report* (1980), p. 1.

12   Bernard Samoff, "The Case of the Burgeoning Load of the NLRB," *Labor Law Journal*, XXII, 10 (October 1971), pp. 611–630.

13   National Labor Relations Board, *Fifty-fifth Annual Report* (1990), p. 2.

14   Subcommittee on Labor-Management Relations, 100th Congress, Second Session, "Oversight Hearings on Practices and Operations Under the National Labor Relations Act," March 9, 1988, p. 10.

15   *Wall Street Journal*, February 13, 1985. See also Bernard Samoff, "What Lies Ahead for the NLRB," *Labor Law Journal*, XXXVIII, 5 (May 1987), p. 263.

16   National Labor Relations Board, *Fifty-fifth Annual Report* (1990), p. 196.

17   Committee on Government Operations, 98th Congress, 2nd Session, House Report 981141, October 4, 1984, "Delay, Slowness in Decisionmaking, and the Case Backlog at the National Labor Relations Board," p. 7.

18   *AFL-CIO News*, October 15, 1990.

19   Steve Gunderson, "Making the Case for a National Commission on American Labor Law and Competitiveness," *Labor Law Journal*, v. 42, September 1991, p. 588.

20   Commerce Clearing House, *Labor Law Reports*, No. 377, December 3, 1993, p. 4.

21   Committee on Government Operations, 98th Congress, 2nd Session, House Report 98-1141, October 4, 1984, *op. cit.*, p. 8

22   National Labor Relations Board, *Fifty-fifth Annual Report* (1990) *op. cit.*, p. 16.

23   *Wall Street Journal*, July 6, 1976.

24   National Labor Relations Board, *Fifty-Fifth Annual Report* (1990), *op. cit.*, p. 15.

25   Frank N. McCulloch and Tim Bornstein, *The National Labor Relations Board* (New York: Frederick A. Praeger, 1974), p. 117, 154.

26   Sheldon Friedman and Richard Prosten, "How Come One Team *Still* Has to Play With Its Shoelaces Tied?" *Labor Law Journal*, v. 44, August 1993, p. 479.

27   *Ibid.*, p. 480.

28   National Labor Relations Board, *Fifty-fifth Annual Report* (1990), p. 196.

29   Sheldon Friedman and Richard Prosten, *op. cit.*, p. 485.

30   *Ibid.*, p. 485.

31   *Ibid.*, p. 186.

32   National Labor Relations Board, *Interim Report*, November 5, 1976, p. 7.

33   *AFL-CIO News*, March 20, 1976, p. 8.

34   *Monthly Labor Review*, CIV, No. 3, March 1981, p. 76.

35   *AFL-CIO News, op. cit.*

36   H.R. 1743, 98th Congress, Labor Law Debarment Act, Commerce Clearing House, *Labor Law Reports*, No. 608, November 4, 1983, p. 3.

37   185 NLRB 107 (1970).

38   *IUE* v. *NLRB (Tiidee Products)*, 426 F. 2d 1243 (D.C. Cir. 1970).

39   *Textile Workers Union* v. *NLRB (J. P. Stevens)*, 475 F. 2d 973 (D.C. Cir. 1973).

40   *Monthly Labor Review*, LVI, No. 5, May 1973, p. 54.

41   *Monthly Labor Review*, CIV, No. 1, January 1981, p. 19.

42   194 NLRB 1234 (1972).

43   *H. K. Porter Co.* v. *NLRB*, 397 U.S. 99 (1970).

44   See Don R. Sheriff and Viola M. Kuebler, eds., *NLRB in a Changing Industrial Society*, Conference Series No. 2 (Iowa City: College of Business Administration, University of Iowa, 1967), p. 43.

45   William N. Cooke and Frederick H. Gautschi III, "Political Bias in NLRB Unfair Labor Practice Decisions," *Industrial and Labor Relations Review*, XXXV, 4 (July 1982), p. 549.

46   "Economic Outlook," *Congress of Industrial Organizations, Department of Education and Research*, XVI, 2 (February 1955), p. 16.

47   Benjamin J. Taylor, *The Operation of the Taft-Hartley Act in Indiana*, Indiana Business Information Bulletin 58 (Bloomington: Bureau of Business Research, Indiana University, 1967), p. 88.

48   *Congressional Record* (Washington, D.C.: Government Printing Office, August 2, 1968), p. S10118.

49   Report of Senate Subcommittee on Separation of Powers of the Committee on the Judiciary, 91st Congress, 1st Session, Congressional Oversight of Administrative Agencies, National Labor Relations Board, 1969.

50   Daniel Yager, "Has Labor Law Failed?" National Foundation for the Study of Employment Policy, Washington, D.C., 1990, p. 3.

51   *AFL-CIO News*, October 27, 1984.

52   *Wall Street Journal*, January 25, 1984.

53   *Wall Street Journal*, January 6, 1984.

54   *AFL-CIO American Federationist*, July 6, 1985, p. 5.

55   *NLRB* v. *Financial Institution Employees of America, Local 1182, Chartered by United Food and Commercial Workers Intl. Union*, 475 U.S. 192 (1986).

56   *AFL-CIO News*, June 1, 1985, p. 3.

57   *AFL-CIO News*, January 16, 1988.

58   Subcommittee on Labor-Management Relations, 100th Congress, *op. cit.*, p. 2.

59   Commerce Clearing House, *Labor Law Reports*, No. 396, April 15, 1994, p. 5.

60   *Wall Street Journal*, May 15, 1994.

Jurisdiction of the National Labor Relations Board

SELF-IMPOSED RESTRICTIONS

Wagner Act Experience

If the NLRB refuses to take jurisdiction over a case, the Taft-Hartley law is not available to the employer, union, or employees involved in the dispute. Only when the NLRB exerts jurisdiction does the law come into play. Also, unlike many other federal agencies, the General Counsel and the NLRB do not take the initiative to start the operation of the law. To activate the provisions of the law, an unfair labor practice charge or an election petition must be filed. In this chapter, we review the evolutionary nature of the Board's self-imposed jurisdictional restrictions, the question of state control of labor relations in areas abnegated by the Board, and the impact of Landrum-Griffin in resolving the gray area of labor relations left by Board and Supreme Court actions. We shall also be concerned with other jurisdictional problems, including a 1974 amendment to Taft-Hartley that brought nonprofit health-care facilities within the coverage of the law. Finally, the relationship between Taft-Hartley and the U.S. Bankruptcy Code will be explained.

The Wagner Act bestowed upon the NLRB authority to assume jurisdiction over unfair labor practices and questions of representation "affecting commerce."[1] Section 2(7) described the phrase so broadly that the Supreme Court held the jurisdictional authority of the Board to be coextensive with the reach of Congress under the commerce power.[2] Recall that the *Jones & Laughlin Steel Corporation* case decided the constitutionality of the Wagner Act and at the same time extended the commerce power of Congress to include production as well as distribution. Once the Wagner Act was upheld, it was the duty of the Board

> to eliminate the causes of certain substantial obstructions to the free flow of commerce . . .[3]

The Board's authority was established more clearly in a 1939 Supreme Court case when it held that it was obviously the intent of Congress

> to exercise whatever power is given to it to regulate commerce.[4]

This broad power of the NLRB to extend coverage of national labor policy to all possible situations was, however, never fully utilized. Authority of the agency to choose its own area of operation was approved by the courts; that is, the Board's jurisdiction did not depend on the volume of commerce involved in a particular situation. The NLRB had discretion as to what cases it would accept. Therefore, at the start of its operation, the Board did not take jurisdiction of cases where the impact on interstate commerce was minimal, concentrating on cases involving a greater impact.[5] It adopted this policy because of a growing case load and insufficient budget, preventing employment of an adequate staff.

The immediate postwar period, 1945–1947, was particularly troublesome for NLRB operations. The nation was in the process of changing to peacetime production of consumer goods; union organizational drives were more active than during the war years; unions were attempting to achieve gains they had forgone because of the war effort; and employer resistance to unions was rising rapidly. The Board's case load swelled, but it did not have staff sufficient to deal with the problem.

Change of NLRB Policy

A much more serious curtailment of Board jurisdiction was revealed in a series of NLRB releases of Board member statements and subsequent decisions in the fall of 1953 and during the first part of 1954. Guy Farmer, then chair of the Board, in a speech after assuming office stated:

> I think perhaps the time has come to accept the proposition that it is not necessary or even desirable for the Federal Government to step into every labor dispute however insignificant it might be. It has always seemed to me, without engaging in any debate of the relative merits of state versus federal rights, that, regardless of the legal scope of the commerce clause the Federal Agencies should, as a matter of self-restraint, impose limits on their own power and thus provide the opportunity for local problems to be settled on a local basis by the citizens of the communities in which these problems arise.[6]

In other words, the Board, dominated by President Eisenhower appointees, justified its retrenchment of jurisdiction on philosophical grounds rather than on those of limited budget and manpower, as had previously occurred. It increased dollar standards or yardsticks for each major branch of industry, ruling it would not take jurisdiction of a case unless the business involved came up to the standard. For example, to be covered by Taft-Hartley, a firm was required to sell $50,000 outside the state instead of $25,000. Purchases from other states were increased from $50,000 to $1,000,000. Data are not available to assess the scope of the retrenchment accurately. The NLRB probably surrendered up to 25 percent of its potential jurisdiction.

Not all Board members agreed with the new jurisdictional standards. A minority dissented vigorously from the self-imposed restrictions. The most-heated aspect of the debate centered on the authority of states to exercise jurisdiction over those business enterprises in interstate commerce denied coverage under federal law by the Board. One reason given for raising the jurisdictional standards in 1954 was the expectation that states would take the initiative by enacting state labor relations laws. Fourteen years later, however, only seventeen states and Puerto Rico had done so.[7] At the present time, approximately the same number of states have such laws.

The reasons the Board gave for decreasing federal authority over enterprises in interstate commerce were (1) the desire for states to regulate the area of labor relations abnegated by it, and (2) its own wish to encourage state labor legislation patterned after the Taft-Hartley Act. It also assumed that states had the constitutional authority to exercise control over the rejected areas.

Federal Preemption: Legislative Aspects of Taft-Hartley

When Congress passed the Taft-Hartley law, the national lawmakers were aware of the supremacy of federal law within interstate commerce. Aware of this state of affairs, but still desiring to provide the states with authority to deal with some labor relations problems within interstate commerce, Congress spelled out with precision those areas in which it desired state regulation to prevail. Perhaps the best illustration of the congressional approach to the federal-state jurisdictional problem involves the manner in which union security is treated in the national law. Whereas the federal law only outlaws the closed shop, the states under express provision of Taft-Hartley may prohibit any form of compulsory union membership.[8] At the time that Congress was considering the passage of Taft-Hartley, several states had already prohibited all forms of union security. Since Congress was determined to preserve this state jurisdiction, it relinquished federal supremacy in this area of industrial relations. In the absence of such a clear statement of federal policy, Congress feared that state law prohibiting union security would have been invalidated because of federal supremacy in matters affecting commerce. In this connection, the House Labor Committee declared:

> Since by the Labor Act Congress preempts the field that the act covers insofar as commerce within the meaning of the act is concerned . . . the committee . . . has provided expressly . . . that laws and constitutional provisions of any state that restrict the right of employers to require employees to become or remain members of labor organizations are valid, notwithstanding any provision of the National Labor Relations Act.[9]

Other areas of Taft-Hartley spell out additional points on which Congress desired the states to control labor relations within interstate commerce. The meticulousness with which these areas are indicated lends additional support to the proposition that, in the absence of national legislation to the contrary, the states were forbidden to operate within interstate commerce once the federal government had occupied the field by the enactment of constitutional legislation. Thus the federal labor law required that parties who were seeking to modify or terminate collective bargaining contracts had to give notice of this fact not only to the Federal Mediation and Conciliation Service but also to any state agency that performed mediation services.[10] The director of the Federal Mediation and Conciliation Service was ordered to avoid attempting to mediate disputes that have only a minor effect on interstate commerce if state or other conciliation services were available to the parties.[11] In addition, the director of the federal mediation agency was empowered to establish suitable procedures for cooperation with state and local mediation agencies.[12] Under authority of another provision of the Taft-Hartley law, employers could sue unions in either federal or state courts for injuries suffered as a result of union action declared illegal in the national law.[13] Obviously, it was in these areas of labor relations that Congress desired the states to have concurrent jurisdiction with the national government. Congress recognized that the doctrine of national preemption would operate to exclude such state regulation of industrial relations within interstate commerce in the absence of clear and specific authority extended by the national government.

Section 10(a): Uniform Application of National Labor Policy

Not only did the Taft-Hartley law establish a system of concurrent federal-state jurisdiction within interstate commerce over certain specified areas of industrial relations, *but it also provided that the NLRB, under certain limited conditions, could cede jurisdiction to state boards in unfair labor practice cases.* This authority was given by Section 10(a) of the law.[14] This provision of the statute has crucial importance in the determination of the question of whether the states may lawfully occupy the area of interstate commerce vacated by the NLRB.

Section 10(a) empowered the NLRB to prevent any person from engaging in any unfair labor practice affecting interstate commerce. It further provided that this power of the Board "shall not be affected by any other means of adjustment or prevention that has been or may be established by agreement, law, or otherwise." With the single exception that the law established a limited procedure whereby the NLRB could cede jurisdiction to the states, this section of Taft-Hartley showed the determination of Congress to reserve for the national labor agency full and exclusive power to enforce the terms of the national labor statute. No other enforcement agency, federal or state, regardless of the circumstances under which a case arose, had any power to implement the provisions of the Taft-Hartley law. This was the clear and unmistakable meaning of Section 10(a). With this one exception, Congress was anxious to ensure the uniform application of national labor policy throughout interstate commerce. Uniform national labor policy within interstate commerce could not have been realized if Congress had permitted a variety of federal and state courts or labor agencies to interpret and apply national labor policy. If Congress had allowed a variety of enforcement channels of the Taft-Hartley law to exist, there might have been as many different versions of its meaning as there are law-enforcement forums within the nation. It was this state of affairs that Congress desired to avoid.

The determination of Congress to ensure the uniform application of the federal law within interstate commerce was not lessened by the limited circumstances under which the NLRB could cede jurisdiction of unfair labor practice cases to state agencies. In the first place, Section 10(a) clearly specified that the only way in which the federal agency could cede jurisdiction to the states was "by agreement." This meant that the Board could not cede jurisdiction to the states merely by declaring that it would not exercise its authority over a certain category of cases. Unless an agreement were entered into by the NLRB with state agencies, Section 10(a) prohibited state exercise of control over labor relations within interstate commerce. Such an agreement was not implied merely by a decline of jurisdiction by the NLRB. *Agreement was possible only if the state law to be applied was identical with the federal law in both language and application stemming from interpretation.*

Obviously, the reason why Congress included the consistency test within Taft-Hartley was to provide for the uniform application of national labor policy within interstate commerce. The objective of uniformity could not have been realized if federal and state law treated the same set of circumstances in an unlike manner. If the consistency standard had not been included in the federal law, a situation could have arisen in which activities unlawful under federal law could be lawful under state law. It was this kind of confusion that Congress meant to avoid when it established the barrier to NLRB jurisdictional cession to the states. In this connection, the Senate Labor Committee, which reported the Taft-Hartley law in 1947, stated: "The provision which has been added to this subsection permits the National Labor Relations Board to allow State labor-relations boards to take final jurisdiction of cases in border-line industries (that is, border line insofar as interstate commerce is concerned) provided the state statute conforms to national policy."[15]

In 1975, the restrictions contained in Section 10(a) prompted the Board to refuse to cede jurisdiction to the state of Minnesota in cases involving nonprofit hospitals. (Below is a discussion of the general problem of Taft-Hartley application to nonprofit hospitals.) Minnesota, which had a law covering that industry, petitioned the Board to cede jurisdiction in this area. The Board refused because of differences between Taft-Hartley and the state law. Under the Minnesota law, strikes and lockouts were prohibited, and binding arbitration was required when nonprofit hospitals and employees had reached an impasse in collective bargaining. No such restrictions were contained in federal law.[16]

Federal Preemption:
The Supreme Court

On several occasions, even before Taft-Hartley, the U.S. Supreme Court had invalidated state laws when they conflicted with national labor legislation. In 1943, Florida enacted a union regulation law that, among other things, required that union officials obtain a license before operating within the state.[17] To satisfy the requirements for the license, a union official had to prove that he or she was a citizen of the United States, had resided in the United States for ten years, had not been convicted of a felony, and was of good moral character. The law also required that the applicant pay a fee before obtaining the license. In 1945, the Supreme Court held that the statute was invalid to the extent that it applied to interstate commerce, on the grounds that it circumscribed the full freedom of choice that employees are given in the selection of bargaining representatives under national labor law.[18] In this connection the Court declared that "the full freedom of employees in collective bargaining which Congress envisioned as essential to protect the free flow of commerce among the states would be, by the Florida statute, shrunk to a greatly limited freedom." Thus the state of Florida could not use a state law to deprive workers of rights protected by the Wagner Act.

The application of the principle of federal supremacy over state law within interstate commerce also involved a case dealing with bargaining rights of supervisors. In May 1943, the NLRB held that it would no longer extend the protection of the Wagner Act to supervisors in the exercise of their collective bargaining rights. Specifically, the Board ruled that supervisors no longer constituted units appropriate for collective bargaining within the meaning of the national law. Under this policy, unions of supervisors could not be certified by the NLRB for collective bargaining purposes. However, while this NLRB policy was in effect, the New York State Labor Relations Board afforded the full protection of the New York State Labor Relations Act to supervisors. Consequently, a union of supervisors, denied access to the NLRB, petitioned and obtained a certification from the state labor agency for purposes of collective bargaining. When this case was heard by the Supreme Court of the United States, the state of New York argued that a state had the authority to act until federal power was actually exercised over the particular employees. However, the Court rejected this argument, declaring that "the State argues for a rule that would enable it to act until the federal board had acted in the same case. But we do not think that a case-by-case test of federal supremacy is permissible here. The federal board has jurisdiction of the industry in which these particular employers engaged and has asserted control of their labor relations in general."[19] The Supreme Court held that the state board did not have the power to permit supervisors to become a bargaining unit under a state labor law because the federal law had denied them this right. Thus the decision demonstrated that a state could not endow employees covered by the national labor law with rights not consistent with federal law.

In 1953, the Supreme Court handed down its decision in the *Garner* case and once again ruled that states were without authority to assume jurisdiction over labor relations disputes that fall within the area of the NLRB.[20] Involved was picketing by a labor organization that violated the laws of Pennsylvania. Without question, picketing was also unlawful under the Taft-Hartley Act. A Pennsylvania court held that the union conduct violated the Pennsylvania Labor Relations Act and enjoined the picketing. However, the Supreme Court of Pennsylvania upset the ruling of the lower court on the grounds that the labor dispute fell within the exclusive jurisdiction of the NLRB. The United States Supreme Court upheld the high court of Pennsylvania, declaring that in enacting the Taft-Hartley law, "Congress did not merely lay down a substantive rule of law to be enforced by any tribunal competent to apply law generally to the parties. It went on to confide primary interpretation and application of its rules to a specific and specially constituted tribunal and prescribed a particular procedure for investigation, complaint and notice, and hearing and decision, including judicial relief pending a final administrative order."

Given these judicial precedents, a 1984 U.S. Supreme Court decision dealing with the 1977 New Jersey Casino Control Act was somewhat surprising. Determined to prevent organized crime from infiltrating the casino industry, the state law imposed qualifications on union officials representing casino industry employees. Not eligible to serve as union officers were those with a criminal record, or with ties to organized crime. By a 4–3 vote, two justices not participating, the high court held the state statute did not conflict with the Taft-Hartley provision under which employees have the right to elect officers of their own choosing.[21] It said that where a state is confronted with crime, corruption, and racketeering, "more stringent state regulation of the qualifications of union officials was not incompatible with the national labor policy as embodied in Section 7."

In any event, despite this aberration, probably justified because of unique circumstances, the U.S. Supreme Court has uniformly held that states could not take jurisdiction of labor disputes falling within the scope of the national law.

The *Guss* Case and the "No Man's Land"

The *Garner* case served notice that the Supreme Court did not look with favor upon state control of labor disputes falling within the scope of national labor legislation. However, it did not conclusively resolve the federal-state jurisdictional problem. Finally, in 1957, the Supreme Court *clearly excluded the states from asserting control over cases declined by the NLRB*. In the light of the language of Taft-Hartley and court precedent, it was only logical to expect such a decision of the high court.

In *Guss* v. *Utah Labor Relations Board*, the Court held that when the Board had jurisdiction, even if it refused to exercise it, states could assert their own laws only when the NLRB ceded jurisdiction under Section 10(a) of the National Labor Relations Act.[22] Recall that Section 10(a) required states to apply law identical to that of the federal statute. Not a single state qualified to accept cases on conditions prescribed by Section 10(a). Denial of state jurisdiction meant the creation of a "no man's land" within which labor relations were subject to neither federal nor state regulation.

The implications of the no man's land were several. First, when the agency declined jurisdiction, it meant that bargaining elections could not be conducted by use of Board machinery to determine whether collective bargaining representatives would be chosen. No method was available to the parties to resolve any conflict arising out of organizational issues. One of the basic purposes of national law is to eliminate organizational strikes. The failure to assert control over some firms would result in strikes seeking to force recognition.

Second, the decision had the effect of allowing employers and unions to engage in activities illegal under national labor law without fear of intervention by either the NLRB or the states. Employers could discharge workers for union activities, refuse to bargain with a majority union, and sponsor company-dominated labor organizations. On the other hand, unions were free to engage in such illegal activities as secondary boycott strikes, jurisdictional strikes, and strikes for closed shops and could refuse to bargain in good faith without fear of restraint. Indeed, when employers and unions recognized that no law would apply, it could be said that they were actually being encouraged to engage in conduct that would otherwise be proscribed under law.

The Supreme Court was aware of the importance of its decision. It pointed out possible alternative solutions to the no-man's-land problem. One was congressional enactment of appropriate legislation. Another was that the Board could reassert its jurisdiction by reevaluating its dollar-volume guidelines.

The *Guss* decision created an immediate response from both Congress and the NLRB. In July 1958, Congress increased the Board's operating budget to permit a lowering of its dollar standards for the purpose of reducing a portion of the no-man's-land area. As a result, the Board revised its jurisdictional standards in October 1958. The policies set forth in 1958 remain in effect at the present time.[23]

Despite the efforts of the Congress and Board, a gray area remained, since many employers, unions, and employees engaged in interstate commerce were still outside the scope of national labor policy. Congressional action on the no man's land was certain, since the controversy was not stilled by the greater budget and Board reevaluation of jurisdictional policies.

Impact of Landrum-Griffin: Title VII

In 1959, Congress attempted to deal with the no-man's-land problem. It enacted an amendment to Section 14 of Taft-Hartley. Two courses of congressional action were available to fill the gap. Congress could require the NLRB to take jurisdiction of all cases defined legally as falling within interstate commerce. Or it could permit states to exercise jurisdiction over those cases declined by the Board. As early as January 1958, President Eisenhower had recommended greater state control, and his preference was known to Congress.

Section 14(c) of the 1959 Landrum-Griffin amendments to Taft-Hartley contained the final decision made from among the alternatives facing the legislators. The section was designed to deal with the no man's land. It reads:

> (c)(1) [The NLRB] is empowered, under certain conditions, to decline jurisdiction] where, in the opinion of the Board, the effect of such labor dispute on commerce is not sufficiently substantial to warrant the exercise of its jurisdiction. . . . (2) Nothing in this Act shall be deemed to prevent or bar any agency or the courts of any State or Territory (including the Commonwealth of Puerto Rico, Guam, and the Virgin Islands), from assuming and asserting jurisdiction over labor disputes over which the Board declines, pursuant to paragraph (1) of this subsection, to assert jurisdiction.[24]

Thus under the new law, the NLRB at its discretion could decline to assert jurisdiction over any case when in its judgment the effect of the labor dispute on commerce was not sufficient to warrant the exercise of its jurisdiction. State courts and agencies had the authority to take jurisdiction of cases the Board declined. Nothing in the new law required the states to take jurisdiction over these disputes. The law was merely permissive in this respect, not compulsory. It is not likely, however, that a state having a general labor relations law similar to Taft-Hartley will decline jurisdiction. *But in states without such a law, the no-man's-land problem still exists.*

The Board could also expand its jurisdiction to reach all cases falling within the area of interstate commerce. To the extent that the federal agency should expand its jurisdiction, the states' rights to intervene in interstate commerce would correspondingly decline. Though the Board could lawfully increase the scope of its jurisdiction, it could not reduce its authority beyond that which was in force as of August 1, 1959. It is also important to note that under the new law, the Board was authorized to decline jurisdiction over an entire industry. Congress provided this power to the Board because the Supreme Court in 1958 had ordered the agency to take jurisdiction over the hotel and motel industry.[25] Before this time, the Board had refused to handle cases involving this industry. Since the Supreme Court decision, the Board has exerted jurisdiction over motels and hotels, provided the enterprise receives at least $500,000 in gross revenue in a year.[26]

Application of Landrum-Griffin Policy

Problems flowed from the congressional policy on jurisdiction. How could the parties determine whether the NLRB would take jurisdiction over a particular case? Could the states apply state law, or could they pick and choose in this respect?

A party involved in a labor dispute can follow two procedures to determine whether the NLRB will accept or decline jurisdiction over a particular case. It can refer to the Board's published standards, which express in money volume the categories of cases the Board will take.[27] Perhaps a more definitive method is to seek an advisory opinion from the NLRB on whether it will take a particular case. The agency made such a procedure available shortly after the passage of the new law.[28] Such advisory opinions, however, deal exclusively with the issue of jurisdiction and will not relate to the merits of the dispute. In addition to the parties involved in a labor dispute, the Board will accept requests for advisory opinions from state courts and labor agencies. Advisory opinions may be filed only if a proceeding is currently pending before an agency or court. In general, the request for an opinion is expected to contain the general nature of the business of the employer involved in the dispute and to present relevant data on commerce. The Board permits the party filing the request for an advisory opinion to withdraw it at any time before the Board issues the instrument.[29]

In regard to the body of law to be applied by a state court or labor agency, it is clear that state law may be applied. A Senate version would have required the states to apply only federal law in all cases affecting interstate commerce. The Conference Committee, however, rejected the Senate proposal so that state law may be applied.[30]

As expected, states having state labor relations laws apply state law, though there is no express prohibition in the 1959 amendment against their applying federal law. Since state laws differ in content and are subject to different construction by state agencies and courts, *the principle and value of uniformity expressed in Section 10(a) no longer apply.* In some competitive categories, depending on circumstances, this situation could be harmful to employees and employers and is a defect of the 1959 amendment. It permits different labor relations policies within interstate commerce.

Employers operating under a strict state law would face a competitive disadvantage over employers in a state with a weak or no organizational law. Likewise, inequitable treatment of employees from one state to another would exist. As noted, another defect of the 1959 amendment is that many states do not have labor relations laws. In those states, the no-man's-land problem is still in effect. In the light of these observations, it would be proper to conclude that Congress did not deal effectively with the problems resulting from NLRB retrenchment of jurisdiction. To this day, Congress has not acted to correct the obvious shortcomings of the 1959 amendment.

Making use of its authority to decline jurisdiction over all cases within an industry, a power conferred upon it in the 1959 amendment, the Board refused to assert jurisdiction over horse and dog racing[31] and over a local doctor's medical practice.[32] In 1979, reversing an earlier policy, the Board asserted jurisdiction over condominiums and cooperative apartments with a gross annual revenue of at least $500,000.[33]

CHANGING NLRB JURISDICTIONAL POLICIES

Private Colleges and Universities

At one time, the agency refused jurisdiction over private colleges and universities.[34] In 1970, it reversed this policy in *Cornell University*,[35] and such educational institutions are now covered by the law. To be covered by Taft-Hartley, the private institution must gross at least $1 million in annual revenue. The modesty of this amount assures that the vast majority of private universities and colleges now fall under the jurisdiction of the NLRB. Not only are nonacademic employees covered by this policy, but faculty members may also use the NLRB to aid them in organizational and collective bargaining efforts.[36] Also, Taft-Hartley applies to private elementary and secondary schools. Provided that a school grosses $1 million annually, the NLRB will take jurisdiction whether or not the school operates for private profit. Public schools and universities, however, are still excluded from the coverage of the federal law because ever since the passage of the Wagner Act, public employees have been excluded from such coverage. Thus, state action is required to provide the legal basis for collective bargaining in public schools.

In 1980, however, in *Yeshiva University*, the U.S. Supreme Court dealt a devastating if not fatal blow to the organizational and collective bargaining rights of faculty members employed by private colleges and universities.[37] What probably came as a shock to some faculty members was that by 5–4, the majority held that faculty members were not professional employees covered by the law but "managerial" employees and hence were excluded from Taft-Hartley. They were managerial employees, said the majority, because they effectively recommended the hiring, promotion, salary, and tenure of the faculty; standards of admission; curriculum; and grading system and graduation requirements; and they participated in the hiring of deans and other administrative officers. In a sharp dissent, Justice Brennan said that faculty members played an entirely different role compared with managers in business in that a faculty exercised "its decision making power in its own interest rather than the interest" of the administration of a university. In other words, Brennan charged that the majority did not understand the role of faculty members within a university.

Soon after the decision, administrations at some private universities used *Yeshiva* to deal with their unionized faculties. They refused to recognize faculty unions, refused to negotiate new contracts when the previous ones expired, and threatened to use the decision as leverage to gain concessions at the bargaining table.[38] Unless protected by tenure rules, faculty members may lawfully be discharged for engaging in union activities by antiunion administrations.

Although not covered by Taft-Hartley, *Yeshiva* could very well chill collective bargaining in the public sector. In 1987, a hearing examiner used its rationale to exclude over 1,500 faculty members at the University of Pittsburgh.[39] This was the first successful attempt to extend the reasoning of *Yeshiva* to a major public university.

Only one hope was held out for union-minded faculty members. Buried in a footnote, the majority stated there may be "institutions of higher learning unlike Yeshiva where the faculty are entirely or predominantly managerial." In other words, a determination would be made on a case-by-case basis. In one decision, the NLRB ruled that faculty members were not managerial employees because they did not effectively formulate and effectuate school policies. Unlike Yeshiva University, faculty member recommendations were frequently overruled by the institution's administration.[40]

In 1984, legislation was proposed in Congress stipulating that faculty members are employees under Taft-Hartley. It did not pass, nullifying the attempt to reverse *Yeshiva* by legislation. Given the current Supreme Court membership, legislative action is the only way for faculty members to regain their status under Taft-Hartley, an unlikely prospect at this time.

Although *Yeshiva* does not apply to public colleges and universities, the doctrine was applied for a time to deny faculties of such institutions collective bargaining rights under some state labor relations laws. In 1987, for example, a hearing officer, dealing with an election petition filed by a faculty union of the University of Pittsburgh seeking to represent 2,200 full-time professors, denied the petition on the grounds they possessed similar conditions and rights as the faculty members at Yeshiva University. In 1990, however, the Pennsylvania Labor Relations Board overturned the hearing officer's decision on the grounds the University of Pittsburgh is covered by state and not federal law.[41]

So far no faculty of a public institution has been denied collective bargaining rights on the basis of *Yeshiva*.

Expansion of NLRB Jurisdiction

In another major reversal of policy, the NLRB in 1976 declared it would take jurisdiction of *nonprofit, noncommercial, and charitable institutions.*[42] For over thirty years, the NLRB had declined jurisdiction over such institutions and, indeed, had affirmed that policy as recently as 1974.[43] A majority of the Board held that the statutory basis for the exclusion disappeared when in July 1974 Congress had amended Taft-Hartley to provide coverage to nonprofit hospitals, a matter that will be discussed later.

Under the new policy, nonprofit enterprises are no longer automatically excluded from the coverage of the law.[44] Institutions such as the Chicago Lighthouse for the Blind are included under the new policy.[45] Under compelling circumstances, however, the Board is prepared to make exemptions, as in *Goodwill Industries*. The Board held that collective bargaining could undermine the goal of Goodwill of hiring handicapped persons for rehabilitation purposes. Higher wages, the Board reasoned, could lead to the hiring of more productive workers and a reduction in Goodwill's work force of handicapped people. Aside from these instances, employees of charitable institutions now have the same protected legal right to organization and collective bargaining as employees in commercial and profit-making firms. A charitable institution's gross revenue must be sufficient, however, to meet the dollar standards established by the Board in order to come within its jurisdiction. In *Rhode Island Catholic Orphan Asylum*, the 1976 precedent case, the institution grossed more than $250,000, sufficient to meet the dollar standard for institutions of that type. In *Chicago Lighthouse for the Blind*, the enterprise earned more than $50,000 per year by performing certain subcontracted work for companies located outside the state of Illinois. In short, under the current policy, a charitable institution that meets the dollar standards established by the Board will not automatically be excluded from its jurisdiction just because it provides a worthy social service.

In 1973, the Board declined all cases arising in law firms.[46] It held that law firms had a minimal degree of impact on interstate commerce and apparently believed that unionization of its employees could compromise the confidentiality between the law firm and its clients. Once again the Board changed its policy, and in 1977, held that *law firms as a class will no longer be excluded from its jurisdiction*.[47] Reversing its position, the Board said:

> Since it is clear that law firms, as a class, do have a substantial impact on interstate commerce, we shall assert jurisdiction over them.

A major factor that induced its change of position about the relationship of law firms to interstate commerce was a U.S. Supreme Court decision in 1975 that law firms are covered by the antitrust laws.[48]

Though the precedent case, *Foley, Hoag & Eliot*, involved an election petition filed by clerks and messengers, attorneys working in large law firms who consider themselves employees rather than managers or owners could use the NLRB for organizational and collective bargaining purposes. Whenever it could be established in a particular case that law firm employees are engaged in confidential activities, the NLRB will probably exclude them from the bargaining unit. However, in 1980, the Board refused to exclude the nonlegal staff members of a law firm just because they had access to the firm's confidential material.[49]

Before 1977, the Board had consistently refused to apply Taft-Hartley to foreign banks and other commercial enterprises operating in the United States *when they were owned by a foreign government*. The issue arose again in the Chicago branch of the State Bank of India, Bombay. At that time, the NLRB reversed its former policy, directing an election among the American citizens working for that bank.[50] To justify this change, the Board stressed that in 1976 Congress had enacted the Foreign Sovereign Immunities Act, which reduced the immunity of foreign commercial enterprises operating in the United States. The NLRB said that this new law manifested a congressional intent to deny "sovereign immunity to a foreign state's private or commercial acts" occurring within the United States. Since under the 1976 law such enterprises are subject to American federal and state court jurisdiction, the Board believed that it would not be consistent to continue its former policy. Thus, *American citizens working for foreign enterprises* have gained legal protection of their organizational and collective bargaining rights and are no longer, in the words of the union involved, "second-class citizens." In 1987, following the *State Bank of India* precedent, the Board applied the law to the U.S. citizens working for a nonprofit German cultural organization.[51] Evidence demonstrated that the German government organization engaged in commercial activities with the United States, including execution of contracts with American cultural institutions and the purchase of supplies for its educational activities.

In short, in the case of law firms, charitable institutions, foreign-operated enterprises, and private educational institutions, the Board in the 1970s shifted its position in favor of extending coverage. It is noteworthy that so far there has been no class of cases in which the Board has declined jurisdiction after it originally asserted jurisdiction. Thus, the NLRB has elected to broaden the coverage of Taft-Hartley rather than to restrict it.

For one class of employees, by a 5–4 vote in 1981, the U.S. Supreme Court specifically approved a Board policy expanding coverage of Taft-Hartley. In *Hendricks County Rural Electric Membership Co.*, the Board held that confidential employees are not generally exempt from Board jurisdiction.[52] *Excluded are only employees who have access to confidential matters directly relating to labor relations*, such as the secretary of an industrial relations manager. Other employees who have access to confidential matters not directly relating to labor relations, such as the secretary of a purchasing manager, are covered by Taft-Hartley. For exclusion, in other words, an employer must show that the employee has access to information relating directly to labor relations matters.

Church-Related Matters

In another highly controversial area, though not involving a change in policy, the NLRB held that it would exert jurisdiction over church-operated commercial enterprises.[53] Like some other religious bodies, the Christian Science Church operates a variety of profit-making commercial enterprises. In the precedent case, the church argued that it should be exempt from the coverage of Taft-Hartley because of the First Amendment to the Constitution calling for the separation of church and state, and it also claimed that the profits it earned from its commercial ventures were used to further the cause of religion. Rejecting these arguments, the NLRB directed an election among employees who worked in the commercial enterprises run by the church.

In another religion-related matter, the Board assumed jurisdiction over private schools operated by the Roman Catholic Church.[54] Though the Board recognized that the schools' admission policies were set to attract future priests, the evidence demonstrated that the schools operated primarily as college preparatory schools with the same curriculum and extracurricular activities as other private and public high schools. Also, it noted that only 16 percent of the graduating class in the year preceding the Board's decision had entered seminary colleges. It would seem, however, that if a religious body operated a school solely for religious instructions, the Board would not apply Taft-Hartley.[55]

In 1979, however, the U.S. Supreme Court by a 5–4 vote in *Catholic Bishop of Chicago*[56] reversed the Board and ruled that lay teachers employed by the church-operated schools are not covered by Taft-Hartley. Writing for the majority, former Chief Justice Warren Burger said that Congress had never intended the NLRB to have jurisdiction over such schools. He believed that the exercise of such jurisdiction would automatically raise serious First Amendment issues entangling the NLRB in religious matters. Therefore, he said, Congress must authorize Board authority over parochial schools by adopting specific language. In other words, Taft-Hartley would have to contain a provision that expressly stipulated that the NLRB had jurisdiction. Since the law does not contain such a provision, the majority of the Court concluded that the Board does not have jurisdiction over parochial schools. In the absence of an "affirmative intention" expressed by Congress, Burger reasoned, the Court should refuse to construe the law in a manner that "could in turn call upon the Court to resolve difficult and sensitive questions arising out of the guarantees of the First Amendment religion clauses."

Justice William Brennan, writing for the minority in a vigorous dissent, argued that the majority had invented a "canon of statutory construction" solely for deciding this case. Never before, he said, had the Court required the affirmative expression of Congress in providing the NLRB with jurisdiction over particular categories of employers. For example, as noted, the Board has asserted jurisdiction over private universities, charitable institutions, law firms, foreign government enterprises, and church-operated commercial enterprises, although Taft-Hartley does not expressly authorize the Board to take jurisdiction over them. Brennan also argued that where Congress had intended to exempt NLRB jurisdiction, it did so by specific exclusionary language, as with government employees, agricultural labor, railroads and airlines, supervisors, and, at one time, nonprofit hospitals. He also stressed that when Taft-Hartley was enacted, Congress had turned down a proposal which would have exempted religious institutions—a clear expression of congressional intent.

Until 1986, the NLRB did not apply *Catholic Bishop of Chicago* to church-related colleges and universities. In *St. Joseph College*, however, the policy changed, with the Board declining jurisdiction over the college.[57] It overruled previous cases to the extent they held that *Catholic Bishop of Chicago* did not apply to church-related institutions of higher learning. So far, however, the Board has ruled that employees of church-operated child-care centers[58] and hospitals[59] are covered by the law on the grounds that religious instruction is not their primary purpose.

In any event, whatever may be said of *Catholic Bishop of Chicago*, as of *Yeshiva*, the U.S. Supreme Court has sharply restricted the application of Taft-Hartley, denying many employees legal protection of their unionization and collective bargaining activities. As a possible consequence, there could be industrial strife. Albert Shanker, president of the American Federation of Teachers, said that if denied the protection of the NLRB, such employees could strike to force their employers into collective bargaining arrangements.[60]

Additional Jurisdictional Matters

A few other jurisdictional matters are of general interest. Under current policy, the Board asserts jurisdiction over professional baseball, and other professional sports;[61] symphony orchestras with an annual revenue of at least $1 million;[62] and the gambling industry, rejecting the contention of the owners of a casino in Nevada that gambling in that state is essentially local.[63] Labor unions as employers also fall within the jurisdiction of the NLRB.[64] Under this policy, union representatives and office employees have been able to form unions of their own to bargain collectively with the union employers.

In a particularly interesting case, the NLRB in 1976 refused jurisdiction over the employees of a business conducted by an *Indian tribe on its reservation.*[65] It held that Indian tribes are sovereign entities insofar as activities on their reservations are concerned, and that the tribal council is equivalent to a government for purposes of NLRB jurisdiction. This decision may come as a surprise to Indians who have had difficulty in other matters with the U.S. government! In 1988, the Board reaffirmed the policy, holding that a health-care clinic operated by a consortium of seven Indian tribes, located on an Indian reservation, was not covered by Taft-Hartley.[66] Therefore, it dismissed a petition filed by the union seeking to represent the clinic employees.

In 1992, however, the Board granted bargaining rights to employees of an Indian tribe who performed their duties at a site located well away from the reservation.[67] Supporting the decision was the fact that the enterprise employed mainly nontribal workers; no proof existed that Congress intended to exempt off-reservation tribal businesses; and assertion of jurisdiction would not abrogate any tribal rights guaranteed by treaty of the United States government.

In 1983, the U.S. Supreme Court held that Taft-Hartley applies to *illegal aliens.*[68] When the Sure-Tan Company's illegal aliens formed a union, the employer in retaliation reported them to the Immigration and Naturalization Service. To avoid deportation, some of them quit their jobs and voluntarily left the United States. Such employer conduct, the high court ruled, amounted to a constructive discharge in violation of the law forbidding discrimination against employees for union activities.

In other words, for purposes of Taft-Hartley, illegal or undocumented aliens are protected just like U.S. citizens. Using the Supreme Court and a federal appeals court for guidance, the Board fashioned a remedy for the employer's violation of the law. For reinstatement to their jobs, the employees had four years to obtain legal entry into the United States. The employer was directed to offer reinstatement in a letter written in Spanish to be sent to their last known address in Mexico. Back pay would depend on the actual economic loss the employees suffered because of the illegal discharges.[69]

In 1992, however, a federal appeals court sharply curtailed the amount of back pay due undocumented aliens.[70] It ruled such persons were not entitled to back pay for the time they were not lawfully entitled to be in the United States. Previously the Board had held an employer was required to pay back pay to undocumented aliens who were unlawfully discharged. Such back pay would include all the time the undocumented aliens resided in the United States. According to the NLRB, the only time of ineligibility would be when they were not in the United States. Not so, said the Chicago federal appeals court in a 2–1 decision, ruling undocumented aliens who unlawfully entered the United States were not eligible for back pay during the time of their unlawful residency.

Union Organizers as Employees

Since 1975 the NLRB has held employers may not lawfully refuse to hire *full-time paid union organizers*.[71] In part it justified its policy by reference to the description of "employee" as established by Section 2(3) of Taft-Hartley. It is broadly defined as including "any employee" except those specifically excluded such as agricultural laborers, persons providing domestic services, and supervisors. Since the law does not specifically exclude union organizers, the Board held it was not the intent of Congress to exclude them from coverage of the statute.

Despite the longstanding policy of the Board, the issue surfaced again in the early 1990s. In *Willmar Electric Service*, a union employee organizer applied for a job at a construction site, telling the employer he intended to use his free time to organize the company's employees. When he was denied employment, the Board ruled the employer discriminated against the union organizer in violation of Taft-Hartley. Eventually a federal appeals court sustained the decision.[72] As with any other employee, however, the employer may lawfully discharge a union organizer should he fail to perform the duties of the job in a proper manner. The union organizer must skillfully juggle job requirements and organization of the firm's employees.

As Crow and Hartman put it:

> . . . The good organizer, usually a competent employee, can perform his or her job and orchestrate the union campaign at the same time. Barry O. Edwards, a professional organizer for the International Brotherhood of Boilermakers, has parlayed his expertise into a career. Many times in the past, Edwards has gone to work for a targeted employer and, much to their chagrin, has performed his work well, coordinated the union campaign, and has adeptly pushed his position to the edge of discharge without going over it . . .[73]

Contrary to the NLRB policy, however, a federal appeals court in 1989 held union organizers were not "employees" entitled to the protection of Taft-Hartley.[74] When there is a disagreement between federal appeals courts, the U.S. Supreme Court normally resolves the issue by reviewing the cases. In regard to union organizers, however, the high court at this writing has not done that.

In 1992, the NLRB carved out an important exception to its policy. It held in *Sunland Construction Co.*[75] that an employer need not hire organizers when a strike is taking place. To justify the exemption, the Board reasoned ". . . the employer had a substantial and legitimate business interest for refusing to hire a paid union agent."

In a concurring opinion, Board member Clifford Oviatt, Jr., remarked:

To many nonunion employers, the organizer's presence in the work place is reminiscent of the Trojan Horse, whose innocuous appearance shields a deadly enemy.

COVERAGE OF HEALTH-CARE INDUSTRY: 1974 AMENDMENT TO TAFT-HARTLEY

Proprietary Hospitals and Nursing Homes

In 1967, the NLRB departed from its policy of declining jurisdiction over proprietary (profit-making) hospitals. In *Butte Medical Properties*, the Board established a new standard for profit-making hospitals that are privately owned.[76] Jurisdiction is asserted if such hospitals have gross revenues of at least $250,000 per year.

The Board justified its action by noting that state regulation of privately owned hospitals is limited in the sphere of labor relations. Also, national health insurance companies and the federal government make large payments to proprietary hospitals. These payments were deemed to have a major impact on interstate commerce. Interstate commerce is also affected by substantial purchases of supplies and services from out-of-state sources. Privately owned nursing homes, operating for a profit, were also placed under the law if the employer receives at least $100,000 in annual gross revenue.[77] The Board justified its action by applying the same reasoning used in *Butte*.

Labor Disputes in Health-Care Industry

Under Taft-Hartley, however, nonprofit hospitals were expressly excluded from its coverage. This placed employees of such hospitals at a significant disadvantage compared with those working for proprietary hospitals. In other words, a different public policy existed for essentially the same group of employees. Given this glaring inequity, Congress in July 1974 amended Taft-Hartley, authorizing coverage of proprietary and nonprofit hospitals and nursing homes. The amendment does not apply to government-operated hospitals. It deals strictly with the private sector. *Both classes of private hospitals and nursing homes, proprietary and nonprofit, are under the same law*.

One consequence of the new legislation is that recognition strikes are no longer necessary in the health-care industry. This serves the public interest, since many long and bitter strikes were formerly undertaken by nonprofit hospital employees because hospital management refused to recognize their unions.

Since hospitals supply a critical public service, unions representing employees in both proprietary and nonprofit hospitals are required to give ninety days' notice before terminating or seeking to modify labor agreements, thirty days more than Taft-Hartley requires in other industries. In addition, a hospital union may not lawfully strike or picket unless it gives ten days' notice. This provision was adopted to give hospital management an opportunity to make arrangements for the continuity of patient care. Furthermore, a labor dispute in a health-care institution is automatically subject to mediation by the Federal Mediation and Conciliation Service. Unlike its authority in other industries, the NLRB is empowered to appoint a fact-finding board to make recommendations to settle hospital labor disputes.

With the passage of the amendment, the NLRB was faced with a series of problems in its application. In 1975, it held that it would apply the same dollar jurisdictional standards to nonprofit health-care establishments as it had previously adopted for profit-making units.[78] As noted, this was $250,000 for hospitals and $100,000 for nursing homes and related facilities. Thus, the same dollar standards for jurisdictional purposes apply to all health-care establishments regardless of whether or not they are operated for profit.

Bargaining Units

A much more complicated problem involved the establishment of appropriate bargaining units for employees who work in hospitals. Of course, this problem had existed even when the NLRB took over jurisdiction of profit-making hospitals. It became much more extensive, however, when Congress brought about 7,000 nonprofit hospitals employing about 5 million workers under the jurisdiction of the NLRB. In addition, the legislative history of the 1974 amendment provided instructions to the Board with regard to hospital bargaining units. The Senate Committee Report said that "due consideration should be given by the Board to prevent proliferation of bargaining units in the health care industry."[79] In other words, Congress did not believe it to be in the public interest to have a multitude of small and narrow bargaining units within a hospital. In carrying out the congressional mandate, the Board grouped hospital employees in terms of their community of interests, training, educational background, professional status, and bargaining history. This was not an easy task, because at times, a particular group on the basis of some of these criteria could reasonably fall within the category of another group.

Before the advent of the Reagan NLRB, six separate bargaining units had been established in the health-care industry. These were registered nurses,[80] physicians employed by a hospital (other than residents and interns),[81] other professional employees,[82] technical employees,[83] clerical employees,[84] and general service and maintenance employees.[85] In this way, the previous Board believed it had struck a reasonable balance between the congressional mandate against proliferation of bargaining units and the desires of employees, based upon their community of interests, to select their own bargaining agent. Under that policy, if all employees within a health-care institution were organized, there could be a maximum of six bargaining units. On the other hand, the collective bargaining rights of one group did not depend upon the organization of other classifications. For example, a bargaining unit composed of registered nurses could be established even though other groups remained nonunion.

The Reagan Board and the Bargaining Unit

In a sharp reversal of policy, the Reagan Board abolished the previous system of bargaining units.[86] Instead of the "community of interest" test, it held that a separate bargaining unit would be established in the heath-care industry only if there was a "disparity of interests" greater than that required in other industries. However, the decision did not establish a standard or guideline demonstrating how a group of health-care employees could prove it had a disparity of interests sufficient to distinguish it from other groups. It seemed that the new policy might be applied to establish only two bargaining units within a health-care institution—professional and nonprofessional. If this in fact resulted, organization within hospitals would be far more difficult, since it is normally easier to unionize comparatively small groups of employees.

Predictably, the Reagan Board's decision was sharply criticized by the labor movement but praised by health-care management and employer groups. Union representatives complained that the new policy was

> outrageous, destroying ten years of legal precedent,

and represented a

> naked political attack on hospital workers' right to organize.[87]

In contrast, the other side supported the new decision, charging that the previous policy was "contrary to the intent of Congress" and stating that the new policy was "a victory for the hospital."[88]

Post-Reagan Board Policy

A surprising development occurred, however, when the initial Reagan members left the NLRB and new ones were appointed. In the fall of 1988, the new Board proposed that the following *eight bargaining units* be established in private hospitals: nurses, physicians, other professional employees, technical employees, skilled maintenance employees, business office clerical employees, guards, and other nonprofessional employees.[89] After announcing the proposed change, the NLRB held hearings, frequently controversial if not bitter, in the major cities, permitting interested parties to voice their views. Needless to say, the American Hospital Association and the AFL-CIO were on opposite sides of the controversy. So contentious was the issue that the Board extended the time of the hearings. Approximately 160 witnesses representing thirteen different organizations testified.

To explain the NLRB position, Chair James Stephens stated that the Reagan Board policies had led to protracted delays and that these delays were

> compounded by more delay. By the time the unit issue is decided, the employees originally interested in union representation, may not even be working in the bargaining unit anymore.[90]

On May 21, 1987, the NLRB put the new policy into effect. A few months later, a federal district court in Chicago enjoined the Board on the grounds that eight units in the health-care industry went beyond the intent of Congress. At that time, about 100 unit cases in the health-care industry were pending in the Board's field offices. As expected, the unions involved appealed the district court's decision. In April 1990, a federal appeals court reversed the district court, upholding the NLRB establishment of eight bargaining units for hospital employees.[91] However, the American Hospital Association appealed the decision to the Supreme Court.

U.S. Supreme Court Upholds NLRB

In April 1991, the U.S. Supreme Court upheld the NLRB decision by a surprising *unanimous* vote.[92] The decision was applied only to acute-care hospitals, excluding nursing homes.

In its attack against the policy, the major argument of the American Hospital Association was that the NLRB does not have the authority to issue an industrywide bargaining policy by adopting a rule. It based its position on Section 9(b) of Taft-Hartley which states:

> The Board shall decide *in each case* whether, in order to assure to employees the fullest freedom in exercising the rights guaranteed by this act, the unit appropriate for the purposes of collective bargaining shall be the employer unit, craft unit, plant unit, or subdivision thereof. . . . (Emphasis supplied)

That is, the Board must decide the appropriate unit on a case-by-case basis. It may not establish bargaining units on the basis of adopting a rule or policy that covers an entire industry.

Rejecting the employer's position, the high court stressed Section 6 of the statute which states:

> The Board shall have the authority from time to time to make, amend, and rescind, in the manner prescribed by the Administrative Procedure Act, such *rules and regulations* as may be necessary to carry out the provisions of this Act. (Emphasis supplied)

In other words, in resolving the policy conflict between the language contained in Section 6 and Section 9(b), the Supreme Court came down on the side of Section 6. Justice John Paul Stevens put it this way:

> . . . [The] more natural reading [of the words] *in each case* was simply to indicate that whenever there is a disagreement about the appropriateness of a unit, the Board shall resolve the dispute. Under this reading [the words] *in each case* are synonymous with whenever necessary. (Emphasis supplied)

Nor did the high court believe the Board policy would result in the proliferation of bargaining units in acute-care hospitals. It said the NLRB gave extensive consideration to the special problems that proliferation might create in hospitals. Finally, the Supreme Court rejected the argument that the rule was arbitrary and capricious because it ignored critical differences among acute-care hospitals in the nation. Instead, it adopted the Board's conclusion that such hospitals did not differ in a material way as related to the appropriateness of bargaining units. Upholding the NLRB, Justice Stevens wrote the agency based its rule on a "reasonable analysis" of an extensive record developed by the public hearings.

The Supreme Court decision did not mean that every hospital would have eight bargaining units. In actual practice, some of the groups would not want unionization. It could be, for example, that whereas the nurses and physicians would select unions to represent them, the other six groups would not desire collective bargaining.

Effects of Policy

During the public hearings, opponents of the NLRB policy of establishing eight bargaining units predicted dire consequences inconsistent with orderly labor relations within the industry. According to hospital employers, wage rates would become excessive, raising costs; work assignments between bargaining units would upset labor relations; and numerous strikes would occur jeopardizing patient care.[93]

At least one careful study based upon research of the problem demonstrates that such predictions and fears proved groundless. Schwarz and Koziara conclude:

> Our findings have several policy implications. First—consistent with other studies, we find that most unionized hospitals have four or fewer bargaining units. It does not appear that Board policies have resulted in bargaining unit proliferation. Considering that the number of potential bargaining units is probably at least several times the number of actual units, the Board seems to have heeded the Congressional admonition to avoid unit proliferation.
>
> Second, fears that multiple units would increase hospital wages and the incidence of work assignment disputes and strikes appear to have been exaggerated. Therefore, the NLRB's proposed eight-unit rule is likely to have few of the negative effects assumed to result from unit proliferation. The only qualification to that generalization suggested by the evidence of this study is that hospitals with multiple units may have more total strikes. Whether an average of one additional strike over an eight-year period is of practical significance, however, involves a value judgment.
>
> This study indicates that the negative consequences of multiple units are relatively small. These consequences should be weighed against the possible benefits of the Board's proposed rules as upheld by the Supreme Court. One significant benefit is decreases in litigation and in the resulting delays that have limited hospital employees' access to collective bargaining. Had an investigation such as this one been conducted prior to the issuance of the Congressional admonition, perhaps litigation could have been avoided and the purposes of the NLRA more speedily fulfilled.[94]

Nursing Homes

As indicated, NLRB policy applies only to profit and nonprofit acute-care hospitals. The Supreme Court expressly stated the decision did not apply to nursing homes since that area of the health-care industry was not before it.

In 1992, the NLRB did not apply the *American Hospital Association* decision to nursing homes.[95] In *Park Manor Care Center*, a regional director of the agency decided licensed practical nurses (LPNs) were technical employees and should be excluded from a service and maintenance unit. The Board remanded the case to the regional office to develop a fuller record to determine whether the LPNs had such a compelling community of interest to justify keeping them in a separate unit.

Given the decision, it would appear the NLRB would determine bargaining units in nonacute health-care facilities on a case-by-case method. As the *Wall Street Journal* stated following *Park Manor Care Center*:

> IT AIN'T NECESSARILY SO: The National Labor Relations Board decided, in a nursing-home case, that it will follow a case-by-case approach for determining proper bargaining units for most health-care facilities. After the Supreme Court upheld an NLRB plan in hospital bargaining cases for expedited rule-making, which benefits unions, some critics warned of a precedent for similar efforts in other fields.[96]

Solicitation of Union Members: Special Rules for Health-Care Industry

In a later chapter, we will discuss the right of unions to solicit employees for membership on employer property, and the corollary right of the employers to ban union solicitation on their premises. However, the NLRB established a special set of rules for hospitals, recognizing that a health-care institution is different from business in general. Hospital management can forbid the right of employees to solicit or distribute union literature on behalf of a union in *patient-care* areas even if the activity occurs during nonworking time.[97] Thus, in order to avoid disturbing patients, hospitals may forbid all such union activity in patient rooms and other patient-care areas such as x-ray, operating, and therapy rooms. On the other hand, the NLRB invalidated a hospital rule that forbade union solicitation in cafeterias and visitors' lounges. It held that even though patients have access to these areas, the possibility of disruption of patient care would be remote. In addition, the NLRB held that off-duty employees have the right to solicit on behalf of a union outside the premises of a hospital. Thus, an off-duty employee had the right to distribute union literature on a rear loading dock and in the front driveway.[98]

In July 1977, a federal appeals court held that hospitals were authorized to ban union solicitation in both *patient-care* and *patient-access* areas, such as hallways, elevators, cafeterias, and waiting rooms. In this case, *St. John's Hospital* v. *NLRB*, the court held that it was "specious" to draw a distinction between patient-care areas and patient-access areas. Unlike the Board, it said that union solicitation in patient-access areas could have an upsetting effect on patients.[99]

Later on, however, the U.S. Supreme Court held that a hospital may not arbitrarily ban union solicitation on all of its premises. In June 1978, the Court held in *Beth Israel Hospital*[100] that a hospital may not forbid distribution of union literature and solicitation in a cafeteria unless it can show that such activities disturb patients. In that case, only 1.56 percent of the cafeteria's patrons were patients. In *Baptist Hospital*[101] the Court modified a no-solicitation rule that had applied to virtually the entire premises of a hospital. Holding that such a rule unreasonably interfered with organizational rights, the Court held that a union could solicit members in areas in which there were no patient rooms, such as cafeterias, gift shops, and lounges located on the lobby floor. On the other hand, the hospital was permitted to ban solicitation in corridors and lounges located on floors occupied by patients. Apparently, for those locations, the hospital had presented sufficient evidence to show that patients would be adversely affected by union activity.

Although these two decisions do not resolve the entire problem with finality, it is safe to say that a health-care institution may not arbitrarily forbid union solicitation in all areas to which patients have access. For a no-solicitation rule to be valid, the burden is on the hospital to prove that union activity in such areas would not be in the best interests of the patients. The presumption is that a ban in nonpatient rooms or care areas is unlawful without a showing that such activity is likely to disrupt patient care or disturb patients.[102]

Strikes and Picketing

Recall that before employees may strike or picket, the union must give ten days' notice to the hospital. With one exception, to be noted below, the Board has applied that requirement literally. In one case, a union complied with the notice requirement and was picketing the hospital. Four union officers of another union joined the picket line to show sympathy. They picketed for only one and one-half hours on one day during a strike that lasted over two weeks. Despite the fact that the sympathy pickets did not place any additional union pressure on the hospital, the Board held that the union that had provided the sympathy pickets had violated the ten-day notice requirement.[103]

Hospital employees who strike or picket without filing the ten days' notice may be discharged by the hospital. It does not matter whether the employees are represented by a union, or whether a union had knowledge of their illegal conduct. The General Counsel dismissed the charges filed by such discharged employees, who had claimed they were engaging in a protected activity under Taft-Hartley.[104]

On the other hand, the General Counsel refused to find that a union violated the ten days' notice requirement in a case where a hospital had committed flagrant and massive unfair labor practices during and after an NLRB election. Though the union filed a notice, it did not meet the technical requirements of the notice, such as stating precisely when picketing and striking would begin. In holding that the union had not violated the notice requirement, the General Counsel stated:

> Although the Union literally breached the [notice] provisions of the Act by striking and picketing after serving upon the Employer and the FMCS a notice which lacked the specificity requirements, the failure to strictly comply with the requirements were deemed excused by the Employer's serious and flagrant unfair labor practices against which the strike and picketing were meant as a protest.[105]

The General Counsel said further that the legislative history of the 1974 amendment demonstrated that unions would not be held to the notice requirement when a hospital commits serious or flagrant unfair labor practices.

These observations demonstrate the way the NLRB and the General Counsel have handled problems growing out of the 1974 amendment. They meet these issues as they arise, and this is by no means the end of the story. It will be interesting to learn how the Board deals with these issues—one hopes in a sound way, because the labor relations program in the health-care industry is vital to the public interest.

Nurses Ruled as Supervisors

In *Health Care & Retirement Corp.*, decided by the U.S. Supreme Court in May 1994, licensed practical nurses were held to be supervisors and excluded from the protection of the Taft-Hartley Act.[106] In the next chapter, we will learn that exclusion from the coverage of the statute means an employer may discharge or otherwise discriminate against persons deemed to be supervisors and who engage in union activities.

This happened to four nurses employed by a nursing home in Urbana, Ohio, who attempted to form a union. After they were fired by the employer, the NLRB held the nursing home violated the law and directed their reinstatement with back pay.[107]

By a single vote, the decision was 5–4, the high court reversed, sustaining the discharge of the nurses. It held the nurses had supervisory authority and served "in the interest of the employer." Writing for the minority that upheld the NLRB, Ruth Bader Ginsburg, recently appointed to the high court, held that the nurses spent only a small fraction of the time exercising supervisory authority and their focus was on the patient. Thus, their authority as supervisors was not exercised in the interest of the employer, but was incidental to the treatment of patients.

In her dissent, Ginsburg stated:

> Through case-by-case adjudication, the Board has sought to distinguish individuals exercising the level of control that truly places them in the ranks of management, from highly skilled employees, whether professional or technical, who perform, incidentally to their skilled work, a limited supervisory role. I am persuaded that the Board's approach is rational and consistent with the Act. I would therefore uphold the administrative determination, affirmed by the Board, that Heartland's practical nurses are protected employees.

In any event, the decision places a formidable obstacle in the organization of nurses in the health-care industry. Though licensed practical nurses were involved in the case, the same legal principle would apply to registered nurses. To be sure, nurses could strike to retaliate against employers who discharge union active nurses or force employers to recognize nurses' unions. Such action could interfere with the orderly operation of a health-care facility and put the patients at risk. Such could be the unfortunate results of the decision denying nurses legal protection in their organizational and collective bargaining rights.

Hospital Interns and Resident Physicians

In *Cedars-Sinai Medical Center*,[108] a majority of the Board sparked an unusual amount of controversy and general interest when it held that hospital interns and resident physicians have no rights under Taft-Hartley. It held that such persons are not "employees" within the meaning of the law but rather students pursuing a graduate medical education. Though interns and residents are paid for their work and devote a great deal of their time to patient care, the Board held that the law does not apply to them. For those who believe that collective bargaining is necessary to improve the conditions of their employment, the Board's decision created a great deal of resentment. The leader of a group of interns and residents promoting collective bargaining said that the Board had

> publicly affirmed that the profits of hospital employers are more important than the welfare of workers or the sick.[109]

During the 1976 congressional hearings concerning NLRB operations, Representative Frank Thompson of New Jersey, who authored the 1974 hospital amendment, said the law should be changed to eliminate *Cedars-Sinai Medical Center*. He feared that residents and interns might strike for union recognition. In bitter criticism of the Board policy, he said:

> And the doctors and interns had to strike for recognition. Now they will appeal that, but the basis of their appeal, I am afraid, is a terribly difficult one. They would have to establish the Board was arbitrary, so that might lead us to amending the act. I discussed this yesterday with my distinguished ranking member and friend Mr. Ashbrook. He is as upset about that decision as I. The Board is human and like all humans, including myself, you make mistakes. Perhaps not as many as I made, but I think to call interns and residents "students" was a very definite mistake and can lead to extreme difficulty in that industry.[110]

However, a bill that would have brought residents and interns within the scope of the law, nullifying *Cedars-Sinai Medical Center*, was defeated in the House of Representatives.[111] Also, a federal appeals court held that the NLRB policy did not violate its authority under Taft-Hartley.[112]

TAFT-HARTLEY AND BANKRUPTCY CODE

NLRB v. *Bildisco*

Here we address a special kind of jurisdictional problem—the relationship between Taft-Hartley and the U.S. Bankruptcy Code. In question is the determination of which statute prevails when the two conflict. The issue was joined in a case involving a small New Jersey building supply distributor, Bildisco and Bildisco. It had a labor agreement with the Teamsters Union that was scheduled to expire in April 1982. Significantly, the contract provided that it was binding on the parties "even though bankruptcy shall supervene."

While the labor agreement was in force, the employer, without bargaining with the union, refused to pay scheduled wage increases, stopped paying the agreed-upon health and pension contributions on behalf of the workers, and refused to turn over union dues that were deducted from the workers' paychecks. Acting favorably on an unfair labor practice charge filed by the union, following its traditional policy, the National Labor Relations Board held that the employer violated Taft-Hartley.[113] The employer was found guilty of an unfair labor practice because it had unilaterally changed the terms of a labor agreement and had failed to bargain with the union before making the changes. From its inception, national labor policy has protected the integrity of labor agreements. Neither employer nor union may unilaterally alter the terms of a labor agreement.

In January 1980, long before the contract was due to expire, Bildisco had filed a voluntary petition for bankruptcy under Chapter 11 of the Bankruptcy Code. Under Chapter 11, a company continues to operate with court protection from creditor lawsuits while it tries to work out a plan to pay its debts. Under these circumstances, the employer is called "debtor-in possession," normally operating the enterprise with the same management personnel under bankruptcy court supervision. In the proceeding before a bankruptcy court, Bildisco received permission to reject the total collective bargaining agreement. On appeal by the union, a federal district court upheld the decision of the bankruptcy court. By this time, the NLRB had held that the employer had violated national labor policy. Thus, when the case was appealed by the NLRB and the union, the federal appeals court was faced with two conflicting decisions: the NLRB had held that Bildisco had violated Taft-Hartley, but the bankruptcy court, upheld by the district court, permitted the employer to reject the entire labor agreement. Upholding the lower court decision, the federal appeals court held that Bildisco had the right to abrogate the labor agreement.[114] In other words, the appeals court ruled that when the two federal statutes in question conflict, the Bankruptcy Code prevails over Taft-Hartley.

Such was the setting as the U.S. Supreme Court was prepared to issue its decision after receiving the appeal from the NLRB. To say the least, the labor relations community awaited this decision by the high court with deep interest. Much more was at stake than the small New Jersey building supply firm. In 1983, Wilson Foods had filed for bankruptcy and immediately cut employees' wages by 40 to 50 percent.[115] In the same year, Continental Air Lines had also filed for bankruptcy under Chapter 11 and had immediately cut wages by about 50 percent.[116] In both cases, strikes occurred, but the firms were able to operate.

On February 22, 1984, in one of the most significant labor cases in modern times, the Supreme Court issued its decision, upholding the decision of the federal appeals court.[117] By a 5–4 vote, the high court held that an employer could abrogate a labor agreement *immediately upon filing for bankruptcy under Chapter 11.* The employer did not have to wait for a bankruptcy court for permission: Mere filing of the petition was sufficient to get rid of the labor agreement.

The second major issue determined by the Court equally shocked the labor movement. By unanimous decision, the Court established standards to guide bankruptcy courts when faced with the problem of determining whether an employer could permanently eliminate a labor agreement. In this respect, the high court ruled that all an employer need show is that the agreement "burdens" the chances for survival under Chapter 11. No requirement was placed on the employer to show that the labor agreement made the difference between survival or extinction of the firm. Indeed, no showing was required to establish whether the contract was the critical factor or even a major reason for the employer's financial difficulties. A firm's financial problems could result from a variety of factors, including the rate of interest, inept management, failure to modernize a facility, poor marketing, insufficient advertising, or changes in consumer demand for a product or service. Obviously any labor agreement burdens an employer in the sense that a low wage is less burdensome than a higher wage. But in arriving at a decision as to whether a contract may be permanently eliminated, a bankruptcy judge had only to determine whether the employer made a "reasonable" effort to negotiate a less burdensome contract. If the employer and union were not able to do that, the bankruptcy court may still cancel the contract.

Obviously, these standards would not make it difficult for employers to use Chapter 11 to be free of labor agreements. Indeed, one bankruptcy lawyer termed the standards as "cosmetic," sending a strong signal to bankruptcy courts to permit employers to abrogate labor agreements.[118]

Reaction to *Bildisco*

Thus, the upshot of *Bildisco* was that an employer would not commit an unfair labor practice by filing under Chapter 11 for bankruptcy and immediately abandoning a labor agreement. The contract could be lawfully eliminated even before a bankruptcy judge had given the employer permission to nullify the contract. In short, the high court held that when Taft-Hartley and the Bankruptcy Code conflicted, the latter statute prevailed. National labor policy was to be subordinated to an employer's use of the bankruptcy statute to break labor agreements.

Needless to say, the labor movement and the business community differed widely in their reactions to *Bildisco*. Unions feared that almost any employer, even those whose financial situations were not critical, could use this decision to break labor agreements and get rid of unions at the same time. Unions do not have a viable role to play in the absence of a labor agreement. Thus:

> The Supreme Court decision drew immediate expressions of shock and dismay from labor leaders and officials, who viewed it as a weapon to aid employers in ousting unions or pressuring them to accept unwarranted concessions on wages, benefits, and work rules. AFL-CIO President Lane Kirkland said, "We're disappointed in the decision and we will pursue a legislative remedy . . ."
>
> William Winpisinger, president of the International Association of Machinists, described the decision as simply "outrageous . . ."[119]

Just as vigorously, the business community hailed the decision. Representatives of management were fulsome in their praise for *Bildisco*. As reported in the *Wall Street Journal* on February 24, 1984,

> . . . a Cleveland bankruptcy lawyer and former federal bankruptcy judge, contends that all labor-intensive companies will have to consider filing for bankruptcy as a result of the Supreme Court decision.
>
> "The officers and directors of any company will be more inclined to consider the bankruptcy alternative as a management tool to answer some of the problems of a troubled company," he said. "It's gotten to the point where management almost has to consider it."

[An] Atlanta lawyer . . . was more direct. "For smaller companies that have been beaten up by unions over the last 10 years," he said, "it may be a way of getting even."

[Another said]: "Chapter 11 is not pleasant . . . It's sort of like going through open heart surgery and brain surgery at the same time. However, the reality is that it is now clear that the option [Chapter 11] is available. If a contract with a union won't allow a company to exist and make a profit, that company doesn't have to wither away."

Congressional Response

On February 22, 1984, the very same day that *Bildisco* was announced by the Supreme Court, the labor movement mounted a massive campaign to nullify *Bildisco* through congressional action. Only twice before in labor history, when Taft-Hartley was enacted in 1947 and Landrum-Griffin in 1959, had organized labor marshalled such a vigorous legislative campaign. Although labor failed in the prior two instances, this time it was successful in persuading Congress to enact legislation in its favor.

As part of a general revision of the Bankruptcy Code, Congress provided the labor movement protection from the *Bildisco* decision.[120] Congress enacted the new law on June 29, 1984, only four months after the Supreme Court action, and it was signed by Reagan on July 10, 1984.

To be sure, under current legislation, employers can still use the Bankruptcy Code to modify or nullify a labor agreement. This was clearly demonstrated when in July 1985, Wheeling-Pittsburgh Steel Corporation received permission from a bankruptcy court to reduce the wages and benefits that had been provided in a labor agreement negotiated with the United Steelworkers of America. When Wheeling-Pittsburgh reduced wages, the workers struck the plant, underscoring the proposition that employees have the legal right to strike when an employer reduces contractual benefits after bankruptcy court proceedings. In June 1986, however, the federal appeals court in Philadelphia reversed the bankruptcy court and a federal district court decision affirming the bankruptcy court, holding that the employer had not complied with the amended Bankruptcy Code.[121]

Restrictions on Abandonment of Labor Contracts

Unlike the situation in *Bildisco*, an employer's opportunity to abandon labor agreements had been sharply restricted. In the first place, no longer may an employer unilaterally repudiate a labor agreement when filing a petition for bankruptcy. A contract can be abolished only when permission is granted by a bankruptcy judge. In 1987, in its first application of the amended Bankruptcy Code, the NLRB held the employer must follow a contract until a bankruptcy court provides permission to abandon the contract. After filing such petition, but before requesting the bankruptcy court to reject a contract, the employer must propose to the union modifications in the labor agreement necessary to keep the firm in business. The company must provide the union with relevant information, financial reports, and the like, so that the union can intelligently evaluate the proposal. Also, the proposal must be fair and equitable to all concerned. For example, if employees are required to take a wage cut, a similar sacrifice must be made by management personnel. In other words, all concerned—employees, management, creditors, and stockholders—must sacrifice equitably. If the firm's proposal is not fair and equitable to all parties, the company will not be permitted to modify or repudiate the labor agreement. After the employer makes a proposal, it must bargain with the union in good faith to reach a mutually satisfactory modification of the labor agreement.

If the parties cannot agree on contractual matters, the employer may then request a bankruptcy court to alter or nullify the contract. Before providing relief, however, the bankruptcy judge must comply with strict standards—far more effective than those established in *Bildisco*. Before authorizing the employer to modify or repudiate the contract, the bankruptcy court must make sure that the employer made an equitable proposal to the union and bargained in good faith, and that the proposal was rejected by the union without good cause. Only when these conditions are fulfilled may the bankruptcy judge permit the employer to modify or abrogate the collective bargaining agreement, provided the court believes the balance of the equities involved in a case clearly requires modification or rejection.

Thus, the new law removes many of the consequences of the Supreme Court decision. Indeed, the AFL-CIO commented that it was "pleased with the measure," which it termed a "vast improvement over what the Supreme Court left us with."[122] No longer may bankruptcy law be used as a license to break labor agreements.

SUMMARY

Following the *Guss* decision, Congress amended Taft-Hartley to deal with the no-man's-land problem. Although state agencies may take jurisdiction of cases declined by the NLRB, the problem still exists because the majority of states do not have state laws. Under the amendment, state agencies may apply state law destroying uniformity of labor relations law in interstate commerce.

In *Yeshiva*, the Supreme Court declared that faculty members of private universities are managers, denying them protection of Taft-Hartley. As a consequence, administrators in antiunion private colleges and universities ceased recognizing faculty unions and otherwise made it difficult for them to exist. In *Catholic Bishop of Chicago*, the Supreme Court held that religious elementary and secondary schools are not covered by Taft-Hartley, denying lay teachers the right to use the NLRB in their union activities.

Over the years, the NLRB has expanded its jurisdiction, applying the law to cover employees formerly held outside its protection. When Congress amended the law in 1974, NLRB jurisdiction was extended to proprietary and nonprofit hospitals and nursing homes. Establishment of the bargaining unit and union solicitation of members in the health-care industry are the most difficult problems the Board faces in applying the amendment.

Fortunately for unions, Congress abolished *Bildisco*, a Supreme Court doctrine that threatened the very existence of the labor movement.

DISCUSSION QUESTIONS

1. What general effect did the NLRB have on Taft-Hartley coverage when it voluntarily declined jurisdiction over certain cases even though it had statutory authority to deal with these cases?

2. How have the courts generally dealt with the problem of supremacy of national labor policy when states have passed conflicting laws?

3. Evaluate the defects of the 1959 amendment of Taft-Hartley designed to resolve the no-man's-land dilemma.

4. Discuss the pros and cons of the *Yeshiva* case.

5. What is the current status of the NLRB jurisdiction over the following: Law firms? Charitable institutions? Foreign-operated enterprises? Private educational institutions?

6. Do you agree with the Board's jurisdictional policy toward church-related schools and church-operated commercial enterprises? Why or why not?

7. Discuss the special policies established for hospitals as they differ from general industry in the areas of (1) permissible bargaining units, (2) special solicitation rules, and (3) strikes and picketing.

8. What is currently permissible under the Bankruptcy Code as amended in 1984, regarding alteration of collective bargaining agreements?

NOTES

1   National Labor Relations Act, Sections 9(c) and 10(a), 49 Stat. 449, 453 (1935).

2   *NLRB* v. *Jones & Laughlin Steel Corporation*, 301 U.S. 1 (1937).

3   National Labor Relations Act, Section 2(7).

4   *NLRB* v. *Fainblatt*, 306 U.S. 601, 607 (1939).

5   National Labor Relations Board, *First Annual Report* (1936), p. 135.

6   NLRB Release R-428, October 21, 1953.

7   As of October 1968, labor relations laws could be found in Colorado, Connecticut, Hawaii, Kansas, Maryland, Massachusetts, Michigan, Minnesota, New Jersey, New York, North Dakota, Oregon, Pennsylvania, Rhode Island, Utah, Vermont, Wisconsin, and Puerto Rico. See "State Laws," *Commerce Clearing House Labor Law Reporter*, October 18, 1968.

8   Section 14(b) of Taft-Hartley provides that nothing in the federal labor law "shall be construed as authorizing the execution or application of agreements requiring membership in a labor organization as a condition of employment in any State or Territory in which such execution or application is prohibited by State or Territorial law."

9   House Report No. 245 on H.R. 3020, 80th Congress, 1st sess., 1947, p. 44.

10   Section 8(d)(3).

11   Section 203(b).

12   Section 202(c).

13   Section 303(b).

14   Section 10(a) of Taft-Hartley provides that "the Board is empowered, as hereinafter provided, to prevent any person from engaging in any unfair labor practice [listed in Section 8] affecting commerce. This power shall not be affected by any other means of adjustment or prevention that has been or may be established by agreement, law, or otherwise: Provided, that the Board is empowered by agreement with any agency of any State or Territory to cede to such agency jurisdiction over any cases in any industry [other than mining, manufacturing, communications, and transportation except where predominantly local in character] even though such cases involve labor disputes affecting commerce, unless the provision of the State or Territorial statute applicable to the determination of such cases by such agency is inconsistent with the corresponding provision of this Act or has received a construction inconsistent therewith."

15   Senate Report No. 105 on S. 1126, 80th Congress, 1st sess., 1947, p. 26.

16   *State of Minnesota*, 219 NLRB 1095 (1975).

17   Laws of Florida, 1943, Chapter 21968, p. 565.

18   *Hill* v. *Florida*, 325 U.S. 538 (1945).

19   *Bethlehem Steel Company* v. *NYSLRB*, 330 U.S. 767 (1947).

20   *Garner* v. *Teamsters Union*, 246 U.S. 485 (1953).

21   *Brown* v. *Hotel and Restaurant Employees, Local 54*, 468 U.S. 491 (1984).

22   353 U.S. 1 (1957).

23   "1. *Nonretail enterprises*: $50,000 outflow or inflow, direct or indirect. Outflow and inflow may not be combined, but direct and indirect outflow or direct and indirect inflow might be combined to meet the $50,000 requirement. 2. *Office buildings*: Gross revenue of $100,000 or more of which $25,000 or more is derived from organizations that meet any of the standards. 3. *Retail concerns*: $500,000 gross volume of business. 4. *Instrumentalities, links, and channels of interstate commerce*: $50,000 from interstate (or linkage) part of enterprise, or from services performed for employers in commerce. 5. *Public utilities*: $250,000 gross volume or meet nonretail standards. 6. *Transit systems*: $250,000 gross volume. Taxi-cab companies must meet the retail standard. 7. *Newspapers and communications systems*: $100,000 gross volume for radio, television, telegraph, and telephone; newspapers, $200,000 gross volume. 8. *National defense*: Substantial impact on national defense. 9. *Business in the Territories and the District of Columbia*: The standards apply in the territories; all firms in the District of Columbia are covered. 10. *Associations*: Treated as single employer." National Labor Relations Board, *Twenty-fourth Annual Report*, 1959.

24   Labor Management Reporting & Disclosure Act, Section 14(c)(1959).

25   *Hotel Employees Local 255* v. *Leedom*, 358 U.S. 99 (1958).

26   *Floridian Hotel of Tampa*, 124 NLRB 261 (1959).

27   See National Labor Relations Board, *Twenty-third Annual Report*, 1958, pp. 8–12, for a discussion of these standards.

28   *New NLRB Rule to Meet Amended Act*, 45 *Labor Relations Reporter* 49 (1959).

29   Address of Stuart Rothman, NLRB General Counsel, before the Association of State Labor Relations Agencies, Detroit, Michigan, November 18, 1959.

30   Conference Report, House Report No. 1147, 86th Congress, 1st sess., 1959, p. 37.

31   *Centennial Turf Club, Inc.*, 192 NLRB 698 (1971).

32   *Alameda Medical Group, Inc.*, 195 NLRB 312 (1972).

33   *30 Sutton Place Corp.*, 240 NLRB 752 (1979).

34   *Columbia University*, 97 NLRB 424 (1951).

35   183 NLRB 329 (1970).

36   *Fordham University*, 193 NLRB 134 (1971).

37   *NLRB* v. *Yeshiva University*, 444 U.S. 672 (1980). This decision generated sharp criticisms among faculty groups. See, for example, John William Gercacz and Charles E. Krider, "NLRB v. Yeshiva University: The End of Faculty Unions?" *Wake Forest Law Review*, XVI, 6 (December 1980), pp. 891–914; American Association of University Professors, "The Yeshiva Decision," *Academe*, Bulletin of the AAUP, LXVI (May 1980), pp. 188–197.

38   Herman Levy, "The Yeshiva Case Revisited," American Association of University Professors, *Academe*, September-October 1987, p. 34.

39   *In the Matter of the Employees of the University of Pittsburgh*, Case No. PERA-R-84-53-W (1987).

40   *The Cooper Union for the Advancement of Science and Art*, 273 NLRB 1768 (1985).

41   *Chronicle of Higher Education*, XXXVII, No. 14 (December 5, 1990), p. 136.

42   *Rhode Island Catholic Orphan Asylum*, 224 NLRB 1344 (1976).

43   *Ming Quong Children's Center and Social Services Union, Local 535*, 210 NLRB 899 (1974).

44   National Labor Relations Board, *Forty-first Annual Report*, 1976, p. 23.

45   225 NLRB 249 (1976).

46   *Bodle, Fogel, Julber, Reinhardt & Rothschild*, 206 NLRB 512 (1973).

47   *Foley, Hoag & Eliot*, 229 NLRB 456 (1977).

48   *Goldfarb* v. *Virginia State Bar*, 421 U.S. 773 (1975).

49   *Kleinberg, Kaplan, Wolf, Cohen, and Burrows, P.C.*, 253 NLRB 450 (1980).

50   *State Bank of India*, 229 NLRB 838 (1977).

51   *Goethe House New York, German Cultural Center*, 288 NLRB No. 8 29 (1988).

52   *NLRB* v. *Hendricks County Rural Electric Membership Co.*, 454 U.S. 170 (1981).

53   *First Church of Christ Scientist in Boston*, 194 NLRB 1006 (1972).

54   *Catholic Bishop of Chicago*, 220 NLRB 359 (1975).

55   *Association of Hebrew Teachers of Metropolitan Detroit*, 210 NLRB 1053 (1974).

56   *NLRB* v. *Catholic Bishop of Chicago*, 440 U.S. 490 (1979).

57   *St. Joseph College*, 282 NLRB 65 (1986).

58   *St. Louis Christian Home*, 251 NLRB 1477 (1980), enf. *NLRB* v. *St. Louis Christian Home*, 663 F. 2d 60 (8th Cir. 1981) and *The Salvation Army of Mass. Dorchester Daycare*, 271 NLRB 195 (1984).

59   *St. Elizabeth Community Hospital*, 259 NLRB 1135 (1981), enf. *St. Elizabeth Community Hospital* v. *NLRB*, 708 F. 2d 1436 (9th Cir. 1983).

60   *Wall Street Journal*, March 22, 1979.

61   *American League of Professional Baseball Clubs*, 180 NLRB 190 (1969).

62   National Labor Relations Board, *Rules and Regulations*, Section 103.2 (March 7, 1973).

63   *El Dorado, Inc.*, 151 NLRB 579 (1965).

64   *Office Employees International Union, Local 11* v. *NLRB*, 353 U.S. 313 (1957).

65   *Fort Apache Timber*, 226 NLRB 503 (1976).

66   *Southern Indiana Health Council, Inc.*, 290 NLRB No. 56 (1988).

67   *Sac and Fox Industries*, 307 NLRB No. 34 (1992).

68   *Sure-Tan, Inc.* v. *NLRB*, 460 U.S. 1021 (1983).

69   National Labor Relations Board, *Fifty-first Annual Report* (1986), p. 135.

70   *Del Rey Tortilleria, Inc.* v. *NLRB*, 976 F. 2d 1115 (1992).

71   *Oak Apparel, Inc.*, 218 NLRB 701 (1975).

72   *Willmar Electric Service, Inc.* v. *NLRB*, 968 F. 2d 1327 (1992).

73   Stephen Crow and Sandra Hartman, "The Fate of Full-Time, Paid Union Organizers as Employees: Another Nail in the Union Coffin," *Labor Law Journal*, v. 44, January 1993, p. 31.

74   *H. B. Zachry Company* v. *NLRB*, 886 F. 2d 70 (1989).

75   *Sunland Construction Company, Inc.*, 307 NLRB No. 160 (1992).

76   *Butte Medical Properties, d/b/a Medical Center Hospital*, 168 NLRB 266 (1967).

77   *University Nursing Home*, 168 NLRB 263 (1967).

78   *East Oakland Community Health Alliance*, 218 NLRB 1270 (1975).

79   Senate Report 93-76, 93d Congress, 2d sess., 5 (1974).

80   *Mercy Hospitals of Sacramento*, 217 NLRB 765 (1975).

81   *Montefiore Medical Center*, 235 NLRB 241 (1978).

82   *Dominican Santa Cruz Hospital*, 218 NLRB 1211 (1975).

83   *Barnert Memorial Hospital Center*, 217 NLRB 775 (1975).

84   *Sisters of St. Joseph of the Peace*, 217 NLRB 797 (1975).

85   *Newington Children's Hospital*, 217 NLRB 793 (1975).

86   *St. Francis Hospital*, 271 NLRB 948 (1984).

87   *AFL-CIO News*, August 18, 1984 and October 13, 1984.

88   *Wall Street Journal*, August 17, 1984.

89   *Monthly Labor Review*, 3, No. 11, November 1988, p. 40.

90   *AFL-CIO News*, November 5, 1988.

91   *American Hospital Association* v. *NLRB*, Case No. 89-2604, 7th Cir., April 11, 1990.

92   *American Hospital Association* v. *NLRB*, 499 U.S. 606 (1991).

93   Joshua Schwarz and Karen Koziara, "The Effect of Hospital Bargaining on Industrial Relations Outcomes," *Industrial Relations Review*, v. 45, No. 3 (April 1992), pp. 577–586.

94   *Ibid.*, p. 586.

95   *Park Manor Care Center, Inc.*, 305 NLRB No. 135 (1991).

96   *Wall Street Journal*, January 28, 1992.

97   *St. John's Hospital and School of Nursing, Inc.*, 222 NLRB 1150 (1976).

98   *Tri-County Medical Center*, 222 NLRB 1089 (1976).

99   *St. John's Hospital* v. *NLRB*, 557 F. 2d 1368 (10th Cir. 1977).

100   *Beth Israel Hospital* v. *NLRB*, 437 U.S. 483 (1978).

101   *NLRB* v. *Baptist Hospital*, 442 U.S. 773 (1979).

102   *St. John's Hospital and School of Nursing, Inc.*, 222 NLRB 1150 (1976).

103   *National Union of Hospital and Healthcare Employees, District 1199*, 222 NLRB 212 (1976).

104   Office of the General Counsel, "NLRB General Counsel's Monthly Report on Health Care Institution Cases," Release No. 1385, March 27, 1975, p. 2.

105   *Ibid.*, p. 6.

106   *NLRB* v. *Health Care & Retirement Corp.*, Case No. 92-1964 (1994).

107   306 NLRB No. 63 (1992).

108   223 NLRB 251 (1976).

109   *Wall Street Journal*, March 23, 1976.

110   Oversight Hearings on the National Labor Relations Board Hearings Before the Subcommittee on Labor-Management Relations, Committee on Education and Labor, House of Representatives, 94th Congress, 2d sess., May 5, 1976, p. 815.

111   H.R. 2222, 96th Congress.

112   *Physicians National House Staff Association* v. *Fanning*, 642 F. 2d 492 (D.C. Cir. 1980).

113   *Bildisco and Bildisco*, 255 NLRB 1203 (1981).

114   *NLRB* v. *Bildisco*, 682 F. 2d 72, (3d Cir. 1982).

115   *Monthly Labor Review*, v. 106, No. 9, September 1983, p. 40.

116   *Monthly Labor Review*, v. 106, No. 11, November 1983, p. 73.

117   *Bildisco and Bildisco*, 465 U.S. 513 (1984).

118   *Wall Street Journal*, February 23, 1984.

119   *Monthly Labor Review*, v. 107, No. 4, April 1984, p. 48.

120   Public Law 98-353.

121   *Wheeling-Pittsburgh Steel Corp.* v. *Steelworkers*, 791 F. 2d 1074 (3d Cir. 1986).

122   *AFL-CIO News*, June 30, 1984.

Control of the Bargaining Unit

Importance of Bargaining Unit

The bargaining unit plays a critical role in the labor relations system. When employees are included in the bargaining unit, the union represents them for all conditions of employment. Whatever benefit the union secures in collective bargaining—be it an increase in wages, seniority, or other job rights—the pensions, medical insurance, and other fringe benefits apply to all employees in the bargaining unit. Grievances filed by such employees are handled by the union, including arbitration of unsettled grievances. On the other hand, employees excluded from the bargaining unit are not covered by a collective bargaining agreement, and they must accept the conditions of employment as determined by the employer.

In addition, when the NLRB conducts a secret election to determine whether a union should be certified for collective bargaining, only employees in the bargaining unit are eligible to vote. Those excluded do not have the right to cast ballots. Indeed, as will be made clear, the determination of the bargaining unit by the Board is one of its most difficult and important problems. Depending on its decision, the bargaining unit may include the workers of a single plant or all employees of a multi-plant corporation. The Board decides whether all employees in the plant constitute the bargaining unit or whether craft or skilled workers should be represented by separate unions.

Wagner Act and Bargaining Unit

Under the Wagner Act, Congress instructed the NLRB in each case to establish appropriate bargaining units

> to insure to employees the full benefit of their right to self-organization and to collective bargaining.

Beyond this mandate, the Wagner Act did not establish any other restrictions on the agency. Whether the unit should be single plant, multiplant, craft, or a subdivision of a plant was a matter of Board discretion.

To implement the policy, the NLRB established a series of standards. It applied these standards under the circumstances of a given case. Early in its career, the agency stated it would not establish

> rigid rules to determine the appropriateness of a unit in each case.[1]

Instead, it said

> the appropriate unit in each case must be determined in the light of the circumstances in the particular case.[2]

The character of the guides that the Board established was related to its fundamental objective: establishing units that would make the collective bargaining process effective. Factors that the agency considered in setting up units included (1) the history, extent, and type of organization of employees in a plant; (2) the history of their collective bargaining; (3) the history, extent, and type of organization and the collective bargaining of employees in other plants of the same employer, or of other employers in the same industry; (4) the skill, wages, work, and working conditions of employees; (5) the desire of employees; (6) the eligibility of employees for membership in the union or unions involved in the election proceedings and in other labor organizations; and (7) the relationship between the unit or units proposed and the employer's organization, management, and operation of the plant.[3]

In practice, frequently employers and unions mutually agreed to the scope of the bargaining unit. In those cases, the Board merely approved the unit that appeared logical to all participants. In fact, during the Wagner Act years, 1935–1947, the Board designated units agreed to by the parties in about three-fourths of all cases.[4] However, when they did not agree, the Board used its power to establish the appropriate bargaining unit. For example, the union might contend that the unit should cover only one plant of a multiplant corporation because it had organized most of the workers. In contrast, the employer might contend that other plants should be included because it was aware the union did not have the support of a majority of employees at all of its plants.

Deferring to the expertise of the Board, federal courts do not disturb units established by the agency. In *Pittsburgh Plate Glass*, the U.S. Supreme Court held that the federal courts should not upset bargaining-unit designations by the Board as long as it exercised its authority reasonably and supported its determinations with evidence.[5] To this day, the courts rarely disturb NLRB bargaining-unit determinations.

Unlike the Wagner Act, Taft-Hartley imposed several restrictions on the Board's authority to establish bargaining units. As treated below, those involve craft or skilled employees, supervisors, plant guards, professional employees, and the extent of organization. We shall also discuss managerial employees other than supervisors and coordinated bargaining, since the NLRB deals with those problems.

CRAFT OR SKILLED WORKERS

Wagner Act Experience

We are concerned here with craft or skilled workers employed in industrial facilities, such as electricians, plumbers, carpenters, bricklayers, and other workers who serve an apprenticeship before attaining journeyman status. The problem arises within industrial facilities, such as manufacturing plants, and not in the building trades where craft workers are employed by building contractors.

The catalyst of the problem concerns the desire of some craft workers to break away from an industrial bargaining unit in order to establish their own unions. They believe their interests will be advanced when they are represented by a traditional craft union rather than by an industrial union. Should they separate, the industrial union represents the production workers, and the craft union or unions represent the craft employees.

To understand the contemporary situation, attention is directed to the treatment of craft-unit problems by the NLRB under the Wagner Act. At the outset, the NLRB lumped together production and craft workers in the same bargaining unit, with the result that the craft group was represented by the industrial union. To say the least, the American Federation of Labor vigorously criticized the Board because its craft union affiliates were denied membership within the industrial area of the nation.

Accommodating craft unions, the NLRB made two major concessions. In 1937, the Board established the *Globe* doctrine.[6] Under this doctrine, the NLRB, under proper circumstances, afforded craft workers the opportunity to decide by secret ballot whether or not they desired to be included in an industrial unit *before* any bargaining unit was established. Thus, the Board was conscious of the craft worker's problem. It recognized that effective collective bargaining and sound industrial relations at times had to be balanced against the freedom of workers to select their own bargaining representatives. In practice, the Board ordered the "Globe election" when it appeared that a group of craft workers constituted a "true" craft, and that this group consisted of a substantial number of employees who had attempted to organize their own union. However, the Board reserved the right to deny craft workers the opportunity to select their own bargaining representatives. When the Board felt that a craft unit would retard effective collective bargaining or impair sound industrial relations, it refused to implement the *Globe* doctrine.

In 1944, the NLRB established the *General Electric* doctrine[7] and therein made a second major concession to craft organizations. Previously, the Board had held that craft workers, once included in a larger industrial unit, would be frozen indefinitely in the industrial classification.[8] This policy, bitterly criticized by the AFL, was established in 1939 in *American Can*. Abandoning this rule, the NLRB decided that it would entertain a representation petition from craft members included in a large industrial unit if it could be shown that (1) the craft employees involved constituted a "true" craft and not a mere dissident faction; and (2) the craft members had maintained their identity throughout the period of bargaining within a more comprehensive unit and had protested their inclusion in such a larger bargaining unit.

When craft members were able to satisfy these prerequisites, the Board was prepared to authorize an election to determine whether the craft workers desired a separate unit or chose instead to remain in the industrial unit. Should such an election take place, and if the craft workers voted for their own union, the Board would certify the craft group as an appropriate bargaining unit. Under these conditions, the craft group would be "carved out" of the wider industrial unit. The larger industrial unit would lose bargaining rights over the craft group, and the employer would be required to bargain with the new unit. Of course, the Board would not undertake to separate craft groups from an industrial unit when it would be inconsistent with effective collective bargaining and sound industrial relations.

Craft Workers under Taft-Hartley: *National Tube* Doctrine

Efforts of the AFL to win favor for craft unions bore some fruit in Taft-Hartley. The 1947 labor law provided in Section 9 that the NLRB could not decide that any craft unit was inappropriate for collective bargaining on the grounds that an industrial unit had been established by a prior Board determination unless a majority of the employees in the proposed craft unit voted against separate representation. By making the *General Electric* doctrine a matter of law, however, Congress prevented the abolition of the policy by the Board regardless of its future membership. In effect, therefore, Taft-Hartley merely incorporated the NLRB policy articulated in *General Electric*.

Under the terms of Taft-Hartley, however, the Board held it still had the right to deny craft workers included in an industrial unit the opportunity to vote in a "self-determination" election. This point was illustrated in *National Tube*, which the Board decided in 1948.[9] The agency refused to permit a group of bricklayers in a steel mill to vote in a craft election on the grounds that inclusion of the bricklayers in the industrial unit was essential for the proper operation of the plant. It was pointed out that bricklaying operations were *closely integrated* into the steelmaking process. Separation of the bricklayers from the industrial unit, the Board concluded, would not be in the interest of sound industrial relations under collective bargaining. This decision underscored the fact that the Board considered it within its discretion to decide under what conditions a group of craft workers would be permitted to vote on the question of separate representation. The 1947 law was taken to mean that the NLRB could not deprive craft workers previously included in an industrial unit of the opportunity to vote in a craft election *on the sole ground that the employees were classified in an industrial unit but might deny the opportunity on other grounds*.

Subsequently, the NLRB applied the principle of integration established in *National Tube* to three other industries: aluminum, lumber, and wet milling. In those four industries, the agency ruled that craft work was so integrated in the production process that separation would be inconsistent with effective labor relations. For example, a strike of any craft group would impair the operation of the plant. Thus, in these four industries, the *Board refused to separate any craft from the industrial unit.*

Where, however, craft workers were not closely integrated into the production process, the agency permitted them to vote in a separate election. For example, it directed a craft election among electricians employed in an aircraft plant. Previously, the Board refused to permit electricians the opportunity to break away from the industrial unit in a locomotive facility. Thus, depending upon circumstances, the Board treated the same craft differently for the purpose of separation.

New Board and New Policy: *American Potash*

In 1954, a different Board membership, appointed by Eisenhower, dramatically changed the craft separation policy. With the exception of the four previously mentioned industries, the new NLRB ruled it would *automatically* permit craft groups to break away from industrial units. Justifying the new policy announced in *American Potash*,[10] it said:

> It is not the province of this Board to dictate the course and pattern of labor organization in our vast industrial complex.

As long as the workers constituted a true craft and a regular craft union was prepared to represent them, the Eisenhower Board automatically directed a craft severance election. To say the least, the new policy was sharply criticized by industrial corporations and industrial unions. The former did not desire to bargain with a multitude of craft unions, and the latter feared a loss of membership. One study put it this way:

> New uncertainty has been introduced by the Taft-Hartley Act which gives preference for craft bargaining units. This could threaten the industry-wide bargaining mechanism which has functioned so successfully in the industry as an instrument of industrial peace. In this complex industry as many as fifteen to twenty individual craft unions might become involved, each with its separate contract and possibly conflicting aspirations. Instead of single negotiations, there might be many negotiations to conduct jurisdictional rivalries, and greater possibilities of strikes.[11]

Determined to expand the *American Potash* doctrine, the Board applied it to integrated industries other than steel, aluminum, lumber, and wet milling, such as glass manufacturing and copper production.[12]

Current Policy: *Mallinckrodt* Doctrine

Again the policy changed with a Board now dominated by Kennedy and Johnson members. In *Mallinckrodt*,[13] a 1966 case, the new Board abolished *American Potash*. The *Mallinckrodt* doctrine is still the current policy, having survived many changes in

Board membership. The new NLRB held that Congress had not intended to deprive it of discretionary authority to find craft unions inappropriate for collective bargaining purposes under all circumstances. In *Mallinckrodt*, the Board held that all relevant factors would be considered in each case. Not only would the interests of craft employees be considered, but also the effect that severance might have on the effectiveness of plant operation. In other words, the NLRB had repudiated *American Potash* and would no longer permit craft employees to break away from an industrial unit on an automatic basis; they might or might not be permitted to do so, depending on the particular circumstances of a case. On the other hand, unions representing craft employees gained a concession from the new policy. When appropriate, the Board would permit craft employees to break away from the industrial unit in the basic steel, aluminum, lumber, and wet-milling industries. In other words, regardless of the industry, the Board would permit severance of skilled employees under appropriate circumstances.

In *Mallinckrodt*, the Board established basic principles and standards to apply to all industries on a case-by-case basis, but it refused to restrict itself to the ones previously mentioned because of the inappropriateness of purely mechanistic rules. Considerations described by the Board as relevant to such a decision were (1) the status of the employees as craft workers working at their craft, or as employees in a traditionally distinct department; (2) the existing patterns of bargaining relationships, their stabilizing effect, and the possible effect of altering them; (3) the separate identity of the employees within the broader unit; (4) the history and pattern of bargaining in the industry; (5) the degree of integration and interdependence of the production system; and (6) the qualifications and experience of the union seeking to represent the employees.

Application of Current Policy

A few examples will demonstrate how the NLRB has applied the *Mallinckrodt* doctrine. It refused to sever the "skilled trades" employees from a production unit.[14] To justify this decision, the agency pointed out that the craft employees were highly integrated in the employer's operation and that severance would probably have a disruptive effect on the operation of the business. On the other hand, in another case, the Board permitted a group of toolroom employees to break away from the industrial unit.[15] One of the chief reasons for the decision was the evidence that the industrial union did not represent the toolroom employees fairly in collective bargaining. Whether or not the industrial union represents craft employees effectively in collective bargaining and in the grievance procedure is one factor that the Board will consider in making the determination of severance.[16] Whenever craft employees receive equal treatment from their industrial union, it is not likely that separation will be permitted unless there are compelling reasons for it. In another case, the Board denied powerhouse employees the opportunity to separate, partly on the basis of a long and stable collective bargaining experience in the company involved.[17] Here the agency pointed out that its decision in that case did not mean that units of powerhouse employees were inherently or presumptively inappropriate and could never be severed. In a later case, powerhouse employees were permitted to have their own union on the basis of special circumstances, including a relatively short bargaining history and the fact that the separation would not necessarily prove disruptive to labor relations.[18] It refused separation of a group of tool-and-die employees from the industrial unit. Among its reasons, the agency pointed to the functional integration of the production process and the high degree of participation by the employees in contract negotiations.[19]

Thus, the Board is attempting to evaluate the rights of all parties involved in such actions. The interests of craft employees are not controlling, and the impact of severance on the larger industrial unit will now be given consideration. In addition, the possible disruptive effect of severance on employer ability to maintain production will also be weighed. The Board further recognizes the effect that technological change has on collective bargaining. In this regard, what is relevant and appropriate for evaluating the collective bargaining process at one point in time may change to render mechanistic rules inappropriate at another point in time.

SUPERVISORS

Wagner Act Experience

With changing personnel, the NLRB shifted its policy with respect to supervisors under the Wagner Act. In 1942, it held that supervisors not only could not be lawfully discharged for union activities but also could be considered appropriate units for purposes of collective bargaining. In other words, the NLRB extended the full protection of the Wagner Act to supervision as it had for rank-and-file workers.[20] When certified for collective bargaining, the employer would be required to recognize the supervisors' union and bargain with it in the same manner as employers did with production and maintenance unions. Guaranteed protection of their bargaining rights, the supervisors' labor movement made rapid progress, spearheaded by the Foreman's Association of America. The number of collective bargaining contracts covering supervisors increased sharply.

The policy, however, only lasted one year, the Board holding in *Maryland Drydock*[21] that supervisors would no longer be covered by the law for collective bargaining purposes. In one way, the new policy was entirely inconsistent because the agency continued to hold that employers could not discharge supervisors for union activities. Logic would dictate that supervisors were employees within the meaning of the Wagner Act for all purposes, or they were not employees for any purpose. Under the policy, employers could not discharge supervisors for union activities, but they were not required to recognize or bargain with their unions.

Denied Wagner Act protection for collective bargaining purposes, supervisors engaged in many strikes for recognition, which seriously hampered wartime production. In 1944, supervisors engaged in 202 strikes causing the loss of 853,118 working days to wartime production.[22] This was considerably higher than 1943 strike activity. Accounting for the large increase, the Bureau of Labor Statistics, U.S. Department of Labor, said it was largely attributable to supervisor recognition strikes.

Given this intolerable situation, the Board changed the policy once again. Affording supervisors the full protection of the Wagner Act in *Packard Motor Car* decided in early 1945,[23] Harry Millis, chair of the agency during the war years, stated the majority (it was a 2–1 vote) "could not shut [their] eyes to these [strike] developments." In early 1947, the U.S. Supreme Court upheld the Board.[24]

Supervisors under Taft-Hartley

Given legal protection of their rights under the Wagner Act, supervisors continued to form their unions. This development was sharply criticized by employers who contended that unionized supervisors would not be loyal to management and would place the interests of the labor union ahead of those of the employer.

When Taft-Hartley was enacted, Congress, deferring to the employers' position, removed supervisors from the jurisdiction of the NLRB. They are no longer employees for purposes of the law. Although Taft-Hartley does not outlaw supervisors' unions, stripping them from the protection of the law made supervisors virtually powerless to force managers to recognize their organizations. Strikes for that purpose were easily broken by employers. For example, shortly after Taft-Hartley was passed, Ford Motor Company ceased recognizing supervisors' unions and refused to renew the contract, breaking a strike undertaken to force Ford to continue to recognize their union. Many other companies refused to renew contracts, the result being that the supervisor unions have virtually disappeared.

Public policy relating to supervisors is not consistent. If having unionized supervisors is deemed undesirable, the law should make supervisors' unions illegal. It is not logical to permit them to exist but take away the only means of making them effective—legal protection under national law. Over the years, unsuccessful attempts have been made in Congress to place supervisors under Taft-Hartley.

Discharge of Supervisors

In addition to relieving employers of any legal duty to bargain collectively with supervisors' unions, Taft-Hartley permits them to discriminate against supervisors who engage in union activities. Thus, employers can discharge or take any disciplinary action against supervisors because of union activities. In this connection, a federal appeals court declared, "It is clear that Congress intended by the enactment of the Labor-Management Relations Act that employers be free in the future to discharge supervisors for joining a union, and to interfere with their union activities."[25] Subsequently, the Supreme Court sustained the decision of the lower federal court when it held that the supervisors' union provisions of Taft-Hartley were constitutional.[26]

As a matter of fact, in only one way does the NLRB find the discharge of supervisors illegal under Taft-Hartley—when such discharges directly interfere with employee union activities. Before *Parker-Robb Chevrolet*,[27] decided in 1982 by the Reagan Board, it reinstated discharged supervisors if their discharge had been part of a *general pattern of employer* unfair labor practices. For example, in *Sheraton Puerto Rico*, supervisors and employees wrote a letter to the employer's home office complaining about working conditions and requested that the hotel's general manager be replaced. In retaliation, the general manager discharged the supervisors and the employees. Given those circumstances, the Board ruled that the discharge of the supervisors discouraged employee union activities, and it ordered the reinstatement of the supervisors and employees.28

In *Parker-Robb Chevrolet*, a supervisor demanded an explanation from the employer about the discharge of employees who attended a union organizational meeting. For this conduct, the employer discharged the supervisor. Though the NLRB recognized the general pattern of unfair labor practices, it upheld the discharge of the supervisor, but ordered the reinstatement of the employees. It said:

> the discharge of supervisors as a result of their participation in union or concerted activity—either by themselves or when allied with rank-and-file employees is *not* unlawful for the simple reason that employees, but not supervisors, have rights protected by the Act.

Thus, under current law, only when the discharge of a supervisor *directly* interferes with employees' union rights will the Board order reinstatement. Direct interference, the Board said, will be found in such circumstances as where a supervisor gave testimony adverse to an employer's interest at an NLRB proceeding or during grievance procedure meetings or arbitration, and when the supervisor refused to commit unfair labor practices to prevent the unionization of the employees. Only under circumstances such as these may an employer not lawfully discharge the supervisor.

MANAGERIAL EMPLOYEES OTHER THAN SUPERVISORS

Bell Aerospace

Unlike supervisors, other managerial employees are not excluded from Taft-Hartley by express language. Under the terms of the law, a supervisor is defined as a person who has the authority to enforce the labor relations program of a company. It would include those who have the authority to hire, transfer, suspend, lay off, recall, promote, discharge, or discipline employees, or effectively to recommend such action. Clearly, there are many managerial employees who do not perform these duties. They are managers, but they do not perform the duties of supervisors as are spelled out in the law.

In this light, it came as a shock to some observers of the labor relations scene when the U.S. Supreme Court in 1974 held that all managerial employees were excluded from the scope of Taft-Hartley.29 Previously, the NLRB had held that managerial employees who were not supervisors were covered by the statute.30 In the Board's view, managerial employees who did not execute the labor relations policy of their employer did not have any conflict of interest should they form a union. It stated that the "fundamental touchstone" in determining whether employees are to be excluded from coverage of the law as managerial personnel is whether their duties

> do or do not include determinations which should be made free of any conflict of interest which could arise if the person was a participating member of a labor organization.

Since the management personnel involved in that case, a group of buyers, did not perform the duties of supervisors or execute labor relations policies of the company, the Board held that there could not be any conflict of interest. Therefore, it held that managerial employees as a group should not automatically be excluded from the law. In short, the Board was prepared to exclude only those managerial employees who participate in

> the formulation, determination, or effectuation of [management] policy *with respect to employee matters*.[31]

But in *Bell Aerospace*, the high court by a 5–4 decision held that managerial employees are not covered by the law, placing them in the same category as supervisors. The majority said that the legislative history of Taft-Hartley supported this decision. Thus:

> The legislative history strongly suggests that there were other employees much higher in the managerial structure, who were likewise regarded so clearly outside the Act that no specific exclusionary provision was thought necessary . . . We think the inference is plain that "managerial employees" were paramount among this impliedly excluded group.

Thus, the Supreme Court ruled that all managerial employees are excluded from protection of the law, and not just those who have positions susceptible to conflict of interest in labor relations, as the Board had previously held.

Minority Position

Four members of the Court sharply dissented, arguing that neither the legislative history of the law, nor its actual statutory provisions, nor the precedents of the NLRB justified the exclusion of managerial employees. They argued that

> there is no reason here to hamstring the Board and deny a broad category of employees the protection of the law.

One feature of the majority's decision requires additional discussion. In the final analysis, the majority held that there was no need for Congress to exclude managerial employees other than supervisors by express language because at one time the Board did exclude this group.[32] The majority reasoned that Congress had no need to exclude managerial employees by literal language, as it did in the case of supervisors, because the Board had already done that. We know, however, that the NLRB frequently changes its policies on many features of the law. Congress was certainly aware of this when it adopted Taft-Hartley. To make sure that the Board would not again deny craft employees the right to self-determination elections because they had previously been included in an industrial unit, Congress by express language told the Board that it no longer had the discretion to adopt such a policy. It would be difficult to defend the majority decision of the Court in *Bell Aerospace* on the basis that Congress believed that it was not necessary to exclude managerial employees expressly as a group because the Board had previously excluded them. To accept the majority's reasoning, one would have to assume that Congress was not aware that the Board shifted its policies in the construction of the statute. The conclusion appears inescapable that if Congress had intended to exclude all managerial employees from the coverage of the law, it would have adopted express language to accomplish this objective. Instead of this approach, it excluded only those supervisors who play a part in the execution of a company's labor relations program.

"True" Managers

Though *Bell Aerospace* excludes all managerial employees from the scope of the statute, the Supreme Court did not define the category. Instead of doing that, it remanded the case to the Board to determine whether buyers, the group involved in this case, were managerial employees. In 1975, the Board held that buyers were not managerial employees and had the protection of the law.[33] It said that buyers are not "true" managerial employees because they did not "formulate and effectuate management policies by expressing and making operative the decisions of the employer." The Board observed that buyers often had only to sign a purchase order or place a telephone call to perform their duties.

In short, managerial employees excluded under *Bell Aerospace* are those who exercise decision-making power to effectuate management policies. These are "true" managerial employees, and they are denied legal protection in union organization and collective bargaining. On the other hand, there are those who are covered by the law because they do not "formulate and effectuate" management policies. It is up to the Board in a particular case to determine whether a group falls within the concept of "true" managerial employees.

In one case, it would seem that the Board had departed from its own definition of managerial employees.[34] Some management trainees tried to form a union and were discharged by their employer. Upon review of the case, the NLRB held that management trainees were managerial employees and refused to reinstate the discharged employees. It ruled that this group were managerial employees within the meaning of *Bell Aerospace*, even though they did not formulate and effectuate management policies. To confuse the issue, however, the agency later ruled that a trainee in a house renovation project was an employee for purposes of Taft-Hartley and directed his reinstatement after he had been discharged for union activities. A federal appeals court upheld the decision.[35] In other words, a trainee may or may not be excluded from the protection of the law. Not much guidance for a trainee who harbors thoughts about engaging in union activities!

PLANT GUARDS

Status under Wagner Act

Plant guards or plant-protection employees are those who enforce plant rules to protect property against theft or sabotage. Almost every company uses guards for that purpose. Under the Wagner Act, guards were fully protected under the terms of the law.

Employers could not discharge them for union activities and were required to recognize and bargain with plant guard unions. Indeed, except for being classified in separate bargaining units, the NLRB held that guards could select the same union that represented production workers. During World War II, the Board applied the full protection of the law to guards who became members of civilian auxiliaries to military police. Even though militarized, the agency ruled that they could also select production workers' unions to represent them provided they were classified in separate bargaining units. When plant guards at Chrysler Motors selected the UAW to represent them, while affirming their right to do so, the Board said: "Freedom to choose a bargaining agent includes the right to select a representative which has been chosen to represent the employees of the employer in a different bargaining unit."[36]

The U.S. Supreme Court upheld the ruling of the NLRB. In 1947, the high court held that the provisions of the National Labor Relations Act were applicable to the collective bargaining activities of plant-protection employees. The decision of the Supreme Court established that plant-protection employees, whether or not militarized or deputized, could form labor organizations and bargain collectively under protection of the Wagner Act. The Court held, moreover, that plant guards classified in separate bargaining units could select production and maintenance employees' labor organizations as their bargaining agents. In commenting on this issue, the Court declared that to prevent guards "from choosing a union which also represents production and maintenance employees is to make the collective bargaining rights of guards distinctly second class."[37]

As with supervision, employers vigorously criticized the policy articulated by the NLRB and Supreme Court. They claimed that unionized guards affiliated with production workers' unions could not perform their duties in an effective and loyal manner. Nothing happened during World War II, however, that would indicate that organized plant-protection employees, classified in units separate from production and maintenance workers, could not perform their plant-security duties effectively. The Supreme Court dealt with this problem when it affirmed the position of the NLRB. It refused to regard as controlling the argument that unionized plant guards might be less loyal to management in the execution of their duties. Nor did the Court give much weight to the contention that rank-and-file labor organizations would make demands upon unionized plant guards or force agreements from management that would lessen the loyalty and efficiency of the guards. The Court stated that the process of collective bargaining is "capable of adjustment to accommodate the special function of plant guards." From this statement, it appears that the Court would look with disfavor upon certification of a bargaining agent that interferes with the proper execution of the plant guards' duties. In addition, it is clear that organized plant guards, discharged because of disloyalty to management, inefficiency, or failure to carry out their duties in an effective manner, would not be reinstated by the Board.

Plant Guards under Taft-Hartley

Under Taft-Hartley, plant guards are denied full protection of the law for collective bargaining purposes. Under its terms, *any union of plant guards affiliated with a production workers' labor organization may not be certified by the NLRB*. It is true that, unlike supervisors, employers may not discharge guards who engage in union activities. It is likewise true that the NLRB will certify a plant guard union provided it is not affiliated in any way with a production workers' labor organization. Nonetheless, Taft-Hartley nullified effective collective bargaining on the part of plant guard unions. Standing alone, these employees have very little bargaining strength. This condition results from two factors: (1) There are comparatively few guards in any one plant, and (2) plant guards either perform tasks that can readily be learned by new employees or can entirely be replaced by guards supplied by a detective agency. As a result of these two conditions, management can easily replace plant-protection employees. Since they are readily replaceable, plant guards cannot employ the strike effectively. This means that plant-guard unions, separated from production employees' labor organizations, cannot make effective use of their economic strength to win concessions. Given this situation, plant-guard unions have not amounted to much after passage of Taft-Hartley.

NLRB Policy

In any event, the NLRB was required to administer the plant-guard provision of Taft-Hartley. Shortly after the passage of the law, the AFL chartered a union to represent plant guards and no other workers. But the NLRB refused to certify the plant-guards' union on the grounds that it was affiliated with the AFL, a parent body composed of production and maintenance workers' unions.

In 1948, the Board greatly expanded the application of the definition of plant guards as contained in Taft-Hartley. Thus, it held in *C. V. Hill* that watchmen are guards within the meaning of the Act, regardless of whether they are armed, uniformed, or deputized.[38] In this case, the watchmen were hourly rated employees and wore the same badges as other employees. Watchmen in some firms are used primarily to check for fires. The effect of this ruling was to deprive a sizable group of employees of the benefits of collective bargaining. Only one qualification was made by the Board with respect to watchmen. The agency originally held that watchmen could be represented by production workers' unions if not more than 50 percent of their time was devoted to watchmen duties.[39] Subsequently, the critical figure was reduced to 25 percent.[40] This means that watchmen who spend 25 percent or more of their time in the enforcement of plant rules fall within the definition of plant guards.

Janitors are not considered guards, even though they may hold the keys to the plant and have the authority to admit people into the plant.[41] Because this group did not have the authority to enforce plant rules to protect property or persons on the premises, the Board rejected the employer's contention that its janitors were guards within the meaning of the law. Previously, the Board had held that to be considered a guard, an employee must enforce against employees and other persons rules to protect the property of the employer's premises.[42] On the other hand, the Board ruled that toll-road security employees are guards within the meaning of the law because they are empowered to enforce against persons seeking to use the toll roads, the state's rules to protect the property and the safety of users of the roads.[43]

To the extent that the Board broadens the definition of "guard," more employees are denied statutory rights. In this respect, the Board has held that armored car and express delivery (Brinks, for example) employees are guards within the meaning of the law.[44] In an article on this subject, one author states:

> The Board has deviated from the legislative intent that prompted the guard exclusion by enlarging the guard definition to cover "driver guards" and other employees in the armored car and express delivery industries. The law in this area has developed in an erratic fashion without providing any rational criteria for distinguishing guards from nonguards. The result has been an unjustified restriction of basic employee rights under the Act and a concomitant disruption of labor-management relations in the affected industries.[45]

In *Wells Fargo Armored Service*,[46] the Board held that it would not require employers to continue to bargain with a mixed unit containing guards and other employees who had previously been recognized on a voluntary basis. Apparently this policy is applicable regardless of the industry involved, and it serves to reduce seriously the statutory protection offered by Taft-Hartley. On the other hand, in 1993 the agency ruled that employer voluntary recognition of a union which admitted guards and nonguards to membership barred an election petition of a rival union which admitted only guards.[47] Understand, however, that under *Wells Fargo, where an employer withdraws its voluntary consent*, the Board will not require the employer to recognize a bargaining unit composed of guards and nonguards.

In a 1991 case, the NLRB ruled a union that admitted nonguards to its membership may be certified as the bargaining representative of an employer's so-called "courier-guards." It determined that those employees did not fit the statutory definition of "guards" under Taft-Hartley and therefore could be represented by a nonguard union.[48]

After the union petitioned for certification as the courier-guards' representative, the employer objected claiming that since the union admitted nonguards into its membership, it could not represent the guard employees under the statute. A regional director of the NLRB agreed with an employer, determining the duties and functions of the courier-guards satisfied the definition of "guards" under national labor law.

Reversing the regional director, the NLRB ruled, after examining the duties of the courier-guards, that they perform duties and functions more closely akin to delivery personnel: their training is minimal; they perform the duties unarmed; security is lax; and they were never instructed to protect their customers' property. In essence, concluded the Board, the duties of the courier-guards merely involved pick-up, transport, and delivery of customer parcels.

About a year later, a federal appeals court in *Pony Express Courier Corp.*[49] upheld the Board's decision concerning courier-guards. Like the NLRB, the St. Louis Circuit Court of Appeals held "courier-guards," the title the employer called its drivers, did not fit the statutory definition of guards. It stated the security aspects of the duties "are common-sense measures and do not require the level of protection that would afford them true guard status under the Act." Noting that the courier-guards did not carry valuables, such as cash or jewelry, the court remarked: "We look to job duties, not job titles."

As with supervisors, unsuccessful congressional efforts have been made to provide full protection to the organization and collective bargaining rights of plant guards. They received consideration in the Labor Law Reform Act of 1977. As part of that law, passed by the House of Representatives in October 1977, the plant guards' opportunity to select a rank-and-file labor organization would have been made available. The measure would have removed the restriction that guards at a plant may be represented only by a union composed exclusively of guards. Had the law passed the Senate, guards could have selected any union to represent them, provided the union did not represent the other employees in the plant.

As stated earlier, a filibuster in the Senate blocked passage of the Labor Law Reform Act.

PROFESSIONAL EMPLOYEES

Multiple-Choice Opportunity

Most of Taft-Hartley was enacted in response to employer pressure. Not so, however, in the case of professional employees. Agitation for special treatment of this group was generated by professional employee organizations. As a result, professionals have rights not enjoyed by any other class of workers.

Unlike supervisors, employers may not discharge professionals when they engage in union activities. Unlike plant guards, they may select a production workers' union to represent them when professional employees believe that kind of representation serves their interests. On the other hand, should they believe a union composed strictly of professionals would be best, they have that right as well. Under the law, *the NLRB may not include professionals in the same bargaining unit with production and maintenance workers unless a majority vote for industrial union representation.* And, of course, they may reject any kind of union representation.

In other words, professional employees have a multiple-choice opportunity: no union; representation by a union composed only of professionals; or representation by a production workers' labor organization. Indeed, Congress provided professionals with the best kind of world—freedom to move in the direction that best serves their interests.

Administration of Provision

Obviously the major problem confronting the NLRB is deciding which employees are professionals. Taft-Hartley sets up general standards in an elaborate definition of the group. The NLRB must decide which specific groups of employees are professional workers.[50]

The Board has held that to be classed as a "professional employee," a worker does not need a college degree. Thus, the NLRB directed that a group of noncollege-trained plant engineers of a telephone company be polled on the question of whether they desired special representation. The Board in another case held that it is not the individual qualifications of employees but rather the character of the work required of them as a group that determines professional status.[51]

Lawyers employed by an insurance company were also classified as professional workers. In this proceeding, the Board rejected the employer's contention that professional employees were removed by Taft-Hartley from its jurisdiction. In a case involving a number of time-study people employed by a pump and machinery company, the Board held that these employees were not supervisors, as the employer urged, but fell within the professional classification. An employer engaged in the designing and construction of office and industrial buildings contended that the "estimators" employed by the firm were not professional workers. The estimators of the company determined the amount of material to be required for the construction of a building and further computed the cost of the material. In rejecting the employer position, the NLRB held that the estimators were included within the professional category on the grounds that they must have a high degree of intellectual ability and a substantial background of training, education, and experience. It was further decided that the estimators performed jobs that required the exercise of a considerable degree of judgment and discretion.

Employees performing accounting work for a manufacturer of window glass were held by the Board as not falling within the professional classification. Training for the job was attained at a local business school and was supplemented by a special training course provided by the company. One employee was engaged in appraising the employer's assets and surveying records with the objective of reorganizing the property record accounting system. Even though he had had three years of college work and performed work requiring a high degree of intellectual ability, the Board held that he was not a professional worker.

On another occasion, a group of editorial employees of a newspaper were held not to be professional workers. In reaching this decision, the NLRB declared that the work they performed did not

> require knowledge of an advanced type in a field of learning customarily acquired by a course of specialized intellectual instruction in an institution of higher learning as distinguished from a general academic education.[52]

Thus, a person with a general college education does not necessarily fall within the professional classification. In another case involving the newspaper industry, the Board refused to classify special editors, rewrite staff, and out-of-town reporters as professional workers. These groups, in the Board's opinion, perform essentially the same duties as regular newspaper reporters, who are a nonprofessional group. In 1976, the Board reaffirmed its policy that newspaper journalists are not professional employees, rejecting the employer's effort to change its longstanding policy on this matter.[53] In this case, the employer attempted to separate the journalists from the other newspaper employees. Commenting on this case, a representative of the Newspaper Guild stated that the case should

> mark the end of a publisher attempt to drive a wedge between newspersons and other newspaper employees . . . a tactic clearly designed to weaken the bargaining positions of both.[54]

Radio announcers, singers, and continuity writers are not professional workers within the meaning of Taft-Hartley. Although it was conceded that these groups are trained and skilled personnel, the Board refused to classify them as professional workers. If a professionally trained worker does not perform the duties of his or her profession, the worker will not be treated as a professional employee. In a case involving a professional chemist, the Board held that he was not a professional worker on the grounds that his job in the plant was the carrying out of duties relating to maintenance electrical work. As a result, he was included in a bargaining unit of maintenance employees.

From the cases reviewed above, it can be seen that the problem of establishing which workers are professional employees for purposes of the Taft-Hartley Act is fraught with difficulty. Objective standards are not available to resolve the problem. The Board has considerable latitude in deciding whether employees are professionals or not.

Judicial Review

In one case, the NLRB did not conduct the professional employees' election, although the group in question appeared to be professionals under the Taft-Hartley definition. It argued that the agency has *exclusive jurisdiction* to establish bargaining units and not to be disturbed by the courts. Not so, said the Supreme Court, holding the bargaining unit was defective.[55] Remanding the case to the NLRB, the high court stated it could not

> lightly infer that Congress does not intend judicial protection of rights against agency action taken in excess of delegated powers.

This was one of the rare instances where the courts upset an NLRB bargaining-unit determination. Nonetheless, *Leedom* v. *Kyne* stands as a compelling precedent demonstrating that federal courts under proper circumstances may review NLRB bargaining-unit determinations.

EXTENT OF ORGANIZATION

Wagner Act Experience

A labor union instituting an organizing campaign in a plant may fail to induce all the workers to join the union. The union may be successful in organizing only a portion of the workers. When the NLRB administered the Wagner Act, it frequently granted legal protection to the collective bargaining rights of those actually organized. For example, in 1941, the Board held that a group of cutters employed by a clothing manufacturer was an appropriate unit, although a larger unit comprising all production employees might likewise constitute an appropriate unit. In reaching its decision, the NLRB declared:

> Self-organization among the Company's employees . . . has not extended beyond the limits of the unit proposed by the Union, nor is any organization here seeking to represent employees of the Company other than the cutters. Under these circumstances, we are of the opinion that the unit sought by the Union herein is appropriate. To find otherwise would deprive the cutters of the benefits of collective bargaining until the remaining production employees had organized.[56]

Thus, when a group of workers, *corresponding to the extent of organization*, by majority vote elected to be represented by a union, the Board under the Wagner Act would certify such a group for the purposes of collective bargaining. The employer was then under legal obligation to bargain collectively with the union representing this group of employees. As noted, the NLRB based this policy on the grounds that the organized workers should not be required to wait until a majority or more of all employees in the wider bargaining unit were unionized before enjoying the benefits of collective bargaining.

Taft-Hartley Restriction

Under the terms of the Taft-Hartley Act, the NLRB may not consider the "extent of organization" *as the controlling factor* in the setting up of the appropriate bargaining unit. This means that the Board may not certify a union to represent a small group of workers of a larger bargaining unit solely on the grounds that a union has been successful in organizing a portion of the larger unit.

The insurance industry received considerable attention regarding the restriction. At one time, the Board ruled that only a statewide or companywide unit of insurance employees was appropriate.[57] The inclusion of insurance employees in such an extensive unit was overruled in 1961, however, when the agency declared that a citywide unit of insurance employees was more appropriate than the statewide or companywide situation.[58] It held that there was no longer a rational basis for applying different organizational rules to the insurance industry than are applied to other industries. For example, there has never been any requirement for a labor organization to organize all plants of a particular manufacturing firm operating within a particular state before a single plant of employees will be certified as a unit appropriate to bargain with an employer. In contrast, the insurance industry was treated differently when the Board required all offices within the state or of a particular company to be organized before bargaining would be permitted. Obviously, such a requirement made it difficult for labor organizations to expand unionization. Some offices in cities might not want to organize, which would prohibit employees in another city from bargaining collectively.

In a series of cases involving the Metropolitan Life Insurance Company, the Board moved away from the statewide unit to single city or district offices and various geographic groupings of district offices in establishing bargaining units. The company challenged the Board and argued in various circuit courts that the extent of organization controlled the agency decision in violation of Taft-Hartley. The First Circuit Court agreed with the employer, but the Third and Sixth Circuit Courts disagreed.[59] The Board appealed to the U.S. Supreme Court for a policy clarification.

NLRB Response: Administrative Entity

In its decision, the high court held that the NLRB may properly consider the extent of organization as one factor in the establishment of bargaining units, *but not as the controlling factor*. It stated:

> Although it is clear that in passing this amendment Congress intended to overrule Board decisions where the unit determined could only be supported on the basis of the extent of organization, both the language and legislative history of 9(c)(5) demonstrate that the provision was not intended to prohibit the Board from considering the extent of organization as one factor, though not the controlling factor, in its unit determination.[60]

The Court, however, refused to sustain the Board's order in *Metropolitan Insurance* because of the agency's "lack of articulated reasons" for its establishment of the smaller bargaining units. The case was remanded to the Board for this purpose, and subsequently the agency articulated its reasons. It explained that each of the insurance company's individual offices constituted an *administrative entity*, and therefore an individual citywide unit was appropriate for collective bargaining under Taft-Hartley. In other words, the controlling factor for the establishment of the smaller unit was its independence and autonomy from the parent company. The extent of organization was a subsidiary and not the controlling factor. So far, the administrative entity reason used as the basis for the Board's policy to establish smaller bargaining units has not been upset by the Supreme Court.[61]

Subsequently, the Board spelled out factors that would make a particular store, restaurant, or office of a parent company an administrative entity. In a precedent-making case, *Haag Drug*,[62] it held that a single store in a chain operation constituted an appropriate bargaining unit because in the day-to-day operation of the restaurant, its manager ordered all of its supplies, contracted for major repairs, did about 60 percent of the hiring, fixed wage rates within the ranges established by central headquarters, trained employees, and had the authority to discharge employees. In another instance, the Board held single stores of a drug chain to be a proper unit for bargaining primarily because of the relatively infrequent visits of representatives of the central management.[63] Later on, in a case involving Michigan Bell Telephone, the Board certified for collective bargaining one of the company's sixty-three commercial offices on the grounds that the office manager had the power to effectuate labor policy. It rejected the employer's position that only a statewide unit of all the commercial department employees should be appropriate. In the Board's view, a single office was appropriate because the manager had the authority and responsibility to recommend promotion and merit increases, to schedule overtime and vacations, to discharge and suspend employees for disciplinary reasons, to issue warnings, and to direct the work of the employees.[64] On the other hand, the Board refused to establish a single store as appropriate, on the grounds that the parent corporation placed sharp limitations on store managers in the matter of personnel policies; considerable employee interchange between stores occurred; and district supervisors of the central headquarters had direct supervision over store departments.[65]

In short, the key to the establishment of a single store or office of a chain operation as a bargaining unit is the autonomy and independence of the unit from control of central headquarters. When this finding is made, the Board applies its administrative entity principle. Each case will be determined on its own merits, since multistore or office operations differ widely in the amount of control exerted by the parent company. In any event, the *Metropolitan Insurance* doctrine has facilitated more organization among white-collar and service employees. Union efforts can be concentrated on smaller units of these employees without the necessity of dealing with a large dispersed unit of identical workers of the same company. Thus, the task of organization is easier within industries such as insurance, chain drug, restaurants, supermarkets, banking, and in other kindred industries that operate on a multistore or office basis.

COORDINATED BARGAINING

Different Unions in Same Corporation

Many corporations operate on a multiplant basis, and by happenstance different unions hold bargaining rights in the various plants. For example, General Electric operates more than one hundred plants and bargains with many different unions, including the International Brotherhood of Electrical Workers (IBEW), International Union of Electrical Workers (IUE), International Association of Machinists (IAM), and United Automobile Workers (UAW). Each of the unions has bargaining rights in one or more plants of the corporation. Unions learned they were at a disadvantage when each union bargains separately for contracts. To avoid the consequences of a strike at one plant, the corporation may simply transfer operations to plants not on strike.

To meet this situation, unions bargain on a *coordinated or coalition basis*. A committee is formed including representatives of the major unions that hold contracts with the corporation at its various plants. They agree on common bargaining goals to be presented at the different plants. The committee first bargains at the plant or plants that have the earliest contract expiration dates and then moves to the other plants as their contracts are up for expiration. The goal is a common expiration date for all the contracts within the corporation.

Legality of Coordinated Bargaining

The legality of coordinated bargaining was tested in a case involving General Electric. Observing a joint union committee, it refused to bargain, claiming the unions were seeking a companywide contract. In fact, the corporation's representatives simply walked out of the negotiating room. Eventually a long strike occurred. Many issues were involved, but coordinated bargaining was a major factor.

The NLRB held that General Electric violated its bargaining obligations under Taft-Hartley. That is, the agency upheld the principle of coordinated bargaining as lawful.[66] Although the joint committee was composed of representatives from different unions, the actual negotiations, the Board found, covered only the employees of the particular plant directly involved in the negotiations. On the basis of the evidence, the Board held that the unions were not attempting to bargain on a companywide basis as charged by General Electric. Thus:

> Such representatives could attempt to bargain for their own unions while serving on the negotiating committee of another, or they might claim to be bargaining for one union when in fact they were locked into an understanding that no union would sign an agreement unless all unions did.
>
> But to recognize the possibility of abuse is quite different from concluding, as does our dissenting colleague, that abuse is inherent in any attempt at coordinated bargaining.
>
> We do not believe that the mere possibility of such abuse without substantial evidence of ulterior motive or bad faith justifies qualification of a union's right to select the persons who will represent it at the negotiating table.

A federal appeals court upheld the Board's decision,[67] and the U.S. Supreme Court did not upset the decision. Coordinated bargaining is a lawful method of collective bargaining. Given the advent of the conglomerate, unions have frequently used coordinated bargaining in the attempt to match the economic power resulting from this form of business enterprise.

SUMMARY

Under the Wagner Act, the NLRB had full authority to establish the unit appropriate for collective bargaining. Taft-Hartley placed limitations on its authority by forbidding the Board to establish supervisors' bargaining units or units of plant guards that are affiliated with a production workers' union. Also, the Board must provide professional employees with the opportunity to vote in a special election before it includes the union in a unit composed of other employees. In 1974, the U.S. Supreme Court held that managerial employees, like supervisors, are not covered by the statute.

Under current policy, the NLRB will determine whether craft employees may separate from an industrial bargaining unit on a case-by-case basis. With respect to the problem of the extent of organization, the Board will certify single stores or offices of an employer's business when it finds that the single unit is an administrative entity. In those cases, the Board held that the extent of organization is not the controlling factor in the establishment of the smaller unit. An employer violates the law by refusing to bargain with different unions on a coordinated or coalition basis.

DISCUSSION QUESTIONS

1. Appropriate bargaining-unit guidelines were established under the Wagner Act to make the collective bargaining process effective. Discuss the factors considered by the Board when units were established.

2. What was controversial about the bargaining-unit appropriateness of the following: craft or skilled employees, supervisors, plant guards, professionals, and the extent of organization? How did Taft-Hartley deal with each of the controversial areas?

3. When may craft workers be separated from an industrial unit into appropriate craft units?

4. Under what circumstances might supervisors receive Taft-Hartley protection from discharge?

5. How does the Board determine if one is a "true" managerial employee who must be denied Taft-Hartley rights?

6. How does a broader definition of what constitutes a plant guard affect the basic Taft-Hartley rights of the workers involved? How valid are arguments that plant guards must be organized separate from all rank-and-file affiliations in order to protect the employer's position?

7. What is the definition of a professional worker for bargaining-unit purposes? What standards are used by the NLRB to classify workers as professionals?

8. Discuss the controversies surrounding coordinated bargaining.

NOTES

1   National Labor Relations Board, *First Annual Report*, 1936, p. 112.

2   *Grace Line et al.*, 2 NLRB 369 (1936).

3   National Labor Relations Board, *Fourth Annual Report*, 1939, p. 83.

4   National Labor Relations Board, *Twelfth Annual Report*, 1947, p. 87.

5   *Pittsburgh Plate Glass Company* v. *NLRB*, 313 U.S. 146 (1941).

6   *Globe Machine & Stamping Company*, 3 NLRB 294 (1937).

7   *General Electric Company*, 58 NLRB 57 (1944).

8   *American Can*, 13 NLRB 1252 (1939).

9   *National Tube Company*, 76 NLRB 1199 (1948).

10   *American Potash & Chemical Corporation*, 107 NLRB 1418 (1954).

11   National Planning Association, *Causes of Industrial Peace Under Collective Bargaining*, Study No. 1, p. 15.

12   *Kennecott Copper Company*, 138 NLRB 118 (1962).

13   *Mallinckrodt Chemical Works*, 162 NLRB 387 (1966).

14   *Firestone Textile Co. Division of Firestone Tire & Rubber Co.*, 222 NLRB 1254 (1976).

15   *Buddy L. Corp.*, 167 NLRB 808 (1967).

16   *Trico Products Corp.*, 169 NLRB 287 (1968).

17   *Mobil Oil Corp.*, 169 NLRB 259 (1968).

18   *Towmotor Corp.*, 187 NLRB 1027 (1971).

19   *LA-Z-Boy Chair Co.*, 235 NLRB 77 (1978).

20   *Union Collieries Coal Company*, 41 NLRB 961 (1942).

21   *Maryland Drydock Company*, 49 NLRB 733 (1943).

22   *Monthly Labor Review*, LX, 5 (May 1945), p. 937.

23   *Packard Motor Car Company*, 61 NLRB 4 (1945).

24   *Packard Motor Car Company v. NLRB*, 67 S. Ct. 789 (1947).

25   *NLRB v. Budd Manufacturing Company*, 138 F. 2d 86 (1948).

26   335 U.S. 908 (1949).

27   *Parker-Robb Chevrolet, Inc.*, 262 NLRB No. 58 (1982), enf. *Food and Commercial Workers, Local 1095, Automobile Salesmen's Union v. NLRB*, 711 F. 2d 383 (D.C. Cir. 1983). For an excellent treatment of this general problem, see Gail Frommer Brod, "The NLRB Changes Its Policy on the Legality of an Employer's Discharge of a Disloyal Supervisor," *Labor Law Journal*, XXXIV, No. 1 (January 1983), p. 13.

28   *Sheraton Puerto Rico*, 248 NLRB 867 (1980).

29   *NLRB v. Bell Aerospace Co.*, 416 U.S. 267 (1974).

30   *Bell Aerospace Co.*, 196 NLRB 827 (1972).

31   *North Arkansas Electric Cooperative*, 185 NLRB 550 (1970).

32   *Swift and Co.*, 115 NLRB 752 (1956).

33   *Bell Aerospace Co.*, 219 NLRB 384 (1975).

34   *Curtis Industries, Division of Curtis Noll Corp.*, 218 NLRB 1447 (1975).

35   *NLRB v. Chinatown Planning Council Inc.*, 875 F. 2d 395 (2d Cir. 1989).

36   *Chrysler Corporation*, 44 NLRB 881 (1942).

37   *NLRB v. Atkins & Company*, 331 U.S. 398 (1947); *NLRB v. Jones & Laughlin Corporation*, 331 U.S. 416 (1947).

38   *C. V. Hill*, 76 NLRB 158 (1948).

39   *Steelweld Equipment Company*, 76 NLRB 813 (1948).

40   *Reynolds Metals Co.*, 198 NLRB 120 (1972).

41   *Meyer Manufacturing Co.*, 170 NLRB 509 (1968).

42   *Petroleum Chemicals, Inc.*, 121 NLRB 630 (1958).

43   *The Wackenhut Corp.*, 196 NLRB 278 (1972).

44   *Teamsters Local 851 (Purolator Courier)*, 268 NLRB 452 (1983); *Brinks, Inc.*, 226 NLRB 1182 (1976).

45   Stephen Kahn, "The NLRB Misinterpretation of the Guard Provision," *Labor Law Journal*, XXXV, No. 6 (June 1984), p. 328.

46   *Wells Fargo Armored Service Corp.*, 270 NLRB 787 (1984).

47   *Stay Security*, 311 NLRB No. 33 (1993).

48   *Purolator Courier Corp.*, 300 NLRB 812 (1990).

49   *Pony Express Courier Corp. v. NLRB*, 981 F. 2d 358 (1992).

50   Section 2(12) defines a *professional employee* as follows: (a) any employee engaged in work (i) predominantly intellectual and varied in character as opposed to routine mental, manual, mechanical, or physical work; (ii) involving the consistent exercise of discretion and judgment in its performance; (iii) of such a character that the output produced or the result accomplished cannot be standardized in relation to a given period of time; (iv) requiring knowledge of an advanced type in a field of science or learning customarily acquired by a prolonged course of specialized intellectual instruction and study in an institution of higher learning or a hospital, as distinguished from a general academic education or from an apprenticeship or from

training in the performance of routine mental, manual, or physical processes; or (b) any employee, who (i) has completed the courses of specialized intellectual instruction and study described in clause (iv) of paragraph (a), and (ii) is performing related work under the supervision of a professional person to qualify himself to become a professional employee as defined in paragraph (a).

51   *Ryan Aeronautical Company*, 132 NLRB 1160 (1961).

52   *Free Press Company*, 76 NLRB 1047 (1948).

53   *Express-News Corp.*, 223 NLRB 627 (1976).

54   *AFL-CIO News*, April 17, 1976.

55   *Leedom* v. *Kyne*, 358 U.S. 184 (1958).

56   *Crescent Dress Company*, 29 NLRB 351 (1941).

57   *Metropolitan Life Insurance Company*, 56 NLRB 1635 (1944).

58   *Quaker City Life Insurance Company*, 134 NLRB 960 (1961).

59   *Metropolitan Life Insurance Company* v. *NLRB*, 327 F. 2d 906 (1st Cir. 1964), denying enf. of 142 NLRB 491 (1964); *Metropolitan Life Insurance Company* v. *NLRB*, 328 F. 2d 820 (3d Cir. 1964), enf. 141 NLRB 337; *Metropolitan Life Insurance Company* v. *NLRB*, 330 F. 2d 62 (6th Cir. 1964), enf. 141 NLRB 1074 (1964).

60   *NLRB* v. *Metropolitan Life Insurance Company*, 380 U.S. 438 (1965).

61   Federal courts have at times reversed the Board when they found that there was not sufficient autonomy of the single store or office. For example, see *NLRB* v. *Purity Foods*, 376 F. 2d 497, (1st Cir. 1967). This case and the subsequent action of the Supreme Court, however, should not be regarded as a reversal of the administrative entity doctrine. Rather, it should be regarded as an instance where the courts have disagreed with the Board's finding that the smaller unit was autonomous from the parent operation.

62   *Haag Drug Company*, 169 NLRB 877 (1968).

63   *Walgreen Company*, 198 NLRB 1138 (1972).

64   *Michigan Bell Telephone Co.*, 216 NLRB 806 (1975).

65   *Star Market*, 172 NLRB 1393 (1968).

66   *General Electric Company*, 173 NLRB 253 (1968).

67   *General Electric Company* v. *NLRB*, 358 F. 2d 292 (2d Cir. 1966).

5

Election Policies of the National Labor Relations Board

NLRB Elections

After the bargaining unit is established and eligible voters are identified, a secret election is conducted to determine whether the employees desire to be represented by the union. These elections are supervised by a field examiner in the NLRB region covering the case. Field examiners must be circumspect in their behavior because the loser may object to the election results, alleging improper conduct of the field examiner. Each side has an observer, and ballots are counted by the field examiner and the partisan observers.

Illustrative of the responsibility and care field examiners must display in conducting elections were the circumstances in *Monte Vista Disposal*.[1] On the day of the election, the parties agreed to set aside four hours for the election. Two employees arrived two minutes after the polls were closed. Nonetheless, the field examiner permitted them to cast challenged ballots. After the union won the election, the employer objected because the late employees were permitted to vote. Overruling previous policies regarding this issue, the NLRB in this 1992 case held employees who arrived late would not be permitted to vote unless extraordinary circumstances were involved. In the case at hand, the Board held, the excuse offered by the employees did not measure up to extraordinary circumstances.

To implement the election procedures under Taft-Hartley, at least 30 percent of the bargaining unit must sign cards authorizing the union to represent them in collective bargaining. In practice, however, unions do not petition for an election unless a much higher percentage than 30 percent sign cards. The reason is that employees who sign the cards may still vote against the union in the poll. Some unions will not proceed with the election unless up to 75 percent of the bargaining unit indicate their desire for representation. Unions understand that once employers enter the election campaign, some employees will be persuaded to vote against the union.

As indicated in a previous chapter, the union will be certified by the NLRB as the exclusive bargaining agent for all employees in the unit for conditions of employment when a majority of those voting select the union. When certified, the employer must recognize and bargain with the union. Should a majority reject the union, the company involved remains nonunion. Normally, the Board will not conduct another election for one year following the election.

Over the years, about 90 percent of the eligible workers cast ballots in the election. For example, in 1990, the NLRB reported that

> of the 261,385 employees eligible to vote, 229,242 cast ballots, virtually 9 of every 10 eligible.[2]

One reason for the high percentage of cast ballots, much higher than that of eligible voters in presidential elections, is that the poll is made convenient for employees. Normally, elections are held on employer property, and polls are conducted on each shift that employees work.

Election Campaigns

Once the election is scheduled, and sometimes before, employers and unions participate in the election campaign. The union attempts to persuade the workers to vote for the union, and the employer attempts to urge the workers to vote against union representation. Spirited and vigorous electioneering is par for the course. As this chapter demonstrates, however, there are lawful and unlawful election tactics. Should either party campaign unlawfully, the NLRB will set the election aside and direct another one, ordering the offending party to cease and desist the unlawful practices.

As the NLRB stated:

> Electioneering is permissible under the Act. However, the Board may invalidate the result of a representation election if the campaign tactics adopted by a party tend to exert a coercive impact. In other words, the employer or the union may attempt to influence the votes of the employees; they may not, however, attempt to coerce the voters to deprive them of freedom of choice.

During an election campaign, the employer or the union might use many forms of conduct in an attempt to influence the employees' votes. In some election campaigns, the parties threaten the employees with reprisals, cajole them with the promise of benefits, or solicit their support through misrepresentations of law or fact. In several significant cases decided during its career, the Board has considered allegations involving each of these types of preelection conduct.

The Board evaluates the permissibility of electioneering tactics, including threats, in terms of whether the conduct tended to prevent free employee expression.[3]

Although employer participation in election campaigns is acceptable and expected, this has not always been true. In the early years of its career, the NLRB imposed a total ban on employers, ordering them to be "neutral." Absolute restriction on the right of employers to participate was difficult to justify within a society that has the constitutional guarantee of freedom of speech. In 1941, the U.S. Supreme Court in *Virginia Electric & Power Company* rejected the Board's policy when it stated:

> The employer . . . is as free now as ever to take any side it may choose on this controversial issue. But, certainly, conduct, though evidenced in part by speech, may amount, in connection with other circumstances, to coercion within the meaning of the Act. And in determining whether a course of conduct amounts to restraint or coercion, pressure exerted vocally by the employer may no more be disregarded than pressure exerted in other ways.[4]

Given the high court's rule on the matter, the Board complied, permitting employers to say anything short of coercion, threats, or promises. Taft-Hartley contains the so-called "free speech" provision authorizing election campaigning by employers and unions. Both sides are free to influence employees in a lawful way. Section 8(c) of the statute states:

> The expressing of any views, argument, or opinion, or the dissemination thereof, whether in written, printed, graphic, or visual form, shall not constitute or be evidence of an unfair labor practice under any of the provisions of this Act, if such expression contains no threat or reprisal or force or promise of benefit.

CONSTRUCTION OF FREE-SPEECH PROVISION

General Shoe Doctrine

One of the Board's most difficult and major problems consists of applying the free-speech provision to the circumstances of a particular case. It must determine whether employers and unions are threatening employees with reprisal or promise of benefits. If so, the election results are set aside; if not, the poll stands.

Early in the game, however, just one year after Taft-Hartley became the law of the land, the Board established a crucial doctrine for the application of the free-speech provision. In *General Shoe*,[5] the agency held that *it would set elections aside under certain conditions even though unfair labor practices were not committed.* That is, the employer or union does not threaten employees with reprisal or promise benefits. Even in the absence of unfair labor practices, the NLRB rejects an election when a party engages in conduct that interferes with the capability of employees to make a free choice. It stated:

> Conduct that creates an atmosphere which renders improbably a free choice in an election may invalidate the election even though such conduct may not constitute an unfair labor practice . . . In election proceedings, it is the Board's function to provide conditions as nearly ideal as possible, to determine the uninhibited desires of the employees.[6]

The Board made clear that the criteria to determine whether certain activities interfered with elections need not be the same as those applied in unfair labor practice cases. Representation cases were intended to be treated differently, and as such, the Board's own standards are relevant in fulfilling the basic objective of extending to employees freedom of choice in selecting bargaining representatives. In *General Shoe*, the Board said that its purpose was to establish "laboratory conditions" wherein employees could express their desires free from events that would prevent them from making a free choice. Perhaps "laboratory conditions" was a poor term to use because the realities of industrial relations are not the same as the conditions that prevail in a pristine scientific laboratory, where all variables are controlled. As the following discussion will disclose, however, the Board over the years has strived to set up these "conditions as nearly ideal as possible."

Under what circumstances have election results been invalidated even though unfair labor practices were not involved?

Application of *General Shoe*: Employee Interviews

In applying *General Shoe*, the Board has held that an election may be invalidated when an employer assembles employees at the focal point of authority, such as calling employees into the office of a supervisor to urge them to vote against the union. The Board, however, will not automatically invalidate the election without evaluating the facts of a particular case. In one instance, an employer interviewed virtually all employees, not as individuals, but in small groups of five or six. The Board noted that there was no reason for any worker to believe he or she had been singled out. The interviews took place in the office of the general manager. However, employees had previously visited with the general manager in his office to discuss grievances and obtain loans. Thus, the Board said that the office and the general manager "had no special impact of awe." Also, the general manager's office was apparently the only place available to the employer for the interviews. Finally, the evidence demonstrated that the general manager's remarks to the employees were temperate and noncoercive. Under these circumstances, the Board held that the election the union had lost would not be set aside.[7] In other words, interviewing employees at the focal point of an employer's authority may or may not invalidate an election. It depends on the size of the group interviewed, the place where the interview is conducted, the status of the interviewer and past relationship to the employees, and the character of the remarks made.

When company officials visit employees' homes to urge them to reject the union, the NLRB upsets the election results.[8] On the other hand, when unions visit employees in their homes during election campaigns, such conduct does not invalidate an election.[9] Though this might appear unfair, the Board reasoned that unions, unlike employers, do not have power over the employees' jobs and working conditions.

Third-Party Intervention

Under certain circumstances, the Board will set aside an election because of the conduct of a third party; that is, people other than the representatives of the employer or the union engage in activities which the Board believes cast substantial doubt on the employees' opportunity to express freely their choice in an election. In one such case, the Chamber of Commerce, the local newspaper, and the bank made it clear that the union was not welcome. The newspaper ran a front-page editorial that said in effect that if the union came in the employer involved in the election would leave. The bank deferred making loans and told applicants that it would talk further about loans if the mill remained nonunion.[10] Concluding that such third-party conduct had created a general atmosphere of fear and confusion, even though there was no clear indication that the employer was responsible, the Board directed a new election after the union lost the first one.

On the basis of the same principle, the Board invalidated an election won by a union. Between the filing of the petition and the day of the election, events occurred that had created fear and confusion. There was extensive damage to property, anonymous telephone threats to eligible voters, a bomb threat, and unruly conduct on the picket line. No credible evidence attributed these events to the union involved in the election, but nonetheless the Board invalidated election results on the grounds that the general atmosphere at the time of the election had made a rational and uncoerced choice impossible.[11]

Thus the third-party principle cuts both ways. It may be used to set elections aside when unions win or lose at the polls. The results will be invalidated even though probative evidence does not establish that the objectionable conduct was attributable to the union or employer involved.

Appeal to Racial Prejudice

At one time the NLRB did not set aside elections despite the use of inflammatory racial propaganda during the election campaign. Although the agency did not condone appeals to racial prejudice, it did not believe such conduct was sufficient grounds for invalidation of the election.

In keeping with the civil rights movement that swept the nation during the 1960s, the Board changed the policy and applied *General Shoe* when an employer or a union initiated racial propaganda in an election campaign that was calculated to inflame racial prejudice of employees and was deliberately designed to overemphasize and exacerbate racial feelings by irrelevant and inflammatory appeals.

In 1962, in *Sewell Manufacturing Co.*,[12] the employer appealed to racial prejudice at its Georgia plants. For example, it sent letters to the employees publicizing an AFL-CIO donation of money to the Committee on Racial Equality to be used to support freedom-rider projects in Alabama and Mississippi. Also included were photographs of a white AFL-CIO official dancing with a black woman. In the case, the Board established standards for future guidance:

> When a party injects racial subjects into an election, it must limit comment to truthful statements of the other party's position on racial matters and must not seek to overstress or exacerbate racial feelings by irrelevant and inflammatory appeals; the party who brings racial statements into the campaign has the burden of establishing that they were both truthful and germane to the election issues.

On these grounds, the Board set aside the election, which the union lost. On the same day, however, the agency issued *Allen Morrison*[13] to demonstrate that appeals to racial prejudice may not invalidate election results. In its campaign, the employer wrote a truthful letter to its employees stating that the national union seeking to represent them had not only given financial support to desegregation activities but had placed one of its locals in trusteeship when its members voted to purchase bonds to finance private white schools to combat forced public school integration. Since the letter was factual, and since racial matters were not the central theme of the employer's antiunion campaign, as they had been in *Sewell Manufacturing*, the Board certified the loss of the union in the election.

Elections won by unions have been set aside where they transgressed the standards established in *Sewell Manufacturing*.[14] When a union, however, appeals to racial pride and does not intend to inflame racial hatred, the agency does not invalidate elections won by the union.[15]

In 1993 the NLRB applied the standards articulated in *Sewell Manufacturing* and *Allen Morrison* to a case involving a Japanese person who had written a letter condemning American workers as lazy and uneducated. On the eve of the election, at a plant partly owned by Japanese, the union circulated the letter among the employees. After the union won the election, the employer asserted the election be set aside and a new one directed.

By a 2–1 vote, the NLRB held the election results should stand on the grounds that the union never stated that the letter in question was either written or endorsed by the employer, and the union at no time used racial epithets against the employer.[16] In addition, the Board majority determined ethnic hostility was not the central issue of the union's election campaign, distinguishing this case from *Sewell Manufacturing* where the employer made race the focus of its campaign against the union.

In dissent, Board member John Raudabaugh said the letter suggested at least that the employer, by being partly Japanese, was in accord with the biased and hostile views expressed in the letter.

Nor did the NLRB set aside an election won by the union because a union representative told employees at a union meeting that an employer representative, probably the general manager, called the workers "dumb niggers."[17] Dismissing the employer's objection, the agency determined the statement was isolated and made in the first of seven union meetings held more than a month before the election, and race was not the significant or central aspect of the union's election campaign.

According to the facts of the case, the general manager apparently told employees prior to the election that they did not know what they had signed on the authorization cards or election petition because some of them could not read or write, and he doubted that the cards and petitions reflected their views about unionization. Several employees complained to the union representative about what the general manager had told them, implying they were dumb and illiterate. In response to those complaints, the union representative made the racial comment in question.

While overruling the employer's objection to the election, the Board made clear the limits of the decision, stating:

We do not condone the use of racial or ethnic epithets such as that at issue here. Had a union representative used such a term in comments attacking a particular racial, ethnic, or religious group, or . . . as part of an inflammatory campaign theme, or . . . in a totally gratuitous way, unconnected to any employees' concerns, we would not hesitate to set aside the election.

In any event, the NLRB has a difficult task in the application of *Sewell Manufacturing* and *Allen Morrison* to the circumstances of a particular case where race, religion, ethnicity, or nationality is involved. There exists no computerlike device that could objectively establish where the line should be drawn. Instead, the decisions are made based upon human judgment and can invite criticism and second-guessing. Although Board members would insist they are objective, the truth of the matter is that subjective judgment stands as the basis of decisions.

Misrepresentation, Distortions, Lies

No better example of NLRB shifting of policy can be found than when the parties use misrepresentation, distortion, and lies during the election campaign. In *Hollywood Ceramics* (1962),[18] the agency held that it would set aside elections when the offending party engaged in such conduct. Although such statements do not constitute an unfair labor practice, the Board held that this kind of electioneering interfered with a fair election under *General Shoe*. Thus, the agency said it would invalidate elections where there has been misrepresentation or other similar campaign trickery that involves a substantial departure from the truth, and at a time that prevents the other party or parties from making an effective reply, so that the misrepresentation, whether deliberate or not, may reasonably be expected to have a significant impact on the election.

In other words, the Board believed that deliberate and substantial lies should not be used in a campaign, particularly when the falsehood was brought into the campaign at the last minute so that the other party could not effectively answer it, and when the lies could reasonably be expected to influence the results of the poll. In one case, an employer created a false impression of the union's bargaining results in another plant owned by the same employer. In effect, it told the employees that the union had given up a Christmas bonus without getting anything in return. Since this declaration was made shortly before the election, in too short a time for the union to reply, the Board held that the employer's conduct was sufficiently material to set aside the election.[19] Another employer told a group of employees that if the union won the election, "the right and the freedom of each of you to come in and settle matters will be gone." Setting aside the election, which the union lost, the NLRB held that the employer had materially misrepresented the employees' statutory right to present their own grievances to the employer.[20]

Like employers, unions have also felt the sting of this policy. In one such case, an employer claimed lack of profits. To counter, the union said that the NLRB requires $50,000 profit by an employer before it will conduct an election. This, of course, was a lie, and the Board upset the election the union had won.[21] Another union had its election victory set aside in part because it sent employees campaign literature that said an employer who commits an unfair labor practice can be fined up to $5,000 and possibly imprisoned up to one year, or both.[22] This was an egregious misrepresentation of the law, because Taft-Hartley does not stipulate criminal penalties for anyone, employers or unions, who commits unfair labor practices.

To be sure, the Board had difficulty in administering the "truth-in-campaign" doctrine. There were frequently tough questions to be determined in its application. For example, did the statement contain a complete lie or was it only an exaggeration or mere election propaganda? If a lie, did the other party have sufficient time to reply? Should employees have known better than to believe the lie? Did the lie reasonably impair the outcome of the election? Though these are weighty questions, the doctrine was rooted in the belief that the standards of conduct of an NLRB election should not sink to the level sometimes associated with political elections. Employees should have the opportunity to vote in an election without being influenced by the "big lie," particularly when at stake are the employees' job protection and working conditions, as well as the interests of the employer and union.

Reversals of Policy

In April 1977, by a 3–2 vote, the Board held that it would "no longer probe into the truth or falsity" of statements made during an election campaign.[23] The particular item involved in the case, *Shopping Kart Food Market*, was the misrepresentation of the employer's profit. A union agent said the firm's profit was $500,000 when the truth of the matter was that profits totaled only $50,000. In the majority's view, employees are

> mature individuals who are capable of recognizing campaign propaganda for what it is and discounting it.

It also justified the new policy by stating that investigating the truth of campaign statements produced a "host of ill effects" including

> extensive analysis of campaign propaganda, restriction of free speech, variance in application as between the board and the courts, increasing litigation, and a resulting decrease in the finality of election results.

The minority said they were

> unwilling to permit the parties to campaign, without challenge, on the basis of misrepresentation and distortion of issues so directly related to the economic security of workers.

Only one year later, 1978, the Board again reversed its position, holding in *General Knit of California*,[24] that it would throw out elections on the basis of material misrepresentations during campaigns. Finally, the Board in *Midland National Life Insurance* (1982)[25] resurrected *Shopping Kart*, holding that deceit, lies, and material misrepresentations would not be sufficient to set aside elections. So, in five years the

NLRB changed policy three times! Maybe by the time this volume is published the agency will again have changed its position.

In any event, under current policy, with the knowledge by the parties that campaign statements will not be policed, it follows that we can expect an escalation of distortions, lies, and other deceit in election campaigns. It would seem that the party that tells the biggest lies would have an edge. Some employees may not have the "maturity" to sort out lies from truth. Even mature people may not have the capability to recognize a lie if it is told in plausible terms. Though the previous policy had its difficulties and disadvantages, some would argue that employees have the right to be protected against deliberate lies in the effort to swing their votes.

That the issue still persists in labor relations is demonstrated by a case decided in 1992. In *ABW Metal*, the union won the representation election. Because the union circulated egregious falsehoods less than twenty-four hours before the election, the employer objected, requesting the NLRB to set the results aside.[26] Refusing to over-rule *Midland National Life Insurance*, the agency reiterated that it does not inquire into the truth or falsity of company material. It said there is no reason to "tamper with Midland" since it is a "clear, realistic rule of each application which lends itself to definite, predictable, and speedy results." What good are these virtues, however, when they are purchased at the expense of the truth?

THREATS TO EMPLOYEES DURING ELECTION CAMPAIGNS

Threats by Employers

Recall that the "free speech" provision places a limitation on what may be told employees during an election campaign. Statements are not privileged if they contain a threat "of reprisal or force or promise of benefit." Should either an employer or a union violate these standards of communication, the Board will set aside an election. Under these circumstances, such conduct constitutes an unfair labor practice because under Taft-Hartley employees may not be restrained or coerced in the exercise of their right to engage in or refrain from union activities. Understandably, the determination of whether statements are privileged or contain threats or promises is one of the most difficult problems confronting the Board. The line between them cannot be drawn with precision. The Board has occasionally shifted its policies on some of the kinds of statements made to employees, and what complicates this vexatious problem is that the courts have not always agreed with the NLRB. Since the Board and the courts have found it difficult to deal with this issue, the task of the authors of this book becomes even more difficult. To illustrate the kinds of statements that fall within the threat and promise categories, some guidelines are presented.

When an employer threatens employees with economic retaliation should a union prevail in the poll, the Board has directed a new election. In one such instance, employer representatives made outright threats of plant closure and loss of employee benefits. It is material that in this case the threats were made to only four employees out of three thousand in the unit, but the Board still ordered a new election because statements made during election campaigns are the subject of discussion and reflection among the electorate.[27]

The following employer statement was also considered a threat:

> . . . if by chance the union were to be voted into this shop, there is no doubt in my mind, because of the terrific demands they are making . . . there will be a strike. Somismo will not be able to cope with that problem; there will be a strike; whether we go out of business or not I am not saying right now. . . . I want to say that the demands of the union cannot and will not be met.[28]

Another employer conveyed to employees the belief that should the union win the election, the company would divert production to a nonunion plant which it also owned. In speeches to the employees, it was intimated that the nonunion status of the plant was responsible for rising employment, and that its continued nonunion status was necessary to avoid a possible drop in employment in the future. In setting aside the election, the Board held that the employer's preelection statements constituted a thinly veiled threat to provide more and better job opportunities at nonunion plants than at organized plants.[29] Also held as a threat was an employer's statement read to assembled employees that the interference of a union would only hinder the company's economic recovery and delay the recall of laid-off employees.[30] The Board noted that the employer did not explain why this would occur nor establish that these adverse economic effects would result from matters beyond employer control.

Economic Predictions

On the other hand, an election will not be set aside when an employer simply predicts the economic consequences of collective bargaining, provided the statement is made in such a way so as not to instill fear in the employees that they will lose their jobs or suffer loss of benefits. The U.S. Supreme Court said that the employer may make

> a prediction as to the precise effect he believes unionization will have on his company. In such a case, however, the prediction must be carefully phrased on the basis of objective facts to convey an employer's belief as to the demonstrably probable consequences beyond his control.[31]

In this regard, the NLRB explained that an employer

> is permitted to present his partisan views of the economic conditions of the company and its competitive position in the industry, as long as these are presented in a noncoercive manner.[32]

Thus, in one case, during the election campaign, a union indicated that it intended to demand a \$3- to \$4-an-hour wage increase. Shortly before the election, the employer expressed to the employees concern for the company's competitive position should the union receive such a high wage increase. The NLRB rejected the union's petition for a new election, reasoning that the employer was making a prediction of the economic consequences of unionization, and in such a way as not to threaten the employees with reprisal.[33]

In addition, an employer has the lawful right to express the opinion that a union would not be in the interests of the employees. Such statements, provided they are made in nonthreatening language, have not resulted in the invalidation of elections. In one such case, the employer's director of industrial relations circulated a letter to the employees which stated that it was his

> sincere belief that if this union were to get in here it would not work to your benefit but to your serious harm.[34]

Since the letter did not threaten employees with retaliation, the Board refused to direct a new election.

Nor did the NLRB in a 1993 case, *Novi American*, hold threatening an employer's statement made during an organizational campaign that if the union called a strike the employees on strike could be permanently replaced and not have jobs.[35] (In Chapter 8 we will deal with the employer practice of permanently replacing strikers.) To the regional director the comment unlawfully failed to distinguish between economic and noneconomic strikers. (It will be explained in Chapter 8 that when employees strike because of employer unfair labor practices the strikers have the permanent right to be reinstated in their jobs.) Board member Clifford Oviatte dissented because the employer did not tell the employees that job loss might not be immediate. Nonetheless, the Board majority held the statement was privileged because employers have the legal right to replace economic strikers on a permanent basis. Thus, the employer was merely sharing with the employees information about its statutory rights. It could be argued, however, that at least some employees might have felt threatened by such an employer statement given the importance of the job to the employee and his or her family. In any event the NLRB by a 2–1 vote refused to set aside the election that the union lost.

During a different election campaign, another employer told the employees that if a union were selected to represent them negotiations would "start from scratch," and in the area of wages, the employer would propose employees start at the minimum wage. Originally the NLRB held that the employer statement was threatening when it demanded negotiations start at substantially reduced wages and fringe benefits. Later on, however, the federal appeals court in Boston reversed the Board, holding the comment (bargaining from scratch) is a lawful bargaining tactic.

Faced with its reversal by the court, the agency was required to comply. So in 1992 the Board held the statement lawful and refused to hold a new election after the union lost the first one.[36]

Futility of Voting for Union

At times, however, an employer's statements have been held to be a threat when the employer in effect tells the employees that it would be futile for them to vote for a union. In this kind of case, the employer tells the employees that it will bargain with the union because the law demands this, but it will not really attempt to bargain in a meaningful manner. In one such case, an employer compared the legal duty to bargain with a "horse being led to water." It said:

> As I mentioned to you before, I am not inclined to be forced to do anything. In a free country, I am a free man, and I believe that I ought to be able to do what I believe I have to do and, that is, I'll bargain; but it's like leading a horse to water. When he's got his head underwater, you don't know for sure he is drinking, but then you've got to practically drown the horse before he drinks enough water, before you bring him out.
>
> The length of negotiations has to do with how long do you hold the horse's head under the water. Finally he wants a drink of water and he comes up, so he talks for a little bit, a little while, and goes back and forth. And, as I pointed out, a lot of it is for show.

Holding the statement to be a threat, the Board said that it included the intent of the employer to engage in sham bargaining.[37] In another instance, the plant being organized was part of a multiplant corporation. Before the election, the employer told the voters that even if the union won the election, their benefits would only be the same as those of the employees in the other plants. While setting aside the election, which the union lost, the Board said the statement indicated that representation would be a futility, and that in no event would a union improve working conditions.[38]

In the light of the preceding observations, it should be obvious that the Board faces a difficult problem in determining when an employer makes a noncoercive prediction of economic consequences resulting from collective bargaining over which the company would have no control should the plant be organized, and when an employer makes an outright threat of economic retaliation should the union win the election. It is equally difficult to establish when an employer offers a noncoercive opinion as to the desirability of unionization, or when it unlawfully instills in the employees' minds that it would be futile for them to vote for a union with which the company does not intend to bargain in good faith. Though the Board and the courts have established some guidelines, the agency must make the determination in the light of the facts of a particular case. As the NLRB said:

> In making this evaluation, the Board treats each case on its facts, taking an *ad hoc* rather than a *per se* approach to resolution of the issues.[39]

Certainly the line between privileged statements and threats cannot possibly be drawn to fit every set of particular facts.

Reagan Board Reversal

Needless to say, the perception of privileged statements and threats, as well as of lawful or unlawful announcements of benefits to influence elections (as treated below), depends to a great extent on Board personnel. It should come as no surprise to learn that the Reagan Board permitted the employer more tolerance in these matters than did its predecessors. Consider, for example, the Reagan Board's reversal of policy dealing with employer interrogation of employees before elections. During organizational campaigns, employers at times question individual employees to learn about union matters, including the employees' sympathy to the union. When the NLRB first addressed this issue, it held that interrogations of any individual employee were per se unlawful as being inherently coercive.[40] Later on, the Board abandoned the per se approach, holding that it would find such interrogation as unlawful only when it was coercive in light of the circumstances of a case.[41] In 1980, the Board returned to the per se rule, finding that questioning of individual employees was coercive regardless of circumstances.[42] In the 1980 case, the employer had questioned an active supporter of the union but had not actually threatened the employee. However, the NLRB said

> the coercive impact of these questions is not diminished by the employees' open union support or by the absence of attendant threats.

In 1984, with the Reagan appointees in place, the NLRB abolished the per se rule, saying

> it completely disregarded the circumstances surrounding an alleged interrogation and ignored the reality of the work place.[43]

In *Rossmore House*, the employer had questioned an active and known supporter of the union and made inquiries about the organizational campaign and other union matters. Finding that the questions were not threatening, and that they implied no promise of benefit, the Reagan Board held the employer's conduct was lawful. Donald Zimmerman, a holdover member from the previous Board, dissented, saying the majority had ignored the fact that employers sometimes use subtle coercion, and that even known union supporters may be intimidated by such coercion. In any event, currently the Board will determine the lawfulness of individual employee interrogation by considering a variety of factors, such as the background of the incident, the nature of the information sought, the identity of the questioner, whether an employee is an open union supporter, and the place and method of interrogation. In 1985, a federal appeals court upheld the NLRB policy established in *Rossmore House*.[44]

Union Threats

At times unions have also seen election victories set aside because they threatened employees. In one of these instances, the NLRB held that the union had shown objectionable conduct prior to the election by threatening employees that if they did not join the union, they would not work.[45] A labor organization interfered with an election when, before the election was held, a union agent threatened that any employee who helped the employer in a strike would be "made an example of" and said further that an employee who had "worked both sides of the fence" during the last strike was in the hospital.[46]

In two other cases, the NLRB held that unions threatened employees. In one case, it held that mass demonstrations organized by a union to harass and imperil workers were unlawful.[47] In the other, setting aside the election in which the union was victorious, the NLRB found that union supporters threatened workers with violence if they did not support the union.[48] A supporter told an employee he would be killed if he worked during a strike. Another threatened an employee with death either by gunfire or by having the life "choked out of him" should he organize an antiunion meeting.

ANNOUNCEMENT OF BENEFITS DURING ELECTION CAMPAIGN

Timing of Announcement

With respect to the proscription against making promises during an election campaign, a federal appeals court remarked:

> Interference is no less interference because it is accomplished through allurements rather than coercion.[49]

To persuade employees to reject a union, employers at times promise benefits, and at times put benefits into effect during an election campaign. If the Board finds such conduct is designed to interfere with the free choice of employees, a new election will be ordered should the union suffer defeat at the poll. The test is the timing of the announcement of the benefits. If no factor other than the approach of the election is involved, the Board has held the benefit was announced to influence the employees' vote. Thus, the Board stated:

> As a general rule, an employer, in deciding to grant benefits while a representation election is pending, should decide that question as he would if a union were not in the picture. On the other hand, if an employer's course of action is prompted by the Union's presence, then the employer violates the Act whether he confers the benefits or withdraws them because of the union.[50]

This means that it is not a per se violation of the law for the employer to announce a benefit while an election is pending. However, the burden is on the employer to show that factors governed the timing of the announcement independent of the election.[51] In one instance, valid business considerations motivated a wage increase, and the final decision to put it into effect was made before the union filed its election petition. Under these circumstances, the NLRB upheld the results of an election in which the union lost.[52] In another instance, the employer was obligated to increase benefits pursuant to its contract with the Tennessee Valley Authority. Even though the increase in benefits occurred while an election was pending, the Board did not invalidate the election because the increase was not motivated by the pending poll.[53] Though an employer may not tell employees that they will lose their present benefits if they elect the union, an employer may lawfully imply that present benefits are not guaranteed but are negotiable.[54] A union told the employees that present benefits are "guaranteed" and the employees "can only gain" from collective bargaining.

The NLRB held that the employer did not interfere with the outcome of the election, which the union lost, when it told the employees that they could actually lose wages and benefits because of the uncertainties at the bargaining table.

Elections Invalidated

On the other hand, the Board has frequently invalidated election results when the employer could not show that any factor other than the scheduled election was the reason for the announcement of the benefits. Elections have been set aside when the employer during the election campaign said that the company would be more generous in granting benefits if the union were not there;[55] announced a profit-sharing plan to the employees prior to the election;[56] granted salary increases when they were not given at any other of the employer's plants besides the one in which the election was conducted, and contrary to past practice;[57] and promised a hospitalization plan to be put into effect after the election was held.[58] In a 1987 case, an employer held a preelection contest offering prizes such as a microwave oven, a food processor, and a color television set to employees who pointed out something positive about the company or a reason why they should vote against the two unions involved in the election. The Board ruled the contest constituted a bribe or benefit interfering with the employees' right to make a free choice in the poll.[59]

Unions and Promises

Though the opportunities for employers to announce benefits during an election campaign are restricted, a union may make almost any promise to the employees. In one campaign, a union promised the employees that there would be a labor agreement containing many benefits, including protection against discharge; pension and dental plans; a credit union; and certain purchases that employees could make at a discount. The employer protested the union victory in the election, citing the making of unlawful promises of benefits by the union. The Board upheld the election on the grounds that employees generally know that a union cannot secure benefits automatically by winning an election but must seek to get them in collective bargaining. It said that the union promises amounted to campaign propaganda, which had already been ruled permissible.[60]

In other words, the Board distinguishes between an employer's promises and those a union makes, because the employer has the power to put benefits into effect unilaterally, whereas the union does not. As the Board said:

> Union promises of the type involved in the case were deemed to be easily recognized by employees to be dependent on contingencies beyond the union's control and do not carry with them the same degree of finality as if uttered by an employer who has it within his power to implement promises or benefits.[61]

If, however, a union has the *power to put a benefit into effect* should it win an election, a promise of a union could upset an election. This issue was raised in a case where the union promised those employees who signed union authorization cards that they would not be required to pay the $10 initiation fee if the union won the election. Though the NLRB ruled that this was not an unlawful promise within the meaning of Taft-Hartley,[62] the Supreme Court held to the contrary, finding that the promise was not authorized and set aside the election, which the union had won by a vote of 22–20. Rejecting the Board's view that the promise to waive the initiation fee was not based on the commitment of the employee to vote for the union, the high court said in *Savair Manufacturing*, the precedent case.[63]

> Whatever his true intentions, an employee who signs a recognition slip prior to an election is indicating to other workers that he supports the union. His outward manifestation of support must often serve as a useful campaign tool in the union's hands to convince other employees to vote for the union, if only because many employees respect their co-workers' views on the unionization issue. By permitting the union to offer to waive an initiation fee for those . . . signing a recognition slip prior to the election, the Board allows the union to buy endorsements and paint a false portrait of employee support during its election campaign . . . We do not believe that the statutory policy of fair elections . . . permits endorsements, whether for or against the union, to be bought and sold in this fashion.

Subsequent to the Supreme Court decision, however, the Board held in *Lau Industries* that it would not invalidate an election won by the union when it promised to waive the initiation fees of all workers, regardless of whether they had signed authorization cards before the election.[64] In *Savair Manufacturing*, the promise was made only to those employees who had signed authorization cards. The Board believed that the promise in *Lau Industries* was lawful because it was extended to all eligible voters.

Application of *Savair*

Since *Savair* the NLRB has struggled to determine when promise of a union benefit would be permissible or unlawful under national law. The outcome depends on the circumstances of a particular case and the view of the members of the agency at the time of the decision. A few examples highlight the Board's dilemma.

In *Mailing Services* the union shortly before the election announced it would make available free of charge screenings for high blood pressure, cholesterol levels, lung function, and diabetes to all employees of the employer's plant. Leaflets were passed out which contained the following heading: "First Union Benefit!"; it also said, "Please take advantage of your First Union Benefit. It's for your health". The following day, two days before the election, about eighty employees took advantage of the program which took place in a large van carrying the union's name and logo. Unlike *Savair*, there was no requirement for any employee to demonstrate preelection support of the union. All employees were eligible for the benefit regardless of union membership.

Nonetheless, the NLRB held the benefit unlawful and invalidated the election which the union had won.[65] It was clear, said the agency, that the union's medical screening was to gain support of the employees in the election. In addition, the Board believed the employees who took advantage of the benefit would feel obligated to vote for the union.

By 1992, with a change of NLRB membership, unions were freer to provide employee benefits before elections. While holding a free picnic luncheon the day before the election, the union handed out free of charge "Union Yes" T-shirts to all employees who signed a pro-union petition urging co-workers to join them in supporting the union. Although the T-shirts cost the union $4 or $5, the employer asserted the shirt for signature swap amounted to a "buying of endorsements" forbidden by *Savair*. An administrative law judge agreed with the employer, holding the union's action in violation of the statute.

The NLRB, however, ruled that the T-shirts were of nominal value and did not amount to action prohibited by *Savair*.[66] While reversing the administrative law judge, the agency said the employees in *Savair* did not know the initiation fee could not be more than $10. Employees who signed the authorization cards could have believed the benefits were much more than $10. In this respect the Board said: ". . . the fee waiver in *Savair* was understood as possibly having significant value." From this supposition, the agency jumped to the conclusion that while economic interest might have motivated *all Savair* employees, the "Union Yes T-shirts would probably have been claimed only by pro-union employees."

In another 1993 case, during a meeting held the night before the election, the union announced it had filed a $20 million class-action lawsuit under the Racketeer Influenced Corrupt Organizations (RICO) statute. It alleged the employer willfully underpaid its employees, union and nonunion. It announced the lawsuit could result in $35,000 per employee if successful, and that the employees "got the support union."

Dismissing the employer's claim to set the election aside, the NLRB determined in the absence of evidence of the cost of filing the case, the action did not bestow any tangible benefits upon the employees.[67] Defending its decision, the agency said employees are aware union campaign promises are contingent on factors beyond the control of the union, so as a matter of public policy the NLRB should not limit a union's ability before an election to seek redress on behalf of employees for alleged employer misconduct. Even though the union waited until shortly before the election to make the lawsuit announcement, the action did not exceed the bounds of privileged campaign propaganda, and the union did not deceive the employees.

James Stephens, Chair of the NLRB at the time of *Nestle Dairy Systems*, dissented, voting to set aside the election won by the union on the grounds that the filing of the lawsuit in combination with the manner of its disclosure had a "reasonable tendency" to interfere with employees' free choice.

Other Reasons for Setting Aside Elections

A company may not conduct an election on its own among employees after an election petition has been filed with the NLRB.[68] The NLRB reasoned that such an employer poll did not serve any legitimate purpose that could not better be served by the pending Board election. A company may conduct its own poll among employees, however, provided that (1) an election petition has not been filed, (2) the employer makes it clear to the employees that the purpose of the poll is only to ascertain the truth of a union's claim of majority status, and (3) employees are given assurances against reprisal and are polled by secret ballot.[69]

Should an employer place employees under surveillance, the NLRB will set aside an election. This occurred in one case when a supervisor five times drove past a union meeting attended by about thirty employees.[70] Obviously, the purpose of the spying was to find out who was attending the meeting. Also, when employees are discharged unlawfully during the campaign period, the Board will automatically set aside the results of an election. In one such case, an employee was discharged on the date upon which the election petition was filed. After the union lost the election, the Board ordered a new one on the grounds that discharge for union activities put fear and confusion into the minds of the employees.[71] Finally, as will be demonstrated below, there are some conditions under which the Board will set aside an election after the employer uses the captive-audience meeting and does not extend an equal opportunity to the union.

CAPTIVE-AUDIENCE PROBLEM

Bonwit Teller Doctrine

The captive-audience rules of the Board, in its attempt to provide a balanced opportunity for unions and employers to conduct their campaigns, have been particularly troublesome. Not only has the NLRB had to deal with the *involuntary assembling* of employees on company property during working time, but it has also had to apply no-solicitation and no-distribution rules invoked by companies to regulate work and nonwork activity on company premises. Bans against solicitation and distribution restrict oral attempts to encourage workers to join a union or to pass out literature for the same purpose. Captive-audience policies are complex, and a variety of approaches have been taken by the NLRB to equalize employer and union rights. The complexity of the issues requires separate treatment of some of the evolving Board doctrines.

The captive-audience doctrine has been subject to considerable change as NLRB membership has shifted over the years. In a 1946 case before Taft-Hartley enactment, the Board dealt with employer meetings with employees on company premises prior to an election.[72] The Board ruled that a captive audience gave the employer an undue amount of control over the election and constituted an unfair labor practice. However, the Second Circuit Court of Appeals modified the Board order somewhat and said that "we should hesitate to hold that he [the employer] may not do this on company time and pay provided a similar opportunity to address them were accorded the union." The case suggested providing equal time for the union's reply. The NLRB did not have time to work out the details involving equal time to reply to captive-audience speeches before the Taft-Hartley Act was passed.

Babcock & Wilcox went before the Board in 1948, one year after Taft-Hartley passage. It provided that the mere use of captive audiences could no longer be the sole basis for a ruling of unfair labor practices.[73] The decision was based on the Taft-Hartley provision dealing with free speech. Union victories at the polls started to decline almost immediately. In 1947, union victories amounted to 81.4 percent of cases reaching the election stage; by 1951, union victories had declined to 71 percent of elections. Such a record may or may not reflect the impact of the captive-audience doctrine. It may well reflect the nature of the bargaining units that unions were attempting to organize by 1951. Possibly the units that were easier to organize were reflected in the 1947 victories, with union efforts centered on more difficult units by 1951. Whatever the reason, union victories started declining at about the same time that the Board announced an easing of employer speech restrictions.

However, a new dimension to the captive-audience doctrine was added in *Bonwit Teller*.[74] Like many other department stores, Bonwit Teller enforced a *privileged no-solicitation rule*, which forbade its employees to urge other employees to join the union on the company's premises on either work or nonwork time, such as during lunch periods and coffee breaks. Department stores have the right to enforce such a rule, and employees who violate it are subject to discharge. The Board and courts have permitted department stores and similar public-access businesses to enforce such a rule because it was recognized that union solicitation on company premises, particularly on selling floors, even on nonwork time, could interfere with sales. On the other hand, other types of businesses may not enforce a privileged no-solicitation rule. In *Republic Aviation Corporation*, the U.S. Supreme Court held that in firms where there is no public access, such as a factory, employees have the right to solicit union members on nonworking time.[75] Under such circumstances, the Court held that denial to employees of the right to engage in such activities on nonwork time constitutes an unfair labor practice.

Thus, *Bonwit Teller* enforced a privileged no-solicitation rule but at the same time used the captive audience in an effort to persuade its employees to reject the union in the coming election. It also denied the union the opportunity of equal time to address the employees in a similar meeting. The union lost the election and filed an unfair labor practice charge. The Board ruled differently than it had in *Babcock & Wilcox*, holding that an unfair labor practice violation had occurred because the employer had not provided the union an equal opportunity to rebut the employer's statements. In short, the NLRB introduced the equal opportunity rule in any industry where a company can enforce a privileged no-solicitation rule.

After *Bonwit Teller*, which was sustained by a federal circuit court of appeals,[76] the Board extended the equal opportunity doctrine *to industry in general*. It ceased to distinguish between department stores, which could lawfully enforce a privileged no-solicitation rule and other companies, which could not. Thus, when an auto parts company and one that manufactured pottery used the captive audience, the Board invalidated the elections, which the unions lost, because the firms had not afforded equal time to the unions to respond under the same circumstances.[77] As noted, such firms, unlike department stores, could not forbid union solicitation on company property on nonworking time. In short, prior to the 1952 national elections, the Board held that the captive audience could not be used by any employer unless the company granted equal time to the union to reply on company time. No longer would the test be whether or not a company could lawfully enforce a privileged no-solicitation rule.

Livingston Shirt and Current Policy

After Eisenhower was elected President in 1952, he appointed new members to the Board. One of the first important decisions of the new members was to upset the equal opportunity doctrine. In *Livingston Shirt*,[78] the new Board held that a union was not entitled to equal time to reply to an employer's antiunion speech delivered to a captive audience. In defending its position, the Eisenhower Board said:

> If the privilege of free speech is to be given real meaning, it cannot be qualified by grafting upon it conditions which are tantamount to negation.

Apparently, it meant by this that the employer's right to free speech was in effect destroyed by giving the union an equal opportunity to respond. Recognizing that the union would have the opportunity to reply, the employer might decide not to use the captive audience. This reasoning is debatable, since it is still in the power of the employer to use or not to use the captive audience. If a company elects to use this right, the question is whether the right to free speech is in effect destroyed if the other side of the story is told under equal circumstances. Also, the Board justified its decision by pointing out that the union had other ways to communicate with employees, such as solicitation on nonwork time (if an employer cannot enforce a privileged no-solicitation rule); visiting employees in their homes and writing them letters (provided that it has their names and addresses); holding a union organizational meeting; taking out advertisements in newspapers; and distributing leaflets at the plant gates. Another method is to use union organizers (nonemployees of the firm) at the company premises to hand out union literature and to speak to employees. This method may be limited by the employer, however, because the U.S. Supreme Court later held that employers could forbid outside organizers from the premises, including the parking lots, if by reasonable effort the union could use other available opportunities to communicate with employees.[79]

Whether or not these alternative methods available to unions measure up to the effectiveness of the employers' use of the captive audience is debatable. Whereas all employees must attend a captive-audience meeting arranged by the employer, attendance at a union organizational meeting is voluntary, and it is not likely that all employees would attend. Probably union organizers would argue that these alternative methods of communication, singly or collectively, do not balance the right of employers to address all the employees in a group on company time.

It should be noted that the Board did not exclude all opportunities for unions to reply to captive audiences. In *Livingston Shirt*, it said that the union had this opportunity if the employer had in effect

> either an unlawful no-solicitation rule, prohibiting union access to company premises on other than working time, or a privileged no-solicitation rule, broad but not unlawful because of the employer's business.[80]

At about the same time that the Board denied unions the equal opportunity to address captive audiences, it held in *Peerless Plywood*[81] that an employer could not use the captive audience within a twenty-four-hour period before an election. It said:

> Such a speech because of its timing, tends to create a mass psychology which overrides arguments made through other campaign media and gives an unfair advantage to the party, whether employer or union, who in this manner obtains the last most telling word.

If the Board was concerned with protecting the right of free speech of employers, *Peerless Plywood* appears somewhat inconsistent, despite the Board's rationale. If free speech is to be protected, it does not seem appropriate on that basis to put a time limitation on it.

Equal Time and Employer Unfair Labor Practices

In 1958, the U.S. Supreme Court sustained the *Livingston Shirt* doctrine, but seemed to hold in abeyance a definitive rule as to whether the union should have an equal opportunity to reply to an employer captive-audience speech when the employer has committed unfair labor practices.[82] The issue arose again in Montgomery Ward & Co., Inc.,[83] in which case the decision of the NLRB was eventually sustained by a federal court of appeals.[84] In this instance, the employer made a captive-audience speech and denied equal opportunity to the union. The company also enforced an unlawful no-solicitation rule which prohibited employees from soliciting union members in nonworking areas during nonwork time. Also, in the captive-audience meetings, the employer made coercive speeches. The NLRB set aside the election and held that the union should have been given equal opportunity to reply because the employer had "created a glaring imbalance in organizational communication."

Thus, the NLRB affords unions equal time to address captive audiences when the employer uses this device as an antiunion weapon and commits serious unfair labor practices. In *Elson Bottling*,[85] the employer made threatening speeches at captive-audience meetings. It also solicited employees to withdraw from the union. Because of these unfair labor practices, the Board directed the employer to provide the union with the opportunity to make a one-hour speech to assembled employees on company time. The Board believed that equal time was justified because its customary remedial orders to stop the employer unfair labor practice would not be sufficient. Thus, it said:

> The possibility is strong that but for [employer's] unlawful conduct the Union would ulti-
> mately have secured the additional support it needed here to achieve majority status. We
> shall require that, upon the request of the union, the employer shall make available to the
> union and its representatives, at a mutually agreeable time within three months of this
> decision, suitable facilities such as are customarily used for employee meetings so that
> the union may speak to the employees assembled on company time.[86]

As a result of J. P. Stevens' long history of unfair labor practices, the NLRB ordered the company to permit the union equal time to respond to any captive-audience address by the employer.[87] The unfair labor practices of J. P. Stevens were so pervasive that the Board also directed a series of extraordinary remedies, including posting, mailing, publishing and reading of compliance notices with copies signed by the company president, board chairperson and directors, and by the highest management officials at the plant, union access to bulletin boards for one year, and access of union organizers to nonwork areas of the plant.

When Employees Ask Questions

In sum, there are limited circumstances under which a union is given an equal opportunity to reply when the employer uses the captive audience as part of an antiunion campaign. Under current law, it would have this opportunity when the employer enforces an unlawful no-solicitation rule; under a privileged no-solicitation rule of the kind permitted in retail department stores, prohibiting solicitation on nonworking time in areas open to the public; and under special circumstances where employers commit serious unfair labor practices. *Other than these conditions, an employer may use the captive audience without giving the union equal opportunity to reply.* Should the union lose an election, it will not be set aside just because the employer denied the union this opportunity.

In 1975, the Board moved further to protect the right of employers to hold captive-audience meetings. At the start of one such meeting held by the J. P. Stevens Company, twenty-two employees got up and asked questions. When the employees refused to sit down and cease asking questions, the employer discharged them. By majority vote, the Board upheld the discharges on the grounds that they viewed the conduct of the employees as a plot to disrupt the meeting with questions that were "loaded, loud, and distracting.[88] In a previous case, the Board had held that an employer could not discharge a single employee who got up toward the end of a captive-audience address to ask a question.[89] In sharp dissent, the minority in the second case stated that the J. P. Stevens

> entire course of conduct in the latter stages of the union campaign clearly reflected its desire to chill concerted partisan activity by inquisitive employees rather than to insure the unencumbered presentation of its speeches.

And:

> There is not a scintilla of evidence of a conspiracy to heckle or otherwise interrupt respondent's speakers so as to prevent an effective presentation of the speech. Nor is there testimony to an agreement among employees, explicit or implicit, to ask disruptive questions.

Needless to say, the discharged workers' union, the Textile Workers, bitterly criticized the Board's decision. Its president, Sol Stetin, said:

> The NLRB has in effect turned its back on workers who had the courage to stand up and challenge company propaganda during the course of a "captive audience" meeting. It now appears to be a crime for pro-union workers to exercise their right of free speech.[90]

Obviously, employers regard the captive audience as an effective antiunion weapon. Why else would they pay workers for their time at meetings? In the proposed Labor Law Reform Act of 1977, the NLRB would have been directed to assure employees an equal opportunity to hear from both sides at captive-audience sessions. As mentioned previously, the legislation was killed in the Senate by a filibuster.

Names and Addresses: The *Excelsior* Rule

In 1966, unions tried once again to persuade the NLRB to provide them equal time when employers used the captive audience. The Board then consisted of members who were appointed by Kennedy and Johnson. The unions felt that with this kind of membership, the Board would return to the policy of equal time and would reverse *Livingston Shirt*. The Board, however, refused to do this, and it sustained the right of employers to use the captive audience without giving unions equal time.[91]

On the same day that the NLRB refused to authorize equal time for unions, it adopted its names-and-addresses policy in its *Excelsior* rule.[92] Under this policy, within seven days after an election is scheduled, the employer must supply to NLRB regional directors the names and addresses of employees eligible to vote. This is called the "Excelsior" list. The regional director then furnishes the list to the union. *Such list must be furnished in all elections, consent or directed, and whether or not the employer used the captive audience.* In effect, the Board said to the unions, "We will not give you equal time to respond at captive audiences, but we will make available to you the names and addresses of the voters." It was a sort of compromise decision that the NLRB believed would balance the scales.

Employers had in their possession the names and addresses of all workers included in the bargaining unit involved in the contest. Possession of such a list made it simple to mail out propaganda dealing with union organizational attempts. Literature could be mailed out in the form of a regular weekly or monthly newsletter to employees, or as a special mailing enabling management to present its views on the pending election. Obviously, the greater accessibility of management to its employees placed unions at a distinct disadvantage in attempting to present views to prospective supporters.

In *Excelsior*, the Board stated that equal access to the names and addresses of eligible bargaining-unit voters "insure[s] the opportunity of all employees to be reached by all parties" even though unions may have other avenues by which they might be able to communicate with employees. Employer refusal to supply such information to the regional directors would be grounds for setting aside elections, if requested by unions, under the *General Shoe* doctrine. *Excelsior* gave unions a more effective organizational tool. Knowledge of employees' names and addresses made it easier for unions to visit employees in their homes and to send them literature. However, it is debatable whether *Excelsior* actually balances the impact of the employer's use of the captive audience. To some employees, reading is painful, and some may resent home visits by union organizers. Oral communication to all employees assembled on company time would probably in most instances outweigh home visits and the reading of literature. Also, given the wide distribution of an employer's labor force, particularly in large cities, it would be difficult to canvass all the employees involved in a pending election.

When the Board rejected the union's petition for equal time and instead announced the names-and-addresses policy, it said that it would delay considering the reversal of *Livingston Shirt* until the effects of the new policy became known. If the NLRB meant by this to determine the relative success of unions in elections, the names-and-addresses policy has not done the unions much good. In 1966, unions won 61 percent of the elections in which they were involved.[93] By 1990, this figure had dropped to below 50 percent.

After a great deal of litigation in the lower federal courts, in 1969 the U.S. Supreme Court sustained the NLRB names-and-addresses policy.[94] The Court said the NLRB has

> wide discretion to ensure the fair choice of bargaining representatives. The requirement that companies furnish worker lists to unions furthers the free-choice objective of encouraging an informed employee electorate by allowing unions the right of access to employees that management already possesses.

THE *GISSEL* DOCTRINE

Development of Policy

If unions sharply criticized the NLRB captive-audience policy, employers sharply criticized the agency's *Gissel* doctrine. As will be made clear, under certain circumstances, unions obtain bargaining rights when *no election is held, and even when they lose representation elections.* As we have learned, the Board invalidates election results and directs a new one when employers commit serious unfair labor practices during the election campaign. Experience demonstrates, however, that in most cases, as high as 75 percent, unions do not prevail in the second election. The impact of the employer unfair labor practices remains pervasive when employees vote in the new poll. For example, it would be difficult for workers to forget the employer's threats to move or shut down the plant should the union win. Understandably, they vote for their jobs rather than for union representation. *Gissel* provided unions with a more adequate remedy when employers interfere with the employees' right to vote free from employer threats and coercion.

Actually, the NLRB originally established the policy in *Joy Silk Mills*,[95] decided in 1949. In that case, before the election was held, a majority of the bargaining unit signed authorization cards designating the union as their bargaining agent. During the election campaign, the employer committed serious unfair labor practices, including interrogation of employees concerning how they would vote, and implied threats of reprisal if the union won the election or if employees voted for the union. On the basis of the employer's unfair labor practices, the Board refused to order a new election but instead ordered the company to bargain with the union. The order to recognize and bargain was based on the evidence that the union had represented a majority of employees in the unit prior to employer interference, restraint, and coercion, which had deprived the union of the margin of votes necessary to win at the poll.

If employers criticized the *Joy Silk* policy, their ire was exacerbated when the NLRB granted unions bargaining rights *after they lost elections.*

In *Bernel Foam*,[96] the employer refused to recognize the union after it offered to prove it had the support of the majority of the bargaining unit. The employer insisted upon a Board election as proof, but in the meantime, engaged in serious unfair labor practices. After the union lost the election, it filed unfair labor practice charges. The company defended itself on the basis of a past Board rule requiring that a union could not file unfair labor practices after elections were held if it had knowledge of the employer conduct prior to the poll.[97]

The NLRB overruled the previous policy on the grounds that such a choice was difficult for a union to make, particularly since the choice was created by employer unlawful conduct. Thus, a union that participates in an election despite illegal employer conduct may, after losing the election, file refusal-to-bargain charges based on the employer's preelection unfair labor practices. The NLRB will require the employer to recognize and bargain with the union provided that it had majority support before the poll and that the employer's unfair labor practices were serious enough to destroy the union's majority status. Three federal appeals courts upheld the Board's policies established in *Joy Silk* and *Bernel Foam*.[98] The U.S. Supreme Court extended its approval in 1969, and this will be discussed subsequently.

Thus, as the law now stands, there are two ways by which unions may obtain Board certification without winning elections. First, there is the *Joy Silk* type of case. This involves unfair labor practices occurring concurrent with a refusal to honor union requests to bargain, destroying the labor organization's card-based majority. Unlike the actual *Joy Silk Mills* case, no election is held in this type of bargaining order. The mere existence of unlawful employer behavior is sufficient to justify a Board order to bargain with the labor organization.

Second, there is the *Bernel Foam* type of case. This involves unfair labor practices existing concurrent with a refusal to bargain, with the result that a union's card-based majority is destroyed. In cases of this nature, an election has been held and lost by the union, but the NLRB still compels collective bargaining. The NLRB justifies such a remedy on the basis that illegal employer action prior to a poll calculated to eliminate the union advantage is not appropriately remedied by forcing a labor organization to go through another campaign. There is no effective way of restoring a union to the same position it was in prior to the illegal conduct, and, as such, a bargaining order is the only appropriate remedy, especially since unions usually lose the second or third election.

In both types, the union *must demonstrate majority support prior to employer unfair labor practices*. They do this by giving the NLRB union authorization cards signed by the majority of the employees in the bargaining unit.

Supreme Court Action: Categories of Unfair Labor Practices

In 1969, by *unanimous* vote, the U.S. Supreme Court upheld the NLRB policies in *Gissel Packing Company*.[99] It dealt with three major issues: whether a union can gain bargaining rights without demonstrating majority support in a representation election; the character of employer unfair labor practices to justify a bargaining order; and whether authorization cards are reliable indicators of employee support for collective bargaining.

The employer argued that under Taft-Hartley, the NLRB is limited to the use of the election as the sole method upon which to base a bargaining order. However, the Supreme Court held that the law does not provide that the election is the exclusive method by which employees may select a union to represent them. It stated that it

> was recognized that almost from the inception of the Wagner Act a union could establish majority status by other means as here by possession of cards signed by the majority of the employees authorizing the union to represent them for collective bargaining purposes.

After establishing the legal basis for bargaining orders based on authorization cards, the Court determined the circumstances under which they may be used for this purpose. It established three categories of employer unfair labor practices that may be committed during an organizational campaign.

From *Conair* to *Gourmet Foods*

In the first category are those acts that are so "pervasive and atrocious" as to call for an order even without inquiry into the union's card-based majority status. In other words, a bargaining order could be issued under these circumstances, *even though the union had not obtained the signatures of a majority of the employees in the bargaining unit.* The Court apparently believed that when the employer commits pervasive and atrocious unfair labor practices, most employees will be afraid to sign cards.

In 1982, for the first time, by a 3–2 vote, the NLRB in *Conair Corporation* granted bargaining rights to a union even though the union had not succeeded in securing a majority of the bargaining unit's authorization cards.[100] In that case, the employer had engaged in massive unfair labor practices during the organizational campaign, including the discharge of union members, threats of plant closure, and promises of additional benefits to employees should the union lose the election. Unanimously the Board agreed that the employer had committed numerous outrageous and pervasive unfair labor practices over a period of nine months, involving every level of management from the highest executive officers to low-level supervisors.

To justify its decision, the majority stated:

> . . . [t]his case is the "exceptional" type envisioned in *Gissel* which warrants the issuance of a remedial bargaining order "without need of inquiry into majority status on the basis of cards or otherwise." Under these exceptional circumstances we find that a remedial bargaining order is the only way to restore to employees their statutory right to make a free and uncoerced determination whether they wish to be represented in collective-bargaining by a labor organization.

In 1984, the Reagan Board reversed *Conair*, holding in *Gourmet Foods* that "under no circumstances" will it order bargaining with a union that did not demonstrate majority support, regardless of the character of employer unfair labor practices.[101] To rule otherwise, the Board said, would thwart the employees' right to select a union of their own choosing. Claiming it did not have the authority to issue a nonmajority bargaining order, the NLRB said the majority rule principle must be maintained even in those "exceptional cases" where an employer committed massive unfair labor practices.

In evaluating *Gourmet Foods*, it should be noted the U.S. Supreme Court had said in *Gissel* that a bargaining order should be issued without inquiry into the union's card-based majority when an employer's unfair labor practices were "pervasive and atrocious." At that time, the high court seemingly implied the NLRB had the authority to issue bargaining orders under those conditions, recognizing that in such a plant environment, employees would be intimidated against signing authorization cards in the first place. In 1980, the federal appeals court in Philadelphia held the NLRB had the authority to issue nonmajority bargaining orders.[102] In contrast, in 1981, the District of Columbia federal court of appeals doubted whether the Board had such authority.[103]

Eventually the U.S. Supreme Court may determine specifically whether the Board has the authority to issue nonmajority bargaining orders. However, even if the court ruled in the affirmative, this would not mean the NLRB would be compelled to do so, because the agency issues such orders on its own discretion.

Second Category of Unfair Labor Practices

In the second category, the Supreme Court placed those unfair labor practices that show a "lesser showing of misconduct." Under these circumstances, the Court held that at some point in its campaign, the union must have demonstrated that it had the support of a majority of the employees. In other words, before a bargaining order would be issued under this category, the employer must be engaged in serious unfair labor practices and the union must have had a card-based majority. In *Apple Tree Chevrolet*,[104] for example, a majority card-based bargaining order was issued. Whereas thirty-five employees had signed union-authorization cards, only twenty-seven voted for the union in the election. During the election campaign, the employer engaged in a variety of unfair labor practices, including preelection announcement of benefits, threats, and interrogation. In a rather creative effort, the employer also used a psychologist who met with employees in small groups to identify their complaints. After receiving the psychologist's report, the employer met with employees to announce that changes would be made. Given the other unfair labor practices, the Board found this tactic to have "a strong coercive effect on the employees' freedom of choice." It also held its effect to be "long lasting, if not permanent."

Though the Reagan Board refused to issue nonmajority bargaining orders, it applied *Gissel* to the second category of unfair labor practices. For example, in a 1984 case, a union at one point in its organizational campaign was supported by the majority of the employees. Later on, it lost majority status, but the Reagan Board nonetheless issued a bargaining order, calling the employer's treatment of employees "sadistic."[105] Representative of the employer's conduct was an incident in which two employees, one of them sixty-two years old, were directed to transfer a large pile of steel pipe from the yard to storage racks in the shop. They picked up one length of pipe, each supporting one end, but were instructed to carry two lengths at a time. On successive trips they were told to take three, then four lengths at a time. When the sixty-two-year-old employee complained that his heart was pounding, the employer asked if he was quitting. The employee responded that he was not and suggested that he could carry two pipes at a time, but not four. Nonetheless, the employer returned to the shop, shouted that the employee had quit, and handed him his paycheck. In addition, the Board found that after the union's demand for recognition, the employer had interrogated employees regarding their union sympathies, threatened to close the shop if they won union representation, required the employees to sign letters renouncing the union, and promised and granted various benefits. Known union supporters were discharged.

In a 1986 case, two supervisors told employees that the employer would close down the plant and discharge all employees rather than allow unionization. The employer discharged two union adherents and also committed several unfair labor practices including unlawfully discharging two strikers and unlawfully interrogating employees. Focusing primarily on the discharges, the Reagan Board found the employer's conduct was more than sufficient to establish the propriety of a *Gissel* bargaining order.[106]

Third Category of Unfair Labor Practices

In the third category, the Court placed those minor employer violations that are likely to have a minimal impact on elections. Under these circumstances, the NLRB will not issue a bargaining order.

Validity of Authorization Cards

In opposition to the authorization-card method as the basis for bargaining orders, some argue that these cards are not reliable indicators of the employees' desire for collective bargaining. Indeed, a federal appeals court stated that

> it would be difficult to imagine a more unreasonable method of ascertaining the real wishes of employees than a "card check" unless it were an employer's request for an open show of hands.[107]

In this respect, it is argued that union organizers coerce employees to sign the cards; employees do not understand what they are signing; group pressure will prompt employees to sign; and union organizers will misrepresent the purpose of the card by telling employees that they are being used only to obtain an election from the NLRB and not for the purpose of authorizing the union to represent them in collective bargaining. As expected, the NLRB has established standards relating to the validity of the cards.[108] To count, a card must plainly state that the employee authorizes the union to represent him or her in collective bargaining. In 1982, a federal appeals court held that a dual-purpose card authorizing the union both to represent employees in collective bargaining and to request an election is valid, provided the union organizer does not tell employees the sole purpose of the card is only to get an election.[109] In short, despite the language on the face of the card, the card will not be counted if it can be proved that the employee was told the card would be used solely for the purpose of obtaining an election. Should the union organizer use coercive tactics, the card will not be deemed valid. As to the employee's intelligence, the Board stated that

> to assume that the employee does not understand what he is signing as long as he can read would be to downgrade his intelligence.[110]

Upon review of these standards, the Supreme Court held that they were sufficient to protect against abuse in the signing of authorization cards. It stated that when cards are obtained in conformance with the NLRB standards, there need be no fear of misrepresentation, and added that "employees should be bound by the clear language of what they sign."

In short, the Supreme Court endorsed the policy of issuing bargaining orders based upon authorization cards. It held that such a remedy is proper when employer illegal conduct makes it unlikely that a fair election could be held. In the absence of such a remedy, the Court stated that the employer

> could continue to delay or disrupt the election process and put off indefinitely his obligation to bargain; and any election held under these circumstances would not be likely to demonstrate the employees' true, undistorted desire.

It is important to understand that should the Board or the federal courts find that authorization cards do not meet the standards for validity, the union will not receive bargaining rights, *regardless of how serious employer unfair labor practices may be.*

In one case, a federal appeals court held the cards invalid when the union had used trickery to obtain them. Each employee was told that all other employees had signed the card. Since that was not true, the court refused to direct bargaining, saying it did not matter that the employer had engaged in serious unlawful preelection conduct.[111]

Another point of interest is that the NLRB will not turn over to employers authorization cards signed by employees. In one case, a company said it needed the cards to challenge their validity in an effort to show there was not sufficient support for the union to justify an election. The company argued that it had the right to the cards under the Freedom of Information Act. While upholding Board policy, a federal appeals court ruled that the law did not apply because disclosure would invade the privacy of the employees.[112] It stated:

> We would be naive to disregard the abuse which could potentially occur if employers and other employees were armed with this information . . .

The appeals court found that the "inevitable result" of disclosure "would be to chill the rights of employees."

In other words, if the employer learned the names of employees who had signed cards, the court implies that they could be discharged. Under these circumstances, employees would be fearful to sign union-authorization cards. Though the issue arose in a regular representation election case, the policy would also be applicable in cases involving the *Gissel* doctrine.

Obey the Law

Most would agree that a secret election conducted by the NLRB is the best way to determine the employees' desire for collective bargaining. When an employer engages in serious unfair labor practices, however, and by this conduct makes a fair election unlikely, the Supreme Court of the United States stressed in *Gissel* that authorization

> cards may be the most effective—perhaps the only—way of assuring employee choice.

In other words, the question arises as to why an employer should be rewarded for illegal acts.

If employers believe the authorization-card method is undesirable, *all they have to do to avoid it is to obey the law*. In the absence of serious unfair labor practices, the NLRB will use the election as the sole method of determining the employer's obligation to bargain collectively. It should be noted that the Board has issued *Gissel* bargaining orders sparingly. It has not issued such bargaining orders in a reckless fashion. Thus, between 1962 and 1975, the Board conducted 114,301 elections and issued 63,198 bargaining orders, the number of elections the unions won. In contrast, for the same period of time, the Board issued only 1,405 bargaining orders based on the *Gissel* doctrine, or only 0.02 percent of the number of the other bargaining orders.[113] This experience prompted a former chair of the NLRB, Betty S. Murphy, to say:

> On both an absolute and a relative basis, requiring an employer to bargain on authorization cards is the exception rather than the rule, and in the overwhelming majority of the instances union bargaining rights are established pursuant to secret ballot elections conducted by the Board.[114]

Though more recent statistical data are not available, it is safe to say the NLRB currently issues *Gissel*-type bargaining orders only under exceptional circumstances.

At times federal appeals courts have reversed the Board's *Gissel* bargaining orders. This does not occur frequently, but it deters the NLRB from issuing such orders in a cavalier manner. For example, in a 1992 case, the agency issued such an order after it determined the employer had committed serious unfair labor practices, including discriminatory discharge, and had threatened to shut down the plant should the union win a representation election. A federal appeals court, however, ruled the discharges were not illegal, and the employer's threat was not sufficient to justify a *Gissel* bargaining order.

In light of the court's reversal, the Board rescinded the bargaining order and directed an election. In the light of the court's decision, there was nothing else the Board could do.[115]

Post-*Gissel* Developments

In 1975, the NLRB made even more meaningful bargaining orders based on *Gissel*. Until that year, the employer's legal obligation to recognize and bargain collectively began on the date the bargaining order was issued. It was recognized, however, that a great deal of time elapsed from the time the employer began a campaign of unfair labor practices to the time the Board issued a bargaining order. As noted in a previous chapter, considerable time elapses between the filing of an unfair labor practice charge and the issuing of the Board's decision. More delay occurs when appeals are made to the federal courts. During this period, the employer could profit from illegal conduct. As the *Wall Street Journal* remarked:

> That allows some guilty employers to freely continue the unfair practices and ignore the union while NLRB and court appeals continue. In this way an employer can "buy time" . . . and gain the benefits of presumably lower labor costs during the interval.[116]

To stop such tactics, the NLRB in *Trading Port*[117] held that the legal obligation of the employer to bargain with the union *began on the date that its unfair labor practices started*. Under this policy, it would be much more costly for an employer to engage in unfair labor practices calculated to destroy the majority status of a union. This retroactive feature of a bargaining order allows a union to try to win backdating of any wage increases or other gains it achieves in collective bargaining that follow the Board's order to bargain. It can lawfully demand such retroactive concessions from the time an employer started its unfair labor practices.

In the precedent case, *Trading Port*, the Board order to bargain was handed down in July 1975. However, the company had started its unfair labor practices in September 1973. In August of that year, the union had signed up 42 of the 49 employees. The company then started a massive and flagrant campaign of unfair labor practices, including threats to close the business. In December 1973, the election was held, but the employer illegal conduct resulted in the union losing the election by 25 to 3. Not only did the NLRB direct the employer to recognize and bargain with the union, but it also held that the obligation of the company to bargain had started in September 1973. The NLRB stated that an employer's bargaining obligation

> should commence as of the time the employer has embarked on a clear course of unlawful conduct or has engaged in sufficient unfair labor practices to undermine the union's status.

Subsequently, in October 1976, a federal court of appeals sustained *Trading Port* in *Ann Lee Sportswear, Inc.*[118] As noted, if an employer desires to be free from a *Gissel*-type bargaining order, as found in *Trading Port*, all the company has to do is to obey the law. If it does not and seeks to destroy a union's majority status by engaging in unfair labor practices, it could be faced with a very costly remedy.

Before the Nixon Board became established, there was another way in which a union could gain bargaining rights without an election. Under these circumstances, the employer had not engaged in any unfair labor practice to destroy the union's majority status. The company had merely refused to recognize or bargain with the union based on a majority of signed union membership cards. The previous Board, however, had held that a bargaining order would be issued if the employer had knowledge of the union's majority status outside the cards.[119] The Nixon Board reversed this policy.[120] It held that a bargaining order would not be issued solely on the basis of authorization cards. In *Linden Lumber Division, Summer & Co.*, a strike took place after the employer refused to recognize the union. Thus, the employer had opportunity to determine from events outside the cards that the union had majority support. Nevertheless, the Board held that an employer

> should not be found guilty of a violation of Section 8(a)(5) [refusal to bargain collectively] solely on the basis of its refusal to accept evidence of majority status other than the results of a Board election.

In 1974, the U.S. Supreme Court upheld the Board's policy by a 5–4 vote.[121] In practice, this means the Board will not direct an employer to bargain with a union on the basis of authorization cards showing the union has majority support, even if the employer has knowledge independent of the cards of the majority status of the union, provided the employer has not engaged in unfair labor practices calculated to destroy the union's majority. Under these circumstances, the union must test its majority status in an election. In the minority view of the Court, however, the union should not be required to go through the election with its inevitable delays, prolonging the time for collective bargaining, because, as they stated:

> The language and history of the act clearly indicate that Congress intended to impose upon an employer the duty to bargain with a union that has presented convincing evidence of majority support, even though the union has not petitioned for and won a Board-supervised election.

In another situation, an employer did not commit unfair labor practices to undermine the union's majority status. It agreed to recognize the union based on authorization cards signed by a majority of the bargaining unit. Later on it reneged, refused to recognize the union, and advised it to seek a representation election. Under these circumstances, the NLRB held that the employer violated Taft-Hartley and ordered it to recognize and bargain with the union without testing the union's majority status in a representation election.[122]

DECERTIFICATION ELECTIONS

Effect of Decertification

Taft-Hartley establishes machinery whereby unions may be decertified. Under its provisions, an NLRB certification normally is valid for one year. After that time, employees within the bargaining unit can petition the Board for a decertification election. If a labor union is defeated in such a referendum, it loses bargaining rights within the unit. In addition, once the Board conducts a decertification election, there can be no additional elections within the bargaining unit for one year. The statute permits only one election per year for certification purposes in a particular bargaining unit. Thus, the defeat of a union in a decertification election relieves the employer from all legal obligation to bargain collectively for at least twelve months. During this period, it is entirely possible that the union might completely disintegrate, thereby precluding collective bargaining on a permanent basis.

The decertification election provides employees with the opportunity to get rid of a union in which they no longer have confidence. One could hardly quarrel with this right of employees. On the other hand, the decertification procedure should be viewed in combination with the "free speech" provision of the law. Employers who desire to avoid collective bargaining can be expected to campaign vigorously for the defeat of the union. They may use the captive audience, or any other lawful method, to seek the demise of the union. Once a decertification petition is filed, the same rules apply as in the original representation election.[123]

Employer Conduct

On the other hand, the NLRB has announced policies that limit employer conduct with regard to decertification elections. An employer may not file a decertification petition. Nor can it help employees file such a petition or induce them to file for decertification. Also, an employer may not conduct a poll of any employees after the expiration of the labor agreement so as to plant a seed for a union decertification movement. In one case, the election was secret, and the employer promised there would be no reprisals. Nevertheless, the NLRB held that the poll was unlawful because the employer did not have a good-faith doubt that employees still wanted a union.[124] In addition, a decertification petition will be dismissed if it is filed while proceedings are being held to deal with employer unfair labor practices.[125] However, an employer may answer employee questions concerning the procedures involved in obtaining a decertification election. When presented with such a question, an employer told the employee to write to the NLRB regional director. Holding the action of the employer to be legal, the Board said the company had only provided the employee with "mere ministerial aid."[126] Also, an employer may lawfully promise employees that the status quo in employment conditions will be maintained if the union loses the election.[127]

In two 1989 cases, the NLRB held employer conduct unlawful and invalidated decertification elections lost by unions. One case involved a $250 prize for the highest score on a test to determine the employees' knowledge of the decertification process.[128] During the election campaign, the employer mailed the test to the employees and listed the sources of the correct answers. Some answers were contained in literature previously sent to employees. Participating employees were required to fill in their names and addresses on the entry form. Completed tests were graded by the employer's director of employee relations. Rejecting the employer's argument that the test was voluntary, the NLRB held that its conduct violated the law.

In the second case, the supervisors of a company promised increased employee benefits should the union be decertified.[129] Such conduct, ruled the NLRB, was not proper during the election campaign.

When an employer changed the conditions of employment immediately after the union lost a decertification election, but before the NLRB formally certified its result, the Board held the employer committed an unfair labor practice.[130] Although the union apparently lost the election, the agency determined the employer may not unilaterally change the conditions of employment before the agency approves the results of an election. Among the unilateral changes: The employer ceased contributing to the employees' pension program; placed the bargaining unit under the company's pension; granted a 6 percent wage increase; and installed a grievance procedure. Given the employer's violation of the statute, the Board directed the status quo be restored until such time it certified the results of the decertification election.

Nor will the NLRB permit employers to cease recognizing and bargaining with the union just because employees filed a decertification petition.[131] In a 1992 case, *the decertification election did not take place.* The employer based its action on the grounds that the union had lost its status as a legal bargaining agent representative for the employees when the petition was filed. Understand, however, the Board did not necessarily rule that an employer may never use the filing of the petition as a basis for withdrawal of recognition and bargaining. Under these circumstances, however, the employer must supply evidence that is "clear, cogent and convincing" to demonstrate the union has lost majority support. In *Laidlaw Waste Systems*, for example, the employer did not know how many employees signed the decertification petition, their names, and the exact number of employees in the bargaining unit. All the employer knew was that employees wanted to "vote on a union." Such evidence, the agency held, failed to measure up to the kind required to use the petition to demonstrate union loss of majority support.

Retaliation against Union Member

A union member who files a decertification petition may be disciplined by a union. The worker may be suspended or expelled from membership but cannot be subject to a fine.[132] The rule permitting expulsion is an exception to general Board policy to protect the integrity of Board processes. For example, the U.S. Supreme Court agreed that it is unlawful to discipline a member for filing unfair labor practices against a union.[133] But the Board held that a decertification petition is a special situation justifying an exception to the general rule.

Expulsion or suspension is permitted because (1) the petition threatens the very existence of the union as an institution; and (2) as a matter of self-defense, the union cannot allow a member to lead an antiunion campaign while retaining the right to attend union meetings, obtain knowledge of union strategy, and even vote on union affairs. Expulsion is probably of little consequence to a member who files a decertification petition, but permitting fines in such cases would be more effective especially since fines are enforceable in the courts in accordance with a 1967 Supreme Court decision.[134]

Decertification Elections: Loss of Union Membership

Understandably, unions lose most of the decertification elections. When employees file a petition for decertification, it indicates dissatisfaction with the union. It should not be surprising, therefore, to learn that unions have lost about 71 percent of the decertification elections. Although the won-lost percentage has remained the same, the number of decertification polls has increased from 229 in the first two years of Taft-Hartley to 587 in 1990.[135]

Decertification election experience, however, is exaggerated by those who believe it is a symptom of the demise of the labor movement. In 1990, the latest data available at this writing, *unions lost only 16,341 members.*[136] The reason is that where unions have lost decertification elections, the average size of the bargaining unit is very small—only 45 employees in 1990. In the same year, unions gained 98,969 new members resulting from victories in representation elections. Given this experience, a writer says:

> . . . it is clear that decertification contests are still not a significant burden to most unions.[137]

EMPLOYER ELECTION PETITIONS

During the first few years of experience under the Wagner Act, employers, regardless of the circumstances, were denied the opportunity to petition the NLRB for representation elections. Widespread discontent over such treatment was expressed in terms of unequal treatment between management and unions. In 1939, the Board permitted employers to petition for elections only when they were faced with two unions seeking recognition in the same bargaining unit.

Taft-Hartley permits employers to file representation petitions even though only one demands recognition for collective bargaining purposes. However, an employer cannot petition for an election before recognition is requested. This restriction keeps employers from obtaining elections before unions are ready to test their strength at the polls. Nor are employers permitted to seek the same result by soliciting employee signatures on election petitions requesting that representation elections be held.[138]

As it has with all other forms, the Board has significant control over employer election petitions. It is required to investigate petitions filed to determine whether "a question of representation exists." An employer's right to seek an election is not a guarantee that the company will obtain an election every time it seeks one. The investigation provides the basis for the Board to reject an employer petition for an election at the close of the first anniversary of an incumbent bargaining agent when it is for the purpose of mere harassment. However, the employer's right to petition for an election at the close of a year on occasion reveals that a union is aware of its minority standing, and it may withdraw from the election. There is no requirement for a labor organization to subject itself to an election if it is unable to run even a close race in a poll. Withdrawal of an incumbent union from election proceedings, of course, relieves an employer from bargaining obligations.

When neither the employer nor the rival unions petition for an election, the NLRB holds that the employer may lawfully recognize one of the unions and execute a labor agreement, provided the union recognized represents a majority of the employees in the bargaining unit. In the precedent case on this issue, handled by the agency in 1983, the employer recognized one of the rival unions based on an authorization-card check conducted by a neutral party.[139]

RUNOFF ELECTIONS

At times more than one union is on the election ballot. After the election, it may be determined that no union received the majority of votes but, on the other hand, neither did a majority of employees vote to reject *all* unions in the election. Under these circumstances, it is necessary to conduct a runoff election.

Under the Wagner Act, the NLRB shifted its policy several times to deal with this problem. When Taft-Hartley was enacted, Congress stipulated that the top two choices are to be placed on the ballot. If the nonunion option ranks in the top two at the original poll, this choice must be on the ballot in the runoff election. On the other hand, the nonunion choice will be dropped from the ballot should two unions be designated as the top two choices. This type of election is not frequent, with the number amounting to only 42 in 1990.[140]

In a related situation, two unions were competing for recognition. Based upon a majority union authorization-card check, the employer, a health-care provider, recognized and negotiated a contract with the seemingly majority union. At this point the rival union petitioned for an election, and the NLRB agreed in order to provide employees the opportunity to choose which of the two unions would represent them.[141] The agency determined that since both unions were actively campaigning, the employer's recognition of one union became ineffective as soon as the rival union filed an election petition.

Denying the recognized union's motion for reconsideration of the election order, the NLRB held its election would be conducted even assuming the recognized union presented bona fide cards to prove a majority of the employees selected the union recognized by the employer.

SUMMARY

The NLRB has considerable responsibility for creating an election atmosphere that provides employees with the greatest range of freedom to select or reject collective bargaining representation. The agency attempts to balance union and employer rights to engage in preelection campaigns by establishing policies in the context of a totality of circumstances. Sole responsibility for establishing effective representation election policies and for developing remedies for violations of such rules has been given the NLRB by Congress. The U.S. Supreme Court reviews Board actions as the last resort but generally supports the agency in its implementation of congressional enactments. Limitations may be placed on employer and union preelection activities to the extent that free elections are advanced by doing so.

Though the *Gissel* doctrine remains controversial, the Supreme Court permits bargaining orders based on authorization cards. The Board requires that unions receive equal time to respond to employer captive-audience speeches under certain circumstances; and names and addresses of eligible bargaining unit voters must be filed with regional directors within seven days after election orders or agreements. The effort to establish the *General Shoe* laboratory conditions continues to be a major problem, complicated by changing NLRB membership that results in some shifting policies.

Employers have been extended the right to petition for elections after they are confronted with a request for recognition. Decertification elections are also possible for employees disenchanted with union representation. Unions lose about 75 percent of these elections, but the total loss of membership is minimal. Runoff elections are also provided to determine employee preference in selecting bargaining representatives. The top two choices of initial polls are currently carried over to the runoff election.

Election policies and procedures remain in a state of change. The Board and courts continue their search for workable policies that will ensure the rights of all parties to election proceedings.

DISCUSSION QUESTIONS

1. How did the Taft-Hartley Act deal with the controversy over employer participation in election campaigns?

2. What is the essence of the *General Shoe* doctrine?

3. Compare the Board's *Shopping Kart* and *General Knit* cases. How might frequent policy shifts affect the parties to an election?

4. How did the Board's *Rossmore House* case impact on the practice of employer interrogation of individual employees during union organizational campaigns?

5. Explain the problems associated with captive-audience rules of the Board. How does the names-and-addresses policy fit into the general framework of captive-audience problems?

6. Explain the doctrine established by *Gissel.* Evaluate the undetermined and controversial feature of *Gissel* concerning the authority of the Board to issue nonmajority bargaining orders.

7. What are some of the problems with bargaining authorization cards?

8. When may an employer petition the Board to conduct an election? Do you see advantages or disadvantages to this right?

9. Do employees have ample choice in runoff elections? Does Taft-Hartley present the possibility that a minority union may be certified because of the requirements for runoff elections?

NOTES

1   *Monte Vista Disposal Co.*, 307 NLRB 531 (1992).

2   National Labor Relations Board, *Fifty-fifth Annual Report*, 1990, p. 11.

3   National Labor Relations Board, *Fifty-first Annual Report*, 1986, p. 48.

4   *NLRB* v. *Virginia Electric & Power Company*, 314 U.S. 469 (1941).

5   *General Shoe Corporation*, 77 NLRB 124 (1948).

6   *Economic Machinery Corporation*, 111 NLRB 947 (1955).

7   *NVF Company, Hartwell Division*, 210 NLRB 663 (1974).

8   *The Hurley Co.*, 130 NLRB 282 (1961).

9   *Plant City Welding and Tank Co.*, 119 NLRB 131 (1957).

10   *James Lees and Sons Co.*, 130 NLRB 290 (1961).

11   *Al Long, Inc.*, 173 NLRB 447 (1968).

12   *Sewell Manufacturing*, 138 NLRB 66 (1962).

13   *Allen Morrison Sign Co.*, 138 NLRB 73 (1962).

14   *NLRB* v. *Schapiro & Whitehouse, Inc.*, 356 F. 2d 675 (4th Cir. 1966).

15   *Baltimore Luggage Co.*, 162 NLRB 1230 (1967).

16   *KI (USA) Corporation*, 309 NLRB 1063 (1992).

17   *Beatrice Grocery Products, Inc.*, 287 NLRB 302 (1987).

18   140 NLRB 221 (1962).

19   *Bausch & Lomb, Inc.*, 185 NLRB 262 (1970).

20   *Lof Glass, Inc.*, 249 NLRB 428 (1980).

21   *Southwest Latex Corp.*, 175 NLRB 1 (1969).

22   *Monmouth Medical Center* v. *National Labor Relations Board*, 604 F. 2d 820 (3rd Cir. 1979).

23   *Shopping Kart Food Market*, 228 NLRB 1311 (1977).

24   239 NLRB 619 (1978).

25   263 NLRB 127 (1982).

26   *AWB Metal, Inc. (Division of Magnode Corp.*, 306 NLRB 109 (1992).

27   *Standard Knitting Mills, Inc.*, 172 NLRB 1122 (1968).

28   *Somismo, Inc.*, 133 NLRB 1310 (1961).

29   *General Electric Co.*, 215 NLRB 520 (1974).

30   *Honeywell, Inc.*, 225 NLRB 617 (1976).

31   *NLRB* v. *Gissel Packing*, 395 U.S. 575 (1969).

32   *TRW, Inc.*, 160 NLRB 21 (1968).

33   *Testing Service Corp.*, 193 NLRB 332 (1971).

34   *Ohmite Manufacturing Co.*, 217 NLRB 435 (1975).

35   *Novi American, Inc.*, 309 NLRB 544 (1992).

36   *Shaw Supermarkets, Inc.*, 303 NLRB 382 (1991).

37   *Donn Products, Inc.* and *American Metals Corp.*, 229 NLRB 116 (1977).

38   *American Telecommunications Corp.*, 249 NLRB 1135 (1980).

39   National Labor Relations Board, *Thirty-eighth Annual Report*, 1973, p. 73.

40   *Standard-Coosa-Thatcher Co.*, 85 NLRB 1358 (1949).

41   *Blue Flash Express, Inc.*, 109 NLRB 591 (1954).

42   *PPG Industries*, 251 NLRB 1146 (1980).

43   *Rossmore House*, 269 NLRB 1176 (1984).

44   *Hotel and Restaurant Employees, Local 11*, 760 F. 2d 1006 (9th Cir. 1985).

45   *Lyons Restaurant*, 234 NLRB 178 (1978).

46   *Sciosa Home and Industrial Disposal Service*, 266 NLRB 100 (1983).

47   287 NLRB No. 74 (1988).

48   *Sequatchie Valley Coal Co.*, 281 NLRB 726 (1986).

49   *Western Cartridge Co.* v. *NLRB*, 134 F. 2d 240 (7th Cir. 1943).

50   *The Great Atlantic & Pacific Tea Co., Inc.*, 166 NLRB 27 (1967).

51   *Performance Measurements Co., Inc.*, 148 NLRB 1657 (1964).

52   *Meir's Wine Cellars, Inc.*, 188 NLRB 153 (1971).

53   *Tennessee Auger Co.*, 169 NLRB 914 (1968).

54   *Ludwig Motor Corp.*, 222 NLRB 635 (1976).

55   *The Borden Manufacturing Co.*, 193 NLRB 1028 (1971).

56   *Hineline's Meat Plant, Inc.*, 193 NLRB 867 (1971).

57   *American Hoist and Derrick Co., Industrial Brownhoist Division*, 184 NLRB 551 (1970).

58   *Cadillac Overall Supply Co.*, 148 NLRB 1133 (1964).

59   *Dynamics Corp. of America, Fremont Division*, 286 NLRB No. 96 (1987).

60   *Smith Co.*, 192 NLRB 1098 (1971).

61   National Labor Relations Board, *Thirty-seventh Annual Report*, 1972, p. 74.

62   *Dic-Amco, Inc.*, 163 NLRB 1019 (1967).

63   *Savair Manufacturing Co.*, 414 U.S. 270 (1973).

64   *Lau Industries*, 210 NLRB 182 (1974).

65   *Mailing Services, Inc.*, 293 NLRB 565 (1989).

66   *Nu Skin International, Inc.*, 307 NLRB 223 (1992).

67   *Nestle Dairy Systems, Inc.*, 311 NLRB 987 (1993).

68   *NLRB* v. *My Store, Inc.*, 345 F. 2d 494 (7th Cir. 1965); *Phillips Manufacturing Co.*, 148 NLRB 1420 (1964).

69   *Struksnes Construction Co., Inc.*, 165 NLRB 1062 (1967).

70   *Wall Colmonoy Corp.*, 173 NLRB 40 (1968).

71   *Ponn Distributing, Inc.*, 203 NLRB 482 (1973).

72   *Clark Bros. Company*, 70 NLRB 802 (1946), 163 F. 2d 373 (1947).

73   *Babcock & Wilcox*, 77 NLRB 577 (1948).

74   *Bonwit Teller, Inc.*, 96 NLRB 608 (1951).

75   *Republic Aviation* v. *NLRB*, 324 U.S. 793 (1945).

76   *Bonwit Teller, Inc.*, v. *NLRB*, 197 F. 2d 640 (2d Cir. 1952).

77   *Metropolitan Auto Parts*, 99 NLRB 401 (1952); *Onondaga Pottery Co.*, 100 NLRB 1143 (1953).

78   107 NLRB 400 (1953).

79   *NLRB* v. *Babcock & Wilcox*, 351 U.S. 105 (1956).

80   National Labor Relations Board, *Nineteenth Annual Report*, 1954, p. 75.

81   107 NLRB 427 (1953).

82   *NLRB* v. *United Steelworkers (Nutone, Inc.)*, 357 U.S. 357 (1958).

83   145 NLRB 846 (1964).

84   *NLRB* v. *Montgomery Ward & Co., Inc.*, 339 F. 2d (889) (6th Cir. 1965).

85   155 NLRB 714 (1965).

86   A federal court of appeals modified this order of the NLRB. It held that the union would have equal time to reply should the employer make captive-audience speeches during future election campaigns (*NLRB* v. *H. W. Elson Bottling Co.*, 379 F. 2d 223 [6th Cir. 1967]). However, it is significant that the court ruled that unions have the opportunity to reply to captive-audience meetings under a particular set of employer unfair labor practices.

87   *J. P. Stevens and Co.*, 245 NLRB 198 (1979).

88   *J. P. Stevens*, 219 NLRB 850 (1975).

89   *Prescott Industrial Products Co.*, 205 NLRB No. 15 (1973).

90   *AFL-CIO News*, August 23, 1975.

91   *General Electric*, 156 NLRB 1247 (1966).

92   *Excelsior Underwear, Inc.*, 156 NLRB 1236 (1966).

93   National Labor Relations Board, *Thirty-first Annual Report*, 1966, p. 20.

94   *NLRB* v. *Wyman-Gordon*, 394 U.S. 759 (1969).

95   *Joy Silk Mills, Inc.*, 85 NLRB 1263 (1949); 185 F. 2d 732 (D.C. Cir. 1950), cert. denied 341 U.S. 914 (1951).

96   *Bernel Foam Products Company*, 146 NLRB 1277 (1964).

97   *Aiello Dairy Company*, 110 NLRB 1365 (1954).

98   National Labor Relations Board, *Thirtieth Annual Report*, 1965, pp. 129–130.

99   *NLRB* v. *Gissel Packing Company*, 395 U.S. 575 (1969).

100   261 NLRB 1189 (1982). For a criticism of the doctrine, see Robert P. Hunter, "*Conair*: Minority Bargaining Orders Usher in 1984 at NLRB," *Labor Law Journal*, XXXIII, No. 9 (September 1982), p. 571.

101   *Gourmet Foods*, 270 NLRB 578 (1984).

102   *United Dairy Farmers Cooperative* v. *NLRB*, 633 F. 2d 1054 (3d Cir. 1980).

103   *Teamsters Local 115* v. *NLRB (Flavor Delight, Inc.)*, 640 F. 2d 392 (D.C. Cir. 1981), cert. denied 102 S. Ct. 141 (1981).

104   237 NLRB 867 (1978).

105   *MMIC, Inc.*, 270 NLRB No. 51 (1984).

106   *Cartridge Actuated Devices*, 282 NLRB 426 (1986).

107   *NLRB* v. *S. S. Logan Packing Co.*, 386 F. 2d 562 (4th Cir. 1967).

108   *Cumberland Shoe Corporation*, 144 NLRB 1268 (1963); *Levi Strauss & Company*, 172 NLRB 732 (1968); *McEwen Manufacturing Company*, 172 NLRB 990 (1968).

109   *NLRB* v. *Keystone Pretzel Bakery, Inc.*, 696 F. 2d 257 (3d Cir. 1982).

110   On this basis, the Board invalidated cards signed by Spanish-speaking employees. It determined that the employees could not speak, write, or read English (*Gate of Spain Restaurant*, 192 NLRB 1091 [1971]).

111   *NLRB* v. *Roney Plaza Apartments*, 597 F. 2d 1046 (5th Cir. 1979).

112   *Pacific Molasses Co.* v. *NLRB*, 577 F. 2d 1172 (5th Cir. 1978).

113   *Oversight Hearings on the National Labor Relations Board*. Hearings Before Subcommittee on Labor-Management Relations, Committee on Education and Labor, House of Representatives, 94th Congress, 1st sess., October 23, 1975, p. 127.

114   Max S. Wortman, Jr., and Nathaniel Jones, "Remedial Actions of the NLRB in Representation Cases: An Analysis of the *Gissel* Bargaining Order," *Labor Law Journal*, XXX, No. 5 (May 1979), pp. 281–288.

115   *Avecor, Inc.*, 309 NLRB No. 9 (1992).

116   *Wall Street Journal*, July 22, 1975.

117   219 NLRB 298 (1975).

118   *Ann Lee Sportswear, Inc.* v. *NLRB*, 543 F. 2d 739 (10th Cir. 1976).

119   *Wilder Manufacturing*, 185 NLRB 175 (1970).

120   *Summer & Company, Linden Lumber Division*, 190 NLRB 718 (1971).

121   *Summer & Co., Linden Lumber Division* v. *NLRB*, 419 U.S. 301 (1974).

122   *Redmond Plastics, Inc.*, 187 NLRB 487 (1970).

123   William A. Krupman and Gregory I. Rasin, "Decertification: Removing the Shroud," *Labor Law Journal*, XXX, No. 4 (April 1979), pp. 231–234.

124   *Mid-Continent Refrigerated Service Co.*, 228 NLRB 917 (1977).

125   *Big Three Industries*, 201 NLRB 197 (1973).

126   *Kono-TV-Mission Telecasting*, 163 NLRB 1005 (1967).

127   *El Cid, Inc.*, 222 NLRB 1315 (1976).

128   *Houston Chronicle Publishing Co.*, 293 NLRB No. 38 (1989).

129   *Weather Shield Mfg., Inc.*, 292 NLRB No. 1 (1989).

130   *W. A. Krueger Co.*, 299 NLRB 914 (1990).

131   *Laidlaw Waste Systems, Inc.*, 307 NLRB 1211 (1992).

132   *International Molders & Allied Workers Local No. 125*, 178 NLRB 25 (1969).

133   *NLRB* v. *Industrial Union of Marine and Shipbuilding Workers of America*, 391 U.S. 418 (1968).

134   *NLRB* v. *Allis-Chalmers Manufacturing Company*, 288 U.S. 175 (1967).

135   National Labor Relations Board, *Fifty-fifth Annual Report*, 1990, p. 11.

136   *Ibid.*, p. 12.

137   Joseph Krislov, "The Increase in Union Decertification Elections," U.S. Department of Labor, Bureau of Labor Statistics, *Monthly Labor Review*, CII, No. 11 (November 1979), p. 31.

138   *Serv-Air, Inc.* v. *NLRB*, 401 F. 2d 363 (10th Cir. 1968).

139   *Great Southern Construction*, 266 NLRB 364 (1983).

140   National Labor Relations Board, *Fifty-fifth Annual Report*, 1990, p. 165.

141   *King Manor Care Center and Healthcare Services Group, Inc.*, 303 NLRB 19 (1991).

6

Collective Bargaining under Taft-Hartley

How Taft-Hartley impacts on bargaining is the focus of this chapter. A fundamental characteristic of the U.S. system of labor relations constitutes the right of employers and unions to negotiate terms and conditions of employment free from government dictation. To an extent, Taft-Hartley is not consistent with the nation's basic philosophy of labor relations. Controls are imposed on union security and the checkoff method of collecting union dues. NLRB and court construction of good-faith collective bargaining limits the freedom of the parties to demand issues at the bargaining table. The right of unions to strike and the concurrent right of employers to lock out may not be implemented when the NLRB and courts classify certain subjects as "voluntary" in the collective bargaining system. Strikes and lockouts are limited to mandatory issues of bargaining. At times the NLRB defers to private arbitrators as to whether the parties have complied with their legal obligation to bargain in good faith. In short, we deal here with a vital area of labor relations. In the final analysis, the labor agreement is the culmination of the bargaining process, and the impact of law thereto moves us into areas of critical concern to employers, employees, and unions.

UNION SECURITY

Character of Controversy

Union security is a primary aim of most labor organizations. It involves some form of compulsory membership as a condition of employment. Very few issues of collective bargaining are more controversial than the problem of union security. Union-security objectives include protection against employer discrimination, worker defection, and rival union-raiding tactics.[1]

Unions contend that compulsory membership as a condition of employment precludes workers receiving the benefits of unionism without bearing the risks and obligations of union activities. A union is the legal bargaining agent for all employees in the bargaining unit whether or not the employees are union members. This means that benefits the union secures in collective bargaining apply to union members and nonunion employees. Also, the union has the legal obligation to represent all employees in the bargaining unit in the grievance procedure. Unions argue, therefore, that nonunion employees are "free riders" and secure the same benefits as union members. Even the courts have recognized the character of this union argument. In a case involving the constitutionality of the union shop, William F. Buckley, the columnist and magazine editor, and M. Stanton Evans, the editor of the *Indianapolis News*, argued that compulsory union membership violates the constitutional right to free speech. For reasons to be made clear later on, the courts held that "free riders" are not required to be members of their union. However, it was held that the union had the right to levy

> mandatory dues on all employees who will reap the benefits of the union's representation of them in the contract negotiations with the employer.[2]

Congress also recognized the service function that unions perform for employees in the bargaining unit. In 1980, it enacted an amendment to Taft-Hartley that exempts from compulsory union membership employees who are members of bona fide organizations which forbid joining labor organizations or financially supporting them.[3] The law says a labor agreement, however, may provide that such persons must make a contribution equal to the amount of dues to a nonlabor nonreligious charity. More pertinent, however, to our discussion is that the amendment provides that if the religious objector requests a labor organization to handle a grievance, the union may charge the employee reasonable costs for such a service.

It is also claimed that in the absence of a union-security arrangement, union leaders must devote a large share of their time to organizing activities, since there is of necessity a constant effort to enlist members. This means there may be less time available for efforts to improve conditions of work in the bargaining unit. Unions also argue that worker morale is improved when union membership is required. Freedom to remain outside the labor organization leads to conflict between union and nonunion workers. Union workers have historically preferred not to work with nonunion workers. It is argued that the production process could be carried out more efficiently if conflicts between the two could be avoided.

It is further contended that union security permits union discipline. A labor organization may be in a better position to enforce contractual provisions if it is able to discipline workers for violating the terms of the collective bargaining agreement. Enforcement is simpler if it is well known that expulsion from the union carries with it loss of job. Thus, union security places unions in a better position to enforce international organizational rules and regulations that result in a more disciplined organization. Essentially, the claim is that union security provides a greater degree of union responsibility.

Arguments presented against compulsory union membership are several. One is that union security may make some union leaders unresponsive to the needs of members. Workers may receive less than the full amount of service they should receive from their union leaders.

Still another argument that is widely discussed in many public circles is that the requirement of union membership as a condition of employment deprives a person of the freedom to work. The influence of this argument on the general public is reflected in the "right-to-work" laws, as will be discussed later in this chapter. The elimination of compulsory union membership is also advanced as one method of dealing with excessive union power.

Though there are variations, for our purposes we are concerned with two types of union security: closed shop and union shop. Under a closed shop, employees must be union members *before* they are hired by the employer. In contrast, under a union shop, the employer has the right *to hire any person it desires.* After being hired, the employee must join the union as a condition of employment. Taft-Hartley provides, however, that the employee may not be forced to join the union until the thirtieth day of hire.

Abuses of Closed Shop

The closed shop extended considerable power to labor unions to regulate the supply of labor. They can restrict the number of workers in a particular occupation to keep wage rates high relative to alternative occupations that do not have such an arrangement. Racketeering has also been associated with unions having a long tradition of requiring the closed shop. It was not uncommon for business agents to demand excessive fees from individuals seeking union cards required for work in occupations such as those associated with the printing and construction industries.

Unfair denial by unions of a worker's opportunity to join unions has been a serious abuse of the closed shop. For example, it was reported in 1949 that thirty-two international unions, consisting of about 2.5 million members, discriminated against black people.[4] Union discrimination operates to deprive qualified workers of the freedom to enter an occupation. Factors such as religion, sex, national origin, and ancestry were likewise utilized by some labor unions to deprive workers of the chance to join their organizations. Unreasonable apprenticeship limitations also operate to deny union membership to qualified employees. When labor unions charged excessive initiation fees, the effect again was to close the door to union membership. Professor Philip Taft found that some labor unions charged initiation fees that would appear excessive to the average worker.[5] This action excluded from membership a number of individuals capable of performing the work required.

Construction workers usually move frequently from one job to another and depend on the union for job information and protection. This permits local unions to control specific job territories for the benefit of members. Theoretically, a craft worker could move from one local labor organization to another with the full job rights enjoyed by any other unionist. In practice, locals often discriminated against members of other locals if unemployment was prevalent in the territory subject to its control. Thus, membership transfer from one local to another was abused, since it was restricted by some unions.

Closed Shop Declared Illegal

Under the terms of the Wagner Act, the issue of the closed shop was left to the determination of the union-management negotiators. It neither required nor forbade the closed shop. As a result of its abuses, Congress outlawed the closed shop when it enacted Taft-Hartley. Under its terms, an employee may not be required to join a union before the thirtieth day of hire. An employer, union, or both violate the law if the employee is forced to join the union before that time. The NLRB took an early position that it would not honor a contract that included a closed-shop provision. Such an agreement would be made unlawful by the mere inclusion of any provision requiring union membership as the prerequisite for obtaining a job. Moreover, strikes or picketing to obtain a closed shop were ruled illegal. In 1950, the NLRB ruled that peaceful picketing or even the threat of it to coerce employers into hiring only union members violated Taft-Hartley.[6] The federal courts have upheld both of these Board decisions.[7]

Events soon proved, however, that the closed-shop principle was so deeply rooted in the industrial relations environment that the passage of a law could not result in its elimination. Working against the successful operation of the 1947 law on the closed-shop issue stood powerful institutional forces. At the time of the passage of the Taft-Hartley Act, millions of employees were working under closed-shop agreements. Some industries—such as printing, building, construction, and maritime—had operated under the closed shop for scores of years.

Many employers cooperated with unions to continue closed-shop arrangements after 1947. They refused to bring charges against unions when they demanded the closed shop. Instead, many employers simply agreed to continue closed-shop provisions in collective bargaining contracts executed subsequent to Taft-Hartley passage. In this connection, the Senate Committee on Labor and Public Welfare in 1949 reported that "notwithstanding the provisions of the Labor Management Relations Act, closed-shop contracts continue to be observed over a wide area of industry."[8] This observation was supported in Buffalo, New York, by a careful study of the closed-shop experience. It was reported that "the most noteworthy fact of all presented by the experience in Buffalo is that the new labor law abolished the closed shop in neither form nor substance."[9]

Many other employers and labor unions, though not renewing closed-shop contractual provisions outright, designed devices that in effect meant that only union members could be hired. Actually, these clauses were a subterfuge to avoid the closed-shop ban. One contract negotiated in 1948 provided that "the employers agree in the hiring of employees to prefer applicants who have previously been employed on vessels of one or more of the companies signatory to the contract.[10] Since the companies and the union, parties to the agreement, had operated under a closed-shop contract for a number of years before the passage of Taft-Hartley, all "previously" employed workers were union members. The contract ensured the continuation of the closed shop, since all employees hired under it belonged to the labor union. Another contract negotiated in 1948 provided that only workers who had successfully completed an apprentice training program conducted in a school sponsored by a labor organization were eligible for employment.[11] Such a contract clause effectively continued the closed-shop arrangement. In still another contract, the employer gave the labor union the inside track in filling job vacancies.[12] It specified that the employer would give the union forty-eight hours' advance notice before interviewing any new applicants. The implication was that the union would send union members to apply for the position. Such a tactic obviously precluded the hiring of nonunion workers.

Brown-Olds Doctrine: A New Board Effort

Aware of these wholesale violations, the NLRB in 1956 attempted to enforce the law by imposing financial penalties on employers and unions that maintained the closed shop. The opportunity was provided in the *Brown-Olds* case involving a collective bargaining agreement that contained several of the union's bylaws, working rules, and regulations requiring employees to obtain union clearance before seeking employment.

An administrative law judge ruled that the specific provisions constituted an unlawful closed-shop agreement. Upon review, the Board decided to use its remedial powers to correct abuse of the closed-shop prohibitions. Union dues were to be returned to members to correct violations. The Board held in *Brown-Olds* that "the remedy of reimbursement of all such monies is appropriate and necessary to expunge the illegal effects of the unfair labor practices found here." A 1943 Supreme Court case in which a company-dominated union was held illegal by its very existence in that it was not formed by employee free choice was used as a precedent. In that case, return of dues had been one means of disestablishing the union.[13] The Board in *Brown-Olds* established the rule that *a union would be required to reimburse employees for dues and assessments collected under illegal closed-shop agreements during a period beginning six months prior to the date unfair labor practice charges were filed.* The doctrine was to affect both unions and management executing illegal closed-shop provisions. When it was determined that the employer had been a willing ally to the illegal arrangement, the company was required to share the costs involved in the refund of dues.

Thus, labor and management were put on notice that they would jointly be held responsible to reimburse all members for dues and other assessments paid from the time a remedial order was issued extending to six months previous to the filing of the charge. For example, if there were 500 union members, all would be reimbursed for all monies paid during this period of time. Financially, the cost could run into thousands of dollars. The doctrine was applied in many cases, but, as will be seen, not a penny was refunded because of the Supreme Court's review of the NLRB policy.

The Board later extended the remedy to hiring-hall arrangements, even if these were not connected with a closed shop. The Board justified the extension by arguing that these arrangements had a coercive influence on work applicants to join the union.[14] That is, if an employer obtained workers exclusively through a hiring hall, the worker's first point of contact would be with the union. Both tacit and overt pressure could be applied to force union membership before a job opening would be made available.

The U.S. Supreme Court reviewed the *Brown-Olds* doctrine in 1961.[15] The case involved a collective bargaining contract with Mechanical Handling Systems, Inc., of Indianapolis, Indiana. In it, the company agreed to provisions requiring it to abide by the union rules and regulations requiring employment of only union members. The case arose when two job applicants, members of another union, were denied employment because they could not obtain referral from the union. The Board upon review applied its *Brown-Olds* doctrine requiring reimbursement to all employees of all dues and assessments collected by the union starting from six months prior to the date unfair labor practice charges were filed.

Upon review, the Supreme Court ruled that the Board's *Brown-Olds* remedy was punitive and not remedial in character. It found that the Board had thus exceeded its statutory powers. The Board had presented no evidence indicating that a single union member had been coerced to join or remain in the labor organization. Indeed, all the workers might have been union members for many years. *Thus, the requirement to pay back all dues and assessments to members benefited union members, but did not provide a remedy to persons denied work in the first place.* The Court held that the only power given the Board was to remedy the harm done to persons denied work because of the illegal union-security provisions. It could only require a company to hire a worker who had been denied employment and order back pay concerning lost wages and benefits. Any other construction of the law was not within the province of the NLRB. Board remedial policy could not be justified solely on its deterrent qualities. Thus, the punitive financial aspect of *Brown-Olds* was held illegal by the Supreme Court.

Hiring-Hall Regulations

The key to the union-controlled and -administered hiring hall is the closed shop, since, to take advantage of its services, a worker had to be a union member. A review of the legislative history of Taft-Hartley establishes that its proponents meant to eliminate the union hiring hall. During debate on the law, Senator Taft, in illustrating the scope of the prohibition of the closed shop, declared that its abolishment "is best exemplified by the so-called hiring halls in the west coast where shipowners cannot employ anyone unless the union sends him to them."[16]

Soon after Taft-Hartley passage, the NLRB ruled the union-controlled hiring hall was unlawful.[17] It was first outlawed in the maritime industry, but the rule applied throughout industry. While commenting on the scope of the prohibition, Robert Denham, former General Counsel, said:

> In the construction industry the matter of the union shop has been the source of much uneasiness ever since the Taft-Hartley Act went on the books. The union shop provision of the law definitely was designed to do away with the closed shop, under which a man was required to be a member of the contracting union before he could ever be considered

for a job. Now, all of that is prohibited, as also is the use of the hiring hall, either directly or indirectly. There simply is no further such thing as the closed shop or the hiring hall, nor any legitimate way by which the employer can contract to prefer union members over nonunion members in the matter of hiring.[18]

In other words, the union hiring hall was per se unlawful. Later on, however, the NLRB shifted its policy, holding a union-operated hiring hall lawful provided it was operated in a manner that did not discriminate against nonunion members. That is, the union and nonunion worker must be treated the same for job opportunities. To be lawful, the employer and union must include the following safeguards in their labor agreements: (1) Selection of applicants for referral to jobs would be without regard to union membership requirements; (2) the employer would retain the right to reject any applicant referred by the union; and (3) standards would be posted in the hiring hall for employee inspection.

If these conditions were not met, the hiring hall would be illegal and subject to the *Brown-Olds* remedy.

NLRB Reversed: *Mountain Pacific*

On the very same day it invalidated the Board's *Brown-Olds* remedy, the Supreme Court also held improper its hiring-hall policy in *Mountain Pacific*.[19] To say the least, the Board did not have a nice day!

In the case, a union and a group of employers had agreed that employees would be hired only by union hiring-hall referral. It was also agreed that referral would be on the basis of seniority and without regard to an employee's union membership. The Board had previously ruled that the hiring arrangement was unlawful because it did not contain the three safeguards mentioned above.

The Supreme Court reversed the NLRB by holding again that it had exceeded its allowable powers. An exclusive hiring-hall arrangement is not per se illegal under the Act, even if it lacks specific safeguards imposed by the Board. Its authority was provided only for remedying cases where discrimination actually occurred.

In short, the NLRB is required to examine the discriminatory nature of each hiring-hall arrangement formally presented to it. It cannot hold such arrangements as illegal just because certain safeguards are not explicitly contained in the contract. The Supreme Court required the Board to look at the administrative operation of each arrangement prior to reaching a decision. If the hiring hall reveals discriminatory hiring practices, each violation must be remedied separately. Thus, should a nonunion person be denied a job because of the hiring-hall operation, the Board may only direct the practice to cease and award back pay.

In any event, though the Board's intention in *Brown-Olds* and *Mountain Pacific* was to implement the Taft-Hartley anti-closed-shop provision, the Supreme Court held the agency could not exercise power not granted by the law. Of course, Congress could have corrected the situation by enacting legislation conferring on the NLRB the authority it tried unsuccessfully to exercise. Congress did not do this, and illegal closed shops and hiring halls undoubtedly still exist today.

LANDRUM-GRIFFIN CHANGES: CONSTRUCTION INDUSTRY

Prehire Contracts

When Congress amended Taft-Hartley by Landrum-Griffin, it gave special treatment to the construction industry because of its relatively short and intermittent nature of employment. Thus, in the construction industry, employees may be required to join the union on the seventh day of hire. In other industries, union membership may be compelled only on or after the thirtieth day of employment.

Of greater significance, the amended law permits contractors and unions to negotiate a *prehire labor agreement*. This means a contract may be negotiated before any worker is hired. When prehire contracts are in place, employees lose the right to select a union to represent them. Elections are not held, and NLRB certifications are not issued. In no other industry are employers and unions permitted to adopt prehire contracts. The employee's right to designate a union was sacrificed to promote a degree of stability within the construction industry.

In its initial application of the prehire provision, the NLRB in *R. J. Smith Construction*[20] held that employers may abandon such contracts at will. No matter that the contract has not expired; contractors may walk away from the agreement. In 1978, the U.S. Supreme Court upheld the Board's policy.[21]

In complete reversal of policy, the NLRB held in *John Deklewa & Sons* (1987)[22] that neither the employer nor the union could abandon prehire contracts. Such contracts may terminate only if they expire or employees reject the union in an NLRB-conducted representation election. In December 1988, the federal appeals court in San Francisco, sitting *en banc*, sustained the new interpretation by the Board in a 6–4 decision.[23] Perhaps the U.S. Supreme Court will review the case, and though predicting decisions of the high court is a risky business, it will probably sustain the Board, deferring to its judgment, just as it deferred to its judgment in *Smith Construction*.

The new policy may make it more difficult for employers to operate on a so-called "doublebreasted" basis. Under this arrangement, the unionized contractor creates a nonunion firm and transfers work from the union members to the nonunion operation. Previously, employers simply abandoned the prehire contract and operated on a nonunion basis. Under the present policy, the employer may not walk away from the prehire contract, and its capability for doublebreasting appears reduced.

When a union struck a contractor to force anti-doublebreasting language in the labor agreement, the NLRB held that kind of strike and picketing was lawful under Taft-Hartley.[24] Construction unions understand, of course, the best protection for doublebreasting would be federal legislation outlawing the practice. Although legislation of this sort has been introduced many times, Congress has not acted on it. In any event, by judicial pronouncements, construction unions have made some, if not considerable, progress toward their goal.

In 1993 the United States Supreme Court gave a considerable boost to prehire contracts. When the state of Massachusetts undertook the cleanup of Boston Harbor, it entered into a prehire contract with the construction trades council, a provision of which specified that each successful bidder for work on the project had to agree to the wages and other conditions of employment contained in prehire contracts. In other words, enforcement of that provision would mean that only union members would work on the project.

A contractors' association representing nonunion construction industry employees filed suit to enjoin that portion of the prehire contract which excluded nonunion labor. The basis of the lawsuit was that federal law, specifically Taft-Hartley, preempted state and municipal laws inconsistent with federal law. A federal district court denied the injunction, but the U.S. Court of Appeals in Boston reversed the district court, issuing an injunction restraining enforcement of the bid specification in question.

Writing for the *unanimous* Court the then Justice Harry Blackmun, reversing the appeals court, distinguished between a situation where states improperly act as regulators and interfere with federal policy, and those in which states are essentially analogous to private business.[25] In other words, here the state was acting as a private consumer, and therefore no conflict existed between state and federal law.

Needless to say the construction unions were delighted by the decision. Construction union chief Robert Georgine proclaimed:

> To say we are elated is an understatement, it [the decision] is a ringing endorsement of the right of states and their subdivisions to participate in union only project labor agreements, just exactly as we have contended all along.[26]

Lawful Contractual Restrictions

In addition to the legality of prehire contracts, Congress extended special privileges to employers and unions in the construction industry. Landrum-Griffin made it more certain—and, indeed, at times almost positive—that only union members would be employed on construction jobs over which a union has collective bargaining rights. In practice, Congress legalized the closed shop in the construction industry despite Taft-Hartley's ban of it.

The 1959 law sanctioned the following kinds of provisions that may be contained in a labor agreement negotiated by a construction union and an employer:

1. Requires the employer to notify a union of employment opportunities.
2. Gives the union the opportunity to refer qualified employees to the employer.
3. Specifies minimum training or experience qualifications for employment.
4. Establishes a priority system for the referral of employees based upon the length of service with the employer in the construction industry or in the geographical area.

Should a labor agreement contain such provisions, only union members are likely to be referred to a job. For example, suppose the labor agreement provided that only employees with two or more years of employment with the particular contractor may be hired; if the union has had a bargaining relationship with the employer over the years, and if the employer previously hired only union members, who else but union members would be eligible for employment?

It could be argued that a construction job covered by a collective bargaining contract should be staffed only by union members. In this way, the problem of strife between union and nonunion employees would be avoided, including the propensity of union members to strike when nonunion employees are hired. If this is sound public policy, Congress should legalize the closed shop in the construction industry and not seek to accomplish this end by the sort of subterfuge that now exists.

Thus the NLRB upheld the legality of a job referral plan in the construction industry contained in a labor agreement that gave preference to employees who had worked with the particular contractor for one or two years in the last four years. It said:

> As is clear . . . Section 8(f)(4) expressly exempts from the strictures of the act and makes lawful an exclusive referral system under which priority in job referrals may be "based on length of service with such employer."[27]

Although receiving substantial benefits from Landrum-Griffin, construction unions are still controlled by other areas of national labor policy. Under certain circumstances, the NLRB held such unions in violation of the law and directed back pay to be awarded by the construction unions to employees harmed by their unlawful conduct. For example, in the case involving the Iron Workers Union, the agency determined that the union threatened and coerced so-called "travelers" into quitting jobs (a "traveler" belongs to a particular local union but goes to another area looking for work under jurisdiction of a different local union, both unions being affiliated with the same national union). Unions engage in this practice in order to protect their own members' jobs. It was undisputed that the union's coercion actually caused the travelers to miss work on many occasions.

As a remedy the Board directed the union to award these employees appropriate back pay. It did so even though the employer involved was not a party to the union's action.[28] Before this decision the agency did not order unions to pay workers for union violations of the law unless employers instigated or acquiesced in the unlawful action.[29] In the case at hand, the NLRB reasoned that merely ordering the offending union to cease and desist from its unlawful conduct would neither remove the "chilling" effect on the victimized employees' willingness to exercise their statutory rights nor restore the status quo. It concluded that only a back-pay remedy would accomplish these ends. To this extent, the agency modified but did not reverse its former policy.

TAFT-HARTLEY AND THE UNION SHOP

Union-Shop Elections

Taft-Hartley legalizes the union shop as a permissible form of union security. The statute, however, controls the circumstances under which the arrangement may be incorporated into collective bargaining contracts and regulates its implementation. The only legal limitation contained in the Wagner Act was that the labor organization negotiating a union-security arrangement had to represent a majority of the bargaining unit.

Until 1951, the most demanding prerequisite for the union shop was that a special election had to be held by the NLRB. The referendum was known as the *union-shop election*. This election should not be confused with the representation or certification election. A certification election refers to a poll to determine whether a labor union represents a majority of workers for the purpose of collective bargaining. The union-shop election was a special referendum to determine whether a majority of bargaining-unit workers approve of their union negotiating an agreement making union membership a condition of employment after the required thirty-day waiting period.

Another distinction between representation and union-shop elections concerned the concept of "majority." For purposes of representation, a labor union is required to win only a majority of the votes cast. But for the union shop, the union was required to receive the votes of a majority of those workers *eligible* to vote in the election. This meant that a worker who did not cast a ballot actually voted against the union shop. Any worker who did not choose to vote, who was laid off, or who failed to vote because of illness or any other reason was counted as voting against union security. It is obvious that Taft-Hartley went beyond normal election procedures to make it difficult for unions to obtain union-security provisions requiring membership as a condition of employment. Even if the union shop was authorized by a majority of the bargaining unit, there was no guarantee that it could be obtained. Authorization by union members merely gave the parties the right to negotiate on the issue.[30]

Not only were elections required to authorize the parties to negotiate union-shop terms, but employees also have the right to petition the NLRB to hold union-shop *deauthorization elections*. A petition including a minimum of 30 percent of the bargaining unit is required. A union loss would mean that the union shop was no longer a valid provision in the collective bargaining agreement. As in union-shop elections, the law provides that to revoke a union shop, a majority of the employees eligible to vote must vote in favor of deauthorization. When the employees vote against the union shop, the effect is to revoke immediately the contractual requirement that employees must hold union membership to work.[31] No other provision of the labor agreement is affected by such a poll. Though deauthorization elections are not frequent, unions lose most of those that do take place. In 1988, the Board conducted 104 of these elections, with the union shop defeated in 56 percent, but covering only 2,300 employees.[32] As with decertification elections, supervisors may not file deauthorization petitions or encourage employees to seek the referendum.[33] Most of the union losses were in small bargaining units with less than 50 employees. Although, as noted below, the union-shop election requirement was repealed in 1951, the union-shop deauthorization election is still part of national labor policy.

Repeal of Union-Shop Election Requirement

The assumption of Taft-Hartley that workers would reject a proposal that required union membership as a condition of employment if given an opportunity to do so in a secret-ballot election was not realized in practice. The union-shop election requirement was repealed on October 22, 1951, by the Taft-Humphrey amendment of Taft-Hartley.[34]

During the four years and two months in which the union-shop election was required, the Board conducted 46,119 polls. Union-shop agreements were authorized in 44,795 of the referendums, or in 97 percent of those conducted. In the polls 6,542,564 workers were eligible to vote, of whom 5,547,478, or 84.8 percent, cast valid ballots. Of those voting, 5,071,988, or 77.5 percent of the workers, voted in favor of union security.[35] In signing the October 1951 amendment, President Truman stated that union-shop elections "have involved expenditures in excess of $3,000,000 of public funds. Experience has proved them to be not only costly, and burdensome, but unnecessary as well."[36]

A state, however, may require a union-shop election before employers and unions are allowed to negotiate arrangements requiring union membership as a condition of employment. In Wisconsin, a union could not lawfully negotiate a union shop unless two-thirds of the bargaining unit voted for it. Though Taft-Hartley no longer provides for union-shop elections, such state laws appear valid. In 1949, the U.S. Supreme Court held the Wisconsin statute lawful.[37] In addition, as will be discussed later in this chapter, the high court in 1963 held that the states under the authority of Section 14(b) of Taft-Hartley may regulate union security provisions.

Taft-Hartley on Nonpayment of Dues

Section 8(a)(3) of Taft-Hartley states that the *only condition whereby a worker may lose his job for nonmembership in a union is for nonpayment of dues*. It has been established by Board cases that unions do not have a right to prescribe rules that interfere with the relationship between employee and employer, except in the case of the nonpayment of dues.[38]

In 1955, the NLRB established a policy prohibiting discharge of a worker if, at any time before the discharge became effective, the employee made full and unqualified tender of dues to the union.[39] This rule was changed in 1962, when the Board held that employee delay of dues payment was at odds with the congressional purpose in permitting the parties to negotiate union-shop agreements.[40] An automatic determination was eliminated in that the Board decided to review the record to determine why an employee had delayed dues payment under a valid union-security agreement. In still another case, the Board held that a union had the duty to inform members upon their joining of what their obligations were.[41] If workers had been informed of their obligations when they became members, they had the responsibility to tender dues in accordance with union rules, or run the risk of discharge.

An employee who offered to pay dues, however, was not in violation of the Act even if the labor organization had expelled him or her for lack of conformity to internal union rules. Union-shop contracts, therefore, *merely offer unions financial security*. In short, Taft-Hartley permitted the union shop as a condition of employment and then proceeded to dilute its enforcement. As early as 1949, the Board held that a worker does not have to join a union even though a union-shop arrangement exists. The employee's obligation under the law is willingness to tender the dues and initiation fees required by the union. If a union imposed any other qualifications and conditions for membership with which an employee was unwilling to comply, the employee could be *excluded from union membership, but not from the job*.[42] Twenty-five years later, in

1973, the NLRB upheld the same principle of law.[43] A union member worked during a strike. He wrote the union he would continue to pay dues under the new labor agreement without being a member. The new contract contained a union shop, and the employer discharged the employee at the request of the union. The NLRB, however, held the discharge of the employee was illegal because he had been willing to pay his dues. When a federal court of appeals upheld the Board, it stressed once again that under Taft-Hartley, *an employee does not have to be a union member to protect the job.* All the employee has to do is to tender the dues required of union members.[44] This feature of the law explains why the courts held, as mentioned earlier, that columnist Buckley and editor Evans were not required to join a union as a condition of employment. They were, however, required to pay the equivalent of union dues.

Thus, it is well established that a union may expel an employee for a violation of its rules, but it may not effect his or her discharge if the expulsion is for any reason other than the refusal to pay an amount equivalent to union dues and initiation fees. Despite a contractual provision requiring union membership as a condition of employment, the individual does not have to be a union member to hold a job. In short, though Taft-Hartley makes lawful a contract provision requiring "membership" in a union as a condition of employment, the word "membership" does not mean actual membership in a union. *For purposes of Taft-Hartley, an employee is a "union member" if he or she is willing to pay dues.*

In an unusual but significant 1993 case, the NLRB was confronted with a situation where a union sought to enforce a union security provision against four employees who were disciplined by the union because they had attempted to transplant seventeen jobs from the bargaining unit to supervisory positions. Needless to say, in union culture they had engaged in conduct which in effect amounts to treason. When the union learned about their action and investigated, they suspended them from participating in most union activities. The suspended employees claimed that the union discriminated against them for engaging in protected activities under Section 7 of Taft-Hartley. Under Section 7 unions may not coerce or force employees to support union activities. They insisted that in effect the union suspended them from membership, and they were no longer required to pay dues under the union security arrangement. In reply the union told the employees that if they ceased paying dues, it would request the employer to discharge them from their jobs.

Rejecting their claim, the NLRB ruled, in *Kaiser Cement*, the union action was lawful.[45] It was lawful because the employees did not resign from the union. If they had resigned prior to engaging in their conduct, the union could not have disciplined them. Since the suspended employees elected to remain in the union, they could not be heard to complain when the union enforced its membership rules. In addition, the Board held because the employees continued to remain in the bargaining unit, they must pay their dues under the union-security arrangement.

That the Board treated the employees properly is manifested by the fact the union had the legal responsibility to provide them fair representation by handling their grievances and provide them other benefits germane in the duty of fair representation. (In Chapter 7 we will deal with the duty of unions to provide fair representation to their members.)

Union Security and the *Paramax* Decision

In another 1993 case, *Paramax*, the NLRB handed down a decision that, if enforced vigorously, could cause unions considerable difficulty.[46] If the labor movement was pleased with *Kaiser Cement*, it had reason to be very concerned with *Paramax*. It placed in jeopardy every union security clause that calls for membership "in good standing" in the union as a condition of employment. At one time the Board recognized that such a clause, ". . . contained in countless labor . . . agreements," is a "traditional term" in labor relations, and Congress intended to permit a requirement of membership in good standing.[47]

Nonetheless, the NLRB held in *Paramax* such clauses are unlawful unless the union informs each and every bargaining-unit employee (union or nonunion) that the only required condition of employment is payment of dues and initiation fees.[48] Failure to do so could lead employees to believe, said the NLRB, that their union-security obligation was greater than what was required by law.

In reaching its decision, the agency said the standard union-security clause in question is ambiguous and could be understood by employees to require full union membership with all its attendant obligations.

To support its decision the NLRB made use of *General Motors* (to be explained later on in this chapter). In that case the high court stated that under union-security provisions, employees need only pay monthly dues and initiation fees to hold their jobs. Thus, in *Paramax*, the Board ordered unions to notify each employee in writing of his or her *General Motors* rights. If unions do not comply, any union-security provision containing the standard language is in violation of Taft-Hartley. Currently, approximately 83 percent of all union agreements contain some kind of union-security provision.[49] Practically all of them contain the traditional language. Given that unions currently represent more than 17 million employees in the United States, this means they would be required to notify about 14 million bargaining-unit employees of their *General Motors* rights. As stated, the impact of *Paramax* depends on the character of enforcement of the doctrine by the NLRB.

A Different Approach: Union Fines

To deal with union members who violate union rules governing their conduct, some unions attempted a different approach. Instead of expelling the disobedient members, unions fined them. Aware that expulsion from a union, despite the existence of a union shop, would not cause these members to lose their jobs, such unions sought to impose a monetary penalty for violation of their rules. In this approach, unions relied upon the feature of Section 8(b)(1) of Taft-Hartley that says:

> This paragraph shall not impair the rights of labor organizations to prescribe their own rules with respect to the acquisition or retention of membership therein.

Such fines are lawful. Of more particular significance, they may be collected through court action instituted by the union against the member. In one case, a union established a rule that limited the amount of incentive earnings that employees could earn through increased production. A member violated the rule, and the union fined him. In *Scofield* v. *NLRB*, the U.S. Supreme Court held in 1969 that the fine was lawful.[50] It said a union is free

> to enforce a properly adopted rule which reflects a legitimate union interest, impairs no policy Congress has imbedded in the labor laws and is reasonably enforced against union members.

It also said the fine was imposed against the person as a "union member" and not as an "employee." In the Court's view, the fine did not disturb the relationship between the union member and the employer.

Despite the legality of such fines, their usefulness to unions in dealing with disciplined members is quite limited. As we shall note later on, the U.S. Supreme Court held in 1972 that fines cannot be imposed if a union member resigns from a union before violating a union rule.[51] Indeed, even in *Scofield*, the high court said that if union members were unhappy about the production ceilings, they were free "to leave the union". Thus, if a member withdraws from a union because of dissatisfaction with a union rule, the employee may not be discharged from the job.

It is clear from this discussion that the nonpayment-of-dues feature of Taft-Hartley undermines the union shop. At the same time, it weakens a union's ability to enforce its internal rules in terms of union members. In a later chapter, we will find that Landrum-Griffin protects a union member against expulsion under unfair procedures. Despite this feature of the 1959 law, Congress left intact the provision of Taft-Hartley that forbids the discharge of an employee from a job because of loss of union membership for any reason other than refusal to pay dues. Either Congress failed to relate its 1959 action to that feature of Taft-Hartley or it believed Landrum-Griffin protection of union membership was not sufficient to deal with the problem of arbitrary and capricious expulsion of members from their unions.

Board Control over Union-Security Clauses

The NLRB established principles to guide it in determining the effect of union-security clauses on representation election petitions. The Board has consistently held that a valid collective bargaining contract will bar an election for at least a twelve-month period.

In 1958, however, the Board held that the existence of a contract would not stop it from holding an election if the agreement did not reflect the limitations placed on union security by Taft-Hartley.[52] But the Supreme Court did not permit this rule to stand. In 1961, in two cases, the Court held that such a mechanistic approach presumed illegality and amounted to a prejudgment of the labor organization.[53] The Board was forced to revise its rules regarding union-security clauses as bars to representation elections.

Revised rules were established in the same year, 1961, in *Paragon Products Corporation*.[54] It was deemed necessary for a union-security clause to be clearly unlawful on its face to permit a representation election before the end of a twelve-month period. The forms of unlawful union security include those that expressly require employers to give union members preference in hiring, layoffs, and seniority. Also, unlawful provisions exist if employees are given less than the thirty-day grace period provided for union membership in Taft-Hartley. Contracts that require employees to pay the union money other than the periodic dues and initiation fees required of all unionists are unlawful. Any other payments required as a condition of employment will not bar the holding of a representation election.

Ambiguous union-security clauses will not necessarily relax the twelve-month rule unless the provision is found illegal by the Board or a federal court. Each case must therefore be investigated and an appropriate remedy provided as a result of findings. Mechanical approaches to the problem of union security are discouraged by the U.S. Supreme Court.

RIGHT-TO-WORK LAWS

Section 14(b) of Taft-Hartley

Right to work is a term used to describe state statutory or constitutional provisions banning the requirement of union membership as a condition of employment. A significant feature of right-to-work laws is that they not only outlaw the execution of union-security arrangements in the area of *intrastate* commerce, but they also forbid the negotiation of compulsory union membership provisions within the area of *interstate* commerce. Taft-Hartley outlawed the closed shop but permitted the negotiation of union shops. However, Section 14(b) of the Act permits states to enact laws applying to the area of interstate commerce that not only outlaws the closed shop but also makes *any form of union security illegal*. This provision of the Taft-Hartley Act states:

> Nothing in this Act shall be construed as authorizing the execution or application of agreements requiring membership in a labor organization as a condition of employment in any State or Territory in which such execution or application is prohibited by State or Territorial law.

In this manner, the federal government invited the states to legislate in the area reserved by the Constitution of the United States to the federal government.

Action of the states to eliminate union-security arrangements began several years before the passage of the 1947 law. In 1944, Arkansas and Florida amended their constitutions to outlaw all agreements making union membership a condition of employment.[55] The Florida amendment provided that

> the rights of persons to work shall not be denied or abridged on account of membership in any labor union or labor organization.

After Florida and Arkansas set the pattern, Arizona, Nebraska, and South Dakota in 1946 passed amendments to their constitutions to prohibit all species of union-security arrangements.[56] In 1947, state prohibition of union security became even more widespread. During early 1947, seven more states banned all forms of union security.[57] In these states, the method of eliminating union security was the enactment of statutes rather than constitutional amendments. Thus, at the time Taft-Hartley was passed, twelve states had already prohibited all types of union security.

Without Section 14(b), no state could lawfully enact right-to-work legislation applying to the area of interstate commerce, since such laws would conflict with the doctrine of national supremacy. National supremacy in the area of interstate commerce was established by the U.S. Supreme Court as early as 1819.[58]

If Congress had so desired when it passed Taft-Hartley, it could have made such state action inoperative in the area of interstate commerce. Even so, a constitutional issue was advanced to test the ability of states to enact laws that in fact become superior to federal law in the area of interstate commerce. In 1949, the U.S. Supreme Court held that Section 14(b) of Taft-Hartley and state right-to-work legislation enacted under its authority were compatible with the federal Constitution.[59] In 1976, unions won minor relief from right-to-work laws when the U.S. Supreme Court held that the Texas law did not apply to marine workers who spend the vast majority of their time on the high seas.[60] Five years earlier, the high court had also nullified a provision of the Georgia right-to-work law that permitted employees to revoke their checkoff authorizations for union dues at any time.[61] The Georgia statute was held to be in conflict with Taft-Hartley on that point because under the federal law, checkoff authorizations may be irrevocable for a maximum of one year. The Court said that if the Georgia law prevailed, it would prevent employers and unions from negotiating a checkoff agreement as authorized by the federal law. Later in this chapter, we will discuss the nature of the checkoff and Taft-Hartley controls. In 1982, a federal appeals court ruled that federal properties were exempt from right-to-work laws.[62] At issue was a union-shop provision negotiated by an employer and union covering employees working at a U.S. Air Force base located in Florida. Holding that the Florida right-to-work law did not apply to federal "enclaves" located in states, the Supreme Court sustained the validity of the union shop by refusing to review the lower court decision. However, the U.S. Supreme Court held it was not unconstitutional for Congress to authorize states to enact right-to-work laws. In effect, the high court told organized labor that if it desired to eliminate Section 14(b) of the law, the proper forum was Congress and not the courts.

Convinced that employees should not get a "free ride," a union attempted to assess nonunion employees for their portion of its collective bargaining costs. Such representation fees would be lower than full dues required of union members. Its effort failed, however, when a federal appeals court ruled that the Mississippi right-to-work law forbade such assessments.[63]

Efforts to Repeal Section 14(b)

Twenty-one states prohibit all forms of union security: Alabama, Arizona, Arkansas, Florida, Georgia, Idaho, Iowa, Kansas, Louisiana, Mississippi, Nebraska, Nevada, North Carolina, North Dakota, South Carolina, South Dakota, Tennessee, Texas, Utah, Virginia, and Wyoming. In 1957, Indiana passed a right-to-work law and gained the distinction of being the only industrial state to have enacted one. As a result of the elections of 1964 and the pressure of the Indiana labor movement, this law was repealed in 1965 and was never again raised as an issue in that state.[64] Where union membership is comparatively large, organized labor has successfully prevented the enactment of such laws. At one time in California, Ohio, and Washington, right-to-work laws were on the ballot for referendum by the public. By large majorities, the proposals were rejected by the voters of those states. In contrast, in November 1976, the citizens of Arkansas voted 387,084 to 192,124 to retain that state's right-to-work law.[65] Between 1978 and 1985, proposed right-to-work laws were defeated in Colorado, Illinois, Kentucky, Maine, Maryland, Missouri, Montana, New Hampshire, Vermont, and West Virginia.[66] In 1979, the New Mexico legislature enacted a right-to-work law, but it was vetoed by the governor of the state. In Missouri, it was generally expected that the right-to-work law would be adopted in a public referendum. In 1978, however, it was decisively defeated (60 to 40 percent) by the voters, largely attributable to a massive public relations campaign mounted by organized labor.

Recognizing it was futile to attempt to repeal laws on a state level, organized labor has sought to eliminate Section 14(b) from Taft-Hartley. Indeed, in President Johnson's administration during 1965–1966, Congress came close to repealing Section 14(b). The House voted twice for repeal, and a majority of the Senate was prepared to do the same. However, Senator Everett M. Dirksen of Illinois led a filibuster to prevent Senate action. Since then, the union movement has continuously tried to knock out Section 14(b), but its efforts have not been successful. It seemed that repeal was assured when President Carter was elected in 1976 along with a large Democratic Party majority in Congress. President Carter said he would not veto a measure to eliminate Section 14(b), nor would he actively promote one.

In the summer of 1977, however, the union movement abandoned its fight to eliminate Section 14(b). Recall that at that time, Carter had agreed to support the Labor Law Reform Act of 1977. The character of the legislation was previously mentioned. To gain Carter's support, the union movement agreed not to press for the repeal of Section 14(b). As the *Wall Street Journal* reported on July 11, 1977:

> To win Mr. Carter's support, and satisfy critical Democratic congressional leaders, the AFL-CIO in May agreed to drop from the bill a proposal to repeal Section 14b of the Taft-Hartley Act, the provision that allows states to ban labor contracts requiring all workers to join the union.

This concession on the part of the union movement, however, did not pay off: a Senate filibuster blocked passage of the Labor Law Reform Act after it was enacted in the House of Representatives.

At the very least, Section 14(b) has created unequal labor relations conditions among the several states. In states without right-to-work legislation, forms of union security are permitted that are outlawed in the states with restrictive legislation. These latter states are located primarily in the south and southwestern parts of the United States and use their restrictive laws on union security to support their drives to attract industry from other sections of the country. The economic effect that these legal differences may have on industry location evades verification. But Congress itself has imposed an atmosphere of potentially unequal competition for industry between the states. However, this is not the case in the railroad and airline industries, since, as we shall soon learn, Congress in 1951 nullified state right-to-work laws as they apply to these two industries.

Enforcement of Right-to-Work Laws

The issue arose as to whether the states or the NLRB had the authority to deal with violations of state right-to-work laws. For understandable reasons, unions argued that the NLRB should have exclusive jurisdiction. Under Taft-Hartley, violators of the federal law do not face imprisonment or fines. On the other hand, under state right-to-work laws, violators may be imprisoned or fined. By unanimous decision, the U.S. Supreme Court held that the states have the right to enforce their own laws.[67] The Court said:

> When Congress gives state policy that degree of overriding authority, we are reluctant to conclude that it is nevertheless enforceable by the NLRB.

In other words, since Congress permitted the states under Taft-Hartley to outlaw union-security arrangements in the area of interstate commerce, the Court held that the states have the corollary authority to punish violators of state right-to-work laws.

Right-to-Work Laws under Railway Labor Act

The Railway Labor Act was enacted in 1926 to regulate labor relations in the railroad industry. The act was amended in 1934, making all forms of compulsory union membership illegal and enforcing violations by imposing criminal penalties. In 1936, it was amended to extend its coverage to air transportation. The major support for prohibiting compulsory union membership came from the railway unions themselves. It was feared that any form of union security would diminish the ability of the legitimate railway unions to compete with company-supported labor organizations for members. By 1951, the contest between the two groups had been resolved sufficiently to change the attitude of railway unions toward compulsory union membership. Nearly 80 percent of the railroad employees were members of labor unions free from company domination.

One amendment in 1951 to the Railway Labor Act provided that

> union shop contracts could be entered into notwithstanding . . . any other statute or law . . . of any state.[68]

Some employees of the Union Pacific Railroad Company challenged the constitutionality of the Railway Labor Act's union-security provision in the Nebraska courts. Nebraska has a right-to-work provision in its constitution, and the workers claimed that compulsory union membership was in violation of the state constitution.

The labor contract signed by the company with the various railway unions required membership within sixty days to be maintained thereafter as a condition of continued employment.

Not only did the Nebraska trial court hold the union-shop agreement in violation of the state's constitution, but it also ruled that compulsory union membership violated the First Amendment of the U.S. Constitution by forcing employees into ideological and political conformity, that is, forcing them to pay dues to support political candidates not of their choosing. When the decision was upheld by the Nebraska Supreme Court, the U.S. Supreme Court reviewed it on appeal.[69]

In *Hanson*, the U.S. Supreme Court by unanimous vote reversed the Nebraska courts, ruling that Congress had the authority to permit the union-shop arrangement, notwithstanding any state laws to the contrary. Federal supremacy over interstate commerce eliminates the ability of states to regulate in this area unless legislation specifically cedes authority to them. Also, the Court reasoned that the union-shop provision of the Railway Labor Act is only permissive. The parties are not compelled to reach agreement on these provisions. Should they desire to include the union shop in the collective bargaining contract, state right-to-work laws would not prevail over the will of Congress.

Thus, Congress has established a dual standard regarding union security. The railway and airline industries are permitted to negotiate union-shop arrangements under the Railway Labor Act. Industry in general is prohibited from doing so where states enact restrictive laws in the form of right-to-work statutes or constitutional amendments. Political pressures account for these differences. There is no rational justification for or against the permissiveness extended to railway and airline employees that could not be applied to employees under Taft-Hartley.

UNION SHOP AND UNION POLITICAL ACTIVITIES

Refund of Union Dues

The Supreme Court's decision in *Hanson* also dealt with the contention that compulsory union membership forced workers into ideological and political conformity. In that case, the Court held that the charge was not supported by the record. In another case, however, the Georgia Supreme Court held that when a union shop was in effect, the use of dues to support political activities was a violation of the U.S. Constitution. It presented unions with a Hobson's choice: The union would have to either give up its union shop or cease engaging in political activities.

Upon review, the U.S. Supreme Court agreed in *Machinists* v. *Street*[70] that Congress had not intended to require workers to support union political activities to which they objected. However, the high court rejected the Georgia court's position that a union shop was illegal just because a union engaged in political activities. Instead, the remedy was to *refund to a complaining member the proportion of the individual's dues money expended on such activities.*

The Court had occasion to deal with the matter again in 1963 under the Railway Labor Act. It then held that a member could "contract out" of all union political activities and need not specify only those that were objectionable.[71] Not only would the member receive a refund of the proportion of dues (the same proportion that union political expenditures were to total expenditures) spent on political matters, but also future dues would be reduced in the same proportion.

The remedy provided was for the purpose of eliminating the ideological and political conformity that a union shop might require if a member was not able to refrain from financial support of union political activities considered contrary to his or her beliefs. All the members of the union were not granted the remedy, only those who actually objected to the use of funds for political purposes. Class-action suits were thus prevented, so that actual drain on a union treasury resulting from a court decision would probably be small.

Efforts of Unions to Comply with Policy

To comply with the new policy, unions tried to establish some practicable and lawful way to rebate that portion of dues that a union spends on political activities. This is not an easy problem, given the difficulty of isolating funds used only for political activities. Indeed, Justice Black, who dissented in *Machinists* v. *Street*, said it would be a "mathematical impossibility" to separate the amount of dues used for collective bargaining purposes from the amount used for political activities. Unions established a variety of dues rebate plans trying to satisfy the policy. In 1975, a union adopted a flat 5 percent rebate plan which it said covered the amount of dues it spent for political campaigns and lobbying.[72] Later, the United Steelworkers put its figure at 3.92 percent,[73] and the United Automobile Workers at 4 percent.[74]

In 1986, however, the U.S. Supreme Court unanimously held in *Chicago Teachers Union*[75] that the union was required to provide a detailed explanation as to how it arrived at the calculation separating collective bargaining and political activities. Previously, the union had announced that 95 percent of its expenditures were related to collective bargaining activities and 5 percent to political matters. Though the case arose in the public sector, the same rule applies to private industry. Given this decision, it appears that unions may no longer establish arbitrarily the percentage of dues allocated to political activities. They must be prepared to demonstrate by competent evidence the amount spent for that purpose.

Expansion of Dues Rebate Policy

So far, the dues rebate requirement has not had much impact upon union treasuries. For example, in 1980, the UAW rebated dues to only 100 disgruntled union members. However, a more serious problem has surfaced, which could cause hardship to the labor movement. Sparked and financed by the National Right to Work Legal Defense Foundation, a well-known antiunion group, many employees have filed court suits demanding rebates covering much more than union political expenditures. These members have claimed *a rebate for any expenditure that is not used for purely collective bargaining and grievance adjustments*, such as for conventions, organization, publications, social and educational activities, and contributions to groups like the NAACP and United Fund.

In 1984, the U.S. Supreme Court addressed this problem in a case that arose under the Railway Labor Act.[76] Involved in this litigation were employees of Western Airlines who were required to pay agency shop fees in lieu of joining the union and paying union dues. They protested the use of their money for purposes other than collective bargaining and grievance procedure proceedings. In *Ellis* v. *Railway Clerks*, the high court established standards governing the use of agency shop fees. It held these payments may properly be used (even if employees object) for conventions where union officers are elected and bargaining goals set; social activities; union publications, except for articles relating to political activity; and litigation expenses, provided they are incurred for purposes of negotiating and administering collective bargaining agreements. However, of critical significance, the Court ruled dissenters' payments may not be used for general organizing purposes. In this respect, it rejected the union's assertion that the degree of organization within an industry or trade has a direct bearing on the ability of unions to negotiate improved wages and working conditions.

One other aspect of the case is of importance. A union may not use agency shop fees for improper purposes and then later rebate that portion to dissenters. Such a procedure, the court held, amounted to a noninterest-bearing loan to the union. To comply, unions must place the dissenters' payments in an interest-bearing escrow account or establish a system of reduced dues payments for them.

In 1988, as expected, the U.S. Supreme Court applied its Railway Labor Act policy to Taft-Hartley. It was expected because both laws contain similar language relating to the legal issue involved in the dispute. In the Taft-Hartley case, decided by the high court in 1988, telephone workers, represented by the Communication Workers of America, protested the use of their dues for activities not related to collective bargaining. They were not union members, but they were forced to pay the equivalent of dues and initiation fees charged to union members under an agency-shop agreement.

In *Communication Workers* v. *Beck*,[77] the high court held the union was obligated to reimburse that amount of dues expended for activities not related to the negotiation of labor agreements and their administration through the grievance procedure and arbitration. The remedy for the union's unlawful conduct was essentially the same that the Court directed in the Railway Labor Act case.

As yet, the full impact of the policy is not certain. It would depend on what proportion of dues money is used by unions for collective bargaining purposes compared with that spent for organization, political activities, community services, charitable donations, publications, and other noncollective bargaining purposes. It would also depend on how many dissenters actually make a claim for reimbursement. Though the labor movement was unhappy with the Supreme Court policy, some union leaders did not believe it would seriously affect unions. In this respect, the president of the Communication Workers of America said:

> Notwithstanding the smoke that will be blown by those organizations which exist solely to deprive workers of their statutory rights to organize and bargain collectively, the Supreme Court decision will have little impact on the CWA and the rest of the labor movement.[78]

Nor did United Automobile Workers of America officials believe the impact of the decision would seriously impair the operation of the union.[79]

Airline Pilots Association: Payment of Dues

In 1993 the federal appeals court in Richmond limited to an extent the dues-rebate policy established by the Supreme Court.[80] Several airlines were struck by the Airline Pilots Association, and to support the strike, the union used dues paid by pilots employed by nonstruck airlines. Forty-two nonunion pilots working for nonstruck airlines were required to pay dues to the union under the agency-shop arrangement. They objected to their dues being used to support strikes at airlines on which they were not employed. They requested the return of that portion of their dues used to support the strike.

In a sharply divided decision reached by the federal appeals court that heard the case *en banc*, the majority held that the Airline Pilots Association need not rebate the dues in question. It stressed the dues expenditures were proper because all pilots would benefit from a favorable strike settlement. According to the court majority, the union would be able to use those settlements to gain similar contracts with other airlines. In other words, because support for the striking pilots was of crucial importance in establishing the union's bargaining position at every airline, the requirement that agency-fee objectors provide funds for the strikers was clearly justified given the bargaining pattern and practice of the entire airline industry.

LEGALITY OF AGENCY SHOP

State Right-to-Work Laws

As indicated earlier, under the agency-shop arrangement, employees need not be union members to hold their jobs. As a condition of employment, however, they must pay the same dues, initiation fees, and special assessment fees as do union members. Labor organizations, of course, prefer the union shop but settle for financial security should the employer object to the union shop but agree to the agency shop. It satisfies the union position concerning "free riders": Employees should not obtain the benefits of collective bargaining without paying their fair share. Though the union shop is far more prevalent in labor agreements, some provide for the agency shop. For example, in 1985, General Electric and the thirteen-union coalition representing 80,000 workers agreed to the agency shop.[81] It was the first time General Electric had agreed to any form of union security.

Unions hoped to negotiate the agency shop in the twenty-one states that had right-to-work laws. Understanding that they could not secure union shops, they attempted to secure agency shops. With the exception of Indiana, the effort proved unsuccessful. Either the right-to-work laws expressly outlawed the agency shop or they were declared unlawful by the state courts or by attorneys general. In Indiana, the state courts held that the agency shop was legal because the law did not expressly forbid it.[82] The agency shop in Indiana, however, became moot after the state repealed its right-to-work law in 1965. Unions that had negotiated the agency shop while the law was in effect went back to the union shop after it was repealed.

Agency Shop under Taft-Hartley

Whereas the state courts dealt with the legality of the agency shop under right-to-work laws, the NLRB and the federal courts were called on to determine whether the agency shop was lawful under Taft-Hartley. Though the NLRB had declared it lawful in 1952,[83] the issue surfaced again because of the changing personnel of the NLRB.

In February 1961, the NLRB, then composed predominantly of Eisenhower appointees, ruled on the legality of the agency shop under the national law.[84] The case involved a General Motors plant located in Indiana. As stated, the agency shop was lawful in Indiana, but the company refused to bargain over the agency shop as proposed by the union on the grounds that the agency shop was illegal under Taft-Hartley. The Board held that the agency shop was unlawful because it was different from a union shop. Under Taft-Hartley, unions may not force employees to engage in any union activity except to require membership as a condition of employment. Section 7 of the law states that employees have the right to refrain from any or all union activities "except to the extent that such right may be affected by an agreement requiring membership in a labor organization as a condition of employment." Since the agency shop does not require union membership as a condition of employment, the NLRB held that the agency shop was illegal because it forced employees to engage in a union activity not authorized by the law. If the Eisenhower Board's decision prevailed, *the agency shop would be illegal throughout the United States.* Whether or not a state had a right-to-work law forbidding the agency shop, a union could not make such a demand on an employer.

By September, 1961, the NLRB was composed predominantly of Kennedy appointees. It reviewed the previous decision and held that the agency shop was lawful under Taft-Hartley.[85] As opposed to the Eisenhower Board, the new Board held that the agency shop was like the union shop, saying that it was a lesser form of the union shop. In 1962, however, the Sixth Circuit Court of Appeals rejected the Board's position and held that the agency shop was illegal under Taft-Hartley.[86] Like the Eisenhower Board, the court said:

> We do not regard the "agency shop arrangement" as being something lesser than a "union shop." We believe it is entirely different. A Union security agreement is premised upon membership in a labor organization. An "agency shop" on the contrary is based upon an employee paying charges in lieu of union membership as a condition of employment.

In other words, the union and the agency shop were different for purposes of Taft-Hartley.

In June 1963, the U.S. Supreme Court had the final word on the matter. It held that the agency shop was lawful under national labor policy and could be negotiated in any state that had not outlawed the agency shop.[87] The Court said that for purposes of Taft-Hartley, *the agency shop and the union shop are the same because under its terms, financial security is the maximum security that a union can achieve.* As an earlier discussion demonstrated, under the nonpayment-of-dues provision, an employee can be discharged from a job only if loss of union membership results from nonpayment of periodic dues and initiation fees. The Court held that under Taft-Hartley, payment of dues—as in the agency shop—is the maximum kind of security that a union can obtain. As noted, an employee need not even join a union despite a union shop, provided that he or she is willing to pay union dues. As the Court said in *General Motors*:

> The burdens of membership upon which employment may be conditioned are expressly limited to the payment of initiation fees and monthly dues.

Section 14(b) and Agency Shop

On the same day that it decided *General Motors*, the Supreme Court also determined whether a state could outlaw the agency shop under Section 14(b) of Taft-Hartley.[88] In *Schermerhorn*, a union located in Florida, where the agency shop was illegal under the state's right-to-work law, argued that the states did not have the authority to outlaw the device under Section 14(b). It said that under Section 14(b), a state could only make illegal arrangements that require union membership as a condition of employment. Section 14(b) says that a state may make illegal "agreements requiring membership in a labor organization as a condition of employment." Thus, unlike the union involved in *General Motors*, the Florida union argued that the union shop and the agency shop were different for purposes of Taft-Hartley. Clearly, the high court could not possibly have accepted the position of the Florida union because to do so, it would have applied the same language found in Section 7 and Section 14(b)—"membership in a labor organization as a condition of employment"—in a highly inconsistent manner. The high court held that the union shop and the agency shop were the same for purposes of Section 14(b), and that a state could make either device illegal under its state right-to-work law.

In short, the unions could not have possibly been successful in both *General Motors* and *Schermerhorn*. They came out the best they could: The agency shop is lawful in any state in which it is not illegal under state law. The Supreme Court could not possibly have held on the very same day that the union shop and the agency shop were the same for purposes of Section 7 and then turn around and hold they were different for purposes of Section 14(b).

In summary, the Supreme Court decisions on the agency shop make it lawful in any state that does not make it illegal. In addition, states may outlaw the agency shop under Section 14(b) of Taft-Hartley. Thus, unions came out the best they could, given the provisions of the law. Indeed, had the high court held that the agency shop violated Taft-Hartley, it would have been illegal in all states and not just in states in which it was prohibited by state law.

TAFT-HARTLEY AND THE CHECKOFF

Character of Checkoff

Checkoff arrangements are included in the large majority of collective bargaining contracts. This dues-collection method, whereby the employer agrees to deduct monthly union dues from the employee's pay (and in some cases initiation fees and special assessments as well) for transmittal to the union, has obvious advantages for labor organizations, not only in terms of time and money but also because the union's institutional needs are further strengthened. Many employers prefer the checkoff compared with the constant visits of union dues collectors to the workplace. Once willing to grant the union shop, employers have rarely made a major bargaining issue of the checkoff per se. And the growth of this mechanism has been remarkably consistent with that of the union security. Whereas in 1946, about 40 percent of all labor agreements provided for the checkoff system of dues collection, by 1954, this percentage had increased to about 75 percent, and the figure is approximately 80 percent today.

As indicated, and contrary to popular notion, many employers favor the checkoff. As the vice-president of the Allis-Chalmers Manufacturing Company once remarked:

> We offered the checkoff to Local 248 because for selfish reasons we do not want a lot of collecting on the company premises.[89]

In other words, from the point of view of plant efficiency, management in large measure favors the checkoff, an important factor for the growth of the checkoff in collective bargaining.

Legal Control of Checkoff

Unions opposed the efforts of Congress and state legislatures to outlaw or regulate the checkoff. When Taft-Hartley was being considered, many labor leaders spoke out against checkoff control. Despite their efforts, however, the 1947 labor law contains two important checkoff restrictions. The effect is to control the ability of the union and management to negotiate checkoff arrangements. Certain basic conditions must be met before a checkoff agreement can become effective.

First, each union member must sign a card authorizing the employer to deduct union dues under the checkoff plan. In the absence of such an authorization, the employer may not deduct union dues despite the existence of a checkoff clause negotiated through the collective bargaining process. The second restriction applies to the length of time for which the authorization can be effective: No authorization of a worker can be irrevocable for more than one year or beyond the termination date of the contract, whichever is shorter. To illustrate, an authorization by a worker signed on January 1, 1991, becomes ineffective on December 31, 1991, regardless of the desires of the union, the management, or the worker. The law provides that any employer that deducts union dues from the wages of employees in violation of these restrictions could be imprisoned for one year and be subject to a fine of $10,000.

Soon after the Taft-Hartley law was enacted, the question arose as to the lawfulness of a collective bargaining provision under which an employer deducts initiation fees, special assessments, and fines as well as regular monthly membership dues. In addition, a question was raised as to whether it was required under the national law that each employee sign a new authorization card each year. On May 13, 1948, the Assistant Solicitor General of the United States issued an opinion that has served to clarify these questions.[90] He ruled that the term *membership dues*, as utilized in the law, includes initiation fees and assessments as well as regular periodic dues. On the other hand, he made no reference to fines assessed against union members for the violation of union rules. Apparently, therefore, checkoff of fines is illegal. An employee is not required to sign a new authorization card each year provided the employee has the annual opportunity to rescind the authorization. This policy serves the interests of the union and the employer. It relieves the union of the burden of having to secure new authorizations each year. Since authorizations are usually signed in the plant, the employer is likewise relieved of the disturbances caused by annual signing of the cards.

As a result, many checkoff provisions now allow for the deduction of initiation fees and assessments as well as for regular monthly membership dues. In addition, it is a common practice in industry for employees to sign one authorization card. Under the latter arrangement, however, both the collective bargaining contract and the authorization card must clearly state that the employee has an annual opportunity, usually lasting for fifteen days, to rescind his or her written authorization. If the employee does not take this opportunity, the authorization card remains in force for another year.

Application of Checkoff Provision

As expected, the NLRB has applied the checkoff language to particular cases. A major issue involved the validity of the checkoff authorization *after an employee resigns from the union*. Cases decided by the agency have seemingly resolved the problem.

When the union accepted and retained membership dues deducted from an employee's wages after he had resigned from the union, the NLRB ruled it violated the employee's rights under Taft-Hartley.[91] Under Section 7 of the statute, as said, a union may not force employees to engage in union activities. By retaining the resigned employee's membership dues, the union unlawfully coerced the employee to support its activities.

When another employee joined a union, he signed a checkoff card authorizing his employer to deduct union membership dues from his wages and remit them to the union. Later the employee requested to be dropped from the union's membership, but the union used the checkoff authorization as its basis for asserting the employee "had a continuing dues obligation after his attempt to resign."

Rejecting the union's position, the agency ruled the employee agreed to pay only while he was a union member. Since the authorization card signed by the employee referred only to an obligation to pay "my initiation fee" and "my regular membership dues," the union violated the law by collecting dues as if the person were still a member of the union.

For a union to collect dues after an employee resigns from the union, the authorization card must state in "clear and unmistakable language" that the employee waives his statutory right not to assist the union while not a union member. This waiver was contained in the dues authorization card signed by an employee in a case involving the United Steelworkers of America.[92] The card stated in explicit and unambiguous language that the employee agreed to pay union dues when leaving the union. Under these circumstances the NLRB held the union did not act unlawfully when it demanded that the employer deduct the employee's dues and transmit them to the union.

BARGAINING IN GOOD FAITH

Employer and Union Obligations

The duty to bargain in good faith is a government requirement that predates the Wagner Act of 1935. The duty was advanced as early as 1921 in a case before the Railway Labor Board.[93] In its interpretation of requirements set forth in the Transportation Act of 1920, the Board held that the negotiating parties must make an honest effort to decide all issues in "conference":

> If they cannot decide all matters in dispute in conference, it is their duty to then decide all that is possible.

The National Labor Board, established by executive order to administer the National Industrial Recovery Act of 1933, held that employers were required to bargain in good faith. This duty involved more than merely meeting and conferring with labor unions. The Wagner Act required the same obligation of employers. Experience under the 1935 law demonstrates that some unions did not bargain in good faith. This led to the inclusion of a provision in Taft-Hartley that required the same set of standards from unions as had been required of employers under the earlier laws.

Congress incorporated the Board's good-faith bargaining requirements into Section 8(d) of the 1947 law. Section 8(d) requires that

> for the purpose of this section, to bargain collectively is the performance of the mutual obligation of the employer and the representative of the employees to meet at reasonable times and confer in good faith with respect to wages, hours, and other terms and conditions of employment, or the negotiation of an agreement, or any question arising thereunder, and the execution of a written contract incorporating any agreement reached if requested by either party, but such obligation does not compel either party to agree to a proposal or require the making of a concession.

This requirement constitutes the congressional framework of good-faith bargaining. The NLRB and the courts took on the responsibility for giving substance to the broad legislative language.

Under the Wagner Act, as with Taft-Hartley, the major task for the Board in each case was to determine whether the parties entered into discussion

> with an open and fair mind, and a sincere purpose to find a basis of agreement . . . and if found to embody it in a contract . . . which shall stand as a mutual guarantee of conduct, and as a guide for the adjustment of grievances.[94]

Decisions are made after a review of the totality of bargaining conduct. Isolated behavior does not generally determine the finding of unfair labor practices.

Good-faith conduct in bargaining requires an assessment of the state of mind of the negotiating parties; all the circumstances in a case must be reviewed to determine their motives. Even though the Wagner Act did not provide for union unfair labor practices, union conduct was reviewed by the Board before holding an employer in violation of the good-faith bargaining requirement. In one Wagner Act case, for example, the NLRB ruled that

> a union's refusal to bargain in good faith may remove the possibility of negotiation and thus preclude the existence of a situation in which the employer's own good faith can be tested. If it cannot be tested, its absence can hardly be found.[95]

The Board and the courts, in their continuing quest to bring about statutory bargaining conformance, have built an enormous set of conditions for good-faith bargaining. Applying to *employers and unions*, these include the following standards:

1. There must be a serious attempt to adjust differences and to reach an acceptable common ground.
2. Counterproposals must be offered when another party's proposal is rejected. This must involve the "give and take" of an auction system.[96]
3. A position with regard to contract terms may not be constantly changed.[97]
4. Evasive behavior during negotiations is not permitted.[98]
5. There must be a willingness to incorporate oral agreements into a written contract.[99]

Employer Bad-Faith Bargaining

In the 1960s, the NLRB and the courts held that General Electric did not bargain in good faith because it practiced what was called "boulwarism," named after its creator Lemuel R. Boulware, a vice-president of the corporation. G.E. submitted a complete labor agreement to the union. It refused to change any of its terms unless the union could prove to its satisfaction that such a change was necessary. In other words, the union realistically had the option to "take it or leave it." At the same time, the corporation mounted a massive publicity campaign directed at its employees. The purpose was to induce the employees to put pressure on the union to accept G.E.'s offer. In 1969, within the context of a long strike, a federal appeals court upheld the Board decision that such a bargaining approach did not meet the good-faith requirement.[100] The court held that a "take it or leave it" approach was not of itself necessarily illegal. What made the G.E. conduct illegal was that, at the same time, it had carried on the employee publicity campaign in the attempt to bypass the union. An employer is not permitted to deal with a union through employees. It is required to deal with employees through a union. In the 1973 contract negotiations, G.E. abolished "boulwarism" and no strike occurred.

Other examples of employer bad-faith bargaining include granting a wage increase to employees over the union's protest and before it bargained with the union to an impasse;[101] refusing to furnish information to a union pertaining to a wage increase granted to nonbargaining unit employees, which the union needed to prepare its wage proposals for upcoming negotiations with the employer;[102] withdrawing from multiemployer bargaining during contract negotiations and refusing to sign and implement the new multiemployer collective bargaining contract;[103] and refusing to grant members of the union's negotiating committee uncompensated leave to permit them to engage in bargaining during working hours while at the same time refusing the union's request to bargain during nonworking hours.[104]

In order to bargain for the health and safety of employees, the Oil, Chemical & Atomic Workers Union demanded that employers disclose generic names of chemical substances used or produced, as well as the medical records of employees. The employers refused, claiming disclosure would invade the privacy of employees and compromise trade secrets. With some limitations, the NLRB in 1982 held that employers did not bargain in good faith when they refused to divulge such information.[105] While upholding the union's request, the Board said few matters could be of greater concern to employees

> than exposure to working conditions potentially threatening their health, well-being or their very lives.

However, before turning over employees' medical records, employers may conceal their identity. Also, employers need not disclose the generic names of chemicals that constitute proprietary trade secrets. Thus, the NLRB attempted to strike a balance between conflicting interests—the employer's desire to protect workers' privacy and protect trade secrets, and the union's need for material information about potentially life-threatening work conditions.

Union Bad-Faith Bargaining

Unions did not bargain in good faith under the following circumstances: The unions amended bylaws, forbidding members to work overtime after they agreed in collective bargaining that employers may require employees to work overtime to meet production requirements;[106] refused to bargain unless there was a merger of two historically separate bargaining units;[107] forbade members to accept temporary supervisory positions when the labor agreement gave employers the right to assign bargaining-unit employees to such jobs;[108] and insisted that persons designated by the union to serve as stewards be hired by the employer.[109]

Agreement Not Required

Though good-faith collective bargaining is a cornerstone of national labor policy, *it does not mean that the parties must reach an agreement*. Its purpose is to encourage the parties to reach an agreement, but the concept does not mean that a strike or lockout cannot occur if they fail to settle their contractual problems. Also, the NLRB is powerless to order the parties to incorporate a particular provision into a labor agreement. In *H. K. Porter*,[110] the NLRB directed the employer to grant the checkoff to the union and incorporate the dues collection device into the labor agreement. The Board felt that this remedy was justified because the company had refused to bargain over the checkoff and generally frustrated the bargaining process. However, the U.S. Supreme Court held that violation of the requirement to bargain in good faith did not authorize the NLRB to insert a provision into the labor agreement as a remedy for the violation.

Underscoring the right of employers and unions to negotiate labor agreements free of judicial control, the U.S. Supreme Court held the courts do not have the power to apply a reasonableness standard in reviewing the provisions of collective bargaining contracts. That is, the judiciary may not substitute its judgment for that of the parties as to what is reasonable.[111]

BARGAINING UNDER *BORG-WARNER*

Limitation on Substance of Bargaining

Congress did not intend for the NLRB and the federal courts to interfere with the substance of collective bargaining. However, by a 5–4 vote in *Borg-Warner*,[112] the Supreme Court approved such interference, opening the door for government control of collective bargaining contracts. Writing the minority opinion, Justice Harlan, quoting Senator Walsh's statement during the debate on the Wagner Act, said:

> When the employees have chosen their organization, all this bill does is to escort them to the door of the employer, and say "here are the legal representatives of your employees." What happens behind these doors is not inquired into, and the bill does not seek to inquire into it.

As we shall see, the government in the form of the NLRB and the courts is firmly implanted in the negotiating room and exercises a veto power over union and employer proposals made in collective bargaining.

Borg-Warner applies Section 8(d) of Taft-Hartley to proposals made by employers and unions during contract negotiations. The provision requires the parties to confer "on wages, hours, and other terms and conditions of employment." Some terms and conditions of employment are outlawed by the statute, for example, the closed shop. Many other items that may be demanded by employers and unions do not fall within the concept of "terms and conditions of employment" according to the subjective judgment of the NLRB and the courts.

Borg-Warner itself involved an employer demand for a prestrike secret vote of employees (union and nonunion) as to the employer's last offer. It also proposed a recognition clause that excluded, as a party to the contract, the international union, which had been certified by the National Labor Relations Board as the employees' exclusive bargaining agent, and substituted for it the uncertified local affiliate.

The UAW refused to agree with either of the company's demands as conditions of contract settlement. A strike resulted, and the union did not prevail. Both clauses were subsequently included in the collective bargaining agreement. Prior to their inclusion, the union filed refusal-to-bargain unfair labor practice charges against the company.

The Board held that the company did not bargain in good faith by insisting on inclusion of these items in the contract. It classified bargaining demands into three major categories. In *Borg-Warner*, the U.S. Supreme Court held that the Board has the power to establish these classifications. At times, however, the courts have upset the agency because they believed that the Board placed a particular demand in the wrong category. What compounds the problem is that the NLRB itself switched the categories of the same demand. In any event, here are the three categories in which the Board will place a particular demand of an employer or a union.

Illegal Category

The first category consists of illegal items. If a demand is made by a party but is illegal under the law, the Board finds a per se violation of the obligation to bargain in good faith. Items unlawful under Taft-Hartley include the closed shop, illegal hiring hall, checkoff for dues collection without employee authorization, representation of guards by a production workers' union, and a union demand to represent supervisors. A demand by either party for these items is prohibited by law. By forbidding bargaining on these subjects, the NLRB is merely enforcing the clear intention of Congress expressed in unambiguous language. Employer or union refusal to bargain over these items does not, of course, constitute an unfair labor practice.

Mandatory Category

Unions and management must bargain in good faith on items in the mandatory category, and they may be bargained to an impasse without violating the unfair labor practice provisions of Taft-Hartley. Unions may strike to obtain mandatory items in the contract. Employers may lock out employees unless their version of the mandatory items is included in the agreement. The NLRB and the courts must ultimately decide which items fall within the meaning of wages, hours, and other terms and conditions of employment.

Many issues have been designated as mandatory subjects for collective bargaining. Some of these include subcontracting;[113] stock purchase plans;[114] profit-sharing plans;[115] pension and employee welfare plans;[116] rental of company housing;[117] Christmas bonuses;[118] work loads and production standards;[119] plant rules;[120] whether union members should be paid by the employer when negotiating a labor agreement during working hours,[121] and a successorship clause that would require a new owner of the business to assume the old employer's contractual obligation.[122] In a significant decision, the U.S. Supreme Court held that employers may lawfully demand that promotions, discipline, and work scheduling be a matter of exclusive management control, and not subject to arbitration.[123]

In an interesting case, a hospital required that employees submit to a polygraph (lie-detector) test as a condition of continuance of employment. Serious vandalism had occurred inside and outside the hospital during a strike. The hospital required such a test as an act of determining which employees, if any, were responsible for the vandalism. The union, however, refused to permit the hospital to test employees under such circumstances. Upon review of the case, the NLRB held that polygraph testing is a mandatory subject of collective bargaining, since if an employee failed the test, he or she could be discharged. The hospital was required to bargain with the union over this issue and could not institute such tests as a matter of managerial prerogative.[124] In 1988, Congress enacted the Employee Polygraph Protection Act, sharply limiting the right of employers to force employees to take polygraph tests. To this extent, the new law largely makes moot the issue of whether such tests are a mandatory subject of collective bargaining.

After considerable litigation, the U.S. Supreme Court sustained the Board position that in-plant food service and prices are mandatory subjects of bargaining. Almost every plant has a cafeteria or vending machines where employees may purchase food. Normally the employer uses an outside vendor to provide such food services. Several federal appeals courts reversed the NLRB, but those decisions were set aside in *Ford Motor Co.*[125] In a unanimous decision, the high court said:

> With all due respect to the courts of appeals that have held otherwise, we conclude that the Board's consistent view that in-plant food prices and services are mandatory bargaining subjects is not an unreasonable or unprincipled construction of the statute . . .

This is an excellent example demonstrating the lack of objective standards in the determination of the *Borg-Warner* categories. If there were, we would not have a conflict among the courts as to whether a particular demand falls in the mandatory or voluntary category.

Since 1966, the NLRB had held that an employer's decision to close a portion of its business and to lay off workers was a mandatory subject for collective bargaining.[126] This did not mean an employer could not shut down a facility or operation that was losing money. Rather, the employer had to bargain with the union to an impasse before closing. The employer could then shut down the facility without violating Taft-Hartley.

Some federal appeals courts, however, refused to sustain the Board policy.[127] As a result, the U.S. Supreme Court agreed to adjudicate the matter. Unions, of course, hoped that the Court would approve the Board position. They did not contend that bargaining over the employer's decision would necessarily persuade it not to close the operation. Instead, they believed collective bargaining could result in an agreement that might minimize the adverse effects on employees.

Whatever merit there might have been in the unions' position, however, did not persuade the U.S. Supreme Court. In June 1981, it held that an employer may lawfully close part of a business for economic reasons without prior bargaining over the decision.[128] While reversing the Board, the Court said in *First National Maintenance* that Congress never intended

> that the elected union representative would become an equal partner in the running of the business enterprise in which the union's members are employed. Management must be free from the constraints of the bargaining process to the extent essential for the running of a profitable business.

In a way, there is irony in this decision. Unions have the right to bargain with employers over many conditions of employment. It appears somewhat ironic for the Court to hold that unions do not have the right to bargain over job security, which is often their members' most pressing need. Employers, however, must still bargain over the effects of a partial closing, including severance pay, pension plans, vacation pay, and preferential hiring rights for laid-off employees.

Voluntary Category

The third category includes items that are voluntary or permissive rather than illegal or mandatory. These items may be discussed at the bargaining table and voluntarily included in the labor agreement, *but they cannot be bargained to an impasse.* Unions may not strike over the item. Employees striking over a voluntary issue *lose their legal right to reinstatement.* This means the NLRB will not direct their reinstatement to their jobs after being discharged by the employer. Of course, the workers do not know in which category the Board will slot the item when they strike. The determination is made for some time in the future, a year or more down the road.

Employers cannot make a voluntary subject a condition for signing a labor contract. If the NLRB finds that an item in the voluntary category was bargained to an impasse, it will hold that a per se violation of section 8(d) has taken place. No further inquiry will be made into the remaining bargaining conduct of the parties. It is a per se violation regardless of the other issues.

Some union demands have been placed in the voluntary category. These include requiring a company to abandon strike insurance plans;[129] requiring a bank to continue a free investment counseling service for its employees whom the bank has terminated;[130] and insisting that an employer association with which the union was negotiating abandon litigation concerning management of a trust fund.[131] In 1971, the U.S. Supreme Court held that unions have no right to bargain for pensions and other insurance programs for persons previously retired. It held that retired persons are not "employees" within the meaning of the law.[132] Previously, the NLRB had held that retired persons were employees under the law and that unions could bargain for them in the area of pension benefits.[133] By the subsequent decision, unions lost the opportunity to improve the living standards of millions of retired persons. In 1985, bills were introduced in Congress that would have explicitly made pension benefits for already-retired employees a mandatory issue of collective bargaining.[134] They were not passed, and the legal situation prevails to this day.

In 1976, the NLRB reaffirmed its longstanding policy that a union could not demand that an employer post a performance bond as a guarantee for the payment of wages and fringe benefits, including pensions.[135] It rejected the union's contention that the Board should change its policy because of the enactment of the 1974 Employee Retirement Insurance Security Act, which provides for federal regulation of employee pension plans.

Employer demands have also been placed in the voluntary category by the NLRB and the courts. These include demanding that a union withdraw fines previously imposed on members who have crossed picket lines during a strike in violation of union rules;[136] insisting that a national union be party to the contract when a local union affiliated with the larger body was the lawful and certified bargaining representative;[137] granting the employer the right to use the union label;[138] requiring a union to post a performance bond;[139] and insisting that nonunion employees have the right to vote on the provisions of the contract negotiated by the union.[140]

Another issue demonstrating the subjective nature of the classification of demands under *Borg-Warner* involved the use of a court reporter to transcribe collective bargaining sessions. For many years, the Board had ruled that the issue was a mandatory bargaining matter. In 1978, however, the Board switched the policy, ruling that the issue fell into the voluntary category.[141] If there were objective standards, we would not find the NLRB changing policies. In any event, as matters now stand, neither employers nor unions may insist on the presence of a court reporter during collective bargaining meetings.

More Recent Cases

When the United States Postal Service unilaterally reduced labor costs by Saturday closings of its operations, window service reductions, and elimination of Sunday mail processing, the NLRB held the employer had committed an unfair labor practice by failure to afford the union the opportunity to bargain over the changes before they were implemented. In 1993, however, the federal appeals court in the District of Columbia reversed the Board, holding that under the circumstances of the case, the Postal Service had the right to make service reductions on a unilateral basis.[142] To support its decision the court stressed the Postal Service was mandated by Congress to reduce operating costs; no employee was laid off; and no reduction of hours by full-time employees occurred. The sole impact on full-time employees was the adjustment of their work schedules. The NLRB ruled the changes were mandatory subjects, and the union had not waived its right to bargain over them. But the federal appeals court countered by ruling the Postal Service had the unilateral contractual right to reduce operations because of a broad managements rights provision that gave the employer the exclusive right "to transfer and assign employees; to determine the methods, means, and personnel of which its operations are to be conducted; and maintain the efficiency of the operations entrusted to it." Although the court's decision appears unassailable, it would not be difficult to support the Board's decision.

At times a union can lose its right to bargain over an issue because it failed to take prompt action when the issue first surfaced.[143] For example, the employer, a health-care provider, adopted a policy about its facilities becoming nonsmoking after April 1, 1990. In late December 1989, the employer sent letters to all employees notifying them of the policy and placed notices on bulletin boards and in the hospital's newsletter. Officials of the hospital held several meetings attended by union representatives regarding implementation of the smoking ban. No union protest was registered until March 31, 1990, the day before the policy was to become operative. At that time the union expressed its desire to bargain over the issue. Believing the union waived its right to bargain by not protesting sooner, the hospital put the policy into effect without bargaining. Holding that the notices and letters issued by the hospital and the meeting did not constitute actual notice of the ban to the union, the NLRB ruled the employer violated the law by its refusal to bargain before it put the ban into effect. Actual notice, said the agency, was not sent to the union until one week prior to the implementation of the policy.

Reversing the Board, however, in a 2–1 decision, the federal appeals court in Cincinnati determined that the union had waived its right to bargain over the matter. In dissent, Judge Ralph B. Guy said the employer did not give the union "clear and unequivocal notice" that it intended to ban smoking in all hospital areas. Since a representative attended a smoke-ban meeting, the majority held sufficient notice was given to the union.

Aside from the conflict between the court and NLRB and a division within the court, one may question whether a statutory right is forfeited by failure to protest in a prompt manner. Even the federal appeals court agreed the union had the legal right to bargain over the issue. In other words, all concerned were satisfied the ban on smoking was a mandatory issue of collective bargaining. It could be argued that passage of time does not erase a protected right established by law.

Additional Cases of Significance: Interest Arbitration

Hardly a day passes that the NLRB or the federal courts do not struggle with the *Borg-Warner* categories. We conclude this inquiry by presenting a number of significant cases. One dealt with so-called "interest arbitration."[144] As opposed to "grievance arbitration," interest arbitration involves the process in which an arbitrator, by prior mutual agreement of the parties, determines the terms of a labor agreement after the parties have reached an impasse in bargaining. Grievance arbitration deals with the arbitration of a grievance under an existing labor agreement. A union demanded that the employer agree to a contract provision that, should a dispute arise in the negotiation of the subsequent contract, arbitration would be used to settle the dispute. The employer refused to agree to such an arrangement. When the union pressed the issue to an impasse, the Board held that the union had violated Taft-Hartley. In short, the Board held that interest arbitration is not a term or condition of employment within the meaning of Section 8(d) of the law. It said that federal policy favors collective bargaining free from outside interference. Submitting an issue to arbitration would remove it from the control of the bargaining process. Showing the subjective nature of making *Borg-Warner judgments*, Betty Murphy, former chair of the NLRB, dissented from her colleagues. In her view, interest arbitration should be a mandatory issue of collective bargaining because it would affect the relationship between employer and employees concerning wages, hours, and other terms and conditions of employment.

Nor did the Board relent from this policy when an expiring contract provided for interest arbitration.[145] It rejected the labor union's contention that pressing the issue to impasse was lawful on the grounds that the employer had previously agreed to interest arbitration. In other words, the NLRB ruled that just because a party has once agreed to a nonmandatory provision, that party does not waive its unilateral right to refuse to bargain on that provision in subsequent negotiations.

Code of Ethics

Another case involved newspaper publishing, but it could reasonably apply to any appropriate industry in which the employer might desire to establish a "code of ethics." The publisher of the *Capital Times* of Madison, Wisconsin, established a code of ethics forbidding its reporters and other news employees to accept gifts, free tickets, trips, or meals from actual or potential subjects of news stories. It also required reporters to inform the management of any personal activity that could create a "potential conflict of interest." The Newspaper Guild supported the goal of ensuring higher ethics but insisted that it wanted an effective input in drafting the code. It also argued that the code of ethics directly affected the wages and working conditions of its members. Therefore, the union believed the code should be a mandatory subject of collective bargaining. In a split decision, however, the NLRB held that the code of ethics fell into the voluntary category.[146] When union demands fall into the voluntary category, employers may implement their rules as a matter of prerogative. Thus, newspaper publishers have the managerial right to establish such codes for their news employees without bargaining with their unions. To justify its decision, the Board said the code of ethics did not change wages and working conditions because

> prohibition of employees from accepting such gifts won't change working conditions

since the newspaper paid for any meals, tickets, or trips deemed necessary for its reporters. The Board stated that loss of the gifts could not be construed as a cut in wages, because the gifts had come from outside the paper rather than from the reporters' employer.

Though the Board held that the publisher could unilaterally establish a code of ethics, the publisher was required to bargain over the penalties for violation of the code. Former Chair John Fanning, who dissented in *Capital Times*, said that the majority was wholly inconsistent, because in his view the substance of the code could not be separated from the penalties. On this point, the union agreed:

> The decision mystifies us. Apparently, we're [the union] supposed to design punishment to fit crimes, without ever mentioning the crimes.[147]

Although it is academic for any employee who may have been disciplined by the *Capital Times* for violation of its code of ethics, a decade later the NLRB, vindicating Fanning, said ". . . as a general principle rules and their constituent penalties should not be artificially severed from each other for purposes of collective bargaining." Actually the Board could not have ruled otherwise because in another case involving the newspaper industry and a code of ethics, a federal appeals court remanded the case to the NLRB and refused to enforce its order.[148] In its remand, the court held rules cannot be reasonably "separated for labor act purposes from the substantive provisions which they are designed to enforce."

In another code of ethics case, American Electric Power established a corporate code of ethics. This time the NLRB held the employer could not put the code into effect without prior bargaining with the union.[149] As its name denotes, the employer's business is the generation and transmission of electricity. Violators of the code could be subject to discipline. In defense of its action, the employer contended the core purpose of its business was "maintaining integrity," and the code of ethics protected the core purpose. On this basis, without prior notice or bargaining, the company put the code of ethics into effect.

Although the Board agreed that integrity is vital to any business, it ruled integrity or ethical conduct is not the core purpose of an enterprise that generates and transmits electrical power. The latter was the core purpose of the business, and not integrity or ethical conduct. Finding the employer violated its bargaining obligation under the law, the NLRB directed the code of ethics be rescinded in its entirety.

Transfer of Bargaining-Unit Work

Reversing a previous policy, the Reagan NLRB in 1984 held that an employer's decision to transfer bargaining-unit work to another location is not a mandatory issue of bargaining.[150] During the term of a labor agreement, United Technologies merged its elevator research and development operations in Mahwah, New Jersey, with a larger operation in East Hartford, Connecticut, resulting in the layoff of office and technical employees. When the employer refused to bargain on the transfer, the NLRB held originally in 1981 that the company had engaged in an unfair labor practice.[151] To justify the abolishment of that policy, the Reagan Board said in *United Technologies*:

> Despite the evident effect on employees, the critical factor to a determination of whether the decision is subject to mandatory bargaining is the essence of the decision itself . . . i.e., whether it turns upon a change in the nature or direction of the business, or turns upon labor costs; not its effect on employees nor a union's ability to offer alternatives.

Thus, as long as an employer's decision to transfer work is not made to reduce labor costs, the company can unilaterally make the change without bargaining with the union. No longer is an employer required to bargain when the transfer of work involves the scope, direction, or nature of the business even though employees lose their livelihood.

Another Reagan Board's reversal of former policy, however, did permit an employer to move operations to a nonunion plant to save on labor costs.[152] During the effective period of a collective bargaining contract, the employer attempted to negotiate a wage cut and reduction of employee benefits. After union members had voted against midterm contract concessions, the employer moved operations from Milwaukee to its nonunion facility in Illinois, resulting in considerable layoffs in the Milwaukee plant. Ruling that the employer's conduct amounted to an illegal unilateral modification of existing contract provisions, the previous NLRB had held the employer to have engaged in an unfair labor practice.[153] Unlike *United Technologies*, the employer in *Milwaukee Spring* had bargained to an impasse. Nonetheless, the impact of both decisions was the same—under both decisions, the capability of unions to provide job security for employees was significantly reduced.

In 1987, with some change among the initial Reagan appointees, the NLRB held that an employer did not bargain in good faith when it relocated some of its assembly-line work without bargaining with the union.[154] It moved the operation from

Minneapolis to Sioux Falls, Iowa, where the wage scale was lower. Since the move was based on labor costs, unlike *United Technologies*, the Board held the relocation decision to be a mandatory bargaining subject.

Another employer closed its largest facility and transferred production to its other plants. It did so without prior bargaining with the union. Despite a broad management rights clause in the labor agreement saying the employer had the right to unilaterally "abandon or discontinue any production methods or facilities," the NLRB held that the matter was a mandatory subject of bargaining.[155] Reversing the decision of an administrative law judge, the agency held that the management rights clause did not cover a situation where production and equipment were not discontinued but were transferred to other plants. As a remedy, the NLRB directed the employer to pay employee moving expenses and to provide jobs for the laid-off employees at its other facilities.

Clarification of Policy: *Dubuque Packing*

In *Dubuque Packing* (1991) the NLRB by unanimous decision clarified and codified legal principles dealing with the relocation of bargaining-unit work.[156] Experiencing substantial monetary losses and looking for a way to cut them, the employer asked its employees to either accept a wage freeze or face relocation of the plant. The union unsuccessfully requested the employer to disclose financial data to demonstrate its distress. Given the company's refusal, the employees voted against the wage freeze. At this point Dubuque Packing transferred its hog-kill and cut-up operations from Dubuque, Iowa, to a nonunion plant in Rochelle, Illinois. Its decision, made without prior bargaining with the union, United Food and Commercial Workers, caused the layoff of about 350 employees. On October 1, Rochelle began operations and Dubuque ceased production two days later.

Claiming the company violated Taft-Hartley because it failed to bargain before transferring the work, the union filed unfair labor practice charges against the employer. In accord with its decision in *United Technologies*, the agency dismissed the charges, holding that the employer's decision to relocate the work was not based on labor costs but represented a change in the nature and direction of the business.[157]

The union appealed the Board's verdict to a federal appeals court. In 1989, the court refused to enforce the NLRB decision remanding the case to the agency with instructions to clarify its reasoning.[158] Complying with the court's order, the NLRB, no longer dominated by the initial Reagan members, articulated the current law governing the transfer of bargaining-unit work.

In the first place, the General Counsel of the NLRB must determine whether the relocation decision represents a basic change in the nature and direction of the business. If the General Counsel finds that this is true, the Board will dismiss the charges. When the General Counsel fails to establish a *prima facie* case, the employer will not be required to bargain and the charges filed by the union will be dismissed. Even when *prima facie* evidence supports the obligation to bargain, the employer may still avoid such a duty by proving one of the three possible defenses: (1) The work performed at the new location differs significantly from the work performed at the previous location; (2) labor costs were not a factor influencing the relocation decision; or (3) if labor costs were a factor, the union could not have offered labor cost concessions that could have changed the employer's decision.

Applying those principles to *Dubuque Packing*, the NLRB held the employer violated its obligation to bargain before making its decision to relocate the hog-kill and cut-up operations. It determined the move did not represent a basic change in the nature or direction of the business. Work carried out at Rochelle was essentially the same as that performed at Dubuque. Given the employer's effort to obtain a wage freeze, labor costs were a factor in the relocation of the bargaining-unit work. Because of the employer's refusal to provide financial data to the union to justify its demand for a wage freeze, Dubuque Packing did not establish that the union would not have offered labor cost concessions that could have changed the decision to relocate.

As a result of the violation, the NLRB ordered the employer to pay the 530 employees back pay for one year. The reason for the one-year limitation was that the employer closed the Rochelle plant after one year of operation.

In 1993 the United States court of appeals in the District of Columbia approved the NLRB decision.[159] Although recognizing the severe financial problems of the employer, the court nonetheless held the move did not represent a basic change in the nature and direction of the enterprise. The appeals court also held bargaining before Dubuque Packing moved its operations would not have been futile. Bargaining could have been productive because the union had requested financial disclosure from the employer to support its claim of financial crisis. By such a request, the union indicated the willingness to bargain over the situation. On April 4, 1994, however, the Supreme Court agreed to review the federal appeals court decision.[160] Among its contentions, Dubuque Packing claims the new NLRB standards do not conform with the Court's ruling in *First National Maintenance*.

Testing for Alcohol and Drugs

In 1989, as was inevitable, the NLRB dealt with compulsory testing of employees for drugs and alcohol, a major problem of the industrial world. Two issues were resolved by the agency: Whether testing of persons applying for a job and testing of current employees are mandatory issues of collective bargaining. With respect to the former, the Board ruled preemployment testing is not a subject of mandatory bargaining.[161] Its rationale was that people applying for a job are not part of the bargaining unit until they are actually hired. It said:

> Job applicants could not properly be joined with the active employees in the unit because they do not share a community of interest broad enough to justify their inclusion in the bargaining unit. Furthermore, even though applicant testing does to some degree affect the composition of the bargaining unit, it does not "vitally" affect the terms and conditions of employment of unit employees or workplace safety.

In the second case, the employer unilaterally established a policy under which any employee injured on the job is compelled to be tested for drugs and alcohol. Holding that the rule changed the terms and conditions of employment, the NLRB said testing of current employees is a mandatory issue of bargaining.[162] The clear implication of the testing program was that employees failing the test would be disciplined, possibly discharged. Before implementing such a rule, the employer must bargain with the union. Undoubtedly, both decisions will be appealed to the federal courts and will ultimately be decided by the Supreme Court. A possible precedent is that in June 1989, the high court held that railroads and airlines may require testing of its employees without prior bargaining with the unions.[163] The employer mandated that drug screening be added to the physical examinations it requires employees to undergo every three years. Of course, there is a vast difference between railroads and airlines and a manufacturing facility in terms of public safety.

Subsequently, the federal courts upheld employer-mandated drug tests for persons seeking law enforcement jobs with the United States Customs Service, Justice Department employees with security clearance, Transportation Department employees, those involved in public health and safety or security, police officers, and jail guards.[164]

Of enormous importance was a 2–1 decision of the United States court of appeals in the District of Columbia upholding a requirement that applicants for all federal employment take a drug test.[165] It makes no difference whether the jobs are related to the public safety or security. Presumably it would apply to any person hoping to be a janitor in a federal building as well as one seeking employment with the FBI. Judge Kikren Henderson, the dissenting member, stated the majority ruling "taken to its logical end . . . sanctions a blanket testing requirement for all federal applicants simply applying for federal employment is too slim a reed to support mandatory testing." As of this writing, the U.S. Supreme Court has not reviewed *Willner* vs. *Thoronburgh.*

In another case involving the United States government the federal appeals court in San Francisco upheld drug testing for the employees suspected of abusing drugs away from the work place.[166] It held testing was constitutional as long as the employer followed the criteria of its drug-testing plan. One requirement was that a federal agency would test only those employees who displayed "reasonable suspicion" showing that they may have been using drugs either on or off duty. It recognized the employee's privacy was invaded by urine analysis testing for illegal drug use but felt the employee's privacy interest was outweighed by drug use which "might impair employees in the performance of sensitive government duties."

In another drug case, the employee in question was a maintenance custodian on a municipal bus line. He was discharged for fighting, but an arbitrator ordered his reinstatement. Before resuming his duties, the employee was required to pass a physical examination which included drug screening. When the drug screen indicated he had used marijuana, the employer discharged the employee.

Upholding a district court decision, the federal appeals court in Philadelphia held the drug screening amounted to a violation of an employee's right under the Fourth Amendment (prohibition against unreasonable search and seizure). To support its decision the court determined the employee did not perform sensitive duties vital to public interest or posed a risk to public safety, and the test was compulsory because the employee's only alternative to refuse the test was loss of his job.[167]

Where an employer establishes a new rule requiring drug testing following a job-related injury, the NLRB held it violated Taft-Hartley because it did not notify or bargain with the union prior to the implementation of the rule.[168] For many years the employer had in effect a preemployment drug testing policy. It decided to expand the policy to employees injured on the job requiring medical treatment. According to the company, this was not a new rule, but merely an expansion of an existing one. Refusing to accept the contention, the NLRB said it was "too far a leap" from existing policies to subject employees to postemployment drug screening for the employer not to have notified and bargained with the union. The agency also rejected another employer argument that a provision in the labor agreement authorized the new rule.

Reviewing NLRB and court decisions, it would appear safe to say an employer without notifying or bargaining with the union may require an employee holding a job vital to the public interest and security to undergo drug testing. This applies to public and private areas of the economy. On the other hand, the employer must notify and bargain with the union prior to making a significant change in drug-testing policy. The latter situation, therefore, is a mandatory issue for collective bargaining while the former falls into the voluntary or nonmandatory category.

Significance of *Borg-Warner*

Borg-Warner authorizes the NLRB and the federal courts to limit the area of free collective bargaining. If a subject is placed in the voluntary category, neither party has the power to insist on its inclusion in a collective bargaining contract. A flat rejection of the issue ends the matter. In other words, once a demand is classified as voluntary, it is not likely to be included in the labor agreement. *Thus, the government controls the substantive content of labor agreements.*

Under the doctrine, it is not a question of who may benefit from a particular decision. Employers and unions may be treated favorably or unfavorably, depending on the decision in a given situation. They both lose, however, since under *Borg-Warner* employers and unions lost their full capability to act within a climate of free collective bargaining. It introduces an element of uncertainty into the collective bargaining process. Would a union demand that management salaries, stock options, "golden parachutes," and other perks be classified in the mandatory or voluntary category? How about a union demand forbidding layoffs as long as the employer operates foreign facilities? Would an employer demand that a portion of the union dues used for medical insurance be mandatory or voluntary? How about union dues being used to retrain workers when their jobs are taken over by automation? This is the problem when government intervenes in the bargaining process. As one writer put it:

> A further criticism can be made that by dividing up the world into two sorts of bargainable subjects, the Court and the Board exercise surveillance of the process of collective bargaining in a manner that is highly intrusive. Parties are likely to have an eye to what the law does and does not permit and are accordingly likely to shape the course of their bargaining based on these factors, rather than on their peculiar needs and interests. This injects a certain artificiality into the course of bargaining . . .[169]

Added to these considerations is that objective standards are not available to determine whether a demand should be placed in the voluntary or mandatory category. Indeed, only the subjective judgment of Board members and judges stands as the basis of the determination. In no way is there a scientific or objective test for the classification of bargaining demands. NLRB decisions are not unanimous, showing that members of the same Board disagree. On the same bargaining issue, the agency has reversed itself. Federal courts have upset NLRB determinations, and the Supreme Court has reversed federal appeals courts. If scientific and objective standards were available, these conditions would not take place.

Free collective bargaining and the interests of the parties would be advanced by the reversal of *Borg-Warner*, which after all became law by only a single vote. Nothing in Taft-Hartley expressly justifies the doctrine. Indeed, where Congress intended to limit the free collective bargaining process, it said so in express terms, the right-to-work provision being a prime example. Unless a demand is expressly illegal, it should be a mandatory issue and permit the bargaining process to settle the matter of inclusion or exclusion in the labor agreement. A researcher said:

> The mandatory-permissive distinction in the scope of the duty to bargain collectively should be abandoned in favor of a policy of classifying all lawful subjects as mandatory . . .[170]

Given the entrenchment of the *Borg-Warner* doctrine in the nation's labor policy, it cannot be expected that the Board or the courts will ever eliminate the doctrine. It would take an act of Congress to do so, which is not very likely at this time. Though the doctrine has been with us for over thirty-seven years, this does not necessarily make it right. As one writer put it:

> The serious question that is left is whether the Board or the Courts should intervene to prevent an impasse over a voluntary subject when the bargaining is being conducted in good faith. The essence of the argument presented herein is that so long as the parties are in good faith, and the demand is legal, the Board and the Courts should keep their hands off.[171]

FIBREBOARD DOCTRINE: EMPLOYER'S DUTY TO BARGAIN DURING CONTRACT PERIOD

Bargaining During Contract Period

Once an issue falls within the mandatory category, the employer has the duty to bargain with the union over the issue while a collective bargaining contract is in effect. Section 8(d) of the law does not limit the obligation of the parties to bargain on the "terms and conditions of employment" only when a new contract is being negotiated. It also establishes an affirmative duty to bargain during the effective period of a collective bargaining contract. This problem arises when an employer desires to change employment conditions during a contract period. To promote efficiency or reduce costs, the employer may desire to eliminate, modify, or add a term or condition of employment.

The employer duty to bargain was established under Taft-Hartley when the U.S. Supreme Court decided the *Fibreboard* case.[172] In that dispute, the employer subcontracted maintenance work during the term of a labor agreement. It did so to save costs and subcontracted without consulting or bargaining with the union. As a result of the subcontract, many employees lost their jobs. Upon its review of the case, the Supreme Court held that the employer had unlawfully refused to bargain collectively under Taft-Hartley. Not only did the Court find that subcontracting was a mandatory issue of collective bargaining, but also that the employer had violated the law by taking action without consulting or bargaining with the union. As to the latter issue, the Supreme Court stated:

> The facts of the present case illustrate the propriety of submitting the dispute to collective negotiation. The Company's decision to contract out the maintenance work did not alter the Company's basic operation. The maintenance work still had to be performed in the plant. No capital investment was contemplated; the Company merely replaced existing employees with those of an independent contractor to do the same work under similar conditions of employment. Therefore, to require the employer to bargain about the matter would not significantly abridge his freedom to manage the business.

After it had made this decision, the Court held that the NLRB had the authority to order the employer to resume the maintenance operation that the company had subcontracted and to reinstate the laid-off employees with back pay. In other words, the Board was authorized *to restore the status quo* because the employer had failed to bargain with the union before it subcontracted the work. As to the power of the Board to direct such a remedy, the Court pointed to Section 10(c) of Taft-Hartley, which empowers the NLRB "to take such affirmative action including reinstatement of employees with or without back pay, as will effectuate the policies of this Act."

Bargaining to Impasse

To understand *Fibreboard*, it should be noted that the law does not forbid an employer to make a change in working conditions. A company may make the change after bargaining with the union to an impasse. After it appears that further bargaining would be fruitless, the employer may make the change. By bargaining to an impasse, a company has discharged its duty to bargain in good faith under the terms of the law. In other words, an employer who has exhausted the bargaining process has the authority to make the change in working conditions that was the subject of negotiations prior to the impasse.[173] Should the union believe that the employer violated the terms of a labor agreement, it then has the opportunity to submit the dispute to arbitration. (We will treat the nature of the arbitration process in full in the next chapter.)

Some employers at times have probably experienced difficulties under the *Fibreboard* doctrine. Before making a change, they had to wait until an impasse was reached. This prevented them from taking immediate advantage of the benefit that would result from the change. If the employer was faced with stiff economic competition, it is possible the doctrine was burdensome. Also, the employer faces a risk under *Fibreboard*, in that the NLRB might subsequently find that no impasse had been reached. Even if the employer waited to make the change after impasse had seemingly been reached, the Board might later find that an impasse had not been reached. Though these appear to be valid criticisms of *Fibreboard*, it would be difficult, if not impossible, to obtain objective evidence to show that this doctrine has been injurious to the business community. At times it is far easier to raise theoretical arguments against NLRB policy than it is to obtain the economic data to evaluate the merits of a charge.

Application of Doctrine

The NLRB frequently applies the *Fibreboard* doctrine. It has decided unfair labor practice cases where the union alleged that the employer did not bargain before the terms and conditions were changed. This does not mean that the Board would find the union charge meritorious in all cases. If it were determined that the employer was authorized to make the change under the language of the labor agreement involved, the union's charge would be dismissed. The Board would consider the management rights clause of the labor agreement and other material provisions contained in it to determine whether the employer was authorized to make the change.

In general, a management rights clause in a labor agreement authorizes an employer to make any decision regarding the labor force and the operation of the plant unless limited by other provisions of the contract. Such a clause would be related to relevant NLRB and court decisions bearing on the case under consideration. In this type of case, the employer would argue that it had such power under the terms of the agreement. Thus, if the employer's position prevailed, the Board would dismiss the union's claim that it did not bargain in good faith. On the other hand, if the NLRB found that the contract did not authorize the employer to make the change in working conditions, it would hold that the employer had not complied with lawful bargaining obligations. Under these circumstances, as noted, it would direct the employer to restore the working conditions and, where appropriate, require the employer to provide back pay to employees who were adversely affected by the unlawful change in working conditions.

THE *COLLYER* DOCTRINE

Deferral to Private Arbitration

In 1971, the NLRB changed the forum for the determination of this type of case by deferring certain unfair labor practice cases to arbitrators. Subject to some restrictions to be discussed below, the Board announced in *Collyer*[174] that it would defer such cases to a private arbitrator to determine whether the employer had violated its bargaining obligations under Taft-Hartley. Under *Collyer*, the Board does not determine the merits of the unfair labor practice charge filed by the union.

Simultaneously, the arbitrator determines whether the employer did not bargain in good faith under Taft-Hartley, and whether it violated the terms of the labor agreement under which the dispute arose. If the arbitrator finds the employer did not violate the contract, he or she would also hold it did not violate its bargaining obligations under the law. On the other hand, should the arbitrator rule the employer did not have the right to make the decision in question under the labor agreement, a violation of Taft-Hartley would be found because the employer did not bargain to an impasse before putting the decision into effect.

This is one of the most controversial policies that the Board has established. *Collyer* and its progeny whipped up a storm of controversy that has not subsided to this day. Indeed, as will be presented below, in February 1990, a federal appeals court ruled the agency did not have the authority to defer a case to arbitration.

Rationale of *Collyer*

One advantage of the *Collyer* doctrine, as claimed by its advocates, is that it reduces the NLRB case load. However, two former Board members have said that *Collyer* has resulted in an "insignificant reduction of the Board's workload."[175] Even if the doctrine substantially decreases the work of the NLRB, it is still controversial, as the following discussion will show.

In the *Collyer* case itself, the employer changed the wage rates of skilled-trade workers as well as the incentive factors used in computing wage rates for certain other employees. It also reassigned job duties among employees. It made these changes unilaterally, without consulting or bargaining with the union. The employer believed that the action was authorized under the terms of the collective bargaining contract. The union filed unfair labor practice charges, alleging that the employer did not fulfill the bargaining obligations of Taft-Hartley. The Board, instead of determining whether the unfair labor practice charge had merit, deferred the matter to arbitration.

In the Board's view, the policy was justified because the arbitration would simultaneously determine the contractual issue and the unfair labor practice charge. It said:

> The contract clearly provides for the grievance and arbitration machinery; where the unilateral action taken is not designed to undermine the union and is not patently erroneous but rather is based on a substantial claim of contractual privilege, and it appears that the arbitral interpretation of the contract will resolve both the unfair labor practice issue and the contract interpretation issue in a manner compatible with the purposes of the Act, then the Board should defer to the arbitration clause conceived by the parties.
>
> In our view, disputes such as these can better be resolved by arbitrators with special skill and experience in deciding matters arising under established bargaining relationships than by the application by this Board of a particular provision of our statute.

The Board deferred to arbitration despite Section 10(a) of Taft-Hartley, which empowers the NLRB to enforce the unfair labor practice program of the statute and which says that

> this power shall not be affected by any other means of adjustment or prevention that has or may be established by agreement, law, or otherwise.

To justify its position, the Board majority pinned its decision to Section 203(d) of Taft-Hartley, which states:

> Final adjustment by a method agreed upon by the parties is hereby declared to be the desirable method of settlement of grievance disputes arising over the application or interpretation of an existing collective-bargaining agreement.

It is material that this provision appears in the section of the law that establishes the Federal Mediation and Conciliation Service. To carry out the policy expressed in the provision, the Federal Mediation and Conciliation Service makes available to employers and unions the names of qualified private arbitrators to enable them to use arbitration as a method for the final adjustment of disputes arising over the application and interpretation of a labor agreement. Since the provision does not appear in those areas of the law that deal with unfair labor practices, however, it could be argued that Congress did not intend Section 203(d) to be used to dilute the exclusive power of the NLRB to prevent unfair labor practices.

The Dissenting View

Collyer was not established by unanimous decision. In the majority were Edward Miller, Ralph Kennedy, and Gerald Brown. Howard Jenkins and John Fanning constituted the minority. None are Board members any longer. With unusual vigor, the minority criticized the majority on the grounds that, in their view, the Board had abandoned its statutory duty to enforce the unfair labor practice provisions of Taft-Hartley. Jenkins and Fanning stated:

> Congress has said that arbitration and the voluntary settlement of disputes are the preferred method of dealing with certain kinds of industrial unrest. Congress has also said that the power of the Board to dispose of unfair labor practices is not to be affected by any other method of adjustment. Whatever else these two statements mean, they do not mean that this Board can abdicate its authority wholesale.
>   . . . The majority is so anxious to accommodate arbitration that it forgets that the first duty of this Board is to provide a forum for the adjudication of unfair labor practices. We have not been told that arbitration is the only method; it is one method.

In short, the minority believed that private arbitrators should not decide unfair labor practice disputes and that the NLRB had improperly conferred this right upon them. They held that once an unfair labor practice was filed, it was the duty of the Board to handle the case and not defer to arbitration. As one study states:

> The Board's contention that it should encourage the use of arbitration is laudable and may very well reflect the rather general, as well as the Congressional, sentiment that the arbitral process is the preferred way to settle contractual disputes, particularly if the alternative is economic strife. However, nowhere in the functions of the Board as described in the collective National Labor Relations Act, as amended, is there mention of encouragement of arbitration as one of those functions either prior to or after entertaining a charge of an unfair labor practice. To be blunt, once the unfair labor practice charge has been

filed by one of the parties (in preference to arbitration) the Board should attend to the statutory business which Congress assigned it and leave the determination of arbitrability of a contractual dispute to the arbitration, and review of the award to the courts.[176]

Despite the language contained in Section 10(a) of the statute, as cited above, federal circuit courts of appeals have upheld the Board's deferral policy.[177] As did the majority of the agency, these courts held that the deferral policy constitutes a legitimate exercise of the discretionary power of the NLRB. A majority of the Board believed that the U.S. Supreme Court has also upheld the Board policy.[178] It should be stressed, however, that though the courts held that the NLRB has the lawful discretion to defer to arbitration, they did not say that the Board must defer.

Cases Deferred

Over the years, the NLRB has deferred many kinds of disputes to arbitration, rejecting the union claim that the NLRB should have jurisdiction over the disputes because of a refusal of the employer to bargain over changed conditions of employment. These cases included such issues as the reduction in crew sizes by an employer, who also increased the wage of apprentices and required that they be high school graduates;[179] discontinuance of the distribution of "turkey" money at Thanksgiving and Christmas;[180] curtailment of the seniority unit for purposes of transfer and promotion;[181] establishment of a separate seniority list for part-time employees;[182] revoking of employee parking privileges;[183] lengthening of Saturday hours and elimination of paid lunch periods;[184] institution of a wage incentive system;[185] and cancellation of a union member's leave of absence to engage in union work.[186]

In each of these cases, the NLRB held that the employer's act was arguably covered by some provision of the labor agreement and/or a past practice. Therefore, it deferred the case to a private arbitrator to determine whether the employer had violated the terms of the labor agreement. The arbitrator would also determine whether the employer had violated the bargaining obligations of Taft-Hartley.

Discharge Cases

Particularly controversial were those cases involving employees' allegations that they were discharged because of their union activities. As we know, discharge for union activities is strictly unlawful. At the outset, the NLRB deferred such cases to arbitration. Deferral of this kind of case was particularly offensive to the minority members of the Board, who stated:

> This case confirms our fears, and again illustrates the extent to which the majority is willing, by its policy of deferring to private tribunals, to abrogate the right of individual employees under the act we administer.[187]

When (former chair) Murphy was appointed to the Board by President Ford, she sided with Fanning and Jenkins and refused to defer discharge cases.[188] She believed that employees allegedly discharged or otherwise disciplined for union activities should receive the full safeguards of the National Labor Relations Act. With the advent of the Reagan Board, however, the NLRB deferred and currently defers such cases to arbitration.[189] In an exception to this policy, the NLRB will not defer to arbitration cases in which an employee has allegedly been discharged because of filing an unfair labor practice charge against an employer.[190]

Given a federal court of appeals decision in 1990, however, it seemed that the original Board minority position would carry the day.[191] A truck driver filed an unfair labor practice charge, alleging the employer retaliated against him for exercising his protected union rights. The NLRB deferred to arbitration on the grounds that the contract contained a provision forbidding discrimination against employees. Also, since the contract contained an arbitration clause, the employee's complaint should have been addressed in arbitration instead of filing unfair labor charges.

Not so, said the court, because it held that the NLRB has the exclusive statutory duty to determine the merits of unfair labor practice charges. It stressed that Section 10(a) of Taft-Hartley confers on the agency the *exclusive* power to remedy unfair labor practices. Thus, the court held that the NLRB abdicated its responsibilities under the statute. It also rejected the Board's position that it retained jurisdiction over the case, and could later review the arbitrator's decision. The court rejected this position because, as we will learn in the next chapter, under the Supreme Court's *Trilogy* doctrine, it is difficult to overturn arbitration decisions.

In 1991, however, this decision was reversed by a federal appeals court sitting *en banc*. It held the NLRB may continue to defer cases involving employee statutory rights.[192]

Cases Not Deferred

A dispute will not be deferred if the labor agreement does not contain a final and binding arbitration provision, or the employer refuses to agree to final and binding arbitration.[193] Also, the changed working condition must arguably be covered by some provision of the labor agreement or by a past practice. Probably this is not an important limitation to deferral, since, as the minority stated in *Collyer*:

> Most unfair labor practices can be connected somehow to contract terms or existing practices, by broad construction of general clauses, by the necessary inquiry into existing practices, by "waiver," or otherwise.

In any event, before the NLRB defers, the case must show that employer conduct is arguably based on contractual provision or practice. If company action is not covered by any provision of the labor agreement or by a past practice, the Board will not defer to arbitration.

In addition, the Board will not defer to arbitration when the evidence shows that the bargaining history between a union and a company has been marred by constant friction. In one case, a dispute was not deferred because of a considerable number of wildcat strikes, distrust for one another, and continual bickering. For example, in one year, the union had filed 301 grievances.[194] Also, the Board will not defer when the employer has engaged in serious unfair labor practices. In one case of this type, the evidence showed the employer's "complete rejection of the principles of collective bargaining" and utter disregard for the organizational rights of its employees.[195]

To understand the significance of *Collyer*, however, one should focus on the Board's policy to defer to arbitration rather than on the limited number of times that it has refused to do so.

NLRB Holds Jurisdiction

When the NLRB does defer to arbitration, it maintains jurisdiction of the case until after the arbitration award is issued. It will take jurisdiction of a case after the award is issued where the arbitrator did not conduct a fair hearing; when the employer refuses to abide by the award should the arbitrator find against it; or if the arbitrator's decision is repugnant to the policies of the NLRB. These are the so-called *Spielberg* standards, which are also discussed in the next chapter.[196] Thus, the Board will take jurisdiction of a case that it deferred to arbitration should the arbitrator not comply with the standards contained in *Spielberg*.

In *Suburban Motor Freight*, decided by the Board in 1980, the Board also held that it would not honor an arbitration decision unless the unfair labor practice issue was expressly presented during the hearing and specifically treated in the arbitrator's decision.[197] The Reagan Board, however, considerably weakened this policy, holding in *Olin Corporation* that it would defer to an arbitrator's award provided the contractual issue was factually parallel to the unfair labor practice issue, and if the arbitrator was presented generally with the facts relevant to resolving the unfair labor practice.[198] No longer, therefore, must the unfair labor practice be expressly raised in the arbitration hearing or treated specifically in the arbitration award. Don Zimmerman, a holdover from the Carter Board and no longer a member, dissented, arguing that under the majority's policy, there was no effective requirement for an arbitrator to give any consideration to statutory protections because the Board would "presume" such consideration even in its total absence. Some arbitrators, however, concerned with the ambivalent policy of the NLRB, still require that the unfair labor practice be presented in the hearing and specifically treat the unfair labor practice in their decisions.

Where the Board revoked deferral, it held that the arbitrator did not meet the *Spielberg* standards, generally because the decision was repugnant to the policies of the NLRB. Not all arbitrators are competent to decide a *Collyer*-type case, because they lack knowledge of NLRB policies. This is a weakness of the doctrine, particularly since the NLRB may hold that though the arbitrator's decision was not exactly consistent with Board policies, it was not altogether repugnant to them. If the NLRB had determined the issue in the first place, without deferral to arbitration, the agency might have rendered a decision unlike the one of the private arbitrator. Recall that in a *Collyer*-type case, the arbitrator must not only apply the terms of a labor agreement but also consider the NLRB policies that bear on the dispute. As Peter Nash, a former General Counsel of the NLRB, stated:

Perhaps the most difficult requirement of *Spielberg* for the arbitrator, again magnified by prearbitration *Collyer* deferral, is that his award may not be repugnant to the purposes and policies of the National Labor Relations Act.

In general terms, this requirement does not mean that the Board must necessarily agree with the arbitrator's final decision. Thus, he may make fact findings with which the Board might well disagree, but which disagreements will not prompt independent Board consideration of the merits of the case. However, the requirement generally does compel an arbitrator to apply correctly Board law upon the facts found, and failure to do so will result in no Board deferral.[199]

Here are some examples where the arbitrators' decisions were not honored. In one instance, the Board refused to sustain an arbitrator's award in which he had held that a Christmas bonus arrangement in effect for many years did not constitute "wages" and could, therefore, be unilaterally terminated at will by the employer. The Board found that the employer had violated Taft-Hartley, and that the arbitrator had "ignored a long line of Board and Court precedent" that clearly established that, as a matter of law, a Christmas bonus system such as that considered by the arbitrator to have existed, did constitute wages and could not be unilaterally terminated by the employer.[200] In another case, an unfair labor practice complaint was issued against an employer after an arbitrator erroneously found that an employer had not violated its collective bargaining obligations when the company unilaterally abolished a wage incentive system.[201] In another case, a group of employees was discharged for allegedly violating the labor agreement's no-strike clause. An arbitrator reduced the penalty to a one-year suspension without back pay. When the General Counsel determined that the employer had not fulfilled its obligations under the same no-strike clause, he issued a complaint seeking to recover from the employer the pay lost by the employees.[202]

While commenting on the instances in which the NLRB or the General Counsel refused to honor an arbitrator's award, Nash warned arbitrators that these examples

> indicate a need for arbitrators to apply Board law accurately; to guard against inconsistent conclusions in their decisions, which conclusions would render the award contrary to Board law; and to view carefully the remedies to ensure that employees' rights under the Act are protected by the arbitrator's award.[203]

Refusal to Enforce Arbitrator's Decision

Though the Board may review an arbitration decision under the *Spielberg* doctrine, it will not enforce an arbitrator's decision of cases in which it deferred to arbitration.[204] Once again, there was a bitter conflict among the members of the Board. As in *Collyer*, the Board split 3–2 on the issue. The majority held that if an employer refused to abide by an arbitrator's decision, the union had the opportunity to go to court for enforcement of the decision. This, of course, results in considerable delay and litigation expenses.

In contrast, the two minority members believed that the arbitrator's award should be enforced by the NLRB. They stressed that if the Board deferred to arbitration, it should enforce the award and not burden the union with court proceedings. In considering this issue, it should be noted that if the Board had not deferred to arbitration in the first place, it would direct a remedy under Taft-Hartley. On this basis, it would seem reasonable that when the Board defers to arbitration, it has the obligation to enforce the arbitrator's award. After all, it was the *Collyer* doctrine that forced the arbitration, and to complete matters, it would seem fair that the Board should enforce the arbitrator's award.

Impact on Labor Relations

One obvious result of the *Collyer* doctrine is that it stimulates more arbitration. Costs of arbitration are substantial. In 1992, the average charge by an arbitrator for services and expenses in a case amounted to $2,110.00.[205] At this writing, this is the most recent data available. By the time this volume is published, the figure will undoubtedly be higher. Normally unions and employers share equally the arbitrator's fees and expenses. Beyond the arbitrator's fee, other costs are involved, including at times the use of an attorney and the making of a stenographic transcript. When workers are used as witnesses, their time lost from the job must be made up, normally by the union involved in the arbitration. Such costs are burdensome to unions, particularly to the smaller unions. Some unions faced with these costs may not proceed to arbitration, with the result that employer conduct allegedly in violation of Taft-Hartley will not be contested. When an employer or union charges a violation of the statute, the charging party does not have to pay for the use of the services of the NLRB. In 1974, the Board took this problem into consideration, holding that it would not defer to arbitration when the expenses of arbitration were beyond the financial resources of the union.[206] When the NLRB in effect forces a union to arbitration, some unions, faced with the financial burden—even those that are not poverty-stricken—might not challenge the employer's decision. It seems somewhat incongruous that a party covered by a federal statute designed to protect its rights must plead poverty to receive the benefits of national labor policy.

In addition, the Board assumes a level of expertise among arbitrators that is not necessarily warranted. Arbitrators differ widely in terms of experience and professional ability. Unfortunately, some arbitrators, one hopes only a few of them, may decide cases on grounds other than the evidence presented to them. There are more uncertainties in arbitration than in NLRB proceedings. As demonstrated earlier, some arbitrators are not qualified to apply NLRB and court law, and when this is so, the process of settlement of the issue is prolonged. Considerable time is involved in processing a case to arbitration, about 225 days from the time that a request for arbitration is made until such time as the arbitrator decides the case.[207] Should the NLRB refuse to honor the award because the arbitrator did not follow the *Spielberg* standards, the case then moves through the normal Board procedures. Under these circumstances, the time and money expended in the arbitration were wasted.

Defenders of *Collyer* argue that it encourages the collective bargaining process. They argue as follows: The employer makes a change in the terms and conditions of employment without consulting or bargaining with the union. The Board defers to arbitration. At this point, the parties have an opportunity to settle the dispute by themselves through the grievance procedure machinery contained in the labor agreement. If the Board did not defer to arbitration, this opportunity would not be available, since the agency would settle the dispute.

The trouble with this argument is that, in the first place, the employer makes the change without consulting and bargaining with the union. It is not likely that an employer will change a decision after making it, despite the wisdom of the union arguments. If the union's input is to have real meaning, it should be made *before* the employer makes the change in the terms and conditions of employment. In the absence of *Collyer*, the employer would be more apt to consult and bargain with the union before making the change, since the company would recognize that failure to do so could result in NLRB proceedings. It could be argued on this basis that *Collyer* discourages collective bargaining rather than promoting it.

SUMMARY

This chapter demonstrated that Taft-Hartley limits the opportunities of employers and unions to negotiate a labor agreement free from government direction. Though the public policy involved in this approach is subject to fair debate, Congress has controlled the substance of the labor agreement. In the area of union security, employers and unions may not negotiate the closed shop, and the opportunity to adopt a union shop is limited. In the right-to-work law states, this opportunity has been extinguished.

The *Borg-Warner* voluntary category of bargaining subjects deprives the parties to collective bargaining of the ability to apply economic pressure to influence the outcome of collective bargaining agreements. Restrictions of this type tend to frustrate the purpose of national labor legislation envisioned in the Wagner Act. The basic purpose of that law and of subsequent amendments in 1947 and 1959 was to balance the powers of labor and management. A balance-of-power approach was supposed to ensure that the parties would be permitted to bargain on issues of interest without undue influence from external forces.

Under *Fibreboard*, employers have an obligation to bargain to an impasse before changing the conditions of employment during the terms of a labor agreement. After the company discharges its bargaining obligations, it may make the change, and the union may challenge the action in arbitration. Before *Collyer*, the NLRB would determine whether the action of the employer was authorized under the labor agreement. With the advent of *Collyer*, the Board defers this kind of case to arbitration. The major argument against *Collyer* is that the NLRB should not permit private arbitrators to determine issues that fall under a national law, a duty that Congress entrusted exclusively to the Board.

DISCUSSION QESTIONS

1. Why is union security such an important issue for American unions?

2. How successful has Congress been in eliminating the closed shop? Of what use were the *Brown-Olds* and *Mountain Pacific* doctrines in pursuit of a policy to do away with the closed shop?

3. Discuss the special privileges granted employers and unions in the construction industry by Landrum-Griffin. What is the justification for these special privileges?

4. Explain how, despite the existence of a union-shop arrangement, a worker need not join a union to hold a job.

5. What is the current legal status of right-to-work laws? How important are such laws to unions? To employers?

6. Discuss the legal status of dues rebates in relation to union-sponsored political activities. How has the general concept of dues rebates been expanded?

7. Discuss the legality of the agency shop in the *General Motors* and *Schermerhorn* cases.

8. Why is the dues checkoff considered a form of union security? What basic conditions must be met for a checkoff arrangement to take effect?

9. How did the Board and Supreme Court construct the congressional language regarding good-faith bargaining in *Borg-Warner*? How has that doctrine been applied in specific bargaining situations?

10. What impact might the Board's *United Technologies* and *Milwaukee Spring* policies have on union ability to provide job security for bargaining-unit employees?

11. How has the issue of compulsory drug testing been treated in terms of the *Borg-Warner* classification of bargaining issues?

12. Explain how *Borg-Warner* has limited the substance of collective bargaining.

13. Does the *Fibreboard* doctrine prevent employers from changing the terms and conditions of employment during the life of a contract?

14. Does the *Collyer* doctrine advance or hinder the good-faith collective bargaining process?

NOTES

1   *Hearings before the Committee on Labor and Public Welfare*, 80th Congress, 1st sess., on S. 55 and S.J. Res. 22, Part III, p. 1204.

2   *Buckley, National Review, Inc. and Evans* v. *AFTRA, NLRB, and American Civil Liberties Union*, 496 F. 2d 305 (2d Cir. 1974), cert. denied 419 U.S. 1093 (1974).

3   Public Law 96-593, 96th Congress, effective December 24, 1980.

4   Joseph Shister, *Economics of the Labor Market* (Philadelphia: J. B. Lippincott Company, 1949), p. 83.

5   Philip Taft, "Dues and Initiation Fees in Labor Unions," *Quarterly Journal of Economics*, February 1946, p. 22.

6   NLRB Release R-336, August 10, 1950.

7   *NLRB* v. *National Maritime Union*, 175 F. 2d 686 (2d Cir. 1949).

8   *National Labor Relations Act of 1947*, Report No. 99 to accompany S. 249, 81st Congress, 1st sess., p. 20.

9   Horace E. Sheldon, "Union Security and the Taft-Hartley Act in the Buffalo Area," New York State School of Industrial and Labor Relations, Cornell University Research Bulletin No. 4, p. 41.

10   Contract negotiated by the Sailors Union (AFL) with a number of shipping operators in 1948.

11   Contract between the New York Local of the International Typographical Union and publishers of that city (1948).

12   Contract between the Milk Wagon Drivers Union and the Milk Industry Association of New York (1948).

13   *Virginia Electric Company* v. *NLRB*, 319 U.S. 533 (1943).

14   *Los Angeles–Seattle Motor Express, Inc.*, 121 NLRB 1629 (1958).

15   *Carpenters, Local 60* v. *NLRB*, 365 U.S. 651 (1961).

16   93 *Congressional Record* 3952, April 23, 1947.

17   *NLRB* v. *National Maritime Union of America, CIO*, 175 F. 2d 686 (2d Cir. 1949), cert. denied 338 U.S. 955 (1950).

18   Hearings before the Senate Subcommittee on Labor-Management Relations, *Hiring Halls in the Maritime Industry*, 81st Congress, 2d sess., p. 168.

19   *Local 357, International Brotherhood of Teamsters* v. *NLRB*, 365 U.S. 667 (1961).

20   *R. J. Smith Construction Company, Inc.*, 191 NLRB 693 (1971).

21   434 U.S. 335 (1978).

22   *John Deklewa & Sons*, 282 NLRB 1375 (1987).

23   *Mesa Verde Construction Co.* v. *Northern California District Council of Laborers*, 861 F. 2d 1124 (9th Cir. 1988).

24   *Painters and Allied Trades District Council No. 51 (Mangenaro Corporation)*, 299 NLRB 618 (1990).

25   *Building Construction Trades Council Of the Metropolitan District* v. *Associated Builders and Contractors of Massachusetts/Rhode Island, Inc., et al.*, 113 S. Ct. 1190 (1993).

26   *AFL-CIO News*, March 15, 1993.

27   *Interstate Electric Co. (IBEW Local 354)*, 227 NLRB 1996 (1977); *Howard Electric Co. (IBEW Local 6)*, 227 NLRB 1904 (1977).

28   *International Association of Bridge, Structural and Ornamental Iron Workers, AFL-CIO, Local No. 111 (Northern States Steel Builders, Inc.)*, 298 NLRB 930 (1990).

29   *Colonial Hardwood Flooring*, 84 NLRB 563 (1949).

30   *Paragon Products Corporation*, 134 NLRB 662 (1961).

31   James D. Dworkin and Marian M. Extejt, "The Union-Shop Deauthorization Poll: A New Look After 20 Years," *Monthly Labor Review*, CII, 11 (November 1979), p. 37.

32   National Labor Relations Board, *Fifty-third Annual Report*, 1988, p. 218.

33   *Rose Metal Products, Inc.*, 289 NLRB No. 146 (1988).

34   Public Law 189, 82nd Congress, approved October 22, 1951.

35   National Labor Relations Board, *Sixteenth Annual Report*, 1951, p. 10.

36   *Monthly Labor Review*, December 1951, p. 682.

37   *Algoma Plywood & Veneer Company* v. *WERB*, 336 U.S. 301 (1949).

38   *International Union, United Automobile, Aircraft, and Agricultural Implement Workers*, 137 NLRB 901 (1962).

39   *Aluminum Workers International Union, Local 135*, 112 NLRB 619 (1955).

40   *General Motors Corporation, Packard Electric Division*, 134 NLRB 1107 (1962).

41   *Philadelphia Sheraton Corporation*, 136 NLRB 888 (1962).

42   *Union Starch & Refining Company*, 87 NLRB 779 (1949); *Union Starch & Refining Co.* v. *NLRB*, 186 F. 2d 1008 (7th Cir. 1951), cert. denied 342 U.S. 815 (1951).

43   *Hershey Foods Corp.*, 207 NLRB 897 (1973).

44   *NLRB* v. *Hershey Foods Corp.*, 513 F. 2d 1083 (9th Cir. 1975).

45   *International Brotherhood of Boilermakers, Iron Shipbuilders, Blacksmiths, Forgers and Helpers, AFL-CIO (Kaiser Cement Corporation)*, 312 NLRB No. 48 (1993).

46   *International Union of Electrical Workers (Paramax Systems Corporation)*, 311 NLRB 105 (1993).

47   *Firestone Tire and Rubber*, 93 NLRB 981 (1951).

48   Wilbur H. Friedman, "The NLRB Suffers Institutional Amnesia: The *Paramax* Decision," v. 44, *Labor Law Journal*, October 1993, p. 651.

49   Arthur A. Sloane and Fred Witney, *Labor Relations* 8th ed. (Englewood Cliffs, N.J.: Prentice Hall, 1993), p. 425.

50   394 U.S. 423 (1969).

51   *NLRB* v. *Granite State Joint Board*, 409 U.S. 213 (1972).

52   *Keystone Coat, Apron & Towel Supply Company*, 121 NLRB 880 (1958).

53   *NLRB* v. *News Syndicate Company, Inc., et al.*, 365 U.S. 645 (1961); *Local 357, Teamsters* v. *NLRB (Los Angeles-Seattle Motor Express)*, 365 U.S. 695 (1961).

54   *Paragon Products Corporation, supra.*

55   Arkansas Constitutional Amendment No. 34, November 7, 1944; Florida Constitutional Declaration of Rights, No. 12, as amended November 7, 1944.

56   Fred Witney, "Union Security," *Labor Law Journal*, IV, 2 (February 1953), p. 118.

57   Georgia, Iowa, North Carolina, North Dakota, Tennessee, Texas, and Virginia.

58   *McCulloch* v. *Maryland*, 4 Wheat. 316 (1819).

59   *Lincoln Federal Labor Union* v. *Northwestern Iron & Metal Company*, 335 U.S. 525 (1949).

60   *Mobil Oil Corporation* v. *Oil, Chemical and Atomic Workers International Union*, 426 U.S. 407 (1976).

61   *Sea Pak* v. *Industrial, Technical and Professional Employees*, 423 F. 2d 1229 (1971).

62   *Lord* v. *Local Union 2088, International Brotherhood of Electronics Workers*, 458 U.S. 1106 (1982), cert. denied U.S. S. Ct. No. 81-8060, June 28, 1982.

63   *Plumbers Locals* v. *NLRB*, 675 F. 2d 1257 (D.C. Cir. 1982).

64   Fred Witney, *Indiana Labor Relations Law* (Bloomington: Bureau of Business Research, Indiana University, 1960), p. 85.

65   *AFL-CIO News*, Washington, D.C., November 6, 1976.

66   *AFL-CIO News*, Washington, D.C., November 18, 1978; February 24, 1979; August 8, 1980; April 11, 1981; May 23, 1981; April 24, 1982; May 11, 1985. *Wall Street Journal*, April 21, 1981.

67   *Retail Clerks, Local 1625* v. *Schermerhorn*, 375 U.S. 96 (1963).

68   68 Stat. 1238, 45 U.S.C. 152 Eleventh, Section 2.

69   *Railway Employees' Dept.* v. *Hanson*, 351 U.S. 225 (1956).

70   367 U.S. 740 (1961).

71   *Brotherhood of Railway and Steamship Clerks* v. *Allen*, 373 U.S. 113 (1963).

72   *Wall Street Journal*, November 23, 1975.

73   *Steelabor*, March 1980.

74   *Wall Street Journal*, April 20, 1981.

75   *Chicago Teachers Union* v. *Lee Hudson*, 475 U.S. 292 (1986).

76   *Ellis* v. *Railway Clerks*, 466 U.S. 435 (1984).

77   *Communication Workers of America* v. *Beck*, 108 S. Ct. 2641 (1988).

78   *AFL-CIO News*, July 2, 1988.

79   *UAW Solidarity*, September 1988.

80   *Crawford* v. *Airline Pilots Association*, 992 F. 2d 1295 (1993).

81   *AFL-CIO News*, July 6, 1985.

82   *Meade Electric Company* v. *Hagberg*, Indiana Superior Court, Lake County, May 19, 1958, No. 158-121. On June 19, 1959, the Second Northern Indiana Division, Indiana Court of Appeals, upheld the decision of the Superior Court.

83   *American Seating Company*, 98 NLRB 800 (1952).

84   *General Motors Corporation*, 130 NLRB 481 (1961).

85   *General Motors Corporation*, 133 NLRB 451 (1961).

86   *General Motors Corporation* v. *NLRB*, 303 F. 2d 428 (6th Cir. 1962).

87   *NLRB* v. *General Motors Corporation*, 373 U.S. 734 (1963).

88   *Retail Clerks International Association, Local 1625* v. *Schermerhorn*, 373 U.S. 746 (1963).

89   *Hearings before the Committee on Labor and Public Welfare*, 80th Congress, 1st sess., on S. 55 and S.J. Res. 22, Part II, p. 839.

90   "Coverage of Checkoff Under Taft-Hartley Act," *Monthly Labor Review*, LXVII, 5 (July 1948), p. 42.

91   *Electrical Workers IBEW Local 2088 (Lockwood Space Operations)*, 302 NLRB No. 49 (1991).

92   *United Steelworkers of America, Local 4671 (National Oil Well, Inc.)*, 302 NLRB 367 (1991).

93   *International Association of Machinists*, 2 RLB 87 (1921).

94   *Globe Cotton Mills* v. *NLRB*, 103 F. 2d 91 at 94 (5th Cir. 1939).

95   *Times Publishing Company*, 72 NLRB 676 (1947).

96   *Majure Transport Company* v. *NLRB*, 198 F. 2d 735 (5th Cir. 1952).

97   *NLRB* v. *Norfolk Shipbuilding & Drydock Corporation*, 172 F. 2d 813 (4th Cir. 1949).

98   *Na-Mac Products Corporation*, 70 NLRB 298 (1946).

99   *Southern Saddlery Company*, 90 NLRB 1205 (1950).

100   *NLRB* v. *General Electric Company*, 418 F. 2d 736 (1969).

101   *Winn-Dixie Stores*, 243 NLRB 972 (1979).

102   *Brazos Electric Power Co-Op.*, 241 NLRB 1016 (1979).

103   *Graham Paper Division, Div. of Jim Walter Paper*, 245 NLRB 1388 (1977).

104   *Indiana & Michigan Electric Co.*, 229 NLRB 576 (1977).

105   *Minnesota Mining & Manufacturing Co.*, 261 NLRB 27 (1982).

106   *Hour Publishing*, 241 NLRB 310 (1979).

107   *Local Union 323, IBEW (Active Enterprises)*, 242 NLRB 305 (1979).

108   *Communication Workers of America, Local 1122 (New York Telephone Co.)*, 226 NLRB 97 (1976).

109   *Local Union 798 of Nassau County, New York (Nassau Div. of Master Painters Assn. of Nassau-Suffolk Counties, et al.)*, 212 NLRB 615 (1974).

110   *H. K. Porter Company* v. *NLRB*, 397 U.S. 99 (1970).

111   *United Mine Workers of America Health & Retirement Funds* v. *Robinson*, 455 U.S. 562 (1982).

112   *NLRB* v. *Wooster Division of Borg-Warner Corporation*, 356 U.S. 342 (1958).

113   *Fibreboard Paper Products* v. *NLRB*, 379 U.S. 203 (1964).

114   *Richfield Oil*, 110 NLRB 356 (1954), enf. 231 F. 2d 717 (D.C. Cir. 1956), cert. denied 351 U.S. 909 (1956).

115   *Dicten & Masch Manufacturing*, 129 NLRB 112 (1960); *Kroger Co.* v. *NLRB*, 399 F. 2d 455 (6th Cir. 1968).

116   *Inland Steel Company*, 77 NLRB 1, enf. 170 F. 2d 247 (7th Cir. 1948), cert. denied 336 U.S. 960 (1949).

117   *Lehigh Portland Cement*, 101 NLRB 529 (1952).

118   *NLRB* v. *Niles-Bemont Pond Company*, 199 F. 2d 713 (7th Cir. 1952).

119   *Beacon Piece Dyeing & Finishing Company*, 121 NLRB 953 (1958).

120   *Miller Brewing Company*, 166 NLRB 831 (1967).

121   *Axelson, Subsidiary of U.S. Industries*, 234 NLRB 414 (1978).

122   *United Mine Workers (Lone Star Steel)*, 231 NLRB 573 (1977).

123   *NLRB* v. *American National Insurance*, 343 U.S. 395 (1952).

124   *Medicenter, Mid-South Hospital*, 221 NLRB 670 (1975).

125   *Ford Motor Company* v. *NLRB*, 441 U.S. 488 (1979).

126   *Ozark Trailers*, 161 NLRB 561 (1966).

127   *NLRB* v. *Transmarine Navigation Corp.*, 380 F. 2d (33 (9th Cir. 1967); *NLRB* v. *Thompson Transport*, 406 F. 2d 698 (10th Cir. 1969); *Royal Typewriter* v. *NLRB*, 533 F. 2d 1030 (8th Cir. 1976).

128   *First National Maintenance Corp.* v. *NLRB*, 452 U.S. 666 (1981).

129   *Operating Engineers, Local No. 12 (Associated General Contractors of America)*, 187 NLRB 430 (1970).

130   *Seattle First National Bank* v. *NLRB*, 450 F. 2d 353 (8th Cir. 1971), rev. 176 NLRB 691 (1969).

131   *NLRB* v. *United Brotherhood of Carpenters, Local 964*, 447 F. 2d 643 (2d Cir. 1971).

132   *Allied Chemical Workers, Local 1* v. *Pittsburgh Plate Glass*, 404 U.S. 157 (1971).

133   177 NLRB 911 (1969).

134   Commerce Clearing House, *Labor Law Reports*, No. 674, January 28, 1985, p. 3.

135   *Columbus Printing Pressmen and Assistants Union 252 (R. W. Page Corp.)*, 219 NLRB 268 (1975). In December 1976, the decision of the NLRB was upheld by a federal circuit court of appeals. *NLRB* v. *Printing Union, Columbus Pressmen and Assistants Union 252*, 543 F. 2d 1161 (5th Cir. 1976).

136   *Universal Oil Products, Norplex Division* v. *NLRB*, 445 F. 2d 155 (7th Cir. 1971).

137   *NLRB* v. *Taormina*, 207 F. 2d 251 (5th Cir. 1953), enf. 94 NLRB 884 (1951).

138   *Kit Manufacturing*, 150 NLRB 662 (1964), enf. 365 F. 2d 829 (1966).

139   *Arlington Asphalt Company*, 136 NLRB 742 (1962).

140   *NLRB* v. *Corsicana Cotton Mills*, 178 F. 2d 344 (5th Cir. 1949).

141   *Bartlett-Collins Co.*, 237 NLRB 770 (1978).

142   *NLRB* v. *United States Postal Service*, 8 F. 3d 832 (1993).

143   *YHA, Inc.* v. *NLRB*, 2 F. 3d 168 (1993).

144   *Lathers Local 42 of Wood, Wire & Metal Lathers International Union (Lathing Contractors Association of Southern California)*, 223 NLRB 37 (1976).

145   *Electrical Workers (IBEW) Local 135, LaCrosse Electrical Contractors Assn.*, 271 NLRB No. 26 (1984).

146   *Capital Times Co.*, 223 NLRB 651 (1976).

147   *Wall Street Journal*, April 9, 1976, p. 8.

148   *Newspaper Guild of Greater Philadelphia, Local 10* v. *NLRB (Peerless Publication)*, 636 F. 2d 550 (1980).

149   *American Electric Power*, 302 NLRB 1021 (1991).

150   *United Technologies, Otis Elevator*, 269 NLRB 891 (1984).

151   *United Technologies, Otis Elevator*, 255 NLRB 235 (1981).

152   *Illinois Coil Spring Co., Milwaukee Spring Division*, 268 NLRB 601 (1984).

153   *Illinois Coil Spring Co., Milwaukee Spring Division*, 265 NLRB 206 (1982).

154   *Litton Systems, Inc., Litton Microwave Cooking Products Division*, 283 NLRB 973 (1987).

155   *The Reece Corporation*, 294 NLRB No. 33 (1989).

156   *Dubuque Packing Company, Inc.*, 303 NLRB 386 (1991).

157   *Dubuque Packing Company*, 287 NLRB 499 (1987).

158   *United Food and Commercial Workers International Union, AFL-CIO, Local 150-A* v. *NLRB*, 880 F. 2d 1422 (1989).

159   *United Food and Commercial Workers International Union, AFL-CIO, Local 150* v. *NLRB*, 1 F. 3d 24 (1993).

160   *Dubuque Packing Company* v. *NLRB*, Dkt No. 93-1103, Cert. Granted April 4, 1994.

161   *Cowles Media Co., Star Tribune Division*, 295 NLRB No. 63 (1989).

162   *Johnson-Bateman Co.*, 295 NLRB No. 26 (1989).

163   *Consolidated Rail Corp.* v. *Railway Labor Executives' Association*, 109 S. Ct. 2477 (1989).

164   *AFL-CIO News*, November 4, 1991, p. 9. (Citations Omitted)

165   *Willner* v. *Thoronburgh*, 928 F. 2d 1115 (1991).

166   *American Federation of Government Employees, AFL-CIO, Local 2391* v. *Lynn A. Martin, Secretary of the United States Department of Labor*, 969 F. 2d 788 (1992).

167   *Russell Bolden* v. *Transport Workers Union of Philadelphia, Local 234*, 953 F. 2d 807 (1991).

168   *Coastal Chemical*, 304 NLRB 556 (1991).

169   E. J. Dannin, "Statutory Subjects and the Duty to Bargain," *Labor Law Journal*, v. 39, No. 1 (January 1988), p. 46.

170   Donna Sockell, "The Scope of Mandatory Bargaining: A Critique and a Proposal," *Industrial and Labor Relations Review*, October 1986, p. 19.

171   Robben W. Fleming, "The Obligation to Bargain in Good Faith," *Public Policy and Collective Bargaining*, eds. Joseph Shister, Benjamin Aaron, and Clyde W. Summers (New York: Harper & Row, 1962), p. 61.

172   *Fibreboard Paper Products Corporation* v. *NLRB*, 379 U.S. 203 (1964).

173   *Television & Radio Artists* v. *NLRB*, 398 F. 2d 319 (1968).

174   *Collyer Insulated Wire*, 192 NLRB 837 (1971).

175   National Labor Relations Board, *Forty-second Annual Report*, 1977, p. 36.

176   D. J. Johannesen and W. Britton Smith, Jr., "*Collyer*: Open Sesame to Deferral," *Labor Law Journal*, XXIII, 12 (December 1972), p. 741.

177   *International Association of Machinists (United Aircraft Corp.)* v. *NLRB*, 525 F. 2d 237 (2d Cir. 1975); *Nabisco, Inc.* v. *NLRB*, 479 F. 2d 770 (2d Cir. 1973); *Associated Press* v. *NLRB*, 492 F. 2d 662 (D.C. Cir. 1974); *Provision House Workers Union Local 274 (Urban Patman, Inc.)* v. *NLRB*, 493 F. 2d 1249 (9th Cir. 1974); *Enterprise Publishing Co.* v. *NLRB*, 403 F. 2d 1024 (1st Cir. 1974).

178   *William E. Arnold Co.* v. *Carpenters District Council of Jacksonville*, 417 U.S. 12 (1974). It should be noted, however, in that case, dealing with other matters, the Court made a passing reference to the Board's deferral policy. Fanning and Jenkins said the Court's reference "was nothing more than dicta in a Section 301 suit rather than an unfair labor practice proceeding." National Labor Relations Board, *Forty-second Annual Report*, 1977, p. 38.

179   *Atlantic Richfield*, 199 NLRB 1224 (1972).

180   *Roadioear*, 199 NLRB 1161 (1972).

181   *Western Electric*, 199 NLRB 326 (1972).

182   *Southwestern Bell Telephone*, 198 NLRB 569 (1972).

183   *Great Coastal Express*, 196 NLRB 871 (1972).

184   *Coppus Engineering*, 195 NLRB 595 (1972).

185   *Peerless Pressed Metal*, 198 NLRB 561 (1972).

186   *Appalachian Power Company*, 198 NLRB 576 (1972).

187   *National Radio Co.*, 198 NLRB 527 (1972).

188   *General American Transportation Corp.*, 228 NLRB 808 (1977).

189   *United Technologies*, 268 NLRB 557 (1984).

190   *International Harvester Co., Columbus Plastics Operation*, 271 NLRB 647 (1984).

191   *Hammontree v. NLRB*, 894 F. 2d 438 (1990).

192   *Hammontree v. NLRB*, 925 F. 2d 1486 (1991).

193   *Tulsa-Whisenhut Funeral Homes*, 195 NLRB 106 (1972).

194   *Borden Inc., Dairy & Services Division*, 196 NLRB 1170 (1972).

195   *Mountain State Construction Company*, 203 NLRB 1085 (1973).

196   *Spielberg Manufacturing Co.*, 112 NLRB 1080 (1955).

197   247 NLRB 146 (1980).

198   *Olin Corp.*, 268 NLRB 573 (1984).

199   Peter Nash, "NLRB and Arbitration: Effect of *Collyer* Policy," *Proceedings of the Twenty-seventh Annual Meeting*, National Academy of Arbitrators, Bureau of National Affairs, Inc. (Washington, D.C.: 1974), p. 119.

200   *Radio Television Technical School, Inc.*, 199 NLRB 570 (1972).

201   Nash, *op. cit.*, pp. 120–121.

202   *Ibid.*, p. 120.

203   *Ibid.*, p. 122.

204   *Malrite of Wisconsin*, 198 NLRB 241 (1972).

205   Federal Mediation and Conciliation Service, *Arbitration Statisics*, October 1992, p. 1.

206   *Local No. 171, Pulp and Paper Workers (Boise Cascade Corp.)*, 165 NLRB 971 (1974).

207   Federal Mediation and Conciliation Service, *op. cit.*, p. 1.

7

Enforcement of the Collective Bargaining Agreement

INTERNAL ENFORCEMENT PROCEDURE: THE GRIEVANCE PROCEDURE

After a labor agreement is negotiated, management and the labor union bargain collectively on a day-to-day basis. Such bargaining does not involve negotiations for a new labor contract. Nor is daily bargaining directed at altering the particular terms of the existing agreement. Collective bargaining on the day-to-day level is the process whereby the labor contract is made a living organism. Many of the day-to-day relations between management and labor involve settling disputes alleging violations of the provisions of the contract. Such settlement is achieved through the *grievance procedure*, a mechanism for self-enforcement of the contract contained in every collective bargaining agreement.

So that the collective bargaining contract will be enforced properly, labor and management rely on the grievance procedure. Both unions and management are aware that charges of contract violation will arise during the contract period. Every day-to-day problem or question that might arise cannot be anticipated in the collective bargaining agreement. The complexities of labor-management relations preclude the drawing up of such a contract. In addition, provisions in an agreement are subject to conflicting interpretations, just as are laws enacted by legislative bodies. In this connection, it should be emphasized that many charges involving contract violations arise merely because union and management representatives do not agree on the meaning of a particular contract provision. The grievance procedure provides management and unions with a mechanism to dispose of charges of contract violations in an orderly and equitable manner.

Control of the Grievance Procedure: Wagner Act Experience

Under the terms of the Wagner Act, a labor union certified by the NLRB became the exclusive representative of all employees within the bargaining unit "for the purposes of collective bargaining in respect to rates of pay, wages, hours of employment, or other conditions of employment."[1] Consequently, an employer was in violation of the Wagner Act if it recognized the majority union as the representative of its members only. A certified labor organization negotiates for all workers within the unit regardless of their union membership status. Apart from conferring this exclusive status upon certified labor organizations, the Wagner Act provided that "any individual employee or a group of employees shall have the right at any time to present grievances to their employers."[2]

For several years, the NLRB had no occasion to render an interpretation of this portion of the Wagner Act. Early in World War II, however, the North American Aviation Company believed that Section 9(a) of the Act gave employees the right to present and adjust grievances individually regardless of the existence of a collective bargaining agreement.[3] The company had previously executed a contract with a union certified by the NLRB. Shortly afterward, copies of the contract were distributed to the firm's employees. In addition, each worker received a notice signed by the company's president which outlined a grievance procedure unilaterally prepared by the company. Such a procedure was inconsistent with the one set forth in the collective bargaining agreement. On the ground that the employer's conduct indicated a refusal to grant exclusive bargaining rights to the certified union, the NLRB subsequently found that the company had engaged in an unfair labor practice. But when the company appealed the Board's decision, a federal circuit court ruled that the "grievance provision" of the Wagner Act conferred upon employers the right to hear and to adjust any grievance presented by individual employees, notwithstanding the existence of a collective bargaining agreement.[4] The court construed the grievance provision to include not only "small out-of-mind grievances" but also all grievances employees might wish to adjust. The court apparently indicated that an employer may lawfully adjust individual grievances relating to all conditions of employment regardless of the terms of a collective bargaining contract.

Beyond reversing the Board's decision, the court's ruling stimulated the first formal NLRB interpretation of the grievance provision. In general, the Board's General Counsel took the position that the provision meant that an individual employee had the technical right to present grievances to an employer, but that representatives of the certified union must be present each time an employee makes such a presentation and must negotiate the settlement of the grievance. Under this construction, the Wagner Act grievance provision extended to individual workers the mechanical right of presentation of grievances but reserved to certified labor organizations the exclusive right to settle the grievances.

Notwithstanding the rule of the federal court in *North American*, the NLRB adopted the interpretation of its General Counsel and ruled in a subsequent case that employers must settle grievances presented by individual workers with the majority union. In one instance, the Board declared that the right of employees to present grievances was not an "empty one." Such a right, according to the Board, ensured to individual employees that the grievances would not be ignored by the majority union.[5] When the exclusive bargaining agent refused to participate in the adjustment of the grievances, the NLRB ruled that the employee could individually negotiate with the employer.

In another case, the Board reaffirmed its policy, even though the certified union involved in the controversy had not yet negotiated a contract. An unfair labor practice was found because the employer had ordered any individual with grievances to take them up directly with management. It is noteworthy that the National War Labor Board also ruled that final adjustment of grievances had to be made with majority unions and not upon an individual basis.[6]

Grievance Procedure under Taft-Hartley

The Taft-Hartley Act nullified the NLRB doctrine established under the Wagner Act dealing with the presentation and adjustment of grievances on an individual worker basis. Under the terms of Taft-Hartley, grievance procedure structures must be broad enough to meet these standards: (1) The individual worker must be permitted to present grievances to the employer on an individual basis; (2) the employer must be permitted to make an adjustment of grievances so presented, provided the adjustment is not inconsistent with the terms of the collective bargaining agreement; and (3) the employer must provide a union official with the opportunity to be present at the time of adjustment.[7]

The first requirement does not greatly change the rulings of the NLRB established under the Wagner Act. Individual workers previously had the opportunity to present grievances to employers. However, it was necessary for employers to invite representatives of the bargaining agent to be present at the time individual workers presented grievances to their employers. Under Taft-Hartley, the labor union holding bargaining rights in the plant does not have to be involved in grievance adjustment but only has to be given an opportunity to be present during the proceedings.

Actually, in this respect, Taft-Hartley did not greatly alter collective bargaining procedures. Many collective bargaining contracts negotiated long before Taft-Hartley provided that the individual worker could choose the method of presentation of the grievance. Scores of agreements gave the worker the freedom to (1) present a grievance on an individual basis; (2) elect to have a representative of the labor union present the grievance for the employee; or (3) go with a union representative to management for the presentation of the grievance. A comparatively small number of agreements went to the extreme of forbidding anyone but the union representative to present workers' grievances, or of requiring that the worker present the grievance on an individual basis.

On the other hand, the second requirement of the 1947 law upset traditional collective bargaining relationships. By providing that the employer may make adjustment of a grievance with a worker on an individual basis, Taft-Hartley destroyed the policies developed by the NLRB under the Wagner Act. As noted, the NLRB had previously required that all grievances must be adjusted with the representatives of the workers' labor union. Only when the collective bargaining agency did not want to adjust a worker's grievance was it permissible for the employer to adjust grievances on an individual worker basis. Obviously, if a labor union refused to do anything about a worker's grievance, the worker and the employer should have the right to make the adjustment. Any adjustment made through this arrangement since the Taft-Hartley enactment, however, must be consistent with the terms of an existing collective bargaining contract. If individuals were permitted to reach agreements inconsistent with the contract, the entire process of collective bargaining could disintegrate. Most unions do not encourage individual processing of grievances because of the apparent implication that the union is not capable of adequately functioning as bargaining agent. However, it should be recognized that some unions are less than enthusiastic about processing nonmember grievances on a par with those raised by members. Regardless of attempts to discourage individual initiative in these matters, unions do not have legal authority to cause the discharge of employees for circumventing the labor organization and directly presenting grievances to employers.[8]

Finally, at the point of adjustment of grievances with individual employees, the employer must provide a union representative the opportunity to be present. In a 1986 case, for example, the employer settled grievances without notifying or inviting the union to be present.[9] It relied on its Equal Opportunity program, which required anonymity of employees involved in those procedures before a complaint was formally filed. Rejecting the employer's position, the NLRB held that confidentiality must yield to the union's statutory right to be present. It noted that the confidentiality rule was to protect employees from management and not the union. In fact, the union was aware of the grievances because it was pursuing them on behalf of the aggrieved employees.

Should an employer adjust a grievance in violation of the labor agreement, the union has a series of options. To remedy the situation, it may appeal to arbitration, file an unfair labor practice charge with the NLRB, or sue the employer in federal court under Section 301 of Taft-Hartley. Its choice would depend on the particular circumstances of a case, the terms of the labor agreement, and the general nature of union-management relations.

DUTY OF FAIR REPRESENTATION

Employee Recourse to NLRB

If a union that holds the position of exclusive bargaining representative of employees declines to process the grievance of a member of the bargaining unit, it has refused representation. Such refusal constitutes restraint and coercion of the worker in the right to representation.[10] As the NLRB stated in *Miranda*:

> . . . Section 7 . . . gives employees the right to be free from unfair or irrelevant or invidious treatment by their exclusive bargaining agent in matters affecting their employment. This right of employees is a statutory limitation on statutory bargaining representatives,

and . . . Section 8(b)(1)(A) of the Act accordingly prohibits labor organizations, when acting in a statutory representative capacity, from taking action against any employee upon considerations or classifications which are irrelevant, invidious, or unfair.

Grievance handling is one aspect of an employee's right to fair and impartial treatment by the exclusive bargaining agent. Popularly this is called the *duty of fair representation.*

Grievance processing is a part of the union's bargaining function. Refusal to process a grievance could constitute a breach of the union's duty to bargain with the employer under the Act's provisions. Any employee who feels aggrieved by a union's refusal to process the grievance may appeal to the NLRB.[11] This means that the Board must judge the substantive aspects of the collective bargaining agreement regarding the rights of employees to fair representation within the unfair labor practice provisions of Taft-Hartley.[12] The Board must evaluate the merits of the grievance and the union's action, as well as the union's motives for disposing of a situation so as to dissatisfy the worker. Failure to convince the NLRB that a worker's grievance was treated in the same fashion as those of other workers could result in unfair labor practice remedies.

Some examples demonstrate how this doctrine has been applied. A union member complained to the international union about the local's violations of the union's bylaws, constitution, and labor agreement. After he was discharged, the local union refused to process his grievance protesting his discharge. It was evident that the grievance was not processed because the union member had evoked the displeasure of the local union when he complained about its transgressions to the international union. Under these circumstances, the Board held that the union had unlawfully refused to accord the union member his right to fair and proper representation.[13] In another case, though a union processed the grievance of a member, it did so without much enthusiasm or sincerity. Under these circumstances, a federal appeals court held that the less than vigorous support of the grievance violated the doctrine of fair representation.[14] Within a bargaining unit, a dissident group was opposed to the union. Two of its supporters were discharged. The union failed to investigate the circumstances of the discharge and did not otherwise pursue the grievance filed by the employees. Under these circumstances, the Board held that the union's conduct was arbitrary and capricious and violated its duty of fair representation.[15] In another case, a union informed a discharged employee that it would request her reinstatement with back pay. When the union, despite its promise to the employee, told the employer it would not seek her reinstatement, the NLRB held the union had violated its duty of fair representation.[16]

Failure to process grievances properly *is not the only way in which unions can violate their duty of fair representation.* A union representing clerical employees and warehouse workers insisted in contract negotiations that both groups receive the same wage increase. Previously, the clericals had requested they receive the same increase as the warehouse workers. However, during contract negotiations, the employer told the union that a wage increase of that magnitude for the clericals would lead to their permanent layoff. The union did not relay that information to the clerical group. After agreeing to the wage increase demanded for the clericals, the employer terminated their employment. Subsequently, the NLRB in *The Emporium* held that the union had violated its duty of fair representation to the clerical workers for its failure to inform that group that the wage increase would jeopardize their jobs.[17] This policy has a great significance for the relationship between unions and their members. Under it, a union must inform its members of employer warnings made during contract negotiations. As the Board pointed out in *The Emporium*, it makes no difference that union representatives might believe an employer is only using a common negotiating scare technique. The union is still obligated to inform its members so they can make an intelligent reassessment of their bargaining demands.

Nonunion Employees

Even nonunion employees are protected under the union's duty to afford all members of the bargaining unit fair and equal representation. In a right-to-work state, a union desired to charge nonunion employees a fee for the processing of grievances. Since the union could not negotiate a union shop or agency shop, it believed that these employees should pay the costs of the handling of their grievances. Despite the apparent equity of this argument, the Board stressed that the union's lawful duty is to represent all employees in the bargaining unit on the same basis. It held that the union had engaged in an unfair labor practice because it could not discriminate against employees in the bargaining unit based on union membership for purposes of the grievance procedure.[18]

In a similar situation, a union did not permit nonunion employees to vote on an employer proposal dealing with vacation scheduling. The employer had said that a system of either fixed or rotating vacation days would be agreeable. The employer was willing to be bound by the vote of the bargaining unit employees. When the union restricted the right to make the choice to union members alone, a federal appeals court, sustaining the Board, held that the union had breached its duty of fair representation.[19]

Remedies for Violations

When the NLRB finds that a union did not provide fair representation, it will direct an appropriate remedy. The Board will order the union to cease and desist from breaches of the duty of fair representation.[20] Of more practical value to a discharged employee, under appropriate circumstances the Board will order reinstatement with full back pay and other contractual rights.[21] When, however, the Board has no jurisdiction over the employer and so cannot direct reinstatement, it will direct the union to pay back pay to the discharged employee. In one such case, a union failed to process a grievance of a discharged employee. The Board required the union to pay back pay from the date of the initial refusal to handle the grievance "until such time as union fulfills its duty of fair representation, or discharged employee obtains substantially equivalent employment, whichever is sooner."[22] In another case, the NLRB held that a union was liable for back pay because it had failed to interview discharged employees before it processed their grievances.[23] It directed the union to request the employer to reinstate the employees. If the employer refused, the union was required to pursue the grievance to arbitration. Should the union be unable to proceed to arbitration because of time limits (labor agreements require an appeal to arbitration to be made within a specified period of time) or for any other reason, the NLRB ruled that the union alone would be liable for back pay.

Under some circumstances, the Board has held that *unions did not violate their statutory duties by refusing grievances.* Two employees were suspended for fighting on the job, one for twenty-five days and the other for four days. Through the grievance procedure, the union managed to reduce the twenty-five day suspension to fourteen days. It refused to process a grievance for the employee who was suspended for four days. While dismissing the latter employee's complaint against the union, the Board held that the union's effort to equalize the penalties was reasonable. Apparently, the union believed that both employees deserved some discipline for their violation of plant rules against fighting on the job.[24] In another case, a union through negligence failed to process an employee's grievance in a timely manner, with the result that the employer denied the grievance on this basis. The affected employee filed unfair labor practice charges against the union, claiming its negligence had denied him the right to fair representation. The Board dismissed the claim on the grounds that negligence alone did not add up to a breach of the statutory obligations of the union. Though the union had been negligent, the Board held that this did not constitute arbitrary, discriminatory, or unfair conduct.[25] In other words, to show that a union has breached its duty of fair and equal representation in the handling of grievances, the evidence must indicate that the union discriminated unfairly against employees and has acted arbitrarily and capriciously. Each case must be determined under its particular set of facts and circumstances.

In order to cut down on the number of cases alleging breach of the duty of fair representation, the General Counsel of the NLRB established guidelines.[26] Union conduct that is "inept, negligent, unwise, insensitive, or ineffectual" does not establish breach of the duty. Complaints will be issued against unions charged with failure to provide fair representation only where union conduct (1) was based upon improper motives such as fraud; (2) was arbitrary; (3) was grossly negligent; or (4) was improperly undercutting an employee's grievance. In this way, it was expected that the Board's case load would be reduced. The guidelines were also established to ease the burden on union representatives. Rather than face employee charges, unions frequently process trivial grievances and even those which are completely devoid of merit. Under the guidelines, union officials will probably be more selective in pursuing employee complaints.

Individual Suits in Federal Courts

Still another avenue is open to employees when a union does not represent them fairly in the collective bargaining process. They have the right to sue unions in federal court under Section 301 of Taft-Hartley.[27] Thus, employees who feel their rights have been violated under collective bargaining agreements may choose to seek relief from the courts or the NLRB. As a matter of fact, in 1989 the Supreme Court specifically held that employees have the right to seek judicial rather than NLRB relief.[28] A union member claimed the union-operated hiring hall discriminated against him in job referrals. A federal appeals court ruled the NLRB had exclusive jurisdiction over fair representation cases. Not so, said the Supreme Court, holding the employee may properly seek judicial relief of the alleged violation of the union's representation.

In a 1990 case (*Teamsters, Local 391* v. *Terry*, 110 S. Ct. 1339), the high court held that employees charging lack of fair representation are entitled to a jury trial. Apparently some employees believe a jury would be more sympathetic to their cause than a judge. Commenting on the case, the *Wall Street Journal* reported a labor law attorney said:

> Most lawyers who bring these kind of cases don't think you can win unless you can get to a jury.

Unions have both the right and the responsibility to represent all bargaining-unit members fairly by evaluating the merits of grievances filed. There is no requirement, however, that a union must process a grievance throughout the entire range of grievance machinery provided by the contract, including arbitration. Financial liability of unions in cases where they may abandon a grievance prior to arbitration is not present *merely because an employee may prove to the courts that it was a meritorious one*. The test for holding labor organizations responsible in court suits is whether the employee can show, as the U.S. Supreme Court said in *Vaca* v. *Sipes*, "arbitrary or bad faith conduct on the part of the union in processing his grievance."[29] Unions have the authority to resolve issues with employers without having to obtain solutions no more advantageous to one employee than to another. Differences are inevitable within bargaining units. A suitable solution to one employee may well be unacceptable to another. Unions cannot bargain effectively with employers unless they can provide reasonable assurances that their actions will not be destroyed legally by dissidents. The Supreme Court has ruled:

> A wide range of reasonableness must be allowed a statutory bargaining representative in serving the unit it represents subject always to complete good faith and honesty of purpose in the exercise of its discretion.[30]

Court Remedies

As a result of litigation costs, most employees would probably seek relief from the NLRB rather than the courts. Where a court finds that a union has breached its duty of fair representation, it will direct an appropriate remedy under the circumstances of a particular case. The court may afford the injured employee injunctive relief, or where appropriate, compensatory damages in the form of back pay. As a matter of fact, in one case a court ordered the union not only to pay the aggrieved employee back pay, but also *future* lost earnings.[31] As a result of the union's failure to represent the employee involved fairly, the employer was able to phase out his job. Under these circumstances, the court held that the award of future damages was the only effective remedy. In 1981, the U.S. Supreme Court made it somewhat easier for union members to sue their organizations. A discharged employee, claiming unfair representation, was denied reinstatement and back pay. Since the employee could not get his job back through internal union procedures, the Court held that he was not required to use that procedure before suing the union.[32] In other words, where an intraunion procedure is not adequate to provide the employee with the relief sought, the union member need not exhaust that procedure as a prerequisite to sue the union.

In a 1983 case, *Bowen* v. *United States Postal Service*, the Supreme Court made it crystal clear that unions are liable for damages when they fail to carry out the duty of fair representation.[33] When a union refused to arbitrate one employee's discharge, the employee sued both the union and the employer. The high court held that the union had failed to comply with its statutory obligation when it did not arbitrate the employee's grievance. As a remedy, the union was directed to pay the lion's share of the back pay award, $30,000, and $23,000 by the employer. The Court rejected the union's argument that only the employer should be responsible for back pay. To avoid the consequences of *Bowen*, some unions may arbitrate cases that do not have merit. As one union officer said, the policy will "create a workload problem for the arbitration system."[34]

Without detracting from the significance of *Bowen*, the U.S. Supreme Court later provided some relief to unions when it held that employees must sue within six months after the union allegedly breached its duty of fair representation.[35] Before the Court established this policy, some courts established time limits as short as thirty days and as long as several years. As the basis of the six-month rule, the high court noted that unfair labor practice charges must be filed under Taft-Hartley within that period of time. Thus, given current case law, an employee who files a lawsuit against a union after more than six months will not be entitled to relief even if the union did in fact fail to provide fair representation.

In their zeal to protect employees, some lower federal courts awarded employees punitive damages beyond the amount of money that they actually lost because of the union's illegal conduct. In 1979, however, the U.S. Supreme Court ruled in *Foust* that under no circumstances could a union be liable for such excess damages in fair representation cases.[36] It held that punitive damages are not consistent with the purposes of national labor policy. In that case, a lower federal court had assessed $75,000 punitive damages. While reversing the lower courts, the high court said punitive awards could

> deplete union treasuries, thereby impairing the effectiveness of unions as collective bargaining agents.

To protect against punitive damages, the court reasoned further, unions "might feel compelled to process frivolous claims or resist fair settlements." Although the issue arose under the Railway Labor Act, the policy also applies to Taft-Hartley. Even in the absence of punitive damages, unions have a sufficient financial incentive to do their best to provide fair representation to their members.

Unions Exculpated

Like the NLRB, federal courts have held that unions have *not* failed to provide fair representation as alleged by employees. Reversing a district court's decision, a federal appeals court ruled that a union was not obligated to pay strike benefits to employees who did not participate in strike activities.[37] Required to pay the equivalent of union dues under an agency shop, an employee was nonetheless denied strike benefits because he did not picket, refused to take a turn in the kitchen to feed picketers, and failed to perform other strike duties. Under these circumstances, the court held the union had not violated its duty of fair representation, limiting such suits to matters that involved an employee's relationship to the employer. Thus, the payment of strike benefits was ruled a purely intraunion matter subject only to the eligibility rules established by a union. In addition, the court noted that the union did not pay strike benefits to union members who had refused to participate in strike activities.

Even when a union failed to appeal a grievance to arbitration within the labor agreement's time limits, a federal appeals court held the Union had not violated its duty of fair representation.[38] The union had simply forgotten the date on which the appeal should have been filed. Forgetting the deadline, the court said, is not the same as a conscious decision to abandon the grievance. In short, the court held that the union's negligence was not arbitrary, discriminatory, or bad-faith conduct.

In a particularly important case, another federal appeals court held that a union had not failed to represent an employee fairly simply because it had refused to seek judicial review to vacate an arbitration award that upheld his discharge.[39] It said the union's obligation to the employee was limited to submitting the grievance to arbitration. Whereas collective bargaining contracts provide for arbitration of grievances and place a fair representation duty upon unions to arbitrate, they do not require unions to appeal unfavorable arbitration awards to the courts for reversal. While denying the employee's charge, the court pointed out that the employee as an individual was free to petition a court for reversal of the arbitration decision. Under these circumstances, the employee and not the union would be liable for litigation and court costs.

More Recent Cases

In more recent cases, a group of guards in 1992 was discharged after the union and employer agreed to subcontract the guards' work for a substantial savings in costs. Finding that the union violated its duty of fair representation, a federal appeals court upheld the decision of a district court in awarding the guards damages including lost wages and additional benefits. Such damages were to be paid by the employer and the union.[40]

An employee completed the thirty-day probationary period and was certified as a union member. Later the union and employer retroactively extended the probationary period. As a result several employees, including the plaintiff in the lawsuit, were fired. Stating that the union acted in bad faith agreeing to a "deceitful scheme to retroactively extend the probationary period," the federal appeals court ruled the union breached its duty of fair representation.[41] Similarly another union violated its representation duty when it agreed to a modification of a labor agreement, establishing a new system for measuring mileage for over-the-road drivers. It did this without asking the membership for approval.[42]

In an extremely important case, the Supreme Court ruled unions have broad latitude to negotiate strike settlements and other labor contracts without facing lawsuits by dissatisfied union members.[43] Continental Airlines filed for Chapter 11 bankruptcy.

With the approval of the bankruptcy court, it repudiated its contract with the Airline Pilots Association. Freed from the contract, Continental slashed wages and benefits by 50 percent. Then a strike took place that lasted over two years.

In October 1985 the pilots union reached an agreement that was clearly unfavorable to the striking pilots. It gave nonstriking working pilots vacant positions and required returning strikers to waive any claim for damages against the airline. It also placed other obstacles in their way to secure employment. Subsequently, the striking pilots sued the union alleging it violated its duty of fair representation.

Reversing a district court verdict to dismiss the lawsuit, the federal appeals court in New Orleans ruled in favor of the plaintiffs. It said the union had breached its duty of fair representation because the union agreed to a contract less favorable to them than simply surrendering to the employer terms to end the strike. It said the settlement "left the striking pilots worse off in a number of respects than complete surrender to [Continental]."

Upon review, the high court held for the union. To justify its decision, the Supreme Court reasoned that even though the contract settlement to end the strike may have been considered "bad" in retrospect, there was no evidence to show that the union's behavior "was so far outside a wide range of reasonableness as to be irrational" or arbitrary. Therefore, the union did not violate its duty of fair representation. In writing for a unanimous Court, Justice John Stevens said: "Congress did not intend judicial review of a union's performance to permit the court to substitute its own view for the proper bargain of that realized by the union."

In other words the decision permits unions to use judgment in negotiating strike settlements, and unions are protected against lawsuits from members as long as the settlement is reasonable and rational and not arbitrary. It gives unions breathing room to negotiate contracts and settle strikes without being second-guessed by federal judges for failing to fairly represent all union members.

COURT ENFORCEMENT OF CONTRACTS

Common Law Doctrine of Agency

The Taft-Hartley Act made it easier for parties to the collective bargaining process to sue each other in courts of law when alleged violations of the labor agreement occur. This is accomplished by expanding the jurisdiction of the federal courts in labor contract violation cases.[44] Before the 1947 law was enacted, labor organizations could be sued for contract violations in the federal courts. However, two conditions had to prevail before the federal courts would assume jurisdiction of the case: (1) The parties involved were required to be citizens of different states, and (2) the amount of damages resulting from the breach of contract had to be at least $3,000. The Taft-Hartley Act removed both of these restrictions on the federal courts. Section 301 provides that

> suits for violations of contract between an employer and a labor organization . . . may be brought in any district court of the United States having jurisdiction of the parties, without respect to the amount in controversy or without regard to the citizenship of the parties.

Proponents of this feature of the 1947 labor law argued that its effect would make labor unions more responsible in the discharge of their obligations under collective bargaining contracts—in particular, that unions would be more prone to respect their no-strike and no-slowdown obligations. In this regard, the National Association of Manufacturers declared: "Now there is less danger that [workers] will suddenly be called out on strike while the contract is in effect."[45] Fearful of being sued in court for damages resulting from strikes violating the collective bargaining agreement, labor unions, it was felt, would exercise caution to prevent such work stoppages.

The Taft-Hartley Act expands the jurisdiction of the federal courts over labor-management disputes. In addition, as noted below, *it sets up a concept of union responsibility quite different from the one in the Norris–La Guardia Act.* Before the passage of Norris–La Guardia, the common-law rules of agency applied to federal court proceedings in which many unions found themselves defendants. *Under the common law, a principal is liable for the unlawful acts of its agents whether or not the principal has knowledge of, has ratified, or has authorized the agents' actions.* For purposes of labor relations, the union, under the common-law doctrine of agency, was responsible for actions of its members and officers.

Although the common-law doctrine of agency may be justified in many areas of judicial proceedings, its application to labor matters works a hardship upon labor organizations. The fundamental reason for this rests upon the nature of the labor union as a functioning institution. Labor unions are composed of large numbers of members. In many unions there are hundreds—in some cases, thousands—of officers, but the employer chooses the union's membership by deciding whom to hire. The union at best exercises a loose degree of discipline over its membership. The imposition of discipline by the union over union members and union officers is usually a difficult process. Union members are not "fired" out of the normal labor organization except after an elaborate procedure. This characteristic of the union movement is not criticized. On the contrary, adequate protection of a worker's union membership is necessary if democracy within the labor union is to be preserved. This merely highlights the fact that the status of union members and officers is well protected. Such insulation provides a basis for conduct that may be inconsistent with the terms of the labor contract.

Finally, it is pertinent to point out that the labor union does not have the control a business firm has in choosing its personnel. Agents of labor unions—such as union officers, stewards, and grievance committee members—are elected by the membership. In contrast with the method employed by the union in obtaining its leadership, the company normally carefully selects representatives of management on the basis of education, experience, aptitude tests, and recommendations.

Congress was aware of these considerations when it passed Norris–La Guardia. It recognized that the application of the common-law rule of agency to labor relations operated to the serious disadvantage of the labor union. The complexities of modern industrial life and a realistic view of the labor union as a living organism militated for a different approach to the problem of union responsibility. As a result, Section 6 of the Norris–La Guardia Act was adopted. This provision required actual authorization or ratification by labor organizations of agents' acts to establish union responsibility. Section 6 declared:

> No officer or member of any association or organization, and no association or organization participating or interested in a labor dispute, shall be held responsible or liable in any court of the United States for the unlawful acts of individual officers, members, or agents, except upon clear proof of actual participation in, or actual authorization of, such acts, or of ratification of such acts after actual knowledge thereof.

Thus, Norris–La Guardia prevented the application of the common-law rule of agency to labor disputes. Under its terms, a labor union, before it could be held liable for illegal action of its members or officers, must have authorized such conduct or ratified the action after it occurred. Proponents of Norris–La Guardia contended that this conception of union responsibility was made necessary by the contemporary industrial relations environment.

Union Responsibility under Taft-Hartley

Under the terms of the 1947 labor law, the rules of agency developed in common law once again govern the issue of union responsibility. The law provides that in determining whether or not any person is acting as an agent of a labor organization so as to make the union responsible for his or her acts, *"the question of whether the specific acts performed were actually authorized or subsequently ratified shall not be controlling."* By this language, the statute makes the labor union responsible for the activities of its members or officers, regardless of whether the union authorized or ratified the conduct. In this connection, the International Association of Machinists pointed out that Taft-Hartley "makes the union responsible for the actions of irresponsible 'agents' who act without authorization. And it subjects the union to legal liability for such unauthorized actions."[46]

At times, strikes and other interruptions to production not authorized by the labor organization occur. These work stoppages, commonly known as *wildcat strikes*, are instigated by a group of workers, sometimes including union officers, without the sanction of the labor union. Under many labor agreements, the employer has the right to discharge such employees or otherwise penalize them for such activities.

An employer may sue a union because of a wildcat strike even if the union has not authorized or ratified it. As a result, unions and employers have negotiated *nonsuability clauses*. Under these arrangements, the company agrees that it will not sue a labor union because of wildcat strikes, provided the union fulfills its obligation to terminate the work stoppage. Frequently, the labor contract specifies exactly what the union must do in order to free itself from the possibility of damage suits. Thus, in some contracts containing nonsuability clauses, the union agrees to announce orally and in writing that it disavows the strike, orders the workers back to their jobs, and refuses any form of strike relief to the participants in such work stoppages.

Danbury Hatters Revisited

Though an employer may sue a union for money damages under Section 301 when employees participate in a wildcat strike, the provision does not authorize employer suits against individual union members.[47] A labor agreement contained a no-strike clause that forbade work interruptions during the period of the contract. Despite this provision, employees went out on strike. The employer sued both the union and the individual members for breach of contract and requested a federal court to assess money damages against the union and its members. The company argued that Section 301 had established the congressional intent that individual strikers, as well as the unions, be held responsible for damages suffered by employers as a result of unauthorized strikes. In rejecting the employer position in *Sinclair Oil Corporation*, a federal appeals court stated:

> The legislative history of the act indicates that the principal concern of Congress was with making unions, as parties to collective bargaining agreements, responsible for breaches of agreements and to avoid subjecting individual union members to fiscal ruin.

In this regard, Section 301 provides that

> any money judgment against a labor organization in a district court of the United States shall be enforceable only against the organization as an entity and *shall not be enforceable against any individual member or his assets*. (Emphasis supplied)

In 1962, the U.S. Supreme Court maintained the integrity of this language when it held that

> when a union is liable for damages for violation of the no-strike clause, its officers and members are not liable for these damages.[48]

Despite the language of the law and the judicial precedent, the issue surfaced once more: An employer requested the federal courts to assess damages against individual union members because of a wildcat strike. In 1981, the U.S. Supreme Court held again that individual union members are not financially liable for the losses suffered by employers resulting from wildcat strikes.[49] Once again the high court explained that Congress had exempted individual union members because it did not want a repetition of the *Danbury Hatters* situation discussed in Chapter 1. In that case, recall that the U.S. Supreme Court held that individual union members were liable for damages assessed against their unions.

What all this means is that union members and officers as individuals are not liable for money damages in the event of wildcat strikes. Action against individual employees is, therefore, limited to discharge or other forms of discipline. Employees who participate in a wildcat strike lose their status as employees for purposes of Taft-Hartley.[50] Thus, if an employer discharges such employees, the NLRB will not direct their reinstatement.

Liability of National Unions

The rule relieving individual union members from the damages of a wildcat strike takes on added significance because of another Supreme Court decision. In *Carbon Fuel*,[51] a unanimous Court held that a national union is not responsible for damages when its local unions are involved in wildcat strikes. Since local unions normally do not have large treasuries, the employer sought damages from the national union. Between 1969 and 1973, local union affiliates of the United Mine Workers of America engaged in forty-eight wildcat strikes. A federal district court held that the national union was liable and ordered it to pay $500,000 to Carbon Fuel.

Reversing the lower court, the U.S. Supreme Court said the national union was not liable because it did not provoke or encourage the wildcat strike. If it had, it would have been liable. The Court also pointed out that the labor agreement did not place an affirmative obligation on the national union to end unauthorized strikes. In other words, the high court said that a national union could be responsible for damages should a labor agreement expressly make the national union liable, or expressly impose an affirmative obligation on a national union to do everything reasonably possible to end wildcat strikes, such as fining or expelling wildcatting employees. Should a national union fail to comply with those contractual obligations, it would be liable for damages. It is extremely unlikely, however, that national unions would agree to these kinds of provisions.

Thus, employers have not fared well with the U.S. Supreme Court in their efforts to obtain damages resulting from unauthorized strikes. Union members and officers as individuals are not liable for damages, and under most circumstances national unions are also exempt.

Where Contracts Do Not Provide for Arbitration

In 1990, the United States Supreme Court broadened its control and enforcement of labor agreements. Although a contract established a grievance procedure, it did not provide for final and binding arbitration when the employer and union fail to settle a grievance. In this respect the contract was sharply different from the custom and practice of the nation's labor relations program.

Two employees were discharged, claiming they were wrongfully deprived of their jobs. They filed grievances, but the parties were unable to resolve them. Normally under these circumstances, the union would appeal to arbitration for final and binding determination of the dispute. As a result the employees filed a lawsuit under Section 301 of Taft-Hartley requesting a remedy from the federal courts. In turn the employer claimed the court had no jurisdiction to hear the dispute because the contract was silent on additional remedies beyond the grievance procedure.

The federal appeals court in Cincinnati agreed with the employer and dismissed the lawsuit. Reversing the lower court, the U.S. Supreme Court ruled there is a "strong presumption" that favors access to a neutral forum—in this case the court system—for peaceful resolution of labor disputes. Contrary to the appeals court, the high court ruled judicial intervention was far preferable to "economic warfare" by the parties in the form of strikes or lockouts. "As a matter of fact," said the Supreme Court, "to keep the judiciary from determining contractual disputes, the parties must clearly agree courts should not intervene in matters of contractual enforcement."[52]

After the decision some persons speculated that final and binding arbitration would be dropped from contracts. This did not happen because arbitration is much swifter and cheaper than litigation in the court system.

ARBITRATION AND THE FEDERAL COURTS

Refusal to Arbitrate

When employers and unions are not able to settle a grievance arising under the terms of an existing labor agreement, arbitration is used to break the deadlock. Practically all collective bargaining contracts contain an arbitration procedure. If it were not for U.S. Supreme Court decisions, however, arbitration would not be used extensively for that purpose. As a matter of fact, until the high court's decision in *Lincoln Mills*, employers did not honor arbitration even though the procedure was incorporated into the labor agreement. Some federal and state courts agreed with employers that they could not be forced to arbitrate contract grievances.

When Lincoln Mills, a large multiplant textile company located in the South, refused to arbitrate a grievance, the union sued it under Section 301 of Taft-Hartley. A federal appeals court held the company was not required to arbitrate even though the labor agreement called for arbitration to resolve unsettled grievances arising under the labor agreement. It said Section 301 of the national law did not provide the federal courts with the authority to force employers to arbitrate.

Upon review, the Supreme Court ruled in *Lincoln Mills* (1957)[53]

that the substantive law to apply in suits under Section 301 (a) is federal law, which the courts must fashion from the policy of our national labor laws.

Thus, arbitration provisions were deemed enforceable in the federal courts under federal law. In practice, what *Lincoln Mills* meant was that when a labor agreement provides that arbitration must be used to determine grievance disputes, the employer must proceed to arbitration. It held also that the Norris–La Guardia Act did not bar injunctive relief, since

the congressional policy in favor of the enforcement of agreements to arbitrate grievance disputes being clear, there is no reason to submit them to the requirements of Section 4 of the Norris–La Guardia Act.

No question that *Lincoln Mills* constituted a major impetus for the use of arbitration. However, other legal issues had to be resolved to establish arbitration as a viable process in labor relations.

The *"Trilogy"* Cases

On June 20, 1960, the U.S. Supreme Court handed down three other decisions that provided even greater integrity to the arbitration process.[54] These decisions are commonly referred to as the *"Trilogy"* cases. Each involved the United Steelworkers of America, and each demonstrates that the system of private arbitration in the United States has received the full support of the highest court in the land.

In *Warrior & Gulf Navigation*, the Court held that in the absence of an express agreement excluding arbitration, it would direct the parties to arbitrate a grievance. To put this in other terms, the Court would not find a case *nonarbitrable unless the parties specifically excluded a subject from the arbitration process.* The Court stated that a legal order to arbitrate would thenceforth not be denied "unless it may be said with positive assurance that the arbitration clause is not susceptible to an interpretation that covers the asserted dispute. Doubts should be resolved in favor of coverage."

More precisely, the courts may not decide that a dispute is not arbitrable unless the parties have taken care to expressly remove an area of labor relations from the arbitration process. This could be accomplished by providing, for example, that "disputes involving determination of the qualifications of employees for promotion will be determined exclusively by the company and such decision will not be subject to arbitration."[55] Needless to say, not many unions would agree to such a clause, since management would then have the unilateral right to make determinations on this vital phase of the promotion process.

Warrior & Gulf Navigation eliminated a course of action that some companies had followed. When faced with union demands for arbitration, some employers had frequently gone to court and asked the judge to decide that the issue involved in the case was not arbitrable. On many occasions the courts had agreed with the company, sustaining the company position in the grievance and denying the union an opportunity to get a decision based on the merits of the case.

In the case at hand, the Warrior & Gulf Navigation Company employed forty-two men at its dock terminal for maintenance and repair work. After the company had subcontracted out some of the work, the number was reduced to twenty-three. The union argued in the grievance procedure that this action of the company violated certain areas of the labor agreement—the integrity of the bargaining unit, seniority rights, and other clauses of the contract that provided benefits to workers. The company claimed that the issue of subcontracting was strictly a management function and relied on the management rights clause in the contract, which stated that "matters which are strictly a function of management should not be subject to arbitration." When the Supreme Court handled the case, it ordered arbitration because the contract did not specifically exclude subcontracting from the arbitration process. It stated:

> A specific collective bargaining agreement may exclude contracting-out from the grievance procedure. Or a written collateral agreement may make clear that contracting-out was not a matter for arbitration. In such a case a grievance based solely on contracting-out would not be arbitrated. Here, however, there is no such provision. Nor is there any showing that the parties designed the phrase "strictly as a function of

management" to encompass any and all forms of contracting-out. In the absence of any express provision excluding a particular grievance from arbitration, we think only the most forceful evidence of a purpose to exclude the claim from arbitration can prevail, particularly where, as here, the exclusion clause is vague and the arbitration clause quite broad.

To understand the significance of this decision, one additional point must be stressed. Though the court may direct arbitration, it will not determine the merits of the dispute. A federal court only decides whether the grievance is arbitrable, but the *private arbitrator has full authority to rule on its merits.* As the Supreme Court stated in *Warrior & Gulf Navigation*:

> Whether contracting out in the present case violated the agreement is the question. It is a question for the arbiter, not for the courts.

This principle was stressed by the U.S. Supreme Court in *AT&T Technologies*.[56] When the union filed a grievance protesting the layoff of seventy-nine employees, the employer refused to submit the grievance to arbitration, contending that its decision to lay off due to a lack of work was not arbitrable. The high court said the question of arbitrability was "undeniably an issue of judicial determination" and remanded the case to the lower federal court to make that decision. At the same time, the Court admonished it "not to rule on the potential merits of the underlying claim" while deciding arbitrability. In other words, the federal courts have the exclusive authority to determine whether a grievance is arbitrable, but the arbitrator has the power to determine whether the grievance has merit.

In the second *Trilogy* case, *American Manufacturing*, the issue of arbitrability was also involved, but in a somewhat different way than in *Warrior & Gulf Navigation*. The American Manufacturing Company argued before a lower federal court that an issue was not arbitrable because it did not believe the grievance had merit. Involved was a dispute on reinstatement of an employee to his job after it was determined that the employee was 25 percent disabled and was drawing worker's compensation. The lower federal court sustained the employer's position and characterized the employee's grievance as "a frivolous, patently baseless one, not subject to arbitration." When the U.S. Supreme Court reversed the lower federal court, it held that the federal courts are limited in determining whether the dispute is covered by the labor agreement and that *they have no power to evaluate the merits of a dispute.* It stated:

> The function of the court is very limited when the parties have agreed to submit all questions of contract interpretation to the arbitrator. It is then confined to ascertaining whether the party seeking arbitration is making a claim which on its face is governed by the contract. Whether the moving party is right or wrong is a question of contract construction for the arbitrator. In these circumstances the moving party should not be deprived of the arbitrator's judgment, when it was his judgment and all that it connotes that was bargained for.

Essentially, this means that the courts may not hold a grievance nonarbitrable even if a judge believes it is completely worthless. It is up to the private arbitrator to make the decision on the merits of a case. He or she may dismiss the grievance as being without merit, but this duty rests exclusively with the arbitrator and not with the courts. Once again the high court affirmed the arbitration process. Employers had previously been able to block arbitration when they could convince a court that a grievance did not have merit. No longer is that avenue available to employers who desire to avoid arbitration.

In the third case, *Enterprise Wheel & Car Corporation*, a lower federal court reversed the decision of an arbitrator on the grounds that the judge did not believe his decision was sound under the labor agreement. The arbitrator's award directed the employer to reinstate certain discharged workers and to pay them back wages for periods both before and after the expiration of the collective bargaining contract. The company refused to comply with the award, and the union petitioned for enforcement. The lower court held that the arbitrator's award was unenforceable because the contract had expired. The U.S. Supreme Court reversed the lower court and ordered full enforcement. In upholding the arbitrator's award, the Court stated:

> Interpretation of the collective bargaining agreement is a question for the arbitrator. It is the arbitrator's construction which was bargained for; and so far as the arbitration decision concerns construction of the contract, the courts have no business overruling him because their interpretation of the contract is different from his.

Thus, neither a union nor a company may use the courts to set aside an arbitrator's award. The decision cuts both ways; it applies to both employers and labor organizations. Whereas the other two decisions definitely favor labor organizations, this one merely serves to preserve the integrity of the arbitrator's award. Even if a judge believes an arbitrator's award is unfair, unwise, or inconsistent with the contract, the court has no alternative but to enforce the award. As long as the award "draws its essence from the collective bargaining contract," said the high court, the federal courts must enforce the arbitrator's decision.

Application of *Enterprise Wheel*

Showing deference to *Enterprise Wheel*, federal courts have enforced arbitration decisions that might very well have been reversed without it. A labor agreement provided that grievances must be filed within ten days after the action to be grieved occurred. The union involved in the dispute did not file its written grievance until fifteen days after the action. The employer, a music college, requested the arbitrator to find that the late filing barred consideration of the merits of the grievance. Nonetheless, the arbitrator granted the grievance, holding the time limitation failure of the union was *de minimis* to the whole dispute. Reversing a district court decision, a federal appeals court in 1988 upheld the award, agreeing with the arbitrator that the contract did not prevent him from making the *de minimis* judgment.[57] To do that, the contract should have specified the consequences of late filing.

Normally, of course, an arbitration does not take place unless the employer and union are present. Alleging that the union did not follow procedural requirements prior to arbitration, the employer in a 1987 case did not show up at the hearing. It was notified, of course, of the date, time, and place of the session. Despite the absence of the employer, the arbitrator conducted an *ex parte* hearing and granted the grievance. The employer successfully persuaded a district court to vacate the award on the grounds of the *ex parte* hearing and alleged further that the arbitrator was biased. On appeal, the San Francisco Court of Appeals reversed the district court and upheld the arbitrator's award.[58] It ruled that when parties to a collective bargaining contract cooperate in the selection of an arbitrator and the absent party has adequate notice of the hearing, the failure to attend does not nullify the award. In addition, the appeals court did not find any bias on the part of the arbitrator.

On the other hand, despite *Enterprise Wheel & Car Corporation*, under limited circumstances, a court may reverse an arbitrator's decision. Reversal could occur because an arbitrator clearly exceeded jurisdiction under a labor agreement, did not "draw the essence" of the award from the contract, failed to conduct a fair hearing, or failed to disclose a conflict of interest relationship to one of the parties. For example, in a 1989 case, a federal appeals court vacated an arbitrator's award because it did not draw its essence from the labor agreement. The arbitrator failed to consider or discuss a contract provision directly involved in the issue of the case. The dispute arose when an employer ceased its meat-slaughtering operations and leased the slaughtering facility to an outside processor who used nonbargaining-unit employees. The union claimed that any slaughtering that took place in the employer's buildings must be performed by union employees. The arbitrator held for the union but neglected to consider and discuss a provision in the labor agreement that covered leasing company operations. Finding the provision relevant to the arbitrator's decision, the appeals court vacated the arbitrator's award.[59]

It should be noted, however, that the instances of court reversal of arbitrators' awards are infrequent when compared with the number of cases where federal courts enforced them under *Enterprise Wheel*. As treated below, however, the U.S. Supreme Court carved out conditions under which federal courts may upset arbitration awards when the basis is not attributable to the conduct of the arbitrator.

Thus, under *Trilogy*, the arbitration process has been strengthened. Arbitration, so to speak, received its "legal diploma" and plays an important role in the nation's labor relations system. In the absence of *Lincoln Mills* and the *Trilogy*, arbitration would not amount to much as the system for resolving contractual grievances arising under labor agreements. In almost every respect, employers and unions must understand that arbitration decisions are final and binding, not to be tampered with by the courts. They must also recognize that when they place arbitration in their contracts, it will be used to determine contractual disputes. Save for the exception noted in *Warrior & Gulf Navigation*, the federal courts will direct arbitration. No longer are the courts available to frustrate the arbitration process.

For arbitrators, the decisions are equally significant. Private arbitrators bear an even greater degree of responsibility as they decide their cases. Not only is the post one of honor, in which the parties have confidence in arbitrators' professional competency and integrity, but arbitrators must also recognize that their decisions are final and binding upon the parties. Indeed, if the system of private arbitration is to remain a permanent feature of the American system of industrial relations, arbitrators must measure up to their responsibilities. Should they fail, companies and unions may delete the arbitration clause from the contract and resolve their disputes by strikes or by going directly to the courts. These are not pleasant alternatives, but the parties may choose them if they believe arbitrators are not discharging their responsibilities in an honorable, judicious, and professional manner.

An example of lack of professional conduct of an arbitrator occurred when the arbitrator contacted a union representative after the hearing was concluded. He reinstated a discharged lead lineman, disclosing in his award that he had contacted a union official "to better reinforce my crane training experience, I have just made inquiry of an International Officer of the Operating Engineer's Union." He asked who was responsible for the operation and safety of the crane. The union official replied it was the crane operator.

When the employer brought suit to vacate the award, the federal appeals court held the arbitrator acted improperly, stating "arbitrators must meticulously refrain from such outside-the-record consultations if the arbitration process is to continue to be respected and used by labor and management."[60]

Although the court ruled the posthearing consultation did not taint the arbitrator's decision and did not deprive the employer of a fair hearing or influence the outcome of the case, the conduct of the arbitrator certainly raises doubt about the integrity of the arbitration process.

After the *Trilogy*

Several major cases dealing with arbitration were decided by the Supreme Court and federal appeals courts after the *Trilogy*. Some supported its basic purpose and philosophy, but others opened the door for court reversal of arbitration decisions.

In *Gateway Coal*,[61] a coal operator refused to suspend two supervisors who had failed to report the collapse of a ventilation structure that reduced the flow of air in the mine. The employees on all three shifts went out on strike, and the union refused to submit the suspension of the supervisors to arbitration in accordance with the National Bituminous Coal Wage Agreement. This agreement provided that "local disputes" will ultimately be settled by binding decision of an impartial arbitrator. It specifically provided arbitration for "any local trouble of any kind [arising] at the mine." Only matters of "national character" were excluded from the arbitration process by express contractual language. A federal district court ordered the union to stop the strike and to arbitrate the dispute. It also directed the employer to suspend the supervisors pending the arbitrator's decision. A court of appeals vacated the injunction, holding that the labor agreement might be construed as excepting safety matters from arbitration.

The Supreme Court reversed the appellate court and held that the arbitration clause covered safety issues. To support its decision, the court referred to *Warrior & Gulf Navigation*, and particularly the following statement contained in it:

> An order to arbitrate the particular grievances should not be denied unless it may be said with positive assurance that the arbitration clause is not susceptible to an interpretation that covers the asserted dispute. Doubts should be resolved in favor of coverage.

Since the arbitration clause in the coal agreement did not expressly exclude local safety matters from its coverage, the Court concluded in *Gateway Coal*:

> We think these remarks are as applicable to labor disputes touching the safety of the employees as to other varieties of disagreement. Certainly industrial strife may as easily result from unresolved controversies on safety matters as from those on other subjects.

Squarely involved in *Nolde Bros.*[62] was the right of a union to arbitrate a dispute after the labor agreement had expired and the employer had gone out of business. As a prerequisite for a strike over new contractual issues, the union terminated the existing labor agreement. Under that contract, there was a provision calling for severance pay upon termination of employment for all employees with three or more years of service. Four days after the strike started, the company closed the bakery permanently. The union then claimed severance pay for all eligible employees. Not only did the company refuse to pay severance benefits, but it also refused to arbitrate the dispute on the grounds that the labor agreement had expired. A federal appeals court held that there was nothing to arbitrate because the right of employees to severance pay ended when the contract was terminated.

In 1977, however, the U.S. Supreme Court ruled that the employer was obligated to arbitrate the issue even though the labor agreement had expired. Fundamental to the decision were two major reasons. In the first place, the high court pointed out that the right to severance pay accrued to employees under the expired labor agreement and was vested in them. In addition, it stated that there was nothing in the broad arbitration clause that expressly excluded from its coverage disputes arising under the contract but based upon events occurring after its termination. Thus, the Court stated that termination of a labor agreement does not automatically extinguish "a party's duty to arbitrate grievances arising under the contract." Any other holding, the Court stated,

> would permit the employer to cut off all arbitration of severance pay claims by terminating an existing contract simultaneously with closing business operations.

In short, the duty to arbitrate survives the termination of a contract when the dispute is over rights created under a labor agreement before it expired.

Fourteen years later in 1991, however, the high court limited the application of *Nolde* by a 5–4 vote. In fact the late Justice Thurgood Marshall filed a dissent stating the majority "turns *Nolde* on its head" and further was "not only unfaithful to precedent, but also it is inconsistent with sound labor law policy."

Litton Financial Printing, the employer, had a labor agreement with the Printing Specialties Union that contained a grievance procedure and final and binding arbitration for unsettled grievances. It expired in October 1979, and a new contract had not been negotiated by December 1980. At that time, without notice to the union, the company shut down its cold-type printing operation, dismissing permanently ten of its most senior employees. The union filed a grievance and, when the dispute was not settled, requested arbitration that was rejected by the employer.

When the issue was handled by the National Labor Relations Board, it ruled the employer had the legal obligation to bargain with the union but refused to direct arbitration on the grounds the dispute did not "arise under" the expired contract. The federal appeals court in San Francisco remanded the case to the Board which in effect directed the NLRB to order arbitration.

In June 1991, the U.S. Supreme Court held the dispute not arbitrable, refusing to direct the employer to arbitrate the layoffs of the senior employees.[63] According to the high court, *Nolde* did not apply because the current dispute did not involve "accrued or vested" rights under the expired contract. It said the layoffs occurred about a year after the expiration of the contract. That is, the laid-off employees had no vested seniority rights once the contract expired.

Not so, held the minority, stressing the laid-off employees had vested seniority rights under the expired contract. These rights survived the contract's expiration and continued undiluted throughout the years. As severance pay in *Nolde* prevailed under the expired contract so did seniority rights survive under the expired contract. However *Litton Financial Printing* may impact on labor relations, it certainly weakens considerably the Supreme Court's decision in *Nolde*.

In *W. R. Grace*,[64] the U.S. Supreme Court in a unanimous decision again upheld the integrity of the arbitration process. The employer entered into an agreement with the Equal Employment Opportunities Commission in which it promised to maintain in the plant the same proportion of women to men when layoffs occurred. When a layoff took place, pursuant to the EEOC agreement, the company laid off male employees who had greater seniority than the retained women. Under the labor agreement, strict seniority governed layoffs, and laid-off male employees filed grievances that were eventually upheld in arbitration. A federal court vacated the arbitrator's award on the grounds that the employer would violate its agreement with the EEOC should it lay off women employees by following the terms of the labor agreement and the arbitrator's award. While reversing the lower court, the high court said the arbitrator's award had to be followed regardless of its conflict with the EEOC agreement. Though the Court recognized the employer's dilemma—to follow the contract and arbitration award would result in the violation of the EEOC agreement, and to follow the EEOC agreement would result in violation of the labor agreement and arbitration award—it said the dilemma was of "its own making" *because the union had not been a party to the EEOC agreement*. If the union had been a party to the EEOC agreement, probably the employer could lawfully have laid off the senior male employees. While upholding the arbitrator's decision, the high court stated:

> Regardless of what this Court's view of the correctness might be of the arbitrator's contractual interpretation, [the parties] bargained for that interpretation, and a federal court may not second-guess it.

Refusal to Enforce Arbitration Awards

In other cases, however, the high court provided the basis for judicial review of arbitrators' decisions. These decisions were inconsistent with the *Trilogy*. In *Gardner-Denver*,[65] to be treated more fully in a later chapter, the Supreme Court held that an arbitrator's decision is not final and binding should Title VII of the Civil Rights Act be involved in a dispute. Though an arbitrator upheld the discharge of a black employee, the case was remanded to the district court to determine whether or not the employee's discharge was motivated by racial considerations. *Anchor Motor Freight*[66] established the principle that an arbitrator's decision is subject to reversal by a court when a union does not provide fair representation of employees involved in the arbitration. An employer discharged eight truck drivers for allegedly submitting inflated motel receipts for reimbursement. The drivers' union took the discharges to arbitration but failed to heed the employees' request to investigate the motel employees. After the arbitration, in which their discharges were sustained, evidence turned up that a motel clerk was originally the guilty party. He had been making false entries in the motel register and pocketing the difference.

Thereupon, the employees sued the employer and the union. A lower federal court upheld the arbitrator's award on the basis of *Enterprise Wheel & Car Corporation*. Consistent with this doctrine, the lower court held the arbitrator's decision to be immune to court reversal. However, the U.S. Supreme Court ruled that when a union fails to provide fair representation to employees involved in arbitration, the employees are entitled to an appropriate remedy. In its decision, the Court held that the remedy would be paid for by both the employer and the union. Thus, any back pay due the employees would be shared equally between them because the employer in error had discharged them in the first place and the union had failed to provide the employees fair representation in the arbitration.

The problem with *Anchor Motor Freight* is not that the employees involved should not receive a remedy. Obviously, they were not discharged for just cause. Elementary fairness should demonstrate that they be returned to their jobs with full back pay. Instead, the real problem is how far the courts will go in applying the doctrine. If employees who lose a case in arbitration discover some evidence that the union may have overlooked, will the arbitrator's award be subject to reversal? Probably in many cases a union may not have dug up every scrap of evidence that may have favored the employees. In other words, if the courts do not use restraint and caution in applying *Anchor Motor Freight*, the integrity and finality of the arbitration process could be threatened. Promiscuous use of the doctrine would make a mockery of the clause invariably contained in an arbitration provision: "The arbitrator's award shall be final and binding." Apparently the Supreme Court recognized this problem when it stated in *Anchor Motor Freight* that

> the grievance process cannot be expected to be error free. The finality provision has sufficient force to surmount occasional instances of mistakes.

The decision puts the unions on notice. In effect, the high court has said that the courts have the authority to upset an arbitration award when a union commits a gross error in the representation of employees in arbitration or when a union is dishonest or shows bad faith in the arbitration process. Not many unions engage in such reprehensible conduct, and probably *Anchor Motor Freight* will not provide the basis for wholesale reversal of arbitration decisions.

Following the *Gardner-Denver* precedent, the U.S. Supreme Court held that an arbitrator's decision involving rights established by the Fair Labor Standards Act may be reviewed and reversed by the federal courts.[67]

Three years later, in 1984, the high court once again determined that an employee's claim, based upon statutory rights, is not finally foreclosed by an arbitration award. In *McDonald* v. *City of West Branch, Michigan*,[68] a police officer, a union steward, was discharged for allegedly participating in a sexual assault on a minor. An arbitrator sustained the discharge, finding that McDonald was discharged for just cause. Asserting that his discharge was in reprisal for his activities as a union steward, the police officer sued in federal district court requesting that damages be assessed against the chief of police and other city officials. His suit alleged a violation of Section 1983 of the Civil Rights Act of 1871, claiming that his discharge violated his First Amendment rights of freedom of speech, association, and freedom to petition the government for redress of grievances. A federal district court permitted McDonald to proceed with his suit, and a jury eventually awarded him an $8,000 judgment against the police chief. On appeal by the city, however, a federal appeals court reversed the lower court's decision, finding that the First Amendment claim was an unwarranted attempt to litigate a matter already decided by the arbitrator.

In a unanimous decision, the U.S. Supreme Court reversed the federal appeals court, finding that arbitration was not the proper forum to address issues involving statutory and constitutional rights. Following its earlier decisions, the high court stated:

> . . . although arbitration is well suited to resolving contractual disputes, our decisions in *Barrentine* and *Gardner-Denver* compel the conclusion that it cannot provide an adequate substitute for a judicial proceeding in protecting the federal statutory and constitutional rights that sec. 1983 is designed to safeguard.

Arbitration Awards and Public Policy: *Misco, Inc.*

With respect to the integrity of arbitration awards as established by the *Trilogy*, there is the problem of their relationship to matters of public policy. The specific issue is whether or not arbitration awards should be vacated by the courts when they conflict with public policy. In *W. R. Grace*, previously discussed, the U.S. Supreme Court held that arbitration awards would not be enforced when they directly violate public policy, stating:

> If the contract as interpreted by [the arbitrator] violates some *explicit* public policy, we are obliged to refrain from enforcing it. . . . Such a public policy, however, must be *well defined* and *dominant*, and is to be *ascertained by reference to the laws and legal precedents* and not from general considerations of supposed public interests. (Emphasis supplied)

Using that pronouncement as the guideline, federal appeals courts have reversed arbitration decisions when they appeared to conflict with public policy. For example, in one case an arbitrator reinstated a truck driver despite the fact that he was discharged for consuming alcoholic beverages on the job.[69]

A federal appeals court held that the arbitrator's decision violated the public policy directed against people who drive when drinking. While vacating the arbitrator's decision, the court stated the public policy of preventing people from "drinking and driving is established in the case law, the applicable regulations, statutory law, and pure common sense."

Another federal appeals court vacated an award reinstating a postal worker who had been discharged for embezzling postal money orders.[70] The court reversed the award even though the arbitrator held the employee had not been terminated for just cause because of his intent to repay, his unusual financial problems, and a previously spotless disciplinary record. To justify its decision, the court cited several statutes relating to the conduct and honesty of postal employees, and it warned that the reinstatement of the employee would imply government condonation of dishonesty.

Additional cases could be cited to show reversal of arbitration awards based on public policy.[71] Indeed, the public policy exception to *Enterprise Wheel* was becoming the most widely used basis by federal courts to set aside arbitration decisions. Lurking in the wings, however, was a case involving Misco Corporation, a paper manufacturing firm located in Monroe, Louisiana. It had a labor agreement with United Paperworkers International Union. The labor agreement stated that management had the right to establish "rules and regulations regulating the discharge of employees [which were to stand] until ruled on by grievance and arbitration procedures as to fairness and necessity." One such rule, in effect for approximately ten years, prohibited intoxicants or controlled substances on plant property. Discharge was the stated penalty for its violation.

During the rest break on the midnight shift, three employees left the plant and went to the automobile owned by Isiah Cooper. It was located in the Misco parking lot. From there they went to another automobile, which was under police surveillance. Two of the men, not including Cooper, left the car. They had been sitting in the front seat and Cooper in the rear seat. He was arrested by the police when a lighted marijuana cigarette was found in the ashtray of the front seat.

Cooper, who operated a slitter-rewinder machine, was discharged for violation of the antidrug rule. Subsequently, an arbitrator reinstated the employee with full back pay, holding the evidence was not sufficient to prove Cooper had in fact been in possession of the marijuana cigarette. At the hearing, the company sought to introduce evidence, obtained several months after the incident, that the police in searching Cooper's car had found traces of marijuana in the dashboard compartment. The arbitrator ruled the evidence was inadmissible because it was not available to the company at the time of the discharge. It was not, therefore, a consideration in the decision to discharge the employee.

Misco filed suit in a federal district court seeking to vacate the award on the grounds, among others, that the reinstatement of the employee was contrary to public policy. The court agreed the award must be set aside as contrary to public policy because it ran counter to general safety concerns that arise from the operation of dangerous machinery while under the influence of drugs. The federal appeals court affirmed, finding also that reinstatement of Cooper would violate the public policy "against the operation of dangerous machinery by persons under the influence of drugs or alcohol."

The labor relations community, of course, awaited the U.S. Supreme Court's review of the case with great interest. At stake were two critical issues: the authority of federal courts to upset arbitration awards under *Enterprise Wheel*, and the circumstances under which the courts could do that on the basis of public policy. Somewhat surprisingly, on December 1, 1987, the high court, *unanimously* in *Misco*,[72] reversed the appeals court's decision. It said:

> The Court made clear almost 30 years ago that the courts play only a limited role when asked to review the decision of an arbitrator. The courts are not authorized to reconsider the merits of an award even though the parties may allege that the award rests on errors of fact or on misinterpretation of the contract.

And further:

> . . . as long as the arbitrator is even arguably construing or applying the contract and acting within the scope of his authority, that a court is convinced he committed serious error does not suffice to overturn his decision. Of course, decisions procured by the parties through fraud or through the arbitrator's dishonesty need not be enforced. But there is nothing of that sort involved in this case.

Nor was the arbitrator's award flawed because he refused to consider the marijuana traces discovered in the employee's automobile. Evidentiary matters are the concern of the arbitrator and not the courts.

Particularly, the high court came down hard on the appeals court's use of public policy to upset the arbitration award. As it did in *W. R. Grace*, previously mentioned, the Supreme Court agreed that arbitrators' awards may be set aside when they conflict with public policy. However, it sharply limited the circumstances when this would be done. Awards may be set aside when they violate "some explicit public policy" that is "well defined and dominant and is to be ascertained by reference to the laws and legal precedent and not from general considerations of supposed public policy." In other words, judges may not use their subjective judgment of what public policy is or should be.

On this basis, the Supreme Court criticized the lower court because it made no attempt to review existing laws and legal precedents in order to demonstrate that they establish a "well defined and dominant policy against the operation of dangerous machinery while under the influence of drugs." The high court agreed that such a judgment is "firmly rooted in common sense," but that is not sufficient to vacate arbitration awards.

Post-*Misco* Developments

Obviously, *Misco* constituted a great victory for the arbitration process. Since the decision was unanimous, the Supreme Court in effect told the lower federal courts, "Look, we meant what we said in the *Trilogy*. You are not to upset arbitration awards just because you don't like the decisions."

Even so, it is up to the lower federal courts to apply the *Trilogy* as reinforced by *Misco*. Not every case can practically be appealed to the Supreme Court.

After the 1987 decision, a federal appeals court found the *Misco* standards for public policy reversal were satisfied in vacating an arbitrator's award. An arbitrator reinstated an employee who was discharged for not properly tightening the lugs on a motor vehicle wheel.[73] It based its public policy reversal on the safety requirements of the California Vehicle Code and the statute creating the California Bureau of Automotive Repair. In a 1988 case, an arbitrator reinstated an airline pilot discharged because he flew a passenger-filled commercial aircraft while intoxicated. A blood test confirmed the presence of alcohol in his system. A federal appeals court reversed the arbitrator's award on the grounds that public policy as expressed through state laws, federal regulations, and case precedent prohibits the operation of commercial aircraft while intoxicated.[74]

On the other hand, a federal appeals court upheld an arbitrator's award reinstating a letter carrier who fired gunshots into his supervisor's unoccupied vehicle. A district court vacated the award, finding a violation of public policy against permitting an employee to direct physical violence at a supervisor, and ruling the arbitrator misconstrued the "just cause" standard for discharge contained in the labor agreement. Reversing the lower court's decision, the appeals court sternly criticized the district judge for "second guessing" the arbitrator's evidentiary conclusions and construction of the contract. It held further that the lower court failed to comply with public policy standards contained in *Misco*.[75]

In sum, aside from judicial reversal resulting from arbitrators' conduct, under current case law, arbitration awards may be reversed when a union fails to provide fair representation to employees involved in arbitration; when statutory or constitutional guarantees are involved; and when arbitration decisions conflict with public policy. Though these exceptions to the *Trilogy* are, of course, significant, it is not a situation where exceptions make a rule meaningless. In the final analysis, the *Trilogy* as reinforced by *Misco* stands as an effective barrier against promiscuous tampering with the arbitration process by the judiciary.

Reversal of Arbitrator Decisions: *Stroehmann Bakeries*

In the 1990s, however, some federal appeals courts reversed arbitration decisions. Most were vacated because they were judged in violation of public policy as the following discloses.

In *Stroehmann Bakeries*, a male delivery driver was discharged when he allegedly violated a company rule prohibiting immoral conduct on the job. During the driver's night delivery of goods to one of the bakery's regular supermarket customers, he allegedly sexually harassed the customer's female night clerk. On the day of the incident, she told two of the driver's supervisors that he had talked to her about sexual matters, tried to pull up her skirt, and grabbed her breasts. She was alone in the store during the night of the incident.

The next day during an interview with the supervisors, the driver denied the allegations and explained "he loved his wife and would not consider jeopardizing his job." At that time, he had worked for the company for seventeen years. After the session the employee was suspended and five days later discharged. Between the time of the suspension and dismissal, Stroehmann made no effort to investigate the case further or attempt to develop its factual setting.

An arbitrator reinstated the driver to his job with full back pay and contractual rights. The labor agreement specified discipline may be given employees only for just cause. The gravamen of the arbitrator's decision was that the driver was not discharged for just cause, because the employer did not make a proper and adequate investigation prior to discharge. Resting his decision on that basis, the arbitrator expressly refused to make a determination whether sexual harassment had occurred.

Upholding the decision of a federal district court, a federal appeals court reversed the arbitrator's decision on the grounds it violated public policy against sexual harassment in the workplace.[76] To support its decision, the court identified Title 7 of the Civil Rights Act of 1964, forbidding employment discrimination on the basis of sex; the U.S. Supreme Court decision in *Meritor Savings Bank*, in which the high court held employers may be held liable for sexual harassment in the workplace under the Civil Rights Act;[77] and documented the definition of sexual harassment by reference to regulations issued by the Equal Employment Opportunities Commission. On this basis the federal appeals court stated the laws establish "a well defined, dominant public policy against sexual harassment in the workplace."

Even if all of this is true, the court's decision in *Stroehmann Bakeries* does not comport with the *Trilogy* as reinforced by *Misco*. True, the arbitrator based his decision on a procedural issue, and not the merits of the case. As the Supreme Court ruled, however, in *John Wiley & Sons* " . . . procedural questions which grow out of the dispute and bear on his final disposition should be left to the arbitrator."[78] No question exists that Stroehmann did not conduct a proper investigation. It amounted to a telephone conversation with the female night clerk, not even a face-to-face interview. The employer did not afford the driver the opportunity to prepare a defense before he was interviewed by supervision. As a matter of fact the company violated its own rules of procedure. In cases of discharge, its policy stated:

> when an immediate action is necessary, supervisors should suspend violators with the intent to dismiss. *This will allow higher management to investigate and collect the facts before a final and official dismissal is declared.* (Emphasis supplied by arbitrator)

Nothing in the record of the case demonstrates this was done.

A cardinal and venerable rule of the arbitration process is that before discharge, employers must make a proper and adequate investigation. This principle has been underscored countless times by scores of professional arbitrators. In short, it was the judgment of the arbitrator in *Stroehmann Bakeries* that the driver was not discharged for just cause. He held the company did not conduct a proper investigation prior to discharge. The arbitrator found no need to determine whether the driver committed sexual harassment against the female clerk. Clearly the federal appeals court substituted its judgment for that of the arbitrator. Under *Trilogy* and *Misco*, it improperly invaded the exclusive authority and the jurisdiction of the arbitrator.

As *Roszkowski and Waland* put it:

> . . . as the Supreme Court has made clear only the arbitrator's interpretation of the contract has legal effect. It is the arbitrator's interpretation for which the parties bargain, and that is the interpretation that is binding on the review court. The Third Circuit Court of Appeals substituted its own construction of the contract for that of the arbitrator.[79]

In another sexual harassment case, no question exists that the discharged male abused a female employee including fondling and patting her buttocks. Although the arbitrator found such conduct clearly "harassment, abusive, and intimidating," he reinstated the employee, apparently without back pay and with a stern warning that any similar behavior would be grounds for immediate discharge. A federal appeals court reversed the decision, because it conflicted with a well-defined public policy against sexual harassment in the workplace.[80]

Although one may quarrel with the wisdom of the arbitrator's decision, the bottom line is that the judiciary may not reverse just because the court finds it to be unwise, or even downright wrong. As the high court said in *Misco*, the courts do not have the authority to upset an arbitrator's award that even rests on "errors of fact or on misinterpretation of the contract."

Drug and Alcohol Reversals

In drug and alcohol cases, federal courts have reversed arbitrators' decisions asserting that they were in conflict with a well-defined and dominant public policy forbidding their use on the job. One instance involved the Railway Labor Act governing labor relations on the railroads and airlines. A railroad employee was discharged because he allegedly was under the influence of alcohol while working. An arbitration panel reinstated the employee asserting his due process rights under the contract were violated by the employer. It did not consider whether the employee was actually under the influence of alcohol. A federal appeals court reversed the arbitrator's decision.[81]

In a very important case where public policy and drugs were *not* involved, a federal appeals court reversed an arbitrator's decision, asserting the arbitrator exceeded his power under the contract. An economic strike occurred and the employer replaced its employees with permanent replacements. As will be explained in the next chapter, employers may lawfully hire replacements to take over the regular employees' jobs during an economic strike. When this takes place, regular employees lose their jobs.

In the case at hand, the union asserted the regular employees, though permanently replaced, should not have been discharged because the employer had the obligation to warn the employees they were risking their jobs by going out on strike. An arbitrator agreed with the union stating "the fundamental right of due process" barred employers from hiring permanent replacements without warning the strikers that they were jeopardizing their jobs. He directed that the discharged employees, about thirty-four, be reinstated in their jobs.

In its reversal of the arbitrator's decision, the federal appeals court ruled that the arbitrator exceeded his authority. It stated that the decision was not based on the expressed or properly implied terms of the contract but rather was improperly based upon "the arbitrator's notion of industrial justice." Rejecting the union's contention that the arbitrator's award was within the bounds of the collective bargaining contract, the court stated that while courts often defer to arbitration decisions, "this deferential standard of review . . . does not amount to a grant of unlimited power to the arbitrator." It further charged the arbitrator with using his "subjective notions of a fair contract."[82]

Despite these reversals it would not be accurate at this time to conclude the lower federal courts have not been faithful to their obligations under the *Trilogy* and *Misco*. Many more arbitration decisions have been enforced than reversed. As one writer put it: "For every case setting aside awards there are twice as many enforcing them. There are even some cases enforcing awards that the court agrees are irrational."[83]

It was unduly alarming for David Feller to state:

> The important conclusion I want to draw now is that there is reason no longer to celebrate the Steelworkers *Trilogy*. The distinction between labor arbitration and commercial arbitration has ceased to have any significance. The two are now the same when the question is whether to compel arbitration. When the issue is enforcement of arbitrators' decisions already made, labor arbitration is disfavored as compared to commercial arbitration.[84]

By any standard there is an overwhelmingly better chance of enforcement by the judiciary since *Misco* and *Trilogy* than before these decisions dramatically changed the courts' response to the arbitration process.

NORRIS–LA GUARDIA AND NO-STRIKE CONTRACT PROVISIONS

Injunctions and Wildcat Strikes

Lincoln Mills and *Trilogy* established a *quid pro quo* approach to the enforcement of agreements. This was thought to have meant that an agreement to arbitrate disputes was entered into in exchange for a union agreement not to strike for the duration of the contract. These cases implied that the no-strike provision of labor contracts was subject to the same rules and treatment as any other contractual provision.[85] Previously, as explained under *Lincoln Mills*, the employer must arbitrate when a labor agreement makes arbitration the final step in a grievance procedure. The question arose as to whether Section 301 of Taft-Hartley would also apply to a union that had struck in violation of a no-strike clause instead of using arbitration to seek relief from an alleged employer violation of a contract.

In 1962, the Supreme Court decided *Sinclair*, which involved a suit for breach of a no-strike clause.[86] The high court refused to enjoin a wildcat strike engaged in by workers during a contractual period, despite the fact that the labor agreement contained no-strike and arbitration clauses. The union could have submitted the grievances that caused the strike to arbitration instead of striking. In its decision, the Court reasoned that it could not issue an injunction to stamp out the strike on the grounds that it was forbidden to do so under the Norris–La Guardia Act. Section 301 of Taft-Hartley had not repealed the Norris–La Guardia Act of 1932. Therefore, the law discriminated against employers, since they had to arbitrate unresolved grievances, whereas a union could bypass arbitration and strike, free from fear that the courts would issue an injunction to stop the strike. It should be recognized, however, that most labor organizations would not strike over grievances rather than making use of the arbitration process.

In *Sinclair*, the high court pointed out that *Congress did not make wildcat strikes an unfair labor practice when it established Taft-Hartley*. Probably Congress believed that it was not necessary to do so, since such activity would be deterred by providing the employer the right to sue unions for damages under Section 301. Since such strikes are not an unfair labor practice, and since the Court held that they constitute a "labor dispute" within the meaning of Norris–La Guardia, it held that the federal courts were not authorized to issue an injunction to stop wildcat strikes. It rejected the employer's argument that an injunction under these circumstances would be compatible with Section 301 and would make that provision meaningful. To say the least, employers were very unhappy with the *Sinclair* decision.

The decision left intact the employer's right to sue unions for damages under Section 301 when a strike in violation of a no-strike provision took place. Also, the company could discharge workers who participated in such strikes, provided it did so without discrimination. However, employers believed that such remedies were not viable, since they would be implemented after the fact. Indeed, as a condition for ending a wildcat strike, unions frequently insisted that employers drop their suits and restore the employees to their jobs.[87] As a practical matter, some employers did so to restore production as quickly as possible. In short, what the employers desired was a legal remedy that would quickly terminate a wildcat strike. Such a remedy could be achieved only through the injunction.

Sinclair Reversed by *Boys Markets*

In any event, unions generally remained in a favored position because they could refuse to honor their no-strike agreements without fear of court enjoinment of their actions. The Supreme Court, in *Sinclair*, had interpreted the use of injunctions in such cases to constitute a violation of Section 4 of the Norris–La Guardia Act. Yet three courses of possible action might provide employers with relief. The first involved a Supreme Court determination of state court authority to issue injunctions. The second involved congressional clarification of the issue. Congress could merely state that arbitration enforcement in the federal courts under federal law was not subject to the equity limitations of the Norris–La Guardia Act. The third approach depended upon the desire of unions and management to avoid industrial warfare. Collective bargaining agreements could have been constructed in a fashion that would subject both parties equally to the equity power of the courts. However, all these issues became moot in the light of the Supreme Court's decision in *Boys Markets* v. *Retail Clerks*.[88] On June 1, 1970, by a 5–2 vote, the Court reversed *Sinclair Refining* and held that employers could obtain injunctions from the federal courts to stop strikes in violation of a no-strike clause. The Supreme Court stated that *Sinclair Refining* was "a significant departure from our otherwise consistent emphasis upon the Congressional policy to promote the peaceful settlement of labor disputes through arbitration."

Though the 1970 decision may be defended on the grounds that employees and unions should not strike to settle their grievances when arbitration is available, the decision was nevertheless sharply criticized because Congress had not changed the

1962 policy, although many bills were introduced in Congress to nullify *Sinclair Refining*. As the *Wall Street Journal* observed on June 5, 1970:

> As a matter of fact such legislation was introduced, but Congress so far has not seen fit to act. Congressional action, of course, would have been much the better way. However desirable the result, the Supreme Court still should restrain itself from assuming the tasks that properly belong to the legislators.

Thus, the basis of the criticism of *Boys Markets* was the change in Supreme Court policy after an eight-year period during which Congress had not seen fit to reverse the *Sinclair Refining* doctrine. Black, writing the minority opinion, stated:

> Nothing at all has changed, in fact, except the membership of the Court and the personal view of one justice.

Nixon's first appointee to the Court, Warren Burger, was Chief Justice at the time of *Boys Markets*, and Stewart was the Justice who changed his mind.

The Court has now provided employers with a potent weapon to stop strikes that violate no-strike agreements. Though objective data indicating the frequency of *Boys Markets* injunctions are not available, it is safe to say that employers have used them on a widespread basis to terminate wildcat strikes. When the decision was announced, there was speculation that unions would refuse to agree to no-strike and arbitration clauses to avoid injunctions. Unless there are no-strike and arbitration clauses in a labor agreement, an employer may not obtain an injunction. These speculations were not realized. There is no evidence that contracts now contain fewer no-strike and arbitration clauses than they did before *Boys Markets*.

Refusal to Issue Injunctions

Despite the advantage that employers receive from *Boys Markets*, federal courts have refused to issue injunctions under certain conditions. Before an injunction will be issued, the court must be satisfied that the issue is arbitrable under the labor agreement and that the employer will proceed to arbitration.[89] A federal appeals court refused to sustain an injunction issued by a district court because the employer refused to concede that certain work assignments were arbitrable under the labor agreement. Also, an injunction will not be issued when a strike took place before the parties agreed to a contract containing no-strike and arbitration clauses. In one case, the negotiating parties had agreed on economic terms, but not on the arbitration clause. By the time of the negotiations, the previous labor agreement containing an arbitration procedure had expired.[90] No injunction was issued. In another case, when an employer could not show that the wildcat strike was causing the company irreparable harm, a court refused to issue an injunction.[91] In a case involving safety in a coal mine, a federal court refused to issue an injunction because the employer did not comply with a contractual provision requiring the company to follow the recommendations of a safety committee to correct an imminently dangerous condition.[92] In this dispute, the court distinguished its circumstances from *Gateway Coal*.

Buffalo Forge Limitation

In 1976, the U.S. Supreme Court placed a significant limitation on the employer's right to a *Boys Markets* injunction. In *Buffalo Forge*,[93] the same union represented the production workers and the office employees of the employer. The dispute arose when a strike occurred during the negotiation of the office employees' first labor agreement. Four days later, the production workers struck in sympathy with the office workers. The production workers' contract contained no-strike and arbitration provisions. The employer applied for an injunction after making it clear that it was willing to arbitrate the dispute under the production workers' arbitration clause.

Affirming lower federal courts' decisions, the U.S. Supreme Court by a vote of 5–4 held that a *Boys Markets* injunction was not proper. At the heart of the majority decision was the finding that the production workers' arbitration provision did not cover sympathy strikes. That is, the production workers' strike was not over a grievance which arose under their contract. Instead, the strike was undertaken to show sympathy with the office employees. Such an event, the majority held,

> was not *over* any dispute between the union and employer that was even remotely subject to the arbitration provisions of the contract.

To put it in other terms, the sympathy strike was not over an arbitrable issue under the production workers' contract. They had agreed only to arbitrate grievances which arose under the contract. They had not agreed to arbitrate the right to engage in sympathy strikes.

In a sharp dissent, the minority argued that the no-strike provision of the production workers' contract should be enforced by an injunction, without regard to whether the cause of the strike was subject to arbitration. In other words, the no-strike clause should be honored and subject to an injunction independent from the reason for the strike. While rejecting this argument, the majority stressed that the Court's decision in *Boys Markets* made a narrow and single exception to the prohibition of injunctions under the Norris–La Guardia Act. The exception is that a union shall not strike over an issue which is covered by a contract's arbitration provision. Otherwise, said the majority, any strike could be enjoined by a court.

Buffalo Forge marks an important restriction in the application of *Boys Markets*, serving to encourage unions to engage in sympathy strikes even if their contracts contain no-strike and arbitration provisions. Employers could defend against such conduct to the extent that they are successful in broadening the language of no-strike and arbitration provisions to cover sympathy strikes.

The Soviet Union's intervention in Afghanistan provided the background for the U.S. Supreme Court dealing with *Boys Markets* injunctions. After President Carter ordered trade restrictions, members of the Longshoremen's Union refused to handle cargo destined for or coming from the USSR. Harmed by the union's action, an employer requested a *Boys Markets* injunction and a judicial order directing the union to arbitrate the issue of whether the work stoppage violated the no-strike provisions of the labor agreement.

Although the high court recognized that the union's action was politically motivated, it held that an injunction could not be issued under the terms of the Norris–La Guardia Act because the work stoppage constituted a "labor dispute" within the meaning of the statute.[94] Nor could the employer obtain a *Boys Markets* injunction, because the issue that had caused the work stoppage was not arbitrable under the labor agreement. It was not arbitrable, the Court held, whether the work stoppage was regarded as protest of Soviet military policy or as expression of sympathy with the people of Afghanistan. Thus, as in *Buffalo Forge*, the U.S. Supreme Court held that a *Boys Markets* injunction may not be issued by the federal courts unless the issue giving rise to a work stoppage is arbitrable under the terms of a labor agreement.

In sum, though a *Boys Markets* injunction will not be issued under some circumstances, this should not detract from the importance of the doctrine. In the absence of some comparatively infrequent circumstances, employers may obtain an injunction to stamp out a strike that violates a no-strike provision. At times exceptions to a rule erase the viability of the rule. This has surely not been the case with respect to the *Boys Markets* injunction.

SYMPATHY STRIKES

Character of Controversy

A sympathy strike occurs when members of one union honor the picket line maintained by a different union at the site of the employer involved in a labor dispute. This activity is a manifestation of the solidarity that is supposed to knit together the different elements of the labor movement. The problem becomes complex because no-strike provisions are contained within virtually every labor agreement. Normally, employers and unions negotiate broad all-inclusive no-strike clauses forbidding the union and its members to engage in any strike or interruption of production during the effective period of a labor agreement. A typical broad no-strike clause was found in *Indianapolis Power* (discussed below):

> the Company and Union agree that during the term of this agreement neither the Union nor its agents nor its members will authorize or instigate any strike or picketing, sit-down, stay-in, slow-down, or the curtailment of work or interference with the operation of the Company's business.

In this light, the issue is whether an employer may discipline employees who refuse to cross a picket line to perform work at the company directly involved in the labor dispute. Employers contend they have this right because these employees violate the no-strike clause.

On the other hand, employees under Section 7 of Taft-Hartley have the right to strike and engage in "other concerted activities for the purpose of collective bargaining or other mutual aid and protection." The NLRB has consistently held Section 7 of the statute, standing by itself without the complication of a no-strike clause, guarantees employees the right to refuse to cross a lawful picket line.[95] On this basis, unions claim employers violate the protected rights of employees should they be disciplined when they engage in a sympathy strike. Not to be undone, employers assert a broad no-strike clause waives the employees' right to engage in such an activity.

Given the conflicting positions, the NLRB was required to determine the legality of sympathy strikes under Taft-Hartley. *It had to establish the circumstances in which a no-strike clause waives the right of employees to engage in such strikes.* If a no-strike clause does not constitute a waiver, sympathy strikes are lawful and employers would be forbidden to discipline employees who exercise their right and engage in such strikes. Where no-strike clauses constitute a waiver, sympathy strikes would not be a protected activity and employers would be free to discipline them.

Original Policy: *Davis-McKee*

In 1978 the NLRB originally addressed the issue in *Davis-McKee*, a case involving a construction company by that name. Some Davis-McKee employees refused to cross the picket line established at the site of another employer and to perform their assigned jobs. Davis-McKee disciplined the employees on the grounds that they violated the broad no-strike provision contained in the labor agreement.[96]

Holding the employer's action was unlawful, the NLRB ruled a no-strike clause does not forbid sympathy strikes unless the provision expressly contains the words "sympathy strikes," or unless extrinsic evidence independently establishes the parties' intent to forbid such strikes. Extrinsic evidence would include the bargaining history of the parties, and past practice relating to whether the employer previously disciplined employees who engaged in sympathy strikes. Since the no-strike clause did not expressly refer to sympathy strikes and since the evidence in the case did not demonstrate the parties' intent to ban them, the employer unlawfully disciplined the employees who engaged in the sympathy strike.

In other words, the NLRB held a broad no-strike clause standing by itself is not a "clear and unmistakable waiver" of the right of employees to engage in sympathy strikes.

Reversal of Policy: *Indianapolis Power I*

With the advent of the Reagan NLRB, the agency in 1985 reversed *Davis-McKee* in *Indianapolis Power Company I*.[97] In a complete change in policy, it held that a broad no-strike clause includes sympathy strikes unless extrinsic evidence indicated the parties *did not* intend it to cover that kind of strike. Unless the record in a case demonstrates such intent, a broad no-strike provision constitutes a waiver of the employees' right to engage in a sympathy strike.

An employee of the power company refused to cross the picket line maintained by another union. He was supposed to read an electric meter on the premises of the company's customer. Claiming the employee violated the no-strike clause, the employer suspended and threatened to discharge the employee.

While sustaining the employer's position, the NLRB held it shall read no-strike clauses

> plainly and literally as prohibiting all strikes including sympathy strikes. If, however, the contract or other extrinsic evidence demonstrates that the parties intended to exempt sympathy strikes, we shall give the parties' intent weight.

Remand by Federal Appeals Court: *Indianapolis Power Company II*

In 1986, a federal appeals court remanded *Indianapolis Power* to the NLRB for consideration of evidence it did not address in its initial decision.[98] Remand was directed because the agency failed to consider compelling evidence that related to the parties' intent when they adopted the no-strike provision, and their practice over the succeeding years as to whether or not the clause included sympathy strikes. Inexplicably the Reagan Board failed to do the very thing it said it must do to apply a no-strike clause: look at the parties' intent establishing whether the clause covers sympathy strikes.

On remand in *Indianapolis Power Company II*, freed from the domination by Reagan initial Board members, the NLRB found extrinsic evidence demonstrating that the parties disagreed whether a provision covered sympathy strikes.[99] Since the union consistently insisted such strikes fell outside the provision's coverage and the employer consistently insisted the provision prohibits sympathy strikes, the NLRB found the parties in reality "agreed to disagree" over the sympathy strike issue. Given that situation, the Board held the union did not "clearly and unmistakably waive the right of employees to engage in sympathy strikes." Accordingly the agency held the employer violated employees' legal right to engage in such activity by suspending and threatening to discharge.

Although they exonerated the disciplined employee, neither the federal appeals court nor the NLRB in *Indianapolis Power II* upset the policy that a broad no-strike clause covered sympathy strikes. In fact, the appeals court said: "Were we faced only with the language of the agreement itself, we would find little trouble upholding the Board's [Indianapolis Power I] order." In its decision, *[Indianapolis Power II]*, the NLRB stated: "To summarize we continue to believe that a broad no-strike clause should probably be read to encompass sympathy strikes."

Understand also that the federal appeals court expressly rejected the union's position based on *Davis-McKee*. It refused to endorse the proposition that a broad no-strike clause does not forbid sympathy strikes unless extrinsic evidence demonstrates the parties' intent to ban them. Under current law, therefore, a broad no-strike clause forbids sympathy strikes unless extrinsic evidence demonstrates the parties' intent that they are not covered. In the absence of such evidence, a broad no-strike provision constitutes a waiver of the employees' right to engage in sympathy strikes.

Aftermath of *Indianapolis Power II*

Following *Indianapolis Power II*, the NLRB reversed other decisions in which it originally held employees could be disciplined for participating in sympathy strikes. The reversals were based on the agency's consideration of extrinsic evidence demonstrating the parties did not intend that the no-strike clause cover sympathy strikes.

Either bargaining history or past practice demonstrated such an intent under the provision.

In *Arizona Public Service*, for example, the Board reversed an earlier decision that sustained suspensions of eight employees who honored the picket line of another union. Evidence disclosed the company recognized there was no agreement with the union that the no-strike clause covered sympathy strikes because it had unsuccessfully proposed the provision be amended to specifically and expressly include such strikes. Also, the employer did not discipline employees who in the past had engaged in sympathy strikes. Such evidence, the NLRB held, demonstrated the parties did not intend that the no-strike provision cover sympathy strikes.[100]

In another case a union threatened its members with fines if they refused to respect the picket line of another union. Originally, the Board held such action unlawful under the federal law because the contract contained a broad no-strike clause.

Reversing that decision, the NLRB held in *Food and Commercial Workers Union Local 1439, (Rosauer's Supermarkets)* that the bargaining history indicated the no-strike provision was not intended to ban such strikes. Reversing the original decision, the Board ruled the union did not unlawfully threaten its members with discipline for refusing to exercise that right.[101]

Private Arbitration

Private arbitrators have used *Indianapolis Power II* in the cases involving the discipline of employees who engage in sympathy strikes. Instead of filing unfair labor practice charges with the NLRB, some unions resort to arbitration in an attempt to nullify such discipline.

One of the authors handled *GTE North, Indiana*, a case involving a midwest public utility and the Communication Workers of America, (CWA).[102] During a strike between GTE North, Michigan, and the International Brotherhood of Electrical Workers, the employer used its Indiana management personnel to replace strikers in Michigan. In retaliation the IBEW stationed picket lines at the GTE reporting centers in Indiana, requesting the employees not to perform their jobs. Many CWA members honored the picket line and refused to work. As a result GTE North, Indiana, sent these employees disciplinary letters charging them with violation of the broad no-strike clause contained in the labor agreement between GTE North, Indiana and the CWA.

While reversing the employer's action, finding the letters to be null and void, the arbitrator in part relied on *Indianapolis Power II*. Extrinsic evidence demonstrated the parties did not intend that the no-strike clause be used to ban sympathy strikes. The evidence demonstrated the employer had twice unsuccessfully tried to include sympathy strikes within the no-strike provision. Although employees had engaged in many sympathy strikes in the previous sixteen years, the company up to the instant dispute never inflicted any kind of discipline on such employees. In short, the bargaining history of the parties and past practice demonstrated they did not intend to forbid sympathy strikes under the no-strike provision.

In light of the record, the arbitrator observed:

> Based on the evidence we find that the no-strike provision in the labor agreement does not prohibit sympathy strikes. This conclusion is consistent with the National Labor Relations Board decision in *Indianapolis Power II.* Indeed based upon the evidence, a contrary decision would be repugnant to the policy established by the National Labor Relations Act as administered by the NLRB and the federal appeals courts.

ADDITIONAL PROBLEMS OF CONTRACT ENFORCEMENT

Metropolitan Edison: Discipline of Union Officers

To deal with unauthorized or wildcat strikes in violation of a no-strike clause, some employers impose stiffer penalties on local union officers, including stewards and grievance committee members, compared with rank-and-file employees who commit the same offense. Disparate discipline is justified because union officials have a greater obligation to comply with and enforce the no-strike clause. In *Metropolitan Edison*, however, the U.S. Supreme Court held that *employers may not impose more severe discipline on union officials who commit the same offense as rank-and-file em-ployees.*[103] If both, for example, instigate a wildcat strike, engage in picketing, or encourage other employees to join the strike, an employer may not discharge the union officials while only suspending the rank-and-file employees. Should a management desire to penalize union officials more severely, it must negotiate a contract provision that specifically authorizes disparate treatment by placing special obligations on the union officials. It is not likely, however, that many unions would agree to such a contractual provision.

Nonetheless, following *Metropolitan Edison*, a U.S. Chamber of Commerce representative stated:

> It is quite likely that employers are going to put some responsibility back where it belongs—on the union stewards and even higher up. Employers will insist during contract talks that the duty of union leaders be spelled out.[104]

No evidence exists that clauses of that kind have been negotiated in collective bargaining. Thus, the decision tends to make it more difficult for employers to enforce no-strike clauses. Obviously, the NLRB has no choice except to follow the high court's policy on this issue. In one case, an arbitrator sustained the discharge of a union steward because the steward failed to end a wildcat strike. However, the NLRB refused to defer to the award because of its conflict with the Supreme Court's decision.[105] Reversing the arbitrator's decision, the NLRB pointed out that the steward had no contractual duty to end unlawful strikes.

Dual Jurisdiction of Arbitrators and NLRB

Despite the existence of no-strike and arbitration clauses in a labor contract, there are situations in which an arbitrator's award might not put an end to a dispute. There is a possibility that some cases may be relitigated before the NLRB if one party is disappointed with the award. These are cases in which Taft-Hartley issues are either directly or indirectly involved. For example, a union may prefer to use arbitration rather than the NLRB in cases that involve Taft-Hartley matters. But under certain circumstances, the NLRB will hear the case if a union loses the arbitration award. Thus, the union could get two chances to win its case. However, with certain important exceptions to be noted below, the NLRB as a matter of general policy defers to arbitration for the resolution of conflicts.[106]

Recall that under the *Collyer* doctrine, treated in the previous chapter, an unfair labor practice is filed, but the NLRB instructs the parties to proceed to arbitration. Under certain circumstances, we learned that the Board might elect to upset the arbitrator's award and find that an unfair labor practice was committed. At this time, we are concerned with an arbitration undertaken by the parties *before* unfair labor practices are filed. The issue here is a determination of NLRB policies, as to whether it will subsequently honor the arbitrator's award, or upset it and find that unfair labor practices have been committed.

The U.S. Supreme Court has extended considerable prestige to the voluntary arbitration process through *Lincoln Mills* and the *Trilogy*, as demonstrated previously. In these cases, the Court recognized that Congress intended that "privately agreed-upon methods of settlement should be favored, the attempt being to restrict administrative supervision of bargaining as much as possible."[107] However, the NLRB may not honor an arbitrator's award if Taft-Hartley unfair labor practices are involved in the case.[108] Thus, the *Trilogy* doctrine will not preserve an arbitrator's decision if it does not conform with Taft-Hartley and its construction by the NLRB.

Taft-Hartley granted the NLRB wide authority to deal with employer-employee relations. One federal court of appeals ruled that the NLRB has exclusive power over unfair labor practices and this authority "shall not be affected by any other means of adjustment or prevention that has been or may be established by agreement, law or otherwise."[109] The power of the Board in the context of existing law is greater than that of any other body in establishing employer and union regulations.[110] Indeed, when the NLRB takes a case after it has been arbitrated, it does so because statutory law is superior to a private labor agreement. In other words, Taft-Hartley takes precedence over any labor agreement, so that unions, employees, and employers do not forfeit any statutory rights under labor agreements. Therefore, the NLRB under certain circumstances will void an arbitrator's award if it finds that the arbitrator deprived someone of rights guaranteed by statute.

As in the *Collyer*-type case, the determination of whether or not the NLRB will defer to an arbitration award issued prior to the filing of unfair labor practice charges depends upon the application of the *Spielberg* standards.[111] To repeat, the NLRB will defer to an arbitration decision where the proceedings appear fair and regular; the parties are in agreement to be bound by the arbitration award; the decision is not clearly repugnant to the purpose and policies of the law; and, as the Reagan Board held—weakening considerably the previous policy—where the contractual issue is factually parallel to the unfair labor practice issue, and if the arbitrator was generally presented with the facts relevant to resolving the unfair labor practice.

Arbitrators must take due care in rendering decisions. Not only are they subject to review by the courts, but by the NLRB as well. Both the courts and the NLRB attempt to give wide latitude to the process that provides a peaceful solution to labor disputes with a minimum of public interference. However, failure of an arbitrator to conform to Board guidelines could result in the reversal of the decision.

In any event, the NLRB has been criticized for its willingness to review cases that have been arbitrated. It is argued that such a policy undermines arbitration and is in conflict with stable labor relations. Indeed, from time to time, professional arbitrators have complained about the NLRB because it will review cases. Actually, like many other issues in labor law, there are two sides to the picture. On the one hand, there is some doubt that a party who has elected to arbitrate instead of going to the NLRB in the first place should be permitted to use the Board to upset an unfavorable arbitration award. The argument is that the party should not get two opportunities to win the same case. On the other hand, the fact is that statutory law takes precedence over private labor agreements. Therefore, the NLRB has the duty to reverse an arbitrator's award when that award deprives an employee, employer, or union of rights guaranteed by Taft-Hartley. Probably there is no satisfactory solution to the problem, and the accommodation between the NLRB and arbitration will have to be resolved on a case-by-case basis.

BARGAINING OBLIGATION
OF SUCCESSOR EMPLOYER

Recognition and the Labor Agreement

In 1970, the NLRB issued a decision that required a successor employer to honor the collective bargaining agreement signed by the predecessor employer.[112] Lockheed Aircraft received security services from Wackenhut. The United Plant Guard Workers had prevailed in a Board-held election and was certified as bargaining agent for Wackenhut employees. A collective bargaining agreement was signed, but four months later, Lockheed awarded the Burns International Detective Agency the contract to provide security services. It was apprised of the collective bargaining relationship Wackenhut had with the United Plant Guard Workers. Burns employed forty-two men on the Lockheed job, of whom twenty-seven had previously worked for Wackenhut. Burns had a bargaining contract with a different union with an accretion clause that was applied to workers on the Lockheed job. Charges were filed against Burns because it did not recognize the United Plant Guard Workers and honor the Wackenhut contract.

In reaching its decision in the *Burns* case, the Board relied on the Supreme Court decision in *John Wiley and Sons* v. *Livingston.*[113] In *Wiley*, a small unionized company was merged into a larger nonunion organization. The union brought a Section 301 suit against the surviving firm to compel arbitration under the terms of agreement with the predecessor. The Supreme Court ordered arbitration, which left the question of applicability of other provisions of the labor contract to the surviving company. In *Burns*, the Board relied on *Wiley* to hold that Burns was obligated under Section 8(a)(5) to honor the Wackenhut agreements. The Board reasoned that a collective bargaining agreement is not an ordinary contract but is a generalized code binding on successors who continue essentially the same enterprise.

Burns appealed the case. The court of appeals upheld the Board on the order to recognize the union but refused to enforce that part of the order requiring Burns to honor the labor contract of the predecessor.[114] The Supreme Court affirmed the appellate court decision.[115] The high court reasoned:

> A potential employer may be willing to take over a moribund business only if he can make changes in corporate structure, composition of the labor force, work, location, task assignment, and nature of supervision. Saddling such an employer with the terms and conditions of employment contained in the old [labor] contract may make these changes impossible and may discourage and inhibit the transfer of capital.

Thus, Burns *tells us the successor employer must recognize the union, but it has no obligation to accept the labor agreement negotiated with the previous employer.*

In 1987, the U.S. Supreme Court sustained the NLRB's application of *Burns,* making it more difficult for companies that acquire the assets of another company to avoid bargaining with incumbent unions.[116] An unprofitable textile firm went out of business. For thirty years, the United Textile Workers had represented its employees. Seven months later, a vice-president of the closed plant and the firm's largest customer acquired the firm and opened for business as the Fall River Dyeing and Finishing Corporation. It hired a majority of the former firm's employees. The dispute arose when the new company refused to bargain with the union. It claimed the seven-month hiatus between employers broke the continuity of the employer-union relationship.

Not so, said the high court, ruling the new company was the successor employer, and ordered it to bargain with the union. It held that there was a substantial continuity between the old company's demise and the new company's start-up. Justifying its decision, the Supreme Court stressed that the successor employer was formed for the express purpose of acquiring its predecessor's assets and taking advantage of that work force. Thus, the employees operated the same jobs, assigned to the same machines in the same production process under many of the same supervisors.

Additional Successor Employer Policies

Burns did not resolve several issues that arose after the decision. Other questions required determination. For a successor employer to have an obligation to recognize the union, the company must continue the same product lines, departmental organization, employee identity, and job functions.[117] So if the new employer changes the business structure in a genuine and fundamental way, the company need not recognize the union. *Also, recognition would depend upon the majority status of the union.* Should the new employer hire a majority of the workers employed by the former owner, the successor employer must recognize the union. A successor employer may raise a good-faith doubt concerning the majority status of the union. However, it must present objective evidence to show that the union no longer represents a majority of the employees. In a 1985 case of this type, a successor employer voluntarily recognized the union and met with it in contract negotiation sessions.[118] Before a subsequently scheduled session, the employer received a petition signed by a majority of the employees stating they no longer desired union representation. At this point, the employer ceased recognizing the union and withdrew from bargaining. Under these circumstances, the NLRB held that the employer's conduct was lawful even though no one had verified the signatures on the petition. The Board held that the petition constituted a sufficient basis to support a good-faith doubt as to the union's majority status.

Also *Burns* did not resolve the issue of when a successor employer can unilaterally institute changes in working conditions. In one case, a union had never been certified by the Board but had won an election supervised by the mayor of the town fourteen years prior to the change of employers. It had a one-year contract with the predecessor employer that was based on an automatic renewal provision.[119] The successor employer refused either to accept the contract in existence or to negotiate a new one. An unfair labor practice was filed by the union. The Board ordered the successor employer to honor the old contract and to recognize and bargain with the union.

A court of appeals overruled the Board order to honor the old contract but did require the successor employer to bargain. It also determined the issue of when a successor employer loses the right to make unilateral decisions. *This right is lost at the moment it becomes clear that most of the predecessor's employees will retain their jobs, and if the nature of the business remains unchanged.* The court reasoned that although there was no obligation to honor the old contract, the employer was not free to make unilateral changes until the two sides had bargained to impasse. If a new employer intends to retain most of the previous employer's workers, the company cannot avoid an obligation to bargain about initial working conditions merely by making employment dependent upon acceptance of unilateral conditions.[120] If a company plans to take most of the employees, bargaining with the incumbent is required before employment conditions are fixed. For example, a former employer paid "year-end bonuses" to employees. Though the benefit was not contained in the labor agreement, it was paid as a matter of practice and was based upon the employees' sales. Therefore, the payment was not really a "bonus," but more realistically a regular portion of the employees' wages. After the successor employer purchased the establishment, the company discontinued the payment without negotiations with the union. A federal appeals court sustained the Board's decision, which held that the successor employer could not end the payment before bargaining with the union.[121]

In June 1974, unions lost some ground in the successor employer controversy. At that time, in *Howard Johnson* v. *Hotel and Restaurant Employees*, the U.S. Supreme Court held that a successor employer did not have the obligation to arbitrate the refusal to hire employees of the seller's work force. In this case, the new employer discharged all supervisors and hired only a small number of the employees who had worked for the former employer.[122] On the other hand, in 1980, unions registered a significant victory. For many years, the Board and courts have held that when a new employer purchases a firm that owes back pay to employees for unfair labor practices, the successor employer becomes responsible for the payment.[123] The U.S. Supreme Court sustained this doctrine.[124] In *International Technical Products*[125] the original employer who owed back pay for committing an unfair labor practice went bankrupt. A bankruptcy court's order permitted the successor employer to purchase the firm "free and clear of all liens, claims, and encumbrances." Based upon these circumstances, the new employer refused to pay the back pay. Rejecting the new employer's position, the Board directed payment on the grounds that its orders may not be modified or eliminated by a bankruptcy court.

SUMMARY

Taft-Hartley established the legal right of unions to negotiate and enforce labor agreements. They could sue employers for compliance but at the same time be sued by employers for violations of labor agreements.

Given the statutory right to represent all employees in a bargaining unit, unions have the corollary duty of fair representation. Unions that fail to perform this duty face NLRB and court proceedings. Case law establishes the circumstances under which unions have failed to carry out this duty.

Lincoln Mills, Trilogy, and *Misco* brought substantial prestige and viability to the arbitration process. In their absence, private arbitration would not play an important role within the nation's labor relations system. Except for limited circumstances, federal courts may not upset arbitration awards.

Reversing *Sinclair,* the Supreme Court in *Boys Markets* held that federal courts may issue an injunction terminating a strike in violation of a no-strike clause. The decision occasioned some surprise because Congress did not act to nullify *Sinclair. Boys Markets* clarifies the complex situation that developed as a result of the courts' attempts to accommodate the Norris–La Guardia Act to violations of union agreements not to strike during the term of a labor agreement. Though congressional action would have been the better method to abolish *Sinclair,* the result of *Boys Markets* is to provide employers with an effective method of making sure that unions will abide by their no-strike pledge when arbitration is available for the final settlement of contract disputes.

The NLRB has jurisdiction over unfair labor practices, and at times this opens the possibility for relitigating an arbitration case if a party is dissatisfied with the award. The Board attempts to accommodate the arbitration process. In so doing, it defers to arbitration if the *Spielberg* standards are not violated.

In the matter of the successor employer, the U.S. Supreme Court's decision in *Burns Detective Agency* still stands. It establishes the legal principle, but the NLRB and courts must deal with the problems on a case-by-case basis. What with the current wave of mergers and voluntary or leveraged buyouts, the successor employer issue takes on added importance in the labor relations legal environment.

DISCUSSION QUESTIONS

1. In what way did a federal appeals court, in the *North American* case, influence the NLRB's Wagner Act policy concerning the right of an individual employee to present grievances directly to an employer? How did Taft-Hartley deal with the same issue?

2. Provide examples of a union's duty of fair representation. What remedies are available to employees when they feel that the duty of fair representation has been breached?

3. How have the Board and the courts treated the common-law doctrine of agency in relation to labor unions? Why does this doctrine work a hardship on labor organizations?

4. What is the primary significance of the *Lincoln Mills* case? In what ways did the *Trilogy* cases amplify the *Lincoln Mills* decision? How have these cases affected the institution of arbitration?

5. Despite the *Trilogy*, under what circumstances have the courts refused to uphold a private arbitrator's decision?

6. Discuss the courts' treatment of arbitration in relation to public policy.

7. Discuss the legal reasoning behind the *Sinclair* and *Boys Markets* decisions. How does *Buffalo Forge* affect the latter?

8. Evaluate the relative impact that the *Metropolitan Edison* decision may possibly have on the collective bargaining process.

9. Under what circumstances does the Board apply the *Spielberg* standards? Does it have flexibility in those applications?

10. Under what circumstances might a successor employer have an obligation to a predecessor's collective bargaining agreement?

NOTES

1   Section 9.

2   Section 9(a).

3   *North American Aviation Company*, 44 NLRB 604 (1942).

4   *NLRB v. North American Aviation Company*, 136 F. 2d 898 (9th Cir. 1943).

5   *Hughes Tool Company*, 56 NLRB 981 (1944).

6   *Douglas Aircraft Company*, 25 War Labor Reports 57 (1944).

7   Section 9(a).

8   *Lakeland Bus Lines, Inc. v. NLRB*, 278 F. 2d 888 (3d Cir. 1960).

9   *U.S. Postal Service*, 281 NLRB 1013 (1986).

10   *Miranda Fuel Company*, 140 NLRB 181 (1962).

11   *Hughes Tool Company*, 147 NLRB 1573 (1964).

12   Reference is made here to Section 8(b)(3) of Taft-Hartley, which says that a labor organization or its agent commits an unfair labor practice by refusing "to bargain collectively with an employer, provided it is the representative of his employees subject to the provisions of Section 9(a)."

13   *Sargent Electric Co.*, 209 NLRB 630 (1974).

14   *Kesner v. NLRB*, 532 F. 2d 1169 (7th Cir. 1976).

15   *General Motors Corp. Delco Moraine Div.*, 237 NLRB 1509 (1978).

16   *Retail Clerks, Local 324, FED Mart Stores, Inc.*, 261 NLRB 1086 (1982).

17   *Warehouse Union, Local 860, IBT (The Emporium)*, 236 NLRB 844 (1978).

18   *International Association of Machinists & Aerospace Workers, Local Union 697 (H. O. Canfield Rubber Co. of Va.)*, 233 NLRB 832 (1976).

19   *Branch 6000, Natl. Assn. of Letter Carriers* v. *NLRB*, 595 F. 2d 808 (D.C. Cir. 1979).

20   *Cargo Handlers, Inc.*, 159 NLRB 321 (1966).

21   *Miranda Fuel Co.*, 140 NLRB 181 (1962).

22   *International Union of Electrical Workers, Local 485 (Automotive Plating Corp.)*, 170 NLRB 1234 (1968).

23   *San Francisco Web Pressmen and Platemakers' No. 4, San Francisco Newspaper Agency*, 272 NLRB 899 (1984).

24   *United Steelworkers of America, Local Union 2610, (Bethlehem Steel)*, 225 NLRB 310 (1976).

25   *General Truck Drivers, Chauffeurs & Helpers Union, Local 692, IBT (Great Western Unifreight System)*, 209 NLRB 446 (1974).

26   National Labor Relations Board, Office of the General Counsel, *Memorandum 79–55*, July 9, 1979.

27   *Humphrey* v. *Moore*, 375 U.S. 335 (1964).

28   *Breininger* v. *Sheet Metal Workers, Local 6*, 110 S. Ct. 424 (1989).

29   *Vaca* v. *Sipes*, 386 U.S. 171 (1967).

30   *Ford Motor Company* v. *Huffman*, 345 U.S. 330 (1953).

31   *Thompson* v. *BHD of Sleeping Car Porters*, 367 F. 2d 489 (4th Cir. 1966).

32   *Clayton* v. *Automobile Workers*, 451 U.S. 679 (1981).

33   *Bowen* v. *United States Postal Service*, 459 U.S. 212 (1983).

34   *AFL-CIO News*, January 15, 1983.

35   *Del Costello* v. *Teamsters*, 462 U.S. 151 (1983).

36   *Electrical Workers* v. *Foust*, 442 U.S. 42 (1979).

37   *Kolinske* v. *Lubbers*, 712 F. 2d 471 (D.C. Cir. 1983).

38   *Hoffman* v. *Lonza*, 658 F. 2d 519 (7th Cir. 1981).

39   *Freeman* v. *Teamsters, Local 135*, 746 F. 2d 1316 (5th Cir. 1984).

40   *Velez* v. *Puerto Rico Marine Management, Inc.*, 957 F. 2d 933 (1992).

41   *Bennett* v. *Local Union No. 66, Glass, Molders, Pottery, Plastics and Allied Workers International Union*, 958 F. 2d 1429 (1992).

42   *Walker* v. *Consolidated Freightways, Inc.*, 930 F. 2d 376 (1991).

43   *Air Line Pilots Association* v. *O'Neill*, 111 S. Ct. 1127 (1991).

44   Section 301.

45   National Association of Manufacturers, *That New Labor Law*, p. 21.

46   International Association of Machinists, *The Truth About the Taft-Hartley Law and Its Consequences to the Labor Movement*, April 1948, p. 26.

47   *Sinclair Oil Corporation* v. *Oil, Chemical and Atomic Workers*, 452 F. 2d 49 (7th Cir. 1971).

48   *Atkinson* v. *Sinclair Refining Company*, 370 U.S. 238 (1962).

49   *Complete Auto Transit, Inc.* v. *Reis*, 451 U.S. 401 (1981).

50   Section 8(d).

51   *Carbon Fuel* v. *United Mine Workers of America*, 444 U.S. 212 (1979).

52   *Groves* v. *Ring Screw Works*, 111 S. Ct. 498 (1990).

53   *Textile Workers Union of America* v. *Lincoln Mills of Alabama*, 353 U.S. 448 (1957).

54   *United Steelworkers of America* v. *American Manufacturing Company*, 363 U.S. 564 (1960); *United Steelworkers of America* v. *Warrior & Gulf Navigation Company*, 363 U.S. 574 (1960); *United Steelworkers of America* v. *Enterprise Wheel & Car Corporation*, 363 U.S. 593 (1960).

55   For other examples of such limiting language, see *To Protect Management Rights* (Washington, D.C.: U.S. Chamber of Commerce, 1961), pp. 7–22.

56   *AT&T Technologies* v. *Communications Workers*, 475 U.S. 643 (1986).

57   *Berklee College of Music* v. *Teachers, Local 4412*, 858 F. 2d 31 (1st Cir. 1988).

58   *Toyota of Berkley* v. *Automobile Salesman's Union, Local 1095*, 834 F. 2d 751 (9th Cir. 1987).

59   *George A. Hormel & Co.* v. *Food and Commercial Workers, Local 9*, 879 F. 2d 347 (8th Cir. 1989).

60   *M & A Electric Power Cooperative* v. *Local Union No. 702, International Brotherhood of Electrical Workers, AFL-CIO*, 977 F. 2d 1235 (1992).

61   *Gateway Coal Co.* v. *United Mine Workers*, 414 U.S. 368 (1974).

62   *Nolde Bros., Inc.* v. *Bakery & Confectionery Workers, Local 358*, 430 U.S. 243 (1977).

63   *Litton Financial Printing Division* v. *NLRB*, 111 S. Ct. 2215 (1991).

64   *W. R. Grace* v. *Rubber Workers, Local 759*, 461 U.S. 757 (1983).

65   *Alexander* v. *Gardner-Denver*, 415 U.S. 36 (1974).

66   *Hines* v. *Anchor Motor Freight*, 424 U.S. 554 (1976).

67   *Barrentine* v. *Arkansas-Best Freight System, Inc.*, 450 U.S. 728 (1981).

68   466 U.S. 284 (1984).

69   *Amalgamated Meat Cutters & Butchers, Local 540* v. *Great Western Food Co.*, 712 F. 2d 122 (5th Cir. 1983).

70   *U.S. Postal Service* v. *Postal Workers Union*, 736 F. 2d 822 (1st Cir. 1984).

71   *Devine* v. *White*, 697 F. 2d 421 (D.C. Cir. 1983).

72   *United Paperworkers International Union* v. *Misco, Inc.*, 108 S. Ct. 364 (1987).

73   *Stead Motors* v. *Automotive Machinists Lodge 1173*, 843 F. 2d 357 (9th Cir. 1988).

74   *Delta Airlines, Inc.* v. *Airline Pilots Assn.*, 861 F. 2d 665 (11th Cir. 1988).

75   *U.S. Postal Service* v. *National Association of Letter Carriers*, 839 F. 2d 146 (3d Cir. 1988).

76   *Stroehmann Bakeries, Inc.* v. *Local 776, International Brotherhood of Teamsters*, 969 F. 2d 1436 (1992).

77   *Meritor Savings Bank* v. *Vinson*, 447 U.S. 57 (1986).

78   *John Wiley & Sons* v. *Livingston*, 376 U.S. 543 (1964).

79   Christy Roszkowski and Robert Waland, "Arbitration Review: Is Public Policy Against Sexual Harassment Sufficient Cause For Vacating An Arbitration Award?" *Labor Law Journal*, November 1993, p. 707.

80   *Newsday, Inc.* v. *Long Island Typographical Union No. 915*, 915 F. 2d 840 (1990).

81   *Union Pacific Railroad Company* v. *United Transportation Union*, 3 F. 3d 255 (1993).

82   *Harry Huffman* v. *Graphic Communications Union Local 261*, 950 F. 2d 95 (1991).

83   David E. Feller, "End of the Trilogy: The Declining State of Labor Arbitration," *Arbitration Journal*, American Arbitration Association, September 1993, p. 22.

84   *Ibid*, p. 23.

85   Thomas J. McDermott, "Enforcing No-Strike Provisions Via Arbitration," *Labor Law Journal*, XVIII, 10 (October 1967), pp. 579–587.

86   *Sinclair Refining Company* v. *Atkinson*, 370 U.S. 195 (1962).

87   McDermott, "Enforcing No-Strike Provisions Via Arbitration," *op. cit.*, p. 2.

88   398 U.S. 235 (1970).

89   *Parade Publications Inc.* v. *Philadelphia Mailers Union No. 14*, 459 F. 2d 369 (3d Cir. 1972).

90   *Emery Air Freight Corp.* v. *Teamsters, Local 295*, 449 F. 2d 586 (2d Cir. 1971).

91   *Ciba-Geigy Corp.* v. *Local 2468, Textile Workers*, 391 F. Supp. 287 (1975).

92   *Jones & Laughlin Steel Corp.* v. *Mine Workers*, 519 F. 2d 1155 (3d Cir. 1975).

93   *Buffalo Forge* v. *United Steelworkers*, 428 U.S. 397 (1976).

94   *Jacksonville Bulk Terminals* v. *Longshoremen*, 457 U.S. 702 (1982).

95   National Labor Relations Board, *Fifty-first Annual Report*, 1986, p. 161

96   *International Union of Operating Engineers, Local Union 18, AFL-CIO*, 238 NLRB 652 (1978).

97   *Indianapolis Power & Light Company I*, 273 NLRB 1715 (1985).

98   *Local Union 1395, International Brotherhood of Electrical Workers, AFL-CIO* v. *NLRB*, 797 F. 2d 1027 (1986).

99   *Indianapolis Power Company II*, 298 NLRB 145 (1988).

100   *Arizona Public Service*, 292 NLRB 144 (1988).

101   *United Food and Commercial Workers Union, Local No. 1439*, (*Rosauer's Supermarkets*), 293 NLRB 26 (1989).

102   *GTE North (Indiana)*, Bureau of National Affairs, *Labor Arbitration Reports*, 1990, vol. 94, p. 1033.

103   *Metropolitan Edison Co.* v. *NLRB*, 460 U.S. 693 (1983).

104   *Wall Street Journal*, April 5, 1983.

105   *John Morrell & Co.*, 270 NLRB 1 (1984).

106   Jay W. Waks, "The Dual Jurisdiction Problem in Labor Arbitration: A Research Report," *The Arbitration Journal*, XXIII, 4 (1968), p. 227.

107   Richard I. Bloch, "The NLRB and Arbitration: Is the Board's Expanding Jurisdiction Justified?" *Labor Law Journal*, XIX, 10 (October 1968), p. 646.

108   *NLRB* v. *Acme Industrial Company*, 385 U.S. 432 (1967).

109   *NLRB* v. *Walt Disney Productions*, 146 F. 2d 44 (9th Cir. 1945).

110   *Shoreline Enterprises* v. *NLRB*, 262 F. 2d 933 (5th Cir. 1959).

111   *Spielberg Manufacturing Company*, 112 NLRB 1080 (1955).

112   *William J. Burns International Detective Agency*, 182 NLRB 348 (1970).

113   376 U.S. 543 (1964).

114   *NLRB* v. *Burns International Detective Agency*, 441 F. 2d 911 (2d Cir. 1971).

115   406 U.S. 272 (1972).

116   *Fall River Dyeing and Finishing Corp.* v. *NLRB*, 482 U.S. 27 (1987).

117   Robert E. Wachs, "Successorship: The Consequences of Burns," *Labor Law Journal*, XXIV, 4 (April 1973), p. 223.

118   *Harley-Davidson Transportation Co., Inc.*, 273 NLRB 1531 (1985).

119   *NLRB* v. *Bachrodt Chevrolet Company*, 468 F. 2d 963 (7th Cir. 1972).

120   *Howard Johnson Company*, 198 NLRB 763 (1972).

121   *NLRB* v. *Pepsi-Cola Distributing Co.*, 646 F. 2d 1173 (6th Cir. 1981).

122   417 U.S. 249 (1974).

123   *Perma Vinyl Corporation*, 164 NLRB 968 (1967).

124   *Golden State Bottling Company, Inc.* v. *NLRB*, 414 U.S. 168 (1973).

125   249 NLRB 1301 (1980).

8

Strikes, Lockouts, and Picketing

Recapitulation

In Chapter 1, we learned that courts frequently limited the right of labor organizations to strike. Judges ruled that certain strikes, such as those for union security, were unlawful. The injunction was the vehicle whereby strikes were stamped out when deemed unlawful. The social and economic predilections of judges provided the basis for the injunction. No action of the legislative branch of government branded these strikes as unlawful. Nevertheless, the judiciary determined the legality of strikes. As the Massachusetts Supreme Court once put it:

> Whether the purpose for which a strike is instituted is or is not a legal justification for it is a question of law to be decided by the court. To justify interference with the right of others the strikers must in good faith strike for a purpose which the court decides to be a legal justification for such interference.[1]

Organized labor protested against a policy that permitted the courts to exercise such power in labor disputes. Union leaders charged that the government via the courts sided with management in labor disputes. They claimed that the indiscriminate use of the labor injunction made it difficult—and at times impossible—for workers to obtain economic concessions from employers.

The legislative branch afforded relief to the nation's labor unions. This was accomplished by stripping the courts of their power to enjoin strikes. In short, judges lost their power to decide whether or not the purposes of strikes were lawful. Peacefully conducted strikes, regardless of objective, were immunized from the injunction. Such a public policy was established by Norris–La Guardia and by a number of state anti-injunction laws. Not only did the federal anti-injunction law protect strikes from the injunction, but it also largely relieved labor unions from prosecution under the antitrust laws. The Wagner Act added still more protection for labor's right to strike, outlawing a variety of strikebreaking practices engaged in from time to time by anti-union employers.

Thus Norris–La Guardia and the Wagner Act protected the right of employees to strike. After World War II, the legal status of the strike underwent a change. A number of states and the federal government regulated and outlawed certain types of strikes. Once again, labor was forbidden to engage in strikes calculated to gain certain objectives. *This time, however, it was the legislative branch of government and not the judiciary that was responsible for the limitations on the exercise of the strike.*

Our task in this chapter is to analyze Taft-Hartley and Landrum-Griffin changes regulating strike activity. How is this limitation accomplished? What enforcement techniques are provided in strike-control legislation? How do these laws affect the operation of collective bargaining? What forms of strikes are completely outlawed? Do these strike-control laws protect the basic interests of the public?

VOTING RIGHTS OF REPLACED ECONOMIC STRIKERS

The Taft-Hartley Act denied replaced economic strikers the right to vote in representation elections. Workers hired to replace economic strikers could vote, but economic strikers for whom the employer had found replacements were not eligible to cast ballots. Such a condition was established in a very short sentence in the law: "Employees on strike who are not entitled to reinstatement shall not be eligible to vote."[2] Organized labor immediately claimed that this fifteen-word phrase threatened the success of every economic strike. More important, union leaders charged that this policy of Taft-Hartley endangered the security of the entire union movement by providing employers with a potent antiunion weapon. In contrast, some people asserted that workers on an economic strike replaced by other employees had severed their employment relationship by the mere act of not reporting to work. Consequently, it was contended, these workers no longer had an interest in the outcome of representation elections.

Economic versus Unfair Labor Practice Strikes

So that the significance of the voting policy of Taft-Hartley may be fully understood, it is first necessary to distinguish between *economic strikes* and *unfair labor practice strikes*. Falling into the economic-strike category are strikes for higher wages, shorter hours, better working conditions, health and welfare plans, and so on. In contrast, an unfair labor practice strike is a work stoppage caused by employer tactics declared unlawful by national labor relations policy. In this classification fall such strikes as those concerning union recognition, discrimination against union members, refusal to bargain collectively, and interference by the employer with the right of workers to organize and bargain collectively. If members of a local union strike because some of their officers are discharged for union activity, they would not be classified as economic strikers. Such a strike falls within the unfair labor practice category. It results from employer action declared unlawful under national law. The strike would not have occurred if the employer had not engaged in an unfair labor practice.

Reinstatement Rights of Strikers

Reinstatement rights of strikers differ depending upon the cause of the strike. Employees engaging in an unfair labor practice strike have the unlimited right to reinstatement. This means that the NLRB has full authority to order the reinstatement of workers, including back pay awards, when this category of strike occurs. Such strikers will be reinstated whether or not the employer replaced them with other workers. An employer must rehire these strikers even though their reinstatement results in the discharge of workers hired to take their jobs.

Indeed, in *Mastro Plastics* the U.S. Supreme Court held that employees are entitled to reinstatement even when they strike in violation of a no-strike clause in a labor agreement, *if they strike because of employer unfair labor practices*.[3] In this case, the Court, while upholding the NLRB, held that there is an

> inherent inequity in any interpretation that penalizes one party to a contract for conduct induced solely by the unlawful conduct of the other, thus giving advantage to the wrongdoer.

In the absence of such a policy, the employer unfair labor practice section of national law would be rendered meaningless. Assume that employers would not be required to rehire unfair labor practice strikers. Now suppose an employer refuses to bargain collectively with a majority union. A strike results. During the course of the strike, the employer permanently replaces the strikers with other workers. Under these conditions, a strike resulting from employer noncompliance with national labor policy could have the effect of eliminating unions. It appears therefore as a matter of industrial justice that unfair labor practice strikers have the unlimited right to reinstatement. However, workers out on strike are generally not entitled to reinstatement when they engage in violence or coercive misconduct. In such a case, it does not matter if an employer had committed unfair labor practices that either caused or prolonged the strike.[4]

As a matter of fact, resulting from a 1983 U.S. Supreme Court decision, employers are placed in a more vulnerable position should they commit unfair labor practices during a strike. In the *Belknap* v. *Hale* case,[5] following an impasse in contract negotiations, the employees struck. At this point, the strike was for economic reasons and the employer hired replacements, assuring them their jobs were permanent. However, during the strike, the employer committed an unfair labor practice by granting a wage increase for nonstriking employees. In a settlement of the strike and the unfair labor practice charge, approved by the NLRB, the employer agreed to reinstate the strikers and lay off the replacements. Asserting a breach of contract and misrepresentation, the "permanent" replacements sued the employer for a total of $6 million damages in state court. The high court held that such suits could properly be adjudicated in state court. Under these circumstances, said the Court, federal preemption did not apply because

> we cannot believe that Congress determined that the employer must be free to deceive by promising permanent employment, knowing that [the employer] may choose to reinstate strikers or may be forced to do so by [the National Labor Relations Board].

Among the implications of this decision is that it will probably be more difficult to settle strikes calling for the reinstatement of the strikers and the discharge of the replacement strikebreakers.

PERMANENT REPLACEMENT OF ECONOMIC STRIKERS

In contrast with unfair labor practice strikers, employees who engage in economic strikes enjoy only a limited right to reinstatement. The NLRB will order their immediate reinstatement *only when the employer does not fill their jobs with permanent replacements.* In the event that economic strikers have been permanently replaced, the NLRB has no authority to direct their reinstatement. Hence, permanently replaced economic strikers have no absolute legal right to reinstatement.

This policy was established by the U.S. Supreme Court under the Wagner Act. In *NLRB* v. *Mackay Radio & Telegraph* (1938),[6] the high court held that employers may not discharge employees who engage in a strike. It reached that decision because employees under the Wagner Act, and later Taft-Hartley, have the fundamental right to engage in strikes. At the same time, however, the Supreme Court held in *Mackay* that *employers may permanently replace the regular employees with strikebreakers.* Whether fired or replaced, employees lose their jobs.

In 1986, the high court reaffirmed that the use of permanent replacements is lawful employer conduct. The Court held that the employer under federal law has no obligation to fire permanent replacements and restore the regular employees to their jobs. More will be said about this case later on in this chapter.[7]

The controversy surrounding the issue is bitter and little chance for compromise appears available. Unions argue permanent replacement of economic strikers impairs their ability to carry out successful strikes. Integrity of the labor movement is at stake when faced with such employer conduct. Likewise the labor movement contends the practice undermines the collective bargaining process. When an employer is determined to use permanent replacements, it will not compromise at the bargaining table and thereby encourage workers to strike. In other words, unions say the strike, the traditional weapon of labor, has ironically been converted to an employer weapon used to destroy unions and lower living standards.

With as much vigor, employers contend forbidding the use of permanent replacements would encourage strikes. Since strikers would be assured of their jobs once the strike is over, regardless of the winner or loser, unions and their members would be more likely to engage in a strike. The employer community also argues the use of permanent replacements advances business capability to compete in a global markets. Fearful of being replaced, workers would be less inclined to strike and would be willing to accept a cheap contract. Pure and simple, argue employers, that to deprive them of the opportunity to use permanent replacements gives unions too much power to the detriment of the employers, employees, and the nation.

It should be said, however, that between 1938, the year of *McKay Radio & Telegraph*, until 1981 when Reagan permanently replaced over 11,000 air traffic controllers, employers rarely replaced economic strikers. And the dire consequences predicted by those who support the current law did not take place. What might soften the controversy would be objective studies showing the effect of permanent replacements on workers, employers, unions, communities, and the nation. So far studies of this kind have been very rare; most have been anecdotal emotional opinions presented within the context of self-interest. One of the very few serious and academic studies of the problem caused John Schnell and Cynthia Gramm to conclude: "Our investigation of the relationship between strike duration and employers' permanent replacement strategy provides evidence that such tactics are associated with longer strikes than occur in their absence."[8]

In recent years, employers have frequently used their right to replace economic strikers to weaken or destroy unions, or at least to obtain significant concessions at the bargaining table. This has been done by nationally recognized firms such as Eastern Airlines, Trans World Airlines, Greyhound Buslines, Magic Chef, Colt Firearms, Phelps Dodge, International Paper, the *Chicago Tribune,* the *New York Daily News*, Diamond Walnut, and Caterpillar. They used as their model Reagan's destruction of the Professional Air Traffic Controllers Organization. In the Caterpillar situation, the threat of the use of permanent replacements broke the UAW strike which lasted about five months. Fearful of losing their jobs, the employees returned to work under conditions of employment imposed by Caterpillar. The General Accounting Office reported permanent replacements were hired in about one-third of all strikes in the two years it studied, 1985 and 1989.[9]

In only one nationally reported instance did a union and its members successfully overcome the use of permanent replacements. This strike involved the Ravenswood Aluminum Corporation, located in West Virginia, and Local 5668, United Steelworkers of America. After a nineteen-month bitter lockout, 1,700 workers returned to work under an agreement which called for the return of the regular employees and the discharge of the replacements. A three-year contract was negotiated that contained very favorable terms for the bargaining unit.[10] At 9:00 A.M., June 29, 1992, the regular employees reported to work; the 1,200 replacements had left the plant at 7:00 A.M. on the same day. It was purposely arranged this way so that "they don't see us [union people] and we don't see them".[11] One reason for the union's success was an international campaign to boycott Ravenswood Aluminum.

Legislative Action

Given the widespread use of permanent replacements, the labor movement sponsored legislation to deal with the situation. At its core would be the prohibition against the use of permanent replacements during strikes, limiting the employer to the use of temporary replacements. After the strike, the regular employees would be reinstated, and the temporary replacements terminated. An effort was made in 1992 to enact such legislation. A bill passed the House of Representatives by a substantial majority, but it was not sufficient to overcome Bush's promise to veto the legislation. In 1993 a new campaign was undertaken, given President Clinton's promise to sign the law if it passed. (During the campaign he had marched with the UAW pickets at the Peoria, Illinois, Caterpillar plant.)

Called the Work Place Fairness Act, it was passed by the House 239–190 on June 15, 1993. On July 13, 1994, the bill's supporters lacked seven votes to stop the filibuster which killed the legislation. This had been forecast by the then Senate Minority Leader Robert Dole. In January 1994, speaking to a group of strikers permanently replaced about twenty-eight months previously by Diamond Walnut, Dole told them that he was not blocking the bill from coming to a vote, but he would filibuster should it come to the floor of the Senate. "The rules have been there a long time," said Dole, "I don't make the rules."[12] The fair question is why should a minority block public policy endorsed by the majority?

To fill the gap created by the failure of Congress to outlaw the use of permanent replacements, the state of Minnesota and the City of New York enacted measures to make the practice illegal within their jurisdictions. Given the doctrine of federal preemption, both efforts did not stand the test of judicial review. In regard to the Minnesota statute, a federal district court ruled federal law permits an employer to hire permanent replacements during an economic strike. Since the state law forbade action permitted under the federal law, the Minnesota statute was unconstitutional.[13]

The City of New York prohibited employers from hiring strikebreakers to replace workers on strike. In defense of its action Greyhound Buslines argued it was not hiring strikebreakers, but rather it was hiring replacement workers. Accepting the employer's position, the New York Supreme Court held the city ordinance invaded an area preempted by the federal government.[14]

National Labor Relations Board Decisions

Over the years the NLRB has applied the employers' right to hire permanent replacements under the circumstances in particular cases. In some, the agency found in favor of the strikers and in others held for the employers. A few examples from each side demonstrate the proposition.

When an employer sent a letter to striking employees threatening to disregard their right of reinstatement to job vacancies after replacement employees departed, the Board held the employer had unlawfully coerced the strikers in the exercise of their protected right to engage in union activities. Strikers have reinstatement rights should their jobs, or positions substantially equivalent to their jobs, become vacant should replacements quit, retire, or be discharged. Because of the employer's violation, the agency ordered the reinstatement of the strikers.[15] When economic strikers make an unconditional application to return to work, the employer must immediately reinstate them to their jobs. The exception, of course, would be when jobs have been filled by permanent replacements. Employees engaged in an economic strike and made an unconditional offer to return to work.[16] Although the employer claimed it had filled their jobs with permanent replacements, the record demonstrated the replacements were temporary. The employer verbally told the replacements they had permanent jobs, but this was contradicted when the employer had them sign temporary agreements. Under these circumstances the NLRB held the employer discriminated against the strikers and ordered their immediate reinstatement.

An employer required prospective employees to take a physical examination, including mandatory drug screening, before being hired. It refused to reinstate economic strikers who made an unconditional application to return to work. The NLRB General Counsel held the employer did not replace the strikers permanently because the new hires had not yet taken the physical examination and drug screening. Overruling the General Counsel, the NLRB held the replacement employees had accepted permanent employment when they agreed to work for the employer. In regard to the preemployment test, the majority of the agency held the replacements were told after they were hired and started working that to retain their jobs they were required to complete the testing "over the next few weeks as the normal work schedule permits."

Striking employees were also denied reinstatement by the NLRB in a case involving a printing establishment. Three skilled employees in the bindery department participated in a companywide economic strike and were replaced. After the union had made an unconditional offer to return to work, the three employees in question were placed on a preferential hiring list. Vacancies arose in the bindery department for an entry level position called "general worker," the lowest paid classification in the department.

The three former strikers were skilled employees, holding jobs requiring the art of preparing publications for final binding, and claimed a high salary. Thus, they had skills and wages much higher than the "general worker" classification. Obviously they had the qualifications to perform the duties of the entry level position. When the employer refused to give them the available jobs in the binding department, the union filed unfair labor practice charges against the company. An administrative law judge ruled for the employees in question. Holding that former strikers were entitled to *any* available position for which they were qualified, the law judge recommended that the NLRB find that the employer unlawfully discriminated against the three former strikers.

In a very important decision, the Board rejected the law judge's recommendation and ruled the employer's obligation to reinstate former economic strikers extends only to vacancies created by the departure of replacements from the *strikers' former jobs or to vacancies in substantially equivalent jobs*.[17] To put it another way, the employer's obligation to reinstate former economic strikers does not extend to any job that a former striker is qualified to perform.

Taft-Hartley Innovation

Returning to the issue of eligibility of economic strikers to vote in elections, the NLRB faced the problem originally under the Wagner Act. The agency ruled economic strikers could be deprived of their jobs by permanent replacements, but not of their right to vote in such elections. Originally it ruled in *Sartorius* that both strikers and their replacements were permitted to vote.[18] Not satisfied with this policy, the NLRB reconsidered the issue and about two months later held replaced economic strikers were permitted to vote, but their replacements were deprived of the right. In its final policy under the Wagner Act, the Board returned to its original *Sartorius* position, finding replacements and strikers had the right to vote.[19] Thus, the policy of voting rights of replaced economic strikers was not first established in 1947 by the Taft-Hartley Act. It was originally set up by the NLRB under the Wagner Act. The innovation of the 1947 labor law was that *replaced economic strikers were denied the right to vote in any representation election held during the course of the work stoppage.* Under the final Wagner Act position, the opportunity to vote was extended to this group of strikers as well as to their replacements.

This aspect of the law generated substantial concern on the part of unions. Suppose the workers of the XYZ Manufacturing Company strike for higher wages. This, of course, is an economic strike. The employer manages to find permanent replacements for the bulk of striking workers. The replacements petition the NLRB for a decertification election.[20] A decertification election could provide the basis for eliminating the bargaining-unit representative and for stabilizing replacement worker jobs. The Board conducts the election but permits only the replacements to vote. The replaced strikers are not eligible to cast ballots. This means that the replacements would win the election. As a consequence, the strikers' union would lose bargaining rights and the employer would no longer need to recognize it or bargain with it.

In short, the union involved in such a situation would be frozen out of the plant. It could no longer demand recognition. The strike is lost and the union is broken. The striking employees could not expect to be rehired. After an economic strike is terminated, a union that maintains its bargaining position will invariably demand that all strikers be reinstated. Such a demand is made as one condition for ending the strike. However, in the illustration, the striking union has lost its status in the plant. It could not extend any protection whatsoever to the striking employees. The company would not be obligated to rehire any of the workers—even those with long years of service. The Board would not hold another election for at least one year. Periods marked by serious unemployment could result in widespread union decline, since replacements

> would be more available. Small bargaining units were particularly vulnerable under Taft-Hartley because of the relatively greater possibility of replacement than in larger units.

Landrum-Griffin Revision

Prior to the 1959 amendments of Taft-Hartley, recommendations were made to either eliminate the Section 9(c)(3) feature or modify it so as to provide replaced economic strikers with an opportunity to vote in representation elections. Among these recommendations were those by President Dwight D. Eisenhower in a speech as early as 1952, and by Senator Robert A. Taft, one of the authors of the 1947 law.

Title VII of Landrum-Griffin changed the language of the 1947 statute. Under the new voting policy

> employees engaged in an economic strike who are not entitled to reinstatement shall be eligible to vote under such regulations as the Board shall find are consistent with the purposes and provisions of this act in any election conducted within twelve months after the commencement of the strike.

Congress apparently believed that replaced strikers would not be interested in the bargaining-unit representative after a period of twelve months. Congress may also have believed that strikers would have obtained other employment after such a long period. Yet it must be considered that many replaced strikers retain a substantial interest in recapturing their former jobs. This is particularly true of workers with long seniority with a company. Even if replaced workers did not have long service records, their ages may have precluded them from finding comparable jobs, or serious unemployment conditions would have made it hard to find a job. Thus, if an employer kept a business operating for more than one year by the use of replacements, unions and employees were no better off than they were before the Landrum-Griffin change was made. In any event, unions received some relief. Probably not many employers could stand a work stoppage for more than a year.

Nonetheless, some employers managed to break unions by decertification elections held twelve months after a strike started. This occurred, for example, at Coors Beer and Kingsport Press. After the strike had continued for more than twelve months, decertification elections were held at Coors Beer and the unions lost their bargaining rights. In the latter instance, at Kingsport Press, the nation's largest textbook manufacturer, out of the 1,309 employees who cast valid ballots, 1,228 voted to decertify the unions that had representation rights in the plant.[21] Since only the strikebreaking replacement employees voted, the results of the election were not surprising. What was surprising, however, was that *twenty-five years later in 1987* the workers voted to be represented by an AFL-CIO affiliated union.[22]

For a time, after *Pioneer Flour Mills*, the NLRB permitted replaced economic strikers to vote in elections held more than twelve months after a strike started.[23] The basis for this decision was that replaced strikers were employees and were entitled to vote for as long as they retained an expectation for future employment by the same employer. As noted later in this section, under the *Laidlaw-Fleetwood* doctrine, replaced economic strikers have a right to a job whenever a job becomes available for them. That is, they have permanent reinstatement rights.[24] The Board held that replaced economic strikers had permanent reinstatement rights, and that an employer could not limit this right to a specific time period. It stated: "We likewise reject the contention that a time limit should be placed on the reinstatement rights of economic strikers." On this basis, the NLRB held in *Pioneer Flour Mills* that replaced economic strikers had the right to vote in elections regardless of when they were held. In 1972, however, Nixon's NLRB ruled that voting rights of replaced strikers were limited to one year.[25] It stated in *Wahl Clipper*:

It seems to us the most reasonable course, as well as the most reasonable interpretation of the statutory language, is to hold that replaced strikers are not eligible to vote in elections held more than 12 months after the commencement of an economic strike.

By this decision, though reasonable under the language of the 1959 law and its legislative history, there is greater opportunity for a motivated employer to get rid of a union, with the expected consequences to the employees.

In contrast to replaced economic strikers, the Board held that unreplaced economic strikers could vote in elections held more than twelve months after the strike began.[26] In its decision, the agency stressed that the original or amended law placed no restrictions on the voting rights of unreplaced strikers. In addition, replaced economic strikers may vote in a *rerun* election held more than twelve months after the strike commenced.[27] In the original election, lost by the union, the results were set aside because of employer misconduct. Under these circumstances, the NLRB ruled that the workers were entitled to a new poll untainted by employer unfair tactics.

NLRB Administration of Policy

The Board was required to establish regulations to implement the economic striker provision of the 1959 law. In 1960, it provided some rules to govern the new policy. The voting eligibility of economic strikers was to be determined by certain tests.[28] Voting privileges are forfeited when (1) the striker obtains permanent employment elsewhere before the election; (2) the employer eliminates a striker's job for economic reasons; or (3) the striker is discharged or refused reinstatement for misconduct rendering him or her unsuitable for reemployment.

An economic striker must be on strike at the time of the election before being entitled to vote.[29] But this does not mean that if a striker gets a new job, he or she automatically forfeits the right to vote. Forfeiture of voting rights occurs only if the new job is substantially equivalent to the struck job.[30] Substantial equivalency depends on such factors as pay, seniority, and working conditions. Even if the new job is substantially equivalent to the struck job, a replaced economic striker does not automatically lose voting rights. The replaced striker may retain the franchise despite the new job if he or she continues to picket or informs the employer that he or she is on strike and intends to return to the struck job if given the opportunity.[31] Thus, it is apparent that the Board weighs the economic gains and losses of replaced strikers when their ballots are challenged in Board elections. There is a recognition that these workers may have a substantial economic interest in their struck jobs. Voting privileges may afford an opportunity to recover the struck job.

On April 17, 1990, the U.S. Supreme Court by a 5–4 vote made it somewhat more difficult for employers to oust a striking union. In *Curtin Matheson Scientific* v. *NLRB*,[32] it ruled that employers may not presume that strikebreaking employees do not support the union on strike. Before the NLRB adopted this policy in 1987, employers would refuse to recognize and bargain with the union after it hired replacements for a majority of the striking employees. They presumed the replacements did not support the striking union.

Under current policy, sustained by the high court, the agency has adopted a neutral approach that the views of the replacements may not be presumed to be either antiunion or prounion. Given another NLRB rule, the employer may not poll its employees about union support until it has evidence that the union lost majority support.

Until that time, the employer must recognize and bargain with the striking union. Although the new policy on the matter serves to protect the union's status, the replacements after one year into the strike may still petition the NLRB for a decertification election, denying the vote to regular employees replaced by strikebreakers. In no way does the new rule erase the strike-voting policy incorporated into Landrum-Griffin.

Laidlaw-Fleetwood Doctrine

In 1968, the NLRB reversed its previous rule governing economic strikers. It held that those who had been permanently replaced still had to be reinstated if their jobs opened up again.[33] This new rule is based on a 1967 decision of the U.S. Supreme Court that requires a company to reinstate strikers not rehired at the termination of a strike because of the low level of production.[34] The Board, following the Supreme Court, reasoned that a striker remains an employee even though not reinstated immediately after the strike is concluded. This is called the *Laidlaw-Fleetwood* doctrine.

In 1971, the Board modified the scope of this doctrine. In *United Aircraft*, the union, as a condition of ending a long strike, "agreed" that reinstatement rights of the strikers would be limited to four and one-half months following the termination of the strike.[35] If they were reinstated after this time, they were to be treated as new employees. Under these circumstances, the employees would have lost their accumulated seniority and other contractual rights. As a matter of fact, 1,500 employees were not rehired at the end of the period. Under this agreement, they had lost reinstatement rights. In reviewing this situation, the NLRB, by this time dominated by Nixon appointees, held that the action of the employer in refusing to reinstate strikers after the four and one-half months and to treat those rehired after this time as new hires, did not violate the law because the union had "agreed" to this arrangement. The Board took the position that an agreement reached under the pressures to end a strike stands as a waiver of employee rights established by federal law. If the scenario in *United Aircraft* is used on a wide scale, the *Laidlaw-Fleetwood* doctrine would not be of much practical value.

JURISDICTIONAL STRIKES: ILLEGAL UNDER TAFT-HARTLEY

A *jurisdictional strike* is a work stoppage resulting from a dispute between two or more unions over the assignment of work. At times, unions strike because of inter-union conflict over the representation of workers. Such strikes do not fall within the jurisdictional strike category. These are representation and not jurisdictional strikes. As John T. Dunlop, a leading authority on labor relations, put it: "In the jurisdictional dispute proper the contending organizations are not seeking new members; they are demanding the work in dispute for existing members."[36] If the character of the jurisdictional strike is understood, it is not difficult to see why such strikes occur. Unions that extend their jurisdiction over new jobs increase their power. A jurisdictional strike does not increase the total amount of work available. It is merely a device to obtain work for one union at the expense of another.

The record reveals that jurisdictional strikes have been a persistent feature of the industrial environment. Despite this, they have accounted for only a minor fraction of all strikes. However, their effect on employers, workers, and the public has been much greater than the figures reveal. In 1981, the NLRB reported 401 alleged union violations of the Taft-Hartley provision making strikes against employer work assignments unfair labor practices.[37] The continuing trend of technological change generates increased friction between unions regarding which one should perform assigned tasks. New materials and new production methods, particularly those affecting the building trades, will promote continued interunion rivalry to obtain controversial work assignments for their own members.

Taft-Hartley outlaws the jurisdictional strike.[38] Unions may not strike against a work assignment of an employer. Jurisdictional strikes in the construction industry are particularly harmful because contractors usually work under specified time limits.

Section 10(k): Settlement of Disputes by NLRB

Not only does Taft-Hartley outlaw the jurisdictional strike, but it also places an affirmative obligation on the NLRB to settle the dispute giving rise to the strike. It is one thing to outlaw such a strike, but a different matter to determine which of two unions has the jurisdiction over the work. Section 10(k) states that the Board "is *empowered and directed* to hear and determine the dispute" that gives rise to a jurisdictional strike unless the parties have adjusted the dispute within ten days, or have agreed upon a method for the voluntary adjustment of the dispute.

After the passage of Taft-Hartley, unions and employers in the construction industry established the National Joint Board for the Settlement of Jurisdictional Disputes. In 1973, that board was replaced by the impartial Jurisdictional Disputes Board. In 1984, that agency was abolished, with the parties agreeing to resolve jurisdictional disputes through private arbitrators. These procedures were adopted to make unnecessary NLRB determination of such disputes.

To say the least, settlement of jurisdictional disputes in the construction industry is a very difficult and complex task. If decisions are to be workable and equitable, they must conform to a large body of precedent established over a long period of time. In addition, arbiters of these disputes must have a firm knowledge of the entire construction industry. Obviously, the parties intimately connected with the construction industry are much better qualified to settle jurisdictional disputes than the NLRB. In this connection, the General Counsel of the NLRB declared:

> We of the Board have plenty to do in the field with which we are familiar, and in which we are properly expected to serve as experts. We frankly do not want to be plunged into this new field that is strange territory to us, in which we would be compelled to become experts almost overnight, but we will do it if we must.[39]

The Board considered itself unqualified to deal with jurisdictional problems and thereby largely ignored such cases unless (1) an employer made a work assignment inconsistent with Board certification of a union or (2) the assignment was inconsistent with the terms of the collective bargaining contract. This NLRB attitude left the actual determination of work assignment in the hands of employers. The possibility of unilateral action in this regard was precisely one of the situations the national labor laws had intended to eliminate.

Supreme Court Intervention

Thus, the Board viewed its function under Section 10(k) as merely that of determining whether a striking union was entitled to the work in dispute under a preexisting Board order or certification, or under a collective bargaining contract. If the striking-union was not entitled to the work on the basis of the two criteria just mentioned, the employer's assignment of work was regarded as decisive. Very often, however, neither the certifications nor the agreements clearly assigned work. This type of problem could lead to constant disputes extending over a period of years. An employer forced to make an assignment would not be immune from work stoppages by dissatisfied labor organizations. A company might attempt to satisfy all the unions involved but usually would end up satisfying none. A strike by one of the unions would leave an employer no recourse but to file an unfair labor practice charge with the NLRB.[40]

These circumstances were presented to the U.S. Supreme Court in a 1961 case.[41] The high court came down hard on the NLRB and explicitly informed it that *it had not been carrying out its statutory duty* to hear and resolve jurisdictional disputes where the parties had not been able to resolve the problem themselves. The Board is required to decide any "underlying jurisdictional dispute on its merits and . . . make affirmative" awards of disputed work in every case before it if the parties have not set up their own machinery to do so within ten days.

The Board has responded in accordance with Supreme Court direction. The *Radio Engineers Union (Columbia Broadcasting System)* decision was fully justified under the law. The legislative history of Section 10(k) makes it obvious that Congress did not intend to permit the Board to ignore such cases.

Employers as "Party" to Dispute

The Supreme Court in 1971 was presented with the problem of NLRB authority to impose a jurisdictional dispute settlement when an employer refused to accept an award agreed to by the unions.[42] The issue centered on whether the employer was a "party" to the "dispute" within the meaning of Section 10(k). The two unions as members of the AFL-CIO's Building Trades Department were required to submit their dispute to the National Joint Board for Settlement of Jurisdictional Disputes. They did so and an award was made. The employers involved had contracts with the union losing the award and refused to accept the National Joint Board's determination. Picketing resulted, and the companies filed unfair labor practice charges with the NLRB. The NLRB accepted the case and made its own award to the Tile Setters and not the Plasterers, as had the National Joint Board. A lower federal court set aside the Board order and held that the employers were bound by the National Joint Board's decision even though they had not agreed to submit the dispute to it.[43] This meant that the NLRB was without authority to settle the dispute. The Supreme Court upheld the NLRB and stated in *Plasterers' Local 79* that "the LMRA requires that the Board defer only when all of the parties have agreed on a method of settlement." In other instances, the Board must settle the dispute.

Thus, the U.S. Supreme Court held in *Plasterers' Local 79* that *an employer is a "party" to a dispute within the meaning of Section 10(k)*. If the employer refuses to submit a jurisdictional dispute to an outside party for determination, the NLRB is required to settle it.

When employers and unions agree by contract that they will take a jurisdictional dispute to a private forum for final determination, they are "parties" to the dispute within the meaning of Section 10(k). They may not avoid this obligation in the effort to involve the NLRB in the settlement of the dispute. On the other hand, if they had not previously and affirmatively agreed and refuse to be parties to such a submission, the NLRB under the *Plasterers' Local 79* doctrine must determine the dispute.

Standards of Determination

The Board has established criteria that it usually observes in making work assignments. These factors are the bargaining agreements and union constitutions, skills and work involved, industry custom and practice, and employer's past practice. It should be noted, however, that these factors do not always permit an assignment. Conflicting results may be obtained when these criteria are applied. This is particularly true when "new work" is involved. The Board has on occasion relied on novel factors to make work assignments. In *Philadelphia Inquirer*, the NLRB applied "substitution of function" and "loss-of-jobs" tests in resolving a jurisdictional dispute.[44] Of critical concern to the Board was what would happen to union members if it assigned work to another organization. Another factor that impressed the Board was that one union had undertaken to train its members in the new technology. Yet similarity of the new techniques to prior processes would have required a different assignment of work.

Generally, however, the Board, when assigning disputed work, adheres to the factors mentioned earlier. Their use provides a greater degree of stability than would determinations made without guidelines. The Board relies on its "experience and common sense" when established tests fail to be adequate. Such an approach is consistent with the Supreme Court's *Columbia Broadcasting System* rule. However, the Board's determination of a jurisdictional dispute may be upset by the courts should it be found that these factors are not applied in a consistent manner. A federal circuit court of appeals reversed a Board decision on the grounds that it applied its standards in an arbitrary and capricious manner. In particular, the court held that the Board did not give sufficient weight to employer preference, a standard that it frequently used in resolving jurisdictional disputes.[45]

Despite the standards established by the NLRB to resolve jurisdictional disputes, a 1985 study reveals that the employer's position is sustained in 90 percent of all work assignment disputes.[46] Given this record, the study concludes:

The apparent routine acceptance of the employer's assignment can be said to be an unwillingness to use or an abdication by the Board of its statutory powers.[47]

Based upon this study, it appears that the situation essentially remains the same as was the case before the Supreme Court's decision in *Columbia Broadcasting System*.

STRIKES AGAINST NLRB CERTIFICATION

Violation of Principle of Majority Rule

The Wagner Act was based on the principle of majority rule. Unions selected by the majority of workers in a bargaining unit were to represent all employees within the unit. Employers were required to recognize and bargain with the majority union and with no other organization. An employer violated the statute by granting any measure of recognition to a minority union. Some labor unions, however, violated the doctrine of majority rule. They refused to respect certifications awarded by the NLRB. Despite the evidence of the ballot box, a number of unions struck against certifications of the NLRB. These unions struck to force employers to violate their legal obligation to recognize majority-designated unions.

Such action resulted when unions were defeated in bargaining elections. Let us assume that Union A and Union B are rivals in a bargaining election. Union A polls a majority vote. Dissatisfied with the election returns, Union B strikes to force the employer to recognize it and not Union A, the majority-designated labor organization. Of course, the employer is under legal obligation to bargain with A. Under the Wagner Act, management would commit an unfair labor practice if it granted any recognition whatsoever to B, the defeated labor organization.

Such strikes are totally indefensible. They violate the most elementary principles of democracy. They are completely inconsistent with the spirit of the Wagner Act. The frequency of such strikes under the Wagner Act was not very great. In the vast majority of cases, unions defeated in elections accepted the results of the polls in good faith. Frequently, this meant that workers were required to change union affiliations. It is to the credit of the union movement that such changes occurred without serious impairment to the productive process.

Ultimate Position of NLRB under Wagner Act

Despite their limited frequency, the fact remains that such strikes did take place in the Wagner Act era. When they did occur, employers and majority-designated unions were placed in an intolerable position. Ultimately, the NLRB did attempt to discourage strikes against its certifications. In the early part of 1947, the Board ruled that employees who participated in a strike with the purpose of compelling an employer to recognize and bargain with the union of the striking employees rather than with a certified labor organization, were not entitled to reinstatement or back pay.[48] Since the Board held the purpose of this form of strike to be unjustified, the strikers were stripped of all benefits of the Wagner Act. This ruling was handed down by the NLRB at about the time the Wagner Act was to expire. The agency had not seen fit to establish this policy earlier in the Wagner Act era.

Treatment under Taft-Hartley

Even the ultimate position of the NLRB on minority strikes, however, was not sufficient to protect the principle of majority rule. At the very best, it merely had the effect of discouraging such strikes. Under the Wagner Act, the NLRB did not have the power to prevent them. In this respect, the law was defective. The Board certified majority unions, but it did not have the authority to protect its certifications against strike action.

The principle of majority rule was included in the Taft-Hartley Act. As in the Wagner Act, employers are required to bargain with majority-designated labor unions. However, when it passed the 1947 labor law, Congress overcame the shortcoming of the Wagner Act. It outlawed strikes for recognition when another union has been certified by the NLRB.[49]

Certification of a union as exclusive bargaining representative makes a strike for recognition by a union other than the one certified an unfair labor practice under Section 8(b)(4)(C). Adequate enforcement procedures were adopted. Injunctions may be obtained against unions that engage in such strikes.

When strikes against NLRB certification occur, Section 10(1) makes it mandatory for the Board to seek injunctions against the strikes. It must give priority to violations of this nature. In addition, whoever is injured by a minority recognition strike may sue the minority union for actual damages. Punitive damages, however, are not permitted[50] under Section 301, which does permit damage suits in federal and state courts.[51] Despite the absence of punitive damages, adequate protection is available to protect employers and certified unions against strikes by minority unions.

LOCKOUT RIGHTS OF EMPLOYERS

The right of unions to strike to influence the outcome of bargaining demands has generally been considered as balanced by the right of employers to lock out employees for the same reason. The NLRB has never upheld the lockout as a legal form of economic pressure when used as an antiunion weapon. Purposes other than to destroy a union may qualify the weapon for legal use.

Essentially, the Board has established three situations under which it permits lockouts. One provides that the weapon is permissible as a defensive device to protect the employer against a sudden strike that might result in unusual economic losses. Another involves a lockout to preserve the institution of multiemployer bargaining. Employers, however, may withdraw from a multiemployer bargaining arrangement only if notice is given prior to contract renegotiations. Later on the company cannot withdraw, even if an impasse is reached. The impasse does not constitute an "unusual circumstance." The U.S. Supreme Court upheld this policy in 1982.[52] Finally, under proper circumstances an employer may use the lockout as an offensive weapon to put pressure upon a union to accept its position when a collective bargaining contract is being negotiated.

Unusual Economic Hardship

Unusual economic hardship might result for a company engaged in custom work that cannot afford to continue to operate on a day-to-day basis for an extended period after contract expiration. This is particularly the case when the timing of a possible work stoppage is not certain. Uncertainty regarding a work stoppage at a firm dealing with custom work could result in loss of considerable goodwill if it were caught with unexecuted orders on hand.

Unusual economic costs might also be involved for a firm that produces a perishable raw material. After a contract has expired, a company may lock out if it has no knowledge of the timing of an expected union strike. Such action is regarded as defensive by the Board, and as such would have nothing to do with an attempt to destroy a union.

Defense of Multibargaining Unit

Buffalo Linen was decided by the Supreme Court in 1957; the case involved a union, the Truck Drivers Local Union No. 449, and eight companies with which it bargained.[53] There was a history of multiemployer bargaining among the parties. The union struck one company and the remaining seven reacted by locking out their employees. The nonstruck companies reacted to prevent whipsawing. Whipsawing refers to successive strikes against one after another of the various members of an employer's association.

Whipsaw action can be highly beneficial to labor organizations in that they may strike one company while all the others continue operations. A single company cannot normally hold out for a long period of time if its competitors continue to supply the market for a particular product. Unions often strike the wealthiest companies first under these circumstances, and then pick off the others at their discretion until all agree to approximately the same contractual terms.

The Board ruled in *Buffalo Linen* that the employers had the right to preserve the traditional multiemployer collective bargaining relationship, which was being threatened by the whipsawing action. A circuit court reviewing the case overruled the NLRB on the basis that it had expanded its "hardship doctrine," which permitted lockouts only if unusual economic costs were likely to be incurred. The U.S. Supreme Court reversed the lower court and upheld Board action on the theory that the pattern of multiemployer bargaining had been established for all purposes. Actually, the doctrine means that the lockout may be used to preserve a multiemployer bargaining arrangement, but only in cases where there is a history of it.

In *A & P*,[54] an employer association used the lockout to attempt to force a change in the pattern of bargaining. Traditionally, bargaining took place on a single-employer basis. During negotiations, the association insisted upon a bargaining change from single units to a multiemployer unit. The union met with the group to discuss the issue and an impasse was reached in negotiations without agreement upon a change to a new procedure. The union struck one of the members whose contract had expired. The other employers locked out their employees as an offensive tactic to secure their objective. The Board held that the employer action was outside *Buffalo Linen* limits, since the lockout in such cases could be undertaken merely to preserve a multiemployer unit from attempted union destruction. This made the lockout an offensive weapon in the Board's view and as such not permissible because of the effect it might have on unionism.

In another case, however, *Evening News Association*, the NLRB held that employer lockout action was protected within the *Buffalo Linen* principle, since the result was to preserve the existing bargaining arrangement.[55]

Lockout and Temporary Replacements

The NLRB was persistent until 1965 in requiring a rigid interpretation regarding what constituted defensive employer lockout behavior. In *Brown Food Store*, the Board held that in locking out their employees, nonstruck employers were exceeding the lawful defensive limits established in *Buffalo Linen* by continuing operations with temporary replacements.[56]

The Tenth Circuit Court of Appeals subsequently refused to enforce the Board's order, and the Supreme Court agreed to hear the case. The high court rejected the Board's reasoning and held that it was not an unfair labor practice for the nonstruck members of a multiemployer unit to continue to operate by using temporary replacements.[57] The companies were permitted to do so as a response to a whipsaw strike against one of the association members. The Court reasoned that

> the continued operations . . . and their use of temporary replacements [no] more imply hostile motivation, nor [is it] inherently more destructive of employee rights, than is the lockout itself. Rather, the compelling inference is that this was all part and parcel [of the employers'] defensive measure to preserve the multi-employer groups in the face of the whipsaw strike.

Thus, multiemployer associations have considerable economic power to deal with labor organizations engaged in whipsaw action. They may lock out workers and replace them temporarily to preserve their bargaining-unit structure.

The Supreme Court was not entirely free to rule differently. It had already ruled in *Mackay Radio* that a struck employer could use replacements to keep a firm open.[58] Since the struck employer has such a right, then the other employers should also be entitled to do so, or they would be placed at a competitive disadvantage relative to the struck firms. Thus, a union may engage in whipsaw action, but if it does, multiemployer unit firms do not have to suffer the economic consequences that would flow from a policy of permitting only a struck firm to continue its operations by replacing employees. It should be noted, however, that the struck firm may *permanently* replace economic strikers, whereas the nonstruck firms may replace them only *temporarily*.

Lockout as an Offensive Weapon

At times employers and unions agree to continue operations after a labor contract has expired. They hope the extra negotiating time will result in settlement. Some employers, however, believe they are at a disadvantage by such a practice. Employees may not exert their best effort, putting pressure on the employer to settle on the union's terms. More important, a union may delay a strike until the employer is in its busy period. This was the background of a case involving the American Ship Building Company. Its busy season was in the winter when lakes are frozen and ships are laid up for repairs. Thus, when contract negotiations with its unions broke down in August, the workers did not strike but waited for winter to do that.

Understanding the unions' stratagem, the employer locked the employees out. That is, it used the lockout not as a defensive weapon to defend a multiemployer collective bargaining contract but as an *offensive weapon* to pressure the unions to accept its contract proposal. Since the lockout did not fit its rule in *Buffalo Linen*, the NLRB held the employer action was unlawful. It said the lockout forced the unions to abandon their wage demands, and by its timing of the lockout the employer deprived the unions of their right to strike.

Overruling the NLRB in *American Ship Building*, the Supreme Court held the lockout was lawful.[59] It said:

> The board has, in essence, denied the use of the bargaining lockout to the employer because of its conviction that use of this device would give the employer "too much power." In so doing, the board has stretched [Labor Act provisions] far beyond their functions of protecting the rights of employee organizations and collective bargaining.

The Court concluded that an employer does not violate the law

> when, after a bargaining impasse has been reached, he temporarily shuts down his plant and lays off his employees for the sole purpose of bringing economic pressure to bear in support of his legitimate bargaining position.

Offensive Lockouts and Temporary Replacements

Under *Buffalo Linen*, *Brown Foods*, and *American Ship Building*, the employer's right to lock out has been significantly expanded. Not only can this weapon be used to defend multiemployer bargaining units against whipsawing, but it can also be used offensively *by a single employer* to pressure unions to accept the employer's bargaining position. One issue, however, was not settled by the Supreme Court in *American Ship Building*: Whether the employer may use temporary replacements to operate after it locks out the regular employees. The Court said:

> We intimate no view whatever as to the consequences which would follow had the employer replaced its employees with permanent or even temporary help.

This issue was not determined by *Brown Foods* because the lockout was used defensively to defend multiemployer collective bargaining.

Inconsistent Decisions by NLRB and Courts

Surprisingly enough, the Supreme Court has not determined the issue at this writing (about thirty years after *American Ship Building*), though there have been inconsistent rulings by the NLRB and the lower federal courts.

In *Inland Trucking*, an employer locked out employees after contract negotiations reached an impasse.[60] Temporary replacements were hired, and the firm continued to operate. The Board and a federal appeals court held the employer in violation of Taft-Hartley. The court ruled that the lockout differed from *American Ship Building* and *Brown* because the use of temporary substitutes during a bargaining lockout was inherently destructive of employee statutory rights. In addition, an appeals court was of the opinion that the employer's motives or reasons for using replacements were unimportant. The desire to avoid a strike that might be called during the busiest season was insufficient by itself to justify use of temporary replacements. An employer's actions cannot be inherently destructive of important employee rights. For example, a union has a statutorily protected right to take initiative with respect to strikes because the right to strike and to refrain from striking are equally guaranteed under Section 7 of Taft-Hartley. Thus, the employer could not use the lockout and temporary replacements for the purpose of forcing agreement to a contract proposed by the employer, nor for the purpose of avoiding a strike that could be called during its busiest season.[61]

In 1972, despite the federal court's decision in *Inland Trucking*, the Board position on use of temporary replacements during lockouts changed. It held by a split vote in *Ottawa Silica* that for a single firm to continue operation with temporary replacements was lawful as a means of getting locked-out workers to act on the company's bargaining proposals.[62] The same circumstances occurred in a subsequent Board decision during the same year.[63] In 1974, a federal circuit court of appeals upheld the right of an employer to use temporary replacements after a company had locked out employees as an offensive weapon. Unlike its sister federal court, it held that such conduct of the employer did not destroy the protected rights of either the employees or the union. It rejected the union's argument that, even in the absence of an antiunion motive, the use of replacements during a lockout was unlawful.[64] In 1976, however, the Board ruled that a lockout becomes illegal when the employer uses *permanent* replacements.[65]

In November 1988, the issue surfaced again before a federal appeals court. Previously, the NLRB had held lawful the use of temporary replacements by an employer that locked out its employees to gain an advantage in collective bargaining. Upholding the NLRB in *Boilermakers, Local 88*, the court ruled the employer action was lawful because it was undertaken to obtain a "legitimate and substantial business"[66] objective. The legitimate objective was to secure a new collective bargaining contract on favorable terms. Though it said the employer's action had a "comparatively slight" adverse impact on the employee right to strike or not to strike, the District of Columbia's federal appeals court held the lockout-replacement conduct was not destructive of those rights.

In the final analysis, whether the use of temporary replacements in offensive lockout situations is destructive of protected employee rights under Taft-Hartley is *strictly a matter of judicial opinion*. As noted, depending on the membership of the NLRB and federal appeals courts, the issue has been resolved inconsistently. At least the Supreme Court should put the matter to rest by reviewing the different decisions of the federal appeals courts.

Locked-Out Employees: Eligibility to Vote in Elections

That an employer may replace locked-out employees with only temporary replacements is the key to determining who may vote in elections held during a lockout.

In *Harter Equipment*,[67] the employer hired replacements during the lockout to take over the jobs of five employees. At that time a decertification petition was filed and the company had hired twelve replacements. At the hearing to determine which group of employees could vote, the regular employees or the replacements, the number of replacements had increased to seventeen.

The NLRB held that only the five locked-out employees were eligible to vote. Even though five years had elapsed since the decertification petition had been filed, the agency determined that there was "no evidence or even allegation" that any of the five employees abandoned his job. It also ruled that because the employer had locked out the bargaining-unit employees in support of its bargaining demands, the employees "were not and could not lawfully be permanently replaced." In other words, though strikers may be permanently replaced and lose their right to vote after one year into a strike, locked-out employees are temporarily replaced and therefore have the right to vote whenever an election is held. To put it another way, whereas permanent replacements have the right to vote in strike situations, temporary replacements may not vote in elections held during the lockout.

EMPLOYEE CONDUCT ON THE PICKET LINE

Section 7: Right of Employees to Refrain from Union Activities

The Taft-Hartley Act also regulates the conduct of workers participating in the picketing process. During strikes, employees normally engage in picket-line activities. Hence, the law on picketing cannot be divorced from that regulating strike action. One would look in vain for specific provisions of the law that deal with strike-related picketing. Nevertheless, the NLRB has inferred from Section 7 of the law that certain picketing patterns are unlawful.

Section 7 of Taft-Hartley provides that

> employees shall have the right to self-organization, to form, join or assist labor organizations, to bargain collectively through representatives of their own choosing, and to engage in mutual other concerted activities for the purpose of collective bargaining or other mutual aid or protection, *and shall have the right to refrain from any or all of such activities.* (Emphasis supplied)

The italicized phrase did not appear in the Wagner Act. Although the Wagner Act guaranteed to workers the right to engage in collective bargaining activities, such as striking and picketing, free from employer interference, it did not protect workers in the right to refrain from such activities. The assumption of Taft-Hartley is that certain workers do not desire to bargain collectively, to strike, or to picket. Hence the law shields these workers from union tactics calculated to force them to participate in concerted employee activities.

Section 7 must be read in conjunction with another provision of Taft-Hartley to gain an understanding of the impact of the statute on picketing.[68] This additional section provides that it shall be unlawful for labor unions or their agents "to restrain or coerce employees in the exercise of the rights guaranteed in section 7." Thus, labor unions violate the law if they coerce or restrain employees in their right to refrain from union activities.

The NLRB has held that certain picketing conduct of labor unions operates to deny workers their right not to engage in union activities. What is the general character of such unlawful picketing? Picketing is illegal under Taft-Hartley when the effect of the picketing denies to employees the opportunity to work during a strike. In short, employees have the protected right to work in the face of a strike. The Board declared in October 1948 that "employees have a guaranteed right to refrain from striking. That right includes the right to go to and from work without restraint or coercion while a strike is in progress."[69] The legislative history of Taft-Hartley fully supports this position of the NLRB. In this connection, Senator Taft declared that Taft-Hartley outlaws "such restraint and coercion as would prevent people from going to work if they wished to go to work."[70] Thus, picketing that prevents employees from working during a strike coerces and restrains workers in the exercise of their right not to engage in collective action.

Substance of Restraint and Coercion

To establish the full effect of the statute on picketing, the NLRB is required to spell out the meaning of the terms *restraint* and *coercion*. What are the circumstances in which a picket line restrains and coerces employees within the meaning of the law? Specifically, what patterns of picketing conduct prevent employees from working during a strike? Actually, this is a much more difficult problem to resolve than the mere establishment of the general character of unlawful picketing. This is necessarily the case because restraint and coercion mean different things to different people.

After the enactment of Taft-Hartley, the Board declared that picketing that forcibly blocks ingress and egress to a struck plant violates the Taft-Hartley Act. For example, during one strike, a union organized a picket line of between 200 and 300 members. The workers massed in front of the driveway leading to the struck plant's parking lot. When cars carrying nonstriking employees reached the driveway, they were blocked by the crowd. Three cars successfully drove into the parking lot, but only through the assistance of local police officers. Two other automobiles started to drive through the picket line but, when instructed by the plant superintendent not to attempt to go through, they drove away. Such picketing, the NLRB held, was unlawful.[71]

A case involving the United Furniture Workers of America is particularly helpful in determining the unlawful area of picketing. In this case, the Board held unlawful a number of picketing tactics that operated to deny employees the right to work, free from restraint and coercion, during a strike. Such conduct included (1) the carrying of sticks by the pickets on the picket line; (2) the piling of bricks for use by the pickets; (3) the blocking of plant entrances by railroad ties, automobiles, raised gutter plates, and tacks; (4) the threat of violence toward nonstriking employees; (5) the warning given one nonstriking employee that "when we get in with the union, you old fellows won't have a job"; (6) the placing of pickets in such a manner as to prevent nonstrikers from carrying out their assigned work of loading cabinets into railroad boxcars on a railroad siding located about a quarter of a mile from the plant; (7) the "goon squad" mass assaults upon various nonstrikers; (8) the overturning of automobiles; and (9) the barring from the plant of a superintendent and a foreman by force and intimidation in full view of nonstriking employees.

Every one of the above acts of violence was held unlawful by the National Labor Relations Board.[72] This policy has been reaffirmed in subsequent cases.[73] However, a new philosophy toward picketing conduct has developed. *Picket violence directed against employer property likewise constitutes unlawful coercion of employees.* Thus, during one work stoppage, striking employees engaged in picketing broke more than 443 windows. This was accomplished by hurling stones, rocks, railroad tieplates, railroad spikes, clubs, and other objects through the windows. The union claimed its activities were not directed at employees but against the employer. Hence, it contended that this action did not coerce or restrain employees in their right not to engage in union activities. This contention was flatly rejected by the Board. It held that the "atmosphere of terror" created by the union in the destruction of the property constituted a threat to employees. The Board observed that nonstrikers would have to risk physical violence if they attempted to enter the struck plant.[74]

Name-Calling Lawful

About a year after Taft-Hartley was enacted, the NLRB was called upon to decide whether or not pickets may lawfully abuse strikebreakers by calling them profane names. Pickets frequently call strikebreakers a variety of foul names as they come through the picket line. It was inevitable that the Board would be called upon to decide this problem. Its decision was handed down in a case that involved a number of pickets and strikebreakers. The facts indicate that six employees who had chosen to abandon the strike and return to work were met at the plant gate by a large group of pickets. The Board reports that "[the strikebreakers] were vilified and verbally abused as scabs—deserters from the strikers' ranks." Some of the pickets called the strikebreakers a variety of obscene epithets besides "scab" and "deserter."

The Board refused to find a violation of the Taft-Hartley Act, declaring that the abuse of the strikebreakers amounted only to name-calling.[75] Thus, vocal resentment by pickets directed against strikebreakers is considered a form of peaceful picketing. Such picketing tactics, according to the Board, do not constitute coercion and restraint of employees within the meaning of the 1947 labor law. To support its position, the Board pointed to the section of Taft-Hartley that provides that

> the expressing of any views, arguments, or opinions, or the dissemination thereof, whether in written, printed, graphic, or visual form, shall not constitute or be evidence of an unfair labor practice under the provisions of this Act, if such expression contains no threat of reprisal or force or promise of benefit.

Ironically, this section, popularly termed the "free speech" clause, as noted in an earlier chapter, was inserted into the law to provide employers with greater opportunity to deliver speeches to employees.[76] It is noteworthy that the Board utilized this section to legalize name-calling on the picket line.

In June 1974, the opportunity to degrade nonmembers of a union was increased. At that time, in *Letter Carriers* v. *Austin*, the U.S. Supreme Court held that publication in a union's newsletter of nonmembers' names in a "list of scabs" that also carried a highly pejorative definition of the term "scab" was protected under federal labor laws. Noting that such laws encourage "uninhibited, robust, and wide-open discussion," the Court reversed the decision of the supreme court of Virginia, which had previously held that the publication was libelous under state law. State courts had found that under state law, the use of "scab" was libelous and had awarded listed nonmembers $165,000 in damages.[77]

Threats on Picket Line

Name-calling constitutes protected conduct. But the Reagan Board changed a previous policy when it ruled that employees who make threats of physical violence to nonstrikers may lawfully be discharged.[78] Previously the Board had held:

> Absent violence . . . a picket is not disqualified from reinstatement despite . . . making abusive threats against nonstrikers.[79]

Later, in *Clear Pine Mouldings, Inc.*, employees directed threats of physical violence against nonstrikers, including threats to break their hands, saying they were taking their lives in their hands by crossing the picket line, and saying: "I am going to kill you . . ." Reversing the previous policy, the Reagan Board rejected "the per se rule that words alone can never warrant a denial of reinstatement in the absence of physical acts." In a 1985 case, the NLRB also upheld an employer's decision to discharge two employees who threatened an employee with bodily harm if he continued to work during a strike.[80]

In 1994, the federal appeals court in Richmond upheld the *Clear Pine Mouldings Doctrine*.[81] It sustained the discharge of a striker when he yelled at a nonstriker: "Hey, scab, ya you . . . sure you can get an early start in the morning, I want to have plenty of time to take care of your home life." The nonstriker stopped and balled up his fist, and the two glared at each other until police intervened.

Such conduct, the court said, not only coerced and intimidated the person in question but also did the same to other employees.

Nonviolent Mass Picketing Unlawful

Picketing by large numbers of workers is commonly termed *mass picketing*. This form of union activity poses no great legal problem when the picket line engages in acts of violence. As noted, the Board ruled that forcible blocking of the entrance to plants constitutes unlawful picketing. This would be true regardless of the number of workers who are picketing.

The perplexing legal problem, however, involves picketing in a peaceful manner by large numbers of workers. Strikebreakers must be allowed entry into the struck plant without violence or threats of violence to their persons or property. What then is the legal status of mass picketing carried out in a peaceful manner?

In 1949, the Board dealt with this extremely difficult problem. The case involved a picket line of some 1,000 to 2,000 persons. The pickets marched back and forth in front of a plant involved in a strike. Apparently, they did not engage in overt acts of violence. However, the Board held that such picketing was unlawful, declaring that "realistically viewed, restraint and coercion were the effect of the mass picketing."[82] It further observed that the "necessary effect of the manner in which the demonstration was conducted was to deny nonstriking employees access to the plant."

The effect of the Board's position was to outlaw nonviolent mass picketing. The Board has not, however, dogmatically stated how many workers can compose lawful picket lines. It avoids this problem by declaring that one definition of mass picketing cannot possibly fit all cases. Hence, the substance of mass picketing must be determined by particular Board decisions. Each case will be decided on its own merits. For example, the Board did not find a violation in one case even though a picket line of about 200 persons assembled near a plant during a strike. What is more, the pickets verbally denounced strikebreakers as they entered the plant. The Board pointed out that "there was no difficulty entering or leaving the plant."[83]

Despite its reluctance to set forth the exact number who may properly picket, the Board has regarded the number of workers on a picket line as relevant in determining the potential or calculated restraining effect of massed pickets in barring nonstrikers from entering or leaving the plant. It has held that some picket parades by mere force of numbers have the effect of coercing employees who want to enter a plant and work. The exact point at which peaceful picketing becomes "massed" and unlawful because of the number of pickets turns on the particular circumstances of each case.

Penalties for Unlawful Picketing

Both unions and employees are subject to penalties for unlawful picketing. Unions that sponsor unlawful picketing face injunction proceedings. Employees who engage in unlawful picketing lose reinstatement rights. Employers have no legal obligation to reinstate a striker found to have engaged in picketing held unlawful under Taft-Hartley. For example, the NLRB has held that workers engaging in violent picketing can expect no relief from the NLRB when discharged. A Puerto Rican firm discharged eighteen strikers who engaged in various acts of violence, threats of force against nonstrikers, and destruction of plant property. The NLRB refused to order the reinstatement of these workers.[84] Actually, the NLRB established this principle under the Wagner Act and has consistently utilized it. In this case, it refused to order the reinstatement of workers who committed extreme acts of violence while on strike, workers found guilty of offenses such as assault and battery, dynamiting, and murder. Under Taft-Hartley, a worker engaging in any act of unlawful picketing loses reinstatement rights. The penalty is not reserved for extreme acts of violence. Thus, the principle of denial of reinstatement has much wider application under Taft-Hartley than was true under the Wagner Act.

The "Clean Hands" Problem

For many years, the NLRB held that unlawful picketing is not excusable because the employer has engaged in unfair labor practices. Even if company unfair labor practices have provoked a strike, the Board has held that unions and employees still violate the 1947 labor law when they prevent strikebreakers from entering a plant during a strike. In 1949, the Board rejected the "clean hands" doctrine in the enforcement of the statute. In this connection, it declared:

> With respect to the "clean hands" defense, we find that the company's alleged unfair labor practices if established, do not lessen the need for vindicating and protecting employees' rights under the Act, which the [union had] infringed.[85]

Some courts, however, did not approve the Board's position that employees should always lose reinstatement rights when they engage in unlawful picketing in the face of employer unfair labor practices. For example, during a long and bitter strike between the UAW and the Kohler Corporation, the employer engaged in serious unfair labor practices. Many strikers committed unlawful acts during the work stoppage. Adhering to its policy, the NLRB refused to direct reinstatement of those employees. However, the federal appeals court in the District of Columbia remanded the case to the Board to weigh the character of the employer's unfair labor practices against the misconduct of employees and determine on that basis whether employees were entitled to reinstatement.[86] Nonetheless, the Board has clung to its traditional policy on this issue. Indeed, in *Clear Pine Mouldings*, as discussed earlier, the agency denied reinstatement to employees even though the employer had apparently committed serious unfair labor practices. In that case, the Board rejected the test that

> balanced the severity of the employer's unfair labor practices that provoked the strike against the gravity of the strikers' misconduct.

Strangely enough, to this day, the U.S. Supreme Court has not expressly adopted a rule establishing the extent to which employer unfair labor practices affect the reinstatement rights of employees who engage in unlawful strike activities. Given the importance of this issue, it would seem that the high court should address it.

UNION ORGANIZER ACCESS TO EMPLOYER PROPERTY

Original Policy

One of the most difficult problems of labor relations law is the extent to which employers may ban outside union organizers (nonemployees) from private property owned by the company. The issue arises because on one hand public policy of the United States expressed in the Norris–LaGuardia, Wagner, and Taft-Hartley acts is the encouragement of collective bargaining and protection of employee rights to organize and select unions of their own choosing. On the other side of the coin are private property rights rooted through a long string of statutes and case law imbedded into the history of the United States. In fact, as one writer put it, "the vanguard of these rights originated in England, a place where land and its ownership became almost sacred in the years prior to the American Revolution."[87]

Given the intensity with which these two propositions are held, it is easy to understand why the problem has proven so contentious. Understand that we are not dealing here with union activities of employees of an employer. The Supreme Court ruled employers must allow their own employees the opportunity to engage in union activities during periods of nonwork time, subject only to reasonable rules of plant efficiency and discipline.[88] Thus employees have the right to solicit members, pass out leaflets, and "talk union" during breaks, lunch, and before and after work-hours. Instead the issue here is the right of union organizers, *not employees of the employer*, to access the employer's property to solicit members.

The first Supreme Court pronouncement on this issue was in *Babcock and Wilcox*.[89] It ruled an employer may ban nonemployee union organizers from its property provided "reasonable efforts by the union through other available channels of communication will enable it to reach the employees with its message."

Jean Country Doctrine

For decades the NLRB and the courts handled the problem by applying what became known as the *Jean Country* doctrine.[90] Under it the agency balanced employer property rights against the employees' right to engage in union activities on company property. Should the balance indicate the employees' rights outweighed the employers' property rights, the NLRB would direct employers to permit union organizers access to company property. Where the reverse was true, the employer could lawfully ban them from the plant, parking lot, or other areas of employer property. In applying *Jean Country*, the Board would consider whether the union had reasonable alternatives to communicate with employees other than access to employer property.

Reversal of Policy: *Lechmere* v. *NLRB*

Thus *Babcock and Wilcox* and *Jean Country* provided the legal precedents under which the Supreme Court established the current policy governing union organizer access to employer property.[91] Lechmere owned a retail store in the Lechmere Shopping Plaza in Newington, Connecticut. The plaza's parking lot was separated from the public highway by a forty-six-foot-wide grassy area, mostly public land through which the plaza's entrance passed. Lechmere and other stores in the shopping plaza owned the parking lot.

In attempting to organize Lechmere's 200 employees, the United Food and Commercial Workers Union ran full-page advertisements in the local newspaper. They generated very little response. Then the union organizers placed handbills on the car windshields in the parking lot area customarily used by employees. Lechmere's manager informed the union representatives that the company prohibited handbill distribution of any kind on its property and asked them to leave. The organizers removed the handbills and left. They repeated the handbill exercise several more times. On each occasion, the manager told them to leave, and they removed the handbills and departed.

Other methods to reach Lechmere employees proved unsuccessful. For example, the union obtained the names and addresses of 20 percent of the bargaining unit employees. It sent them mailings and made home visits and phone calls. These efforts resulted in only one signed union authorization card.

Subsequently the union filed successful unfair labor practice charges with the National Labor Relations Board. Applying the *Jean Country* test, the NLRB determined organizers' access to the parking lot would not substantially impair Lechmere's property rights because the parking lot was open to the public. By limiting their activities to the parking lot, the union organizers would not interfere with the store's business or inconvenience its customers. To support its decision the NLRB held the union lacked a reasonable alternative to reach the employees.[92] On these grounds the Board directed Lechmere to permit organizers access to the parking lot. Subsequently a federal appeals court upheld the NLRB decision.[93]

In a 6–3 vote, the Supreme Court reversed the NLRB and the federal appeals court. The majority held that Section 7 of Taft-Hartley "confers rights only on employees so that non-employees [union organizers] have no rights under the statute, and therefore no right of access to enter an employer's property to engage in union activities." The high court ignored the finding of the Board and the federal appeals court that the parking lot was open to the public, and organizers did not disturb Lechmere's business. In only one way would union organizers have access to employer property. The majority said this would be a situation where employees actually *live on employer property.* Since the employees went home every day, the majority reasoned the union could reasonably find the means to contact them away from the store.

In reaching its decision, the Supreme Court abolished *Jean Country* and previous union organizer access cases. As long as the union can communicate with employees, it is improper to balance property and employee organizational rights. And as long as employees do not reside on employer property, as was the case in the era of the legendary Pullman Car Company strike, and are free to go home each day, the union can reach them. Therefore employers are not under any legal obligation to permit union representatives access to employer property.

Instead of *Jean Country*, the majority used *Babcock and Wilcox* as the legal precedent. True, in that case, the high court did say "an employer may validly post his property against non-employee distribution of union literature." It also stated, however, access to employer property should be granted when no other reasonable means exist for unions to communicate with the employees. To say, as the majority did in *Lechmere*, that unions have that capability as long as employees do not reside on employer property ignores the realities of modern labor relations and demographics. The majority also stated outside union organizers should be permitted access to employer property only "when unique obstacles" prevent other means of communication. It made much of the showing that the union was able to contact 20 percent of the bargaining unit. This demonstrated "unique obstacles" did not stand in the way of the union's capability to reach employees. The high court reasoned access to employees other than on company property was the issue—not success in organization.

But the majority refused to recognize that lack of success is critically relevant to determining whether reasonable access to employees existed.

Aftermath of Lechmere

Lechmere does not ban all access to employer property by outside union organizers. The NLRB has held employers may not ban them when an employer permits other organizations to solicit on its property. Where the employer forbids union access but permits, say, church, school groups, boy scouts, or little league teams to solicit on employer property including placing handbills on the cars in the employer parking lot, the Board has held the employer discriminated against unions and ordered an appropriate remedy.[94]

In addition *Lechmere* did not ban union officials access to a job site when the contract between a construction union and subcontractors called for job site access for union officers.[95] A general contractor's subcontracting agreements required that subcontractors fully abide by all labor agreements. The Board reasoned that the union could not possibly know whether the contracts were being honored unless its officials visited the job site. To defend its denial of union visitation, the general contractor relied on *Lechmere*. Rejecting that position, the Board stressed that under *Lechmere* the employer lawfully denied union access because outside organizers were involved. In the case at hand, and in contrast, the union's officials wished to communicate with represented employees and the contract permitted access. In addition the agency pointed out the union did not have any other reasonable means to contact workers at the large fenced-in job site.

In another interesting case, an employer's handbook of shop rules contained a section requiring visitors and off-duty employees to register with the receptionist before entering the plant. Rules banned solicitation/distribution by employees during working time, and by nonemployees at any time on company property. An employee distributed union literature in a nonwork area prior to his regular shift. The company applied the antisolicitation rule to the employee. Its action, the employer argued, was protected by *Lechmere*. Not so, ruled the NLRB because *Lechmere* applied to nonemployee access to company property. Unlike outside organizers, said the agency, an off-duty employee remains an employee under law even if not scheduled to work at the time he sought access to the employer property.[96]

These few exceptions to *Lechmere* should not be exaggerated. In the final analysis *Lechmere* is a formidable obstacle to union organization, contributing to the decline of the American labor movement. It stands very high on the list of legal barriers making it difficult to expand union membership.

FINES AGAINST UNION MEMBERS WORKING DURING A STRIKE

Allis-Chalmers: Fines Lawful

The NLRB held in 1964 that a union has the authority to impose fines against members who cross picket lines while they are on strike.[97] This Board position was rejected by the Seventh Circuit Court of Appeals, however, and was accepted for review by the U.S. Supreme Court. The high court sustained the Board's position in a close 5–4 decision in *Allis-Chalmers*.[98] In doing so, it stated that the "economic strike against the employer is the ultimate weapon in labor's arsenal for achieving agreement upon its terms and the power to fine or expel strikebreakers is essential if the union is to be an effective bargaining agent." The Court argued further "that Congress did not propose any limitations with respect to the internal affairs of unions, aside from barring enforcement of a union's internal regulations to affect a member's employment status." Thus, rules are legal that impose fines on members for crossing picket lines, because unions have the right to preserve their integrity during a time of crisis. Section 7 does not insulate employees from all consequences flowing from their choice of actions. Employees may legally cross a picket line to work during a strike, but they may have to pay a fine for doing so if it is administered without discrimination by a labor organization. The ability to deal with a worker as a union member is therefore established by law. Court suits may be initiated by unions to collect fines assessed against members. This authority is found in Section 8(b)(1) which states that "this paragraph shall not impair the right of a labor organization to prescribe its own rules with respect to the acquisition or retention of membership therein." This language prompted five Supreme Court justices to hold that a fine for crossing a picket line was a legitimate union action. However, the other four were of the opinion that such union action forced employees to engage in union activities against their will.

Though the high court held that a union may fine union members who work during a strike and sue such members for the collection of the fines in state courts, it stated that the amount of the fines must be "reasonable." The question arose as to whether or not the NLRB has jurisdiction to determine the reasonableness of a fine. Thus, if the Board has authority over such a problem, it could hold that a union would commit an unfair labor practice if the fine was deemed unreasonable. However, in 1973, the Supreme Court held that the NLRB is without authority to determine the reasonableness of such fines.[99] What this decision means is that state courts have jurisdiction to establish whether a fine levied against a union member for strikebreaking is reasonable. If a union member feels that the fine levied is too high, he or she must seek relief from the state courts and not from the Board.

Application to Supervisor-Union Members

In June 1974, the *Allis-Chalmers* doctrine was applied to supervisors who were members of a union. At that time, the U.S. Supreme Court in *Florida Power and Light* v. *Electrical Workers* held that a union may properly fine supervisor-members who cross picket lines during a strike and perform bargaining-unit work.[100] However, such fines would not be lawful when supervisor-members represented their employer in collective bargaining or in the grievance procedure. To justify its decision, the Court reasoned that supervisor-members do not carry out their supervisory duties when during a strike they take over the jobs normally performed by striking employees.

However, the Board has had particular difficulty in applying the Supreme Court decision. In a dozen or so cases that followed the decision, the Board reached its decision by split votes.[101] A majority held that supervisor-members could not be fined if they performed only the following types of work: managerial work; a minimal amount of bargaining-unit work in connection with their managerial duties; or a large amount of bargaining-unit work if the supervisor-members had performed that amount of work prior to the strike. As long as the amount of such work did not increase during the strike, a fine could not be imposed. In practically every case, former Board member Fanning dissented on the grounds that the Board majority had not properly applied the *Florida Power & Light* doctrine. In his view, a supervisor-member could lawfully be fined regardless of the amount of bargaining-unit work he or she performed, or whether the amount increased during the strike. The situation became so confused that the U.S. Supreme Court agreed to review the problem.[102]

In *American Broadcasting* v. *Writers Guild of America*,[103] decided in June 1978, the high court held that a union may not fine supervisor-members who cross a picket line and perform regular supervisory duties, including the adjustment of grievances. To permit fines when the supervisors' duties involve the handling of grievances, the court reasoned, meant that a supervisor "might be tempted to give the union side of a grievance a more favorable slant while the threat of discipline remained, or while his own appeal of a union sanction was pending." Thus, the U.S. Supreme Court said that under such circumstances, union-imposed fines unlawfully coerced employers in the selection of their grievance-adjustment representatives. On the other hand, it would appear that the decision authorizes fines should supervisor-members perform struck work. The high court stated that a union has "ample leeway" to discipline members, including supervisors, for performing tasks at issue under a union contract. In its decision, the court expressly noted that the supervisors did not perform any struck work. Fines, however, may not be levied against a supervisor-member when the bargaining unit work in question was traditionally performed by the employer's supervisory personnel.[104]

By virtue of another Supreme Court decision, unions obtained added control over the activities of supervisor-members.[105] A union levied fines against two supervisor-members who took supervisory positions with a building contractor not under contract with the IBEW, the union involved in the case. Since a union did not exist there, the supervisor-members obviously did not participate in collective bargaining action, including the adjustment of grievances. For this reason, the high court rejected the employer position that the fines had the effect of depriving it of the right to select collective bargaining representatives.

In the *Electrical Workers Local 340* case, the supervisor-members did not work during a strike, but they violated a union rule prohibiting its members from working with employers who did not have a collective bargaining contract with it. Justice William Brennan, writing the majority opinion, stated: "When there is no contract between the union and employer, the union has no incentive to affect a supervisor's performance of his duties. The law was designed only to prevent a union engaged in a long-term relationship with an employer from dictating the latter's choice of representative or the form that representation would take." In addition, the Supreme Court did not question the union rule, common within the construction industry, designed to curb the practice of its skilled members taking jobs with nonunion contractors.

In 1993 the NLRB, guided by *Electrical Workers Local 340*, ruled a union *lawfully* fined an employer's superintendent and twelve supervisors for violating its constitutional provision forbidding its members, including supervisor-members, from working for an employer not a party to a collective bargaining contract with the union.[106] The employer filed charges against the union, alleging the union was attempting to coerce the supervisors by fining them because of the company's nonunion status. The NLRB determined, however, that the union was not trying to organize the employer's employees, disclaimed any interest in representing them, did not solicit authorization cards, or otherwise attempt to seek a collective bargaining relationship with the company. Under these circumstances the union lawfully fined its members in accordance with its constitution even though they were supervisory personnel.

Passing of *Allis-Chalmers* Doctrine

Severe criticism was leveled at the *Allis-Chalmers* decision.[107] It was argued that union rules designed to prevent employees from crossing picket lines have an effect on their job status. To avoid a fine, employees may avoid work, and hence, lose wages. If employees do work, the union may fine them in the amount of the wages that they earned. Fines in this amount would probably be deemed reasonable by state courts. Under these circumstances, the union members would in effect work at their jobs without pay. On the other hand, the enforcement of a union rule against strikebreaking preserves the integrity of the union and the wishes of the majority during a strike.

In any event, the sharp criticisms against *Allis-Chalmers* prompted the Supreme Court in a subsequent case to undermine the policy. The question was whether a union may fine a union member who resigns from the union before crossing the picket line. In determining this important issue, the high court held by an 8–1 majority in *Granite State Joint Board* that a fine under these circumstances violates Taft-Hartley.[108] Thus, a union member who desires to engage in strikebreaking may simply resign from the union before crossing the picket line, and the union may not levy fines for this activity. Justice Blackmun, the sole dissenter, stated in his opposition to the majority:

> I cannot join the Court's opinion, which seems to me to exalt the formality of resignation over the substance of the various interests and national labor policies that are at stake here. Union activity, by its very nature, is group activity, and is grounded on the notion that strength can be garnered from unity, solidarity, and mutual commitment. This concept is of particular force during a strike, where the individual members of the union draw strength from the commitments of fellow members, and where the activities carried on by the union rest fundamentally on the mutual reliance that inheres in the "pact."

Limitations on Right to Resign

One question, however, was not determined by the majority in *Granite State Joint Board*. The constitution of the union involved in that case did not expressly forbid resignations of members during a strike. It was silent on this issue. In its decision, the Court majority made special note of this omission. It stated: "We do not now decide to what extent the contractual relationship between union and member may curtail the freedom to resign." For a time it appeared that a union could lawfully place a reasonable restriction upon a member's right to resign. In *Dalmo Victor*,[109] the NLRB said a reasonable restriction would be a rule stating that a union member must wait thirty days after tendering a resignation notice before actually resigning. This limitation would apply regardless of whether there was a strike in progress. Members who violated this rule would be subject to fines.

Predictably, however, the Reagan NLRB upset this policy, holding that any restriction on a union member's right to resign unlawfully interfered with the right to refrain from union activities.[110] In *Neufeld Porsche-Audi*, the union's constitution said that resignation from the union would not relieve a member from the obligation to refrain from working during a legal strike or lockout. After a member tendered a letter of resignation and returned to work for the struck employer, the union imposed a fine of $2,250. Imposition of the fine was illegal, ruled the Reagan Board, regardless of the union's constitution. In a later case, the NLRB held it was unlawful for a union to refuse to accept a member's resignation until his "anniversary date" of becoming a union member.[111] In other words, a union may not lawfully place a time limitation on the member's right to resign.

By providing union members with the unfettered right to resign, despite restrictions contained in a union's constitution or bylaws, the NLRB ignored the portion of the law that states that the Section 7 rights of employees to refrain from union activities do not impair the right of a labor organization to adopt its internal rules. In addition, the Reagan Board did not recognize that the absolute right of members to resign interferes with the protected right of other employees to engage in a lawful strike. Obviously, *Neufeld Porsche-Audi* will make it more difficult for unions to implement successful strikes, thereby interfering with the Section 7 right of employees to engage in

> concerted activities for the purpose of collective bargaining or other mutual aid or protection.

The current policy does not balance the right of employees to refrain from union activities with the corresponding right of employees to engage in concerted activities.

In *Pattern Makers' League*, the U.S. Supreme Court in 1985 by a 5–4 vote sustained the Board's policy permitting union members to resign at any time and under any circumstances, free from union fines.[112] The Court said it deferred to the Board's expert judgment, suggesting that if the NLRB had upheld reasonable restrictions against a union member's right to resign during a strike, it would also have sustained such a policy. Thus, whatever protection unions received in *Allis-Chalmers* has been eliminated by the high court's pronouncements in *Granite State Joint Board* and *Pattern Makers' League*.

It would not be accurate, however, to believe court deferral to the NLRB has always worked against employees and unions. Indeed, in 1994 the Supreme Court unanimously upheld the agency's decision reinstating an employee with full back pay under unusual circumstances.[113] The employee was discharged for being late to work after having received prior warnings pursuant to the employer's tardiness policy. He told his employer, and later an administrative law judge, that his car had had a breakdown on the freeway, and that he had been assisted by an officer whom he named.

In the hearing before the law judge, the officer testified the employee was stopped for speeding at a time after he should have reported to work. The law judge recommended that the NLRB uphold the discharge, specifically finding the employee had lied.

Despite the lie, the Board reinstated the employee, ruling he was discharged because of union activities. While emphasizing strong disapproval of his dishonesty, the high court held that fired employees who lie during administrative hearings held by law judges should not automatically be denied reinstatement. Justice John Stevens, writing for the Court, said the judiciary should "rarely second guess" the judgment of executive branch agencies, such as the NLRB, given authority by Congress to make such policy decisions.

THE SUPREME COURT AND THE RIGHT TO STRIKE

Given the membership of the Supreme Court in the 1980s, it was not overly sympathetic to the workers' right to strike. Aside from *Pattern Makers' League*, the high court hampered that right in other cases. In 1981, Congress amended the Food Stamp Act, which stated that no members of a household are eligible for food stamps during the time when any member of the family is on strike. In 1988, the high court, reversing a lower federal court, upheld the constitutionality of the amendment.[114] Though the Court recognized denial of food stamps pressures workers "to abandon their union," it refused to recognize that the policy interfered with the right of workers to engage in strikes as protected by Taft-Hartley. Sharply criticizing the Supreme Court's decision, the labor movement said labor relations matters should not be settled on the basis of hunger.

In 1986, the Independent Federation of Flight Attendants unsuccessfully struck against Trans World Airlines (TWA). To maintain operations, TWA hired 2,350 replacements and used 1,300 members of the union who did not strike or who returned to work during the work stoppage. At the end of the seventy-two-day strike, TWA gave job preference to union-represented employees who either did not strike or returned to work during the strike. This meant those employees had job preference over longer-seniority flight attendants who did not work during the entire strike period.

Upholding the TWA action in a 6–3 vote, the majority of the Supreme Court said:

> We see no reason why those employees who chose not to gamble on the success of the strike should suffer the consequences when the gamble proved unsuccessful.[115]

In contrast, the minority charged the majority engaged in "inarticulated hostility toward strikes" and went too far in siding with employers. The decision makes it more difficult for unions to carry out successful strikes. It encourages union members to serve as strikebreakers. Though the case arose under the Railway Labor Act, it applies to employers and unions covered by Taft-Hartley.

CONCEPT OF "CONCERTED ACTIVITY"

Aside from applying Taft-Hartley to strikes engaged in by employees, the NLRB addressed the problem involving a *single employee's* refusal to work. The key to this problem involves Section 7 of the law, which states in part:

> Employees shall have the right . . . to engage in other concerted activities for the purpose of . . . mutual aid or protection.

For many years, the NLRB protected employees from discharge when a single employee refused to work for a purpose of group concern. For purposes of the law, a concerted activity existed, since other employees would presumably have supported the individual employee's refusal to work. For example, in *Alleluia Cushion Co.*,[116] an employee complained to the employer about safety matters. Not satisfied with the employer's response, the employee reported the employer to the California Occupational Safety and Health Administration (OSHA).

The employee had not expressly sought the support of other employees in the matter of safety. He did not request their help or advice in the drafting of the letter to OSHA. He acted by himself, not as part of any group. Despite the individual nature of his action, the NLRB held the discharge to be illegal on the premise that "safe working conditions are matters of great and continuing concern for all within the work place." That is, the employee *had* engaged in concerted activities within the meaning of Section 7 *because other employees, also concerned with safety matters, would have supported his activities had they been requested to do so.*

Reversal of Policy: *Meyers Industries I*

In *Meyers Industries*[117] the Reagan Board reversed this concept of concerted activity. To be protected from discharge, *an employee must expressly act in concert with other employees to protest employer conduct.* The facts of the case demonstrated that the employer's mechanic failed to correct defects on a tractor-trailer truck assigned to the employee. When on the highway, the trailer's brakes malfunctioned. The driver stopped at an Ohio roadside inspection station where the vehicle was cited for several defects, including the brakes. The employee sent the citation to the company.

Subsequently, while in Tennessee, the employee, driving the same vehicle, had an accident caused by the defective brakes on the trailer. The employee then contacted the Tennessee Public Service Commission. Upon inspection of the vehicle, an official of the agency cited the vehicle, directing the employee not to move it until repairs had been made. Faced with this situation, the employer decided to sell the trailer for scrap.

When the employee returned to company headquarters, he was discharged, the employer telling him, "We can't have you calling the cops like this all the time."

Reversing *Alleluia Cushion*, the Reagan NLRB upheld the employee's discharge, ruling that he had not engaged in concerted activity within the meaning of Section 7 of Taft-Hartley because he had acted by himself and not with other employees when he had reported the defective vehicle to the state authorities.

Although expressing "outrage" at the employer's conduct, the Board said that to be engaged in concerted activities for purposes of the law, and so to be protected from discharge, the employee must be "engaged in with or on the authority of other employees, and not solely by and on behalf of the employee himself."

Subsequently, the Reagan NLRB applied its construction of concerted activities to other situations, sustaining the discharge of the employee in each instance. For example, in one case a truck driver refused to drive more hours than permitted by federal regulations. Upholding his discharge, the NLRB said that the employee had acted by himself and not with other employees, nor did he have their authorization when he had refused to drive the excess hours.[118]

Remand to NLRB

In 1985, a federal appeals court remanded *Meyers Industries* to the NLRB with instructions that its literal and narrow construction of concerted activities was not mandated by Taft-Hartley.[119] It said that the NLRB had erred when it decided that its new definition of "concerted activities" was mandated by the National Labor Relations Act. It suggested that the NLRB may lawfully apply the concept of concerted activities in a more broad and realistic manner so as to afford employees statutory protection.

In support of its decision, the federal appeals court made reference to the U.S. Supreme Court's decision in *City Disposal Systems*.[120] In that case, by a 5–4 vote, the high court held that an individual employee's refusal to drive what he believed to be an unsafe truck constituted concerted activity within the meaning of Section 7 of Taft-Hartley. However, a significant difference existed between *Meyers Industries* and *City Disposal Systems*. Unlike the former case, the latter involved a collective bargaining contract that provided employees with the right to refuse to drive unsafe vehicles. No union or collective bargaining contract was involved in *Meyers Industries*. In *City Disposal Systems*, though the employee did not make specific reference to the labor agreement when he refused to drive, nor discussed his conduct with other employees, nor had their express support and authorization, the high court held that the employee had nonetheless engaged in concerted activity in the sense that he was attempting to enforce the labor agreement. It pointed out that as long as the nature of an employee's complaint is reasonably clear and refers to a reasonably perceived violation of a contract, the employee is engaged in the enforcement of the contract and engages in concerted activity under the statute. Other drivers are also concerned with the proper enforcement of the labor agreement.

Meyers Industries II

Despite the federal appeals court remand, the NLRB in *Meyers Industries II* upheld its previous interpretation of concerted activity.[121] Although it agreed its construction of the concept was not mandated by Taft-Hartley, it nonetheless believed its construction was a reasonable interpretation of Section 7. When *Meyers Industries II* was appealed to the same federal appeals court, this time it upheld the Board's construction of concerted activity.[122] It said that by "requiring that workers actually band together, the [Board] has adopted a reasonable—*but no means the only reasonable*—interpretation of Section 7 [that] is consistent with the history of the Act." (Emphasis supplied) In other words, the court was prepared to affirm the pre-Reagan construction of concerted activity had the NLRB accepted that interpretation. If nothing else, the issue raised in *Meyers Industries* is a classic example of the importance of membership makeup of the National Labor Relations Board. Under *Alleluia Cushion* the worker would be reinstated to his job, but under *Meyers Industries* his discharge, because he had called "the cops" about the unsafe vehicle, was affirmed by the Reagan Board.

RECOGNITION PICKETING

Unions frequently picket employers to gain recognition and to persuade employees to join the organization. Picketing for this purpose was protected under the Norris–La Guardia Act and Wagner Act. Taft-Hartley did not expressly regulate recognition picketing. Given the lack of legal restraint, unions could picket employers indefinitely and inflict serious damage, particularly in consumer-oriented industries, such as department stores, hotels, and restaurants. Some consumers dislike crossing picket lines, refusing to patronize a business being picketed.

The issue came to a head under circumstances where the Supreme Court held that recognition picketing carried out by a union that lost a representation election conducted by the NLRB was lawful. Despite the results of the poll, the union immediately picketed the employer's premises. The Board held the picket line illegal on the grounds that it tended to coerce employees to join the union in violation of their Section 7 right not to engage in union activity. The high court, however, ruled the NLRB did not have the authority to curb minority-union picketing undertaken to achieve recognition.[123]

Landrum-Griffin Changes

Landrum-Griffin makes it unlawful for unions to picket for recognition under the following three conditions: (1) when the employer has lawfully recognized another union and a representation question may not appropriately be raised; (2) when a valid election has been held by the NLRB within the preceding twelve months; or (3) when picketing has been conducted for a reasonable period of time, "not to exceed thirty-days from the commencement of such picketing," without filing an election petition with the Board. These restrictions do not apply to unions that are the certified bargaining agents of employees. In short, recognition picketing is illegal should the picketing continue beyond the maximum thirty-day period without the union filing an election petition.[124]

Not only must a union file an election petition within thirty days, but the NLRB must also expedite the election. These so-called "quickie elections" serve to resolve the representation issue in a prompt manner. If the union wins, it is certified as the legal bargaining representative of the employees. If the union loses, it may not petition for another election for twelve months. This means the employer is relieved from a picket line for at least one year.

When an election petition is filed under the terms of the provision, the law directs the Board to process the petition under the expedited procedure. The agency does not follow the general procedures that guide it in other elections. It does not require a showing that at least 30 percent of the bargaining unit supports the petitioning union as proof that it represents a substantial number of employees. The Board is required to make a rapid determination of bargaining-unit appropriateness for collective bargaining purposes.[125]

Despite the legal constraints on recognition picketing, not all picketing is unlawful after thirty days in the absence of an election petition. To satisfy the requirements of the First Amendment to the U.S. Constitution, unions may picket for *informational* purposes after the thirtieth day. A union may picket beyond thirty days for the purpose of *truthfully* advising the public, including consumers, that an employer does not employ members of, or have a contract with, the labor organization engaged in picketing. This picketing, however, is prohibited when it has the effect of interfering with services or the flow of goods to and from the picketed company. The NLRB is required to obtain federal court injunctions when violations occur.

Implementation of Policy

Over the years, the NLRB and the federal courts have interpreted and applied the recognition picketing policy contained in Landrum-Griffin. The Board held that a union may picket lawfully to publicize the fact that the employer was not paying the prevailing wage rates in the area even though another union was certified to bargain with the employer. It held that picketing for this limited purpose was not the same as recognition picketing.[126] Another minority union, the Board held, may lawfully picket to protest the discharge of an employee without at the same time seeking recognition. Reinstatement could be achieved without the employer recognizing or consulting with the union.[127]

In applying the informational picketing exception previously mentioned, the NLRB held that it prevailed in cases where there are only isolated instances of drivers refusing to cross picket lines.[128] A federal appeals court upheld the informational picketing provision, saying a "quantitative test concerning itself solely with the number of deliveries not made and/or services not performed is an inadequate yardstick for determining whether to remove informational picketing from" the protection of the publicity section of the law.[129] For informational picketing to be illegal, the employer must prove not only that delivery stoppages occurred but also the extent to which such stoppages disrupted business.

Under current law, there is no presumption that an original recognitional or organizational motive continues as the basic motive of unions after picketing becomes informational. There must be proof that the original motive remains the basic aim.[130] Proof may be available if a picket line is shifted from, for example, a restaurant's public entrance to its employee entrance. A shift of the picket line provides a signal to employees to leave their jobs. Thus, the Board will not protect picketing of this nature, which is viewed as an appeal to other union members as opposed to consumers. The mere shift is deemed unlawful, and the fact that employees do not leave their jobs does not control the decision.[131]

In 1992, the NLRB applied that portion of Landrum-Griffin that bans picketing for recognition within twelve months after a valid election. The union's picket signs demanded recognition and bargaining by the employer being picketed. At the time of the picketing, the union was not certified as a collective bargaining agent of the employees because it had recently lost a decertification election. Once the union lost the election and the results were certified by the NLRB, the union lost the right to picket for recognition and organization purposes for twelve months. The NLRB determined the union's picket signs bore precisely the same legend as signs used in the earlier picketing in support of bargaining. Thus the union was not picketing for informational purposes, and the agency also noted the pickets persuaded several truck drivers not to make deliveries or pick-ups at the employer's facility. Under these circumstances the Board held the picket line was unlawful and directed the union to cease picketing. It was unlawful because the union picketed for recognition within twelve months after it had lost an election, and further because the union was not picketing for informational purposes.[132]

Employer Unfair Labor Practices

Shortly after the recognition picketing section was enacted into law, the question was raised as to whether a union may picket toward this end, without violating the provisions, when employers commit unfair labor practices. Congress did not expressly permit a union to picket for recognitional or organizational purposes beyond thirty days without filing a representation petition, even when an employer engages in unfair labor practices. The Eisenhower Board searched the legislative history of the 1959 law and concluded that Congress had not intended to permit recognitional and organizational picketing beyond thirty days even if employer unfair labor practices occurred.[133]

Alternatively, it should be recalled that the U.S. Supreme Court held in *Mastro Plastics* that the Taft-Hartley penalties against a union striking during a contractual period do not apply when it strikes against an employer unfair labor practice.[134]

In *Blinne*, a union sought to represent three common laborers employed by a construction company.[135] All three had signed bargaining authorization cards. The employer transferred one worker to another building site in an effort to destroy the union's majority status. The labor organization afterward engaged in recognitional picketing for more than thirty days without filing an election petition. Unfair labor practice charges were filed against the employer about three weeks after the picketing started. The union advanced the argument that the recognitional and organizational regulations should not be enforced when employer unfair labor practices were alleged.

The Board in its first consideration of *Blinne* held that the employer unfair labor practices did not legalize the union's picketing. Despite the merit of such charges, congressional intent was interpreted as being opposed to lifting organizational and recognitional picketing prohibitions under such circumstances.[136]

Blinne was reconsidered in 1962 after a change in Board personnel.[137] The new rule was only slightly changed from the one set forth in 1961. A union may picket beyond the thirty-day limit without filing an election petition only when an employer is in violation of the refusal-to-bargain provision of Taft-Hartley. *Election petitions must be filed within the thirty-day limit when other unfair labor practices are committed.* The NLRB set forth the reason for the distinction between unfair labor practices when recognition picketing is involved. The reason is based entirely on Board procedure. For unfair labor practice charges other than refusal to bargain, the Board holds a representation petition in abeyance until the allegations have been remedied or dismissed. Under these circumstances, the Board will accept an election petition and will not dismiss one already filed. However, the election will not be conducted until such time as the unfair labor practice charges have been remedied or dismissed.

Refusal-to-bargain charges are handled differently: An election petition will not be accepted or, if already submitted, will be dismissed. This distinction is based on the idea that a representation petition assumes an unresolved question concerning representation. A refusal-to-bargain charge presupposes that no question of representation exists and that the employer is wrongfully refusing to recognize or bargain with a statutory bargaining representative.

On the whole, it seems appropriate to conclude that the NLRB and federal courts have struck a fair balance between the employer's right to be protected against recognition picketing for an indefinite period of time and the union's right to engage in recognition and informational picketing. Of course, it is a difficult problem, but given the provisions of Landrum-Griffin and the congressional intent, current law on the issue appears to treat both sides equitably.

SUMMARY

No area in labor relations law is more controversial than industrial conflict. Given the high stakes involved, this is understandable. The right of employers to conduct profitable businesses and the right of employees to a decent economic life through collective bargaining are rooted to the fundamental basis of society. How the law should balance these objectives in a fair and satisfactory manner is a never-ending debate and has no universal solution. In large measure, it depends on the perspective from which one views the industrial conflict. Employers, workers, and unions obviously have their own agenda of what law should be. Even though the NLRB and the courts strive to be impartial, their decisions must favor one side or the other in a particular case. In the final analysis, fairness and equity are in the eye of the beholder.

In this chapter, we have traced the elements of industrial conflict under Taft-Hartley as applied by the NLRB and the federal judiciary. Included in the analysis have been the voting rights of replaced economic strikers, jurisdictional disputes, strikes against NLRB certifications, employers' right to lockout, conduct of the picket line, union capability to fine union members who work during strikes, fate of the individual employee who refuses to work, and recognition picketing. It is difficult if not impossible to find a common thread connecting these matters. Employers, unions, and employees will find much in NLRB and federal court decisions to either agree or disagree with them. What complicates the problem are the changing policies of the Board and the federal courts on exactly the same issues.

Clearly, the developing law requires constant study and analysis. It certainly is not static or dull.

DISCUSSION QUESTIONS

1. What is the difference between economic strikes and unfair labor practice strikes? What rights to reinstatement exist in each case?

2. Discuss the significance and implications of *Belknap* v. *Hale* for economic striker reinstatement rights.

3. Trace the development of NLRB policy regarding voting rights in representation elections of permanently replaced economic strikers. What changes were made by Taft-Hartley? By Landrum-Griffin?

4. What is the NLRB policy for determining the voting eligibility of replaced economic strikers?

5. How important is the Taft-Hartley prohibition against jurisdictional strikes? In which industry are such strikes most likely to prove harmful?

6. How have construction industry unions responded to the Taft-Hartley requirement obliging the NLRB to settle jurisdictional disputes? To what purpose?

7. What is the significance of the Supreme Court's decision in *Plasterers' Local 79*? Is it likely to be stabilizing or destabilizing of collective bargaining in the construction industry?

8. Discuss the tests applied by the NLRB when it is required to assign disputed work. How well has the Board performed in this category?

9. How effective are Taft-Hartley and Board decisions in dealing with strikes against NLRB certification?

10. What are the current lockout rights of employers?

11. How have the courts and the Board dealt with the issue of temporary replacements in the case of defensive lockouts? Offensive lockouts?

12. Briefly outline the range of prohibited conduct on the picket line.

13. Do employees always lose reinstatement rights when they engage in illegal picketing, even when an employer commits unfair labor practices?

14. Discuss the legality of fining union members who continue to work during a strike under *Allis-Chalmers*. How did *Granite State Joint Board* affect *Allis-Chalmers*? *Pattern Makers' League*?

15. Discuss the Board and courts' handling of the concept of "concerted activity" as it relates to individual employees.

16. Under what conditions does Landrum-Griffin make it unlawful for unions to picket for recognition?

17. May unions ever picket for recognitional or organizational purposes beyond thirty days without filing a representation petition when an employer engages in unfair labor practices?

NOTES

1   Edwin E. Witte, *The Government in Labor Disputes* (New York: McGraw-Hill Book Company, 1932), p. 20.

2   Section 9(c)(3).

3   *Mastro Plastics Corporation* v. *NLRB*, 350 U.S. 270 (1956).

4   *NLRB* v. *Fansteel Metallurgical Company*, 306 U.S. 240 (1939).

5   *Belknap* v. *Hale*, 463 U.S. 491 (1983).

6   *NLRB* v. *Mackay Radio & Telegraph Company*, 304 U.S. 333 (1938).

7   *Trans World Airlines* v. *Independent Federation of Flight Attendants*, 489 US 426 (1989).

8   John Schnell and Cynthia Gramm, "The Empirical Relations Between Employers' Striker Replacement Strategy and Strike Duration," *Industrial and Labor Relations Review*, v. 47, No. 2 (January 1994), p. 189.

9   *Wall Street Journal*, February 5, 1991.

10   *Monthly Labor Review*, v. 15, September 1992, p. 94.

11   *AFL-CIO News*, June 22, 1992.

12   *AFL-CIO News*, January 17, 1994.

13   *Employer Association, Inc.* v. *United Steelworkers of America*, 803 F. Supp. 1558 (1992).

14   *Transit Union Local 1202* v. *Greyhound Buslines*, 561 N.Y.S. 2d 118 (1990).

15   *Gibson Greetings, Inc.*, 310 NLRB No. 221 (1993).

16   *Harvey Manufacturing, Inc.*, 309 NLRB No. 71 (1992).

17   *Rose Printing Company*, 304 NLRB 1076 (1991).

18   *A. Sartorius & Company*, 10 NLRB 493 (1938).

19   *Rudolph Wurlitzer*, 32 NLRB 163 (1941).

20   Recall the discussion of decertification elections in Chapter 5.

21   *Louisville Courier-Journal*, April 28, 1967.

22   *Monthly Labor Review*, v. 110, No. 10 (October 1987), p. 49.

23   *Pioneer Flour Mills*, 174 NLRB 1202 (1969).

24   *Brooks Research & Manufacturing*, 202 NLRB 634 (1973).

25   *Wahl Clipper Corporation*, 195 NLRB 634 (1972).

26   *Gulf States Paper Corp., EZ Packaging Division*, 219 NLRB 806 (1975).

27   *Jeld-Wen of Everett, Inc.*, 285 NLRB 118 (1987).

28   *W. Wilton Wood, Inc.*, 127 NLRB 1675 (1960).

29   *Bright Foods, Inc.*, 126 NLRB 553 (1960).

30   *National Gypsum Company*, 133 NLRB 1492 (1961).

31   National Labor Relations Board, *Twenty-seventh Annual Report*, 1962, p. 80.

32   *Curtin Matheson Scientific* v. *NLRB*, 110 S. Ct. 1542 (1990).

33   *Laidlaw Corporation*, 171 NLRB 175 (1968).

34   *NLRB* v. *Fleetwood Trailer Company*, 389 U.S. 375 (1967).

35   *United Aircraft Corporation*, 192 NLRB 62 (1971).

36   John T. Dunlop, "Jurisdictional Disputes," *Proceedings of New York University Second Annual Conference of Labor*, p. 479.

37   National Labor Relations Board, *Forty-sixth Annual Report*, 1981, p. 192.

38   Section 8(b)(4).

39   Bureau of National Affairs, *Taft-Hartley After One Year* (1948), p. 101.

40   Section 8(b)(4)(D) makes it an unfair labor practice for a union to strike or to refuse to perform services when the object is "forcing or requiring any employer to assign particular work to employees in a particular labor organization or in a particular trade, craft, or class rather than to employees in another labor organization or in another trade, craft, or class, unless such employer is failing to conform to an order or certification of the Board determining the bargaining representative for employees performing such work."

41   *NLRB* v. *Radio Engineers Union*, 364 U.S. 573 (1961).

42   *NLRB* v. *Plasterers' Local 79, Operative Plasterers (Texas State Tile and Terrazzo Company)*, 404 U.S. 116 (1971).

43   *NLRB* v. *Plasterers' Local 79, Operative Plasterers (Texas State Tile and Terrazzo Company)*, 440 F. 2d 174 (D.C. Cir. 1970), cert. granted 71 S. Ct. 1195 (1971).

44   *Philadelphia Typographical Union, Local No. 2 (Philadelphia Inquirer, Division of Triangle Publications, Inc.)*, 142 NLRB 36 (1963).

45   *NLRB* v. *International Longshoremen's and Warehousemen's Union, Local 50 (Pacific Maritime Association)*, 504 F. 2d 1209 (9th Cir. 1974).

46   Bruce Simmons, "Jurisdictional Disputes: Does the Board Really Snub the Supreme Court?" *Labor Law Journal*, XXXVI, 3 (March 1985), p. 183.

47   *Ibid.*, p. 191.

48   *Thompson Products, Inc.*, 72 NLRB 886 (1947).

49   Section 8(b)(4).

50   *United Mine Workers* v. *Patton*, 211 F. 2d 742 (4th Cir. 1954), cert. denied 348 U.S. 824 (1954).

51   *Dairy Distributors, Inc.* v. *Western Conference of Teamsters*, 294 F. 2d 348 (10th Cir. 1961).

52   *Charles D. Bonanno Linen Supply* v. *NLRB*, 454 U.S. 404 (1982).

53   *NLRB* v. *Truck Drivers Local Union No. 449, et al. (Buffalo Linen Supply Company)*, 353 U.S. 87 (1957).

54   *Great Atlantic & Pacific Tea Company*, 145 NLRB 361 (1963).

55   *Evening News Assn., Owner and Publisher of Detroit News*, 145 NLRB 996 (1964).

56   *Brown Food Store*, 137 NLRB 73 (1962), enf. denied 319 F. 2d 7 (10th Cir. 1963), cert. granted 375 U.S. 962 (1965).

57 *NLRB* v. *Brown et al.*, d/b/a *Brown Food Store et al.*, 380 U.S. 278 (1965).

58 *NLRB* v. *Mackay Radio & Telegraph Company*, 304 U.S. 333 (1938).

59 *American Ship Building Company* v. *NLRB*, 380 U.S. 300 (1965).

60 *Inland Trucking Company* v. *NLRB*, 440 F. 2d 562 (7th Cir. 1971).

61 *Local 155, International Molders and Allied Workers Union (U.S. Pipe and Foundry Company)* v. *NLRB*, 442 F. 2d 742 (D.C. Cir. 1971).

62 *Ottawa Silica Company*, 197 NLRB 449 (1972).

63 *Intercollegiate Press, Graphic Arts Division*, 199 NLRB 177 (1972).

64 *Intercollegiate Press, Graphic Arts Division* v. *NLRB*, 486 F. 2d 837 (8th Cir. 1973).

65 *Johns-Manville Products Corp.*, 223 NLRB 1317 (1976).

66 *Boilermakers, Local 88* v. *NLRB*, 858 F. 2d 756 (D.C. Cir. 1988).

67 *Harter Equipment, Inc.*, 293 NLRB 647 (1989).

68 Section 8(b)(1).

69 *Sunset Line & Twine*, 79 NLRB 1487 (1948).

70 *Congressional Record*, XCIII, 4563.

71 *Sunset Line & Twine, supra.*

72 81 NLRB 886 (1949).

73 *Local 761, International Union of Electrical, Radio & Machine Workers, AFL-CIO (General Electric Company)*, 126 NLRB 123 (1960).

74 *North Electric Manufacturing Company*, 84 NLRB 136 (1949).

75 *Sunset Line & Twine, supra.*

76 See chapter dealing with election policies of the NLRB.

77 *Letter Carriers (Old Dominion Branch No. 496, National Association of Letter Carriers)* v. *Austin*, 418 U.S. 264 (1974).

78 *Clear Pine Mouldings, Inc.*, 268 NLRB 1044 (1984).

79 *Coronet Casuals*, 207 NLRB 304 (1973).

80 *Georgia Kraft Company, Woodcraft Division*, 275 NLRB 636 (1985).

81 *Newport News Shipbuilding and Dry Dock Company* v. *NLRB*, 738 F. 2d 1404 (1984).

82 *Cory Corporation*, 84 NLRB 972 (1949).

83 80 NLRB 47 (1948).

84 NLRB Release R-321, May 27, 1950.

85 84 NLRB 972 (1949).

86 *Local 833, United Automobile, Aircraft & Agricultural Implement Workers of America, UAW-CIO* v. *NLRB*, 300 F. 2d 699 (D.C. CCA 1962), cert. denied 370 U.S. 911 (1962).

87 Robert T. Schupp, "Employer Property Rights v. Union Rights to Access," *Labor Law Journal*, v. 44, June 1993, p. 361.

88 *Republic Aviation Corporation*, 324 U.S. 793 (1945).

89 *NLRB* v. *Babcock and Wilcox Company*, 351 U.S. 105 (1956).

90 *Jean Country*, 291 NLRB 11 (1988).

91 *Lechmere, Inc.* v. *NLRB*, 112 S. Ct. 841 (1992).

92 *Lechmere, Inc.*, 295 NLRB No. 15 (1989).

93   *Lechmere, Inc.* v. *NLRB*, 914 F. 2d 313 (1990).

94   *New Jersey Bell Telephone*, 308 NLRB No. 32 (1992); *Susquehanna United Super, Inc.*, 308 NLRB No. 43 (1992); *Davis Supermarkets, Inc.*, 306 NLRB No. 86 (1992).

95   *CDK Contracting Company*, 308 NLRB No. 162 (1992).

96   *Automotive Plastic Technologies, Inc.*, 313 NLRB No. 50 (1993).

97   *Local 248, UAW (Allis-Chalmers Manufacturing Company)*, 149 NLRB 67 (1964).

98   *NLRB* v. *Allis-Chalmers Manufacturing Company*, 388 U.S. 175 (1967), rev. 358 F. 2d 656 (7th Cir. 1966).

99   *NLRB* v. *Boeing*, 412 U.S. 67 (1973).

100 *Florida Power and Light* v. *Electrical Workers*, 417 U.S. 790 (1974).

101 National Labor Relations Board, *Fortieth Annual Report*, 1975, pp. 113, 115.

102 *Wall Street Journal*, April 26, 1977, p. 4.

103 437 U.S. 411 (1978).

104 *Teamsters, Local 296, Northwest Publications, Inc.*, 263 NLRB 778 (1982).

105 *NLRB* v. *Electrical Workers, Local 340*, 481 U.S. 573 (1987).

106 *Plumbers Local 597*, 308 NLRB No. 101 (1992).

107 Hearings before the Subcommittee on Separation of Powers, *Congressional Oversight of Administrative Agencies (National Labor Relations Board)*, Part II, U.S. Senate (Washington, D.C.: Government Printing Office, 1968), p. 1115.

108 *NLRB* v. *Granite State Board*, 409 U.S. 213 (1974).

109 *Machinists, Local 1327, Dalmo Victor*, 263 NLRB 984 (1982).

110 *Machinists, Local 1414, Neufeld Porsche-Audi, Inc.*, 270 NLRB 1330 (1984).

111 *Letter Carriers, United States Postal Service*, 283 NLRB 644 (1987).

112 *Pattern Makers' League* v. *NLRB*, 473 U.S. 95 (1985).

113 *A.B. Freight Systems* v. *NLRB*, 114 S. Ct. 835 (1994).

114 *Lyng* v. *Automobile Workers*, 485 U.S. 360 (1988).

115 *Trans World Airlines* v. *International Federation of Flight Attendants*, 489 U.S. 426 (1989).

116 *Alleluia Cushion Co.*, 221 NLRB 999 (1979).

117 *Meyers Industries, Inc.*, 268 NLRB 493 (1984).

118 *Moyer Trucking & Garage Service*, 269 NLRB 958 (1984).

119 *Prill* v. *NLRB*, 755 F. 2d 241 (D.C. Cir. 1985).

120 *NLRB* v. *City Disposal Systems, Inc.*, 465 U.S. 822 (1984).

121 *Meyers Industries (II)*, 281 NLRB 882 (1986).

122 *Prill* v. *NLRB*, 835 F. 2d 1481 (D.C. Cir. 1987).

123 *NLRB* v. *Drivers Local Union*, 362 U.S. 274 (1960).

124 National Labor Relations Board, *Twenty-eighth Annual Report*, 1963, p. 115.

125 Fred Witney, "NLRB Membership Cleavage: Recognition and Organizational Picketing," *Labor Law Journal*, XIV, 5 (May 1963), pp. 434–458.

126 *Calumet Contractors Association*, 133 NLRB 512 (1961).

127 *United Automobile Workers, Local 259 (Fanelli Ford Sales, Inc.)*, 133 NLRB 1468 (1961).

128   *Retail Clerks, Locals 324 & 770 (Barker Bros.)*, 138 NLRB 478 (1962).

129   *Barker Bros. Corporation v. NLRB*, 328 F. 2d 431 (9th Cir. 1964).

130   *Retail Clerks International Association, Local 344*, 136 NLRB 478 (1962).

131   *Atlantic Maintenance Company*, 136 NLRB 1104 (1962).

132   *Graphic Communications International Union, Local IM*, 305 NLRB No. 168 (1991).

133   *Legislative History of the Labor-Management Reporting and Disclosure Act of 1959*, II, 1383, 1384.

134   *Mastro Plastics Corporation v. NLRB*, 350 U.S. 270 (1956).

135   *C. A. Blinne Construction Company*, 130 NLRB 587 (1961).

136   Discussion of Elliott bill as reported by the House, H.R. 8342, 86th Congress, 1st sess., 1959, and Kennedy-Irvin bill in the Senate, S. 1555, 86th Congress, 1st sess., 1959.

137   *C. A. Blinne Construction Company*, 135 NLRB 1153 (1962).

9

Secondary Boycott Pressures

Recapitulation

In Chapter 1, we investigated the legal status of the secondary boycott under the antitrust laws. Reference was made to famous labor cases such as *Danbury Hatters* and *Bedford Cut Stone*. In these cases, the Supreme Court held union secondary boycott activities unlawful under the Sherman Act. This meant that a union could not call or induce a strike when the objective would be to force one employer to cease doing business with another. Frankfurter and Greene defined the device as "a combination to influence A by exerting some sort of economic or social pressure against persons who deal with A."[1] This definition of a secondary boycott is not nearly as simple as implied, as will be seen subsequently.

In discussing the relationship of unions to the antitrust laws, close attention was paid to the economic factors that caused labor unions to resort to the secondary boycott. Consequently, there is no need to review these aspects again, except to point out that employees involved in labor antitrust cases resorted to the secondary boycott to preserve the status of their labor unions. The alternative to the secondary boycott could have been their disintegration.

Congress enacted the Clayton Act in 1914, but this legislation did not prove to be the labor's Magna Charta that it was hailed to be. The position of organized labor under the antitrust statutes was not improved. It was not until the Norris–La Guardia Act was passed in 1932 that the union objective was realized. The law protected secondary boycott activities from prosecution under antitrust provisions. This protection remained until Taft-Hartley was enacted in 1947. It outlawed secondary boycotts, not under the antitrust statutes but under the 1947 law. Thus, public policy has come full circle—from unlawfulness to lawfulness back to illegality.

SECONDARY BOYCOTTS UNDER TAFT-HARTLEY

Congressional Intent

The legislative history of the Taft-Hartley Act makes it clear that the congressional objective was to protect neutral employers and neutral employees from economically injurious union pressures stemming from labor-management disputes. Protection was to be extended to these groups when they were neutral parties to the dispute.

In the Taft-Hartley hearings in 1947, Congress determined that the secondary boycott—the union practice of striking, picketing, or otherwise boycotting one employer in order to exert pressure on another—was unjustifiable and should be removed from the labor scene. Congress drew up the Section 8(b)(4) language to accomplish its objective. In pertinent part the provision provided:

> It shall be an unfair labor practice for a labor organization or its agents—(4) to engage in, or to induce or encourage the employees of any employer to engage in, a strike, or a concerted refusal in the course of their employment to use, manufacture, process, transport, or otherwise handle or work on any goods, articles, materials, or commodities, or to perform any services, where an object thereof is: (A) forcing or requiring . . . any employer or any other person to cease using, selling, handling, transporting, or otherwise dealing in the products of any other producer, processor, or manufacturer, or to cease doing business with any other person.

The scope of the section was explained by Senator Robert Taft during the debates. He stated:

> This provision makes it unlawful to resort to a secondary boycott to injure the business of a third person who is wholly unconcerned in the disagreement between an employer and his employees. . . . It has been set forth that there are good secondary boycotts and bad secondary boycotts. Our committee heard evidence for weeks and never succeeded in having anyone tell us any difference between different kinds of secondary boycotts. So we have so broadened the provision dealing with secondary boycotts as to make them an unfair labor practice.[2]

The intent of Congress in enacting the provision appeared clear. As detailed below, however, the NLRB and federal courts while applying the law opened up loopholes by permitting unions to continue using secondary boycotts under certain circumstances. In 1953, a congressional committee reviewed the loopholes that were considered so large that "a truck can be driven through them."[3] The loopholes included:

1. Direct coercion of employers to cease doing business with another person. Strikes were not used to accomplish this end.

2. "Hot-cargo" contracts whereby employers agreed not to do business with firms considered "unfair" by unions.
3. Exemption from the secondary boycott provision of "employers," "persons," and "employees" not considered as coming within the Act's definitions.
4. Union ability to influence the nonconcerted activities of employees. That is, the ability to deal with an employee as a single individual.
5. Union inducement to engage in consumer boycotts.
6. Union refusal to allow members to accept jobs from secondary employers.
7. Boycotts taking place at the location of the primary dispute.
8. Picketing trucks at secondary locations.
9. Boycotts of secondary employers who are allied with primary employers.[4]

Congress reviewed the secondary boycott loopholes of Taft-Hartley during the Landrum-Griffin Act hearings. It reaffirmed its intention to outlaw secondary action. Senator John F. Kennedy, then chairman of the Senate conferees on the Landrum-Griffin bill, explained the intent of the secondary boycott provision amendments as follows:

> The chief effect of the conference agreement, therefore, will be to plug loopholes in the secondary boycott provisions of the National Labor Relations Act. There has never been any dispute about the desirability of plugging these artificial loopholes.[5]

Ally Doctrine

The legislative history of Taft-Hartley makes it clear that Congress intended to prohibit union inducement of work stoppages for the purpose of forcing B to cease doing business with A only when B *was in fact neutral in the dispute*. The assumption implicit in the language of the law was that the two employers were independent.[6] Senator Taft during a debate on the section remarked that it "is not intended to apply to a case where the third party is, in effect, in cahoots with or acting as a part of the primary employer."[7] That is, the secondary boycott provisions do not apply when the third party is not really neutral but is in fact a willing *ally* of the primary employer.

The ally doctrine is applicable when a primary employer is struck and then subcontracts work to another company that is aware of the existence of the labor dispute.[8] Indeed, this form of boycott was often permitted under the common law even when other secondary activity was held unlawful. Unionists are permitted to protect themselves against such offensive employer actions. The primary employees have a self-interest in the work in dispute and do not have to sit idly by while their economic position deteriorates as a result of subcontracting. The NLRB ruled in *Kable Printing Co.* that an "orchestrated" maneuver by a firm to have its customers contract directly with other companies during a strike does not make them neutral to the dispute.[9]

The secondary employer in such cases is not completely powerless to resolve the underlying dispute. Such a company could refuse to handle the struck work that is not handled by it under normal circumstances, with the result that significant economic pressure would be placed back on the first point of union concern. Since this is the case, the "secondary employer" is in fact treated as a primary employer by the Board. The ally doctrine has been consistently applied by the NLRB and was not a topic for

1959 remedial action by Congress. *The ally doctrine is not and has never been a loophole of the secondary boycott provisions of Taft-Hartley.* The intent of Congress was made clear by the Conference Committee Report revealing that "no language has been included with reference to struck work because the committee conference did not wish to change the existing law as illustrated by such decisions as *Douds* v. *Metropolitan Federation of Architects*."[10]

Taft-Hartley Loopholes

Under the 1947 law, for secondary boycott activity to be unlawful, there had to be *union pressure to induce the employees of the neutral employer* in the course of their employment to engage in a *concerted refusal* to perform services. The refusal had to be for the purpose of interfering with a business relationship between the secondary and primary employers. The basis for loopholes included the key phrases "induce the employees" of the neutral employer and "a concerted refusal" to perform services. Interpretation of this language had to be made within the statutory definition of *employer* under Taft-Hartley, which excluded such users of labor as agencies of federal, state, and municipal governments. In addition, railroads and airlines were among the organizations not defined as employers. Consequently, unions were lawfully permitted to *exert pressure on the employees of these organizations for the purpose of effecting a secondary boycott.* It would have been highly inconsistent to have ruled that some sections of law applied to these organizations while other sections did not. The Board and the courts responded to the total public policy and not to fragmented parts of it.

It was also lawful for a union to induce key employees of the neutral employer to cause a secondary boycott. This situation was made clear by the U.S. Supreme Court in *International Rice Milling*[11] when a union persuaded two truck drivers of the neutral employer to refuse to cross a picket line at the site of the primary employer. Holding that such action did not constitute a *concerted refusal to work*, the high court ruled the union action lawful.

On the basis of the decision, unions could lawfully pressure key employees of neutral employers within the context of secondary boycott activities. Depending on the circumstances of a dispute, such pressure could force the primary employer to yield to union demands.

Another loophole developed when the union put pressure on the secondary or neutral employer itself. *Since the target was the employer and not its employees,* the NLRB and courts held such union action lawful. The union was not inducing the secondary employees to withhold their services. This tactic would be particularly effective when the union held a contract with the neutral employer. By threatening that the union intended to take a hard line in the next contract negotiations, the secondary employer might cease doing business with the primary employer. Even when unions did not hold bargaining rights with the secondary employer, the tactic was used successfully.

Under original Taft-Hartley language, unions could lawfully persuade the public not to buy from a firm doing business with the primary employer.[12] This was the same tactic taken by the union involved in *Danbury Hatters*. The NLRB and courts held such boycott activity lawful because the *pressure was directed solely against the secondary employer*. The union did not interfere with the right of the secondary employer's employees to work.

To say the least, the business community sharply criticized the NLRB and court policies. Employers believed Taft-Hartley protected the neutral firm from the impact of the secondary boycott. Much to their chagrin here was loophole after loophole, which permitted the labor movement to escape from the ban. The business community wanted the loopholes plugged up. Congress responded to the business point of view when Landrum-Griffin was enacted.

LANDRUM-GRIFFIN CHANGES

Closing of the Loopholes

Congress closed the loopholes generated by the 1947 statutory language. Two clauses were adopted to achieve this end. Clause (i) of Section 8(b)(4) of Landrum-Griffin forbids unions to strike or to induce or encourage strikes or work stoppages by *any individual employed by any person* for a secondary boycott purpose. Thus, it is unlawful for unions to pressure any individual to participate in secondary boycotts. Unlike the prior situation, unions may not pressure key individuals of the neutral employer.

Clause (ii) makes it unlawful for a union to threaten, coerce, or restrain *any person* engaged in commerce or in an industry affecting commerce for a secondary boycott objective. "Any person" refers to government agencies and other organizations not defined as employers by Taft-Hartley. Thus, such employers as railroads and airlines are now covered by the law, since they are "persons" even if they are not legally defined as employers. Also, the new language outlaws union pressure on secondary employers themselves, since now the pressure need not be exerted against the employees of an employer to fall within the unlawful area. *It is now illegal to exert pressure against the employees of the neutral employer or against employers themselves*. The amendment also makes secondary consumer boycotts unlawful, since such union pressure is directed against the secondary employer.

In short, Landrum-Griffin plugged the loopholes of permitting unions to put pressure (1) directly on employers, (2) directly on key individuals, and (3) directly on organizations not considered employers under Taft-Hartley. Ironically, however, the NLRB and the courts found some loopholes even in the new language. Despite these new loopholes, the opportunity for unions to engage in secondary boycotts is far less than it was before the adoption of the Landrum-Griffin changes.

Landrum-Griffin Loophole: Managers of Neutral Employers

In *Servette*,[13] the U.S. Supreme Court held that union appeals to managers or supervisors of neutral employers to cease doing business with the primary employer were lawful *provided they have the managerial discretion to grant the union appeal*. Even though managers are "individuals employed by any person," the high court ruled the legal test of union action was whether the appeal was to the exercise of managerial discretion or was an appeal for managers to cease performing services for the secondary employer, as long as it dealt with the employer with whom the union had the primary dispute.

The case involved the union's appeal to chain store managers to cease handling products supplied by Servette. Since the managers had such discretion and authority—they could purchase the same products elsewhere—the union's action was lawful. If the union requested the managers to cease working for the chain stores, such appeals would be unlawful. It may well be that union "appeals" to management to pressure other employers, however politely stated, carry with them implicit threats of economic reprisal if refused. This is particularly the case if the union has a bargaining relationship with the firm to which it makes an appeal.

Servette opened a loophole in the Landrum-Griffin secondary boycott ban. To escape the proscription, unions need only be careful that they do not request the supervisors or managers to cease working for the secondary firm and make sure they have the discretion to grant the appeal. Depending on the circumstances of a particular situation, such appeals to managers of the secondary firms could effectively gain the union a definite advantage in its dispute with the primary employer.

Divisions of the Same Corporation

On the other hand, the Board construed the word "person" to limit boycott activities in a dispute involving two divisions of the same parent corporation. In a case that concerned the Hearst Corporation, the NLRB forbade the picketing of one division of the enterprise when a union had a dispute with another division of the same corporation. Hearst owned a TV station and a newspaper division. The direct labor dispute concerned the TV operation. During the dispute, the union picketed the offices of the newspaper. The Board held that the picketing of the newspaper was illegal under the secondary boycott provisions of the law, since it was calculated to solicit support of the newspaper employees to aid the union in its dispute with the TV station. In upholding the Board decision, a federal court stated that the two enterprises, though owned by the same parent corporation, were separate "persons" within the meaning of the law.[14]

On the basis of the record, the NLRB found that the divisions were separate and autonomous, with independent control vested in the officers of the respective divisions. Though the court acknowledged that the Hearst president could replace division heads and had the power to approve large corporation expenditures, it also determined that in practice Hearst vested active control in the respective division heads. For example, the division heads set their own news policies, could reject news services offered by Hearst, handled collective bargaining on an independent basis, and established their own financial and accounting systems. In short, it was found that there was a sufficient degree of autonomous control to warrant their treatment as separate "persons" for purposes of the secondary boycott provision.

In any event, the *Hearst* case has important implications for labor policy in these days of the conglomerate business enterprise. Though owned by the same parent corporation, different divisions of the same enterprise could be regarded as separate "persons" for purposes of federal labor law.

Landrum-Griffin Loophole: Consumer Secondary Boycotts

Landrum-Griffin does not outlaw all union activities to publicize that neutral employers are selling or otherwise distributing products produced by the employer with whom the union has the primary dispute. A flat ban on all informational activities probably would not satisfy the constitutional guarantee of free speech. Concerned with that problem, Congress added a publicity proviso in Landrum-Griffin. It states:

> For the purpose of this paragraph, only, nothing contained in such paragraph shall be construed to prohibit publicity, *other than picketing*, for the purpose of truthfully advising the public, including consumers and members of a labor organization, that a product or products are produced by an employer with whom a labor organization has a primary dispute and are distributed by another employer. (Emphasis supplied)

During the debate on Landrum-Griffin, Senator John F. Kennedy, then chair of the Senate Labor Committee, said unions may publicize the secondary employer's relationship with the primary employer by handbilling, newspaper advertisements, radio, and TV.[15] Given the unambiguous language of the publicity provision, it appears just as clear that picketing at the site of the secondary employer was per se unlawful. It says unions may lawfully make public the neutral employer's relationship with the primary employer by means *"other than picketing."*

Following the literal language of the provision, the NLRB originally held that union picketing was unlawful when undertaken at the site of the secondary employer, a retail store, that was selling products produced by the primary employer struck by the union. The purpose of the picketing, of course, was to persuade the public not to purchase the struck product.[16]

Ignoring the clarity of the language, however, the U.S. Supreme Court held in *Tree Fruits* that Congress did not intend to outlaw all picketing at the site of the secondary employer.[17] The essence of the decision was that picketing does not coerce the secondary employer when the target of the picketing is directed solely *at the struck product* and not to persuade the public to cease buying any of its products.

To justify its decision, the high court said the legislative history of Landrum-Griffin "does not reflect with the requisite clarity a congressional plan to proscribe all peaceful consumer picketing at secondary sites." The record merely revealed that such picketing was unlawful if the labor organization attempted to persuade customers not to buy any of the products at the neutral store. Customers may be persuaded through picketing not to buy the struck product. Thus, picketing confined to persuading customers to cease buying the product of the primary employer with whom the dispute exists is not prohibited secondary action. In most cases, the Court reasoned, if secondary stores drop the item in dispute from their counters, they would not be hurt economically. This view of the Court may be correct in terms of grocery stores or department stores that handle a large range of goods. Presumably, the *Tree Fruits* doctrine rationale would not hold when specialty shops are involved. That is, a store that specializes in a particular good supplied by a single producer could be dealt a severe economic setback if consumer picketing were permitted.

At the same time, however, it should be realized that unions may be legally within their rights to use forms of publicity other than picketing to appeal to customers not to patronize a secondary store. Consider this statement of the Court in *Tree Fruits*:

> Peaceful consumer picketing to shut off all trade with the secondary employer unless he aids the union in its dispute with the primary employer is poles apart from such picketing which only persuades his customer not to buy the struck product.

The Court said that picketing may not be used to stop all customer trade with a neutral employer, but that other forms of publicity may be used even if they accomplish this end. All that is required is that the information on handbills, for example, be truthful and not misleading to the public.

In short, the Supreme Court has held that all picketing of secondary employers is not per se illegal. This doctrine provides a basis for unions to exert secondary pressure and creates a loophole in the provisions of Landrum-Griffin. Carefully worded picket signs permit unions to effectuate consumer boycotts on particular goods.

Application of *Tree Fruits*

After a number of inconclusive rulings by the NLRB and the lower federal courts, the Supreme Court in *Safeco*[18] held the extent of damages to the secondary employer must be considered for the proper application of *Tree Fruits*. That is, the legality of secondary employer picketing depends on the amount of loss suffered by it.

The primary employer involved in the strike was Safeco, a title insurance underwriter. It sold its product to land title firms. In addition to picketing Safeco's place of business, the union also picketed and passed out handbills at the offices of five land title companies. These companies obtained 90 percent of their total revenue from the sale of Safeco's insurance policies. Holding the picketing at the site of the neutral employers unlawful, the high court said "the union's secondary appeal against the central product sold by the title companies is reasonably calculated to persuade customers not to patronize the neutrals at all." Thus, a union that desires to picket a product at a secondary site will be required to calculate whether the primary product makes up such a substantial proportion of the firm's business that the Board and courts will not approve of the action.

Handbilling under *De Bartolo Corporation*

In *De Bartolo*,[19] a 1988 case, the U.S. Supreme Court expanded the lawfulness of union secondary boycott activity. To this extent, another loophole was created in the Landrum-Griffin antisecondary boycott provisions. Unlike *Tree Fruits*, this case involved handbilling, not picketing, at a shopping mall located in Tampa, Florida. De Bartolo, which owned the mall, hired a contractor to build a new department store in the mall. Unlike its previous practice, the mall owner used a nonunion firm. Being unorganized, the contractor did not pay union rates and fringe benefits.

In protest, building trades unions handbilled entrances to the mall. They requested the public not to shop *at any store* located therein. The union action was limited to handbilling. Unions did not picket, patrol, or prevent employees from reporting to work at the stores, no violence occurred, and customers were not intimidated. The handbills requested the public not to shop at the mall because of the "Mall's Ownership's Contribution To Substandard Wages."

De Bartolo filed charges with the NLRB alleging the unions engaged in illegal secondary boycott action. Its charge contended that the union by handbilling coerced the mall store tenants to cease doing business with De Bartolo in order to force the mall owner to cease doing business with the nonunion contractor.

Upsetting a previous NLRB decision, the Reagan Board held the union's activity was illegal and ordered the handbilling stopped.[20] *By unanimous vote*, the Supreme Court reversed the NLRB, holding that the handbilling was lawful. Rejecting the Board's ruling, the high court stated:

> We [do not] find any clear indication in the relevant legislative history that Congress intended to proscribe peaceful handbilling, unaccompanied by picketing urging a consumer boycott of a neutral employer.

And further:

> The handbills involved here truthfully revealed the existence of a labor dispute and urged potential customers of the mall to follow a wholly legal course of action, namely not to patronize the retailers doing business in the mall.

Needless to say, *De Bartolo* provoked sharp criticism from the employer community. For example:

> This conclusion, however, seems contrary to the idea that Congress intended to protect secondary employers. It makes little difference to a secondary employer whose business is ruined what method was used to do it, picketing or handbills; nor is it important to him if the customers were persuaded rather than coerced, a distinction which could thrust future courts into a quagmire of semantics.[21]

Regardless of the controversy, within shopping malls, the predominant source of consumer spending, *De Bartolo's* significance goes far beyond the Tampa mall. It provides building trades unions with an important tool to maintain union standards in the construction of shopping malls.

Products Produced for Publicity Purposes

Another feature of the publicity provision required attention by the NLRB and the federal courts. It says a union may publicize that a company is distributing or selling "*products produced* by an employer with whom the union has the primary dispute."

The issue arises as to whether products produced by the primary employer constitute strictly a physical product, an automobile for example, or whether the concept includes a service provided by the primary employer. Depending on the construction, the scope of the publicity provision would be determined. If products produced related exclusively to physical products, the opportunity of unions to publicize the primary dispute would be restricted. On the other hand, the opportunity would be greater should the concept include services provided to the neutral employer.

Relying on the economic definition of production, the NLRB consistently held that the publicity provision includes intangible services rendered by the primary employer. In economic terms, value is added to a product at each stage of production or distribution. In *Lohman Sales Company*,[22] the union struck a wholesaler that distributed candy, cigarettes, and other sundry items to drug stores. Obviously, Lohman, the primary firm, did not physically produce the candy or cigarettes. Nonetheless, the Board held the union involved could lawfully pass out handbills at the drug stores publicizing the fact that they were distributing products of the struck employer.

This interpretation was carried over to *Middle South Broadcasting*. A union had a dispute with a radio station. A blacklist with the names of several firms that advertised over the station was circulated. One of the firms listed was an automobile agency that advertised over the Middle South station. The Board overruled an administrative law judge to hold that the radio station was a producer of the product it advertised. The Board justified its position by stating that

> as found in [Lohman Sales], labor is the prime requisite of one who "produces" and therefore an employer who applies his labor to a product, whether of an abstract or physical nature, or in the initial or intermediate stages of the marketing of the product, is one of the "producers" of the product.[23]

In *Servette*, previously mentioned, the U.S. Supreme Court upheld the Board's construction of the publicity proviso. Unfortunately, the record of Landrum-Griffin does not reveal what Congress intended by the words "products produced." Lacking such information, it would appear reasonable for the NLRB and high court to apply the language in terms of the economic definition of production. If the construction did not satisfy employers, it would probably satisfy at least some economists.

American and Japanese Unions: Secondary Boycott

This is probably the first instance in United States labor history where a secondary boycott was arranged by an American labor organization with the cooperation of a foreign trade union. Given the current global state of international trade and communication, it is understandable why the situation occurred and, indeed, it may very well be the harbinger of more international cooperation among labor unions in future years.

The players in the case were an American union, Longshoremen; a Japanese Dock Workers' Union; Stevedoring Companies (operating in Florida); and Florida citrus fruit growers and shippers. For many years Florida citrus fruit products were loaded for shipment to Japan at the Florida ports of Fort Pierce and Cape Canaveral located on the east coast of the state. They were loaded by two nonunion stevedoring companies. For an equally long period of time the American union had had an ongoing dispute with the nonunion companies: It had unsuccessfully attempted to persuade the companies to hire employees represented by the union.

When a frontal approach was not successful, the union decided to use indirect means, the secondary boycott. Understand that the primary dispute was between the American union and the American nonunion stevedoring companies. The union requested the Japanese dock workers to refuse to unload citrus fruit in Japan that was loaded in the United States by nonunion employees. It received the full cooperation of the Japanese union. Indeed, it advised the Florida growers and shippers that the Japanese union workers would refuse to unload Florida citrus fruit unless it had been loaded in the United States by the unionized longshoremen. The Japanese warning was successful—vessels coming to Florida to pick up citrus fruit for delivery to Japan were diverted to Tampa, located on the west coast of Florida, 150 miles from Fort Pierce.

This, of course, is a textbook scenario of a secondary boycott. The primary dispute was between the American Longshoremen's Union and the nonunion stevedoring firms, and the neutral employers were the growers and shippers of Florida citrus fruit products. At the urging of the American union, the Japanese Dock Workers' Union exerted economic pressure and coercion on the neutral employers to cease doing business with the nonunion stevedoring companies. Such activities would have been unlawful under Taft-Hartley's original language as well as the provisions of Landrum-Griffin amendments.

In fact the American Longshoremen's Union readily admitted the arrangement would have been an unlawful secondary boycott had all the players been American, and if it had been conducted within the geographic territory of the United States. Under these circumstances, the NLRB held the only issue to be determined was whether the fact that a foreign union put the actual pressure on the neutral employers, growers and shippers of Florida citrus products, makes lawful what otherwise would have been unlawful. In a unanimous decision, the Board responded in the negative because the Japanese union acted as the agent of the American union. Indeed, after the Japanese Dock Workers' Union served the American Longshoremen's Union's interest, the latter wrote a letter to the Japanese union expressing gratitude for its assistance in the secondary boycott, requesting that such assistance continue. Although the NLRB did not have authority over the Japanese union, it directed the American Longshoremen's Union to cease and desist requesting help from the foreign union.[24]

HOT-CARGO AGREEMENTS

Landrum-Griffin Prohibition

At times employers and unions agree to what is called a *hot-cargo agreement*. Under this arrangement, contained in labor agreements, the employer agrees not to handle products of another company that the union identifies as unfair. In practice, "unfair" means the employer is nonunion. Labor organizations, particularly the Teamsters, have used the device as an effective organizational tool. For example, the union is attempting to organize Employer A, a trucking firm. The products are to be shipped to Employer B, which uses the products for whatever purpose. The union informs B that A is unfair. B refuses to accept the products being hauled in A's trucks. This puts pressure on A to recognize the union.

Obviously, the hot-cargo agreement implements a secondary boycott. In the example, the union exerts pressure on B to cease doing business with A. Despite the secondary boycott ban in Taft-Hartley, the NLRB held that not only were hot-cargo agreements lawful, but the union could also use economic pressure to enforce them.[25] Thus, in the example, the union could lawfully strike B to force it to cease doing business with A.

With a change in membership, the NLRB eventually held that hot-cargo agreements could be negotiated, but the union could not engage in prohibited secondary boycott action to enforce them.[26] Not content with only that restriction, Congress in Landrum-Griffin completely outlawed hot-cargo agreements in all industries except clothing and construction. Under existing law, a union commits an unfair labor practice should it attempt to persuade an employer to negotiate a hot-cargo agreement. Such agreements are illegal whether made in writing or orally.

Attempts to Circumvent the Law

Some unions attempted to get around the provisions of the 1959 law. Soon after the Taft-Hartley amendments became effective, a union attempted to circumvent the restrictions by obtaining a "Refusal to Handle" clause in the labor agreement. This required an employer to agree that it would not discharge or discipline any employee because he or she refused to work on nonunion or struck goods. The Board held that such clauses were an attempt to evade the law and as such were illegal.[27]

In another case, a contractual clause forbade subcontracting to other employers of any work unless their employees "enjoy the same or greater wages" as the companies that were parties to the agreement paid.[28] The Board held the clause illegal because it went further than merely restricting subcontracting "for the purpose of the preservation of jobs and job rights of the unit employees." This type of clause was viewed as an attempt to prohibit an employer from doing business with another firm and as such violated the law.

Thus, the NLRB has been steadfast in preventing unions from subverting the prohibitions against hot-cargo arrangements. It has carefully reviewed such clauses in the light of the intent of Congress and has repeatedly struck down subterfuges designed to circumvent the hot-cargo proscription. The ingenuity of unions has not been so sharp as to delude the Board into believing that violations did not exist.

Hot-Cargo Exemption: Construction and Clothing Industries

Congress extended special privileges to labor unions operating in the construction and clothing industries. This policy was motivated by the peculiarities of these industries.

In a qualification to Section 8(e), the anti-hot-cargo provision, the law states that "nothing in this section shall apply to an agreement between a labor organization and an employer in the construction industry relating to the contracting or subcontracting of work to be done at the site of the construction, alteration, painting, or repair of a building, structure or other work." Several important problems are involved in this exemption. One concerns the interpretation of the phrase "at the site." May an employer and a construction union lawfully execute a hot-cargo arrangement for work that *could be done at the site*, or does the exemption apply only to work *actually done at the site of construction*?

A source of the problem is that in the construction industry, certain work could be done either at the site or in firms located off the construction site. These off-site shops are frequently owned by employers not involved in the actual construction of the building site. Some work—such as the threading, bending, or fabrication of pipe, for example—can be done either in the shop or at the construction site. One of the Senate members of the Conference Committee debating the Landrum-Griffin changes of Taft-Hartley stated that the exemption was meant to apply to any work that "could be" done at the construction site.[29] Against this position, however, there is substantial evidence that the exemption was to apply only to work actually done at the site.

In 1963, the Board gave attention to the issue. It ruled that the hot-cargo exemption applies only to work done at the site.[30] Otherwise, the NLRB held, a subcontractor that performs work away from the site would be effectively deprived of its contract to fulfill a work assignment. A supplier of materials to an employer at the site was deemed the primary target of the union's conduct, which constituted secondary action. Thus, nonunion labor may perform work off the site at lower wages, even though the work could be done at the site. Contract clauses that attempt to cover subcontractor operations away from the site were found unlawful. This policy reflects the intent of Congress when the exemption was granted to the construction industry. When this issue was being debated in the Senate, then Senator John Kennedy stated:

> It should be particularly noted that the proviso relates only to the contracting or subcontracting of work to be done at the site of construction. The proviso does not cover boycotts of goods manufactured in an industrial plant for installation at the job site, or suppliers who do not work at the job site.

On the other hand, in 1982, a unanimous U.S. Supreme Court held that it is lawful for construction unions and employers to negotiate a clause that requires a general contractor to subcontract work at *any of its sites* only to employers who recognize the union.[31] Upholding an NLRB decision on this issue, the high court rejected the employer's argument that the exemption applied only to a particular job site where both union and nonunion workers may be employed. As long as the hot-cargo clause was adopted in the normal course of collective bargaining, such provisions may lawfully apply to all job sites of the general contractor.

Unions and employers in the clothing industry may lawfully negotiate a hot-cargo provision limiting subcontracts to employers who recognized the union. This exception was adopted to prevent clothing manufacturers from subcontracting work to so-called "sweat shops" where substandard labor conditions prevail.

Strikes to Obtain and Enforce Hot-Cargo Clauses

In addition, within the clothing industry, no doubt exists as to the right of unions to use economic force to secure and enforce hot-cargo provisions. Given the language of Section 8(e), however, the right of construction unions to use strikes and picketing to obtain and enforce hot-cargo provisions remains somewhat unsettled. At the outset, the NLRB held that unions in the construction industry were forbidden to use economic pressure to obtain or enforce agreements to cease doing business with nonunion contractors.[32] However, federal appeals courts have consistently held that construction unions may strike and picket to secure hot-cargo provisions, though courts have also held that it is not legal to use economic pressure to enforce such provisions.[33] This principle was explained in a court case involving the issue:

> Secondary subcontracting clauses in the construction industry are lawful, under the proviso to Section 8(e), and economic force may be used to obtain them notwithstanding Section 8(b)(4)(A), because Section 8(b)(4)(A) incorporates that proviso by reference. But under Section 8(b)(4)(B) such secondary clauses may be enforced only through lawsuits, and not through economic action. . . .[34]

The language used by Congress in Section 8(e) prompted the courts to construe the proviso as they did. Congress referred to the third qualification of the hot-cargo clause as "nothing in this Act shall prohibit the enforcement of any agreement that is within *the foregoing exception.*" (Emphasis supplied) The exception referred to has been interpreted to include the clothing industry, but not the construction industry.

At this writing, the Supreme Court has still not ruled whether construction unions may use force to secure hot-cargo provisions. In *Woelke & Romero Framing*, the employer argued that even if the subcontract clause in question was legal, unions could not strike or picket to force contractors to agree to such a provision. However, the high court refused to deal with this issue, saying that the employer involved did not raise the issue when the case was before the NLRB.

PRESERVATION OF BARGAINING-UNIT WORK

National Woodwork

The Board has long held with court approval that a union strike to preserve bargaining-unit work does not violate the secondary boycott prohibitions even though there may be consequences for neutral employers.[35] Work "historically and regularly" performed by employees is not involved in the secondary boycott proscription if a labor organization attempts to force an employer to abide by a contractual clause to preserve bargaining-unit work.[36]

In *National Woodwork*, the NLRB and Supreme Court sustained the right of unions to enforce work-preservation clauses.[37] The carpenters' union had a clause in its contract that provided that union members would not handle or install prefitted doors. That is, the labor agreement provided that only the carpenters on the site would fit the doors with the necessary hardware. Hence the union and the contractor agreed that such work fell under the jurisdiction of the union. It was a work-preservation clause. A strike was called to enforce the clause after the contractor purchased prefitted doors and the carpenters refused to install them.

The NLRB ruled in *National Woodwork* that a product boycott taken to enforce a work-preservation clause did not violate the hot-cargo or secondary boycott provisions of amended Taft-Hartley. The Board reasoned that *union action was taken to preserve bargaining-unit work for members of the construction union and was not aimed at the suppliers of the prefabricated product.* This was deemed legal even though the effect was to force the contractor to boycott the products of suppliers.

The Supreme Court in a 5–4 decision upheld the NLRB position. Thus, the work-preservation doctrine of the Board and Supreme Court recognizes that a literal reading of the boycott prohibitions of Taft-Hartley would render unions helpless in attempts to protect bargaining-unit work at the job site. The Court reasoned that the clause was included in the contract for the sole benefit of bargaining-unit members and was not directed against a secondary employer. The strike was provoked by the employer's unilateral decision to purchase prefabricated doors in violation of a collective bargaining agreement designed to protect the traditional job-site work of craft workers against the inherent danger of factory-fitted building materials. There is no doubt that this interpretation may well slow down efforts to utilize new and improved materials and methods of production. However, unions must also be given the opportunity to attempt by use of economic pressure to prevent unilateral decisions to subcontract traditional work. A failure to distinguish between primary and secondary activity could lead to a demise of union action that other portions of the same law purport to protect. There is no absolute union right to preserve bargaining-unit work, but a labor organization's express legal right should be protected in order to enable it to bargain effectively on problems vital not only to its existence but to the jobs of members as well. *National Woodwork* permits strikes to preserve bargaining-unit work and, as such, is an important exception to the secondary boycott and hot-cargo prohibitions found in the amended Taft-Hartley Act. Appropriately written work-preservation clauses are permissible in general industry as well as in construction.

Right-of-Control Test

The practical significance of *National Woodwork*, however, is related to the so-called "right-of-control" test that the NLRB stressed in the case. In the precedent case, the employer had the right to use either prefitted or unfitted doors. Thus, it controlled the kind of product that could be used. When the employer has no option as to the kind of product to be used, the NLRB has held that employees may not refuse to install the product called for by job specifications. In short, the right-of-control test establishes that if an employer controls the use of prefabricated products, union pressure tactics to stop use of the product are lawful. *But if the owner of the building or general contractor specified a prefabricated product, the employer lacks control of its use and union pressures directed at it constitute illegal secondary boycott activity.*

It is easy to see why the right-of-control test is significant in establishing the potential value of *National Woodwork*. To get around this decision, prefabricated materials could be specified in construction contracts. For example, the builder's architect could establish that prefitted doors be used. Under the right-of-control test, the employees assigned to the installation of the doors could not refuse to install them because their employer has no control over what kind of doors might be used. In fact, should the NLRB right-of-control test prevail, much of the protection that construction workers receive from *National Woodwork* would be lost. On the other hand, under this test, economies in construction could be realized by the use of prefabricated products. In this respect, an attorney for the Associated General Contractors warned that if the right-of-control test is abandoned, "You'll see housing costs go higher, since cheaper prefabricated material would be kept off the market."[38]

The Supreme Court approved the right-of-control doctrine in *Plumbers, Local 638*.[39] In doing so, it limited the right of construction unions to enforce agreements containing work-preservation clauses. Furthermore, the decision makes it more difficult for construction unions and employers to negotiate solutions to disputes arising out of technological change, bringing with it greater reliance on prefabricated materials that might eliminate or diminish jobs at the site of construction. A negotiated work-preservation clause can be avoided by a subcontractor who merely permits a general contractor to specify that a special type of material or equipment must be used. Should a union refuse to install the equipment or use the material because it violates their agreement, such refusal is considered to be secondary, with the general contractor the illegal target. The *Plumbers* decision can be interpreted to mean that a union has a right to negotiate a work-preservation clause under *National Woodwork*, but it has only a limited right to enforce it, depending on how the Board and courts interpret the right-of-control doctrine.

Language Must Be Specific

For a work-preservation clause to be valid, the language must be specific and not written in a way to accomplish objectives other than preserving work traditionally performed by employees. Also, a work-preservation clause will not protect union conduct if it is used in a manner other than to protect unit work. Two cases demonstrate these conditions. In one case, the clause stated "all work . . . will be done on material, equipment, and apparatus owned by the Employer." The union argued that this clause preserved work for employees because ownership of the equipment would facilitate the contractor's control of the work assignments. In finding this provision invalid, the Board held that the language was too broad, aimed primarily at the ownership of equipment and not at work to be done at the job site.[40] In the second case, union conduct was held to be illegal in its use of the following clause: "All merchandise for resale which is delivered to a retail outlet owned by the Employer . . . shall be delivered from the warehouses of the Employer covered by the Collective Bargaining Agreement." The union involved used this clause to prevent retail outlets from purchasing soft drinks directly from a soft drink firm. In holding the union action illegal, the Board found that the provision was not being used to preserve work but rather to force the employees of the soda pop companies to join the Teamsters union.[41] In the case, the Board was not impressed with the union's argument that its conduct did not cause the employer to terminate completely its business relationship with the soda pop company. By changing the point of delivery, the Board held that this would mean that the soda pop company would be required to reduce the number of its drivers. As the Supreme Court has held, Taft-Hartley does not require a union to demand a complete cessation of business before a secondary boycott violation can be found.[42]

In any event, the *National Woodwork* doctrine has been bitterly criticized in many circles. The criticisms became more intense as the doctrine was applied to several products. Work-preservation clauses protected employees against the installation of prefabricated fireplaces,[43] precut steel bands,[44] and prefitted boilers.[45] As stated, the controversy involves job protection as against economy in construction. Ignoring employee concern for their jobs, the *Wall Street Journal* remarked:

> If the labor unions, with the labor board's help, continue successfully to plumb these depths of inefficiency, the outlook for even minor economies in construction seems very dim too. If their theories are sound, they ought to go all the way and come out foursquare for making things like nails by hand.[46]

SUMMARY

When originally passed, Taft-Hartley outlawed secondary boycotts. However, many loopholes developed based on the language of the antisecondary boycott provisions. Most of these loopholes were closed by Landrum-Griffin. Ironically, however, the U.S. Supreme Court carved a few loopholes in the new language. Unions may appeal to managerial discretion to implement secondary boycotts. As long as a union pickets against a particular product, unions are free to use picketing to persuade the public not to purchase that product. However, should the boycott result in excessive monetary damage to the neutral employer, such picketing is not lawful.

Under Supreme Court interpretation, unions may handbill a shopping mall to try to persuade the public to boycott all stores and force the owner to use unionized construction workers to build new stores. This strengthens the building trades unions' ability to maintain union standards for shopping mall construction.

Although Congress outlawed hot-cargo agreements, it exempted the construction and clothing industries from its ban. Work-preservation clauses contained in labor agreements are lawful, but their effectiveness is limited to the extent contractors do not have the right to exclude prefabricated materials.

In the final analysis, the problem is to protect neutral employers from the impact of union action but at the same time protect unions in their right to use effective economic action to achieve their goals. This, of course, is a difficult balance, but Congress, the NLRB, and the federal courts should strive for a workable and equitable solution to the problem. To tip the scale unreasonably in favor of the neutral employer would undermine the nation's public policy supporting unions and collective bargaining. To ignore unreasonably the interests of the neutral employer would likewise be a misuse of law.

DISCUSSION QUESTIONS

1. Define *secondary boycott.*

2. What did Congress intend in the secondary boycott language provided in the Taft-Hartley Act?

3. Why was the ally doctrine excluded from the secondary boycott provisions of Landrum-Griffin in 1959?

4. Discuss the secondary boycott loopholes that developed after the 1947 law was passed.

5. How did Landrum-Griffin close the secondary boycott loopholes created after Taft-Hartley?

6. Explain how the Supreme Court created a loophole in the Landrum-Griffin legislation with its ruling in *Servette.*

7. Explain the significance of *Hearst.*

8. How did *Tree Fruits* create a loophole in Landrum-Griffin's secondary boycott prohibitions? How did the high court's ruling in *Safeco* relate to *Tree Fruits*?

9. May a union that has a dispute with the contractor at a shopping mall request through handbills that consumers boycott *all* stores within the mall and not be in violation of Landrum-Griffin? Why or why not?

10. What is a "hot-cargo" agreement? Are these agreements ever legal? If so, when?

11. Use *National Woodwork* and *Plumbers, Local 638* to illustrate the extent to which unions may negotiate and enforce bargaining-unit work-preservation clauses.

NOTES

1   Felix Frankfurter and Nathan Greene, *The Labor Injunction* (New York: The Macmillan Company, 1930), p. 43.

2   *Legislative History*, Taft-Hartley Act, p. 1106.

3   *Hearings Before Committee on Education and Labor*, on H.R. 115, 83d Cong., 1st sess., 1953, p. 3441.

4   Melvin J. Segal, "Secondary Boycott Loopholes," *Labor Law Journal*, X, No. 3 (March 1959), p. 175.

5   *Legislative History*, Landrum-Griffin Act, p. 1431.

6   Section 8(b)(4)(B) in part makes it an unfair labor practice for a union to induce a work stoppage in order to force a secondary employer to cease doing business with a primary employer.

7   95 *Congressional Record* 8709 (1947).

8   *AFL-CIO Brewery Workers Union (Adolph Coors Company)*, 121 NLRB 271 (1958).

9   *Graphic Arts International Union* and *Kable Printing Co.*, 225 NLRB 1253 (1976).

10   *Douds* v. *Metropolitan Federation of Architects*, 75 F. Supp. 672 (S.D.N.Y., 1948).

11   *NLRB* v. *International Rice Milling Company*, 341 U.S. 665 (1951).

12   *NLRB* v. *Brewery Workers*, 272 F. 2d 817 (1959).

13   *NLRB* v. *Servette, Inc.*, 377 U.S. 46 (1964).

14   *Radio Artists, Washington-Baltimore Local* v. *NLRB*, 462 F. 2d 887 (D.C. Cir. 1972).

15   105 *Congressional Record*, 17898–17899 (1959).

16   *Upholsterers Frame & Bedding Workers Twin City Local 61 (Minneapolis House Furnishings Company)*, 132 NLRB 40 (1961).

17   *NLRB* v. *Fruit & Vegetable Packers & Warehousemen, Local 760 et al. (Tree Fruits, Inc.)*, 377 U.S. 58 (1964).

18   *NLRB* v. *Retail Store Employees Union, Local 1001 (Safeco)*, 444 U.S. 1011 (1980).

19   *De Bartolo Corp.* v. *Florida Gulf Coast Trades Counsel*, 485 U.S. 568 (1988).

20   273 NLRB 1431 (1985).

21   Samuel A. DiLullo, "Secondary Boycotts: Had the Court Gone Too Far or Maybe Not Far Enough," *Labor Law Journal*, v. 40, No. 6 (June 1989), p. 386.

22   *Local 537, Teamsters (Lohman Sales)*, 132 NLRB 901 (1961).

23   *Local 662, Electric Workers (Middle South Broadcasting Company)*, 133 NLRB 1698 (1961).

24   *Longshoremen International Association (Coastal Stevedoring Company)*, 313 NLRB No. 53 (1993).

25   *Conway's Express*, 87 NLRB 972 (1949), aff. *Rabouin* v. *NLRB*, 195 F. 2d 906 (2d Cir. 1952).

26   *Local 1976, United Brotherhood of Carpenters (Sand Door & Plywood Company)*, 113 NLRB 1210 (1955), enf. *NLRB* v. *Local 1976*, 241 F. 2d 147 (9th Cir. 1957), aff. 357 U.S. 93 (1958).

27   *Brown* v. *Local No. 17, Amalgamated Lithographers of America (Employing Lithographers Division)*, 180 F. Supp. 294 (DCN, Calif.), 1960.

28   *Meat & Highway Drivers, Local 710 (Wilson & Company)*, 143 NLRB 1221 (1963).

29   *Labor Relations Reporter*, 132 (1959).

30   *Ohio Valley Carpenters District Council (Cardinal Industries)*, 144 NLRB 91 (1963).

31   *Woelke & Romero Framing* v. *NLRB*, 456 U.S. 645 (1982).

32   *Construction, Production & Maintenance Laborers Union Local 383 (Colson & Stevens Construction Company)*, 137 NLRB 1650 (1962).

33   323 F. 2d 422 (9th Cir. 1963).

34   *Building & Construction Trades Council of San Bernadino* v. *NLRB*, 328 F. 2d 540 (D.C. Cir. 1964).

35   The proviso to Section 8(b)(4)(B) reads: "Provided, that nothing contained in this clause (B) shall be construed to make unlawful, where not otherwise unlawful, any primary strike or primary picketing." See *International Association of Heat & Frost Insulators (Houston Insulation Contractors Association)*, 148 NLRB 866 (1964), sustained 386 U.S. 664 (1967).

36   *Local 1332, ILA (Philadelphia Marine Trade Association)*, 151 NLRB 1447 (1965).

37   *National Woodwork Manufacturers Association* v. *NLRB*, 386 U.S. 612 (1967).

38 *Wall Street Journal*, June 26, 1972.

39 *Plumbers, Local 638* v. *NLRB*, 429 U.S. 507 (1977).

40 *IBEW, Local 1186 (Pacific General Contractors)*, 192 NLRB 254 (1971).

41 *Teamsters, Local 688 (Schnuck Markets)*, 193 NLRB 701 (1971).

42 *NLRB* v. *Operating Engineers, Local 825*, 400 U.S. 297 (1971).

43 *Bricklayers & Stone Masons, Local 8 (California Concrete Systems)*, 180 NLRB 43 (1969).

44 *Houston Insulation Contractors Association*, 148 NLRB 866 (1964).

45 *American Boiler Manufacturers Association*, 167 NLRB 602 (1967).

46 *Wall Street Journal*, October 27, 1967.

10 ❧

Labor-Management Reporting and Disclosure Act of 1959

The Labor-Management Reporting and Disclosure Act of 1959, commonly referred to as the Landrum-Griffin Act, is concerned primarily with the internal practices of unions.[1] Its major purpose is to protect union members from improper union conduct. Still another purpose of the law is to eliminate arrangements between unions and employers that would deprive members of proper union representation. A few provisions of the Act are directed at management. The 1959 law was the direct outgrowth of Senate investigations revealing unsatisfactory internal practices of a small but strategically located minority of unions. The first six of seven titles in the statute introduce controls on the powers that union officials exercise over funds, internal union affairs, and the membership. This chapter reviews the background and treats the major areas of the 1959 law. They are (1) "the bill of rights," (2) reports to the Secretary of Labor, (3) union trusteeships, (4) conduct of union elections, and (5) financial safeguards.

In addition to an analysis of the provisions of the 1959 statute and its application by the courts, experience with it will be discussed to the extent that information is available. How the law operates in practice provides the necessary basis for its understanding and evaluation.

Background of Regulation of Internal Union Affairs

Growth of the U.S. labor movement from a position of relative weakness in the early 1930s to one of relative strength by the 1950s led to greater public attention devoted to internal union practices. Union membership grew from about 9 million in 1941 to

17 million in the 1950s. The logical extension of concern with strikes and picketing was to the perceived power of those directing such actions. The war years and the period of adjustment thereafter did not represent the first period of time the public was conscious of internal union operations. Concern with internal union affairs was prevalent even before the period of government protection of the right to organize and bargain collectively as provided by the Wagner Act of 1935.

By 1900, racketeering was revealed in the building trades, longshore workers, and teamsters unions. Graft, violence, extortion, and mishandling of funds by union leaders are some practices reported in these organizations. Labor organizations were also criticized for improper use of trusteeships, discrimination against black people by barring them from membership or placing them in separate auxiliary locals, and lack of disciplinary protection of members.[2]

Scrutiny of union activities was intensified after World War II. In 1954, Congress began investigating the administration of employee benefit plans. Discovery of widespread abuses in the labor field led to the creation of the Senate Select Committee on Improper Activities in the Labor or Management Field, better known as the McClellan Anti-Racketeering Committee. Between 1957 and 1959, the McClellan committee held numerous hearings dealing with patterns of union behavior. Several findings and recommendations were presented as a result of the three-year effort. It should be noted that the committee concentrated on only five national unions of the 200 or so that operate in the nation. These were the International Brotherhood of Teamsters, Bakery and Confectionery Workers, United Textile Workers, Operating Engineers, and Allied Industrial Workers of America. Some attention was devoted to other unions, including those in the building trades, but the five mentioned accounted for the largest share of the committee's efforts. As a result of the inquiry, the Teamsters were expelled from the AFL-CIO, and, subsequently, its president, James Hoffa, was convicted and jailed for tampering with a jury and mail fraud. Prior to the 1972 national elections, Nixon permitted Hoffa to leave prison, but he was forbidden to hold a union office until 1980. After being released from jail, Hoffa engaged in litigation to set aside the ban and began a campaign to return as president of the Teamsters, a job then held by Frank Fitzsimmons. Ironically, Hoffa had handpicked Fitzsimmons for the top job when he went to jail. However, once established in office, Fitzsimmons did not look with favor on Hoffa's effort to regain control of the union, to say the least. In 1976, Hoffa disappeared; allegedly, he was murdered by elements that opposed his efforts to gain control of the union. At this writing, no one has been indicted for the alleged crime committed against Hoffa.

McClellan Committee Findings and Recommendations

The labor movement anticipated government intervention into its internal affairs. In 1957, the AFL-CIO adopted a series of six codes of ethical practices to regulate the behavior of its affiliates. The codes dealt with paper locals, health and welfare funds, subversives and racketeers, business interests of union officials, union financial and proprietary activities, and union democratic processes.[3] The self-regulated effort proved too late. The McClellan committee, after many hearings and thousands of pages of testimony, uncovered these facts:

1. Rank-and-file members have no voice in union affairs, notably in financial matters, and frequently are denied secret ballot.
2. International unions have abused their right to place local unions under trusteeship by imposing the trusteeship merely to plunder the local's treasury or boost the ambitions of candidates for high office.
3. Certain managements have bribed union officials to get sweetheart contracts or other favored treatment.
4. Widespread misuse of union funds through lack of adequate inspection and audit.
5. Acts of violence to keep union members in line.
6. Improper practices by employers and their agents to influence employees in exercising the rights guaranteed them by NLRA.
7. Organizational picketing misused to extort money from employers or to influence employees in their selection of representation.
8. Infiltration of unions at high levels by criminals.
9. A no man's land in which employers and unions could not resort either to the NLRB or state agencies for relief.

On the basis of the findings, the McClellan committee recommended legislation to deal with abuses in five areas. They were:

1. Legislation to regulate and control pension, health, and welfare funds.
2. Legislation to regulate and control union funds.
3. Legislation to ensure union democracy.
4. Legislation to curb activities of middlemen in labor-management disputes.
5. Legislation to clarify the no man's land in labor-management disputes.[4]

As presented in previous chapters, Title VII of the 1959 law dealt with amendments to Taft-Hartley. We are concerned here with the first six titles of the law; as will be disclosed, they were broad and ambitious.

BILL OF RIGHTS OF UNION MEMBERS

Member and Union Rights

Senator McClellan was largely responsible for the "bill of rights" section that was written into the 1959 law. He stated that "racketeering, corruption, abuse of power and other improper practices on the part of some labor organizations" could not be prevented

> until and unless the Congress of the United States has the wisdom and the courage to enact laws prescribing minimum standards of democratic process and conduct for the administration of internal union affairs.[5]

The resulting bill of rights for union members is an ambitious and wide-sweeping one. It attempts to legislate into internal union constitutions and bylaws certain basic rights contained in the Bill of Rights of the United States Constitution. Title I provides for equality of rights concerning the nomination of candidates for union office, voting in elections, attendance at membership meetings, and participation in business transactions—all, however, "subject to reasonable union rules and regulations" as contained in constitutions and bylaws. It lays down strict standards to ensure that increases in dues and fees are responsive to the desires of the union membership majority. It affirms the right of any member to sue the organization, once "reasonable" hearing procedures within the union have been exhausted. Provision is also made that no member may be fined, suspended, or otherwise disciplined by the union except for nonpayment of dues, unless the member has been granted such procedural safeguards as being served with written specific charges, given time to prepare a defense, and being afforded a fair hearing. And the provision obligates union officers to furnish each of their members with a copy of the collective bargaining agreement, as well as full information concerning the Landrum-Griffin Act itself.

Considerable controversy broke out almost immediately after passage of the 1959 law. The underlying premise of the bill of rights was that labor organizations should function in a democratic fashion. The question was, however, could such a standard be imposed on unions externally? Union members are often viewed as apathetic to internal operations as long as they remain reasonably satisfied with collective bargaining results. Revolt against the leadership may be forthcoming only when there is a widespread feeling that contractual terms obtained are less than could have been received. Furthermore, some allege that union responsibility and internal democracy are often in conflict within the context of collective bargaining.6

Congress intended to give individual members the right to assert themselves more fully in matters dealing with their employment relationships. At the same time, it recognized the union right to represent a majority of workers in collective bargaining matters. Unions must have authority to enforce a labor contract entered into with an employer. For this reason, the exercise of individual rights is subject to "reasonable" union rules. Members have some responsibilities to the labor organization to which they belong. Recognition of this fact prompted Congress to provide that nothing in this section of the law should be construed to

> impair the right of a labor organization to adopt and enforce reasonable rules as to the responsibility of every member toward the organization as an institution and to his refraining from conduct that would interfere with its performance of its legal or contractual obligations.

In a significant 1987 case, *Carothers* v. *Presser*, a federal appeals court upheld union rights over those of a group of dissident members.7 At issue was their demand that the Teamsters Union turn over to them the mailing list of the entire membership. They wanted the list so that they could contact the membership if the dissidents opposed collective bargaining contracts negotiated by the national union. The court held the union did not violate the bill of rights of Landrum-Griffin by refusing to supply the list. It said "a union having committed no violation of the law may not be ordered to supply the means by which [dissidents] might seek to frustrate the performance of its collective bargaining responsibilities." Aside from that, the court pointed out that the dissidents had other means to communicate their views to union members. Only if the facts of the case demonstrated that the union specifically violated the rights of the dissidents would the court direct the union to supply the mailing list. These Landrum-Griffin rights would be violated, said the court, where the union advocated voting for the contract while denying others the opportunity to express contrary views through mailings or in the union newspaper, or a union's presentation of misleading information to members. Since the record did not show such union misconduct, the dissidents could not have the right to the mailing list.

On the other hand, in a 1991 case, a union member wanted to inspect *all* collective bargaining contracts negotiated by her local union. It refused to comply, claiming she was entitled only to the contract negotiated with her direct employer. The union based its denial on Section 104 of Landrum-Griffin. In pertinent part the provision states the employee has a right to a copy of the contract ". . . whose rights as such employee are directly affected by such agreement . . . ."

In the union's view the language restricted the right of inspection to union members whose rights were affected by the agreement. That is, the right is restricted to the collective bargaining contract of the member's direct employer because that is the only contract affecting the member's rights. Nonetheless, a federal district court upheld the employee's right to inspect all contracts negotiated by the member's union.[8] It reasoned the statute's democratic purpose did not reasonably permit an interpretation of Section 104 that would permit union members access only to agreements that directly affected the employees. It rejected the ancillary argument that the members' knowledge of all their local union agreements would cause divisiveness within the union. The court ruled the union did not present any facts to support its allegation.

Here are the major problems and experience of the bill of rights area of Landrum-Griffin.

Equal Rights

The law grants equal rights and privileges to every union member with regard to nomination of candidates, voting in elections and referendums, attendance at union meetings, and voting at such meetings. The section made no attempt, however, to regulate union admission standards. The procedural safeguards did not prohibit labor organizations from refusing membership or segregating members on the grounds of race, religion, color, sex, or national origin. This aspect was made clear by Representative Phillip Landrum when he stated that

> we do not seek in this legislation to tell the labor unions of this country whom they shall admit to their unions.

Congressman Adam Clayton Powell attempted to remedy this defect in Title I but was unsuccessful by a vote of 215 to 160. A remedy to the problem was not available until it was provided by Title VII of the Civil Rights Act of 1964.[9]

Race was not the only form of discrimination permissible under Title I. The practice of filial preference has also been recognized as a basis for closing the door to union membership.[10] Only sons and close relatives are admitted under this practice which has the blessing of the courts, including the New York Court of Appeals.[11] Thus, the law permits union action designed to restrict the supply of labor available under some circumstances. Union democracy is limited to the extent that membership may be denied to qualified applicants. The view is taken by many that unions are no longer voluntary associations, but quasi-public organizations. Prevailing technology, it is argued, does not lend itself to monopolistic control over labor supply. Thus, the internal restrictive membership practices artificially restrict the supply of labor.[12]

The Title I political rights of union members are closely connected with Title IV of Landrum-Griffin. Title I guarantees equal rights and privileges to nominate candidates and vote in union elections. Title IV extends to members a reasonable opportunity to nominate candidates. It also provides that every member, subject to some qualifications, shall be eligible to hold office. The member also has the opportunity to support candidates and vote for them without interference or reprisals.

Benjamin Aaron reveals that the courts have given these titles narrow interpretations.[13] Title I rights may be enforced prior to the holding of elections, but Title IV rights are enforceable only after an election is held. After an election, only the Secretary of Labor has authority to seek relief in the courts. The full range of litigation required to secure member rights may take so long that the full term of office in dispute may be served out completely before a decision may be obtained. Little practical relief from a violation, therefore, may be forthcoming.

A union may deprive members of their equal rights to nominate, to vote, and to participate in internal affairs. It may do so by the way it frames its eligibility rules. A union may do as was done by the National Marine Engineers' Beneficial Association. The association constitution provided that a member could nominate only himself or herself for office, but no one was eligible to hold office unless he or she had been a member of the national union for five years. Also, eligibility was conditioned by the requirement that a member had to have served at least 180 days at sea in two of the preceding three years prior to the election. Sea service had to be on ships covered by labor contracts with the national or its locals. The U.S. Supreme Court sustained a motion to dismiss the case filed against the union in *Calhoon* v. *Harvey*.[14]

Despite its authority to adopt reasonable rules, a federal appeals court held that a union may not deprive a laid-off union member of the right to vote and participate in union affairs.[15] Under a union constitution, laid-off union members were forbidden to pay dues. Since they could not pay dues, they were not members in good standing. So they were denied the opportunity to vote on an issue dealing with recall rights. Only actively employed union members were permitted to vote. Under those circumstances, the court held that the union had violated the equal rights section of Landrum-Griffin. It pointed out that the union's "good standing" provision permitted one group of union members to benefit and protect itself at the expense of laid-off members who were not permitted to vote, or even speak, on the recall issue.

Freedom of Speech and Assembly

Landrum-Griffin provides for both individual and organizational rights. Every member is granted the right to meet and assemble freely with other members to express views, arguments, and opinions. Such activity may be at union meetings or some other place. The rights of members are subject to two qualifications. One permits unions to apply their established and reasonable rules pertaining to the conduct of meetings. For example, time limits may be placed on debate and measures may be taken to maintain order. The ability to conduct business in an orderly fashion is necessary to efficient operation. Dissident members could call the tune at union meetings without this organizational safeguard.

The second limit placed on member rights to speech and assembly is that a union has the right "to adopt and enforce reasonable rules as to the responsibility of each member toward the organization as an institution and refraining from conduct that would interfere with its performance of its legal or contractual obligations." The union member therefore is extended the right to dissent from established or advocated union policies, but that right is not without limit.

Courts, however, tend to rule in favor of individual speech and assembly rights as opposed to union rights. Salzhandler v. Caputo was a case posing the issue of whether a union member's allegedly libelous statements regarding the handling of union funds by union officers justified disciplinary action against the member.[16] The case also involved the issue of whether the union could exclude the member from any participation in union affairs for a period of five years, including speaking and voting at meetings and even attending meetings. A district court ruled in favor of the union. Upon appeal, the Second Circuit Court of Appeals reversed the lower court and remanded the case for further proceedings.

In upholding individual over organization rights, the appeals court stated:

> We hold that the LMRDA protects the union member in the exercise of his right to make such charges without reprisal by the union; that any provisions of the union constitution which make such criticism, whether libelous or not, subject to union discipline are unenforceable; and that the Act allows redress for such unlawful treatment.

The court pointed out that libelous statements may be made the basis of civil suit between those concerned, but a union governing board may not subject a member to disciplinary action for his or her statements.

Two more examples demonstrate that the courts lean toward supporting individual rights over union rights. A union member was expelled for publicly urging the membership to refuse to pay an assessment levied by the union. He claimed that the levy violated federal law. A federal appeals court directed his reinstatement in the union, holding that he was protected by the free speech section of Landrum-Griffin.[17] Some members who belonged to the union by virtue of a union-shop agreement were fined for supporting a rival union in a representation election. Even though they sought to destroy the bargaining rights of their union, courts held that their activities were protected by the free-speech provision.[18]

In 1973, the U.S. Supreme Court made it easier for union members to sue their organizations.[19] It held that a union is liable for the attorneys' fees when a union member's suit prevails in court. It said that "to the extent that such lawsuits contribute to the preservation of union democracy," they benefit the entire membership. On these grounds, unions are responsible for attorneys' fees. Of course, should a union's position prevail in court, union members would be required to pay their attorneys' fees.

In 1985, a federal appeals court affirmed the obligation of unions to pay attorneys' fees and costs when union members prevail in a lawsuit.[20] In a federal district court, union members had won a lawsuit against their union for wrongful expulsion from the organization. Not content with the decision of the federal district court, the union appealed, including a petition for *certiorari* to the Supreme Court that was later denied. Requiring the union to pay the attorneys' fees and costs of the union members in the amount of $5,000, the appeals court said if their claim were denied:

> Situations would develop where union officials could wilfully violate the law, yet recognize an inability on the part of their membership to challenge the Local hierarchy in court due to a lack of funds. Union members would decide to bring suit based on financial considerations rather than merit. Hence, due to the uneven bargaining positions of the parties, the purpose of the LMRDA would be frustrated.

Dues, Initiation Fees, and Assessments

Certain democratic procedures must be followed by a union in increasing dues, initiation fees, or assessments. This policy is intended to stop unscrupulous union officers from imposing higher dues upon members against their will. The McClellan committee hearings and reports had revealed such actions in a few unions.

A local union has different procedural requirements than a national union. A local union may raise dues, initiation fees, or assessments by *secret ballots* in two ways so long as the determination is based on a majority of those members voting who are in good standing. The vote may be (1) taken at a membership meeting after reasonable notice that the issue will be put to the members, or (2) in a membership referendum. Posted notices on bulletin boards in union halls and where work is performed, as well as an announcement at one regular monthly meeting that a vote on the issue will be held at the next regular monthly meeting, would meet the reasonable-notice requirement. There may be no better way to get a large membership turnout to a meeting than to announce that a vote will be taken on whether to increase union dues! Union leaders have to present valid reasons for desiring an increase in dues. Failure to do so will inevitably lead to a rejection of the proposal by the membership.

A national union may use one of three different ways to increase its income from members. It may require (1) a majority vote of the delegates voting at a regular convention, or at a special convention held upon thirty days' written notice to each local union, provided *delegates are selected by secret vote of the local unions*; (2) a majority vote of the members voting by secret ballot in a membership referendum; or (3) a majority vote of the members of the executive board or similar governing body, if they are expressly granted such authority by the union's constitution and bylaws. The latter approach is subject to repeal at the next regular convention, and for this reason may not be a politically feasible approach for increasing national union income.

Federations of national unions, such as the AFL-CIO, however, do not fall within the Landrum-Griffin prohibitions on increases of dues, initiation fees, and assessments.

In *American Federation of Musicians*, the U.S. Supreme Court was faced with the issue of whether the law prohibits the vote of delegates at a national convention of the union, in accordance with its constitution, to be weighed and counted according to the number of members in the local the delegates represent.[21] The Court ruled that the legislative history of the section makes it clear that weighted voting was not one of the abuses of union government found by the McClellan committee. Many large unions vary voting strength according to the size of the locals.

A union may not, however, impose an increase in dues and assessments unilaterally and then proceed to obtain member ratification after the fact.[22] Also, a local union's bylaws that in effect delegated to union officers the authority to increase dues were declared a violation of the statute.[23] In that case, the San Francisco federal appeals court stressed that under the statute, a majority vote of the union membership by secret ballot is required to increase membership dues. A union in violation of the procedural safeguards concerning dues and assessments must return the excess of dues unlawfully collected.

Protection of the Right to Sue

Unions are prohibited from limiting the right of a member to bring suit against a labor organization, even when the leaders may be involved. Congress, however, placed two qualifications on member rights to engage in such action. The first is that a member "may be required" to exhaust "reasonable hearing procedures [but within a four-month lapse of time] within such organization" before initiating action. The second qualification is as follows:

> No interested employer or employer association shall directly or indirectly finance, encourage, or participate in, except as a party, any such action, proceeding, appearance, or petition.

In June 1977, however, a federal district court held this provision to be unconstitutional.[24] The National Right to Work Legal Defense & Education Foundation, a notorious antiunion organization, solicited money from antiunion employers. These funds were used to support legal action by dissident union members against their unions. On these facts alone, the court held that the foundation violated the law. The judge declared that "by financing union members in litigation against their labor organizations, the foundation had violated" the 1959 law. He cited the foundation as "an agent and conduit" for employers seeking to weaken unions.

Though the district court held that the employer-financed foundation violated the law based on the facts of the case, it said that the provisions of the law violated the First Amendment rights of the foundation and the employers who contributed to it. In 1978, a federal appeals court sidestepped the constitutional issue *and held that the foundation did not violate the law, since the statute was not intended to cover legitimate legal aid associations, even though they received money from interested employers.*[25] As long as the employer contributors have no control over the litigation that the foundation seeks to pursue on behalf of union members, the statute is not violated. Unless reversed by the U.S. Supreme Court, this decision means unions can be expected to defend themselves from more lawsuits. To date, the high court has not treated the matter. Naturally unhappy about this state of affairs, a union attorney commented:

> Our entire American labor policy has been based on keeping employers out of union affairs. This decision reverses 80 years of history.[26]

With respect to the first qualification, the one dealing with the exhaustion of internal union procedures before union members have the right to sue, the issue quickly arose as to how the courts would apply this limitation.

Typical union constitutions contain procedures that provide for an appeal of local decisions to the national officers and then ultimately to the national convention. The section provides that a member may be required to exhaust internal remedies available *within a four-month period* before permitting suit against a union or its officers. Questions arose immediately after the law was enacted. Does a member have to exhaust all internal remedies available within a four-month period before initiating proceedings? Does a member have the right to bring suit after four months of effort even though all internal procedures have not been exhausted?

The legislative history of the Act sheds light on the issue of the members' right to bring suit after four months of internal effort to deal with a problem. Then Senator John F. Kennedy was of the opinion that the section did not automatically permit a suit after a four-month period. He stated:

> The purpose of the law [was not] to eliminate existing grievance procedures established by union constitutions for redress of alleged violation of their internal governing laws. Nor is it the intent or purpose of the provision to invalidate the considerable body of State and Federal court decisions of many years standing, which require, or do not require, the exhaustion of internal remedies prior to court intervention depending on the reasonableness of such requirements in terms of the facts and circumstances of a particular case. So long as the union member is not prevented by his union from resorting to the courts, the intent and purpose of the "right to sue" provision is fulfilled, and any requirements which the court may then impose in terms of pursuing reasonable remedies within the organization to redress violation of his union constitutional rights will not conflict with the statute.[27]

The magnitude of the particular problem of a member and the appropriateness of internal appeals machinery have a great deal to do with a court's judgment of particular cases. Some courts may require an exhaustion of internal remedies before allowing judicial relief, whereas others may permit a suit despite the availability of internal procedures that would exceed four months.

The issue of exhausting all internal remedies available within a four-month period has been litigated on several occasions since 1959. Congress intended to permit unions an opportunity to correct their own wrongdoing by stimulating them to independently establish democratic appeal procedures.[28] A safeguard against union abuse was provided by not requiring exhaustion of union remedies if the procedures exceed four months in duration. As stated by Representative Griffin, "It should be clear that no obligation is imposed to exhaust procedures where it would obviously be futile or would place an undue burden on the union member."[29]

In 1961, an appellate court reversed a district court decision that imposed upon a union member an absolute duty to exhaust union remedies before applying to the federal courts.[30] In so doing, it made a review of the legislative history of the section and held:

> Taking due account of the declared policy favoring self-regulation by unions, we nonetheless hold that where the internal union remedy is uncertain and has not been specifically brought to the attention of the disciplined party, the violation of federal law clear and undisputed, and the injury to the union member immediate and difficult to compensate by means of a subsequent money award, exhaustion of union remedies ought not to be required. The absence of any of these elements might, in light of Congressional approval of the exhaustion doctrine, call for a different result.

In a case decided by the U.S. Supreme Court, *Industrial Union of Marine & Shipbuilding Workers*, it was decided that the four-month period was not a grant of authority to unions to require exhaustion of internal remedies.[31] Instead, it was merely a statement of policy that the courts may refuse to intervene for this period of time. Courts may prefer to consider whether a procedure is reasonable and should be exhausted, or if they should entertain the complaint. Each case therefore appears to revolve about the particular issues involved and the particular procedures available to which members may appeal.

Safeguards against Improper Disciplinary Action

The "bill of rights" in Landrum-Griffin provides that a union member may not be "fined, expelled, or otherwise disciplined," except for nonpayment of dues, unless certain procedural steps are taken to ensure due process. The member must be "(A) served with written specific charges; (B) given a reasonable time to prepare his or her defense; (C) afforded a full and fair hearing." When a union violates these standards, the union member has the right to challenge the action taken against him or her in the courts. In 1971, however, the U.S. Supreme Court held that the courts do not have the power to construe union rules to determine the offenses for which discipline may be imposed.[32] When a union official did not refer a union member to an available job, the member struck the official. Subsequently, the union member was disciplined by his union, and the lower federal courts held that the union rule in question could not be used as the basis for expulsion. By its reversal of these decisions, the U.S. Supreme Court has held that unions may interpret union rules for which members may be disciplined. In other words, *the law's protection is limited to the procedure for discipline and not to the substantive character of union rules and their interpretation by the organization.*

Should a court find, however, that a union member was fined, expelled, or otherwise disciplined without due process, it will direct an appropriate remedy. For example, under appropriate circumstances, a court will direct reinstatement of an expelled member in the union and award damages.

This principle of the law was demonstrated in 1992 by the Chicago federal appeals court. A union member was convicted of a felony and served time in prison. The union's constitution contained an expulsion procedure requiring that members be of "good moral character." While the member was in jail, the union sent a letter notifying him that he was expelled from union membership. Nothing in the letter told the member the reason for the expulsion or offered him an opportunity of a hearing in the event he elected to contest his expulsion.

Stressing the provisions in Landrum-Griffin requiring procedural due process safeguards for discipline of members, the court held the union in violation of those standards.[33] In its decision the court determined the union failed to demonstrate that a felony conviction, in itself, established lack of "good moral character." Nor did the union establish that its disciplinary board did not have discretion to impose a penalty short of expulsion. On these grounds the federal appeals court vacated the decision of a federal district court which had previously dismissed the expelled member's claim. Despite its decision, however, the appeals court said the union was still free to comply with Landrum-Griffin procedures and could still possibly expel the member.

Due-Process Rights for Whom?

The problem arose concerning the relationship of unions to their officers. Thus, may a union summarily remove an officer from office without affording due process? As noted above, a union member may not be fined, expelled, or otherwise disciplined unless due process is afforded. Is a union officer "otherwise disciplined" when removed from office? To resolve this problem, courts distinguish among the reasons why an officer is removed. If removal is caused by malfeasance, the officer is not entitled to due process. For example, in one case, a business agent was removed because he showed favoritism in work assignments. A federal appeals court upheld that removal.[34]

In contrast, when a union officer exercises rights protected by the bill of rights, a federal appeals court held that the union must comply with the due-process requirements. A group of officials were summarily removed from their offices because they actively supported an unsuccessful candidate for union office.[35] A federal appeals court upheld the dismissed officers and ruled that

> nothing in the statutory language excluded members who are officers. Nor is there any intimation in the legislative history that Congress intended these guarantees of equal political rights and freedom of speech and assembly to be inapplicable to officer members.

As another federal court pointed out:

> The statutory distinction between officers and members of a union organization seems to be, for the most part, confined to the summary discharge of officers for alleged malfeasance. However, by contrast, when rights are asserted under [the bill of rights], no member "may be fined, suspended, expelled, or otherwise disciplined" without observance of . . . the due process section.[36]

Finnegan v. *Leu*

In 1982, however, the U.S. Supreme Court in *Finnegan* v. *Leu* held that a union president lawfully dismissed *appointed* union officers (business agents).[37] They supported the challenger who had unsuccessfully run against the incumbent union president. The Court pointed out that Landrum-Griffin is designed to protect the interests of rank-and-file union members, not the job security of appointed union officers or employees. It ruled that the statute does not preclude an elected union officer from selecting staff members who hold compatible views with his or her own. In a footnote, however, the Court left open the question of whether a different result might be reached in a case involving "a nonpolicymaking and nonconfidential" employee.

Following the high court's precedent, a federal appeals court held that a union could lawfully discharge a secretary employed in its office because of her perceived lack of loyalty to a newly elected union administration. During the election campaign, the secretary remained neutral at least outwardly, supporting neither the incumbents nor the challengers. Her apparent neutral stance, however, did not provide her with a valid suit under the law. Since she had almost unlimited access to confidential and sensitive union information, she did not fall within the exemption expressed by the high court.

Another federal appeals court held that the removal of a dissident union officer from an important union committee was lawful.[38] Noting that the operation of the group from which he was removed, the Nuclear Safety Committee, played a significant role in union affairs, the court held that the removed officer did not fall within the "nonpolicymaking" exemption expressed in the precedent case.

Understand that *Finnegan* v. *Leu* dealt with *appointed union officers and not persons who are elected to union office.* Nothing in the decision appears to authorize the removal of elected union officers who exercise their rights established in the statute. Indeed, should the decision be interpreted to cover elected union officers, the result would deal a serious blow to internal union democracy. In the past, national union presidents defeated in elections almost always lost to officers serving under them. To say the least, union democracy would be undermined if the successful candidate had the power to remove the elected officers who supported the loser. One example was the loss of the United Steelworkers presidency by David MacDonald to I. W. Abel, former secretary-treasurer of the national union. Also, in 1969, Joseph Yablonski, a United Mine Workers official for twenty-seven years, challenged W. A. (Tony) Boyle for the presidency. Yablonski lost the election and later his life, along with the lives of his wife and daughter. The Secretary of Labor challenged the election after Yablonski's murder, which is one of the most notorious blots on union history. The fact that Yablonski was successful in even running for the UMW presidency is considered almost miraculous and marks the first attempt in about forty years to challenge the incumbent president of the UMW. In December 1972, Arnold R. Miller decisively defeated Boyle for the union presidency in an election ordered by the courts and supervised by the Department of Labor. Miller, a reform candidate, headed an insurgent group called "Miners for Democracy." Several UMW officials who had served under Boyle were convicted for the Yablonski murders, and subsequently Boyle was convicted of the crime. Miller was embroiled in considerable internal political problems during the 1978 bituminous coal strike and subsequently resigned his office.

Nonetheless, two federal court of appeals' decisions permitted the removal of elected union officers. In 1984, the New Orleans federal appeals court upheld the removal of eleven elected union officials.[39] In the same year, the Atlanta federal appeals court ruled that the removal of the union president did not violate Landrum-Griffin.[40]

Sheet Metal Workers, Local 75 v. Lynn

In 1989, the U.S. Supreme Court finally laid the matter to rest, holding that *elected union officers may not be removed from office because they speak out against policies advanced by higher-level union officers.* After union members elected a business agent for a three-year term, a union trustee removed him from office because the newly elected business agent spoke out against a proposed dues increase. Relying on *Finnegan*, a federal district court upheld the union, ruling that the business agent could be removed from office.

In *Sheet Metal Workers, Local 75* v. *Lynn*,[41] the high court *unanimously* ruled that to sustain the union's position, union members would lose the right to select officers of their own choice if elected officials could be discharged for speaking out against union leadership. Distinguishing the case at hand from *Finnegan*, the Court held that the free speech guarantee established by Landrum-Griffin applies to elected union officers. Aside from that, *Finnegan* involved appointed union officers not elected officials, a distinction unbelievably not recognized by the district court. Thus, not only are union members guaranteed the right to free speech under the statute, but also elected union officers. In fact, the high court stated that the "potential chilling effect on the law's free speech rights is more severe" when elected officials are removed in retaliation for stating views not held by union leadership.

Enforcement of Bill of Rights

Union members on their own must enforce allegations of violations of the bill of rights by suing their unions or officers in civil court. In contrast, the Secretary of Labor investigates and enforces violations of the other areas of the statute. Individual members might not have the financial resources to sue their unions. Although the problem may be eased somewhat by class action lawsuits, the financial burden may deter members from suing their unions. Also, union members may be subject to group pressure militating against their using court action.[42] In this way, the full benefits of the bill of rights may not be available to union members. On the other hand, to permit the Secretary of Labor to intervene at the request of union members may result in an unreasonable amount of litigation, which could impair the effective operation of labor organizations. Dissident groups could use the section to harass union officers if union members did not bear the burden of enforcement. It was these considerations that prompted Congress to forbid the Secretary of Labor to enforce the bill of rights.

Despite the difficulty of union member enforcement, however, the fact is that private suits alleging violations of the bill of rights are filed in court. Between 1959 and 1974, 1,559 private suits were filed by union members against their unions or officers, and a majority of them alleged violations of the bill of rights.[43] By 1977, the number had increased to 2,072,[44] or an average of about 188 per year since Landrum-Griffin was enacted. As noted above, the number should increase given the current court policy on the activities of the National Right to Work Legal Defense & Education Foundation.

An added incentive was provided union members to sue their unions. Earlier we pointed out that the Supreme Court had held under Taft-Hartley that punitive damages could not be assessed against a union that violated its members' right of fair representation. In contrast, under Landrum-Griffin, a federal appeals court held that punitive damages could be assessed when a union violates its members' rights protected by the bill of rights section of the statute.[45] The court, however, restricted its own rights in this respect, saying that punitive damages should be awarded only in the most egregious cases, where the conduct involved is malicious, and the amount should not be so great as to cripple a union financially. Unlike fair representation cases under Taft-Hartley, no blanket prohibition of punitive damages exists so far under Landrum-Griffin.

REPORTS TO SECRETARY OF LABOR

Union Requirements

Within ninety days of the time a union first becomes subject to the 1959 law, it must file an initial report with the Secretary of Labor. The report must be signed by the principal union officers such as the president and secretary and must include specific information on the following:

1. Union name and address where records are kept.
2. Names and titles of officers.
3. Initiation fees for new members or other fees for transferred members as well as for working permits.
4. Dues and fees required of members.

The union must also indicate where information may be found in documents filed that contain provisions and procedures for

1. Membership qualifications.
2. Assessment levies.
3. Participation in insurance and other benefits.
4. Authorization for disbursement of funds.
5. Financial audits.
6. Calling of regular or special meetings.
7. Selection of officers and representatives.
8. Discipline or removal of officers or agents.
9. Imposition of fines, suspensions, and expulsion of members.
10. Authorization for bargaining demands.
11. Ratification of contract terms.
12. Strike authorization.
13. Issuance of work permits.

Any change in information filed in the initial report must be reported once a year when the annual financial report is filed. A union that is terminated for reasons such as merger or consolidation and dissolution must file a terminal report within thirty days after loss of identity or existence. The report must state (1) circumstances and effective date of termination; and (2) name and address of the union into which it was consolidated, merged, or absorbed.

A labor organization is also required to file an annual financial report within ninety days after the end of each fiscal year. The report must show

1. Assets and liabilities at the beginning and end of the fiscal year.
2. Receipts of any kind and the sources thereof.
3. Salaries, allowances, and other direct or indirect payments to each officer, irrespective of amounts, and also to each employee who received a total of more than $10,000 during the year from the reporting organization and any other affiliated union.
4. Direct and indirect loans to any officer, employee, or member that aggregated more than $250 during the fiscal year, together with a statement of the purpose, security, and arrangements for repayment.
5. Direct and indirect loans to any business enterprise, together with a statement of the purpose, security, and arrangements for repayment.
6. Other disbursements made by it and the purposes thereof.

Although the reporting requirement imposes a heavy burden on union officers, they faced the inevitable and complied with the law. Between 1959 and 1977, the Secretary of Labor filed 115 civil court actions to compel compliance with the reporting sections of the law, or an average of only six per year.[46] Considering, however, that 53,265 unions were covered by the law in 1977,[47] compliance appears excellent. A problem still exists over the application of the reporting duty to small unions. They received some relief when the Secretary of Labor permitted them to file simplified reports.

Landrum-Griffin requires reporting unions to make information contained in reports available to their members. The right of members to examine the union's books and records to verify the report is enforceable in any state court or in an appropriate federal district court. The provision also stipulates that a union member successful in a court suit may be allowed to recover costs and reasonable attorneys' fees. Thus, proper administration of union funds is advanced because of the provision.

Conflict-of-Interest Reporting

Every union officer or employee, other than those performing clerical or custodial services exclusively, is required to file an annual report within ninety days after the end of the fiscal year if he or she, a spouse, or a minor child had any specified financial transaction that might constitute a possible conflict of interest. The obvious reason for such a requirement was to discourage the kinds of transactions that might constitute a conflict of interest. Apparently not many union officers are involved in this kind of activity. Only one reported action has been brought against a union officer for refusal to file the necessary reports, and that occurred in 1964.[48] Union officers and employees who do engage in conflict-of-interest transactions must at least disclose their activity. Should the membership learn that an officer receives income from a company in which the union holds bargaining rights (one example of a conflict-of-interest transaction), such an officer would probably be defeated in the next election or quickly removed pursuant to the internal rules of the organization.

Criminal Penalties under Landrum-Griffin

Union officers who willfully violate the reporting section of the law may he fined up to $10,000 and imprisoned for one year. A violation could involve a union officer who fails to report, files a false report, or withholds material information. Between 1959 and 1974, about 900,000 reports were filed by union officers. In 1977, they filed about 93,000 reports.[49] Data after 1977 are not available.

Other areas of the law also provide for criminal penalties. It is necessary to understand that several hundred thousand union officers are in a position to commit Landrum-Griffin violations. As noted earlier, in 1977 the law applied to about 53,000 labor organizations. Each union averages about seven officers, or a total of about 370,000. Beyond the reporting requirements, a union officer may be convicted under the law for many crimes, including failure to secure union bonds; embezzlement; bribery; making union loans to union officers or employees in excess of $2,000; payment of any fine imposed on a union officer or employee convicted of violating the law; depriving union members of their rights by coercion or violence; wrongful transfer of funds of a local union to the national union under a trusteeship arrangement; and serving as a union official after being convicted of specified crimes.

Between 1959 and 1977, approximately 933 union officers were convicted for *any* criminal offense under the law.[50] This amounted to an average of fifty-one convictions per year. The most frequent offense involved embezzlement, theft, or conversion of union funds. Violation of the reporting requirements was the second most prevalent offense. Given the small number of convictions, it would appear that union officers have faithfully complied with their obligations under the law.

Employer Reports

Employers are also required to file reports with the Secretary of Labor. Willful violations call for fines up to $10,000 and a year in prison. In general, these reports must be filed when employers engage in activities or make expenditures that undermine the integrity of the collective bargaining process or interfere with employee rights protected by Taft-Hartley.

To be reported are any payments or loans made to any labor organization or union officer. One purpose is to prevent the negotiation of "sweetheart contracts," in which the employer pays off union officers to settle on cheap or obviously substandard labor agreements. This employer requirement is the counterpart of the obligation of union officers to report any receipt of money or things of value from an employer, and the obligation of union officers to report any conflict-of-interest transaction.

An employer must also report any payment to any of its employees for the purpose of persuading other employees not to exercise their right to organize and bargain collectively. So if an employer makes a payment to an employee, for example, to persuade other employees not to vote for a union, such an expenditure must be reported. Payments to the employer's regular officers or supervisors, however, would be exempt. So the employer would not be required to report the salary, for example, of its personnel manager or labor relations director who as part of their regular duties may persuade employees not to join or vote for a union.

An employer must also report expenditures made to *anyone* hired from outside the company to interfere with lawfully protected employee rights or to obtain information about its employees or labor organization involved in a labor dispute with the employer. For example, such expenditures must be reported should the employer engage the services of so-called "consultants," who may or may not be attorneys, for the purpose of persuading employees not to vote for a union, or to decertify a union. (The issue of consultants will be discussed further.) Exempt would be payments to obtain information to be used in proceedings with a government agency, arbitration, or court proceedings. Also, an employer need not report payments made to any person engaged to represent it in collective bargaining negotiations or in arbitration, government agency, or court proceedings.

Labor Relations Consultants

The law imposes a duty on an employer to report any arrangement and payment made to an outside consultant when used to persuade employees not to join a union, or to decertify a union. It imposes the same duty on the consultant to report the arrangement and payment as well. Two separate reports are required of the consultant. One involves arrangements made with the employer, and the other is a report on receipts and disbursements made as a result of the arrangements. The report on arrangements must be filed within thirty days after entering into an agreement. It must contain:

1. Name under which the person making the report is engaged in doing business and the address of the principal office.
2. Detailed statement of the terms and conditions of the agreement or arrangement.

The basic reason for this requirement is to obtain reports from those consultants hired to (1) influence employees regarding their organizational and bargaining rights, or (2) supply an employer with information regarding union activities similar to those that employers are required to report.

When consultants provide such services to employers, they must report the following financial data:

1. Receipts of any kind from employers on account of labor relations advice or services, and the sources of the receipts.
2. Disbursements of any kind in connection with labor relations services and the purposes thereof.

Nothing in law, of course, forbids consultants from engaging in such activities. It is only that they must report the information. However, willful failure to report, or false reporting, could result in criminal penalties, a fine up to $10,000 and a year imprisonment. Regardless of whether the consultant is an attorney, a report must be filed should the consultant persuade employees not to exercise their organizational and collective bargaining rights protected by Taft-Hartley. A federal appeals court held that an attorney must report such activities and financial data, and is not exempt from doing so on the basis of the attorney-client relationship.[51] In 1984, another federal appeals court ordered a law firm to report its persuasion activities, though the attorneys did not commit any violation of Taft-Hartley on behalf of their employer-clients.[52] The law firm contended reports are required only when a consultant engages in unfair labor practices, for example, industrial espionage or threatening employees should they vote for a union. Rejecting this position, the court stated:

> Congress did not distinguish between disclosed and undisclosed persuaders or between legitimate and nefarious persuasive activities.

Nor are consultants relieved from the reporting requirements because they may infringe upon the First Amendment rights of free speech, association, or privacy.[53] A trade association published a magazine and other documents "unabashedly antiunion," which were distributed to employer members and employees. Holding that the trade association was required to report such activities, the court said any encroachment on its free speech right was speculative and was not substantially breached. In other words, any infringement on the association's First Amendment right was outweighed by the public interest of protection of employees in the exercise of their union rights. It also rejected the argument that the reporting requirement constituted a prior restriction on free speech, *observing that the association is free to publish and distribute whatever material it desired as long as it complied with the reporting requirements of the law.*

Increased use of consultants by antiunion employers has generated growing attention.[54] As reported in the *Wall Street Journal*:

> The number of specialists—including lawyers, consultants and social scientists—who are on the companies' side in these fights has ballooned, though statistics are sketchy. Last year, the Labor Department chronicled the involvement of such specialists in 159 labor disputes, a 127% increase from 1975.[55]

An AFL-CIO study published in 1984 revealed that consultants were directing management antiunion strategy in *70 percent of organizing campaigns conducted in 1982–1983.*[56]

In a congressional investigation of the subject, an AFL-CIO official said:

> So let me turn now to examining the nature of union-busting in 1979.
> The fact is that today the phenomena of union-busting is very different from 1959. Unfair labor practices of all kinds have skyrocketed. Our records show that out of 6,000 organizing campaigns of 10 or more workers, two-thirds involve some form of outside

anti-union expertise. By some estimates there are more than 1,000 firms directly and indirectly involved in union-busting activities with more than 1,500 individual practitioners engaged in the full-time activity of preventing unionization efforts. Union-busting is now a major American industry with annual sales well over one-half billion.

These firms and consultants have almost all emerged within the last ten years. The conclusion must be drawn that there is a direct link between the professionalization of union-busting and the skyrocketing abuse of the law. In fact, many consultants openly claim credit for the meteoric rise in decertification and deauthorization elections.

Union-busting is no longer as blatant as the blunt-end of a billyclub. It is a sophisticated science spanning the field of psychology, law, and personnel administration. The practice of union-busting, like any of these component professions, involves the dissemination of expertise for practical application. We have identified five principal delivery systems by which this union-busting technology is disseminated from the expert into the midst of the workplace. They are: (1) The seminar lecturer who gives companies a two or three day crash course in the art of antiunionism. (2) The consulting firm composed of psychologists and industrial relations experts. (3) The anti-union law firm which handles the legal strategies of union-busting, including delays, discharges, bargaining to impasse and decertification. (4) The industrial psychologist who develops and administers the surveys and psychological testing of anti-unionism. (5) The trade association which combines all of these functions and specifically tailors them to the labor relations of an industry.[57]

Though the AFL-CIO official may have been hyperbolic and not completely accurate, the statement nevertheless highlights the growing use of the consultant as part of an employer's antiunion campaign.

Advice or Persuasion

Should consultants merely give advice directly to employers, they have no obligation to report their activities or financial data. Landrum-Griffin states:

> Nothing in this section shall be construed to require any employer or other person to file a report covering the services of such person by reason of his giving advice to such employer. . .

As long as the consultant does not deal directly with employees but provides antiunion counsel directly to the employer and its supervisors, no reports need to be filed. Given the growing use of consultants, unions claim that this is a weakness in the law and should be corrected. Thus:

> The House Subcommittee on Labor-Management Relations issued in March 1981 a report on labor relations consultants that was based on extensive hearings in 1979 and 1980. A key recommendation was that the Labor Department should be more diligent in enforcing the reporting requirements for consultants under the Landrum-Griffin Act. "Virtually every union is required to and does report its activities under the provisions of the Act," the report says. "It is inequitable that the Department does not require consultants, even in instances when they are clearly running management's anti-union campaign, to disclose their involvement."[58]

One study on this issue stated:

> That there has been general noncompliance with the Act's employer and consultant reporting provisions is agreed upon by all observers. Indeed, a report entitled *The Forgotten Law—Disclosure of Consultant and Employer Activity under the LMRDA* was issued by the Subcommittee on Labor-Management Relations of the House Education and Labor Committee in December 1984. It concluded that the Labor Department had "systematically dismantled its employer and consultant reporting enforcement program."[59]

The legal issue involved in this matter is the correct interpretation of "advice" and "persuade" for purposes of Landrum-Griffin. As noted, employers and consultants need not report payment when the consultant gives advice to the employer. However, Section 203 of the statute requires a financial accounting when the consultant "directly or indirectly [persuades] employees to exercise or not exercise . . . the right to organize and bargain collectively through representatives of their own choosing."

In a case decided by a federal district court, a consultant drew up the employer's antiunion campaign, including the training of supervisors to use antiunion tactics. The consultant, however, did not deal face-to-face with employees. The UAW, the union in the case, argued that payments to the consultant should be reported because at least the consultant *indirectly* persuaded employees not to join the union. Involved in the case was the regulation of the Secretary of Labor that exempts reporting when consultants provide antiunion advice to the employer and its supervisors. Reports are required only when consultants directly persuade employees to reject the union. Rejecting the Labor Secretary's position, the court held the payments must be reported on the grounds that the *objective of the consultant's activities was to persuade employees to remain nonunion.*[60]

In 1989, however, a federal court of appeals reversed the district court, ruling the Secretary of Labor's position was correct.[61] It held the consultant's action was advice given the employer, and not persuasion of employees to reject the union. It refused to accept the union's position that at least the consultant indirectly persuaded employees not to exercise their organizational and collective bargaining rights. Defending its ruling, the appeals court said the employer was free to accept or not accept the consultant's advice. If so, why did the employer hire a consultant to map out its antiunion strategy? The issue is important enough for Supreme Court review, though at this writing it has not done so.

In an NLRB proceeding, however, a labor consultant had a track record of committing serious unfair labor practices on behalf of employers who engaged his services. Excluding the employer party to the case at hand, he had engaged in violations of Taft-Hartley for seven other employers. To stop the practice, the Board issued a very broad order. It not only directed him to cease and desist carrying out his illegal conduct for the employer in the case (who terminated his services) but also all *future employer clients.* Rejecting the consultant's argument that the agency order was unlawful because it was "unprecedented," a federal appeals court upholding the NLRB order stated: "It does not follow the agency can never do anything that it has not done before."[62] While noting the employer involved in the case had terminated the consultant's services, the court held an order merely forbidding the commission of further unfair labor practices on behalf of that employer "would be a nullity."

CONTROL OF TRUSTEESHIPS

Legitimate and Unlawful Trusteeships

Trusteeships are normally used by national unions to prevent or eliminate malpractices in subordinate local unions. House Committee Report No. 741 explained the operation of trusteeships as follows:

> Constitutions of many international unions authorize the international officers to suspend the normal processes of government of local unions and other subordinate bodies, to supervise their internal activity and assume control of their property and funds. These "trusteeships" (or "receiverships" or "supervisorships," as they are sometimes called) are among the most effective devices which responsible international officers have to insure order within their organization. In general, they have been widely used to prevent corruption, mismanagement of union funds, violation of collective bargaining agreements, infiltration of Communists; in short, to preserve the integrity and stability of the organization itself.

The McClellan committee found, however, various misuses of the trusteeship arrangement. Some national unions without justification imposed trusteeships. *At times, a local was taken over and its officers removed because the local union officers were opposed to the national union officers. National unions used the device to plunder local treasuries. Also, the corrupt nature of the trusteeship arrangement was displayed in some instances wherein local union funds were diverted to national-union-appointed trustees for their personal use. Once the arrangement was imposed, some continued under national control for as long as thirty years.*

The McClellan committee devoted a great deal of attention to the trusteeship abuses of three unions: the Bakery and Confectionery Workers Union, the Operating Engineers, and the Teamsters Union. Widespread publicity was devoted to union trusteeship abuses. The result was that the 1959 Landrum-Griffin Act provided three types of regulation of trusteeships. *The first permits the establishment of trusteeships only if they are to achieve legitimate union goals*:

1. To correct corruption.
2. To correct financial malpractices.
3. To assure the performance of union contracts.
4. To assure the performance of a bargaining representative's duty.
5. To restore democratic practices.
6. To carry out the legitimate objects of the labor organization.

The constitution and bylaws of a union imposing a trusteeship must establish the administrative procedure to be used. This requirement limits the freedom of a parent body to impose its own rules as it pleases.

The second statutory regulation prohibits a local under trusteeship to cast votes at an international convention, "unless the delegates have been chosen by secret ballot in an election in which all members in good standing . . . were eligible to participate." This restriction makes it more difficult for parent bodies to keep locals under their control to further their political objectives.

Reports Required

The third regulation is that parent unions are required to file reports on each trusteeship upon its imposition, periodically while it is in effect, and upon its termination. Once a labor organization imposes a trusteeship over a subordinate body, it must report the action within thirty days to the Secretary of Labor. Detailed information is required on the following items:

1. Name and address of the subordinate body.
2. Date the trusteeship was established.
3. Detailed statement of reasons for establishing the trusteeship.
4. Nature and extent that the subordinate body's membership participates in regular or special conventions or other policy-making sessions.
5. Full and complete account of the financial condition of the local at the time the trusteeship was established.

Much of the information listed must be filed every six months while the trusteeship remains in effect. A trusteeship imposed in accordance with a parent union's constitution and bylaws and for the allowable purposes enumerated above are presumed to be valid for a period of eighteen months. However, if union officials feel the arrangement should continue beyond the eighteen-month period, the presumption of validity is reversed, if challenged, and the national officers must show "clear and convincing proof" for the need to continue the device.[63] Even before a trusteeship arrangement may be considered valid for eighteen months, it must be ratified "after a fair hearing before the executive board or before such other body as may be provided in accordance with its constitution or bylaws."

A regular annual financial report is required of the national union president, the treasurer, and the trustee in order to account for the use of the funds of the seized local.

Another report is required under the trusteeship provisions. A financial report must be filed at the time a trustee arrangement is terminated, in order to protect the integrity of the finances of a trusteed organization. *Should a national transfer funds from the local, the responsible union officials are subject to a fine up to $10,000 and one year of imprisonment.*

Enforcement Procedures

A local union or any member may file a complaint with the Secretary of Labor alleging violation of the prohibitions regarding (1) transfer of funds, (2) delegate voting, or (3) improper imposition of the trusteeship. The Act requires an investigation when a complaint is filed alleging any violation of these three conditions. A civil suit is brought in a federal district court if the Secretary finds a violation.

A complaining union member or a trusteed labor organization apparently has the right to bring suit in a federal district court. Court cases are divided on the issue of whether a union member could choose between filing a complaint with the Secretary of Labor or filing a suit in a district court. One court ruled that a review of trusteeship had to be made first through the Secretary of Labor as the primary remedy.[64] Another court, however, reasoned that a union member could seek relief from either source.[65] Remedies for trusteeship violations are available under state or local courts. However, if the Secretary of Labor files a complaint, the action takes precedence over one that may be pending in any court.

Experience under the Law

Up to 1975, the Department of Labor instituted lawsuits to compel compliance with Landrum-Griffin trusteeship provisions on only five occasions.[66] More recent data are not available. One case was particularly noteworthy because it dealt with a subterfuge to cover up an illegal trusteeship. A federal appeals court ruled a trusteeship was in effect merely on the basis of a showing that a *de facto* loss of autonomy was in effect.[67] The court rejected the national claim that a trusteeship was not in effect because the national union did not formally suspend the autonomy of the local. Undoubtedly, the court's judgment was influenced by the fact that the local in effect lost its autonomy for *twenty years*. This decision indicated the courts will sweep aside subterfuges to conceal violations of the trusteeship provisions.

In 1973, however, a federal appeals court held that the courts do not have the authority to terminate a trusteeship when the subordinate body is limited to state public employees.[68] The basis for the court's decision was its finding that the local union, composed solely of public employees, was not a "labor organization" within the meaning of the law. In one way, the decision seems somewhat strange because the national union itself, American Federation of State, County and Municipal Employees, is subject to the provisions of Landrum-Griffin.

It would appear that abuses involving the trusteeship arrangement have abated as a result of the legislation. In 1959, the year in which Landrum-Griffin was enacted, there were about 500 trusteeships in effect. It is quite possible that these involved abuses in at least some cases, since the locals had been placed in trusteeship prior to enactment of the law. By 1966, only 19 of the 500 were still under an active trusteeship arrangement.[69]

As noted, the law permits trusteeships for specified and legitimate purposes. For example, in 1987, a federal appeals court approved a trusteeship when the local union engaged in a long and bitter strike not authorized by the national union.[70] Thus, since the enactment of the law, national unions have continued to place locals under this arrangement. Indeed, between 1959 and 1972, about 2,200 trusteeships were reported to the Secretary of Labor. By June 1972, however, the most recent data available, only 351 of these were still in effect.[71] This is not a large number when one considers that there were more than 50,000 local unions in the nation; and, further, since the trusteeships were put into effect under the stringent provisions of the law, the national unions probably acted lawfully.

GOVERNMENT CONTROL OF UNION ELECTIONS

Election Abuse

Landrum-Griffin deals with internal union elections. The relevant section establishes requirements concerning the frequency of elections, and it sets forth minimum standards relating to such things as nomination and election procedures, candidate eligibility to vote, campaign rules, and fund expenditures. It also establishes provisions to enforce the requirements.

Concern with union election procedures predates the Taft-Hartley Act, although the interest was at the state level and not in Congress. Indeed, by 1943, five states had passed laws with the purpose of regulating the election of officers among other internal practices.[72] One state supreme court held the election provisions to be unconstitutional (Texas), and another held them to be valid (Colorado).[73] However, most "state legislatures and courts were reluctant" to regulate internal union procedures prior to 1959.[74]

Malpractices in union election procedures were disclosed by the Bureau of Labor Statistics, the National Industrial Conference Board, and the McClellan committee. The committee found various violations of democratic principles in union elections. These were:

1. Disregard for the [union] constitutional provisions regulating elections.
2. Prevention of members from participating in elections.
3. Prevention of opponents from nomination by violence and intimidation.
4. Use of checkoff system to disfranchise membership.
5. Giving no advance notice to membership of balloting.
6. Not using secret ballots.
7. Use of union money for the election of incumbent officers.
8. Rigging elections by stuffing ballot box.
9. Removal of duly elected officers without due process.[75]

Two studies found that only a small percentage of unions were in violation of democratic internal practices. In 1958, the Bureau of Labor Statistics study revealed that only 5 percent of unions did not hold presidential elections at least every five years.[76]

A study by Philip Taft, however, was far more devastating to unions. Taft found that during the period 1900–1948, 81 percent of 202 national union presidential elections were uncontested. The reason was either lack of membership interest or political strength of incumbents.[77] Membership apathy, therefore, was an element in lack of membership participation in internal union affairs. The federal government proceeded to deal with the election abuses with the aim of establishing democracy in the election procedures used by unions.

Frequency of Elections

Election provisions of Landrum-Griffin apply to national unions, intermediate bodies, and local unions. Federations and state or local central bodies were not included in its coverage. *National unions are required to hold elections at least once every five years.*

Voting must be by secret ballot among members of good standing, or at a convention of delegates chosen by secret ballot.

Local union elections must be held at least every three years. Secret balloting must proceed among members in good standing. Intermediate bodies must hold elections at least every four years. Balloting is on the same basis as that required of national unions. The credentials of convention delegates and all election records must be preserved for one year.

Many union constitutions and bylaws may call for more frequent elections than are required under the statute. Labor organizations may also legally establish stricter requirements for the election of officers. Title IV merely provides minimum standards, not maximum. Also, it would appear that the states under the federal preemption doctrine are forbidden to impose requirements stricter than those in Landrum-Griffin. Greater uniformity of internal union behavior is provided by federal control as opposed to state control of elections. For example, the too-frequent holding of elections could generate uncertainty in the collective bargaining process.

Minimum Election Procedures

A union's constitution and bylaws control elections if they are not in conflict with the following Landrum-Griffin standards:

1. An election notice must be mailed to the last known address of a member within at least fifteen days prior to an election.
2. Each member in good standing is entitled to one vote.
3. No member shall be ineligible to vote or to be a candidate because of alleged default or delay in payment of dues if his or her dues have been withheld by the employer pursuant to a voluntary dues checkoff established in the labor agreement.
4. Votes by members of each local union must be counted and the results published, separately.
5. Election records must be kept for at least one year.
6. Any candidate has a right to have an observer at the polls and at the counting of ballots.
7. A reasonable opportunity must be given to nominate candidates and every member in good standing is eligible to be a candidate and entitled to vote without fear of reprisal.

Exceptions to Right to Hold Office

Congress prohibited some persons from holding office in Title V of the 1959 law. Persons are barred from holding most union offices and jobs for five years after the end of their conviction or imprisonment for such crimes as robbery, bribery, extortion, embezzlement, grand larceny, burglary, arson, violation of narcotics laws, murder, rape, assault with intent to kill, and assault that inflicts grievous bodily injury. The five-year ban on holding office runs from the date of prison sentence expiration, not from parole date.[78] A union office, however, may be held by a banned person prior to the end of the five-year period if either U.S. citizenship has been regained or a Certificate of Exemption has been issued by the Board of Parole, U.S. Department of Justice.

Originally disqualified from being a union officer was any individual who was a member of the Communist Party, who was excluded for five years after Communist Party membership termination. The Landrum-Griffin anticommunist provision was intended to replace the provision of Taft-Hartley that required principal union officers to sign noncommunist oaths before they could use National Labor Relations Board facilities. The labor movement fought such a requirement and argued that it stigmatized union leaders as anti-American. Furthermore, some critics argued that Communists holding union offices could easily sign such an oath. Others, however, pointed out that refusal of known Communist union leaders to sign the oath prevented their unions from using NLRB facilities. This paved the way for noncommunist unions to raid their membership and therefore weaken the Communist hold on the labor movement.

In any event, the noncommunist oath requirement of Taft-Hartley was held constitutional by the U.S. Supreme Court in 1950.[79] The Court pointed out that Taft-Hartley denied the use of NLRB facilities to unions whose officers refused to sign the affidavit. The 1947 law did not deny them the right to hold office.

Landrum-Griffin, as mentioned, denied Communists the right to hold union office for a five-year period after termination of party membership. The U.S. Supreme Court, however, held the provision unconstitutional in 1965.[80] The high court admitted that Congress has power to deal with the problem of Communists occupying positions of power and trust in labor unions. It was not willing, however, to permit Congress to deal with Communist Party members under criminal sanctions through general legislation.

Thus, there are no longer prohibitions on a Communist holding union office. It should be recognized, however, that the number of Communists holding union offices has sharply declined over the years. There is no apparent need for a statutory prohibition on such individuals. In the unlikely event that a threat should arise, Congress, despite the Supreme Court decision, would appear to have the power to deny Communists the right to hold union office. As stated, the Court held the Landrum-Griffin anticommunist provision unconstitutional because the law dealt with Communists as a class. Legislation designed to prevent Communists or members of other political groups from holding union office would probably stand the test of constitutionality if a law established specific standards upon which to judge the fitness of such individuals to serve as union officers.

Qualifications to Run for Union Office

Under Landrum-Griffin, all union members in good standing are eligible to run for local and national office, subject "to reasonable conditions uniformly imposed." As noted earlier, the U.S. Supreme Court in 1964 held in *Calhoun* v. *Harvey* that the limitations placed on union members' quest for office were reasonable. Since the union covered the maritime industry, the requirements for a candidate to serve at sea and be a member for five years were held to be lawful. In two other cases, however, the high court invalidated qualifications placed upon the opportunity of union members to run for office. One case required a union member to have held prior office and the other required attendance at a certain number of meetings.

Local 6, Hotel, Motel and Club Employees Union established a requirement that candidates for office had to be prior officeholders as a condition of eligibility. A district court held the requirement an unreasonable restriction on the right of union members to hold office and as such a violation of the Act. It refused, however, to set aside the election and order a new one because of lack of evidence that the prior officeholding requirement affected the election outcome. The trial court merely enjoined the local from using the requirement for candidacy in future elections. An appellate court deemed the union-imposed requirement reasonable and reversed the lower court.

The Supreme Court reversed the prior decisions and held that an eligibility requirement that rendered 93 percent of the membership ineligible for office could hardly be deemed reasonable.[81] Further, exclusion of candidates from the ballot was *prima facie* evidence that the violation "may have affected the outcome." Disqualified candidates might have won an election. Such a restriction was viewed as a deviation from the congressional model for democratic union elections. The members themselves were deemed the best judges of candidacy qualifications as expressed in their actions at the polls.

In 1977, the high court by a split vote upset a rule requiring candidates to have attended at least one-half of a local's regular meetings for the three years preceding the election.[82] Under the union's rule, 96.5 percent of the members of the local were disqualified from union office. In its decision, the Court stressed that the 1959 law was designed to promote union democracy without interfering unduly with union internal affairs. It said:

> Applying these principles to this case, we conclude that . . . the anti-democratic effects of the meeting attendance rule outweigh the interests urged in its support. . . . An attendance requirement that results in the exclusion of 96.5 percent of the members from candidacy for union office hardly seems to be a "reasonable qualification" consistent with the goal of free and democratic elections. A requirement having that result obviously severely restricts the free choice of the membership in selecting their leaders.

The minority believed the attendance rule to be a reasonable qualification. It criticized the majority for using a statistical test. The rule was reasonable, said the minority, because it could encourage attendance at meetings, guarantee that candidates for office had a meaningful interest in the union, and assure that the candidates had a chance to become informed about union affairs.

In *Marshall v. Illinois Education Association*, a federal appeals court held unlawful a union's bylaw reserving a bloc of seats on its board of directors for members of specified minority groups: American Indians, black people, Hispanics, and Asians. It said that the policy conflicted with the purpose of the statute.

In 1982, a federal appeals court protected the rights of dissidents to run for office.[83] Attempts to discipline a dissident received widespread publicity throughout the union, the members gaining the impression that the dissident member was not eligible to run for office because disciplinary action had been taken against him or her. To correct this situation, the court directed the union to send a letter to each member stating that the dissident was a union member in good standing and the disciplinary action taken against him or her did not bar candidacy for union office. The court, however, did not deal with the merits of the charges alleged against the dissident member.

To be eligible to run for office, unions require members to be in good standing. One union, however, required continuous dues payment for twenty-four consecutive months to be in good standing. No grace period was permitted. Thus, should a member not pay his or her dues, say, in the twenty-third month, the member would be ineligible to run for office. This rule conflicted with a Department of Labor regulation establishing an automatic grace period for dues payment.

In *Masters, Mates & Pilots*, sustaining the union's rule as reasonable, a federal appeals court said the continuous good standing requirement depends on the circumstances of a particular case.[84] The problem with the government policy was its inflexible character, precluding consideration of the facts of a given case. In the case at hand, ruled the court, the union's policy did not have an antidemocratic effect on the union. Only 10 percent of the total union membership would have been disqualified. The members were well paid, and prompt payment of dues was not difficult. Also, the union rule provided a waiver for ill or inactive members. *Masters, Mates & Pilots*, as well as other cases, *demonstrate that the Secretary of Labor does not have exclusive power to void union elections*. Under proper circumstances, the federal courts will reject the complaint and uphold the union election.

Some unions have established a strict age limit for union officers, mostly sixty-five years. Members older than that age are not eligible to run for union office. In 1987, however, the Department of Labor abolished the age restriction as a valid criterion for union office.[85] The reason is that effective January 1, 1987, Congress made illegal, with a few exceptions, compulsory retirement at any age. To comply with the law, called the Age Discrimination in Employment Act, the Department of Labor prohibits a labor organization from establishing a compulsory retirement age for officers or as a restriction on candidacy.

A provision in the constitution of the National Association of Letter Carriers forbade union members who had applied for a supervisory position from seeking union office for two years. After being nominated for the office of vice-president, a union member was declared ineligible to run for office pursuant to the union's constitution. He had applied unsuccessfully for a supervisory position with the United States Postal Service.

Upon review of the case, a federal district court held the restriction was an unreasonable qualification.[86] According to the court the constitutional provision conflicted with the statute's fundamental purpose of fostering the broadest possible participation in union affairs. It was also entirely speculative that the union member would ever obtain a managerial position so as to create a conflict of interest. Consequently, because of the invalid eligibility standard, the court declared the reelection of the previous vice-president to be null and void and directed the union to conduct a new election under the supervision of the Secretary of Labor.

Undoubtedly, other qualifications for union office will be reviewed by the courts. In this type of case, the question becomes the reasonableness of the rule in question, and the problem of balancing the right of the union to run its internal affairs against the right of union members to seek union office. Not all union rules are designed to limit unfairly the opportunity for union office. Some serve to maintain the integrity and viability of the organization. On the other hand, rules that are arbitrary and capricious should not be permitted, since they would be inconsistent with the general philosophy of the 1959 law assuming maximum participation of union members in the organization's affairs.

Conduct of Campaign

A candidate for union office can be at a distinct disadvantage during a campaign if he or she does not have access to the membership on a par with all other candidates. The law therefore provides that within thirty days prior to an election, a candidate can inspect a list of the last-known addresses of the union's members. Discrimination in the use of such lists is forbidden. The list must be available to all candidates at a union's main office, and if one candidate is permitted to copy the membership list, then all must be afforded the same right.

The distribution of campaign literature is treated in similar fashion. Unions must comply with any reasonable request by a candidate to distribute campaign literature. The candidate, however, *must bear the expense.* This applies to the incumbent officers as well as to those who may be challenging the present officers. Any distribution arrangement made on behalf of any candidate must be made available to all upon request.

In a case decided by the Supreme Court in 1991, a candidate for union office requested mailing labels to assist in mailing campaign literature before the nominating convention. The union, however, had a rule prohibiting a mailing before the nominating convention. On this basis the union denied the candidate's request for the labels.

In a unanimous decision, the high court directed the union to furnish the labels for the candidate.[87] In reaching its decision the Court stressed that under Landrum-Griffin, a union must comply with all reasonable requests of any candidate to distribute campaign literature at the candidate's expense. The request was reasonable because of the statute's promotion of the democratic election process. Also, complying with the candidate's request, reasoned the Supreme Court, would not cause the union undue hardship since the candidate would have paid for the actual mailing. The labels would merely facilitate the mailing of the campaign literature.

Union funds and employer contributions cannot be used to promote any candidate for election. A labor organization, however, has authority to use its funds to operate election machinery. It may pay for such items as ballots and notices publicizing the election date, place, time, and candidates. It may even publish factual statements of election issues as long as the names of the candidates are not included.

Mine Workers' Election

On the basis of wholesale violations of these campaign standards, a federal court invalidated the 1969 United Mine Workers' election, in which the incumbent Boyle defeated Yablonski, the challenger. It was determined that the union journal, financed wholly out of union member dues, had given extensive and favorable coverage during the election campaign to Boyle and his slate, printing their speeches, statements, and pictures. The journal, sent to all union members, did not even note the candidacy of Yablonski or credit him for his efforts to secure the enactment of mine safety legislation. Union funds were used in other ways to support the election of the incumbents. Salary increases were provided to persons on the union's payroll to secure their support of Boyle and his slate. It was expected that these salary increases out of union funds would be turned over to Boyle to finance his campaign. Yablonski was denied the right to have observers at polling places. These and other serious campaign irregularities prompted a federal district court to say:

> . . . to find for the union [Boyle] the court would be forced to swim upstream against the tide of evidence too strong to resist.[88]

Ironically, these were the same charges that Yablonski had made before the 1969 election took place. If the government had acted on these charges and had forbidden the election to take place, it is possible that the Yablonski murders would not have occurred. As it turned out, Yablonski was not alive to enjoy the fruits of victory when his supporters defeated Boyle in the 1972 court-ordered election. In any event, the law did provide the basis for the new election and the restoration of democracy in the union.

Source of Campaign Funds

In a hotly contested election for national president of the United Steelworkers of America in 1977, the challenger, Edward Sadlowski, obtained substantial financial contributions from nonmembers of the labor organization. Though the incumbent, Lloyd McBride, won the election by about 80,000 votes, the union later amended its constitution forbidding a candidate to solicit or accept funds from anyone not a member of the organization. Sustaining a lower court, a federal appeals court held the restriction to violate Landrum-Griffin.[89] It said that the outside contribution restriction

> . . . unreasonably impinges on the right of free speech and association guaranteed by section 10(a)(2) . . .

of the bill of rights provision of the 1959 statute. In *United Steelworkers of America* v. *Sadlowski*, however, the U.S. Supreme Court by 5–4 held that unions can bar candidates for union offices from accepting contributions from individuals or groups outside the union so that outside individuals and groups cannot influence union elections by their cash contributions.[90]

Removal of Officers

Elected union officers may be removed for serious misconduct.[91] If a union's constitution or bylaws do not provide an adequate procedure for removal, the Act provides a procedure. A union member may file a complaint with the Secretary of Labor. The

Secretary then holds a hearing to determine the adequacy of internal union machinery for such matters. If inadequate procedures are found, proper notice must be given that a hearing will be held on the charges. If the hearing discloses that serious misconduct occurred, a secret-ballot election will be held. The Secretary can force such an election by a civil suit. If a court orders a vote, the Secretary certifies the results. The court will decide from the results whether or not an officer is removed.

Enforcement of Election Procedures

There are three preliminary steps involved in the enforcement of election provisions based on a union member's complaint to the Secretary of Labor. The steps are as follows:

1. The complaining union member must have exhausted internal union procedures, at local and parent union levels, or must have invoked them without a final decision within three calendar months.
2. The complaint must be filed within one calendar month thereafter.
3. The Secretary of Labor must investigate the complaint.

A challenged election is presumed valid unless found to the contrary. Elected officials perform their regular duties during the investigation. If the Secretary of Labor finds probable cause to believe a violation has occurred, a suit must be filed in a federal district court within sixty days after the complaint is filed. If the district court agrees with the Secretary of Labor and directs a new election, *it will be held under the direct supervision of the Department of Labor.*

Challenge of Election

It is important to note that the union member must challenge an election through the Secretary of Labor and not through the courts. In 1984, this policy was upheld by the U.S. Supreme Court in *Teamsters, Local 82.*[92] Union members alleged that an election was not held in conformance with the Landrum-Griffin standards. After the union dismissed the complaint, they successfully persuaded a district court to enjoin the election and direct a new poll to be conducted by an impartial arbitrator.

Reversing a district and a federal appeals court, the high court held that the union members' exclusive remedy, after exhaustion of internal union procedures, was to file a complaint with the Secretary of Labor. Only the Secretary of Labor after an investigation has the authority to petition a federal district court to void an election and order a new one. Though the Supreme Court noted that union members may appeal directly to the courts for alleged violations of the bill of rights section of the statute, it held that election matters fall within the exclusive jurisdiction of the Secretary of Labor. Should a federal court direct a new election, as said, it is to be held under the Secretary of Labor's supervision.

In 1992, the federal district court in Maryland determined whether losing candidates in a Department of Labor supervised rerun election could intervene to protest the court's acceptance of the Secretary of Labor's certification of election results. A rerun election was held under the supervision of the Department of Labor because the original election was tainted by violations of Landrum-Griffin election standards. After the new election, the two losing candidates filed a protest with the Secretary of Labor alleging violations during the election campaign. Although the Secretary found minor violations, it was determined that they did not adversely affect the outcome of the election. When the Secretary of Labor filed a certification of election petition with the court, the two losing candidates sought to intervene to protest the court's acceptance of the Secretary's certification.

The court ruled the losing candidates did not have standing to object to the Secretary of Labor's certification of the results of a supervised election.[93] According to the court, complaints of irregularities that the Secretary determined as being without merit were the types of claims that Congress intended to be barred when it made the Secretary's actions the exclusive means of challenging election results. The district court's ruling on the issue, however, may not be the last word on the matter. Indeed, as the district court itself recognized, federal appeals courts have split on this issue, making it ripe for Supreme Court action.

Additional Supreme Court Decisions

The question arose as to whether a decision by the Secretary of Labor *not to set an election aside could be reviewed by the courts*. This was a particularly difficult issue because, under the 1959 law, the Secretary of Labor has wide powers to determine the circumstances under which to challenge an election. Mindful of this congressional purpose, the U.S. Supreme Court held in 1975 that the courts do not have the authority to order a trial-type inquiry into the factual basis of the Labor Secretary's refusal to upset an election.[94] On the other hand, *the high court rejected the contention of the Secretary of Labor that the courts have no authority whatsoever to review such a decision*. It pointed out that nothing in the 1959 law explicitly makes such a decision immune from judicial review. In short, the high court said a decision of the Labor Secretary not to challenge an election will not be disturbed unless the reasons are so "irrational as to be arbitrary and capricious." In other words, the Secretary of Labor must provide the court and the complaining union member with a statement of the supporting reasons for the refusal to challenge an election. If in a particular case the court determines the Secretary acted capriciously or arbitrarily, it has the authority to direct the Secretary of Labor to run a new election.

The Secretary will not bring suit in every case where violations are found, but only in cases where there is evidence that violations "may have affected the outcome of an election." The Department of Labor adopted this policy because a district court is required by law to make a similar finding before ordering a new election. An appeal of a district court's decision is available, but an ordered election must be held while the appeal is pending. Otherwise, the period required for final litigation could be—and usually is—longer than the term of office challenged.

The U.S. Supreme Court ruled that a district federal court must direct a new election when the Secretary of Labor has demonstrated that violations of Landrum-Griffin standards may have affected the outcome of an election. To assure compliance with the law, the Court also held that another election held by the union after the original one was challenged does not stay the Secretary of Labor's power to conduct one under his or her supervision. The Court stated:

> The intervention of an election in which the outcome might be as much a product of unlawful circumstances as the challenged election cannot bring the Secretary's action to a halt. Aborting the exclusive statutory remedy would immunize a proved violation from further attack and leave unvindicated the interests protected [by law].[95]

Thus, a union may not eliminate a pending Title IV action by conducting an unsupervised election of officers after the original one was challenged.

In still another case before the Supreme Court, it was held that the Secretary of Labor's investigative powers are not limited to the specifics of a union member's complaint. The Court stated:

> We reject the narrow construction adopted by the District Court and supported by respondent limiting the Secretary's complaint solely to the allegations made in the union member's initial complaint. Such a severe restriction upon the Secretary's powers should not be read into the statute without a clear indication of congressional intent to that effect . . . [when] the indications are quite clearly to the contrary.[96]

A union member may file a complaint based on incomplete information. The Department of Labor has machinery at its disposal to look at the totality of election conduct, and the Supreme Court upholds that right to do so. However, the high court limited the power of the Secretary of Labor to police union elections.[97] It held that the Secretary can bring suit in court only against the union practices that *a union member protests to the union before filing charges with the Department of Labor.* While investigating a member's complaint, it was discovered that the union allegedly committed another violation of the law. The union member, however, did not attempt to correct this condition through internal union procedures, but only through the complaint filed with the Labor Department. On this basis, the Supreme Court held that the district court could consider only that complaint that the union member had unsuccessfully attempted to correct through internal union procedures. Thus, it was the judgment of the high court that a union should be given the opportunity to correct undemocratic procedures before a court takes action. If the Secretary of Labor could file suit against union practices that the union itself had not been given the opportunity to correct, the Court stated that union "self-government . . . would be needlessly" weakened.

Usage of Election Provisions

The election provisions of the 1959 law have been used much more frequently by union members than have any other features of Landrum-Griffin. Between 1965 and 1974, union members filed 1,296 complaints alleging violations of the election standards contained in the law.[98] Though this number appears substantial, it should be noted that in that period, there were about 57,000 labor organizations covered by the law. Since local unions must conduct an election at least once every three years, intermediate bodies at least once every four years, and national unions at least every five years, it follows that in that nine-year period more than 150,000 elections were held. Actual violations of the law were found in only a small number of the cases alleging wrongdoing. Of the 1,296 complaints, the federal courts ordered only 165 new elections.[99] In 767 instances, complaints were dismissed because no violations were found, or because of the lack of evidence to demonstrate that alleged violations affected the outcome of the elections. In 239 of the cases, unions agreed to take corrective measures, such as recounting the ballots, amending the election provisions of their constitutions and bylaws, or installing winning candidates whom they had previously refused to install for some reason.

Essentially the same experience occurred between 1975 and 1977.[100] Of the 742 complaints filed by union members in those three years, 443 were dismissed because no violation had occurred, or because of lack of evidence to show that alleged violations had affected the outcome of the elections. Federal courts ordered new elections in only 70 instances. Unfortunately, later data are not available, though there is no sound reason to believe the previous experience would not be repeated.

In short, in the light of the numerous elections held by union groups, it appears that the vast number of labor organizations hold regular and fair elections. Undoubtedly, union members frequently challenge elections because of internal political differences rather than on the basis of genuine wrongdoing by incumbent union officials. On these grounds, it is understandable why the AFL-CIO remarked that Landrum-Griffin election investigations

> produced only harassment and disruption, with justifiable bitterness against unnecessary governmental intrusion into internal union affairs.[101]

On balance Landrum-Griffin election standards are salutory because they provide an effective remedy whenever incumbent union officers fail to provide for a fair election. Also, the existence of the law serves as a deterrent to unions that may be inclined to deprive members of the opportunity to elect officers of their own choice on a regular and fair basis.

FINANCIAL SAFEGUARDS FOR LABOR ORGANIZATIONS

Title V contains some of the most important provisions of Landrum-Griffin on internal union operations. It includes (1) fiduciary responsibilities of union officers; (2) embezzlement of union funds; (3) general bonding; and (4) loans and payment-of-fines standards.

Fiduciary Responsibilities of Union Officers

Union officers and representatives occupy positions of trust in relation to the union and its members. Under Landrum-Griffin, they have a duty to use the union's money and property in accordance with its constitution and bylaws "solely for the benefit of the organization and its members."

A *fiduciary* may be defined as a person who undertakes to act in the interest of another person.[102] Congress codified the common law applicable to trust relations in Title V. Persons responsible for union funds must manage, invest, and expend such funds and property in strict accordance with a labor organization's constitution, bylaws, and governing body resolutions. They must refrain from (1) dealing with their own union as an adverse party, and (2) holding or acquiring pecuniary or personal interests that conflict with the union's interests. Also, such persons must account to the union for any profits received by them in any transaction conducted under their direction on behalf of the union. The prohibitions extend beyond money transactions but include other deals, as well as some that could evolve out of the collective bargaining process. This basic language was intended "to aid members of labor organizations in their efforts to drive criminals from the trade union movement."[103] Supreme Court Justice Cardozo captured the primary fiduciary responsibility well when he stated:

> Many forms of conduct permissible in a workaday world for those acting at arm's length, are forbidden to those bound by fiduciary ties. A trustee is held to something stricter than the morals of the market place. Not honesty alone, but the punctilio of an honor the most sensitive, is then the standard of behavior. As to this there has developed a tradition that is unbending and inveterate. Uncompromising rigidity has been the attitude of courts of equity when petitioned to undermine the rule of undivided loyalty by the "disintegrating erosion" of particular exceptions. . . . Only thus has the level of conduct for fiduciaries been kept at a level higher than that trodden by the crowd.[104]

It is not at all strange in light of the attention that Congress devoted to the common law that a section was included preventing a union from freeing its personnel from liability of trust duties. Any attempt to do so by the inclusion of provisions in constitutions or bylaws is void because it is against public policy.

Congress made no attempt to tell unions how to spend their money. It merely intended that funds and assets be used in accordance with the direction of the membership. Then Senator John F. Kennedy made this clear when he remarked that

> the bill wisely takes note of the need to consider the special problems and functions of a labor organization in applying fiduciary principles to their officers and agents.[105]

A local union, for example, may pass a resolution to use union funds to pay an officer's defense in court litigation. Should a local do so, however, the courts may enjoin the resolution as *ultra vires* in violation of the Act's purpose.[106] The resolution itself does not have the effect of relieving a person from his or her trust duties.

The fiduciary feature of the law becomes more meaningful when considered in the light of the reporting features discussed in the earlier part of this chapter. As noted, union officers must report all expenditures of union funds and specify the purpose. If a union officer does not report such expenditures, or reports falsely, the officer would be subject to criminal penalties. If the officer expends funds not in the interest of the union and reports the transaction, this information is available to union members. For example, suppose a union officer caused union funds to be spent for an item for personal use, say a boat, and truthfully reports the expenditure. Under these circumstances, the union or its members can by suit in court force the union officer to return the money with interest to the union treasury. The suit would be based upon the charge that the union officer breached fiduciary responsibilities. Unfortunately, there are no data available to demonstrate experience under this section of the law.

Recovery of Assets

Landrum-Griffin provides that in the event a labor organization or its governing board of officers refuses or fails to proceed against union agents who violate their fiduciary responsibilities, a union member may file a civil suit in a federal or state court for appropriate relief under certain circumstances. A request must first be made of the officers. If they fail to correct the situation within a reasonable period of time, the member may file suit. An individual suit may be brought only "upon leave of the court obtained upon verified application and for good cause shown." If a court permits an individual suit, it may be for damages, an accounting of the assets in question, or "other appropriate relief" for the benefit of the labor organization. Upon request, a trial judge may allot to an individual the counsel fees and expenses incurred in the litigation. Recovery of such costs to the individual is usually allotted from any recovery of assets resulting from the action. However, the District of Columbia Circuit Court of Appeals has ruled that the Act does not limit the courts to the amount of assets recovered through litigation.[107] Thus, unions that become lax maintaining internal control over officers could find themselves liable for litigation costs that far exceed the value of assets in question. In still another case, an appellate court held that the monetary recovery may constitute a source from which litigation costs of a member are paid.[108] The award of costs, in the court's view, should be based on the benefits realized by the union as a result of the suit.

A union member is not required to exhaust internal union remedies prior to bringing suit.[109] In *Giordani*, the union argued unsuccessfully that it had not refused or failed to sue its officers within a reasonable time after being requested to do so. Nearly a year had passed from the time the member had requested union officials to proceed to obtain appropriate relief. In another case, *Purcell* v. *Keane*, a trial judge relying on the *Giordani* case ruled that "since exhaustion of remedies is not mandatory, a court does not have to find exhaustion in order to find good cause."[110]

It is still not known exactly what is meant by "within a reasonable period of time," but the courts in the *Giordani* and *Purcell* cases referred to about one year. The period of time, however, could depend largely upon the procedures initiated by particular unions after members request action of them. Many union officers, particularly those who remember the court proceedings during and prior to the 1930s, prefer to keep union affairs out of court. This may account for some reluctance to initiate action. Some officers may have convinced their members to forget violations of fiduciary responsibility. The courts have proved themselves less kind in such matters.

Embezzlement of Union Funds

Under Landrum-Griffin, it is a federal crime for anyone to embezzle, steal, or unlawfully and willfully convert union assets to personal or someone else's use. The section goes further than placing a limit on union officers. Any *officer or employee* who siphons off union funds to third parties violates the law. Apparently, it is no violation of the section for a nonmember to behave in such fashion. However, it is unlikely that a nonmember would be in a position to violate the law without assistance from a member. A person convicted of such a violation may receive a maximum sentence of a $10,000 fine or five years' imprisonment, or both. The basic issue involved at an embezzlement trial is whether an official misused union funds, not whether personal benefit was gained from the assets.[111] The courts deal sharply with officials convicted of this crime. For example, a New York federal district court fined a union official $25,000 on two counts of embezzlement and one of absconding with union fund records.[112] A five-year prison sentence was also imposed. A union business agent was imprisoned for two and one-half years because of embezzlement.[113]

General Bonding

All union personnel who "receive, handle, disburse, or otherwise exercise custody or control of the funds or other property of a labor organization or a trust in which a labor organization is interested" must be bonded. Union officers, agents, shop stewards or other representatives, and union employees are included in the requirement. Bonding is not required of personnel, however, if their union has property and annual financial receipts of less than $5,000. The amount of bond required of a person is not less than 10 percent of the funds handled by the person in the previous fiscal year. The law does not require any bond to exceed $500,000. If there is no previous fiscal-year experience upon which to calculate the bond, it shall be (1) not less than $1,000 in the case of a local union, and (2) not less than $10,000 in the case of any other kind of union.

Bonds must be obtained from a surety company authorized by the Secretary of the Treasury as a surety on federal bonds. They cannot be obtained from a broker or surety company in which any labor organization or any union representative has a direct or indirect interest. The bond can be either individual or schedule in form. An *individual* bond is a single bond covering a single named individual. A *schedule bond* covers particular positions. A single position may be involved, or the bond may designate several positions. Each position may carry quite different coverage in accordance with the amount of funds handled. Most unions prefer schedule bonds because under this system, they are relieved from the expense and trouble of obtaining a new bond each time a new officer is elected or appointed to a position.

The bonding enforcement provision makes any person who willfully violates the requirements subject to a fine of not more than $10,000 or imprisonment for not more than one year, or both. Unintentional violations may merely result in a prohibition on an individual's function in a capacity for which bonding is required.

Loans and Payment of Fines

Landrum-Griffin limits the amount of loans unions can make to their personnel. It also forbids both unions and employers from paying a fine for any officer or employee convicted of any willful violation of the Act.

Total indebtedness of union officers and employees cannot exceed $2,000. This safeguard was provided to eliminate the misuse of union assets under the guise of bona fide loans.

Willful violations are subject to fines up to $5,000 and imprisonment of up to one year.

SUMMARY

The basic aim of Landrum-Griffin is to assure fair treatment to union members, and guarantee to them rights that are expressed or implied by the United States Constitution. At this writing, the law has been in effect for about thirty-seven years. Despite the original protest of organized labor against the law and its continued opposition in some respects, unions have learned to live with and adjust to the law. Its provisions have proved burdensome at times. Particularly with regard to the election standards, unions have often been burdened with defending themselves against false or trivial charges. However, when there is evidence of abuse and wrongdoing and the interests of people are placed in jeopardy, it is commonplace that government does intervene.

Certainly the vast number of union leaders are honest and have integrity. As in any large institution, however, there are those who would use the union movement for their personal aggrandizement and not in the interest of the members. In this light, the law fulfills a public purpose and constitutes a valuable feature of our social fabric. No law, of course, can possibly result in a utopian kind of democracy in which all participants are treated equally and fairly. Despite Landrum-Griffin, some corruption and undemocratic practices undoubtedly still exist in the union movement.

Undoubtedly, some unions are dominated and controlled by organized crime. The best evidence is the Teamsters Union agreement with the U.S. Department of Justice in 1989 regarding wide-ranging reforms, including election of top officials by the rank and file and oversight by a court-appointed review board. In 1992, a permanent three-person independent review board was established to investigate and discipline corruption within the union. This was a last-minute agreement by the Teamsters to avoid prosecution under the Racketeer Influenced Corrupt Organization Act (RICO).

Based on a congressional investigation, one writer put the figure of organized crime domination of local unions at about 300.[114] In 1990, the *Wall Street Journal* reported the Mafia controlled "as many as 400 individual local unions nationwide," which it estimated to be less than 1 percent of the total number of local unions in the United States.[115] It is true that some of those local unions are strategically located, giving organized crime the power to disrupt important areas of the economy. Based on the facts, any perception of widespread organized crime control of the labor movement is clearly erroneous.

Understand also that for the purpose of money-laundering, organized crime has infiltrated and seized control of business enterprises. To condemn all union and business leaders because of racketeering on the part of some of them clearly flies in the face of fairness and common sense. In any event, Landrum-Griffin has eliminated some of the more flagrant abuses, and it has served to educate officers on their responsibilities to the membership. Clearly, it has served as a deterrent for the unscrupulous who would be inclined to treat the rights of members with contempt.

DISCUSSION QUESTIONS

1. Were internal union abuses sufficient to warrant passage of the Landrum-Griffin Act?

2. The "bill of rights" in Landrum-Griffin attempts to achieve a balance between what competing rights? How does it do so?

3. True or false: Labor unions may legally discriminate against individuals in admitting members to unions under Landrum-Griffin. Explain.

4. Do courts tend to support unions or individuals in cases dealing with individuals' rights to free speech and assembly? Give an example.

5. What checks or controls were placed on unions regarding dues, initiation fees, and assessments?

6. What qualifications did Congress place on the rights of members to bring suits against their unions? How have the courts construed this provision?

7. What due-process protections do members have against improper disciplinary action? How do these due-process protections apply to elected union officers? To appointed union officers or employees?

8. What enforcement procedure is available to union members who allege violations of the "bill of rights" provision of Landrum-Griffin? What is the weakness in the procedure?

9. Why do unions feel that the portion of Landrum-Griffin dealing with employer reporting is a weakness that needs correcting?

10. What relief has been provided to local unions from trusteeship abuses of national unions? Have they been effective?

11. How have the courts interpreted union rights to impose qualifications on members who seek union offices? Give examples.

12. If a union violates Landrum-Griffin election standards, what remedy is available to members who seek relief?

13. What financial safeguards are provided by Title V to protect unions from fiduciary violations on the part of officers and employees?

NOTES

1   73 Stat. 519.

2   Joel Seidman, "Emergence of Concern with Union Government and Administration," in *Regulating Union Government*, eds. Marten S. Estey, Philip Taft, and Martin Wagner (New York: Harper & Row, 1964), pp. 22–3.

3   Robert D. Leiter, "LMRDA and Its Setting," in *Symposium on the Labor-Management Reporting and Disclosure Act of 1959*, ed. Ralph Slovenko (Baton Rouge, La.: Claitor's Bookstore Publishers, 1961), p. 13.

4 Interim Report of the Senate Select Committee on Improper Activities in the Labor or Management Field, Report No. 1417, 85th Congress, 1958.

5 105 *Congressional Record* 5806 (daily ed.), April 22, 1959.

6 C. Peter Magrath, "Democracy in Overalls: The Futile Quest for Union Democracy," *Industrial and Labor Relations Review*, XII (1959), p. 503.

7 *Carothers* v. *Presser*, 818 F. 2d 926 (D.C. Cir. 1987).

8 *Elizabeth Dole, Secretary of Labor* v. *International Union of Electrical, Radio and Machine Workers, Local 427*, 760 F. Supp. (1991).

9 Benjamin Aaron, "Employee Rights and Union Democracy," *Monthly Labor Review*, U.S. Department of Labor, Bureau of Labor Statistics, XVII, 3 (March 1969), p. 50.

10 *Ibid.*, p. 50.

11 *Ibid.*

12 *Phalen* v. *Theatrical Protective Union No. 1 International Alliance of Theatrical & Stage Employees, AFL-CIO*, 22 N.Y. 2d 34 (1968).

13 Aaron, *op. cit.*, pp. 50–51.

14 *Calhoon* v. *Harvey*, 379 U.S. 134 (1964).

15 *Alvey* v. *General Electric Co.*, 622 F. 2d 1279 (7th Cir. 1980).

16 *Salzhandler* v. *Caputo*, 316 F. 2d 445 (2d Cir. 1963).

17 *Farowitz* v. *Associated Musicians of Greater New York, Local 802*, 330 F. 2d 999 (2d Cir. 1964).

18 U.S. Department of Labor, Labor-Management Services Administration, *Compliance, Enforcement, and Reporting* (Washington, D.C.: Government Printing Office, 1975), p. 49.

19 *Hall* v. *Cole*, 412 U.S. 1 (1973).

20 *Asbestos Workers, Local 17* v. *Young*, 775 F. 2d 870 (7th Cir. 1985).

21 *American Federation of Musicians* v. *Wittstein*, 379 U.S. 171 (1964).

22 *Peck* v. *Associated Food Distributors of New England*, 237 F. Supp. 113 (D. Mass 1965).

23 *Burroughs* v. *Operating Engineers, Local 3*, 686 F. 2d 723 (9th Cir. 1982).

24 *Auto Workers* v. *National Right to Work Legal Defense & Education Foundation*, 584 F. Supp 1219 (D.D.C. 1984).

25 *Automobile Workers* v. *National Right to Work Legal Defense & Education Foundation*, 590 F. 2d 1139 (D.C. Cir. 1978).

26 *Wall Street Journal*, June 3, 1977, p. 2.

27 105 *Congressional Record* 16414 (daily ed.), September 3, 1959.

28 Archibald Cox, "The Role of Law in Preserving Union Democracy," *Harvard Law Review*, LXXII (1959), pp. 609, 615.

29 105 *Congressional Record* A7915 (daily ed.), September 4, 1959.

30 *Detroy* v. *American Guild of Variety Artists*, 286 F. 2d 75 (2d Cir. 1961).

31 *NLRB* v. *Industrial Union of Marine & Shipbuilding Workers, AFL-CIO, Local 22*, 391 U.S. 418 (1968).

32 *Boilermakers* v. *Hardeman*, 401 U.S. 233 (1971).

33 *English* v. *Cowell*, 10 F. 3d 434 (1993).

34   *Sheridan* v. *United Brotherhood of Carpenters*, 306 F. 2d 152 (3d Cir. 1962).

35   *Grand Lodge of International Association of Machinists* v. *King*, 335 F. 2d 340 (9th Cir. 1964), cert. denied 85 S. Ct. 274 (1964).

36   *DeCampli* v. *Greeley* (November 1968); see *Monthly Labor Review*, U.S. Department of Labor, Bureau of Labor Statistics, XCII, 3 (March 1969), pp. 62–63.

37   *Finnegan* v. *Leu*, 456 U.S. 431 (1982).

38   *Cotter* v. *Owens*, 753 F. 2d 223 (2d Cir. 1985).

39   *Adams-Lundy* v. *Association of Professional Flight Attendants*, 731 F. 2d 1154 (5th Cir. 1984).

40   *Dolan* v. *Transport Workers*, 746 F. 2d 733 (11th Cir. 1985).

41   *Sheet Metal Workers, Local 75* v. *Lynn*, 488 U.S. 347 (1989).

42   Russell A. Smith, "The Labor-Management Reporting and Disclosure Act of 1959," *Virginia Law Review*, XLVI, 2 (March 1960), p. 210.

43   U.S. Department of Labor, Labor-Management Services Administration, *Compliance, Enforcement, and Reporting* (1974), p. 43.

44   *Compliance, Enforcement, and Reporting*, 1977, *op. cit.*, p. 61.

45   *Quinn* v. *DiGiulian*, 739 F. 2d 687 (D.C. Cir. 1984).

46   *Compliance, Enforcement, and Reporting, 1977, op. cit.*, p. 22.

47   *Ibid.*, p. 39.

48   *Compliance, Enforcement, and Reporting*, 1968, *op. cit.*, p. 11.

49   *Compliance, Enforcement, and Reporting*, 1977, *op. cit.*, p. 39.

50   *Ibid.*, p. 25.

51   *Price, Nelson & Sears* v. *Wirtz*, 412 F. 2d 647 (5th Cir. 1969).

52   *Humphrey, Hutcheson and Moseley* v. *Donovan*, 755 F. 2d 1211 (6th Cir. 1984).

53   *Master Printers of America* v. *Donovan*, 751 F. 2d 700 (4th Cir. 1984).

54   *Hearings Before Subcommittee on Labor-Management Relations Committee on Education and Labor, House of Representatives*, 96th Congress, First Sess., *Pressures in Today's Work Place*, I and II, October, December, 1979.

55   *Wall Street Journal*, November 19, 1979.

56   *AFL-CIO News*, February 11, 1984.

57   *Pressures in Today's Work Place, op. cit.*, I, p. 410.

58   AFL-CIO, Industrial Union Department, *Viewpoint* (Spring 1981), p. 6.

59   Jules A. Bernstein, "The Evolution of the Use of Management Consultants in Labor Relations: A Labor Perspective," *Labor Law Journal*, XXXVI, 5 (May 1985), p. 297.

60   *Automobile Workers* v. *Secretary of Labor*, 678 G. Supp. 4 (D.C. Dist. 1988).

61   *Auto Workers* v. *Dole*, 869 F. 2d 616 (D.C. Cir. 1989).

62   *Blankenship and Associates, Inc.* v. *NLRB*, 999 F. 2d 248 (1993).

63   Sar A. Levitan, "The Federal Law of Union Trusteeship," *in Symposium on the Labor-Management Reporting and Disclosure Act of 1959*, ed. Ralph Slovenko (Baton Rouge, La.: Claitor's Bookstore Publishers, 1961), p. 453.

64   *Rizzo* v. *Ammond*, 182 F. Supp. 456 (D.C.N.J. 1960).

65   *Local 28* v. *IBEW*, 184 F. Supp. 649 (D.C. MD 1960).

66   *Compliance, Enforcement, and Reporting*, 1977, *op. cit.*, p. 22.

67   *Lavender* v. *United Mine Workers of America*, 285 F. 2d 869 (1968).

68   *State, County, and Municipal Employees, New Jersey and Municipal Council 61* v. *State, County, and Municipal Employees*, 478 F. 2d 1156 (3rd Cir. 1973), cert. denied 414 U.S. 975 (1973).

69   U.S. Department of Labor, *Summary of Operations, 1966, LMRDA*, pp. 15–17.

70   *Hansen* v. *Guyette*, 814 F. 2d 547 (8th Cir. 1987).

71   *Compliance, Enforcement, and Reporting*, 1972, *op. cit.*, p. 5.

72   The states were Colorado, Florida, Kansas, Minnesota, and Texas.

73   See Julius Rezler, "Union Elections: The Background of Title IV of MLRDA," in Slovenko, ed., *op. cit.*, pp. 475–494.

74   *Ibid.*, p. 482.

75   *Ibid.*, pp. 485–486.

76   *Ibid.*, p. 483.

77   *Ibid.*, p. 483.

78   *Serio* v. *Liss*, 189 F. Supp. 358 (D.C. N.J. 1960), aff. 300 F. 2d 386 (3d Cir. 1961).

79   *American Communications Association* v. *Douds*, 339 U.S. 382 (1950).

80   *United States* v. *Archie Brown*, 381 U.S. 437 (1965).

81   *Wirtz* v. *Hotel, Motel & Club Employees Union, Local 6*, 391 U.S. 492 (1968).

82   *Local 3489, United Steelworkers* v. *Usery*, 429 U.S. 305 (1977).

83   *Rollison* v. *Hotel and Restaurant Employees, Local 879*, 677 F. 2d 741 (9th Cir. 1982).

84   *U.S. Department of Labor* v. *Masters, Mates & Pilots*, 842 F. 2d 70 (4th Cir. 1988).

85   *Federal Register*, 53 F.R. 8750, March 17, 1987.

86   *Martin* v. *National Association of Letter Carriers, Branch 419, AFL-CIO*, 1991 WL 315138 (E.D. Tenn.).

87   *Masters, Mates, and Pilots* v. *Brown*, 498 U.S. 406, (1991).

88   *Wall Street Journal*, April 3, 1972.

89   *Sadlowski* v. *United Steelworkers of America*, 645 F. 2d 1114 (D.C. Cir. 1981).

90   *United Steelworkers of America* v. *Sadlowski*, 457 U.S. 102 (1982).

91   Section 401(h).

92   *Teamsters, Local 82 Furniture & Piano Movers* v. *Crowley*, 467 U.S. 526 (1984).

93   *Martin* v. *Masters, Mates, and Pilots*, 786 F. Supp. 1230 (1992).

94   *Dunlop* v. *Backowski*, 421 U.S. 560 (1975).

95   *Wirtz* v. *Local 153, Glass Bottle Blowers Association of the United States & Canada, AFL-CIO*, 389 U.S. 463 (1968).

96   *Wirtz* v. *Local Union No. 125, Laborers International Union of North America, AFL-CIO*, 389 U.S. 477 (1968).

97   *Hodgson* v. *Steelworkers, Local 6799*, 403 U.S. 333 (1971).

98   *Compliance, Enforcement, and Reporting*, 1974, *op. cit.*, p. 4.

99   *Ibid.*, p. 5.

100   *Compliance, Enforcement, and Reporting*, 1977, *op. cit.*, p. 8.

101   AFL-CIO, *American Federationist*, XXVII, 11 (November 1970), p. 21.

102   Albert B. Barbutton, Jr., "The Fiduciary Responsibility of Officers of Labor Organizations Under the Common Law and LMRDA," in Slovenko, ed., *op. cit.*, p. 514.

103   Samuel Duker, "Fiduciary Responsibility of Union Officials," in Slovenko, ed., *op. cit.*, p. 521.

104   *Meinhard* v. *Salmon*, 249 N.Y. 464 (1928).

105   *History of the Labor-Management Reporting and Disclosure Act*, NLRB, II (1959), p. 1433.

106   *Local 107, Highway Truck Drivers & Helpers* v. *Cohen*, 182 F. Supp. 608 (1960), aff. 284 F. 2d 162 (3d Cir. 1960), cert. denied 365 U.S. 833 (1961).

107   *Ratner* v. *Bakery Workers*, 394 F. 2d 780 (D.C. Cir. 1968).

108   *Local 92, Iron Workers* v. *Norris*, 383 F. 2d 735 (5th Cir. 1967).

109   *Giordani* v. *Hoffman*, 277 F. Supp. 722 (ED Pa. 1967).

110   *Purcell* v. *Keane*, 277 F. Supp. 252 (ED Pa. 1967).

111   *United States* v. *Harrelson*, 223 F. Supp 869 (ED Mich. 1963).

112   *United States* v. *Davis*, (SD N.Y., September 12, 1963), Nos. 63 Criminal 164 and 293.

113   *Compliance, Enforcement, and Reporting*, 1977, *op. cit.*, p. 115.

114   Baker Armstrong Smith, "Landrum-Griffin After Twenty-One Years: Mature Legislation or Childish Fantasy," *Labor Law Journal*, XXXI, 5 (May 1980), p. 276.

115   *Wall Street Journal*, May 27, 1990.

11 ❧

Discrimination and Equal Employment Opportunity

Title VII of the Civil Rights Act of 1964 started machinery into motion throughout the entire economy toward equal employment opportunities for all persons without regard to race, religion, sex, color, or national origin. Employers and unions fall under the jurisdiction of agencies and laws as well as those created by the Civil Rights Act of 1964 as amended in 1968, 1972, and 1991. This chapter will focus on the essential features of Title VII of the Civil Rights Act as amended, Landrum-Griffin, and the operations of the National Labor Relations Act, as administered respectively by the Equal Employment Opportunity Commission (EEOC) and the National Labor Relations Board. Policies, regulations, and remedies of both will be analyzed in the context of court decisions affecting them.[1] Discussed are EEOC guidelines and court construction of them; NLRB treatment of discrimination cases; and the economic impact that antidiscrimination laws may have on public and private employers, unions, and workers. The chapter closes with a brief discussion of the Age Discrimination Act.

EVOLUTION OF RACIAL DISCRIMINATION POLICY

Both employers and unions practiced discrimination in employment, reflecting society's general attitude toward women and minorities. The CIO recognized the need to include black persons in unions and courted them more so than did the AFL. Even so, few black people progressed through the ranks to better union positions after the right to represent the bargaining units was achieved. Indeed, the government participated in racial discrimination under both the Railway Labor Act of 1926 and the National Labor Relations Act of 1935. The National Mediation Board certifies unions under the Railway Labor Act and, in this function, certified unions that expressly prohibited black people from membership. It did so until the Civil Rights Act was passed in 1964.

The NLRB, prior to 1964, generally took the position that the Taft-Hartley Act did not contain a mandate from Congress to deal with union discrimination practices. The duty to represent fairly all workers in the bargaining unit was a vehicle made available by the U.S. Supreme Court in *Syres* v. *Oil Workers Union*, 1955.[2] The Court ruled that a union certified by the NLRB could not engage in racial discrimination. The Board did not move quickly to use the power to certify and decertify unions practicing racial discrimination. As was often the case during the 1950s and part of the 1960s, the Court was running well ahead of other institutions in society in attempts to provide fundamental rights to all citizens. The judiciary has rarely taken the initiative in providing such rights because of the web of rules developed for its own purposes. Not even the Thirteenth and Fourteenth Amendments to the U.S. Constitution deterred the Supreme Court from applying its rules of precedent until 1954, when in *Brown* v. *Board of Education*[3] it held that its separate-but-equal rule of 1896 for public education no longer applied.[4] The landmark case of 1954 slowly led to changes in the racially discriminatory practices of other institutions, including unions, despite their reluctance. The NLRB was no exception.

The Duty of Fair Representation

The U.S. Supreme Court declared in the 1944 *Steele* and *Wallace Corporation* cases that Section 9(a) of the Wagner Act imposed upon unions the duty to provide "fair representation" of all employees in an exclusive bargaining unit.[5] Neither the Wagner Act nor Taft-Hartley mentioned the duty of fair representation. Since a union is the legal bargaining agent, however, the Court held that it could not discriminate against any employee in the bargaining unit. Enforcement of this duty was treated as if it fell within the exclusive jurisdiction of the courts until 1962, when the Board considered that it had the responsibility to employees and union members to assure them of fair representation in all aspects of collective bargaining. The Second Circuit Court of Appeals disagreed with the Board and denied enforcement.

The Board was not deterred by the adverse treatment it received, and in a 1964 case involving racial discrimination, ruled that the union had by discrimination refused to bargain, since a majority union has the statutory obligation to represent fairly *all* employees in a collective bargaining unit.[6] The *Hughes Tool Company* case arose when a local union comprised of only white employees refused to consider a grievance filed by a member of a jointly certified local union comprised entirely of black workers. Refusal to process an employee's grievance was solely for reasons of race. Refusal to consider the grievance for processing was held to be, in effect, a situation where the local had acted for the benefit of only its white members. But the local had the statutory duty to represent all employees in the bargaining unit, irrespective of membership. The Board held further that there was no statutory language limiting a union's bargaining obligation as owed only to employers.[7] The obligation to bargain was a duty owed equally to employees. The Board decision was not controlled by the reversal in the court of appeals, but by the Supreme Court opinion handed down after that case. Determination of the question of the duty of fair representation as redressable by unfair labor practice charges was held open by the Supreme Court.[8] The Board interpreted this as granting it the authority to rule on the issue. It was suggested in the case that the employer owed an obligation under Section 8(a)(5) not to enter into contracts permitting invidious discrimination.

The Board further declared in a later case that perpetuation of discriminatory provisions in a collective bargaining agreement was "ground upon the irrelevant, invidious, and unfair considerations of race or union membership." Such a situation was adjudged in violation of union responsibility under the Act, in that the labor organization was in effect causing an employer to discriminate against employees in violation of Section 8(a)(3). It was clear that the Board did not intend to free employers from responsibility for attempting to alleviate racial injustice in employment.

In 1966, the Fifth Circuit Court of Appeals reviewed a determination by the NLRB that a labor union had engaged in unfair labor practices when it refused to process grievances of black workers in the bargaining unit.[9] Local 12 had been the exclusive bargaining agent for employees of a Goodyear Alabama plant since 1943. Three separate seniority lists had been maintained until 1962. Separate rolls were provided for white males, black males, and females. It was the custom that black employees with greater seniority had no rights over white employees with less seniority with respect to promotions, transfers, layoffs, and recalls. Separate facilities were also maintained on the basis of race. Eight black workers approached the president of Local 12 and requested grievance action to remedy their being laid off while white workers with less seniority remained on the job. Additionally, it was alleged that new employees were being hired while the black workers were still on layoff status. The black employees asked for back pay. The local union refused to process the grievances, which the Board held was an unfair labor practice. The issue before the court of appeals was to determine whether a breach of the duty of fair representation in itself constituted an unfair labor practice within the framework of the Taft-Hartley Act.

The Fifth Circuit Court of Appeals, contrary to the Second Circuit Court of Appeals, held that "the duty of fair representation was implicit in the exclusive representation requirement of Section 9(a) of the act . . . as guaranteed in Section 7." As such, remedial action was considered available to the Board through the unfair labor practice provisions of national labor laws. Also, the Fifth Circuit Court agreed that breaches of the duty to provide fair representation were within the primary jurisdiction of the Board.[10]

It is significant that the Fifth Circuit Court upheld the Board requirement that the employer in the *Rubber Workers* case should incorporate provisions in the collective bargaining contract aimed at prohibiting continued racial discrimination in terms and conditions of employment. It is obvious that the Board had invoked unfair labor practice charges against both unions and employers for the purpose of dealing with racial discrimination. The unfair labor practices of refusal to bargain and discrimination with regard to hire and tenure were to be utilized to achieve the goal of racial justice in collective bargaining relations. It had taken the Board nearly thirty years to move forcibly into this area. In a 1969 case, the District of Columbia Circuit Court of Appeals upheld and went beyond a Board decision that the existence of racial discrimination was a proper subject for bargaining.[11] The federal court also ruled that discrimination may be an unfair labor practice in and of itself. The Supreme Court refused to review the decision. As noted above, the NLRB has long held that racial discrimination by unions violates the Taft-Hartley Act. The *Farmers' Cooperative Compress* case meant that both employer and union racial discrimination cases could be decided by the NLRB.[12]

An example of this is contained in a Supreme Court decision handed down in 1975, ruling that employees cannot bypass their exclusive bargaining representative to present grievances to an employer separate from the prescribed contractual grievance procedure.[13] If minority workers picket for separate recognition along racial lines, they may be discharged under Taft-Hartley. Justice Thurgood Marshall, writing the 8–1 majority opinion, stated that the whole concept of collective bargaining would be negated if a dissident handful of workers were able to compel employers to bargain only with them and not with the union charged with the statutory responsibility of representing the entire bargaining unit. However, as the Supreme Court majority pointed out in *Emporium*, a basis for discharge under Taft-Hartley might not be the end of the matter, because remedies against discrimination on the job are available through a variety of orderly means. Instead of picketing, the black workers could have taken action through the NLRB's unfair labor practice procedures, used Title VII machinery, or ultimately sued in court. The remedial provisions of Section 704(a) of Title VII provide the means by which discharged workers in the case might recover their jobs with back pay.[14] This decision, plus others of kindred types, has provided the basis for union liability in discrimination cases under Title VII. When a union is a codefendant in fair representation cases and the evidence demonstrates that the union has violated the principle of fair representation, the courts have held that unions and employers are jointly liable for damages.

Once discrimination is proved under the Equal Pay Act of 1963 and Title VII of the Civil Rights Act of 1964, an employer cannot force a union to share back pay liability under a "right to contribution" doctrine available under other statutes. Congress did not permit this means of enforcement as a remedy available to workers under the two laws. Arguments before the Court in *Northwest Airlines* generally were along the lines that liabilities of employers and unions should be kept separate to encourage vigorous antidiscriminatory bargaining.[15]

Equal Rights under Landrum-Griffin

In a previous chapter, we dealt extensively with the first six titles of Landrum-Griffin. Some of the provisions relate to the material of this chapter and should be stressed at this point. We learned that Title I of the 1959 law, the "bill of rights" provision, grants equal rights and privileges to every union member with regard to nomination of candidates, voting in elections and referendums, attendance at union meetings, and voting at such meetings. The section made no attempt, however, to regulate union admissions standards. The procedural safeguards did not prohibit labor organizations from refusing membership or segregating members on the grounds of race, religion, color, sex, or national origin. Representative Adam Clayton Powell attempted to remedy this defect in Title I but was unsuccessful by a vote of 215 to 160. A remedy to the problem was not available until Title VII of the Civil Rights Act of 1964.[16]

Racial discrimination was permissible under Title I of Landrum-Griffin, but not under the Civil Rights Act. Other forms of discrimination under Title I involved the practice of filial preference, which was a basis for closing the door to union membership. Only sons and close relatives are admitted under this practice, which has the blessing of the courts. The practice has been approved by the New York Court of Appeals. Thus, the law permits union action designed to restrict the supply of labor available under some circumstances. Many take the view that unions are no longer voluntary associations, but quasi-public organizations. Internal restrictive membership practices are viewed as antisocial because they may work against public attempts to achieve and sustain high levels of employment.[17] On the other hand, it should be realized that restrictive admission practices have been responses to excessive unemployment in labor markets in which these unions operate, as well as attempts to protect wage rates and to pass on high skill levels to relatives. A public policy not committed to full employment cannot hope to attain it by changing union admission.

EQUAL EMPLOYMENT OPPORTUNITY: ESSENTIAL FEATURES OF TITLE VII

Scope of Title VII

Title VII of the Civil Rights Act of 1964, as amended in 1968, 1972, and 1991, is designed to prohibit discrimination in hiring, firing, wages, terms, and conditions or privileges of employment. The law covers employers, employment agencies, and labor unions whose activities affect interstate commerce. The protected classes of Title VII are race, sex, religion, and national origin.

Coverage under Title VII is broader than that of Taft-Hartley because the employer for its purposes includes individuals, state and local governments, government agencies, political subdivisions, labor unions, partnerships, associations, corporations, legal representatives, mutual companies, joint-stock companies, trusts, unincorporated organizations, trustees, and trustees in bankruptcy, or receivers. The enforcement agency (Equal Employment Opportunity Commission) has not established dollar guidelines eliminating certain categories from coverage, as has the NLRB. Agricultural workers, supervisors, and state and local government employees also fall within the Civil Rights law. Successor employers may be liable to remedy past discrimination on the same basis as these employers assume the bargaining duties of succeeded employers under Taft-Hartley.

Educational institutions since 1972 face all of the same provisions of law as do private employers. The only exception is that religious institutions are not covered by the prohibition on religious discrimination, which means, for example, that preference in employment may be given to a member of a given denomination over others. (Religious organizations are exempt only from the Act's prohibition on religious discrimination but must comply with other provisions of the law, such as race or sex discrimination.)

Employers who are covered by Taft-Hartley are also covered by Title VII. Federal civil service employees fall under the provisions of the Act, but enforcement of the law against discrimination based on race, color, religion, sex, or national origin is in the hands of the U.S. Civil Service Commission. State and local governments on the other hand are covered on the same basis as employees in the private sector. Indian tribes and elected officials, along with their personnel and policy-making staffs, do not come under the Act.

Enforcement and Procedure of Title VII Complaints

The Equal Employment Opportunity Commission consists of five members charged with responsibility for administering the law. Regional or state offices have been established to administer the Act, in addition to the commission's main location in Washington, D.C. In 1972, the office of General Counsel, similar to the office created by Taft-Hartley, was created. The General Counsel is responsible for all cases before the courts except those in the U.S. Supreme Court, which are handled by the Attorney General. The commission may assign other duties to the General Counsel, and the office shares responsibility with the commission chair for appointing and supervising regional attorneys.

An Equal Employment Opportunity Coordinating Council was established by the 1972 amendments. It consists of the Secretary of Labor, EEOC chair, Attorney General, chair of the U.S. Civil Service Commission, and chair of the U.S. Civil Rights Commission. The council is required to coordinate the operations, functions, and jurisdictions of the various departments. An annual report to the President and Congress is required by July 1 of each year and should include recommendations for administrative or legislative changes.

The commission has issued rules and regulations to guide compliance with the law. Those covered by the Act must keep records and file any reports that might be required by the EEOC. A notice must be posted by those covered containing information and summaries of the law that have been prepared and approved by the commission.

In general, the procedure followed in fair employment practice cases is as follows: A charge must first be filed with an approved state or local agency if the state in which the alleged violation occurs has a fair employment practice law. After a specified time, a written charge may be filed with the EEOC by a person who claims discrimination, or since the 1972 amendments, by someone else who may file on behalf of the person aggrieved. A member of the commission may file a charge if there is reasonable cause to believe a violation has occurred. Within ten days, the commission must inform an employer, union, or employment agency that a charge has been filed against them. The public is not informed of the charge at this time. Under certain circumstances, the EEOC will defer to a state or local fair employment practices law if there is an agency to deal with discrimination in employment practices.

A state or local fair employment practices agency operating under legislation approved by the EEOC may request what is known as a "706 agency" designation. If

EEOC requirements are met, the EEOC will defer charges to the state or local agency and give substantial weight to its findings and final order. An agency that does not meet EEOC standards will merely be advised that a complaint has been filed in its jurisdiction. The state agency must keep the information confidential, whether it merely receives notice or has the complaint deferred to it.

Procedure in Non-Deferral States

The procedure used when there is no comparable state agency is as follows:

1. The charge must be filed with the EEOC within 180 days following the incidence of an unlawful employment practice.
2. After the charge has been filed, the EEOC must serve notice of the charge on the company within 10 days.
3. An investigation must be made within 120 days, if practicable, to determine whether there is reasonable cause to believe that the charge is true.
4. If it is found that there is no reasonable cause, the EEOC must dismiss the charge. If reasonable cause is found, the EEOC will attempt to conciliate the case.

Procedure in Deferral States

In states with their own agencies, the following procedure is used:

1. The charge may be filed with the EEOC first, but then it is automatically deferred to the state agency for 60 days.
2. If the initial charge is filed with a state agency, it must be filed within 240 days of the unlawful practice.
3. The state agency has at least 60 days to act on the charge, but the charge must be filed with the EEOC within 300 days.
4. The EEOC procedure then progresses from step 2 in the non-deferral state procedure.

The accompanying chart shows the essential ingredients of the procedure.

Civil Suits

The EEOC can file a suit in federal district court if it is unable to obtain voluntary compliance within thirty days after a charge is filed. The U.S. Attorney General must initiate any legal action that is taken against a government, government agency, or political subdivision. The aggrieved person has a right to intervene.

There is no time limit on the EEOC's right to sue, which is likewise not affected by any statute of limitations that may be written into federal or state laws.[18] The individual may bring suit after 180 days if the EEOC has not done so, but the commission may also bring suit of its own later. As noted, the EEOC is required to engage in conciliation efforts, and a time limit might frustrate those efforts.

The commission or the Attorney General must notify individuals filing charges within 180 days of the filing that a conciliation settlement has not been made or a

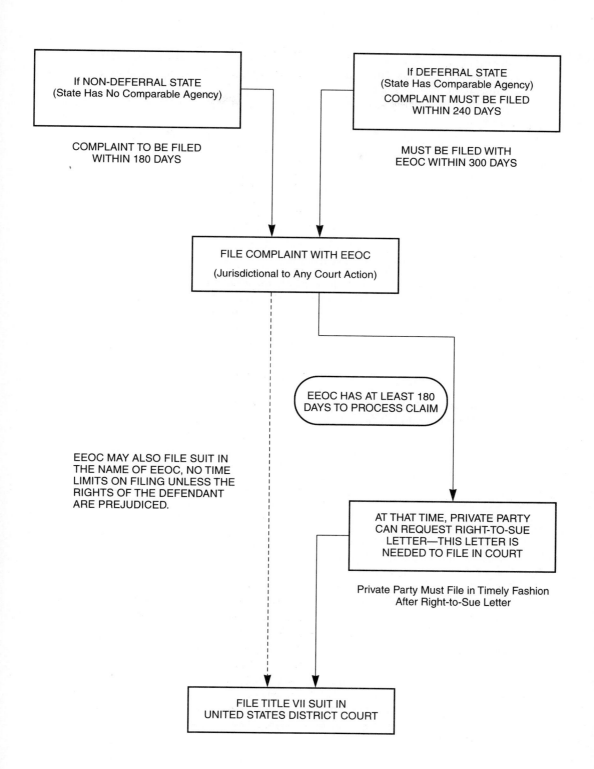

If NON-DEFERRAL STATE
(State Has No Comparable Agency)

COMPLAINT TO BE FILED
WITHIN 180 DAYS

If DEFERRAL STATE
(State Has Comparable Agency)
COMPLAINT MUST BE FILED
WITHIN 240 DAYS

MUST BE FILED WITH
EEOC WITHIN 300 DAYS

FILE COMPLAINT WITH EEOC

(Jurisdictional to Any Court Action)

EEOC HAS AT LEAST 180
DAYS TO PROCESS CLAIM

EEOC MAY ALSO FILE SUIT IN
THE NAME OF EEOC, NO TIME
LIMITS ON FILING UNLESS THE
RIGHTS OF THE DEFENDANT
ARE PREJUDICED.

AT THAT TIME, PRIVATE PARTY
CAN REQUEST RIGHT-TO-SUE
LETTER—THIS LETTER IS
NEEDED TO FILE IN COURT

Private Party Must File in Timely Fashion
After Right-to-Sue Letter

FILE TITLE VII SUIT IN
UNITED STATES DISTRICT COURT

suit filed. The individual then has ninety days after receipt of the notice to bring court action on his or her own. Suits are brought in the most appropriate U.S. district court.

Three standards are applied by the courts in deciding Title VII discrimination cases.

Individual Disparate Treatment

Under this standard, one person has been treated differently than others merely for being a member of a protected class. For example, if five employees are habitually late to work, but only the black person is fired, this constitutes discrimination under this standard. However, an intent to discriminate must be shown.

Systematic Disparate Treatment

The employment system as a whole must have treated a protected class differently under this standard. For example, if Hispanics or blacks are only rarely promoted from blue-collar to white-collar jobs, this constitutes discrimination under this standard. Statistics may be used to prove discrimination in these cases; intent to discriminate need not be shown.

Adverse Impact

In this classification, an employment policy may be neutral on its face but in application have an adverse impact on the protected classes. For example, height and weight restrictions may appear to be neutral, but in practice eliminate women from consideration for certain jobs. Intent to discriminate does not need to be proven under this standard.

Remedies

The EEOC can seek court enforcement of its orders. Remedial action may be quite varied, depending on the nature of the violation. Reinstatement or hiring of employees, or other appropriate affirmative action may be ordered. Back pay less interim earnings may be a part of the remedy.

The courts have determined that punitive damages are not allowed in Title VII suits. Punitive damages are allowed in civil rights cases under section 1983 and private suits.[19]

A discriminating party may be required to proceed through more than one forum on the same issue. An employer might go through arbitration or NLRB unfair labor practice procedures, and then through state machinery. In rare but conceivable circumstances, the same action could advance through the EEOC and ultimately to the courts.

The U.S. Supreme Court in 1977 decided two cases that set forth procedures for using statistics in Title VII suits that allege a pattern or practice of illegal discrimination.[20] A person bringing suit has to show that comparative general population figures are drawn from the relevant labor market area. In addition, general statistics would have to demonstrate that the discriminatory behavior was "long-lasting and gross." The burden of proof to show discriminatory motive is on the one bringing action.

Though discrimination problems have been handled by the NLRB, civil rights legislation endorsed by Congress constitutes the cornerstone of national policy calculated to provide equal opportunity in employment and union membership. The Civil Rights Act of 1964 was passed to deal with a variety of discriminations in employment. Title VII of the 1964 law was at first not very effective because of the lack of enforcement machinery.

The Equal Employment Opportunity Act of 1972 was passed to correct some of the deficiencies of the original law. The Equal Employment Opportunity Commission was reorganized along the lines of the NLRB. An independent General Counsel was named and made responsible for litigation. Three new groups of employers were also brought under the law. These were (1) public and private educational institutions, (2) state and local governments, and (3) employers and unions with fifteen or more members, and unions as employers without regard to numbers.

The Equal Employment Opportunity Commission set forth guidelines in 1965 to deal with discriminatory employment practices. These guidelines became far more meaningful because of the 1972 amendments to Title VII; they are used in all of the commission's deliberations. Some of the more controversial guidelines are discussed.

Recruitment, Selection, and Conditions of Employment Advertisements

Title VII enjoins any advertisement that indicates a preference, limitation, specification, or discrimination based on sex. The EEOC holds it a violation for Help Wanted advertisements to indicate a sex unless sex is a bona fide occupational qualification for the particular job involved. A preference for race can never be a bona fide occupational qualification, but on occasion the law permits such a qualification concerning religion, sex, or national origin.

However, newspapers are not employment agencies within the meaning of the law and therefore may publish classified ads under "Male" and "Female" columns.[21] Employers must publish in both columns or in only one labeled "Help Wanted—Male or Female." Otherwise the employer is considered to have expressed a preference, limitation, specification, or discrimination based on sex.

Employment Records

At first, the EEOC held it discriminatory even to indicate on employment records a person's race, sex, or marital status. Later, it was realized that such information was necessary in order to develop statistical evidence of discrimination. Now such questions may be asked when a person fills out the initial employment application.

Physical Examinations and Business Necessity

A requirement that a job applicant pass a physical examination is not discriminatory per se. For example, if 20/20 vision is required, an employer must show that the requirement is necessary for the person to perform a job, or that it is a reasonable safety requirement. Physical requirements must be justified on the basis of the particular job to be performed. Disqualification must be made on a case-to-case basis, because some women might be able to perform a given job, even though a majority of them might not.[22] The same restriction applies to stereotyped views of certain jobs traditionally labeled "men's work" or "women's work."

Height and weight requirements for jobs must be shown to be related to the task to be performed. The Supreme Court in *Dothard* held that such requirements posed unnecessary barriers to employment.[23] The decision eliminated women from employment as prison guards in men's prisons in Alabama, however, on the sex bona fide occupational qualification (BFOQ) provision of Title VII. The majority felt that the job itself posed a threat to women in general.

Justices Brennan and Marshall disagreed with the majority on the BFOQ rule, because any attack on a guard of either sex should require immediate punitive action. Justice White disagreed with the height and weight decision because he was not convinced that a large percentage of females would fail to meet the requirements set by Alabama law, which were a height of between 5'2" and 6'10" and a weight of between 120 and 300 pounds.

The Court emphasized that physical requirements would be considered on a case-to-case basis, and that they could be established.

"Sex-Plus" Qualifications

A rule to hire unmarried women is only discriminatory if there is no rule against hiring married men. Any rule that affects married women but not married men is discriminatory. The fact that such a rule does not affect all women does not eliminate sex as a factor in the employment decision. Sex plus some other factor, whether it is marital status or family responsibility, is an unlawful hiring restriction. An employer may, however, have a rule against hiring any relative of an employee, as long as the rule is applied without sex discrimination. For example, newlyweds in a plant could be given the right to decide who would quit his or her job, or employment policy could require the one with the least seniority to quit.[24]

Testing and Educational Requirements

Regarding testing and educational requirements, the basic case for guiding equal employment actions is *Griggs* v. *Duke Power Company*, a U.S. Supreme Court decision.[25] In it, the Court held that the requirement to successfully pass an invalidated ability test or to require a high school education as a condition of employment or a prerequisite for promotion was in violation of Title VII, because such requirements discriminated against black people and were not job-related.

Extension of coverage of Title VII to government employees in 1972 led to substantial revision of civil service examinations. In fact, the Federal Service Entrance Examination was eliminated by the Civil Service Commission, largely because of a court case charging that the test discriminated against black people.[26]

More females than males have high school diplomas, which raises the question of whether such a requirement discriminates against males. Another question is involved: Do such requirements perpetuate discrimination that started in the past?

The EEOC developed its guidelines on testing after conducting a study on their uses and obtaining a report from a panel of psychologists. The guidelines issued in 1970 were revised in 1978. General agreement on the Uniform Guidelines was reached with the Office of Personnel Management, the EEOC, the Justice Department, and the Department of Labor. The U.S. Supreme Court in the *Griggs* case held that not only tests, but any employment practice "which operates to exclude [minority groups] and cannot be shown to be related to job performance," is prohibited. *The employer must prove that a test is job-related in any action brought contesting its validity.*

Validation studies that show a given test to be valid for minority groups as well as for nonminorities may be required of employers. The EEOC makes every effort to require equal opportunity for employment, and if a test's validity is questionable, an employer may be required to seek some alternative method of selection. Unions that desire to examine test scores of individual employees are not entitled to do so without the written consent of the persons involved, according to the U.S. Supreme Court in *Detroit Edison.* The 1979 decision may make it more difficult for unions and workers to pursue complaints of discriminatory tests. Companies have increasingly turned to aptitude and *skill* tests as substantial factors in hiring and promotions, in order to protect themselves from Title VII liability if statistical data show inadequate minority representation.[27] The cloud of secrecy provided by the Court over union access to these data was to protect test access.

Business necessity can justify employment practices that have discriminatory impact, but demonstrating the business necessity basis for tests is not an easy task. About the most that can be said in this regard is that if serious consequences result from hiring an unqualified applicant, an employer bears a correspondingly lighter burden to show that employment criteria are job-related.[28] In one case, the District of Columbia Court of Appeals declined to consider the validity of tests that were used by a company to refuse to hire a black person because his commitment to a career in its sales force was doubted.[29]

The *Griggs* case also held that educational requirements were subject to the same scrutiny as tests. They must be job-related and the employer must prove it.

Minorities placed into lower paid jobs and departments as a result of past discrimination cannot be locked into those positions by imposing tests for promotion or transfer. The *Griggs* case makes it clear that when the majority of white employees had a chance at better-paying jobs without tests, then even nondiscriminatory tests could not be used as a basis for promotion after the illegal discrimination had ended. Tests may be used by employers only if they apply equally to everyone.

The Equal Pay Act and Comparable Worth

The Equal Pay Act of 1963 requires equal pay for equal work. The only protected class under this act is sex. The Act permits wage differentials if based on (1) seniority, (2) merit, (3) quantity or quality of production, or (4) any other factor except sex.[30] An employer cannot pay different rates of pay for the same job on the basis of sex. Violations of this standard transgress the Equal Pay Act of 1963 as well as Title VII of the Equal Employment Opportunity Act. The Wage and Hour Division enforces the Equal Pay Act of 1963, taking the position that the work need only be substantially the same in order to require equal pay. The EEOC guideline with respect to wages states that the commission will give appropriate consideration to the interpretation of the Wage and Hour Division, but it will not be bound thereby, even though Section 703(h) of the Civil Rights Act states that wage differentials between sexes are not illegal if they are authorized by the Equal Pay law.

It was thought that the Equal Pay Act would solve the problems of pay differentials between men and women. Instead, most suits under the Act involve questions of whether the work is equal. It is legal under the Equal Pay Act for employers to pay differentially to employees if they perform different work. Title VII of the Civil Rights Act of 1964 seemingly forbids discrimination in any of the terms and conditions of employment as well as pay that may have comparable worth to the firm.

Pay differentials exist in part because of occupational segregation, whereby women are concentrated in lower-paying jobs. The average wage differential between women and men hovers around 60 percent. The concept of comparable worth was born out of concern over the persistence of the pay differential over time. *The assumption of comparable worth is that women should be paid wages comparable to men for work that is comparable.* Implementing this principle would eliminate wage differentials based on occupational segregation of the sexes, so that the wage structure would reflect the worth of jobs to the firm.

In 1981, the Supreme Court in a 5–4 decision gave women more grounds to challenge pay discrimination than had been provided under the Equal Pay Act of 1963. The question of comparable worth was raised in the case *County of Washington* v. *Alberta Gunther*.[31] Four female prison guards brought suit against the county under Title VII of the Civil Rights Act of 1964. Part of their claim was that since they received less pay than did males performing a similar job, they were being discriminated against due to their gender.

During the court proceedings, it was made clear that although the jobs the female guards performed were similar to those of the male guards, the positions and duties were not equal. According to past court decisions and interpretations of the amendment to the Civil Rights Act of 1964, commonly called the Bennett Amendment, the matrons appeared to have a good case.

The Bennett Amendment had been interpreted in the past as simply incorporating the affirmative defenses of the Equal Pay Act into Title VII. The *Gunther* decision, however, interpreted the amendment quite differently. The Court determined that the amendment ensured that the equal pay standard specified in the Equal Pay Act would also apply to wage compensation claims filed under Title VII but would not limit discriminatory wage suits to the equal pay for equal work standard of the Equal Pay Act. In *Gunther*, the Court held that an action for wage discrimination can be brought under Title VII even if the work is not equal. The "equal work" standard of the Equal Pay Act will not apply to Title VII wage discrimination suits. *Though the high court held in Gunther that wage discrimination suits may be filed under Title VII, it did not hold that discrimination may be proved based upon comparable worth. To prevail under Title VII, a successful suit must demonstrate intentional discrimination against women.*

It appears clear that Title VII suits filed by women on the basis of comparable worth will not be successful. Based upon a 1983 job evaluation of 15,000 public sector employees in the State of Washington, it was determined that on the average, job classifications dominated by women were paid 20 percent less than those classifications in which men dominated though both classes of jobs were given the same number of points in the study. Faced with this situation and to reduce the disparity, the state legislature appropriated funds to be paid to women-dominated jobs. However, given the pace of the projected legislative action, the inequity would not be corrected until 1993. State officials admitted the pay inequity but claimed lack of financial ability to correct the situation at a faster rate. A Washington State federal district court in 1983 held that the state's plan to eliminate the inequity was much too slow. Rejecting the state's position, the court held that cost and ability to pay is not a valid defense for a Title VII violation. In *AFSCME* v. *State of Washington* (578 F. Supp. 846 [DC-Wash]), the court directed the state to pay almost a billion dollars to wipe out the inequity. Thus, the district court upheld comparable worth valid to prove a Title VII violation.

No money was paid, however, while the case was appealed. In 1985, a federal appeals court in a case involving the same parties, reversed the district court's decision (770 F. 2d 1401 [CA-9] 1985). It specifically rejected comparable worth for purposes of Title VII. As long as an employer can hire women at lower rates than men for comparable jobs, it does not violate Civil Rights statutes. In other words, *the free labor market system prevails over matters of equity*. The federal appeals court said:

> . . . Neither law nor logic deems the free market system a suspect enterprise . . . The State of Washington's initial reliance on a free market system in which employees in male-dominated jobs are compensated at a higher rate than employees in dissimilar female-dominated jobs is not in and of itself a violation of Title VII, notwithstanding that the [job evaluation] study deemed the positions of comparable worth.

Other federal courts held that a violation of Title VII could not be proved by comparable worth, and the U.S. Supreme Court denied *certiorari*.

Despite its failure in the judiciary, women's groups, including their unions, press comparable worth in collective bargaining and state legislatures. After a prolonged strike at Yale University, which completely disrupted the campus for several months, the union successfully used comparable worth to obtain substantial wage increases for jobs held predominantly by women. Indeed, unions have increasingly made comparable worth a bargaining goal. Sparked by women's groups, several states and their political subdivisions have enacted comparable worth statutes. By no means is comparable worth dead just because it has not met the judicial test.

Sexual Harassment

Courts were initially reluctant to view sexual harassment as actionable under Title VII but later recognized that it was because of a person's sex that she—or he—was being harassed. Not until 1976 was the first case involving sexual harassment found actionable under Title VII. This was in *Williams* v. *Saxbe*.[32] The EEOC defines sexual harassment as unwelcome sexual advances, requests for sexual favors, and any other verbal or physical conduct of a sexual nature, under the following guidelines:

1. when submission is a term or condition of employment;
2. when sexual conduct is used as a basis for employment decisions, such as hiring or promotion;
3. when the conduct has the purpose or effect of interfering with the work environment.

An adverse job reaction such as termination of employment was often necessary in order to prove sexual harassment. In *Fisher* v. *Flynn*, a college professor was required to show that she had been fired because she rejected the department chair's sexual advances.[33] Since she had no proof that she had been terminated because of the advances, the advances were deemed merely an "unsatisfactory personal encounter."

Sexual harassment was found to exist under Title VII for the first time in *Bundy* v. *Jackson*[34] without the requirement of proof that employment or job benefits were lost by rejecting the overtures. It is important to note that if a supervisor or manager sexually harasses an employee, the company or agency is absolutely liable under Title VII. If an employee views behavior as sexually harassing, it is actionable under Title VII even if the supervisor lacked intent. Men may also be sexually harassed by a member of the same sex or by women and obtain relief under Title VII.

A work environment made hostile because of sexual harassment is judged on the totality of circumstances. Some behavior such as vulgar language may be merely annoying, but insufficient to create a hostile work environment in violation of the law. Teasing and touching, comparisons of the person to nude pictures, and requests that a person strip have been held as sufficient to find an employer guilty of providing a hostile work environment. Once again, the employer is responsible for providing a work climate that is free from sexual harassment. Immediate and appropriate corrective action must be taken by employers to protect themselves from liability.

Homosexuals

While homosexual advances are subjects for remedy as sexual harassment under Title VII, homosexuals themselves may be discriminated against by employers on the basis of affectional preference. A court of appeals ruled in *DeSantis* v. *Pacific Telephone and Telegraph Co., Inc.*, that Title VII's prohibition of "sex" discrimination applies only to discrimination on the basis of gender.[35] In *DeSantis*, it was charged that the employer refused to hire or promote a person who preferred sexual partners of the same sex. The court ruled that homosexuals are not a protected class within the meaning of the civil rights statute. It also ruled that employment discrimination because of effeminacy, like discrimination because of homosexuality or transsexualism, is not protected by the law.

Pregnancy

The treatment of pregnancy as unlawful discrimination on the basis of sex has developed in stages. The EEOC guideline is that pregnancy must be treated as any other temporary disability. It states that disabilities caused or contributed to by pregnancy, miscarriage, abortion, childbirth, and recovery therefrom, for all job-related purposes, are temporary disabilities and should be treated as such under any health or temporary disability insurance or sick leave plan available in connection with employment. Written and unwritten employment policies and practices involving matters such as the commencement and duration of leave, the availability of extensions, the accrual of seniority and other benefits and privileges, reinstatement, and payment under any health or temporary disability insurance or sick leave plan, formal or informal, shall be applied to disability due to pregnancy or childbirth on the same terms and conditions as they are applied to other temporary disabilities.

Thus, the EEOC guideline was that pregnancy would require the collecting of sick leave pay; therefore, it did not really matter when the leave started or how long it lasted. However, the length of the leave can determine whether or not disability pay will be available, since some employers have little or no short-term disability coverage. The U.S. Supreme Court has hinted that a woman with the advice of her physician will decide when to leave a job due to pregnancy and when to return after childbirth.[36] The Court also decided that a state could not deprive all women of unemployment compensation for a prescribed period of time under the assumption that they are unable to work due to pregnancy.[37] Some are able to work much longer than are others prior to delivery, and some return to work earlier.

In 1976, in *General Electric Co.* v. *Gilbert*, the U.S. Supreme Court voided the essential part of the EEOC guideline.[38] The exclusion of pregnancy from an employer's disability insurance plan was not viewed as sex discrimination. The *Gilbert* ruling was similar to the Court's earlier decision that a state disability insurance law could exclude disabilities arising from pregnancy.[39] The Court's *Gilbert* decision was overturned when Congress amended Title VII by the 1978 Pregnancy Amendment. Now, according to the EEOC, pregnancy must be treated as any other disability. *The best policy appears to be a maximum number of weeks for employee coverage under a disability plan. This limit would apply to all physical disabilities, including pregnancy.*

Fringe Benefits in General

Fringe benefits include medical, hospital, accident, life insurance, and retirement benefits. In addition, profit-sharing and bonus plans, leaves, and other terms, conditions, and privileges of employment are included in EEOC guidelines. The EEOC makes it an unlawful employment practice for an employer to discriminate between men and women with regard to fringe benefits. This means that when an employer makes benefits conditional on whether the employee is head of a household, or the principal wage earner in the family unit, it is assumed that the benefits tend to be available primarily to male employees and their families. As such, there is discrimination against the rights of female employees. Further, it is held that the head of household or principal wage earner status bears no relationship to job performance and, consequently, such conditions discriminate against females. It is also an unlawful employment practice for an employer to make benefits available to wives and families of male employees if the same benefits are not made available to the husbands and families of female employees. In addition, the EEOC will not permit an employer to defend a practice under Title VII when charged with sex discrimination on the basis that the cost of such benefits is greater with respect to one sex than the other.

Maternity is not grounds for termination but must be treated as a leave of absence. Reinstatement poses a different situation. The problem is whether a woman is entitled to exactly the same job she held when she left, or only to the vacancies that exist at the time of reinstatement. The particular circumstances of each case arising under the guidelines should determine each answer without a mechanistic approach.

Pension and Retirement Plans

Pension and retirement plans pose critical difficulties for employers. The problem with them is that, in fact, men and women are not "equal," because women live longer. The Wage and Hour Division takes the position, under the Equal Pay Act, that there is no violation if the employer contribution for both sexes is equal, or if the benefits paid are equal even though the cost is different. However, the Wage and Hour Division has not prohibited different retirement ages for men and women. The EEOC operates differently. It states: "It shall be an unlawful employment practice for an employer to have a pension or retirement plan which establishes different optional or compulsory retirement ages based on sex, or which differentiates in benefits on the basis of sex." So far, the courts have agreed.[40]

A critical problem in pension discrimination cases is that normally the number of female employees covered by such plans is comparatively small. To extend additional benefits to male employees has the effect of increasing benefits to a very high level. Because of the high cost involved in these benefit cases, employers faced with pension litigation seek to bring unions in as codefendants. Understandably, unions do not want to be involved in these cases, despite the fact that they, along with employers, may have negotiated a pension plan favoring women. In any event, discrimination in pension plans more favorable to women is not permitted under EEOC guidelines.

State workers' compensation laws are forbidden from differentiating death benefits based on sex.[41] The laws of seven states—Missouri, Pennsylvania, Michigan, Indiana, Georgia, Idaho, and Mississippi—gave automatic death benefits to widows in job-related deaths, but no benefit was given to the widowers.

In July 1983, the Supreme Court held it is unlawful to differentiate between sexes for purposes of pension payments. No longer may pension plans penalize women be-cause they live longer.[42]

Reverse Discrimination

Male employees have filed many complaints alleging sex discrimination under Title VII. For example, the EEOC has held that an employer hiring females with long hair may not discriminate against males with long hair.[43] A very controversial type of case involves pension and profit-sharing plans, as mentioned above. These plans usually provide for different retirement ages for female and male employees. A circuit court of appeals held in *Rosen* v. *Public Service Electric Company* that males who were penalized by reduction in pension, if retiring before sixty-five, were entitled to recover the amounts necessary to equalize them with females, who were permitted to retire at age sixty-two on full pension without actuarial reductions.[44]

ARBITRATION AND TITLE VII RIGHTS

Rios and Hutchins

In 1972, in *Rios* v. *Reynolds Metals Company*,[45] a circuit court of appeals ruled that federal courts may defer to arbitration cases involving employees' rights protected by Title VII of the Civil Rights Act. The conditions set by the court of appeals for accepting arbitration awards for cases involving Title VII rights are more specific and demanding than the NLRB's.[46] These are as follows:

> . . . First, there may be no deference to the decision of the arbitrator unless the contractual right coincides with rights under Title VII.
>
> Second, it must be plain that the arbitrator's decision in no way violates the private rights guaranteed by Title VII, nor of the public policy which inheres in Title VII. In addition, before deferring, the District Court must be satisfied that (1) the factual issues before it are identical to those decided by the arbitrator; (2) the arbitrator had power under the collective agreement to decide the ultimate issue of discrimination; (3) the evidence presented at the arbitral hearing dealt adequately with all factual issues; (4) the arbitrator actually decided the factual issues presented to the Court; and (5) the arbitration proceeding was fair and regular and free of procedural infirmities. The burden of proof in establishing these conditions of limitation will be upon the respondent as distinguished from the claimant.

A question also raised in *Rios* involved whether an aggrieved employee could seek relief under Title VII without first invoking or exhausting available alternative legal or contractual remedies. That is, could an aggrieved employee submit a grievance to arbitration and also take it before the court? It was decided in *Caldwell* v. *National Brewing Company* that employees may seek relief under Title VII without invoking or exhausting available alternative legal or contractual remedies.[47] Further, in *Hutchins* v. *United States Industries, Inc.* it was held that even where an employee does pursue an alternative remedy, such as arbitration in cases involving Title VII rights, the federal court is the final arbiter.[48] In *Rios*, however, the circuit court stated that

> it does not follow, however, that the policies of Title VII require that an employee who has submitted his claim to binding arbitration must always be given an opportunity to relitigate his claim in court. In some instances such a requirement would not comport with elementary notions of equity for it would give the employee but not the employer a second chance to have the same issue resolved.

Alexander v. *Gardner-Denver*

In February 1974, the U.S. Supreme Court resolved the inconsistency created by the lower courts in *Rios* and *Hutchins*. At that time, in *Alexander* v. *Gardner-Denver*, the high court held that an arbitrator's decision is not final and binding when an employee claims that he or she was discharged because of racial reasons in violation of Title VII of the Civil Rights Act. An arbitrator sustained the discharge of a black employee on the grounds that the employee had been terminated for just cause. A district court upheld the arbitrator's decision and did not inquire into the question of whether the discharge was in violation of the Civil Rights Act. However, the U.S. Supreme Court remanded the case to the lower court with instructions that it determine whether the employee's rights under Title VII had been violated. What *Gardner-Denver* means, therefore, is that even if an employee loses a case in arbitration, appeal for relief may be made from the courts provided that Title VII rights are involved; as stated, the employee has two bites at the apple. In other words, the finality of an arbitrator's award as established under *Enterprise Wheel*, discussed in an earlier chapter, does not apply.

Religious Discrimination

The problem of direct discrimination because of an individual's religion has taken several forms. It has involved outright refusal to hire, segregation after employment, and job classification and assignment according to religion. Special problems have also been observed, such as observance of religious holidays and the Sabbath that differ from the majority observances.

The 1972 amendments to the Civil Rights Act accepted the position of the EEOC guidelines, which was that "the term 'religion' includes all aspects of religious observance and practice, as well as belief, unless an employer demonstrates that [it] is unable to reasonably accommodate to an employee's or prospective employee's religious observance or practice without undue hardship on the conduct of the employer's business." The Fifth Circuit Court of Appeals ruled that the 1972 amendments endorsed EEOC's guidelines on relitigation.[49]

The EEOC has a wide range of standards regarding its construction of what is meant by "reasonable accommodation" and "undue hardship." It has held, among many decisions, that a company could not (1) discharge a Saturday Sabbath observer without proving that rotation of other employees would result in an undue hardship to the firm; (2) apply a rule that vacations had to be taken at a certain time for a worker who had requested leave to attend a compulsory religious convention, even though other employees would be discontented; and (3) apply a policy of a whole weekend of overtime or none at all to a person whose religion prohibited working on one of the two days. The burden of proof is on the employer to show that accommodation to one's religious beliefs would impose an undue hardship on the firm.

Collective bargaining agreements combine the dimension of conflict and the need for accommodation of the Taft-Hartley law and the Equal Employment Opportunity Act of 1972. In 1977, the U.S. Supreme Court ruled that an employer was not obligated to go very far in seeking to accommodate a worker's religious beliefs.[50] In *TWA*, it held that Title VII does not require an employer to violate a collective bargaining agreement so that a few employees may observe their Sabbath. The seniority system protects the rights of all employees; therefore, an employer does not have to put up with the cost of being shorthanded or pay overtime to accommodate an employee's religious beliefs. It was held that the Civil Rights law was designed to eliminate discrimination against the majority as well as minorities. To pay overtime to some employees in order to give others the days off they wanted, when no such costs were required for the majority of workers, was viewed as unequal treatment of employees on the basis of religion.

Justices Marshall and Brennan, in dissent, argued that the Court majority had gutted the Civil Rights Act without declaring it illegal.

Still another troublesome area is found in union-security arrangements. Union-shop agreements provide that an employee can be discharged for nonpayment of dues. Circuit courts have taken the position in several cases, with *Gray* denied Supreme Court review, that workers may be discharged under Taft-Hartley for failure to pay union dues even if the refusal is due to religious objections to unions.[51] The EEOC has ruled that both a company and union violate Title VII if they discharge a worker for refusing to pay union dues for religious reasons.[52] An attempt to accommodate the employee's belief is required before discharge is permissible.

The *TWA* decision of the Supreme Court in 1977 has essentially said that not much of an accommodation for religious beliefs is required under Title VII. It did not say, however, that the provision was unconstitutional.

It was pointed out in an earlier chapter that Congress amended Taft-Hartley in 1980 and exempted from compulsory union membership employees who have bona fide religious beliefs against joining or financially supporting labor organizations.

National Origin

Discrimination based on national origin is unlawful. The national origin provision of Title VII does not apply to aliens unless a firm's employment policy applies only to aliens of certain national origins, or if it is used to refuse jobs to certain nationalities.[53] A rule that employees must be U.S. citizens is not in violation of the law.

EEOC guidelines require that violations occur when (1) employment tests are given in English to persons whose native language is not English and whose language skill has nothing to do with job performance; (2) height and weight requirements are applied that have nothing to do with job performance and certain groups fall outside the national norms; and (3) rules are instituted against persons who belong to organizations identified with national groups.

The U.S. Supreme Court ruled in *Espinoza* v. *Farah Manufacturing Co.*[54] that the term "national origin" does not mean citizenship. An employer has the right to deny employment to noncitizens. Discrimination in hiring noncitizens may occur where employment policies are based on whether employees are U.S. citizens. If a firm hired noncitizens from one national origin but refused to hire the same of some other ancestry, that would be a violation of the law. But the Civil Rights Act of 1964 does not make it illegal to formulate a hiring policy based on citizenship.

Justice Douglas entered a vigorous dissent from the majority opinion, which construed the congressional interpretation of "national origin" to exclude citizenship. Douglas noted that legal permanent resident aliens are most vulnerable to discrimination and exploitation and chided the court for its inconsistency with other cases. He viewed citizenship as much an artificial, arbitrary, and unnecessary barrier to equal employment opportunity as those barriers addressed in *Griggs* v. *Duke Power Co.*

AFFIRMATIVE ACTION PROGRAMS

Federal Contract Compliance

Affirmative action means active efforts toward redressing any racial, sexual, or other minority imbalances that may exist in an employee work force. Executive Orders 11246 and 11375, along with related regulations of the Office of Federal Contract Compliance (OFCC), brought affirmative action programs into existence. The Civil Rights Act does not contain language that requires a program of affirmative action. The OFCC affirmative action program requirements apply to all employers, contractors, and subcontractors of the federal government, whether the contract is direct or is only financed or assisted by federal funds. Employers are not under a strict obligation to seek racial balance for its own sake. Neither must future job openings be necessarily reserved for minority groups. However, affirmative action requires employers to evaluate their work forces, analyze their employment needs, and actively solicit to obtain more minority employees. The primary requirement is a written stipulation of good-faith efforts to achieve more rapid change than would occur from Title VII alone. At a minimum, such efforts must include (1) an analysis of deficiencies in the utilization of minorities; (2) a timetable for correcting such deficiencies, together with their expected goals; and (3) a coherent and reasonable plan for achieving these goals.

The analysis of the work force should include an analysis of all major job categories, by establishment, to determine where minorities are being underutilized, along with an explanation of why they are being underutilized and a further explanation of how this can be corrected. Goals and timetables must be couched in terms of actual commitment. Also, they must be cast in terms of correcting identifiable conditions, and support data must be furnished to show that the goals and timetables are realistic. Specific means set forth in a plan for reaching equal employment goals must include internal and external dissemination. Internally, the company should publicize its commitment to equal employment by placing appropriate notices on company bulletin boards, by setting forth its goals in company newspapers, and by verbal expression during meetings held with company employees. Externally, a company must actively recruit employees from minority groups. After a contractor with the federal government has established an affirmative action policy, he or she must then disseminate that policy.

In 1971, the OFCC set up a number of factors that have to be considered in order to determine whether an employer is guilty of underutilization. These considerations are (1) minority population of the labor area in the plant locale; (2) size of the minority unemployment force in that locale; (3) percentage of minority work force compared with the total work force of that locale; (4) general availability of minorities with the necessary skills, both in the immediate location and within a reasonable recruiting radius; (5) availability of promotable minorities within the employer's work force; (6) existence of training institutions capable of training minorities with the requisite skills; and (7) amount of training that the contractor is reasonably able to undertake to make all job classifications available to minorities.

Later in this chapter, several U.S. Supreme Court decisions will be presented dealing with affirmative action within a context of negotiated seniority provisions contained in labor agreements.

Negotiated Consent Decree

In employment discrimination cases, the parties to a court action may enter into a negotiated consent decree for purposes of working toward affirmative action plan objectives. If a labor organization is not a named party to the action, it is nevertheless usually given an opportunity to intervene in proceedings to protect its interests. Failure to do so within the time frame allowed by a court may exclude it from input in the initial proceedings before a negotiated consent decree is approved.

The negotiated consent decree approach is a temporary remedy designed to end when the targeted racial or sex imbalances have been corrected. Specific statistical promotion and hiring goals and ratios are permissible elements of the plan. A consent decree of this nature has certain court-imposed restrictions placed on its content.

In order to approve a negotiated consent decree, the trial court must find that several ingredients are present, namely, that it is *reasonable*, which means that it provides a fair and adequate solution to the complaints raised. The solution must also be fair and reasonable to nonminorities affected by it. Reverse discrimination challenges to the solution are viewed as impermissible secondary attacks if the consent decree is found to be reasonable. For a decree to be found reasonable, the court must consider all objections to the decree, as well as alternative approaches to secure equal employment opportunity.

The court maintains jurisdictional administration over reasonable consent decrees and is empowered to issue further orders to achieve the statistical goals and ratios of the order as they may be necessary over the life of the agreement. These bargained affirmative action decrees may be terminated when the court is convinced that the objectives of the agreement have been achieved. At that time, the essence of employment relations is returned to the original parties to collective bargaining agreements.

The Secretary of Labor has extensive powers to enforce the nondiscrimination policy of the executive orders. A failure to develop an affirmative action program can lead to possible cancellation of existing contracts and debarment from future contracts. The OFCC will grant a conference to a contractor who has not developed an acceptable affirmative action program. The purpose of the conference is to make every effort to assist in developing an acceptable affirmative action program. If the contractor remains in noncompliance, the OFCC will move to set a hearing date that will serve to make the contractor ineligible for future contracts and subcontracts. If there is no program at all, or one that is unacceptable, the agency can issue notice, giving the contractor thirty days to show cause why enforcement proceedings should not be instituted. If the situation is not corrected within the thirty days, the compliance agency, with authorization, will commence formal proceedings leading to the cancellation or termination of existing contracts or subcontracts. In reality, very few contract terminations have occurred.

If an employer's discrimination is caused by union practices in referral or membership, the Secretary of Labor can refer union violations to the EEOC or the Attorney General for action. It is the employer who contracts directly with the government, not the unions.

Preferential Treatment

The issue of preferential treatment or reverse discrimination has been narrowly construed by the U.S. Supreme Court. In the celebrated *Bakke*, case,[55] it was ruled that the University of California had practiced reverse discrimination against Bakke by denying admission to him and at the same time declaring that race could be taken into account in establishing the medical school's special admissions program. In another case involving selection of workers, the Court in *Weber* ruled that *voluntary affirmative action agreements could be reached through collective bargaining*.[56] As such, race-conscious affirmative action plans were permissible to correct or eliminate conspicuous racial imbalance in traditionally segregated job categories. The Court refused to distinguish between lawful and unlawful voluntary affirmative action plans. It stressed that voluntary collective bargaining accords well reflected the intent of Equal Employment Opportunity.

The United Steelworkers and Kaiser Aluminum and Chemical Corp. agreed to require one black worker for every white worker to enter into a new job training program *regardless of seniority*. The intent was to increase minority representation in craft jobs. There was no constitutional question in *Weber*, and because there was no state action involved, there was no possible violation of the Equal Protection Clause of the U.S. Constitution. The negotiated plan was to continue in force only until the target percent of black people in skilled jobs equaled the percentage of black people in the local labor force. Thus, the Supreme Court reasoned, white people were not unduly harmed, since they were not locked out of job training programs. The EEOC issued a policy statement in 1980 that voluntary union-management efforts should be the preferred solution. However, if only one party is willing to advocate measures to deal with discrimination, the EEOC would recognize the good faith efforts of that party in any subsequent discrimination actions.

Title VII does not require employers to hire women and racial minority members just because they are as qualified as white men competing for the same jobs.[57] Employers do not have to restructure employment practices to maximize the number of minorities and women hired.

Equal Employment Opportunity and Labor Unions

Labor unions are covered by the fair employment practices provisions of the Civil Rights Act of 1964, if they are in an industry affecting commerce. A union is deemed to affect commerce if (1) it operates a hiring hall, or (2) has fifteen or more members. The EEOC has ruled that a union is covered by the law regarding its own employees, even though it may have fewer than fifteen members. The Act in Section 703(c) prohibits a union from excluding or expelling from its membership or otherwise discriminating against any individual because of race, color, religion, sex, or national origin. Thus, EEOC has ruled that the Act's language is broad enough to prohibit a union from discriminating against its employees without regard to numbers. In addition, a union must meet one of several additional requirements to be covered by the Act. In essential part, the possibilities are (1) the union must be certified under the NLRA or Railway Labor Act; (2) if not certified, the union must represent employees of an employer covered by the Act; (3) the union has chartered a local or subsidiary that represents or seeks to represent employees falling under (1) or (2) above; (4) the organization has been chartered by a union that represents or seeks to represent employees falling under (1) or (2) above; or (5) the group is a conference, general committee, joint or system board, or joint council subordinate to a national or international union that includes a union covered under any of the tests set out in (1) to (4) above.

Discrimination under Taft-Hartley and Equal Employment Opportunity

As noted, a union is guilty of an unfair labor practice under Taft-Hartley if it causes or attempts to cause an employer to discriminate against an employee who has been denied union membership on any ground other than nonpayment of dues. The Civil Rights Act prohibits a union from causing or attempting to cause an employer to discriminate against any person because of race, color, religion, national origin, or sex. Thus, a union may be in violation of both the NLRA and Civil Rights Act if it causes or attempts to cause discrimination for any reason other than nonpayment of dues.

Unions as employers are covered under the same provisions of equal employment opportunity as employers generally. Selected categories have been identified below to provide information on how labor unions are affected by the Civil Rights Act.

SENIORITY AND CIVIL RIGHTS

Remedies for Past Discrimination

The law provides that "it shall not be an unlawful employment practice for an employer to apply different standards of compensation, or different terms, conditions or privileges of employment pursuant to a bona fide seniority . . . system . . . provided that such differences are not the result of an intention to discriminate because of race, color, religion, sex, or national origin." Any collective bargaining contractual clause that conflicts with the Act is void.[58] The seniority system itself cannot be discriminatory. Both unions and employers are held responsible when discriminatory seniority practices are found.

Seniority systems that maintain the results of past discrimination can place some unions in serious situations. If an employer attempts to champion the cause of the minority worker and proposes to revise long established discriminatory seniority systems, unions may face a dilemma, depending on the nature, severity, and timing of the practices as discussed below.

Title VII prohibits seniority clauses in labor agreements that perpetuate discrimination against minorities where a history of discrimination has been shown. In *Griggs*, it was held that Title VII required the removal of any artificial, arbitrary, and unnecessary barriers to employment. The Court stated that such barriers included not only those that were overtly discriminatory, but also those that were fair in theory but discriminatory in practice. With respect to construction industry union employment barriers, the courts have indicated a willingness to require affirmative action in any situation where a deliberately discriminatory employment practice has been discovered.[59]

It is intended that employees keep all benefits of their seniority. However, a problem of substantial proportions arises in attempts to correct seniority systems that had been discriminatory in the past. Congressional debate shows that the 1964 law was not intended to permit the firing of whites to hire blacks, or to grant blacks special seniority rights at the expense of whites with longer years of service.[60] One court has held that this point was not controlling over remedies to systems containing past discrimination, because the debate took place before the Act's seniority provision was introduced to the Senate.[61] The possibility of reverse discrimination and, indeed, charges of such have been popular in recent years. Reverse discrimination seems to be prohibited by Section 703(j), which says in brief: "Nothing in this title . . . [shall require the granting] of preferential treatment to any individual or group because of race, color, religion, sex, or national origin . . . on account of an imbalance which may exist with respect to the total number or percentage of [such] persons."

Several theories for remedying the effects of past discriminatory systems have been advanced. The "status quo" approach is one usually called for by some union leaders, who argue that employers today follow fair employment practices and may even prefer minorities when federal or state contracts are involved. Thus, the negative effects of past discrimination should be ignored. Others at the opposite end of the "status quo" argument advanced a "freedom now" proposition, that all remains of past discrimination should be eradicated immediately. The Fifth Circuit Court of Appeals took a position between the "status quo" and "freedom now" positions, advancing its "rightful place" theory.[62] Some lower courts accepted the "status quo" and "freedom now" theories, but most found the "rightful place" theory more acceptable.[63]

The "rightful place" theory provides that future awarding of vacant jobs based on a seniority system that locks in past discrimination is unlawful. White employees should not lose positions held, however, even though minorities continued at a disadvantage. The Fifth Circuit Court of Appeals held, "Where a seniority system has the effect of perpetuating discrimination, and concentrating or 'telescoping' the effect of past years of discrimination against Negro employees into the *present* placement of Negroes in an inferior position for promotion and other purposes, the present result is prohibited, and a seniority system which operates to produce that present result must be replaced with another system." The court argued further that the fact that Title VII of the Act referred to an effective date was no defense for expanding a discriminatory, departmental seniority system into a plantwide system. White employees were not deprived of seniority accrued before passage of the Act. Black employees would no longer be locked into dead-end departments but would become eligible for promotion into better jobs on a par with white workers on a plantwide basis.

Precisely how far a remedy may go under particular circumstances depends upon the court ordering the remedy. For example, a federal district court in Virginia ordered that *all* nonsupervisory jobs must be opened for bidding, with the only qualifications for a position being a willingness to learn the job and seniority.[64] The court ordered this remedy because vacancies seldom occurred in the tobacco industry, plagued by static employment because of automation. Any incumbent employees demoted as a result of the remedy, however, were not to have their wages reduced. Demotions were ordered because the details of the case revealed that future job openings would probably not occur in sufficient number to correct past practices. Employers maintain that such orders can seriously affect the financial welfare of businesses.

The Fifth Circuit Court of Appeals introduced still another dimension into seniority cases evidencing past discrimination with present effects.[65] It set forth a twofold test: (1) Does the present policy perpetuate the past discrimination? (2) Is the present policy justified by a showing of business necessity?

The question then becomes, what constitutes justifiable business necessity? It means more than attempting to avoid inconvenience or additional costs. An employment policy must be related to job performance before a business necessity policy that affects any group adversely will be acceptable.[66] Employee preferences for a given policy will not justify an employer's discriminatory practice.[67] A medical examination for the purpose of determining the ability of a person to physically perform a job is justifiable under the business necessity doctrine if the standard used is in fact essential for attaining the goals of the specific job. A physical standard not necessary for the specific job, such as a minimum height requirement, is considered discriminatory.

In 1976, the U.S. Supreme Court in *Franks* v. *Bowman Transportation* utilized the "rightful place" theory in dealing with a make-whole remedy for rectifying the victims of unlawful employment discrimination.[68] Seniority was ordered from the date that employment was wrongfully refused. Thus, the blacks involved got seniority from the date of discrimination and would jump ahead of whites who were hired after that date and who had actually worked, whereas those discriminated against did not actually work. The Court held that Section 706(g) provided for an award of seniority as a remedy even though the court of appeals reasoned that Section 703(1) prohibited tampering with a bona fide seniority system. Section 703(g) provides that the courts could

> order such affirmative action as may be appropriate which may include, but is not limited to, reinstatement or hiring of employees, with or without backpay . . . , or any other relief as the court deems appropriate.

The Supreme Court went on to say that a refusal to provide seniority relief on the grounds that it would diminish the expectations of other employees would frustrate the objective of Title VII. Majority employees must share the burden of past discrimination, even when it requires a modification of their expectations arising from a seniority system agreement. The Court then dampened the inclusiveness of the decision by granting trial courts initial control over the remedy required in seniority cases. General tampering with the seniority system was not required.

Majority employees may therefore expect to have their seniority rights modified in cases where discrimination in employment has been found in the past with present and future implications.

T.I.M.E.-D.C. and Alteration of *Griggs*

In 1977, the U.S. Supreme Court handed down a decision on bona fide seniority systems which runs counter to thirty decisions by six federal courts of appeals on similar issues.[69] The Court ruled that it is *not* unlawful for a bona fide seniority system to perpetuate the effects of Title VII discrimination. Retroactive seniority after the law became effective may be ordered in appropriate cases under the *Franks* v. *Bowman Transportation Co.* case.[70] However, the *T.I.M.E.-D.C.* case addressed itself to discrimination in seniority systems that occurred prior to the effective date of Title VII. Employees who suffered from pre-Act discrimination are not entitled to relief, and retroactive seniority cannot be awarded to a date earlier than the effective date of Title VII. Discriminatory intent in negotiating or administering seniority systems is required to win suits.

It is recalled that *Griggs* made any employment practice that was "fair in form, but discriminatory in operation," unlawful. As such, then, any practice that perpetuated the effects of past discrimination was governed by *Griggs*. *T.I.M.E.-D.C.* released bona fide seniority systems in existence before Title VII from the *Griggs* doctrine because of the language of Section 703(h) of the Act protecting bona fide seniority systems.

The Court was convinced that Section 703(h) prevented the courts from outlawing existing seniority lists and tampering with the vested rights of workers simply because their employer had engaged in discrimination prior to passage of the Civil Rights Act. Blacks and Chicanos had been hired for years by a Texas trucking firm, the subject of the *T.I.M.E.-D.C.* case, only for local hauls; they were excluded from the higher-paying hauls between cities. When the minority workers were finally accepted to drive the intercity routes, they were not permitted to take their intracity seniority to the other division. The result was that blacks and Chicanos received the less desirable routes and were more vulnerable to layoffs than were whites.

Justices Marshall and Brennan dissented from the majority view that workers suffering from pre-Title VII discrimination should be denied relief. They argued that Congress did not intend this result, because it did not overturn the courts of appeals decisions on the issue when Title VII was amended in 1972. Thus, a system that contains pre-Title VII discrimination can nevertheless continue to be bona fide, with no relief available. Past discrimination, if committed prior to the effective date of the Civil Rights Act, cannot lead to relief for workers who suffered from the system.

Supreme Court Decisions: 1984–1986

In a series of decisions issued between 1984 and 1986, the U.S. Supreme Court continued to address the problem of affirmative action and negotiated seniority programs contained in collective bargaining agreements. In *Firefighters* v. *Stotts* (467 U.S. 561 [1984]), the high court held an affirmative action program may not be used to lay off senior white employees and retain junior service black workers. Under a federal court decree, the City of Memphis was required to increase the number of black firefighters from 4 percent to 11 percent. Subsequently, the city laid off senior white employees ahead of junior service black employees to maintain the balance between white and black firefighters. Reversing a federal appeals court which sustained the layoff procedure, the U.S. Supreme Court held that Title VII was violated by such preferential treatment afforded black employees. As in *T.I.M.E.-D.C.*, the high court held the seniority system as it applies to layoffs was bona fide and not intended for discrimination against black employees.

In May 1986, the high court again held that junior service black employees may not be retained and senior white employees laid off (*Wygant* v. *Jackson Board of Education*, 476 U.S. 267). In Jackson, Michigan, the board of education negotiated a labor agreement with the teachers' union which stipulated that junior service black teachers would be kept on while senior white teachers would be laid off. Such a system was negotiated to keep black teachers as "role models." By a 5–4 majority, the high court held that the white teachers were denied equal protection of the law, ruling the affirmative action program to maintain black teachers as role models could not alone justify laying off the senior white teachers. That the Court found the issue to be perplexing and highly controversial is demonstrated by the fact that five separate opinions were written, none of them joined by more than three justices. Nonetheless, the Court did not slam the door on all aspects of affirmative action as the following two 1986 cases will demonstrate. As a matter of fact, even in the matter of layoffs, it hinted in *Wygant* that under special circumstances white employees senior to minority employees may be laid off. Apparently there was sufficient agreement among the justices that such a condition might prevail should the facts of a case prove the employer historically discriminated against minority group employees.

In 1980, a group of black firefighters sued the City of Cleveland contending discrimination because only 4.5 percent of the lieutenants and higher officers were black while nearly one-half of the city's population was black. Subsequently, lower federal courts approved a voluntary settlement of the suit calling for promotion of black firefighters on a one-to-one ratio with white firefighters. That is, 50 percent of the promotions were to be filled by blacks regardless of their seniority and test scores compared with whites.

By a 6–3 vote, the United States Supreme Court on July 2, 1986, upheld the promotion system which obviously provided affirmative action for black employees (*Local 98, International Association of Firefighters* v. *City of Cleveland*, 106 S. Ct. 3063). It rejected the Firefighters Union position that the plan was illegal under Title VII. Differentiating the case from *Stotts*, the high court pointed out that case dealt strictly with layoffs and not with voluntary affirmative action programs providing preference to black employees for promotion purposes. Justice Brennan, who wrote the majority opinion, observed the Memphis case involved the integrity of a bona fide seniority system governing layoffs, and nothing in that decision prevented federal courts from ordering race-conscious programs "to dismantle prior patterns of employment discrimination and to prevent discrimination in the future."

On the same day, July 2, 1986, the high court, this time by a 5–4 vote, upheld a federal court order establishing a 29 percent minority membership goal for a sheet metal workers' union in New York which for many years had excluded nonwhite applicants (*Local 28, Sheet Metal Workers' International Association* v. *EEOC*, 478 U.S. 421). Justice Brennan, again writing the majority opinion, stated:

> A court may have to resort to race-conscious affirmative action when confronted with an employer or labor union that has engaged in persistent or egregious discrimination. Or such relief may be necessary to dissipate the lingering effects of pervasive discrimination.

Of course, the final word on affirmative action has not been written. Given the controversy on this problem and the divided court (no less than nine opinions were issued in the July 1986 cases), only time will tell as to its ultimate outcome. Nonetheless, at this writing, it would be safe to say that affirmative action programs may not supersede negotiated seniority systems governing layoffs. It appears equally safe to say that affirmative action is alive and well when the program deals with hiring, promotions, and apprenticeship programs.

Indeed, the July 1986 decisions dealt a stinging rebuke to the Reagan Department of Justice. Starting in 1981, the Department of Justice contended that only actual victims of discrimination may prevail in civil rights suits. It denounced race-conscious remedies and numerical goals as morally wrong. Throughout the nation, the Department of Justice attempted to nullify programs in which state and local governments agreed to use employment goals to undo the effects of discrimination against black employees, Hispanic workers, and women. Given the July 1986 Supreme Court pronouncements, the Reagan administration was not successful—at least not at that time.

THE REAGAN COURT AND CIVIL RIGHTS

The preceding observations that appeared in a previous edition of this book proved to be prophetic. With the Reagan Court firmly in place, it sharply curtailed civil rights for minority and women workers. Four decisions issued in 1989 severely limited the use of law to defend against discrimination. Taken as a whole, it became clear that the judiciary could no longer be counted on to protect minorities and women against employer discrimination.

City of Richmond: Set-Aside Programs

In the first of these cases (*Richmond* v. *J. A. Cruson*, 109 S. Ct. 707), the Supreme Court held the City of Richmond set-aside program unconstitutional. It enacted an ordinance requiring prime contractors working on city projects to subcontract at least 30 percent of the dollar amount to minority-owned businesses. Before establishing the program, a public hearing was held to determine the extent of discrimination in awarding public contracts. No direct evidence was discovered to prove the city or prime contractors actually discriminated against minorities. Evidence, however, was presented demonstrating that only 0.67 percent of the city's prime contractors had been awarded to minority businesses in past years despite the fact that 50 percent of the city's population was black. In other words, the purpose of the set-aside program was to remedy past discrimination in the awarding of construction contracts.

Not persuaded by the imbalance between contracts to blacks and their percentage of the city's population, the Supreme Court held the program violated the "equal protection" clause of the Fourteenth Amendment of the U.S. Constitution. It ruled that way because evidence was not presented to demonstrate specific instances of minority discrimination. In other words, a set-aside program can meet the constitutional test only if it is designed to correct demonstrable acts of past discrimination. The Court did not take into account the difficulty of obtaining such evidence. Indeed, the task would at times prove to be insurmountable.

In a sharp dissent, Justice Thurgood Marshall said the majority decision was a "deliberate and giant step backward in this Court's affirmative action jurisprudence." Unlike the majority, Marshall viewed the Richmond program as an effort "to eradicate the effects of past discrimination." It is somewhat ironic that the Fourteenth Amendment, designed to assure equal treatment for former slaves, was used to frustrate a legislative effort to protect minority groups against discrimination. In any event, the Supreme Court's decision jeopardized set-aside programs in 36 states and 190 cities across the nation.

Wards Cove: The Shifting Burden of Proof

Recall that in *Griggs*, the high court held the employer must prove that criteria in the hiring process (testing and educational requirements) are job-related and a business necessity. Since *Duke Power* did not supply such proof, it ruled the impact of such criteria discriminated against minority groups in violation of Title VII of the 1964 Civil Rights Act. While upholding Griggs and other black employees, the Supreme Court proclaimed:

> According to this ruling, it is the employer who has the burden of proving that the specific practices in question have a manifest relationship to the jobs in question. The touchstone is business necessity.

In *Wards Cove Packing Co.* v. *Atonio* (490 U.S. 642), the Supreme Court in effect reversed *Griggs* by *shifting the burden of proving discrimination to minorities*. Under it, minorities or women for that matter must prove that an employment practice that discriminated against them was not a business necessity.

Wards Cove Packing operated a salmon cannery in Alaska where the jobs were classified into two types. Unskilled cannery jobs were predominantly held by nonwhites—Filipinos and Alaskan natives. The noncannery jobs, mostly skilled, including managerial, were predominantly filled by whites. Noncannery positions paid higher wages compared with cannery jobs. Also, living and eating quarters were separate according to job group, which meant that white employees were treated much better than nonwhites.

Given their disparate treatment, the nonwhite cannery workers claimed a violation of Title VII of the Civil Rights Act of 1964. The basis of the legal action was the allegation that employer hiring and promotion policies, including nepotism, a rehire preference, and separate hiring channels, as well as other employment practices, caused the racial stratification of the work force. Reversing a federal district court's decision holding the nonwhites' allegations lacked sufficient proof, a federal appeals court, relying on *Griggs*, held that once a *prima facie* case of discrimination was existent, the employer must prove the job-related practices were a business necessity.

By a 5–4 vote, the Supreme Court upset the federal appeals court decision. As already mentioned, the lower court held for the nonwhites because of the racial imbalance of the work force. Reversing that decision, the majority ruled that the racial imbalance of the work force in the absence of additional evidence does not demonstrate a violation of Title VII. Such evidence must be supplied by the nonwhites to prove a specific employment practice operated to discriminate against them. Also, nonwhites bear the burden of refuting the employer's defense that employment practices were a legitimate business necessity. No longer is the employer required to prove the business need for hiring and employment practices that resulted in discrimination. Under *Wards Cove*, coming about twenty years after *Griggs*, minority employees must now prove that specific hiring and promotion practices were not a business necessity. Never mind that such proof would be difficult, if not impossible, to obtain.

Needless to say, the minority sharply criticized the majority. At the core of the dissent, the minority asserted it was not the intent of Congress under Title VII to place the burden on minorities or women to identify and prove a specific employment practice caused discrimination. It was not the intent of the Civil Rights Act to require them to disprove an employer's claim that discriminatory practices were a business necessity. Justice Harry Blackmun, writing for the minority, captured its sense of bewilderment and frustration when he said:

> [We wonder] whether the majority believed that race discrimination against nonwhites is a problem in our society, or remembers that it ever was.

AT & T Technologies: **Discriminatory Seniority Systems**

Not content with *Richmond* and *Wards Cove* as being destructive of the civil rights of minorities and women, the high court on June 12, 1989, issued two additional decisions to further reduce legal protection of their civil rights. In *Lorance v AT & T Technologies* (490 U.S. 228), the employer and union adopted a new seniority system under which three female employees claimed discrimination in violation of Title VII. Under the new system, the jobs held by the women had been converted from coverage by department seniority preference to coverage by plantwide seniority preference. Because of the change, they were eventually assigned lower-paying jobs.

Under the Civil Rights Act of 1964, an aggrieved employee has 180 days to file the complaint with the Equal Employment Opportunity Commission after the alleged unlawful employment practice occurred, or 300 days if the employee initially instituted proceedings with a state or local agency authorized to grant relief from an alleged discriminatory employment practice. In the case at hand, *AT & T Technologies*, the women were not aware of the new seniority system until they had been demoted to lower-paying jobs. By that time, the 180–300-day time limits had expired. On this basis, by a split vote the Supreme Court ruled the women forfeited their rights under Title VII. According to the majority, the time limits started on the day the new seniority system was adopted.

Unpersuaded by the majority's highly technical construction of the time limits provision, the minority unsuccessfully asserted the limitations should not have started until the women actually suffered adverse effects. In the practical world of labor relations, employees are seldom aware of changes in a labor agreement until months or even years after the new language has been adopted. Before being harmed by the new language, they have no reason to believe the change will operate to discriminate against them. Even if they are aware, they do not file grievances or lawsuits until they have actually been harmed. Why protest before the actual damage occurs?

In other words, the majority was completely oblivious of the way labor relations actually operates. As a matter of fact, as the minority stressed, nothing in the Civil Rights Act requires employees to complain before they are in fact harmed. Clearly, the minority construction of the time limits provision was compatible with its terms. In any event, the majority decision deprived the women of substantive rights under Title VII based on a highly technical and unrealistic construction of the time limits requirement.

Wilks: **Reverse Discrimination**

In what may prove to be the major setback to minority and women's civil rights, the Supreme Court in *Martin* v. *Wilks* (490 U.S. 755), by a 5–4 vote, upheld the right of whites *to upset affirmative action plans approved by federal district courts by consent decree*. Earlier in this chapter, the nature of the consent decree was discussed. At its essence, federal district trial courts approve those plans that are negotiated by minority or women's groups and employers and work toward a goal to eliminate racial or sexual imbalance in the work force. Consent decrees end when the goals of the affirmative action program have been realized.

The National Association for the Advancement of Colored People (NAACP) and individual black persons filed lawsuits against the City of Birmingham, Alabama, charging blatant discrimination against the hiring and promotion of black firefighters in violation of Title VII. The federal district court held a fairness hearing where all concerned, including white firefighters, had an opportunity to express their views. Following the hearing, the federal district court in 1981 approved two consent decrees for the hiring and promotion of black persons. In marked contrast to *AT & T Technologies*, white firefighters waited two years before filing a lawsuit to attack the consent decrees. Despite the hiatus, federal courts accepted their action.

In their lawsuit, the white firefighters claimed the affirmative action plan denied them promotions because of their race, a violation, they contended, of Title VII of the Civil Rights Act and the Fourteenth Amendment of the U.S. Constitution. They charged the decrees illegally discriminated against them in the matter of promotions because of their skin color while less-qualified blacks were promoted. The federal district court dismissed the lawsuit on the grounds that the Birmingham Fire Department promotion policies were required by the consent decrees, and, therefore, it was not guilty of illegal racial discrimination. As the majority acknowledged in *Wilks*: "The great majority of federal appeals courts have rejected challenges to consent decrees by secondary parties," such as the white firefighters.

Nonetheless, the Supreme Court held the white firefighters had the right to attack the consent decrees. The basis of the decision was that they were not parties to the affirmative action plan negotiated by the employer and blacks even when approved by a federal district court. According to the majority, the white firefighters' lawsuit must be allowed because a voluntary settlement between a group of employees and the employer "cannot possibly settle . . . the conflicting claims of another group of employees who do not join in the agreement."

In their dissent, the minority of the Court said the majority decision was "unfathomable" and would subject employers "who seek to comply with the law to a never-ending stream of litigation and potential liability." Although the affirmative action plans, by their very nature, had an adverse impact on white firefighters and seemingly were unfair because they were not responsible for the discriminatory employment practices, the minority said it should not be forgotten that some of the same white individuals also benefited from the employer's past discriminatory practices. The minority also stressed that the white firefighters had the opportunity to be heard at the fairness hearing and chose not to be heard. Finally, the minority asserted that the affirmative action goals were fair and reasonable given the nature and extent of the discrimination that resulted in the consent decrees in the first place.

Wilks jeopardized every affirmative action plan already established and approved by consent decree. Also, the decision will decrease the willingness of employers to provide equality to minorities and women. As the minority said, the consequences of *Wilks* are indeed "unfathomable."

Given these four decisions, the Supreme Court has seriously impaired the right of minority and women employees to use the law for equal and fair employment opportunities. Considered as a whole, they reopen the door for widespread employer discrimination and just about nullify affirmative action as a matter of public policy. With the 1990 resignation of Justice William Brennan, a champion of civil rights and social justice, the current drift of the Supreme Court will undoubtedly be accentuated. Minority and women employees can no longer count on it to defend them against discrimination.

Congressional Response and Veto

If discrimination in employment is to be effectively reduced, the policy must come from legislation and not the judiciary. Understanding this proposition, Congress by substantial majorities in the House and Senate enacted the Civil Rights Act of 1990. It would have reversed or sharply modified the Supreme Court's decisions in question. In addition, for the first time, all victims of blatant and intentional racial, sexual, and religious discrimination would have the right to sue for compensatory and punitive damages.

To address concerns of the business community, the final version of the statute stated that it shall "not be construed to require or encourage an employer to adopt hiring or promotion quotas," and "the mere existence of statistical imbalance in an employer workplace [is] not alone sufficient to establish a *prima facie* case of discrimination."

Nonetheless, Bush vetoed the bill because he believed its impact would result in employment quotas. Despite language in the law to the contrary, he felt employers would hire and promote minorities and women to avoid being sued for discrimination employment practices. Bush was not impressed by the fact that during the eighteen-year period since *Griggs*, employers had complied with the Civil Rights Act of 1964 without evidence of employment quotas.

In the Senate, the effort to override the veto fell *one vote* short of the required two-thirds majority. Given the closeness of the vote, efforts to pass the law took place in the 1991 session of Congress.

THE CIVIL RIGHTS ACT OF 1991

After a two-year political struggle between Congress and the White House, Bush signed the Civil Rights Act of 1991[71] on November 21, 1991. For our purposes, we are concerned with the content of the legislation and not with the political maneuvering or its numerous compromises. The statute is a complex law dealing with employment practices beyond the previously discussed Supreme Court decisions that focused public and congressional attention to civil rights. To be sure, the Supreme Court will be called upon again to interpret and apply the new law, particularly in the congressional effort to deal with *Wards Cove.* Since 1989, there have been membership changes in the high court, and perhaps a change of attitude of holdover justices toward civil rights. Although predicting how the court will rule on any issue is risky business, it is possible the Supreme Court as currently constituted may be more favorable to a public policy providing minority groups and women fair treatment in the workplace.

Women and Punitive Damages

The 1991 statute addresses a problem that women's groups felt was unfair and discriminatory under existing legislation. Victims of racial discrimination could claim compensatory and punitive damages. *Compensatory damages* mean the actual amount of money lost because of discriminatory employment policy. *Punitive damages* is a sum of money beyond actual damages imposed by courts to deter such conduct in the future. Unlike victims of racial discrimination, women were limited to compensatory damages resulting from employer illegal conduct.

Under the 1991 legislation, this disparity and unequal treatment were remedied to an extent. A woman can collect punitive damages when a private-sector employer (government agencies are exempt) engages in discriminatory employment practices including sexual harassment "with malice or with reckless indifference to the federally protected rights of the aggrieved individual." Unfortunately, the law does not define the meaning of "malice or reckless indifference," requiring judicial construction of the concepts.

In the event punitive damages are assessed against the employer, the statute *limits money awards* to a particular amount based upon the size of the firm. Size is measured by the number of workers a company employs in each of twenty or more calendar weeks in the current or previous year. Employer liability ranges from $50,000 for firms of 15–100 employees to $300,000 for firms employing more than 500 workers. Thus, caps were placed on employer liability.

Hardly was the ink dry on the law when women's groups condemned the caps. An officer of the Women's Law Center, noting an absence of caps for punitive damages for unlawful racial discrimination, put it this way: "We will never accept a situation where women have second-class remedies under the law, and to the extent that President Bush has been insisting that second-class treatment is the price of civil rights legislation, that is a price that is indefensible to defend."[72]

Although Senator Edward Kennedy, civil rights groups, and the AFL-CIO backed legislation to remove the caps, it has not been passed as of this writing.

Civil Rights Act of 1866: *Patterson* v. *McClean Credit Union*

As a part of Reconstruction legislation, Congress enacted the Civil Rights Act of 1866, not to be confused with the Civil Rights Act of 1964. In pertinent part, the 1866 statute (Section 1981) provided all persons within the jurisdiction of the United States shall have the same right in every State and Territory "to make and enforce contracts as enjoyed by white citizens." Obviously the purpose of the law was to place black and white persons on the same footing to make and enforce contracts. Though restricted to racial discrimination, the 1866 law "increasingly has been used to challenge employment discrimination." Part of its popularity can be ascribed to the fact that (prior to the Civil Rights Act of 1991) this statute contains provisions allowing for punitive damages.[73] Under the 1866 civil rights statute black people were able to sue for racial discrimination and collect punitive damages.

In *Patterson* v. *McClean Credit Union*,[74] the Supreme Court sharply limited the scope of the 1866 legislation. It ruled that the law only applies to the *hiring* of individuals. Section 1981 does *not* apply to discriminatory practices after the person is hired. Promotions, wage matters, working conditions, sexual harassment, or discharge, even if the action is discriminatory, do not fall within the scope of the law. According to the high court, those employment practices are actionable under the Civil Rights Act of 1964 and not under the one passed during the Reconstruction era.

To erase *McClean Credit Union*, Congress amended the 1866 statute in the Civil Rights Act of 1991. Now the concept of "make and enforce contracts" includes activities on the job, such as benefits, privileges, and terms and conditions of the contractual relationship.

Given the broad coverage of the 1866 statute as amended by the 1991 Civil Rights Act, more suits of minority groups and women will probably be filed. Since the 1991 law does not apply to firms of fifteen or fewer employees, the workers in those small shops will probably make use of their rights under the amended 1866 legislation. Since there are no limits to punitive damages in the post–Civil War law, women now under punitive damage caps in the 1991 statute will also probably make use of the 1866 legislation.

Understand, however, the Civil Rights Act of 1991 specifically states that an employee alleging employment discrimination is limited to the use of *either* the 1991 or 1866 statute. Thus if an employee seeks compensation and punitive damages under the 1866 statute, he or she may not also file suit under the one passed in 1991.

Multiple Reason Lawsuits

Price Waterhouse refused to grant Ann Hopkins a partnership. Some of the reasons for its actions were legitimate, such as lack of interpersonal skills; other reasons, however, were clearly discriminatory based upon sexism, such as not being feminine enough. In *Price Waterhouse* v. *Hopkins*,[75] the Supreme Court ruled in 1989 in favor of the employer, dismissing Hopkins' claim that it unlawfully discriminated against her in violation of Title VII of the Civil Rights Act of 1964. It accepted the employer's argument that it would have denied her the partnership *even in the absence of whatever illegal conduct it may have committed.* In other words, even if some of the employer's conduct was illegal, to escape liability all it had to show was that some of its conduct was lawful.

Addressing this issue, Congress declared in the Civil Rights Act of 1991 that employers' conduct would be unlawful if the employee could show that race, color, religion, sex, or national origin was *a reason* for the decision even if other reasons were lawful. In pertinent part, it states:

> an unlawful employment practice is established when the complaining party demonstrates that race, color, religion, sex, or national origin was a motivating factor for any employment practice, even though other factors also motivated the practice.

It would seem the language is clear enough to nullify *Price Waterhouse*. An additional provision, however, appears to weaken the apparent purpose of this area of the statute. Should the employer prove to the court that it would have made the same decision in the absence of race, color, religion, sex, or national origin reasons, the judge and/or jury *may not* "award damages or issue an order directing hiring, reinstatement, promotion, or payment of benefits." If the employer is found to have violated the Civil Rights Act of 1991, the court may direct it to pay court costs, attorney fees, issue injunctive relief but not to order the employer to hire, promote, pay benefits, or reinstate the employee. Given this qualifying provision, it is difficult to see how the statute sets aside *Price Waterhouse*. The only practical action an employee can take is to sue the employer in state court, using violation of the federal law as part of the case. Of course, not all states have laws that forbid employer discriminatory employment practices. In the alternative, the employee may try to prove the employer's action was in truth based upon an unlawful reason, and the other legitimate reasons advanced by the employer were merely used to cover up the real reason. This would place a very heavy burden upon the employee.

Application to Foreign Nations

The far-reaching scope of the Civil Rights Act of 1991 is demonstrated by its application to American companies operating in foreign nations. Under the statute, compliance with Title VII is mandatory unless compliance causes the employer to violate the laws of the foreign nation. It appears that such laws must be written and not a matter of custom. In other words, if local custom does not forbid the employment practice, but the foreign nation's written legal code does, the American company is bound by the written law.

Dealing with the 1989 Decisions

If there was one 1989 decision that galvanized attention to civil rights it was *Wards Cove*. No question exists that congressional effort to deal with that decision constitutes the most controversial feature of the 1991 statute. Delaying consideration of that decision and the congressional aftermath, the other three decisions claim our attention at this point.

Consent Decrees: *Martin* v. *Wilks*

Recall that the Supreme Court decision in *Martin* v. *Wilks* jeopardized each and every consent decree existing in the nation. White firefighters in Birmingham, Alabama, objected to a court decree between the city and the NAACP providing for an affirmative action program relating to the hiring and promotion of black firefighters. Despite a fairness hearing held by the federal district court, the white firefighters boycotted the hearing. The Supreme Court held the consent decree invalid because the white firefighters were not a party to it.

To get around the high court's decision, the Civil Rights Act of 1991 declares consent decrees may not be challenged, provided interested parties were notified of the fairness hearing, and had "a reasonable opportunity to present objections" to a pending consent decree. To put it in other terms, if white firefighters have the opportunity to present objections to a consent decree, the white firefighters may not attack their legality in federal courts.

Judicial review will likely be required to establish what constitutes reasonable notification and "the opportunity to object" to a proposed consent decree. Although these appear to be simple concepts to establish, attorneys and judges at times convert simple issues into ones of great complexity.

Seniority Systems: *Lorance* v. *AT&T Technologies*

In *Lorance* v. *AT&T Technologies*, the high court ruled that female plaintiffs alleging a seniority plan to be discriminatory could not file a Title VII lawsuit because their action was not filed soon enough after the seniority plan was adopted by the employer and union. It ignored the women's claim that the time limit should not start until they were actually harmed by the plan.

Addressing the problem, Congress amended the pertinent provisions of the Civil Rights Act of 1964 to allow lawsuits to be filed timely within 180 days that start "when the seniority plan is adopted; when a person becomes covered by the seniority system; or a person is harmed or injured by the application of the seniority system or a provision of the system."

Advising management of the impact of the change, one writer stated

> a review of existing seniority systems is necessitated to assess compliance. If any component of the system indicates that it may harbor a discriminatory intent that component should be corrected immediately and voluntary remedial action taken. Otherwise, the employer runs the risk of having the courts impose a remedial action at some future date. An ounce of prevention is the best adage to follow regarding flawed systems.[76]

City of Richmond

For reasons not articulated by Congress, the Civil Rights Act of 1991 does not deal with the *City of Richmond*. In that case the Supreme Court held the minority set-aside program was in violation of the "equal protection" clause of the Fourteenth Amendment of the U.S. Constitution. It ruled that way because the record of that case did not demonstrate specific instances of minority discrimination.

Probably Congress did not address the *City of Richmond* because the high court seemed to signal that a set-aside program would be constitutional if it were designed to correct actual and demonstrable acts of past discrimination. Thus, in that kind of situation, minority or women's groups would be required to search for evidence that demonstrates actual and specific acts of past discrimination. It would not be sufficient for plaintiffs to use generalized statistical data to demonstrate unlawful conduct. Recall in the *City of Richmond* that the record demonstrated only 0.67 percent of the city's prime contracts had been awarded to minority businesses, despite the fact that 50 percent of the city's population was black. In other words, general statistical data do not demonstrate unlawful discrimination. It must be proved by specific instances of violations of Title VII.

Wards Cove Packing and Civil Rights Act of 1991

This brings the discussion to *Wards Cove Packing,* the most controversial and celebrated of the Supreme Court's civil rights decisions of 1989. Previously the core of that decision was presented: the shifting of the burden of proof to the plaintiff-employees, reversing *Griggs* and its progeny. The high court ruled once a complaining party proves that an employment practice has a disparate impact on a minority or female group, "the employer carries the burden of producing evidence of business justification for his employment practice." The burden of proof, however, remains with the disparate impact plaintiff-employee. Thus, after the employer says a disparate impact arises from a business justification (*not business necessity*), the employee must prove the employer was wrong—that there was no business justification.

Divorced from reality, the majority in *Wards Cove* disregarded a principle of our legal system: "A determination of which party should bear the burden of proof of a particular fact should be based upon such common sense considerations as which party has access to the underlying information and which party is arguing from a disadvantaged position. *Griggs* properly allocated the burden of proof in a disparate impact case and *Wards Cove* did not."[77] Clearly in the overwhelming number of situations, it is the employer and not the employee who has access to the necessary data and circumstances of employment practices that result in disparate impact in the workplace.

Section 105 of the Civil Rights Act of 1991 returns the burden of proof to the employer. Entitled "Burden of Proof and Disparate Impact Cases," it says:

> an unlawful employment practice based upon disparate impact is established under this title only if a complaining party [employee] demonstrates that respondent [employer] uses a particular employment practice that caused a disparate impact on the base of race, color, religion, sex, or national origin and the respondent fails to demonstrate that the challenged practice is job related for the position in question and consistent with business necessity.

Thus, the minority or women's group must present a *prima facie* case demonstrating that an employer's hiring, promotion, benefit, or other particular employment practice caused a disparate impact upon the labor force. This burden imposed on the employee is not insignificant. If the employee fails to demonstrate a particular employee practice caused a disparate impact, the employer is not required to prove that practice is consistent with business necessity. In addition, employers would probably have the right to attack the data offered by the plaintiff to demonstrate a disparate impact. As stated by one writer:

> ... employers would apparently be able to defend their [employment] practices by showing the complaining parties statistics are either flawed or insignificant. This statement only reinforces previous court precedent in this area as employers have long been able to challenge disparate impact allegations based upon fallacies and deficiencies in the complaining parties' data. Such challenges typically involve demonstrating flaws in statistical methodology used, errors and data used, or comparisons with irrelevant labor markets.[78]

This means the minority or women's group must be careful in alleging disparate impact. They must make sure that an employer practice results in disparity and take equal care in the selection of the evidence to demonstrate a disparate impact.

In *Wards Cove*, the nonwhite cannery workers adequately demonstrated employment practices that resulted in disparate impact on the labor force. They cited several employment practices, including hiring and promotion policies, nepotism, rehire preferences, and separate hiring channels, that caused the racial stratification of the workplace—unskilled jobs held by Filipinos and Alaskan natives. The better-paid skilled or managerial positions were held by white males, and with significant difference between the two groups' living and eating quarters. The Supreme Court did not rule against the nonwhite groups because they did not present a *prima facie* case or failed to demonstrate employment practices caused the disparate impact in the workplace. It held for the employer because the nonwhite groups could not adequately refute its contention that business necessity or justification resulted in a disparate impact.

If a minority or women's group establishes a *prima facie* case demonstrating a specific employment practice caused a disparate impact on the labor force, Section 105 of the 1991 statute shifts the burden of proof back on the employer. Unless the employer presents compelling evidence to demonstrate the *challenged employment practice is job related for the position in question and consistent with business necessity*, the court must find the employer violated Title VII of the Civil Rights Act of 1964 as amended in 1991.

One final word about the 1991 statute is in order. Strangely enough, Congress excluded the 2,000 workers employed by Wards Cove Packing from the coverage of the law. Other employees may collect damages under the statute, but not the Wards Cove employees whose treatment sparked the Supreme Court decision in the first place. One can only wonder how such a discriminatory exclusion would appear in civil rights legislation. Early in 1993 the AFL-CIO announced its support of a bill to eliminate the exclusion. At this writing Congress has not acted on the proposal.

Problems of Interpretation

To be sure the Supreme Court will interpret and apply the new civil rights statute. It does not establish standards to be used by plaintiff-employees to establish a *prima facie* case demonstrating specific employment practices that cause disparity in the workplace. Nor does the statute explain the meaning of the concept of "business necessity."

The question of retroactivity was not handled in the law, whether it applies to lawsuits filed before the statute became effective or after November 21, 1991, the date the Civil Rights Act of 1991 went into effect. This problem arose because Congress apparently wanted the courts to decide the issue. Some federal district courts have applied the statute retroactively, but federal appeals courts generally have not done so.[79]

In April 1994, the Supreme Court by an 8–1 vote resolved the issue. It held the law will not be applied retroactively.[80] At the time of the decision, as many as 8,000 lawsuits seeking millions of dollars in damages were pending.[81] Although it is not very likely, Congress could nullify the decision by enacting legislation specifying the 1991 law shall be applied retroactively. In any event, the business community was understandably very pleased with the decision, while civil rights activists were disappointed. Former Justice Harry Blackmun, the only dissenter, said:

> . . . there is nothing unjust about holding an employer responsible for injuries caused by conduct that has been illegal for almost 30 years . . .

What concerned civil rights groups is that the 1994 decision could be a harbinger of the undermining of the law.

Finally the courts will be required to determine the extent to which the 1991 statute applies to affirmative action. Section 116 of the statute expressly states that nothing in the Civil Rights Act of 1991 shall be construed to affect "court-ordered remedies, affirmative action, or conciliation agreements *in accordance with the law.*" (Emphasis supplied) As indicated in *Webber, Johnson* and *Sheet Metal Workers*, the Supreme Court approved affirmative action programs. The provision, however, does not say "in accordance with *existing* law"; it says only "*in accordance with the law.*" (Emphasis supplied) If it said existing law, the high court would probably hold affirmative action is consistent with the 1991 statute. Since it only says in accordance with the law, the Supreme Court *can change the law at any time* and hold that affirmative action is not permitted under the Civil Rights Act of 1991.[82]

In large measure, the impact of the Civil Rights Act of 1991 depends on its treatment by the Supreme Court. As the story unfolds, case by case, we will be in a better position to judge whether the statute affords benefits to minority and women's groups. What would appear to be a welcome signal to these groups was the high court's verdict in a 1993 sexual harassment case.[83] In a unanimous decision, it reversed the requirement imposed by a lower federal court that to prevail in lawsuits, women must demonstrate that they suffered severe psychological harm. An alleged victim's emotional distress, said the Supreme Court, may be relevant, but she does not have to prove extreme psychological distress to prevail. The woman in the case had worked in a hostile environment for about two years, so hostile that she was forced to quit her job because of the firm's president's continuous offensive sexual remarks, such as, "You're a woman what do you know?"; and an invitation to go to a nearby motel with him "to negotiate her raise."

AGE DISCRIMINATION

In 1980, Congress enacted the Age Discrimination Act, forbidding mandatory retirement before seventy years of age. It was followed by a 1986 amendment making it unlawful to require retirement at *any* age with the exception of college professors, law enforcement officers, and airline pilots. It applies to employers, labor organizations, and employment agencies. Coverage of the Act also extends to federal employees. Age discrimination is the only type of discrimination that all workers face at some point. The Act prohibits an employer to fail or refuse to hire, to fire any individual, or otherwise to discriminate with respect to pay, terms, conditions, or privileges of employment because of age. It is permissible, however, for an employer to make it attractive for an individual to retire. Thus, voluntary retirement plans are acceptable. However, the Act provides an exception "where age is a bona fide occupational qualification reasonably necessary to the normal operation of the particular business."

Under the Age Discrimination Act, employers are to evaluate employees on their merits and not on their age.

SUMMARY

This chapter deals with minority and women employees' quest for fair and equal opportunity for jobs. It focuses on government effort to provide them with the same employment rights that white males take for granted. In the absence of effective legal protection of their employment rights, the historical record clearly establishes that employers and unions engaged in blatant discrimination, making minorities and women second-class citizens.

Starting with halting uneven progress under the National Labor Relations Act, the apex of legal protection was embedded in the 1964 Civil Rights Act. Under the former, the National Labor Relations Board and federal courts eventually held labor unions may not discriminate against their black members and were required to afford them fair representation.

With the passage of the Civil Rights Act, equal employment opportunity for minorities and women became a matter of national policy. Title VII makes it illegal for an employer, including unions, to discriminate against employees on the basis of race, color, sex, religion, or national origin. To administer the law, Congress created the Equal Employment Opportunity Commission (EEOC). Given the complexity of the statute, the EEOC had difficulty establishing standards of conduct for employers so that they could determine illegal and legal practices under the law. Enforcement and remedies under the statute became a particularly serious problem. In addition, since the federal courts have the final authority to apply the law, they at times upset policies developed by the agency.

Areas of the law requiring interpretation and application included advertisements for hiring, employment records, testing and educational requirements, physical examinations, national origin, sexual harassment, homosexuality, pregnancy, fringe benefits including pensions and retirement plans, arbitration awards that involved Title

VII rights, religious discrimination, and the conditions of seniority within the context of discrimination.

By far the most controversial and difficult job facing the EEOC and federal courts concerned affirmative action. Although affirmative action as a weapon to deal with discrimination is not expressly mentioned in the Civil Rights Act, it became a matter of national policy. Supreme Court decisions on the issue, however, were not consistent. For a time it appeared that hiring and promotions were subject to affirmative action plans, but layoffs of white males would not be permitted to achieve balance in the racial and sexual composition of the work force. Supreme Court decisions in 1989, however, in effect made illegal any affirmative action plans. In 1990, Congress attempted to nullify those decisions.

Although the quest by minority and women employees for fair and equal employment opportunity has made significant progress under the Civil Rights Act, it would be erroneous to believe racism and sexism no longer exist. In the final analysis, the question facing the nation is: How far should public policy go to achieve true equality and fairness for employment opportunity by minority and women employees? To what extent should public policy be implemented to achieve that goal recognizing the competing interests of employers and white males?

The Civil Rights Act of 1991 appears to answer those hard questions in favor of minorities and women. At the present time, however, grave doubt exists as to whether that trend will continue. Indeed, as this volume goes to press, the conflict of affirmative action has reached a new level of intensity. White males voted overwhelmingly for Republican party candidates in the 1994 elections giving the Republican Party control of Congress for the first time in decades. No question exists that the Republican Party, looking at the presidential election of 1996, will either abolish or seriously undermine affirmative action.

Aware of the political realities of the situation, President Clinton announced that all regulations giving preference to minorities and women will be reviewed. He said the regulations that "work" will be retained, and those that "do not work" will be scrapped.

DISCUSSION QUESTIONS

1. Prior to 1964, could the NLRB have used national labor legislation or Supreme Court decisions to deal with employment discrimination against women and minorities? What was available for use in such cases prior to 1964? After 1964? After 1991?

2. Explain the procedures necessary to file Title VII complaints. Distinguish between *non-deferral* and *deferral* cases.

3. Three standards are applied by the courts in deciding Title VII discrimination cases. How might each standard affect the outcome of a case?

4. Explain how the Equal Employment Opportunity Commission deals with classified ads seeking job applicants.

5. What might constitute a bona fide occupational qualification (BFOQ) based on sex? Religion? Race?

6. In which important areas do you think that *Griggs* v. *Duke Power Co.* has had the most impact?

7. If the Equal Pay Act of 1963 was designed to deal with the issue of equal pay for equal work, how did the concept of comparable worth develop? Explain the concept of comparable worth, and discuss the impact that it might have on internal and external markets.

8. How does *Bundy* v. *Jackson* differ from *Fisher* v. *Flynn*? How might employers protect themselves from liability under *Bundy*?

9. Do you agree with the decision in *DeSantis*? Why or why not?

10. The treatment of pregnancy as any other disability is still a subject for debate and experimentation. What do you think should be included in a model policy on the issue?

11. What major economic problems are associated with nondiscriminatory pension plans?

12. A protected class under Title VII is national origin. Evaluate the *Espinoza* case in the context of that objective.

13. Evaluate affirmative action programs with respect to reverse discrimination and the integrity of collective bargaining agreements. (Hint: *Bakke* and *Stotts* may provide useful information.)

14. What theory do you consider most important to apply as a remedy to the effects of past discriminatory seniority systems? What effect would each have on all the impacted parties?

15. What is the significance of *Wards Cove*?

16. What are the implications for affirmative action of the *Wilks* decision?

17. Under the 1980 Age Discrimination Act, may an employer ever require an employee to retire because of age? If so, under what conditions?

NOTES

1   Included are the 1989 U.S. Supreme Court decisions relating to civil rights and the aftermath.

2   350 U.S. 892 (1955).

3   347 U.S. 483 (1954).

4   *Plessy* v. *Ferguson*, 163 U.S. 537 (1896).

5   *Wallace Corporation* v. *NLRB*, 323 U.S. 248 (1944); *Steele* v. *Louisville and Nashville Railroad*, 323 U.S. 197 (1944).

6   *Independent Metal Workers (Hughes Tool Company)*, 147 NLRB 166 (1964).

7   *Humphrey* v. *Moore*, 375 U.S. 335 (1964).

8   *Local 1367, International Longshoremen's Association (Galveston Maritime Association),* 148 NLRB 897 (1965), enf. 368 F. 2d 1010 (CA 5, 1966), cert. denied 389 U.S. 837 (1967).

9   *Local 12, Rubber Workers* v. *NLRB,* 368 F. 2d 12 (CA 5, 1966), cert. denied 389 U.S. 837 (1967).

10   See *San Diego Building Trades Council* v. *Garman,* 359 U.S. 236 (1959), whereby the U.S. Supreme Court held that "when an activity is arguably subject to sections 7 or 8 of the Act, the states as well as the federal courts must defer to the exclusive competence of the National Labor Relations Board."

11   *Farmers' Cooperative Compress* v. *United Packinghouse, Food and Allied Workers Union,* 416 F. 2d 1126 (1969), cert. denied 396 U.S. 903 (1969).

12   *Farmers' Cooperative Compress,* 194 NLRB 185 (1972).

13   *Emporium Capwell Co.* v. *Western Addition Community Organization,* 420 U.S. 50 (1975).

14   420 U.S. 72.

15   *Northwest Airlines, Inc.* v. *Air Line Pilots and Transport Workers,* 447 U.S. 920 (1981).

16   Benjamin Aaron, "Employee Rights and Union Democracy," *Monthly Labor Review,* XCII, 3 (March 1969), p. 50.

17   *Phalen* v. *Theatrical Protective Union No. 1, International Alliance of Theatrical & Stage Employees AFL-CIO,* 22 N.Y. 2d 34 (1968).

18   *Occidental Life Ins. Co.,* 14 FEP Cases 1718 (1977).

19   *EEOC and Hugh Stone III* v. *Gladdis,* 733 F. 2d 1373 (1984); *EEOC* v. *Detroit Edison Co.,* 515 F. 2d 301 (1975).

20   *Teamsters* v. *United States,* 431 U.S. 324 (1977) and *Hazelwood School District* v. *United States,* 433 U.S. 299 (1977); see J.P. McGuire, "The Use of Statistics in Title VII Cases," *Labor Law Journal,* XXX, 6 (June 1979), p. 361.

21   *Brush* v. *San Francisco Newspaper Printing Co.* (N D Calif.) 315 F. Supp. 577, 1970, affd. (9 Cir.), 469 F. 2d 89, 1972.

22   *Weeks* v. *Southern Bell Telephone and Telegraph Co.,* 409 F. 2d 228 (CA 5, 1969).

23   *Dothard* v. *Rawlinson,* 433 U.S. 321 (1977).

24   *Harper* v. *TWA, Inc.,* 525 F. 2d 409 (CA 8, 1975).

25   401 U.S. 424 (1971).

26   *Douglas* v. *Hampton,* CDC CA, February 27, 1975, Case No. 72-1376 (case remanded to Civil Service Commission).

27   *Detroit Edison Co.* v. *NLRB,* 440 U.S. 301 (1979).

28   *Spurlock* v. *United Airlines, Inc.,* 475 F. 2d 216 (CA 10, 1972).

29   *Kinsey* v. *First Regional Securities, Inc.* (DC CA), No. 75-1224, April 18, 1977; EEOC Decision No. 71-1504, March 25, 1971.

30   Unpublished paper by Karen S. Koziara, David A. Pierson, and Russell E. Johannesson, "The Comparable Worth Issue: Current Status and New Directions," Department of Industrial Relations and Organizational Behavior, Temple University, 1985.

31   *Washington County* v. *Alberta Gunther,* 452 U.S. 161 (1981).

32   *Williams* v. *Saxbe*, 413 F. Supp. 654 (D.C. 1976), reversed on other grounds *Williams* v. *Bell*, 587 F. 2d 1240 (D.C. Cir. 1978).

33   *Fisher* v. *Flynn*, 598 2d 663 (1st Cir. 1979).

34   *Bundy* v. *Jackson*, 641 F. 2d 934 (D.C. Cir. 1981).

35   *DeSantis* v. *Pacific Telephone and Telegraph Co., Inc.*, 608 F. 2d 327 (1979).

36   *Cleveland Board of Education* v. *La Fleur*, 414 U.S. 632 (1974).

37   *Turner* v. *Department of Employment Security*, 423 U.S. 44 (1975).

38   *General Electric Co.* v. *Gilbert*, 429 U.S. 881 (1976).

39   *Geduldig* v. *Aiello*, 94 U.S. 2485 (1974).

40   See *Bortmess* v. *Drewry's U.S.A., Inc.*, 444 F. 2d 1186 (1971), cert. denied, 92 U.S. 274 (1971); *Rosen* v. *Public Service Electric and Gas Co.*, 477 F. 2d 90 (CA 3, 1973).

41   *Wengler* v. *Druggists Mutual Insurance Co.*, 446 U.S. 142 (1980).

42   *Arizona Governing Commission* v. *Norris*, 463 U.S. 1073 (1983).

43   EEOC Decision No. 6-8-6654, M EPG Section 6021 (1969).

44   409 F. 2d 775 (1969).

45   467 F. 2d 54 (1972).

46   In Chapter 6, there is discussion of the circumstances under which the NLRB defers to arbitration under the *Collyer, Spielberg*, and *Banyard* doctrines.

47   443 F. 2d 1044 (1971).

48   428 F. 2d 303 (1970).

49   *Riley* v. *Bendix Corp.*, 464 F. 2d 1113 (CA 5, 1972).

50   *Trans World Airlines, Inc.* v. *Hardison*, 432 U.S. 63 (1977).

51   *Gray* v. *Gulf, Mobile and Ohio Railroad Co.*, 429 F. 2d 1064 (CA 5, 1970), cert. denied 401 U.S. 1001 (1971).

52   EEOC Decision No. 74-107, April 2, 1974.

53   *Espinoza* v. *Farah Manufacturing Co., Inc.*, 94 U.S. 334 (1973), aff. 462 F. 2d 1331 (CA 5, 1972).

54   *Espinoza* v. *Farah Manufacturing Co.*, 414 U.S. 86 (1973).

55   *Regents of the University of California* v. *Bakke*, 438 U.S. 265 (1978).

56   *United Steelworkers of America* v. *Weber*, 440 U.S. 193 (1979).

57   *Texas Department of Community Affairs* v. *Burdine*, 450 U.S. 248 (1981).

58   *U.S.* v. *Local 189, Papermakers*, 416 F. 2d 980 (5th Cir., 1969), cert. denied 397 U.S. 919 (1970).

59   *Heat, Frost and Asbestos Workers, Local 53* v. *Vogler*, 407 F. 2d 1047 (1969).

60   *Congressional Record*, April 8, 1964, p. 6992.

61   *Watkins* v. *United Steelworkers*, 369 F. Supp. 1221 (1974).

62   *U.S.* v. *Local 189, United Papermakers and Paperworkers*, 282 F. Supp. 39 (ED La., 1968), aff. 416 F. 2d 980 (5th Cir., 1969), cert. denied (U.S. S. Ct.) 397 U.S. 919 (1970).

63   Irving Kovarsky, *Discrimination in Employment* (Iowa City: Center for Labor and Management, 1976), pp. 84–85.

64   *Patterson* v. *The American Tobacco Co.* (ED Va., September 26, 1974), No. 104-73-R.

65   *Bing* v. *Roadway Express, Inc.*, 444 F. 2d 245 (1970), cert. denied 401 U.S. 954 (1971).

66   *Johnson* v. *Pike Corp. of America*, 332 F. Supp. 490 (1971).

67   EEOC Decision, Case No. CL-68-431 EU, December 16, 1969.

68   *Franks* v. *Bowman Transportation Co.*, 424 U.S. 747 (1976).

69   *International Brotherhood of Teamsters* v. *U.S.*; *T.I.M.E.-D.C., Inc.* v. *U.S.*, 431 U.S. 324 (1977).

70   424 U.S. 747 (1976).

71   Civil Rights Act of 1991, 102 Public 166, 105 Stat. 1071 (1991).

72   *Louisville Courier Journal*, Thursday October 17, 1991.

73   Robert Robinson, et al., "Equal Employment Requirements for Employers: A Closer Review of the Effects of the Civil Rights Act of 1991," *Labor Law Journal*, v. 43, November 1992, p. 725.

74   491 U.S. 1604 (1989).

75   490 U.S. 228 (1989).

76   Robinson, et al., *op. cit.*, p. 750.

77   Randall Kammeyer, "Disparate Impact Cases Under the Civil Rights Act of 1991," *Labor Law Journal*, v. 43, October 1992, p. 649.

78   Robinson, et al., *op. cit.*, p. 727.

79   Frederick Douglass, "The Civil Rights Act of 1991: Continual Allocation and the Retroactivity Controversy," *Labor Law Journal*, v. 44 March 1993, p. 153.

80   *Rivers* v. *Roadway Express, Inc.*, 114 S. Ct. 1510 (1994).

81   *Wall Street Journal*, April 27, 1994.

82   Roland Turner, "Affirmative Action and the Civil Rights Act of 1991," *Labor Law Journal*, v. 44 October 1993, p. 615.

83   *Forklift* v. *Harris*, 114 S. Ct. 367 (1993).

12 ❧

Labor Relations in the Public Sector

The issue of public employee collective bargaining reached unprecedented proportions in the decades of the sixties and seventies, primarily for two reasons. One was the rapid growth of government employment. The other was the issuance of Executive Order 10988 by President John F. Kennedy, as well as legislative action in many states. The Executive Order established the basic framework for collective bargaining in agencies under the executive branch of the federal government. All of these factors ushered in a new era of labor relations in the public sector. The new federal attitude toward employees prompted the states to reconsider many of their own employment practices. In fact, the federal government transferred employee bargaining rights from the executive orders to the Civil Service Reform Act of 1978.[1]

The public sector has experimented extensively with the issues, which have grown with the level of public-sector employment. This fact is revealed in the diverse pattern of treatment extended to workers in the fifty states and in the federal government. Some states have passed labor legislation to protect the collective bargaining rights of some state and local employees. Labor relations systems are generally governed by a wide variety of state laws, local ordinances, and federal statutes. For identical jobs, the collective bargaining rights of workers in the same locale are usually quite different for a state or local employee, a federal employee, and an employee in the private sector.

This chapter will focus on the diverse patterns of the states and the federal government for dealing with the employment conditions confronting workers in their jurisdictions.

Basis of Denial of Government Employee Bargaining

The doctrine of sovereignty has been used by government bodies as a basis for denying the collective bargaining process to public employees. Sovereignty may be defined as the supreme, absolute, and uncontrollable power by which any independent state is governed. Unionization of government workers is still viewed in some jurisdictions as interference with sovereign authority because it could lead to joint determination of wages, hours, and terms and conditions of employment. But the sovereignty doctrine is no longer as important as it once was.

The extension to public employees of the right to join unions was traditionally viewed as a surrender of power and a dereliction of duty. President Franklin Roosevelt made a distinction between public and private bargaining rights in 1937. He has often been quoted:

> The employer is the whole people, who speak by means of laws enacted by their representatives in Congress. Accordingly, administrative officials, and employees alike, are governed and guided, and in many instances restrained, by laws which establish policy procedures or rules in personal matters.[2]

Both the Wagner Act and the Taft-Hartley Act deliberately excluded all government employees from coverage under their provisions. Public Law 330 (1955) made a felony of federal employee strike activity.[3]

It has been advanced in recent years that a government has the authority to abandon traditional approaches to public employee bargaining. This may be done either by the legislative or executive branches of government. One writer concluded that

> the [sovereignty] doctrine does not preclude the enactment of legislation specifically authorizing the government to enter into collective bargaining relationships with its employees.[4]

Indeed, the concept of sovereignty has not prevailed as a hard and fast political concept over time. The federal government has long deviated from a policy of absoluteness.

It is frequently argued that the public is deprived of essential services if strikes result from bargaining impasses. One member of the House Post Office and Civil Service Committee assessed the public-interest argument this way:

> The trouble with the "public interest" concept is that it is only triggered in time of crisis. There's no "public interest" generated ahead of time, no particular show of concern for meeting the genuine economic and social needs of the public employee—whether he's a teacher, a fireman, a policeman, a clerk or a laborer. It's not until there is a direct, adverse effect on the body politic that the "public interest" is invoked—and then, of course, it's invoked against the public employee and on the side of the public administrator.[5]

A second argument that is used to deny public employee collective bargaining is known as the special status concept. Such workers are viewed as virtually immune from unemployment imposed by business cycles. Furthermore, it is alleged that their pensions and other fringe benefits are superior to those available in the private sector. The late 1970s and early 1980s revealed that public employees were more susceptible to problems experienced in the private sector than had been so in earlier years.

The doctrine of sovereignty is no longer capable of generating acceptance of the denial of collective action in the public sector. Various approaches have been used to deal with the employment difficulties of public employees.

COLLECTIVE BARGAINING AMONG FEDERAL EMPLOYEES

Early Development

Unionization of federal employees reportedly existed as early as 1800 in naval yards.[6] The Departments of Defense and Interior have a long history of collective bargaining. Wage-rate negotiations have occurred among various levels of TVA employees, ranging from those classed as production workers through the professional ranks. Negotiations have occurred despite the general understanding that wages are set by law.

Federal policy toward employee organizations dates back to 1883, when the Pendleton Act was passed. This Act is commonly known as the Civil Service Act. Under its terms, only Congress had the authority to regulate wages, hours, and other terms and conditions of employment.

President Theodore Roosevelt in 1902 banned federal employees from seeking legislation that would benefit them directly or indirectly through their associations, except through the departments in which they were employed. A violation of the order was grounds for dismissal.[7] In 1906, President Roosevelt broadened the earlier order, stating that

> all officers and employees of the United States of every description, serving in or under any of the Executive Departments or independent Government establishments, and whether so serving in or out of Washington, are hereby forbidden, either directly or indirectly, individually or through associations, to solicit an increase of pay or to influence or attempt to influence in their own interest any other legislation whatever, either before Congress or its Committees, or in any way save through the heads of the Departments or independent Government establishments, in or under which they serve, on penalty of dismissal from the Government service.[8]

Congress took up the question of federal employee organization in 1912. It rejected the approach of President Theodore Roosevelt in the Lloyd-La Follette Act.[9] The statute became the basis for the principle that federal employees in general had the right to join any organization that did not assert the right to strike against the government.[10] If a literal interpretation is made of it, the Act limited protection of union membership to postal employees. Despite that fact, other employees gained the right to organize on the basis of its language. The right to organize, however, is of limited value if procedures are not provided to guarantee an effective collective bargaining process. The Lloyd-La Follette Act did not provide such machinery.

Construction of the Alaskan railroad, which began in 1914, provided another boon to federal employee bargaining. Most of the construction workers on the railroad had already been organized prior to the time work was to start. The government negotiated its first written labor agreement, with these workers, in 1920.[11]

The Boston police officer's strike in the 1920s slowed the drive toward more effective collective bargaining machinery among all public employees—federal, state, and local alike. However, instances of collective bargaining arrangements occurred throughout the period of the thirties despite the damage done by the Boston strike. Renewed efforts to obtain more favorable bargaining legislation started in the 1940s.

The Rhodes-Johnston Bill was introduced in 1949 as a measure to protect the right of unions to represent federal employees. It failed to pass in that year and was debated for fourteen years.[12] Essentially, the bill was designed primarily to provide for the resolving of grievances within the various federal agencies. A large number of weaknesses in the bill were partially responsible for its not being passed.

The Classification Act of 1949 contained a section that facilitates union influence on wages. It provides that wage board employees' compensation

> shall be fixed and adjusted from time to time as nearly as is consistent with the public interest in accordance with prevailing wages.

The provision makes it possible to affect wage rates by negotiating on the items that determine the outcome. These are (1) the geographic area to be covered; (2) the firms to be included or excluded in the survey; (3) key jobs to be used as a basis for gathering wage information; and (4) the number of jobs to be surveyed. The 1949 provisions therefore enhanced the power of some unions to influence the wage rates paid their members.

The Postal Service

The U.S. Postal Service is not subject to Title VII of the Civil Service Reform Act of 1978. It was removed from cabinet status to that of an independent government agency by the Postal Reorganization Act of 1970. Postal employees were removed from coverage under executive order labor policy and given collective bargaining rights comparable to those governing private industry.

The pay comparability principle covering federal workers was retained in the law, and progression through the pay grades was compressed from 21 to 8 years. The process of collective bargaining was designated to guide the operation of these provisions.

The National Labor Relations Board was authorized to determine the appropriateness of bargaining units, supervise representation elections, and enforce unfair labor practice provisions permitted in the 1970 law. Even though the Act authorized collective bargaining on wages and working conditions under laws that apply to private industry, it continued the prohibition against strikes. Final and binding arbitration could be utilized only after an impasse had persisted for 180 days after the start of bargaining.

Postal employees have never had a statutory right to strike, even though some have engaged in work stoppages. As a matter of fact, one federal court ruled that the right to strike could not be denied if the right had never existed in the first place.[13] There was a two-week strike by 225,000 postal workers in 1970. The 1975 and the 1981 National Postal Agreements were signed only after postal workers threatened strike action. The six-month delay on submitting issues to arbitration by virtue of law may not provide an adequate alternative to strike action. In 1978, the no-strike provision was again tested.

Union-shop arrangements are prohibited; in this regard the Postal Reorganization Act retained the basic union security limitations of the executive orders.

Overall, federal collective bargaining is evolving closer to private-sector practices. Postal Service experiences will undoubtedly have some influence over practices adopted under the executive orders. On the other hand, state and local collective bargaining rights continue to remain varied, with no significant pattern in the relaxation of traditional restrictions.

Federal Reserve System

The Federal Reserve System remains under its own bargaining system, separate from the Civil Service Reform Act of 1978. On May 9, 1969, the Board of Governors of the Federal Reserve System issued a statement of policies concerning employee-management relations within the system.[14] The statement was patterned after the executive order system but took into account the special responsibilities of the system under the terms of the Federal Reserve Act and related statutes. It recognized the right of certain classes of employees to join or to refrain from joining labor organizations. Procedures were provided for recognition of labor organizations, bargaining-unit determinations, and elections. Grievance machinery was established, along with a list of unfair labor practice prohibitions.

The Board of Governors issued its "Policy on Unionization and Collective Bargaining for the Federal Reserve Banks," because of the exclusion of the system from both the Taft-Hartley Act and the Executive Order.

A few features of the policy require comment. Professional employees are given the right to organize, as long as they belong to bargaining units separate from those that represent the other bank employees. Bank guards also have the right to organize into separate labor organizations. Therefore, some of the NLRB policies dealing with bargaining units have been incorporated into the policy statement.

Exclusive recognition of a labor organization is available after an election is held. At least 30 percent of employees of an appropriate bargaining unit must sign representation request cards. Once this is achieved, an election is held under the auspices of the American Arbitration Association. A union will receive exclusive recognition if a majority of at least 60 percent of eligible bargaining-unit employees cast votes for representation. Discontinuance of a labor organization's exclusive status is determined by the same procedure; however, only one election may be held in any unit in a twelve-month period.

Unfair labor practice prohibitions are fashioned after those contained in Taft-Hartley. Both parties are required to bargain collectively and are prohibited from interfering with employee organizational rights guaranteed by the system's policy.

Administration of the provision is vested in a three-member Federal Reserve System Labor Relations Panel. The panel is fashioned after the Federal Labor Relations Council established by Executive Order 11491. Two of the panel members are from the Board of Governors and one is a public member. All three are selected by the Board of Governors. The panel is charged with the responsibility for establishing regulations and procedures similar to those applicable to unions and management in the private sector. The Board of Governors reserves the right to amend its labor relations policies without notice, provided that all labor organizations are informed of any changes. Amendments will not be applied retroactively.

The Federal Reserve System's labor relations policy has the strength of incorporating many of the essential features of both the Taft-Hartley Act and the Executive Order. The potentially most serious weakness is the possibility of considerable shifts in policy as the membership of the Board of Governors changes. It may be that pressures will continue to be placed upon Congress to provide statutory rights for Federal Reserve employee collective bargaining, as is the case with federal employees organized under executive order provisions.

CIVIL SERVICE REFORM ACT OF 1978: TITLE VII

The current framework within which collective bargaining is structured in federal agencies evolved from the initial Executive Order 10988 issued by President Kennedy in January 1962, through President Nixon's revision in 1970 (Executive Order 11491, entitled "Labor-Management Relations in the Federal Service"), and up to President Ford's further amendment in 1975 in Executive Order 11838. The essential features of the executive order framework, procedures, and practices provided the basis for the Civil Service Reform Act of 1978. Title VII of the law superseded E.O. 11491 in January 1979. The State Department continued to operate under the Executive Order until the Foreign Service Act of 1980 was passed.

Administrative Structure

Title VII gave federal labor relations the stability of law. It organized the bargaining system into the Office of Personnel Management (OPM), the Merit System Protection Board (MSPB), and the Federal Labor Relations Authority (FLRA).

The Office of Personnel Management has delegated functions that are subject to further delegation to agency heads. Rule-making of the OPM is subject to consultation with labor organizations over any substantive changes made in personnel regulations.

The Merit System Protection Board was granted authority to review Office of Personnel Management regulations and to invalidate them if in violation of the prohibited personnel practices detailed in Title I of the Civil Service Reform Act of 1978. A three-member board is empowered to obtain testimony and evidence to decide issues before it. It may order corrective action of any agency found in violation of the Act's provisions. Also, the Merit System Protection Board may discipline federal employees prosecuted by the Special Counsel to the Board. Such actions may include removal, reduction in grade, or reprimands, among others.

The Federal Labor Relations Authority took over the functions previously performed by the Federal Labor Relations Council under the former executive orders. The Authority was made independent from the executive branch by protecting tenure of its three members for five-year terms. In large measure, the Authority is modeled on the National Labor Relations Board, and includes a General Counsel to prosecute unfair labor practice complaints.

The Authority administers the law to meet the special needs of the federal system. It has somewhat the same powers as its predecessor, the Federal Labor Relations Council. The Council functioned under the executive orders and members were ex officio part time. Members were the Secretary of Labor, the Director of the Office of Management and Budget, and the chair of the Civil Service Commission.

The Department of State remained under Executive Order 11636 until the Foreign Service Act of 1980 was passed. A Federal Labor Relations Board was established to administer labor relations in the State Department. Other employees covered by this law work in the International Communications Agency, the International Development Cooperation Agency, and the Departments of Commerce and Agriculture. The Foreign Service Relations Board has a connection with the Federal Labor Relations Authority through a common chair. Board decisions must by law be consistent with decisions of the Authority under the Civil Service Reform Act of 1978.

The Federal Service Impasse Panel's authority under Executive Order 11491 to "take any action it considers necessary to settle an impasse" remains virtually the same under the 1978 law. The Federal Mediation and Conciliation Service provides its services, and in practice it determines "under what circumstances and in what manner it shall proffer its services." Generally, the panel becomes involved in disputes only after the FMCS has bowed out of them.

The Assistant Secretary of Labor for Labor-Management Relations during the executive order era had authority to resolve disputes over the makeup of bargaining units and representation rights, to order and supervise elections, and to disqualify unions from recognition because of corrupt or undemocratic influences. The Assistant Secretary of Labor function was terminated in the 1978 law because the Federal Labor Relations Authority has its own staff.

Recognition and Elections

Exclusive recognition is the only form that is available to unions representing federal employees. Such recognition must be established in a secret ballot election by a majority of employees in an appropriate bargaining unit. The Authority may withhold exclusive recognition from a labor organization if it is subject to corrupt influences, fails to represent at least 30 percent of the unit, or if there is an election bar to such recognition. There are other comparatively minor circumstances when recognition may be withheld.

Unit Appropriateness

The Authority determines the appropriateness of a bargaining unit. It will consider several factors in arriving at a determination, such as extent of organization, an identifiable community of interest among employees, and whether a union will promote an effective relationship with the agency. National consultation rights provided by the Act were not available under the executive orders. If an organization with exclusive rights does not exist, then one that represents a substantial number of employees of the agency may obtain national consultation rights from the Authority. The Authority has the power to determine criteria for national consultation designation. Essentially, an exchange of views is provided for, with the agency involved obligated to inform the labor organization of reasons why a given action was finally undertaken.

Employee Categories in Unit Determinations

Managerial employees are not eligible for bargaining unit inclusion except in cases where they were represented by labor organizations that historically or traditionally represented management workers in private industry. Also, the specialized organization had to have held exclusive rights at the time the 1978 law became effective in 1979.

Confidential employees, or those in positions of trust with supervisors and management officials, are not to be placed into bargaining units. The fear is that the agency could be compromised by such inclusion. Professional employees may not be placed into units with any other employees unless they vote to be included with nonprofessionals.

Employees who administer any provisions of the labor relations law may join unions if such unions are separate from those that represent other workers. These unions may not even be indirectly affiliated with other organizations.

Employees who are engaged in work that directly affects national security or internal security are not eligible for membership in an appropriate bargaining unit. Guards do not fall within these general prohibitions. The excluded categories must be involved in administration of security matters, such as deciding whether duties are discharged honestly and with integrity.

Military personnel are forbidden from union membership in the United States by the Thurmond Act of 1979. The Teamsters and the American Federation of Government Employees once threatened to organize enlisted military personnel. Their motive, perhaps as much as anything else, could have been to influence the outcome of the Civil Service Reform Act, which was under consideration by Congress at the time. The Thurmond Act makes it a felony for (1) enlisted personnel to join a union; (2) anyone to solicit enlisted personnel to join a union; (3) military officers or designees to recognize or bargain with a union; and (4) a union to attempt to bargain for enlisted personnel.

Actually, the Department of Defense has a long history of bargaining with civilian employees, dating back to approximately 1830. Many civilians in the Department of Defense perform jobs comparable to some in the military, and these employees do have bargaining rights.

In situations where there are two or more units in an agency for which a labor organization is the exclusive representative, consolidation into a larger single unit may be permitted by the Authority. The Authority may be petitioned for such by either the labor organization or the agency, or both. The Authority may permit the petition with or without an election if it considers the proposed larger unit appropriate.

Bars to Elections

The Act identifies three bars to elections. One is an election bar, which means that if an election has been held within the previous twelve months, a new one will not be approved.

A second is a certification bar to an election. This bar exists if exclusive rights have been granted to another labor organization through an election held within the previous twelve months.

The third bar to an election is a contract bar. The Act defines a contract bar as a lawful written agreement in effect for less than three years.

Labor Organizations and Recognition

Agencies may only grant exclusive recognition to labor organizations that are "free from corrupt influences and influences opposed to basic democratic principles." In this respect, several Landrum-Griffin provisions applicable to unions in the private sector are prescribed for federal employee representatives. These include the holding of periodic elections, member rights to participate in internal organization affairs, and the filing of financial and other reports with the Assistant Secretary of Labor for Labor Management Relations.

A labor organization may not be extended exclusive bargaining status by the Authority if it is involved willfully or intentionally in a strike, slowdown, or work stoppage. It must take positive corrective action in such events or be subject to the Authority's rescinding exclusive status and legal representation rights. It is an unfair labor practice for a labor organization to call or participate in strikes, picketing, or work stoppages or slowdowns, or even to condone such activity.

In October 1981, the Federal Labor Relations Authority revoked the right of the Professional Air Traffic Controllers Organization (PATCO) to represent air traffic controllers. The reason for the decertification order was a strike called by the union in August 1981. Striking air controllers were dismissed by the Reagan administration for violation of strike prohibitions in federal employment. The decertification order marked the first time that a union lost its status as legal representative of a group of federal workers. The permanently replaced strikers were denied reinstatement. Programs to train replacements were developed after the wholesale dismissals, in order to support the administration's stated resolve not to recall strikers to duty or declare them eligible for alternative federal employment.

Union Conduct

The Civil Rights Act of 1964, Title VII, plus the 1972 amendments to it, establish Equal Employment Opportunity requirements for unions. Labor organizations representing government workers are prohibited from discriminating in their terms or conditions for membership on the basis of race, color, creed, sex, age, or national origin.

Communists are excluded from "office holding as are persons affiliated with other totalitarian movements." Persons identified with corrupt influences are also prohibited from office holding.

Scope of Bargaining

The parties must bargain in good faith on negotiable issues. The basic scope of bargaining remains about the same as it was under the executive orders. The 1978 law expanded labor organization rights in this regard by permitting negotiations without regard to agency regulations. The Act specifies and clarifies management rights. Agency officials have the right to make unilateral decisions on items not subject to bargaining. These include determination of the agency's mission, budget, organization, number of employees, and internal security. Management is also given the full right to determine whether work will be performed within the unit or subcontracted to personnel outside of the agency. Permissible items for bargaining are specified, and include methods, means, and technology of conducting agency operations.

Illegal items for bargaining are also covered. Some of these include retirement, life and health insurance, and suspension or removal for national security reasons.

Considerable concern developed over possible conflicts between internal agency regulations and conflicting bargaining proposals presented by unions. The 1975 Ford Order changes were designed to broaden the scope of permissible negotiations at local levels by restricting the regulatory authority of federal agencies. The view of the Federal Labor Relations Council in its recommendations to President Ford was that in many situations, higher-level agency regulations were not critical to effective agency management or to the public interest and, therefore, were unduly restrictive of negotiations.[15] After 1975, agency regulations would bar negotiations only if a compelling need for the regulations could be established. The council decided on a case-by-case basis whether a compelling need existed in the context of its rules outlining permissible limits. The overall effect was to broaden the scope of collective bargaining at the local agency levels. The 1978 law reaffirmed these developments.

Federal labor relations under the statute differ from those in the private sector in that some items may not be bargained on (e.g., budget, mission) under any circumstances. Management rights *may* be bargained, but management is not required *initially* to bargain on these issues. However, if bargaining on management rights *is* initiated, the defense that it is a management right is not controlling, and an unfair labor practice may result. Thus, some issues are mandatorily bargainable, some are mandatorily nonnegotiable, and some are, in effect, "optionally" bargainable.

The use of work time to negotiate agreements has been controversial. The 1962 order permitted a wide range of practices for allowing union negotiators to be paid while negotiating a contract. In 1969, union negotiators could not be paid at all for negotiating during working hours. The 1971 modification permitted the parties to agree to pay union representatives a maximum of forty hours of official time, or a maximum of one-half the total time spent in negotiations. The issue of whether or not to permit negotiators to be paid within the allowable limits of forty hours of official time required substantial negotiation time to determine and left little if any clock time to settle other matters. The law now requires that union representatives be on official time and be paid for time spent in negotiations equal to the official time and compensation provided to management officials.

Grievance and Arbitration Procedures

From 1962 to 1970, the parties could negotiate a grievance procedure to apply the terms of an existing labor agreement. The capstone step, however, provided only for advisory arbitration, not for final and binding arbitration, as is common in the private sector. There was, therefore, no impartial procedure for breaking deadlocks in contract negotiations. The federal agency involved in the negotiations made the final decisions concerning all disputes.

In 1970, the amended order required that a grievance procedure must be negotiated by the parties. Applicable grievances were to be exclusively resolved through the negotiated device. Grievable issues were limited to interpretation or application of the contract. The order excluded matters from the negotiated grievance procedure which were subject to a statutory appeals system, as well as issues concerned with the application or interpretation of agency policy. The 1975 amendments excluded only matters subject to statutory appeals. Since 1975, grievances over agency policies and regulations have been processed through the negotiated system. The 1975 Executive Order amendments opened up considerably the range of potential coverage of a negotiated grievance procedure. Except for statutory appeals rights, the potential to negotiate was left to the parties.

In 1962, the Civil Service Commission issued standards limiting the procedures that could be negotiated by agencies and unions. Advisory arbitration was permitted, but only if the employee concerned gave approval, and even then it was limited to an interpretation or application of negotiated agreements or agency policy. Dual systems were permissible in that a negotiated grievance procedure and a separate agency grievance system could exist side by side. In 1970, dual grievance systems could be eliminated through negotiation. They remained permissible. Whichever system was negotiated, it had to conform to the requirements established by the Civil Service Commission. Since 1975, there were no restrictions on negotiated grievance procedures as long as they did not conflict with the statute or Executive Order. If, for example, the order did not specifically exclude an item from the bargaining process, it was a matter for determination through the negotiated grievance system, even if the issue involved an agency policy or regulation not contained in the collective bargaining contract.

The 1978 law says that negotiated grievance procedures must be the exclusive ones for resolving grievances available to bargaining-unit employees, except in the case of adverse action and Equal Employment Opportunity (EEO) cases, when the employee may use either the negotiated procedure or the statutory appeals procedure—but not both. Employees not in the bargaining unit or employees eligible but not represented by a union have access only to the agency procedure. The applicability of *Alexander* v. *Gardner-Denver* (treated in Chapter 11), which permits the use of both procedures in EEO cases, is uncertain as far as unrepresented employees are concerned.

Arbitration is the final step of negotiated grievance procedures. The process may be invoked by either the labor organization or the agency. The arbitrator's award may be appealed to the Authority for review, but it will not be overturned unless the award is

1. contrary to any law, rule, or regulation; or
2. inconsistent with federal court standards or those applied by the NLRB in its *Spielberg* standards.

Exceptions to an arbitrator's award must be taken within thirty days, or else the award will be final and binding.

Union Security

Title VII of the Civil Service Reform Act forbids arrangements requiring union membership as a condition of employment. Exclusive recognition requires that a union represent all employees in the bargaining unit, even if they do not hold membership in the labor organization. In the private sector, as we learned, federal law permits the union shop or lesser arrangements unless the states prohibit them.

Dues checkoff, a form of financial union security, is permitted if the employee has authorized the union as the exclusive representative. Once allowed, dues checkoff is not revocable for one year. No charge is assessed for the service. Unions in units with 10 percent or more membership, but where no exclusive representative exists, also have dues checkoff rights.

Unfair Labor Practices and Their Resolution

Unfair labor practices largely reflect those established under the Taft-Hartley law. A government agency violates the terms of the order if it interferes with the right of employees to join unions; encourages or discourages membership in a union by discrimination in regard to hiring, tenure, promotion, or other conditions of employment; refuses to recognize a union qualified for recognition; or refuses to negotiate with a union that has secured exclusive bargaining rights. A union engages in an unfair labor practice if it interferes with the right of employees not to join a union; coerces or

fines a member as punishment for the purpose of impeding his or her work performance, productivity, or duties as a government employee; engages in strikes or slowdowns or fails to take appropriate action to prevent or stop a strike; or refuses to
bargain collectively.

Union unfair labor practices are expanded beyond those of Taft-Hartley in that a
union cannot interfere with a member's performance as an employee. Unions also
cannot discriminate on the basis of race, color, creed, national origin, sex, age, preferential or nonpreferential civil service status, political affiliation, marital status, or
handicapping condition. To do so constitutes an unfair labor practice.

Informational picketing that does not interfere with an agency's operations is
expressly eliminated from being an unfair labor practice. It is, however, an unfair
labor practice to call, or to participate in, a strike, slowdown, or the picketing of an
agency in a labor-management dispute if such picketing does interfere with an
agency's operations.

Labor organizations have a right to set reasonable admission standards without
committing an unfair labor practice if these standards are uniformly required and
administered. Thus, a person may be denied membership if occupational standards
for admission are not met and may be denied membership or expelled for nonpayment
of dues.

The Federal Labor Relations Authority interprets unfair labor practices that
come before it in the same way that the NLRB interprets the Taft-Hartley law. Regional
directors and administrative law judges are appointed by the Authority to apply its
rules and policies in cases that come before them.

An unfair labor practice charge is investigated by the General Counsel's office.
If a complaint is issued, then the case is set for a formal hearing. The labor organization or agency involved has a right to answer the complaint at the hearing. Informal
methods of resolution are available in the Authority's regulations. Formal orders are
issued to support the findings demanding corrective action.

*Final orders of the Authority may be appealed to the appropriate court of
appeals, and judicial enforcement may be requested by the Authority.*

Contract Negotiation Impasses

Impasses between labor organizations and agencies are provided for in the 1978
statute. The Federal Mediation and Conciliation Service decides under which circumstances and in what manner it will provide services and assistance as it did under the
former executive order. If other efforts also fail, either party may request that the
Federal Service Impasse Panel consider the matter. Prior to this step, though, the
parties may seek binding arbitration of the impasse, subject to Panel approval.

Once the Impasse Panel is involved, it holds a prehearing meeting and then may
proceed along various courses of action to deal with the dispute. *Fact finding, recommendations for settlement, and directed settlement may be required.* The arsenal of
weapons approach is utilized by the Federal Impasse Panel, the only federal dispute
settlement agency that does so.

The Panel is able to settle most disputes prior to formal recommendations for settlement. So-called "informal settlements" are actually mandatory. Moreover, if the parties have not sought and secured mediation, this too will be directed and the recommendation followed. The Federal Service Impasse Panel is generally effective in its mission.

A special expedited procedure for most negotiability disputes is provided in the law to determine whether an item is subject to negotiation. The matter may be taken to the Authority to decide whether a compelling need exists for any rule or regulation of the agency. Impasses that occur in this category may be resolved quickly by the Authority, without General Counsel involvement in the procedure.

Assessment

Collective bargaining experience was gained in the federal sector under the Executive Orders. Periodic reviews made the system more viable. The Civil Service Reform Act of 1978 provided a statutory basis for the federal labor relations program. The Office of Personnel Management has estimated that approximately 70 percent of eligible federal employees are represented by labor organizations, whereas less than one-half of these are members. Collective bargaining practices in the federal sector have grown closer to those of the private sector, though there remain some sharp differences. In any event, the new law made a number of changes that have improved labor relations in general.

COLLECTIVE BARGAINING AT THE STATE AND LOCAL LEVELS

Right to Join Unions

Whereas federal civilian employment has remained more or less constant, state and local government employment has more than doubled.[16] Total public-sector employment is about 16 million of which federal civilians amount to about 3 million. In general, there are many more local government workers than at the state level. There is generally no uniform pattern to bargaining rights available through state and local governments. For example, some states have no policy whatever. At the local level, New York, Detroit, and San Francisco have had across-the-board bargaining for decades. It may well be that as many as 8 million workers, or well over one-half of all state and local government employees, are represented by unions. They are represented by the National Education Association affiliates, American Federation of Teachers, Fraternal Order of Police, International Association of Fire Fighters, American Federation of State and Municipal Employees, County Laborers, Teamsters, and a large number of unaffiliated independent labor organizations. Many states dwell on collective bargaining controls through statutes, court pronouncements, or attorneys' general opinions, such as prohibitions on work stoppages.

In 1969, a federal court of appeals determined the right of public employees to join unions.[17] The issue presented to the appellate court in the *Woodward* case was whether public employees discharged because of union membership have a right to seek injunctions and sue for damages those public officials who discharged them. A solution to the basic issue required a determination of whether public employees have a constitutionally protected right to belong to a union.

The court ruled unanimously that union membership is protected by the right of association under the First and Fourteenth Amendments. The court quoted an earlier ruling that the right of assembly protects more than the right to attend a meeting. It includes "the right to express one's attitudes or philosophies by membership in a group or by affiliation with it or by other lawful means."[18]

Public officials who violate the public employees' constitutional right of association are subject to court action for damages. A different appellate court decision was quoted in reaching this conclusion. It stated:

> It is settled that teachers have the right of free association, and unjustified interference with teachers' associational freedom violates the Due Process clause of the Fourteenth Amendment . . . Public Employment may not be subjected to unreasonable conditions, and the assertion of First Amendment rights by teachers will usually not warrant their dismissal. . . . Unless there is some illegal intent, an individual's right to form and join a union is protected by the First Amendment.[19]

The guaranteed right to join a union may be important to a worker, but that right is not effective if there is no procedure to protect it—such as required recognition of a labor organization representing a majority of bargaining-unit workers and, thereafter, good-faith collective bargaining. Other courts will not necessarily rule the same as the Seventh and Eighth Circuit Courts of Appeals. Conflicting rules may eventually result in a Supreme Court decision on the issue. In the meantime, the states vary in their interpretation of public employee collective bargaining rights.

Status of State Laws

Some states have enacted comprehensive public sector labor relations laws covering state, county, and municipal employees. These laws reflect Taft-Hartley but contain provisions designed to deal with problems in the public sector. As of 1994, twenty-nine states had in effect comprehensive public-sector laws. In 1992 New Mexico enacted its legislation of this type, having the distinction of being the last state passing such a law.[20] There would have been thirty states with such laws, but the Indiana Supreme Court held the general legislation invalid under the state's constitution limiting the public sector law to teachers.

As of 1994 the following states were without comprehensive public employee labor relation laws: Alabama, Arizona, Arkansas, Colorado, Georgia, Idaho, Indiana, Kentucky, Louisiana, Maryland, Mississippi, Missouri, Nevada, North Carolina, North Dakota, Oklahoma, South Carolina, Tennessee, Texas, Virginia, and West Virginia. With the exception of Kentucky and Indiana these are the right-to-work states demonstrating labor's political power is not effective in those states.

Some states have enacted labor relations laws which apply to a specific class of employees, such as the Indiana law which covers only teachers. Aside from teachers, other special groups, mainly police and firefighters, are covered by special public-sector laws. Most states outlaw strikes but only a comparatively small number have procedures to resolve labor disputes.

Dispute settlement provisions vary. A few states require compulsory arbitration if other methods fail. However, the requirement of compulsory arbitration is often limited to certain groups, such as police officers, teachers, and firefighters. Some states permit voluntary, binding arbitration of interest items, including the states of Delaware, New York, and Vermont. Final and binding arbitration is authorized in some states, although some employee classifications are exempted and it is not unusual to limit arbitrable items. Wages and salaries are often subject to arbitration. Consequently, for the majority of states, there is no adequate dispute settlement machinery designed to deal with the economic issues that most trouble public employees.

Bargaining is authorized but not required in some states. There is no penalty, however, for refusals to bargain or for refusals to meet and confer. Usually the "meet and confer" laws are enforced by state lower courts rather than by a specialized labor agency. For employees in several states, as in Arkansas and Mississippi, there are no provisions whatever on either bargaining permissiveness or meeting and conferring. Obviously, some states, through silence, encourage power conflicts between public employers and employees. Work stoppages may thus force legislative action. Once meetings and conferences are forced by such pressures, it may be more difficult to establish conditions within which constructive negotiations can prevail.

Considerable uncertainty regarding bargaining rights faces public employees in a large number of states. In some cases, rights are spelled out for certain categories of workers, but not for others. Even if public employees are dealt with uniformly in a particular state or lesser political jurisdiction, the mere difference of treatment in other states is enough to create instability in employment relations. Union organizers supply the comparative information to workers. This situation may be termed a "demonstration effect." Public workers in a municipality, or in a state that does not protect collective bargaining, become malcontents when bargaining rights are observed for employees performing similar tasks in other states. Indeed, the ability of federal employees to engage in limited and growing bargaining activities within the same state serves also to frustrate state and local employees deprived of the same right.

Agitation for equal bargaining rights is likely to persist among public employees. Public pressure forces government agencies to maintain a constant flow of public services, and there is considerable pressure to expand and improve services when per capita income rises. It is difficult to adhere to traditional practices in the face of widespread employee dissatisfaction. Disruption of services could invoke the wrath of the general public, which in turn could lead to losses at the polls, and eventually to new public employers. These factors, including widespread strikes among public employees, will probably result in more and more recognition of public employee unions.

Selected categories of state and local treatment of collective bargaining are provided to permit comparisons with private and federal practices.

The Right to Strike

There is no more explosive issue in the public sector than the right of public employees to strike. A majority of states have outlawed strikes through legislation, court decisions, or attorney-general opinions. A lesser number either permit a limited right to strike or have relaxed strike penalties to the point that in effect, a deterrent does not exist. The states that permit a limited right to strike are Illinois, Vermont, Montana, Pennsylvania, Hawaii, Alaska, Minnesota, Oregon, Rhode Island, and Wisconsin. Alaska permits strikes by employees in the nonessential category and extends a limited right to semiessential workers. The problem is in the definition of which public employees are nonessential, and which are essential or semiessential. Hawaii extends a limited right to strike; strikes endangering public health and safety are prohibited. The determination of which strikes endanger public health and safety is made by the Public Employment Relations Board. Thus, in Hawaii, strike legality depends on the basic philosophy of Board personnel which, of course, can change over relatively short periods of time. Pennsylvania law also extends a limited right to strike to state and local employees. Many strikes have occurred, however, with minimal interference. The courts may prohibit strikes that they deem to constitute a clear and present danger or threat to health, safety, or welfare of the public.

It is obvious that the right to strike is not as liberal in those states that permit a limited version as might be thought on the face of the laws. Most public bodies with authority to decide strike legality will hold generally false conceptions of the effect that public employee strikes will have and will prohibit them far beyond any real need to do so. In this respect, the politics of the moment may prevail over rational economic judgment. It has been demonstrated that because of technology, excess capacity, and the ability to substitute and postpone demand for services often performed by the public sector, most public employee strikes will impose little or no economic cost, only some inconvenience in substituting or in delay. State legislatures should spend more time developing strike safeguards instead of evading the problem by merely outlawing strikes.

An increasing number of unions and employee organizations are changing their traditional policy of no-strike pledges. In 1963, the American Federation of Teachers issued a policy statement supporting strikes under certain conditions. The American Federation of State, County, and Municipal Employees Union followed this example in 1966. In one study it was found that, of twenty unions composed primarily of public employees, eight had constitutional bans on strikes and eight others did not refer to the issue in their union constitutions.[21]

Public employee union leaders contend that without the right to strike employers will not negotiate in good faith. A former union official, speaking for the International Association of Fire Fighters, remarked:

> Certain arbitrary public officials knowing that we cannot and will not strike because we voluntarily gave up the right in 1918 when we were founded, have certainly taken advantage of the professional firefighters across the land. As a matter of fact, the record will show we have been exploited by such arbitrary public officials who oft time dared us to strike, knowing that we would not.[22]

Various penalties have from time to time been imposed upon striking employees. In 1947, New York passed the Condon-Wadlin Act, which permitted reemployment of strikers but eliminated their pay increases for a period of three years. Reinstated strikers were also considered temporary employees for a period of five years. The 1967 New York Taylor Act eliminated the ban on pay raises but provided instead for dismissal or fines. A labor organization is subject to loss of dues checkoff privileges for as long as eighteen months, plus fines, for engaging in strikes. In effect, strike activity is no longer subject to serious restraints in New York, although as a practical matter, any striker runs the risk of losing a job, whether in public or private employment.

In Michigan, state employees are subject to discharge or financial penalties for striking. Massachusetts provides that striking municipal workers may be fined $100. Most states reserve the right to discharge striking public employees, although this is not clearly spelled out in legislation.[23] In the 1970s, Wisconsin, Maine, and South Dakota either lowered or eliminated strike penalties.

Laws prohibiting public employee strikes have not been successful in their objective. In 1966, the first full year after Michigan amended its public employee relations act, there were twenty-three strikes in the public sector. This number of strikes was more than had occurred in the previous twenty years.[24] In the next year, the number of strikes in Michigan almost doubled. Other states have experienced increased strike threats even if actual work stoppages have not materialized. Part of the problem can be traced to the nature of bargaining structures, which delay agreements. Even if the parties come to agreement, the appropriate legislative body has to pass a law on the subject. If it does not, or the law is different, difficulties result.

Government employee strikes increased between 1960 and 1980. Over 90 percent of all government strikes occur at the local level. In 1960, there were 33 stoppages at the local level, but in 1980, there were 493. There was a substantial increase in strike activity after 1965, but by 1994, the level of strike activity had fallen dramatically. Teachers account for more than one-half of local government strikes.[25] Most strikes occur in public education. Local school boards tend not to resolve teacher employment problems but merely discuss them without providing answers. Past practices of school boards will have to be altered if relative peace is to be achieved in public education. In general, public employees are expressing a growing dissatisfaction with their wages and conditions of work. States without adequate provisions for resolving disputes or establishing bargaining relationships should expect work stoppages caused by the lack of alternatives for dealing with employee problems.

Union Security Practices

As noted earlier, union-security agreements are forbidden under the Civil Service Reform Act of 1978 for federal employees, except for dues checkoff. The states have a variety of practices. Alaska, Kentucky, Vermont, and Washington permit the union shop. In Washington, the agency shop is authorized for employees who object to union membership on religious grounds.

The states of Alaska, Hawaii, Massachusetts, Michigan, Montana, Oregon, Rhode Island, Vermont, and Wisconsin authorize the agency shop. As long as the fee paid to a union is not used for political activity in case the employee objects, the U.S. Supreme Court has authorized agency-shop clauses in public employee contracts.[26] New Mexico prohibits the arrangement. Only Pennsylvania law expressly permits maintenance of membership for state and local employees. There may, in fact, be many other forms of union security negotiated at the state and local levels, but they probably take the form of tacit understandings as opposed to written agreements in a majority of cases. The union-security issue is, at times, an issue in long strikes involving public employees. It would seem, therefore, that the public interest would best be served if state legislatures would address themselves to the problem of union security and permit negotiation to resolve the issue.

Resolution of Disputes

One of the most significant issues facing the public sector is machinery for resolving disputes in the face of prohibitions on the right to strike. Many states have some limited provisions for dispute settlement. Some limit machinery to specific categories of workers, such as firefighters or teachers. When legislation has been passed, it almost always states that there can be no conflict with civil service provisions or other statutes setting employment standards. The major difficulty seems to come from legislative bodies, even when economic issues are negotiable. These bodies have to appropriate funds to cover the agreements and are usually unwilling to abide by decisions denied outside the traditional legislative processes.[27]

There are at least three types of disputes in the public employment field. The first, organizational, involves the issue of determining employee desires for union representation. Some states have labor relations boards to make bargaining-unit determinations.

The second type involves the terms and conditions of employment that are usually included in written collective bargaining agreements. Resolution may result from such devices as mediation or fact-finding boards with authority to offer recommendations.

The third type involves interpretation and enforcement of existing collective bargaining agreements. The usual method of resolving such disputes in private industry is an internal grievance procedure, with impartial third-party arbitration as a final step.

It seems probable that strikes in the public sector could be decreased if certain steps were clearly provided. Some possible steps that could result in better labor-management relations include:

1. The right of employee representation by a union of employees' own choice.
2. Independent third-party mediation and fact finding to deal with bargaining impasses.
3. Written contracts with detailed clauses dealing with wages and other working conditions.
4. Final and binding arbitration as the last step in a grievance procedure involving contractual interpretation.
5. Final and binding arbitration to resolve an impasse in negotiations for a new labor agreement.

Mediation and fact-finding boards are utilized by some states to resolve bargaining impasses. Connecticut made them available in its Municipal Employee Relations Act of 1965. Michigan also provides for fact finding and nonbinding recommendations by its State Labor Mediation Board to resolve bargaining impasses. Wisconsin utilizes the fact-finding approach, which may be initiated by its Employment Relations Board to break deadlocked negotiations. Generally, public employees tend to strike over wages and fringe benefits. Mediation and fact-finding boards are utilized by a large number of states to resolve bargaining impasses.

Fact finding is more formal than mediation. Fact finders hear the positions of both parties, informally collect information during hearings, and then make settlement recommendations.

Referendums may be used to deal with disputes, but several problems are associated with this procedure. Delay and voter misunderstanding are primary problems that must be overcome if impasses are to be settled on election ballots.

Arbitration

Interest arbitration is different from grievance arbitration in that it involves determination of the content of contracts as opposed to interpretation and application of an existing agreement. In the private sector, the strike and other economic sanctions have been the preferred methods of determining contract content. Public employees in most jurisdictions are prohibited from using the strike for any purpose. Several states have legalized some public employee strikes under controlled conditions.[28] Because of the widespread prohibition on strikes, alternatives for dispute settlement became important. Many states have passed legislation permitting arbitration for settling unresolved issues as a substitute for strikes.

Final-offer arbitration refers to the process of limiting the third-party umpire to selection of the final offer of one party or the other, but not to a pick-and-choose of the best features from both positions. It has been tried in Michigan, Wisconsin, and Iowa. Each state has imposed its own peculiar description of guidelines that must be followed in selecting the final offer that will become the parties' contract. In Michigan, the arbitrator assumes the role of mediator in carrying out her or his function. Final-offer arbitration may have the effect of forcing unions and employers to deal with each other in good faith at the bargaining table. Failure to do so may result in selection of a final package, not a combination of the final offers, that would not have materialized from good-faith bargaining. Most of the twenty-nine states with comprehensive collective bargaining legislation provide fact finding with recommendations as a final step in impasse procedure. Mediation is usually required before the fact-finding stage. One study concluded that the longer the fact-finding procedures required, the greater the probability that illegal strikes will occur.[29]

Voluntary binding arbitration is available in about fourteen states. A few place limits on the bargaining units involved, or on the issues subject to a binding award. Binding arbitration, where it was available, has been used more often than work stoppages to settle interest disputes.[30]

Another variation is "advisory arbitration" which actually means fact finding with recommendations. Several states take the position that judicial or legislative bodies are prohibited from delegating their powers to some other body. Hence, a negotiating team or tripartite arbitration group may only recommend to a city council any terms arrived at for inclusion into an agreement.

Mediation and arbitration combined place authority in a given third party to mediate and then to arbitrate, if mediation fails. The same person is empowered to function in both processes. The arbitrator will have greater familiarity with the case than if different persons are involved in the two processes. Wisconsin utilizes the combined mediation and arbitration form of dispute settlement. A final and binding arbitration award may be more agreeable to the parties because of the greater involvement of one person in the entire proceedings. If legislatures desire to avoid strikes, they will need to furnish acceptable substitutes. Binding arbitration seems to be strongly preferred over fact finding with recommendations.

It does not make sense to outlaw public employee strikes while failing to provide an effective substitute. In Indiana, for example, teacher strikes frequently occur despite their prohibition simply because an effective method is not available to break impasses when the parties are unable to agree on the terms and conditions of a new contract. As matters stand, teachers are compelled to accept the final offer of school boards. This makes as much sense as compelling the school boards to accept the final offer of the teacher unions.

Clearly, there must be an effective procedure when the other methods (mediation, fact finding, nonbinding recommendations) do not work. Obviously, the only method that makes sense is compulsory and binding arbitration. Like the experience in Indiana demonstrates, public employee strikes will occur despite their illegality. In this regard, it should be noted that state courts generally uphold the constitutionality of statutes requiring compulsory arbitration.[31]

SUMMARY

Labor relations policies in the federal services are developing as experience is gained with the collective bargaining process. Changes were made in the Executive Orders and policies under them to facilitate changing conditions. Collective bargaining under the Executive Orders was superseded by passage of the Civil Service Reform Act of 1978. State and local practices vary from comprehensive statutes defining collective bargaining rights to outright prohibition of collective bargaining.

Unilateral determination of wages and employment conditions is increasingly being questioned by government employees. Employers are finding their decisions questioned not only by unions representing their employees but also by associations that have traditionally been somewhat passive in the area of collective bargaining. Competition between unions and associations has resulted in the use of more aggressive tactics to obtain wages and other working conditions that more nearly approach those of the private sector. Experimentation with impasse procedures is necessary for the development of stability in public-sector collective bargaining.

Several years of sustained high levels of employment, coupled with increased demand for public services, have placed employers in a position whereby they must reevaluate their traditional management practices. The general public is intolerant of inconveniences resulting from stoppages in the flow of services performed by the various agencies of government. Placed between their employees and the general public, a growing number of state and local governments have been forced to spell out more clearly the collective bargaining rights of workers. Once the process begins, there is little possibility of reversing it. The rights established in one state may be expected to spill over into adjoining states and then to spread still further. The process may be expected to continue for as long as relatively high levels of employment exist. Otherwise, work stoppages and high turnover rates may be expected to persist. The general public may react more against work stoppages than against the high turnover rates, although both are costly in terms of taxes. The public may not approve of government employee strikes and may therefore treat such workers in harsh fashion— but probably for a short period of time only. The greatest cost of a failure to provide a workable labor-management policy is likely to fall on the elected officeholders. Thus, there are incentives for state and local governments to deal with their employees on a basis more comparable with the private sector.

DISCUSSION QUESTIONS

1. Discuss the sovereignty doctrine in the context of essential services in the public sector. Compare services in the public sector with those in the private sector as to which sector's services are more essential.

2. Trace the development of collective bargaining in federal employment. How effective were the various laws in achieving their stated purposes?

3. Outline the structural framework of collective bargaining prodded by Title VII of the Civil Service Reform Act of 1978.

4. How are bargaining impasses dealt with under the Civil Service Reform Act of 1978?

5. What was the statutory basis for discharge of striking air traffic controllers in 1981?

6. Discuss the range of permissible bargaining items under the 1978 law. How are management rights handled?

7. How important are negotiated grievance procedures in federal agencies as compared with statutory appeals procedures?

8. Discuss the unfair labor practice procedure used in federal employment compared with that of the NLRB in its interpretation of Taft-Hartley.

9. Do you detect any trends in the development of collective bargaining at the state and local levels?

10. To what extent is the strike permissible at the state and local levels? How important is the strike weapon to successful bargaining results in the public sector?

11. What category of state or local public employees is most likely to resort to strikes as a method of resolving impasses? Why?

12. Identify and discuss the most popular methods used by state and local governments to resolve impasses. Do you prefer other methods? Why?

NOTES

1   Title VII, Civil Service Reform Act, P.L. 95-454, effective January 1, 1978.

2   Committee on Public Employer-Employee Relations, *Employee Organizations in the Public Service* (New York: National Civil Service, National Civil Service League, 1946), p. 16.

3   69 Stat. 624 (1955).

4   Wilson R. Hart, *Collective Bargaining in the Federal Civil Service* (New York: Harper & Row, 1961), p. 44.

5   *Collective Bargaining in the Public Sector, An Interim Report.* Prepared for Executive Board, AFL-CIO Maritime Trades Department, February 13, 1969.

6   H. Roberts, *A Manual for Employee-Management Cooperation in the Federal Service* (Honolulu, Hawaii: Industrial Relations Center, University of Hawaii, 1964), p. 4.

7   Sterling Denhard Spero, *Government as Employer* (New York: Remsen Press, 1948), p. 122.

8   Kurt L. Hanslowe, *The Emerging Law of Labor Relations in Public Employment*, ILR Paperback No. 4 (Ithaca, N.Y.: New York State School of Industrial and Labor Relations, Cornell University, 1967), p. 35.

9   5 U.S.C. 642 (1912).

10   Charles B. Craver, "Bargaining in the Federal Sector," *Labor Law Journal*, IX, 9 (September 1968), p. 570.

11   *Ibid.*

12   Hart, *op. cit.*, p. 168.

13   *Postal Clerks v. Blount*, 325 F. Supp. 879 (D-D.C.) (1971), aff. 404 U.S. 802 (1971).

14   Federal Reserve Press Release, "Policy on Unionization and Collective Bargaining for the Federal Reserve Banks," May 9, 1969.

15   United States Federal Labor Relations Council, *Labor-Management Relations in the Federal Service* (Washington, D.C., 1975), p. 32.

16   U.S. Department of Labor, Bureau of Labor Statistics.

17   *American Federation of State, County, and Municipal Employees, AFL-CIO v. Woodward*, 406 F. 2d 137 (1969).

18   *Ibid.*, p. 139.

19   *McLaughlin v. Tilendis*, 398 F. 2d 287 (CA 7, 1968).

20   *AFL-CIO News*, September 2, 1992.

21   James E. Young and Betty L. Brewer, *State Legislation Affecting Labor Relations in State and Local Government*, Labor and Industrial Relations Series No. 2 (Kent, Ohio: Kent State University Bureau of Economic and Business Research, 1968), p. 16.

22   William Buck, former president of the International Association of Fire Fighters, as quoted by Eric Polisor in "Strikes and Solutions," Public Employee Relations Report No. 7, Public Employee Personnel Association, 1968.

23   Anne M. Ross, "Public Employee Unions and the Right to Strike," *Monthly Labor Review*, XCII, 3 (March 1968), p. 15.

24   John Bloedorn, "The Strike and the Public Sector," *Labor Law Journal*, XX, 3 (March 1969), p. 157.

25   Richard C. Kearney, *Labor Relations in the Public Sectors* (New York: Marcel Dekker, Inc., 1984), p. 210.

26   *Abood* v. *Detroit Board of Education*, 431 U.S. 209 (1977).

27   *Collective Bargaining in the Public Sector*, Interim Report, Executive Board, AFL-CIO Maritime Trades Department, 1969, p. 42.

28   Robert E. Dunham, "Interest Arbitration in Non-Federal Public Employment," *The Arbitration Journal*, XXXI, 1 (March 1976), pp. 45–46. States that permit public-employee strikes are Alaska, Hawaii, Minnesota, Montana, Oregon, Pennsylvania, and Vermont. Others, as noted, have minimal penalties and therefore impose few constraints to strikes.

29   *Ibid.*

30   *Ibid.*

31   Paul D. Standohar, "Constitutionality of Compulsory Arbitration Statutes in Public Employment," *Labor Law Journal*, XXVII, 11 (November 1976), p. 675.

13 ❧

Evolution and Problems of Labor Relations Law

EVOLUTION OF PUBLIC POLICY

From the inception of unionism in the United States until the advent of the New Deal era, organized labor operated in a legal environment that had not accepted unionism as a permanent and responsible institution. As a result, unions played a minor role in the affairs of the nation. Union membership was small. With few exceptions, the bargaining power of unions was weak. The basic industries were essentially nonunion. By 1932, unions were freed from the effects of the conspiracy doctrine as developed in the pre-*Commonwealth* v. *Hunt* period. However, the courts were still heavily utilizing the injunction. By use of the injunction, the courts stamped out union economic activities calculated to influence and expand the collective bargaining process. Unions that engaged in secondary boycott activities risked prosecution under the Sherman Act, a statute ostensibly enacted to curb the growth of big business. The yellow-dog contract was still enforceable in the courts, owing to the pronouncement of the Supreme Court in the *Hitchman* decision.

While the courts blocked the progress of unions and collective bargaining, the legislative branch of government made some attempts to encourage the growth of unionism. Congress and some states passed laws calculated to prevent the employer from interfering with the right of employees to self-organization and collective bargaining. Congress limited its action to the railroad industry, though some states passed union protection legislation that applied to general industry. These laws forbade employers to discharge workers because of their membership in labor unions. To check abusive use of the labor injunction, Congress and some states attempted to curb the power of the judiciary. The injunction provided the means whereby government aided management at the most crucial points of industrial relations conflicts.

It is noteworthy that the legislative branch of government was more favorable to organized labor than were the courts. This condition resulted from the more responsive character of the legislative branch to social change. Protected in tenure, the judiciary was more concerned with legal formalism and precedent than with social and economic realities. For many years, the legislative and judicial branches of government were in sharp conflict over the labor issue. The employees of the nation stood by, hoping for a favorable outcome to the struggle so that they might realize a better socioeconomic existence. But for decades, the courts refused to confirm legislation calculated to promote unions or, for that matter, any laws which promoted the welfare of the working population. Social legislation was blocked by a Supreme Court that ignored the most obvious facts of economic life. As late as 1937, there was substantial reason to doubt that the Court would change its views on social legislation and approve the Norris-La Guardia and Wagner acts.

However, the period 1929–1937 was characterized by sweeping changes in the attitude of the American people toward the proper role of government in the area of economic activity. Stimulated by the effects of the Great Depression, the climate of opinion of the nation underwent great change. Many people came to believe that government had an important part to play if the national economy were to be restored to conditions of relatively full employment. Previously, only a small group had held this view, the majority having faith in the operation of "natural" economic laws to maintain a healthy industrial environment. Indeed, prior to the Great Depression, the nation generally believed that "the government governs best that governs least." The depression changed this attitude, and great segments of the people welcomed government intervention in the economic sphere. The people saw in this approach the cure for many of the problems of the national economy. In short, the people became government-minded, supporting government efforts to restore the national economy to a relatively higher level of operation.

This change in the climate of opinion had great implications for organized labor. If weak unions had not prevented a depression, there was reason to believe that a strong and widespread union movement might contribute to economic recovery. A strong and growing union movement depended on the action of government. It was necessary to establish a legal framework in which the collective bargaining process could function effectively. This produced the logic underlying the Norris–La Guardia and Wagner acts, the laws that set the tone of the labor policy of the New Deal. These laws were products of the Great Depression. They rested not only on the assumption that effective unionism would insure workers a greater measure of social justice, but also on the idea that an effective and growing labor movement would promote economic stability. In short, a strong union movement would fit nicely into the scheme of New Deal economics; hence, the unqualified support of legislation calculated to protect the right of employees to self-organization and collective bargaining.

Since 1937, the Supreme Court has permitted the legislative branch the widest latitude to shape labor policy. Congress and state legislatures are judicially free to determine the elements of the framework of labor law. Only upon rare occasions has the Court invalidated labor legislation on the ground of unconstitutionality. Actions of the legislative branch are struck down only when the statute clearly and unmistakably violates the terms of the Constitution.

Such was the status of organized labor in 1947. In that year, Taft-Hartley became the law of the land, and many changes occurred in the character of national labor policy. A variety of factors produced this legislation, but not the least important was the fact that society felt that the power of unionism was excessive. The law was an effort to provide collective bargaining balance between unions and management. Unions were to be made more responsible.

The Carter administration proposed considerable changes in Taft-Hartley to Congress in 1977. Among the proposals were the acceleration of NLRB elections; immediate reinstatement of employees discharged for union activity during an organizational campaign; financial penalties against the employer who refused to bargain in good faith; loss of federal contracts to employers who flaunt NLRB and court orders; and increasing the number of NLRB members. Though the Carter program was passed in the House, action in the Senate was forestalled because of filibustering during the summer of 1978.

The demand for more union responsibility did not end with the Taft-Hartley Act. Between 1957 and 1959 the McClellan Anti-Racketeering Committee held numerous hearings dealing with patterns of union behavior. Several findings and recommendations were presented to Congress as a result of the three-year effort. The Labor-Management Reporting and Disclosure Act was enacted in 1959. Its primary concern is with the internal practices of unions. The law attempts to protect union members from improper union conduct. Proper union representation is the vehicle by which labor organizations are expected to respond to the desires of members. The election provisions of Title IV have been utilized more heavily than other sections seeking to regulate internal union affairs. The loose organizational structure of the AFL-CIO resulted in government intervention into union internal affairs. Its adoption of six codes of ethical practices to regulate the behavior of its affiliates in 1957 proved to be too little, too late.

Continued public concern with the general operation of economic institutions is reflected in efforts other than Landrum-Griffin. President Kennedy issued an Executive Order that touched off a wave of reexamination of traditional attitudes toward public employee organizations. Subsequent presidents, from Nixon through Ford, also issued Executive Orders to strengthen the right of federal civilian employees to organize and bargain collectively. The Civil Service Reform Act of 1978 was passed, which superseded the Executive Orders. State and local jurisdictions continued their efforts to define the collective bargaining rights of their employees. To help minority and women employees in their quest for fair treatment and equal employment opportunity, Congress enacted the Civil Rights Act of 1964 and amended it in 1991. This effort is reflected at the state and local levels.

PUBLIC POLICY AND FREE COLLECTIVE BARGAINING

This volume has highlighted numerous issues of controversy in the labor relations area. Some of them can be mentioned at this time. If free collective bargaining is to be the cornerstone of public policy, radical changes must be made in the character of labor relations law. Free collective bargaining is generally acclaimed by all, but partisan interests encourage departure from the principle. Their attitude is "free collective bargaining is good, except when it hurts us." Here we are speaking of principle, and not policies, to satisfy the agenda of any partisan group. At the rock bottom of traditional American philosophy is that management and labor unions are in the best position to define what is suitable for them, and government intervention for that purpose is the antithesis of free collective bargaining.

Right-to-work laws are totally inconsistent with the principle of free collective bargaining. Management and workers' representatives should be permitted to negotiate a union shop or agency shop when they believe it suits their institutional needs. Government should no more forbid the union shop than require union membership as a condition of employment.

Borg-Warner seriously intervened with the free process, placing government in the middle of the collective bargaining table. It would depend on the ruling of the NLRB and the courts to establish whether a particular policy would benefit the union or the employer. Although an employer or a union may benefit by a particular policy, they both lose to the extent government diminishes their capability to fashion a labor agreement free from its control. Unless a demand is unlawful, all other demands should be in the mandatory classification, permitting collective bargaining to determine whether an issue will be included in a labor agreement. Checkoff controls by government likewise are not compatible with the free collective bargaining principle.

By no means does this mean government should withdraw completely from labor relations. Workers and unions need NLRB and court protection for their organizational and collective bargaining rights. Employers need legal protection against union activities that are clearly antisocial. Union members need legal protection against antidemocratic practices of their organizations.

OTHER CONTROVERSIAL ISSUES

Employees should have the right to hear and read employer and union views before a representation election. In this regard, the law should treat both sides fairly so that they are fully informed before they cast their ballots. Fairness does not allow for the captive-audience doctrine any more than workers should be paid to learn only the union's side of the story without giving the employer an equal opportunity to reply.

Exclusion from NLRB jurisdiction in effect means employees are denied self-organization and collective bargaining rights. From this point of view, the Supreme

Court decisions in *Catholic Bishop of Chicago, Yeshiva University*, and *Bell Aerospace* are inconsistent with the national policy of promoting the collective bargaining process. Nor does the Taft-Hartley policy of excluding supervisors from the scope of the law square with the policy.

Current policies in the area of industrial conflict must be addressed to promote equity to employers, employees, and unions. If employers are to be protected from the secondary boycott, the policy adopted by the Supreme Court in *Tree Fruits, Servette*, and *De Bartolo* should be reversed. Employers and employees need more adequate protection against violent conduct displayed by some unions on the picket line. By the same token, the employees' right to strike is not treated fairly when employers have the right to replace strikers with permanent replacements and to permit permanent replacements and not striking employees to vote in decertification elections held during the course of the work stoppage.

EFFICIENCY AND INTEGRITY OF THE NLRB

Employers, employees, and unions are not fairly treated given the interminable delays involved in the processing of unfair labor practices by the National Labor Relations Board and the federal courts. Specific time limits should be placed at each level of adjudication to assure prompt processing of those cases. If some employers believe long delays favor their side, they should also understand that their own interests will be jeopardized if the NLRB and courts award employees large back pay awards that could undermine the financial stability of the business.

Stability in labor relations becomes a casualty given Board reversals of policies with the changing personnel of the agency. The Eisenhower Board altered policies of the Board appointed by Roosevelt and Truman. In turn, the Kennedy-Johnson Board reversed policies established by the previous agency. In the Reagan years, the NLRB overturned more precedents than has any other Board in its fifty-odd-year history. Aside from the partisan acclaim or criticism depending on which Board was in place, reversal of policies is incompatible with stability in labor relations. No sooner do employers and unions adjust to a policy than it is changed by another Board.

To deal with this problem, NLRB members should be appointed for life in the same manner as federal court judges. Though there are some disadvantages to lifetime appointment, they are by far outweighed by the certainty and predictability of Board policy.

PUBLIC RESPONSIBILITY

The citizen should become more informed on the operation of trade unions and collective bargaining. Since he or she will determine the ultimate status of unions, judgment as to their merits should be based on accurate information and sound analysis. Too many people judge the overall program and functioning of unions by information purveyed by sources of doubtful reliability. The citizen owes it to the nation to gain the sound knowledge that will place him or her in a position to intelligently appraise the operation of unions and collective bargaining.

Such a search will not lead to the conclusion that legal curbs on unions are undesirable. On the contrary, some limitations on union activities are perfectly compatible with strong and militant unionism. However, the quest for accurate knowledge, if faithfully carried out, will lead to one obvious conclusion: In the modern profit economy, characterized by institutional forces not contemplated or given adequate weight by the classical or neoclassical school of economics, collective bargaining offers the American worker the only effective means whereby he or she can realize social and industrial justice. This factor underlies the nation's labor union movement. It is the major justification for unions.

Unions themselves can do much to influence the climate of opinion and thereby the character of the law of labor relations. Acts of social irresponsibility on the part of unions will result in the enactment of restrictive measures. In some areas of organized labor, the growth of union power has not been matched by the development of social responsibility. Unions that are socially responsible do not have to be servile or weak. Rather, union responsibility means the orientation of collective bargaining and union practices for the public good. Responsible unions are democratic unions. They scrupulously adhere to the letter and spirit of collective bargaining contracts. Such unions are vitally concerned with the overall prosperity of the firm, the industry, and the national economy. They recognize and understand the problems of management, and they expect management to recognize and understand the problems of the union and its members. Within the framework of effective collective bargaining, responsible unions are a force for national progress. In short, the responsible union is social-minded.

If this attitude of organized labor prevails, and if employers accept in good faith the principle of collective bargaining, the reliance upon law to enforce a viable and responsible collective bargaining system would decrease. It could lead to the end of the adversarial relationship between management and unions and be replaced by a program of genuine cooperation and mutual accommodation. If past history is any guide, however, it is doubtful that such a desirable change of attitude on the part of unions and management will take place. At this writing, therefore, the safe prediction is for increasing government intervention in labor relations and the growing complexity of labor relations law.

Appendix

LABOR RELATIONS ACT, 1947

Act of June 23, 1947, 61 Stat. 136, as Amended by Act of September 14, 1959, 73 Stat. 519*

KEY TO AMENDMENTS

Portions of the Act which have been eliminated by the Labor-Management Reporting and Disclosure Act of 1959, Public Law 86-257, are enclosed by black brackets; provisions which have been added to the Act are in italics, and unchanged portions are shown in roman type.

An Act

To amend the National Labor Relations Act, to provide additional facilities for the mediation of labor disputes affecting commerce, to equalize legal responsibilities of labor organizations and employers, and for other purposes.

Be it enacted by the Senate and House of Representatives of the United States of America in Congress assembled,

SHORT TITLE AND DECLARATION OF POLICY

SEC. 1. (a) This Act may be cited as the "Labor Management Relations Act, 1947."

(b) Industrial strife which interferes with the normal flow of commerce and with the full production of articles and commodities for commerce, can be avoided or substantially minimized if employers, employees, and labor organizations each recognize under law one another's legitimate rights in their relations with each other, and above all recognize under law that neither party has any right in its relations with any other to engage in acts or practices which jeopardize the public health, safety, or interest.

---

*Section 201 (d) and (e) of the Labor-Management Reporting and Disclosure Act of 1959 which repealed Section 9(f), (g), and (h) of the Labor Management Relations Act, 1947, and Section 505 amending Section 302(a), (b), and (c) of the Labor Management Relations Act, 1947, took effect upon enactment of Public Law 86-257, September 14, 1959. As to the other amendments of the Labor Management Relations Act, 1947, Section 707 of the Labor-Management Reporting and Disclosure Act provides:

The amendments made by this title shall take effect sixty days after the date of the enactment of this Act and no provision of this title shall be deemed to make an unfair labor practice, any act which is performed prior to such effective date which did not constitute an unfair labor practice prior thereto.

It is the purpose and policy of this Act, in order to promote the full flow of commerce, to prescribe the legitimate rights of both employees and employers in their relations affecting commerce, to provide orderly and peaceful procedures for preventing the interference by either with the legitimate rights of the other, to protect the rights of individual employees in their relations with labor organizations whose activities affect commerce, to define and proscribe practices on the part of labor and management which affect commerce and are inimical to the general welfare, and to protect the rights of the public in connection with labor disputes affecting commerce.

AMENDMENT OF NATIONAL LABOR RELATIONS ACT

SEC. 101.   The National Labor Relations Act is hereby amended to read as follows:

Findings and Policies

SEC. 1.   The denial by some employers of the right of employees to organize and the refusal by some employers to accept the procedure of collective bargaining lead to strikes and other forms of industrial strife or unrest, which have the intent or the necessary effect of burdening or obstructing commerce by (a) impairing the efficiency, safety, or operation of the instrumentalities of commerce; (b) occurring in the current of commerce; (c) materially affecting, restraining, or controlling the flow of raw materials or manufactured or processed goods in commerce; or (d) causing diminution of employment and wages in such volume as substantially to impair or disrupt the market for goods flowing from or into the channels of commerce.

The inequality of bargaining power between employees who do not possess full freedom of association or actual liberty of contract, and employers who are organized in the corporate or other forms of ownership association substantially burdens and affects the flow of commerce, and tends to aggravate recurrent business depressions, by depressing wage rates and the purchasing power of wage earners in industry and by preventing the stabilization of competitive wage rates and working conditions within and between industries.

Experience has proved that protection by law of the right of employees to organize and bargain collectively safeguards commerce from injury, impairment, or interruption, and promotes the flow of commerce by removing certain recognized sources of industrial strife and unrest, by encouraging practices fundamental to the friendly adjustment of industrial disputes arising out of differences as to wages, hours, or other working conditions, and by restoring equality or bargaining power between employers and employees.

Experience has further demonstrated that certain practices by some labor organizations, their officers, and members have the intent or the necessary effect of burdening or obstructing commerce by preventing the free flow of goods in such commerce through strikes and other forms of industrial unrest or through concerted activities which impair the interest of the public in the free flow of such commerce. The elimination of such practices is a necessary condition to the assurance of the rights herein guaranteed.

It is hereby declared to be the policy of the United States to eliminate the causes of certain substantial obstructions to the free flow of commerce and to mitigate and eliminate these obstructions when they have occurred by encouraging the practice and procedure of collective bargaining and by protecting the exercise by workers of full freedom of association, self-organization, and designation of representatives of their own choosing, for the purpose of negotiating the terms and conditions of their employment or other mutual aid or protection.

DEFINITIONS. SEC. 2.   When used in this Act—

(1) The term "person" includes one or more individuals, labor organizations, partnerships, associations, corporations, legal representatives, trustees, trustees in bankruptcy, or receivers.

(2) The term "employer" includes any person acting as an agent of an employer, directly or indirectly, but shall not include the United States or any wholly owned Government corporation, or any Federal Reserve Bank, or any State or political subdivision thereof, or any corporation or association operating a hospital, if no part of the net earnings inures to the benefit of any private shareholder or individual, or any person subject to the Railway

Labor Act, as amended from time to time, or any labor organization (other than when acting as an employer), or anyone acting in the capacity of officer or agent of such labor organization.

(3) The term "employee" shall include any employee, and shall not be limited to the employees of a particular employer, unless the Act explicitly states otherwise, and shall include any individual whose work has ceased as a consequence of, or in connection with, any current labor dispute or because of any unfair labor practice, and who has not obtained any other regular and substantially equivalent employment, but shall not include any individual employed as an agricultural laborer, or in the domestic service of any family or person at his home, or any individual employed by his parent or spouse, or any individual having the status of an independent contractor, or any individual employed as a supervisor, or any individual employed by an employer subject to the Railway Labor Act, as amended from time to time, or by any other person who is not an employer as herein defined.

(4) The term "representatives" includes any individual or labor organization.

(5) The term "labor organization" means any organization of any kind, or any agency or employee representation committee or plan, in which employees participate and which exists for the purpose, in whole or in part, of dealing with employers concerning grievances, labor disputes, wages, rates of pay, hours of employment, or conditions of work.

(6) The term "commerce" means trade, traffic, commerce, transportation, or communication among the several States, or between the District of Columbia or any Territory of the United States and any State or other Territory, or between any foreign country and any State, Territory, or the District of Columbia, or within the District of Columbia or any Territory, or between points in the same State but through any other State or any Territory or the District of Columbia or any foreign country.

(7) The term "affecting commerce" means in commerce, or burdening or obstructing commerce or the free flow of commerce, or having led or tending to lead to a labor dispute burdening or obstructing commerce or the free flow of commerce.

(8) The term "unfair labor practice" means any unfair labor practice listed in section 8.

(9) The term "labor dispute" includes any controversy concerning terms, tenure or conditions of employment, or concerning the association or representation of persons in negotiating, fixing, maintaining, changing, or seeking to arrange terms or conditions of employment, regardless of whether the disputants stand in the proximate relation of employer and employee.

(10) The term "National Labor Relations Board" means the National Labor Relations Board provided for in section 3 of this Act.

(11) The term "supervisor" means any individual having authority, in the interest of the employer, to hire, transfer, suspend, lay off, recall, promote, discharge, assign, reward, or discipline other employees, or responsibly to direct them, or to adjust their grievances, or effectively to recommend such action, if in connection with the foregoing the exercise of such authority is not of a merely routine or clerical nature, but requires the use of independent judgment.

(12) The term "professional employee" means—

(a) any employee engaged in work (i) predominantly intellectual and varied in character as opposed to routine mental, manual, mechanical, or physical work; (ii) involving the consistent exercise of discretion and judgment in its performance; (iii) of such a character that the output produced or the result accomplished cannot be standardized in relation to a given period of time; (iv) requiring knowledge of an advanced type in a field of science or learning customarily acquired by a prolonged course of specialized intellectual instruction and study in an institution of higher learning or a hospital, as distinguished from a general academic education or from an apprenticeship or from training in the performance of routine mental, manual, or physical processes; or

(b) any employee, who (i) has completed the courses of specialized intellectual instruction and study described in clause (iv) of paragraph (a), and (ii) is performing related work under the supervision of a professional person to qualify himself to become a professional employee as defined in paragraph (a).

(13) In determining whether any person is acting as an "agent" of another person so as to make such other person responsible for his acts, the

question of whether the specific acts performed were actually authorized or subsequently ratified shall not be controlling.

(14) The term "health care institution" shall include any hospital, convalescent hospital, health maintenance organization, health clinic, nursing home, extended care facility, or other institution devoted to the care of sick, infirm, or aged persons.

NATIONAL LABOR RELATIONS BOARD

SEC. 3.   (a) The National Labor Relations Board (hereinafter called the "Board") created by this Act prior to its amendment by the Labor Management Relations Act, 1947, is hereby continued as an agency of the United States, except that the Board shall consist of five instead of three members, appointed by the President by and with the advice and consent of the Senate. Of the two additional members so provided for, one shall be appointed for a term of five years and the other for a term of two years. Their successors, and the successors of the other members, shall be appointed for terms of five years each, excepting that any individual chosen to fill a vacancy shall be appointed only for the unexpired term of the member whom he shall succeed. The President shall designate one member to serve as Chairman of the Board. Any members of the Board may be removed by the President, upon notice and hearing, for neglect of duty or malfeasance in office, but for no other cause.

(b) The Board is authorized to delegate to any group of three or more members any or all of the powers which it may itself exercise. *The Board is also authorized to delegate to its regional directors its powers under section 9 to determine the unit appropriate for the purpose of collective bargaining, to investigate and provide for hearings, and determine whether a question of representation exists, and to direct an election or take a secret ballot under subsection (c) or (e) of section 9 and certify the results thereof, except that upon the filing of a request therefor with the Board by any interested person, the Board may review any action of a regional director delegated to him under this paragraph, but such a review shall not, unless specifically ordered by the*

Board, operate as a stay of any action taken by the regional director. A vacancy in the Board shall not impair the right of the remaining members to exercise all of the powers of the Board, and three members of the Board shall, at all times, constitute a quorum of the Board, except that two members shall constitute a quorum of any group designated pursuant to the first sentence hereof. The Board shall have an official seal which shall be judicially noticed.

(c) The Board shall at the close of each fiscal year make a report in writing to Congress and to the President stating in detail the cases it has heard, the decisions it has rendered, the names, salaries, and duties of all employees and officers in the employ or under the supervision of the Board, and an account of all moneys it has disbursed.

(d) There shall be a General Counsel of the Board who shall be appointed by the President, by and with the advice and consent of the Senate, for a term of four years. The General Counsel of the Board shall exercise general supervision over all attorneys employed by the Board (other than trial examiners and legal assistants to Board members) and over the officers and employees in the regional offices. He shall have final authority, on behalf of the Board, in respect of the investigation of charges and issuance of complaints under section 10, and in respect of the prosecution of such complaints before the Board, and shall have such other duties as the Board may prescribe or as may be provided by law. *In case of a vacancy in the office of the General Counsel the President is authorized to designate the officer or employee who shall act as General Counsel during such vacancy, but no person or persons so designated shall so act (1) for more than forty days when the Congress is in session unless a nomination to fill such vacancy shall have been submitted to the Senate, or (2) after the adjournment sine die of the session of the Senate in which such nomination was submitted.*

SEC. 4.   (a) Each member of the Board and the General Counsel of the Board shall receive a salary of $12,000* a year, shall be eligible for reappoint-

---

*AUTHOR'S NOTE: All salaries quoted in this Act are now increased periodically as a result of the Government Employees Salary Reform Act of 1964, 88th Congress, Public Law 88–426. 78 Stat. 400.

ment, and shall not engage in any other business, vocation, or employment. The Board shall appoint an executive secretary, and such attorneys, examiners, and regional directors, and such other employees as it may from time to time find necessary for the proper performance of its duties. The Board may not employ any attorneys for the purpose of reviewing transcripts of hearings or preparing drafts of opinions except that any attorney employed for assignment as a legal assistant to any Board member may for such Board member review such transcripts and prepare such drafts. No trial examiner's report shall be reviewed, either before or after its publication, by any person other than a member of the Board or his legal assistant, and no trial examiner shall advise or consult with the Board with respect to exceptions taken to his findings, rulings, or recommendations. The Board may establish or utilize such regional, local, or other agencies, and utilize such voluntary and uncompensated services, as may from time to time be needed. Attorneys appointed under this section may, at the direction of the Board, appear for and represent the Board in any case in court. Nothing in this Act shall be construed to authorize the Board to appoint individuals for the purpose of conciliation or mediation, or for economic analysis.

(b) All of the expenses of the Board, including all necessary traveling and subsistence expenses outside the District of Columbia incurred by the members or employees of the Board under its orders, shall be allowed and paid on the presentation of itemized vouchers therefor approved by the Board or by any individual it designates for that purpose.

SEC. 5.   The principal office of the Board shall be in the District of Columbia, but it may meet and exercise any or all of its powers at any other place. The Board may, by one or more of its members or by such agents or agencies as it may designate, prosecute any inquiry necessary to its functions in any part of the United States. A member who participates in such an inquiry shall not be disqualified from subsequently participating in a decision of the Board in the same case.

SEC. 6.   The Board shall have authority from time to time to make, amend, and rescind, in the manner prescribed by the Administrative Procedure Act,

such rules and regulations as may be necessary to carry out the provisions of this Act.

RIGHTS OF EMPLOYEES. SEC. 7.   Employees shall have the right to self-organization, to form, join, or assist labor organizations, to bargain collectively through representatives of their own choosing, or to engage in other concerted activities for the purpose of collective bargaining or other mutual aid or protection, and shall also have the right to refrain from any or all of such activities except to the extent that such right may be affected by an agreement requiring membership in a labor organization as a condition of employment as authorized in section 8(a)(3).

UNFAIR LABOR PRACTICES. SEC. 8.   (a) It shall be an unfair labor practice for an employer—

(1) to interfere with, restrain, or coerce employees in the exercise of the rights guaranteed in section 7;

(2) to dominate or interfere with the formation or administration of any labor organization or contribute financial or other support to it: Provided, That subject to rules and regulations made and published by the Board pursuant to section 6, an employer shall not be prohibited from permitting employees to confer with him during working hours without loss of time or pay;

(3) by discrimination in regard to hire or tenure of employment or any term or condition of employment to encourage or discourage membership in any labor organization: Provided, That nothing in this Act, or in any other statute of the United States, shall preclude an employer from making an agreement with a labor organization (not established, maintained, or assisted by any action defined in section 8[a] of this Act as an unfair labor practice) to require as a condition of employment membership therein on or after the thirtieth day following the beginning of such employment or the effective date of such agreement, whichever is the later, (i) if such labor organization is the representative of the employees as provided in section 9(a), in the appropriate collective-bargaining unit covered by such agreement when made [and has at the time the agreement was made or within the preceding twelve months received from the Board a notice of compliance with section 9(f), (g), (h)], and (ii) unless following

an election held as provided in section 9(e) within one year preceding the effective date of such agreement, the Board shall have certified that at least a majority of the employees eligible to vote in such election have voted to rescind the authority of such labor organization to make such an agreement: Provided further, That no employer shall justify any discrimination against an employee for non-membership in a labor organization (A) if he has reasonable grounds for believing that such membership was not available to the employee on the same terms and conditions generally applicable to other members, or (B) if he has reasonable grounds for believing that membership was denied or terminated for reasons other than the failure of the employee to tender the periodic dues and the initiation fees uniformly required as a condition of acquiring or retaining membership;

(4) to discharge or otherwise discriminate against an employee because he has filed charges or given testimony under this Act;

(5) to refuse to bargain collectively with the representatives of his employees, subject to the provisions of section 9(a).

(b) It shall be an unfair labor practice for a labor organization or its agents

(1) to restrain or coerce (A) employees in the exercise of the rights guaranteed in section 7: Provided, That this paragraph shall not impair the right of a labor organization to prescribe its own rules with respect to the acquisition or retention of membership therein; or (B) an employer in the selection of his representatives for the purposes of collective bargaining or the adjustment of grievances;

(2) to cause or attempt to cause an employer to discriminate against an employee in violation of subsection (a)(3) or to discriminate against an employee with respect to whom membership in such organization has been denied or terminated on some ground other than his failure to tender the periodic dues and the initiation fees uniformly required as a condition of acquiring or retaining membership;

(3) to refuse to bargain collectively with an employer, provided it is the representative of his employees subject to the provisions of section 9(a);

(4) (i) to engage in, or to induce or encourage [the employees of any employer] *any individual employed by any person engaged in commerce or in an industry affecting commerce* to engage in, a strike or a [concerted] refusal in the course of [their] *his* employment to use, manufacture, process, transport, or otherwise handle or work on any goods, articles, materials, or commodities or to perform any services [,]; or *(ii) to threaten, coerce, or restrain any person engaged in commerce or in an industry affecting commerce*, where in *either case* an object thereof is:

(A) forcing or requiring any employer or self-employed person to join any labor or employer organization or [any employer or other person to cease using, selling, handling, transporting, or otherwise dealing in the products of any other producer, processor, or manufacturer, or to cease doing business with any other person] *to enter into any agreement which is prohibited by section 8(e)*;

(B) *forcing or requiring any person to cease using, selling, handling, transporting, or otherwise dealing in the products of any other producer, processor, or manufacturer, or to doing business with any other person, or* forcing or requiring any other employer to recognize or bargain with a labor organization as the representative of his employees unless such labor organization has been certified as the representative of such employees under the provisions of section 9[;]: *Provided, That nothing contained in this clause* (B) *shall be construed to make unlawful, where not otherwise unlawful, any primary strike or primary picketing*;

(C) forcing or requiring any employer to recognize or bargain with a particular labor organization as the representative of his employees if another labor organization has been certified as the representative of such employees under the provisions of section 9;

(D) forcing or requiring any employer to assign particular work to employees in a particular labor organization or in a particular trade, craft, or class rather than to employees in another labor organization or in another trade, craft, or class, unless such employer is failing to conform to an order or certification of the Board determining the bargaining representative for employees performing such work:

Provided, That nothing contained in this subsection (b) shall be construed to make unlawful a refusal by any person to enter upon the premises of any employer (other than his own employer), if the employees of such employer are engaged in a strike ratified or approved by a representative of such employees whom such employer is required to recognize under this Act [;]: *Provided further,*

That for the purposes of this paragraph (4) only, nothing contained in such paragraph shall be construed to prohibit publicity, other than picketing, for the purpose of truthfully advising the public, including consumers and members of a labor organization, that a product or products are produced by an employer with whom the labor organization has a primary dispute and are distributed by another employer, as long as such publicity does not have an effect of inducing any individual employed by any person other than the primary employer in the course of his employment to refuse to pick up, deliver, or transport any goods, or not to perform any services, at the establishment of the employer engaged in such distribution;

(5) to require of employees covered by an agreement authorized under subsection (a)(3) the payment, as a condition precedent to becoming a member of such organization, of a fee in an amount which the Board finds excessive or discriminatory under all the circumstances. In making such a finding, the Board shall consider, among other relevant factors, the practices and customs of labor organizations in the particular industry, and the wages currently paid to the employees affected; [and]

(6) to cause or attempt to cause an employer to pay or deliver or agree to pay or deliver any money or other thing of value, in the nature of an exaction, for services which are not performed or not to be performed [.]; *and*

(7) *to picket or cause to be picketed, or threaten to picket or cause to be picketed, any employer where an object thereof is forcing or requiring an employer to recognize or bargain with a labor organization as the representative of his employees, or forcing or requiring the employees of an employer to accept or select labor organization as their collective bargaining representative, unless such labor organization is currently certified as the representative of such employees:*

(A) *where the employer has lawfully recognized in accordance with this Act any other labor organization and a question concerning representation may not appropriately be raised under section 9(c) of this Act,*

(B) *where within the preceding twelve months a valid election under section 9(c) of this Act has been conducted, or*

(C) *where such picketing has been conducted without a petition under section 9(c) being filed within a reason-* *able period of time not to exceed thirty days from the commencement of such picketing: Provided, That when such a petition has been filed the Board shall forthwith, without regard to the provisions of section 9(c)(1) or the absence of a showing of a substantial interest on the part of the labor organization, direct an election in such unit as the Board finds to be appropriate and shall certify the results thereof: Provided further, That nothing in this subparagraph (C) shall be construed to prohibit any picketing or other publicity for the purpose of truthfully advising the public (including consumers) that an employer does not employ members of, or have a contract with, a labor organization, unless an effect of such picketing is to induce any individual employed by any other person in the course of his employment, not to pick up, deliver or transport any goods or not to perform any services.*

Nothing in this paragraph (7) shall be construed to permit any act which would otherwise be an unfair labor practice under this section 8(b).

(c) The expressing of any views, argument, or opinion, or the dissemination thereof, whether in written, printed, graphic, or visual form, shall not constitute or be evidence of an unfair labor practice under any of the provisions of this Act, if such expression contains no threat of reprisal or force or promise of benefit.

(d) For the purposes of this section, to bargain collectively is the performance of the mutual obligation of the employer and the representative of the employees to meet at reasonable times and confer in good faith with respect to wages, hours, and other terms and conditions of employment, or the negotiation of an agreement, or any question arising thereunder, and the execution of a written contract incorporating any agreement reached if requested by either party, but such obligation does not compel either party to agree to a proposal or require the making of a concession: Provided, That where there is in effect a collective-bargaining contract covering employees in an industry affecting commerce, the duty to bargain collectively shall also mean that no party to such contract shall terminate or modify such contract, unless the party desiring such termination or modification—

(1) serves a written notice upon the other party to the contract of the proposed termination or modification sixty days prior to the expiration date thereof, or in the

event such contract contains no expiration date, sixty days prior to the time it is proposed to make such termination or modification;

(2) offers to meet and confer with the other party for the purpose of negotiating a new contract or a contract containing the proposed modifications;

(3) notifies the Federal Mediation and Conciliation Service within thirty days after such notice of the existence of a dispute, and simultaneously therewith notifies any State or Territorial agency established to mediate and conciliate disputes within the State or Territory where the dispute occurred, provided no agreement has been reached by that time; and

(4) continues in full force and effect, without resorting to strike or lockout, all the terms and conditions of the existing contract for a period of sixty days after such notice is given or until the expiration date of such contract, whichever occurs later.

Whenever the collective bargaining involves employees of a health care institution, the provisions of this section 8(d) shall be modified as follows:

(A) The notice of section 8(d)(1) shall be ninety days; the notice of section 8(d)(3) shall be sixty days; and the contract period of section 8(d)(4) shall be ninety days.

(B) Where the bargaining is for an initial agreement following certification or recognition, at least thirty days' notice of the existence of a dispute shall be given by the labor organization to the agencies set forth in section 8(d)(3).

(C) After notice is given to the Federal Mediation and Conciliation Service under either clause (A) or (B) of this sentence, the Service shall promptly communicate with the parties and use its best efforts, by mediation and conciliation, to bring them to agreement. The parties shall participate fully and promptly in such meetings as may be undertaken by the Service for the purpose of aiding in a settlement of the dispute.

The duties imposed upon employers, employees, and labor organizations by paragraphs (2), (3), and (4) shall become inapplicable upon an intervening certification of the Board, under which the labor organization or individual, which is a party to the contract, has been superseded as or ceased to be the representative of the employees subject to the provisions of section 9(a), and the duties so imposed shall not be construed as requiring either

party to discuss or agree to any modification of the terms and conditions contained in a contract for a fixed period, if such modification is to become effective before such terms and conditions can be reopened under the provisions of the contract. Any employee who engages in a strike within the sixty-day period specified in this subsection shall lose his status as an employee of the employer engaged in the particular labor dispute, for the purposes of sections 8, 9, and 10 of this Act, as amended, but such loss of status for such employee shall terminate if and when he is reemployed by such employer.

(e) It shall be an unfair labor practice for any labor organization and any employer to enter into any contract or agreement, express or implied, whereby such employer ceases or refrains or agrees to cease or refrain from handling, using, selling, transporting or otherwise dealing in any of the products of any other employer, or to cease doing business with any other person, and any contract or agreement entered into heretofore or hereafter containing such an agreement shall be to such extent unenforceable and void: Provided, That nothing in this subsection (e) shall apply to an agreement between a labor organization and an employer in the construction industry relating to the contracting or subcontracting of work to be done at the site of the construction, alteration, painting, or repair of a building, structure, or other work: Provided further, That for the purposes of this subsection (e) and section 8(b)(4)(B) the terms "any employer," "any person engaged in commerce or an industry affecting commerce" and "any person" when used in relation to the term "any other producer, processor, or manufacturer," "any other employer," or "any other person" shall not include persons in the relation of a jobber, manufacturer, contractor, or subcontractor working on the goods or premises of the jobber or manufacturer or performing parts of an integrated process of production in the apparel and clothing industry: Provided further, That nothing in this Act shall prohibit the enforcement of any agreement which is within the foregoing exception.

(f) It shall not be an unfair labor practice under subsections (a) and (b) of this section for an employer engaged primarily in the building and construction industry to make an agreement cover-

ing employees engaged (or who upon their employment, will be engaged) in the building and construction industry with a labor organization of which building and construction employees are members (not established, maintained, or assisted by any action defined in section 8[a] of this Act as an unfair labor practice) because (1) the majority status of such labor organization has not been established under the provisions of section 9 of this Act prior to the making of such agreement, or (2) such agreement requires as a condition of employment, membership in such labor organization after the seventh day following the beginning of such employment or the effective date of the agreement, whichever is later, or (3) such agreement requires the employer to notify such labor organization of opportunities for employment with such employer, or gives such labor organization an opportunity to refer qualified applicants for such employment, or (4) such agreement specifies minimum training or experience qualifications for employment or provides for priority in opportunities for employment based upon length of service with such employer, in the industry or in the particular geographical area: Provided, That nothing in this subsection shall set aside the final proviso to section 8(a) (3) of this Act: Provided further, That any agreement which would be invalid, but for clause (1) of this subsection, shall not be a bar to a petition filed pursuant to section 9(c) or 9(e)*

(g) A labor organization before engaging in any strike, picketing, or other concerted refusal to work at any health care institution shall, not less than ten days prior to such action, notify the institution in writing and the Federal Mediation and Conciliation Service of that intention, except that in the case of bargaining for an initial agreement following certification or recognition the notice required by this subsection shall not be given until

_____
*Section 8 (f) is inserted in the Act by subsection (a) of Section 705 of Public Law 86-257. Section 705 (b) provides:

Nothing contained in the amendment made by subsection (a) shall be construed as authorizing the execution or application requiring membership in a labor organization as a condition of employment in any State or Territory in which such execution or application is prohibited by State or Territorial law.

the expiration of the period specified in clause (B) of the last sentence of section 8(d) of this Act. The notice shall state the date and time that such action will commence. The notice, once given, may be extended by the written agreement of both parties.

REPRESENTATIVES AND ELECTIONS. SEC. 9. (a) Representatives designated or selected for the purpose of collective bargaining by the majority of the employees in a unit appropriate for such purposes, shall be the exclusive representatives of all the employees in such unit for the purpose of collective bargaining in respect to rates of pay, wages, hours of employment, or other conditions of employment: Provided, That any individual employee or a group of employees shall have the right at any time to present grievances to their employer and to have such grievances adjusted, without the intervention of the bargaining representative, as long as the adjustment is not inconsistent with the terms of a collective-bargaining contract or agreement then in effect: Provided further, That the bargaining representative has been given opportunity to be present at such adjustment.

(b) The Board shall decide in each case whether, in order to assure to employees the fullest freedom in exercising the rights guaranteed by this Act, the unit appropriate for the purposes of collective bargaining shall be the employer unit, craft unit, plant unit, or subdivision thereof: Provided, That the Board shall not (1) decide that any unit is appropriate for such purposes if such unit includes both professional employees and employees who are not professional employees unless a majority of such professional employees vote for inclusion in such unit; or (2) decide that any craft unit is inappropriate for such purposes on the ground that a different unit has been established by a prior Board determination, unless a majority of the employees in the proposed craft unit vote against separate representation; or (3) decide that any unit is appropriate for such purposes if it includes, together with other employees, any individual employed as a guard to enforce against employees and other persons rules to protect property of the employer or to protect the safety of persons on the employer's premises; but no labor organization shall be certified as the representative of employees in a bargaining unit of guards if such organization admits to membership, or is affiliated directly or indirectly with an organization which admits to membership, employees other than guards.

(c) (1) Whenever a petition shall have been filed, in accordance with such regulations as may be prescribed by the Board—

(A) by an employee or group of employees or any individual or labor organization acting in their behalf alleging that a substantial number of employees (i) wish to be represented for collective bargaining and that their employer declines to recognize their representative as the representative defined in section 9(a), or (ii) assert that the individual or labor organization, which has been certified or is being currently recognized by their employer as the bargaining representative, is no longer a representative as defined in section 9(a); or

(B) by an employer, alleging that one or more individuals or labor organizations have presented to him a claim to be recognized as the representative defined in section 9(a);

the Board shall investigate such petition and if it has reasonable cause to believe that a question of representation affecting commerce exists shall provide for an appropriate hearing upon due notice. Such hearing may be conducted by an officer or employee of the regional office, who shall not make any recommendations with respect thereto. If the Board finds upon the record of such hearing that such a question of representation exists, it shall direct an election by secret ballot and shall certify the results thereof.

(2) In determining whether or not a question of representation affecting commerce exists, the same regulations and rules of decision shall apply irrespective of the identity of the persons filing the petition or the kind of relief sought and in no case shall the Board deny a labor organization a place on the ballot by reason of an order with respect to such labor organization or its predecessor not issued in conformity with section 10(c).

(3) No election shall be directed in any bargaining unit or any subdivision within which, in the preceding twelve-month period, a valid election shall have been held. Employees [on] *engaged in an economic* strike who are not entitled to reinstatement shall [not] be eligible to vote [.] *under such regulations as the Board shall find are consistent with the purposes and provisions of this Act in*

any election conducted within twelve months after the commencement of the strike. In any election where none of the choices on the ballot receives a majority, a run-off shall be conducted, the ballot providing for a selection between the two choices receiving the largest and second largest number of valid votes cast in the election.

(4) Nothing in this section shall be construed to prohibit the waiving of hearings by stipulation for the purpose of a consent election in conformity with regulations and rules of decision of the Board.

(5) In determining whether a unit is appropriate for the purposes specified in subsection (b) the extent to which the employees have organized shall not be controlling.

(d) Whenever an order of the Board made pursuant to section 10(c) is based in whole or in part upon facts certified following an investigation pursuant to subsection (c) of this section and there is a petition for the enforcement or review of such order, such certification and the record of such investigation shall be included in the transcript of the entire record required to be filed under section 10(e) or 10 (f), and thereupon the decree of the court enforcing, modifying, or setting aside in whole or in part the order of the Board shall be made and entered upon the pleadings, testimony, and proceedings set forth in such transcript.

(e) (1) Upon the filing with the Board, by 30 per centum or more of the employees in a bargaining unit covered by an agreement between their employer and a labor organization made pursuant to section 8(a)(3), of a petition alleging they desire that such authority be rescinded, the Board shall take a secret ballot of the employees in such unit and certify the results thereof to such labor organization and to the employer.

(2) No election shall be conducted pursuant to this subsection in any bargaining unit or any subdivision within which, in the preceding twelve-month period, a valid election shall have been held.

[(f) No investigation shall be made by the Board of any question affecting commerce concerning the representation of employees, raised by a labor organization under subsection (c) of this section, and no complaint shall be issued pursuant to a charge made by a labor organization under subsection (b) of section 10, unless such labor organization and any national or international labor organization of which such labor organization is an affiliate or constituent unit (A) shall have prior thereto filed with the Secretary of Labor copies of its constitution and bylaws and a report, in such form as the Secretary may prescribe, showing—

(1) the name of such labor organization and the address of its principal place of business;

(2) the names, titles, and compensation and allowances of its three principal officers and of any of its other officers or agents whose aggregate compensation and allowances for the preceding year exceeded $5,000, and the amount of the compensation and allowances paid to each such officer or agent during such year;

(3) the manner in which the officers and agents referred to in clause (2) were elected, appointed, or otherwise selected;

(4) the initiation fee or fees which new members are required to pay on becoming members of such labor organization;

(5) the regular dues or fees which members are required to pay in order to remain members in good standing of such labor organization;

(6) a detailed statement of, or reference to provisions of its constitution and bylaws showing the procedure followed with respect to, (a) qualification for or restrictions on membership, (b) election of officers and stewards, (c) calling of regular and special meetings, (d) levying of assessments, (e) imposition of fines, (f) authorization for bargaining demands, (g) ratification of contract terms, (h) authorization for strikes, (i) authorization for disbursement of union funds, (j) audit of union financial transactions, (k) participation in insurance or other benefit plans, and (l) expulsion of members and the grounds therefor;

and (B) can show that prior thereto it has—

(1) filed with the Secretary of Labor, in such forms as the Secretary may prescribe, a report showing all of (a) its receipts of any kind and the sources of such receipts, (b) its total assets and liabilities as of the end of its last fiscal year, (c) the disbursements made by it during such fiscal year, including the purposes for which made; and

(2) furnished to all of the members of such labor organization copies of the financial report required by paragraph (1) hereof to be filed with the Secretary of Labor.]

[(g) It shall be the obligation of all labor organizations to file annually with the Secretary of Labor, in such form as the Secretary of Labor may

prescribe, reports bringing up to date the information required to be supplied in the initial filing by subsection (f)(A) of this section, and to file with the Secretary of Labor and furnish to its members annually financial reports in the form and manner prescribed in subsection (f)(B). No labor organization shall be eligible for certification under this section as the representative of any employees, and no complaint shall issue under section 10 with respect to a charge filed by a labor organization unless it can show that it and any national or international labor organization of which it is an affiliate or constituent unit has complied with its obligation under this subsection.]

[(h) No investigation shall be made by the Board of any question affecting commerce concerning the representation of employees, raised by a labor organization under subsection (c) of this section, and no complaint shall be issued pursuant to a charge made by a labor organization under subsection (b) of section 10, unless there is on file with the Board an affidavit executed contemporaneously or within the preceding twelve-month period by each officer of such labor organization and the officers of any national or international labor organization of which it is an affiliate or constituent unit that he is not a member of the Communist Party or affiliated with such party, and that he does not believe in, and is not a member of or supports any organization that believes in or teaches, the overthrow of the United States Government by force or by any illegal or unconstitutional methods. The provisions of section 35A of the Criminal Code shall be applicable in respect to such affidavits.]

PREVENTION OF UNFAIR LABOR PRACTICES. SEC. 10. (a) The Board is empowered, as hereinafter provided, to prevent any person from engaging in any unfair labor practice (listed in section 8) affecting commerce. This power shall not be affected by any other means of adjustment or prevention that has been or may be established by agreement, law, or otherwise: Provided, That the Board is empowered by agreement with any agency of any State or Territory to cede to such agency jurisdiction over any cases in any industry, (other than mining, manufacturing, communications, and transportation except where predominantly local in character) even though such cases may involve labor disputes affecting commerce, unless the provision of the State or Territorial statute applicable to the determination of such cases by such agency is inconsistent with the corresponding provisions of this Act or has received a construction inconsistent therewith.

(b) Whenever it is charged that any person has engaged in or is engaging in any such unfair labor practice, the Board, or any agent or agency designated by the Board for such purposes, shall have power to issue and cause to be served upon such person a complaint stating the charges in that respect, and containing a notice of hearing before the Board or a member thereof, or before a designated agent or agency, at a place therein fixed, not less than five days after the serving of said complaint: Provided, That no complaint shall issue based upon any unfair labor practice occurring more than six months prior to the filing of the charge with the Board and the service of a copy thereof upon the person against whom such charge is made, unless the person aggrieved thereby was prevented from filing such charge by reason of service in the armed forces, in which event the six-month period shall be computed from the day of his discharge. Any such complaint may be amended by the member, agent, or agency conducting the hearing or the Board in its discretion at any time prior to the issuance of an order based thereon. The person so complained of shall have the right to file an answer to the original or amended complaint and to appear in person or otherwise and give testimony at the place and time fixed in the complaint. In the discretion of the member, agent, or agency conducting the hearing or the Board, any other person may be allowed to intervene in the said proceeding and to present testimony. Any such proceeding shall, so far as practicable, be conducted in accordance with the rules of evidence applicable in the district courts of the United States under the rules of civil procedure for the district courts of the United States, adopted by the Supreme Court of the United States pursuant to the Act of June 19, 1934 (U.S.C., title 28, secs. 723–B, 723–C).

(c) The testimony taken by such member, agent, or agency or the Board shall be reduced to writing and filed with the Board. Thereafter, in its discretion, the Board upon notice may take further testimony or hear argument. If upon the preponderance of the testimony taken the Board shall be of the opinion that any person named in the complaint has engaged in or is engaging in any such unfair labor practice, then the Board shall state its findings of fact and shall issue and cause to be served on such person an order requiring such person to cease and desist from such unfair labor practice, and to take such affirmative action including reinstatement of employees with or without back pay, as will effectuate the policies of this Act: Provided, That where an order directs reinstatement of an employee, back pay may be required of the employer or labor organization, as the case may be, responsible for the discrimination suffered by him: And provided further, That in determining whether a complaint shall issue alleging a violation of section 8(a)(1) or section 8(a)(2), and in deciding such cases, the same regulations and rules of decision shall apply irrespective of whether or not the labor organization affected is affiliated with a labor organization national or international in scope. Such order may further require such person to make reports from time to time showing the extent to which it has complied with the order. If upon the preponderance of the testimony taken the Board shall not be of the opinion that the person named in the complaint has engaged in or is engaging in any such unfair labor practice, then the Board shall state its findings of fact and shall issue an order dismissing the said complaint. No order of the Board shall require the reinstatement of any individual as an employee who has been suspended or discharged, or the payment to him of any back pay, if such individual was suspended or discharged for cause. In case the evidence is presented before a member of the Board, or before an examiner or examiners thereof, such member, or such examiner or examiners, as the case may be, shall issue and cause to be served on the parties to the proceeding a proposed report, together with a recommended order, which shall be filed with the Board, and if no exceptions are filed within twenty days after service thereof upon such parties, or within such further period as the Board may authorize, such recommended order shall become the order of the Board and become effective as therein prescribed.

(d) Until the record in a case shall have been filed in a court, as hereinafter provided, the Board may at any time, upon reasonable notice and in such manner as it shall deem proper, modify or set aside, in whole or in part, any finding or order made or issued by it.

(e) The Board shall have power to petition any court of appeals of the United States, or if all the courts of appeals to which application may be made are in vacation, any district court of the United States, within any circuit or district, respectively, wherein the unfair labor practice in question occurred or wherein such person resides or transacts business, for the enforcement of such order and for appropriate temporary relief or restraining order, and shall file in the court the record in the proceedings, as provided in section 2112 of title 28, United States Code. Upon the filing of such petition, the court shall cause notice thereof to be served upon such person, and thereupon shall have the jurisdiction of the proceeding and of the question determined therein, and shall have power to grant such temporary relief or restraining order as it deems just and proper, and to make and enter a decree enforcing, modifying, and enforcing, as so modified, or setting aside in whole or in part the order of the Board. No objection that has not been urged before the Board, its member agent, or agency, shall be considered by the court, unless the failure or neglect to urge such objection shall be excused because of extraordinary circumstances. The findings of the Board with respect to questions of fact if supported by substantial evidence on the record considered as a whole shall be conclusive. If either party shall apply to the court for leave to adduce additional evidence and shall show to the satisfaction of the court that such additional evidence is material and that there were reasonable grounds for the failure to adduce such evidence in the hearing before the Board, its member, agent, or agency, the court may order such additional evidence to be taken before the Board, its member, agent, or agency, and to be made a part of the record. The Board may modify its findings as to the facts, or make new findings, by reason of additional evidence so taken and filed, and it shall file such modified or new findings, which findings with respect to questions of fact if supported by substantial evidence on the record considered as a whole shall be conclusive, and shall file its recommendations, if any, for the modification or setting

aside of its original order. Upon the filing of the record with it the jurisdiction of the court shall be exclusive and its judgment and decree shall be final, except that the same shall be subject to review by the appropriate United States court of appeals if application was made to the district court as hereinabove provided, and by the Supreme Court of the United States upon writ of certiorari or certification as provided in section 1254 of title 28.

(f) Any person aggrieved by a final order of the Board granting or denying in whole or in part the relief sought may obtain a review of such order in any circuit court of appeals of the United States in the circuit wherein the unfair labor practice in question was alleged to have been engaged in or wherein such person resides or transacts business, or in the United States Court of Appeals for the District of Columbia, by filing in such court a written petition praying that the order of the Board be modified or set aside. A copy of such petition shall be forthwith transmitted by the clerk of the court to the Board, and thereupon the aggrieved party shall file in the court the record in the proceeding, certified by the board, as provided in section 2112 of title 28, United States Code. Upon the filing of such petition, the court shall proceed in the same manner as in the case of an application by the Board under subsection (e) of this section, and shall have the same jurisdiction to grant to the Board such temporary relief or restraining order as it deems just and proper, and in like manner to make and enter a decree enforcing, modifying, and enforcing as so modified, or setting aside in whole or in part the order of the Board; the findings of the Board with respect to questions of fact if supported by substantial evidence on the record considered as a whole shall in like manner be conclusive.

(g) The commencement of proceedings under subsection (e) or (f) of this section shall not, unless specifically ordered by the court, operate as a stay of the Board's order.

(h) When granting appropriate temporary relief or a restraining order, or making and entering a decree enforcing, modifying, and enforcing as so modified, or setting aside in whole or in part an order of the Board, as provided in this section, the jurisdiction of courts sitting in equity shall not be limited by the Act entitled "An Act to amend the Judicial Code and to define and limit the jurisdiction of courts sitting in equity, and for other purposes," approved March 23, 1932 (U.S.C., Supp. VII, title 29, secs. 101–115).

(i) Petitions filed under this Act shall be heard expeditiously, and if possible within ten days after they have been docketed.

(j) The Board shall have power, upon issuance of a complaint as provided in subsection (b) charging that any person has engaged in or is engaging in an unfair labor practice, to petition any district court of the United States (including the District Court of the United States for the District of Columbia), within any district wherein the unfair labor practice in question is alleged to have occurred or wherein such person resides or transacts business, for appropriate temporary relief or restraining order. Upon the filing of any such petition the court shall cause notice thereof to be served upon such person, and thereupon shall have jurisdiction to grant to the Board such temporary relief or restraining order as it deems just and proper.

(k) Whenever it is charged that any person has engaged in an unfair labor practice within the meaning of paragraph (4) (D) of section 8(b), the Board is empowered and directed to hear and determine the dispute out of which such unfair labor practice shall have arisen, unless, within ten days after notice that such charge has been filed, the parties to such dispute submit to the Board satisfactory evidence that they have adjusted, or agreed upon methods for the voluntary adjustment of the dispute. Upon compliance by the parties to the dispute with the decision of the Board or upon such voluntary adjustment of the dispute, such charge shall be dismissed.

(l) Whenever it is charged that any person has engaged in an unfair labor practice within the meaning of paragraph (4) (A), (B), or (C) of section 8(b), *or section 8(e) or section 8(b)(7)*, the preliminary investigation of such charge shall be made forthwith and given priority over all other cases except cases of like character in the office where it is filed or to which it is referred. If, after such investigation, the officer or regional attorney to whom the matter may be referred has reasonable cause to believe such charge is true and that a complaint should issue, he shall, on behalf of the Board, petition any district court of the United States (including the District Court of the United States for the District of Columbia) within any district where the unfair labor practice in question has occurred, is alleged to have occurred, or wherein such person resides or transacts business, for appropriate injunctive relief pending the final adjudication of the Board with respect to such matter. Upon the filing of any such petition the district court shall have jurisdiction to grant such injunctive relief or temporary restraining order as it deems just and proper, notwithstanding any other provision of law: Provided further, That no temporary restraining order shall be issued without notice unless a petition alleges that substantial and irreparable injury to the charging party will be unavoidable and such temporary restraining order shall be effective for no longer than five days and will become void at the expiration of such period [.]: Provided further, That such officer or regional attorney shall not apply for any restraining order under section 8(b)(7) if a charge against the employer under section 8(a)(2) has been filed and after the preliminary investigation, he has reasonable cause to believe that such charge is true and that a complaint should issue. Upon filing of any such petition the courts shall cause notice thereof to be served upon any person involved in the charge and such person, including the charging party, shall be given an opportunity to appear by counsel and present any relevant testimony: Provided further, That for the purposes of this subsection district courts shall be deemed to have jurisdiction of a labor organization (1) in the district in which such organization maintains its principal office, or (2) in any district in which its duly authorized officers or agents are engaged in promoting or protecting the interests of employee members. The service of legal process upon such officer or agent shall constitute service upon the labor organization and make such organization a party to the suit. In situations where such relief is appropriate the procedure specified herein shall apply to charges with respect to section 8(b)(4)(D).

(m) Whenever it is charged that any person has engaged in an unfair labor practice within the meaning of subsection (a)(3) or (b)(2) of section 8, such charges shall be given priority over all other cases except cases of like character in the office where it is filed or to which it is referred and cases given priority under subsection (1).

INVESTIGATORY POWERS

SEC. 11. For the purpose of all hearings and investigations, which, in the opinion of the Board, are necessary and proper for the exercise of the powers vested in it by section 9 and section 10—

(1) The Board, or its duly authorized agents or agencies, shall at all reasonable times have access to, for the purpose of examination, and the right to copy any evidence of any person being investigated or proceeded against that relates to any matter under investigation or in question. The Board, or any member thereof, shall upon application of any party to such proceedings, forthwith issue to such party subpoenas requiring the attendance and testimony of witnesses or the production of any evidence in such proceeding or investigation requested in such application. Within five days after the service of a subpoena on any person requiring the production of any evidence in his possession or under his control, such person may petition the Board to revoke, and the Board shall revoke, such subpoena if in its opinion the evidence whose production is required does not relate to any matter under investigation, or any matter in question in such proceedings, or if in its opinion such subpoena does not describe with sufficient particularity the evidence whose production is required. Any member of the Board, or any agent or agency designated by the Board for such purposes, may administer oaths and affirmations, examine witnesses, and receive evidence. Such attendance of witnesses and the production of such evidence may be required from any place in the United States or any Territory or possession thereof, at any designated place of hearing.

(2) In case of contumacy or refusal to obey a subpoena issued to any person, any district court of the United States or the United States courts of any Territory or possession, or the District Court of the United States for the District of Columbia, within the jurisdiction of which the inquiry is carried on or within the jurisdiction of which said person guilty of contumacy or refusal to obey is found or resides or transacts business, upon application by the Board shall have jurisdiction to issue to such person an order requiring such person to appear before the Board, its member, agent, or agency, there to produce evidence if so ordered, or there to give testimony touching the matter under investigation or in question; and any failure to obey such order of the court may be punished by said court as a contempt thereof.

(3) [Repealed.]

(4) Complaints, orders, and other process and papers of the Board, its member, agent, or agency, may be served either personally or by registered mail or by telegraph or by leaving a copy thereof at the principal office or place of business of the person required to be served. The verified return by the individual so serving the same setting forth the manner of such service shall be proof of the same, and the return post office receipt or telegraph receipt therefor when registered and mailed or telegraphed as aforesaid shall be proof of service of the same. Witnesses summoned before the Board, its member, agent, or agency, shall be paid the same fees and mileage that are paid witnesses in the court of the United States, and witnesses whose depositions are taken and the persons taking the same shall severally be entitled to the same fees as are paid for like services in the courts of the United States.

(5) All process of any court to which application may be made under this Act may be served in the judicial district wherein the defendant or other person required to be served resides or may be found.

(6) The several departments and agencies of the Government, when directed by the President, shall furnish the Board, upon its request, all records, papers, and information in their possession relating to any matter before the Board.

SEC. 12. Any person who shall willfully resist, prevent, impede, or interfere with any member of the Board or any of its agents or agencies in the performance of duties pursuant to this Act shall be punished by a fine of not more than $5,000 or by imprisonment for not more than one year, or both.

LIMITATIONS

SEC. 13. Nothing in this Act, except as specifically provided for herein, shall be construed so as either to interfere with or impede or diminish in any way the right to strike, or to affect the limitations or qualifications on that right.

SEC. 14.   (a) Nothing herein shall prohibit any individual employed as a supervisor from becoming or remaining a member of a labor organization, but no employer subject to this Act shall be compelled to deem individuals defined herein as supervisors as employees for the purpose of any law, either national or local, relating to collective bargaining.

(b) Nothing in this Act shall be construed as authorizing the execution or application of agreements requiring membership in a labor organization as a condition of employment in any State or Territory in which such execution or application is prohibited by State or Territorial law.

(c) (1) The Board, in its discretion, may, by rule of decision or by published rules adopted pursuant to the Administrative Procedure Act, decline to assert jurisdiction over any labor dispute involving any class or category of employers, where, in the opinion of the Board, the effect of such labor dispute on commerce is not sufficiently substantial to warrant the exercise of its jurisdiction: Provided, That the Board shall not decline to assert jurisdiction over any labor dispute over which it would assert jurisdiction under the standards prevailing upon August 1, 1959.

(2) Nothing in this Act shall be deemed to prevent or bar any agency or the courts of any State or Territory (including the Commonwealth of Puerto Rico, Guam, and the Virgin Islands), from assuming and asserting jurisdiction over labor disputes over which the Board declines, pursuant to paragraph (1) of this subsection, to assert jurisdiction.

SEC. 15.   Wherever the application of the provisions of section 272 of chapter 10 of the Act entitled "An Act to establish a uniform system of bankruptcy throughout the United States," approved July 1, 1898, and Acts amendatory thereof and supplementary thereto (U.S.C., title 11, sec. 672), conflicts with the application of the provisions of this Act, this Act shall prevail: Provided, That in any situation where the provisions of this Act cannot be validly enforced, the provisions of such other Acts shall remain in full force and effect.

SEC. 16.   If any provision of this Act, or the application of such provision to any person or circumstances, shall be held invalid, the remainder of this Act, or the application of such provision to persons or circumstances other than those as to which it is held invalid, shall not be affected thereby.

SEC. 17.   This Act may be cited as the "National Labor Relations Act."

SEC. 18.   No petition entertained, no investigation made, no election held, and no certification issued by the National Labor Relations Board, under any of the provisions of section 9 of the National Labor Relations Act, as amended, shall be invalid by reason of the failure of the Congress of Industrial Organizations to have complied with the requirements of section 9(f), (g), or (h) of the aforesaid Act prior to December 22, 1949, or by reason of the failure of the American Federation of Labor to have complied with the provisions of section 9(f), (g), or (h) of the aforesaid Act prior to November 7, 1947: Provided, That no liability shall be imposed under any provision of this Act upon any person for failure to honor any election or certificate referred to above, prior to the effective date of this amendment: Provided, however, That this proviso shall not have the effect of setting aside or in any way affecting judgments or decrees heretofore entered under section 10(e) or (f) and which have become final.

INDIVIDUALS WITH RELIGIOUS CONVICTIONS

SEC. 19.   Any employee of a health care institution who is a member of and adheres to established traditional tenets or teachings of a bona fide religion, body, or sect which has historically held conscientious objections to joining or financially supporting labor organizations shall not be required to join or financially support any labor organization as a condition of employment; except that such employee may be required, in lieu of periodic dues and initiation fees, to pay sums equal to such dues and initiation fees to a nonreligious charitable fund exempt from taxation under section 501(c)(3) of the Internal Revenue Code, chosen by such employee from a list of at least three such funds, designated in a contract between such institution and a labor organization, or if the contract fails to designate such funds, then to any such fund chosen by the employee.

EFFECTIVE DATE OF CERTAIN CHANGES*

SEC. 102. No provision of this title shall be deemed to make an unfair labor practice any act which was performed prior to the date of the enactment of this Act which did not constitute an unfair labor practice prior thereto, and the provisions of section 8(a)(3) and section 8(b)(2) of the National Labor Relations Act as amended by this title shall not make an unfair labor practice the performance of any obligation under a collective-bargaining agreement entered into prior to the date of the enactment of this Act, or (in the case of an agreement for a period of not more than one year) entered into on or after such date of enactment, but prior to the effective date of this title, if the performance of such obligation would not have constituted an unfair labor practice under section 8(3) of the National Labor Relations Act prior to the effective date of this title, unless such agreement was renewed or extended subsequent thereto.

SEC. 103. No provisions of this title shall affect any certification of representatives or any determination as to the appropriate collective-bargaining unit, which was made under section 9 of the National Labor Relations Act prior to the effective date of this title until one year after the date of such certification or if, in respect of any such certification, a collective-bargaining contract was entered into prior to the effective date of this title, until the end of the contract period or until one year after such date, whichever first occurs.

SEC. 104. The amendments made by this title shall take effect sixty days after the date of the enactment of this Act, except that the authority of

---

*The effective date referred to in Sections 102, 103, and 104 is August 22, 1947.

the President to appoint certain officers conferred upon him by section 3 of the National Labor Relations Act as amended by this title may be exercised forthwith.

CONCILIATION OF LABOR DISPUTES IN INDUSTRIES AFFECTING COMMERCE: NATIONAL EMERGENCIES

SEC. 201. That it is the policy of the United States that—

(a) sound and stable industrial peace and the advancement of the general welfare, health, and safety of the Nation and of the best interest of employers and employees can most satisfactorily be secured by the settlement of issues between employers and employees through the processes of conference and collective bargaining between employers and the representatives of their employees;

(b) the settlement of issues between employers and employees through collective bargaining may be advanced by making available full and adequate governmental facilities for conciliation, mediation, and voluntary arbitration to aid and encourage employers and the representatives of their employees to reach and maintain agreements concerning rates of pay, hours, and working conditions, and to make all reasonable efforts to settle their differences by mutual agreement reached through conferences and collective bargaining or by such methods as may be provided for in any applicable agreement for the settlement of disputes; and

(c) certain controversies which arise between parties to collective bargaining agreements may be avoided or minimized by making available full and adequate governmental facilities for furnishing assistance to employers and the representatives of their employees in formulating for inclusion within such agreements provision for adequate notice of any proposed changes in the terms of such agreements, for the final adjustment of grievances or questions regarding the application or interpretation of such agreements, and other provisions designed to prevent the subsequent arising of such controversies.

SEC. 202.   (a) There is hereby created an independent agency to be known as the Federal Mediation and Conciliation Service (herein referred to as the "Service," except that for sixty days after the date of the enactment of this Act such term shall refer to the Conciliation Service of the Department of Labor). The Service shall be under the direction of a Federal Mediation and Conciliation Director (hereinafter referred to as the "Director"), who shall be appointed by the President by and with the advice and consent of the Senate. The Director shall receive compensation at the rate of $12,000* per annum. The Director shall not engage in any other business, vocation, or employment.

(b) The Director is authorized, subject to the civil-service laws, to appoint such clerical and other personnel as may be necessary for the execution of the functions of the Service, and shall fix their compensation in accordance with the Classification Act of 1923, as amended, and may, without regard to the provisions of the civil service laws and the Classification Act of 1923, as amended, appoint and fix the compensation of such conciliators and mediators as may be necessary to carry out the functions of the Service. The Director is authorized to make such expenditures for supplies, facilities, and services as he deems necessary. Such expenditures shall be allowed and paid upon presentation of itemized vouchers therefor approved by the Director or by any employee designated by him for that purpose.

(c) The principal office of the Service shall be in the District of Columbia, but the Director may establish regional offices convenient to localities in which labor controversies are likely to arise. The Director may by order, subject to revocation at any time, delegate any authority and discretion conferred upon him by this Act to any regional director, or other officer or employee of the Service. The Director may establish suitable procedures for cooperation with State and local mediation agencies. The Director shall make an annual report in writing to Congress at the end of the fiscal year.

(d) All mediation and conciliation functions of the Secretary of Labor or the United States Conciliation Service under section 8 of the Act entitled "An Act to create a Department of Labor," approved March 4, 1913 (U.S.C., title 29, sec. 51), and all functions of the United States Conciliation Service under any other law are hereby transferred to the Federal Mediation and Conciliation Service, together with the personnel and records of the United States Conciliation Service. Such transfer shall take effect upon the sixtieth day after the date of enactment of this Act. Such transfer shall not affect any proceedings, pending before the United States Conciliation Service or any certification, order, rule, or regulation theretofore made by it or by the Secretary of Labor. The Director and the Service shall not be subject in any way to the jurisdiction or authority of the Secretary of Labor or any official or division of the Department of Labor.

FUNCTIONS OF THE SERVICE

SEC. 203.   (a) It shall be the duty of the Service, in order to prevent or minimize interruptions of the free flow of commerce growing out of labor disputes, to assist parties to labor disputes in industries affecting commerce to settle such disputes through conciliation and mediation.

(b) The Service may proffer its services in any labor dispute in any industry affecting commerce, either upon its own motion or upon the request of one or more of the parties to the dispute, whenever in its judgment such dispute threatens to cause a substantial interruption of commerce. The Director and the Service are directed to avoid attempting to mediate disputes which would have only a minor effect on interstate commerce if State or other conciliation services are available to the parties. Whenever the Service does proffer its services in any dispute, it shall be the duty of the Service promptly to put itself in communication with the parties and to use its best efforts, by mediation and conciliation, to bring them to agreement.

(c) If the Director is not able to bring the parties to agreement by conciliation within a reasonable time, he shall seek to induce the parties voluntarily to seek other means of settling the dispute without resort to strike, lockout, or other coercion, including submission to the employees in the bargaining unit of the employer's last offer of settlement for approval or rejection in a secret ballot. The failure or refusal of either party to agree to any procedure suggested by the Director shall not be deemed a violation of any duty or obligation imposed by this Act.

(d) Final adjustment by a method agreed upon by the parties is hereby declared to be the desirable method for settlement of grievance disputes arising over the application or interpretation of an existing collective-bargaining agreement. The Service is directed to make its conciliation and mediation services available in the settlement of such grievance disputes only as a last resort and in exceptional cases.

Sec. 204. (a) In order to prevent or minimize interruptions of the free flow of commerce growing out of labor disputes, employers and employees and their representatives, in any industry affecting commerce, shall—

(1) exert every reasonable effort to make and maintain agreements concerning rates of pay, hours, and working conditions, including provision for adequate notice of any proposed change in the terms of such agreements;

(2) whenever a dispute arises over the terms or application of a collective-bargaining agreement and a conference is requested by a party or prospective party thereto, arrange promptly for such a conference to be held and endeavor in such conference to settle such dispute expeditiously; and

(3) in case such dispute is not settled by conference, participate fully and promptly in such meetings as may be undertaken by the Service under this Act for the purpose of aiding in a settlement of the dispute.

Sec. 205. (a) There is hereby created a National Labor-Management Panel which shall be composed of twelve members appointed by the President, six of whom shall be selected from among persons outstanding in the field of management and six of whom shall be selected from among persons outstanding in the field of labor. Each member shall hold office for a term of three years, except that any member appointed to fill a vacancy occurring prior to the expiration of the term for which his predecessor was appointed shall be appointed for the remainder of such term, and the terms of office of the members first taking office shall expire, as designated by the President at the time of appointment, four at the end of the first year, four at the end of the second year, and four at

the end of the third year after the date of appointment. Members of the panel, when serving on business of the panel, shall be paid compensation at the rate of $25 per day, and shall also be entitled to receive an allowance for actual and necessary travel and subsistence expenses while so serving away from their places of residence.

(b) It shall be the duty of the panel, at the request of the Director, to advise in the avoidance of industrial controversies and the manner in which mediation and voluntary adjustment shall be administered, particularly with reference to controversies affecting the general welfare of the country.

NATIONAL EMERGENCIES

Sec. 206. Whenever in the opinion of the President of the United States, a threatened or actual strike or lockout affecting an entire industry or a substantial part thereof engaged in trade, commerce, transportation, transmission, or communication among the several States or with foreign nations, or engaged in the production of goods for commerce, will, if permitted to occur or to continue, imperil the national health or safety, he may appoint a board of inquiry to inquire into the issues involved in the dispute and to make a written report to him within such time as he shall prescribe. Such report shall include a statement of the facts with respect to the dispute, including each party's statement of its position but shall not contain any recommendations. The President shall file a copy of such report with the Service and shall make its contents available to the public.

Sec. 207. (a) A board of inquiry shall be composed of a chairman and such other members as the President shall determine, and shall have power to sit and act in any place within the United States and to conduct such hearings either in public or in private, as it may deem necessary or proper, to ascertain the facts with respect to the causes and circumstances of the dispute.

(b) Members of a board of inquiry shall receive compensation at the rate of $50 for each day actually spent by them in the work of the board, together with necessary travel and subsistence expenses.

(c) For the purpose of any hearing or inquiry conducted by any board appointed under this title, the provisions of sections 9 and 10 (relating to the attendance of witnesses and the production of books, papers, and documents) of the Federal Trade Commission Act of September 16, 1914, as amended (U.S.C. 19, title 15, secs. 49 and 50, as amended), are hereby made applicable to the powers and duties of such board.

SEC. 208.   (a) Upon receiving a report from a board of inquiry the President may direct the Attorney General to petition any district court of the United States having jurisdiction of the parties to enjoin such strike or lockout or the continuing thereof, and if the court finds that such threatened or actual strike or lockout—

(i) affects an entire industry or a substantial part thereof engaged in trade, commerce, transportation, transmission, or communication among the several States or with foreign nations, or engaged in the production of goods for commerce; and

(ii) if permitted to occur or to continue, will imperil the national health or safety, it shall have jurisdiction to enjoin any such strike or lockout, or the continuing thereof, and to make such other orders as may be appropriate.

(b) In any case, the provisions of the Act of March 23, 1932, entitled "An Act to amend the Judicial Code and to define and limit the jurisdiction of courts sitting in equity, and for other purposes," shall not be applicable.

(c) The order or orders of the court shall be subject to review by the appropriate circuit court of appeals and by the Supreme Court upon writ of certiorari of certification as provided in sections 239 and 240 of the Judicial Code, as amended (U.S.C., title 29, secs. 346 and 347).

SEC. 209.   (a) Whenever a district court has issued an order under section 208 enjoining acts or practices which imperil or threaten to imperil the national health or safety, it shall be the duty of the parties to the labor dispute giving rise to such order to make every effort to adjust and settle their dif-

ferences, with the assistance of the Service created by this Act. Neither party shall be under any duty to accept, in whole or in part, any proposal of settlement made by the Service.

(b) Upon the issuance of such order, the President shall reconvene the board of inquiry which has previously reported with respect to the dispute. At the end of a sixty-day period (unless the dispute has been settled by that time), the board of inquiry shall report to the President the current position of the parties and the efforts which has (sic) been made for settlement, and shall include a statement by each party of its position and a statement of the employer's last offer of settlement. The President shall make such report available to the public. The National Labor Relations Board, within the succeeding fifteen days, shall take a secret ballot of the employees of each employer involved in the dispute on the question of whether they wish to accept the final offer of settlement made by their employer as stated by him and shall certify the results thereof to the Attorney General within five days thereafter.

SEC. 210.   Upon the certification of the results of such ballot or upon a settlement being reached, whichever happens sooner, the Attorney General shall move the court to discharge the injunction, which motion shall then be granted and the injunction discharged. When such motion is granted, the President shall submit to the Congress a full and comprehensive report of the proceedings, including the findings of the board of inquiry and the ballot taken by the National Labor Relations Board, together with such recommendations as he may see fit to make for consideration and appropriate action.

COMPILATION OF COLLECTIVE-BARGAINING AGREEMENTS, ETC. SEC. 211.   (a) For the guidance and information of interested representatives of employers, employees, and the general public, the Bureau of Labor Statistics of the Department of Labor shall maintain a file of copies of all available collective-bargaining agreements and other available agreements and actions thereunder settling or adjusting labor disputes. Such file shall be open to inspection under appropriate conditions prescribed by the Secretary of Labor, except that no specific information submitted in confidence shall be disclosed.

(b) The Bureau of Labor Statistics in the Department of Labor is authorized to furnish upon request of the Service, or employers, employees, or their representatives, all available data and factual information which may aid in the settlement of any labor dispute, except that no specific information submitted to confidence shall be disclosed.

EXEMPTION OF RAILWAY LABOR ACT. SEC. 212. The provisions of this title shall not be applicable with respect to any matter which is subject to the provisions of the Railway Labor Act, as amended from time to time.

CONCILIATION OF LABOR DISPUTES IN THE HEALTH CARE INDUSTRY

SEC. 213. (a) If, in the opinion of the Director of the Federal Mediation and Conciliation Service a threatened or actual strike or lockout affecting a health care institution will, if permitted to occur or to continue, substantially interrupt the delivery of health care in the locality concerned, the Director may further assist in the resolution of the impasse by establishing within 30 days after the notice to the Federal Mediation and Conciliation Service under clause (A) of the last sentence of section 8(d) [which is required by clause (3) of such section 8(d)], or within 10 days after the notice under clause (B), an impartial Board of Inquiry to investigate the issue involved in the dispute and to make a written report thereon to the parties within fifteen (15) days after the establishment of such a Board. The written report shall contain the findings of fact together with the Board's recommendations for settling the dispute. Each such Board shall be composed of such number of individuals as the Director may deem desirable. No member appointed under this section shall have any interest or involvement in the health care institutions or the employee organizations involved in the dispute.

(b) (1) Members of any board established under this section who are otherwise employed by the Federal Government shall serve without compensation but shall be reimbursed for travel, sub-

sistence, and other necessary expenses incurred by them in carrying out its duties under this section.

(2) Members of any board established under this section who are not subject to paragraph (1) shall receive compensation at a rate prescribed by the Director but not to exceed the daily rate prescribed for GS-18 of the General Schedule under section 5332 of title 5, United States Code, including travel for each day they are engaged in the performance of their duties under this section and shall be entitled to reimbursement for travel, subsistence, and other necessary expenses incurred by them in carrying out their duties under this section.

(c) After the establishment of a board under subsection (a) of this section and for 15 days after any such board has issued its report, no change in the status quo in effect prior to the expiration of the contract in the case of negotiations for a contract renewal, or in effect prior to the time of the impasse in the case of an initial bargaining negotiation, except by agreement, shall be made by the parties to the controversy.

SUITS BY AND AGAINST LABOR ORGANIZATIONS

SEC. 301. (a) Suits for violation of contracts between an employer and a labor organization representing employees in an industry affecting commerce as defined in this Act, or between any such labor organizations, may be brought in any district court of the United States having jurisdiction of the parties, without respect to the amount in controversy or without regard to the citizenship of the parties.

(b) Any labor organization which represents employees in an industry affecting commerce as defined in this Act and any employer whose activities affect commerce as defined in this Act shall be bound by the acts of its agents. Any such labor organization may sue or be sued as an entity and in behalf of the employees whom it represents in the courts of the United States. Any money judgment against a labor organization in a district court of the United States shall be enforceable only against the organization as an entity and against its assets, and shall not be enforceable against any individual member or his assets.

(c) For the purposes of actions and proceedings by or against labor organizations in the district courts of the United States, district courts shall be deemed to have jurisdiction of a labor organization (1) in the district in which such organization maintains its principal office, or (2) in any district in which its duly authorized officers or agents are engaged in representing or acting for employee members.

(d) The service of summons, subpoena, or other legal process of any court of the United States upon an officer or agent of a labor organization, in his capacity as such, shall constitute service upon the labor organization.

(e) For the purposes of this section, in determining whether any person is acting as an "agent" of another person so as to make such other person responsible for his acts, the question of whether the specific acts performed were actually authorized or subsequently ratified shall not be controlling.

RESTRICTIONS ON PAYMENTS TO EMPLOYEE REPRESENTATIVES. SEC. 302.   (a) It shall be unlawful for any employer *or association of employers or any person who acts as a labor relations expert, adviser, or consultant to an employer or who acts in the interest of an employer* to pay, *lend*, or deliver, or [to] agree to pay, *lend*, or deliver, any money or other thing of value—

(1) to any representative of any of his employees who are employed in an industry affecting commerce [.]; *or*

(2) to any labor organization, or any officer or employee thereof, which represents, seeks to represent, or would admit to membership, any of the employees of such employer who are employed in an industry affecting commerce; or

(3) to any employee or group or committee of employees of such employer employed in an industry affecting commerce in excess of their normal compensation for the purpose of causing such employee or group or committee directly or indirectly to influence any other employees in the exercise of the right to organize and bargain collectively through representatives of their own choosing; or

(4) to any officer or employee of a labor organization engaged in an industry affecting commerce with intent to influence him in respect to any of his actions, decisions, or duties as a representative of employees or as such officer or employee of such labor organization.

(b) (1) It shall be unlawful for any [representative of any employees who are employed in an industry affecting commerce] *person* to *request, demand,* receive, or accept, or [to] agree to receive or accept, [from the employer of such employees] *any payment, loan, or delivery* of any money or other thing of value[.] *prohibited by subsection* (a).

(2) It shall be unlawful for any labor organization, or for any person acting as an officer, agent, representative, or employee of such labor organization, to demand or accept from the operator of any motor vehicle (as defined in part II of the Interstate Commerce Act) employed in the transportation of property in commerce, or the employer of any such operator, any money or other thing of value payable to such organization or to an officer, agent, representative or employee thereof as a fee or charge for the unloading, or in connection with the unloading, of the cargo of such vehicle: Provided, That nothing in this paragraph shall be construed to make unlawful any payment by an employer to any of his employees as compensation for their services as employees.

(c) The provisions of this section shall not be applicable (1) [with] in respect to any money or other thing of value payable by an employer *to any of his employees whose established duties include acting openly for such employer in matters of labor relations or personnel administration or to any representative of his employees, or to any officer or employee of a labor organization* who is *also* an employee or former employee of such employer, as a compensation for, or by reason of, his service[s] as an employee of such employer; (2) with respect to the payment or delivery of any money or other thing of value in satisfaction of a judgment of any court or a decision or award of an arbitrator or impartial chairman or in compromise, adjustment, settlement, or release of any claim, complaint, grievance, or dispute in the absence of fraud or duress; (3) with respect to the sale or purchase of an article or commodity at the prevailing market price in the regular course of business; (4) with respect to money deducted from the wages of employees in payment of membership dues in a labor organization: Provided, That the employer has received from each employee, on whose account such deductions are made, a written assignment which shall not be irrevocable for a period of more than one year, or beyond the termination date of the applicable collective agreement, whichever occurs sooner; [or] (5) with respect to money or other thing of value paid to a trust fund established by such representative, for the sole and exclusive benefit of the employees of such employer, and their families and dependents (or of such employees, families, and dependents jointly with the employees of other employers making similar payments, and their families and dependents): Provided, That (A) such payments are held in trust for the purpose of paying, either from principal or income or both, for the benefit of employees, their families and dependents, for medical or hospital care, pensions on retirement or death of employees, compensation for injuries or illness resulting from occupational activity or insurance to provide any of the foregoing, or unemployment benefits or life insurance, disability and sickness insurance, or accident insurance; (B) the detailed basis on which such payments are to be made is specified in a written agreement with the employer, and employees and employers are equally represented in the administration of such fund, together with such neutral persons as the representatives in the administration of such fund, together with such neutral persons as the representatives of the employers and the representatives of [the] employees may agree upon and in the event the employer and employee groups deadlock on the administration of such fund and there are no neutral persons empowered to break such deadlock, such agreement provides that the two groups shall agree on an impartial umpire to decide such dispute or in event of their failure to agree within a reasonable length of time an impartial umpire to decide such dispute shall, on petition of either group, be appointed by the district court of the United States for the district where the trust fund has its principal office, and shall also contain provisions for an annual audit of the trust fund, a statement of the results of which shall be available for inspection by interested persons at the principal office of the trust fund and at such other places as may be designated in such written agreement; and (C) such payments as are intended to be used for the purpose of providing pensions or annuities for employees are made to a separate trust which provides that the funds held therein cannot be used for any purpose other than paying such pensions or annuities [.]; *or (6) with respect to money or other thing of value paid by any employer to a trust fund established by such representative for the purpose of pooled vacation, holiday, severance or similar benefits, or defraying costs of apprenticeship or other training programs; Provided, That the requirements of clause (B) of the proviso to clause (5) of this subsection shall apply to such trust funds.* [; or] (7) With respect to money or other thing of value paid by any employer to a pooled or individual trust fund established by such representative for the purpose of (A) scholarships for the benefit of employees, their families, and dependents for study at educational institutions, or (B) child care centers for preschool and school age dependents of employees: Provided, That no labor organization or employer shall be required to bargain on the establishment of any such trust fund, and refusal to do so shall not constitute an unfair labor practice: Provided further, That the requirements of clause (B) of the proviso to clause (5) of this subsection shall apply to such trust funds; or (8) with respect to money or any other thing of value paid by any employer to a trust fund established by such representative for the purpose of defraying the costs of legal services for employees, their families, and dependents for counsel or plan of their choice: Provided, That the requirements of clause (B) of the proviso to clause (5) of this subsection shall apply to such trust funds: Provided further, That no such legal services shall be furnished: (A) to initiate any proceeding directed (i) against any such employer or its officers or agents except in workman's compensation cases, or (ii) against such labor organizations, or its parent or subordinate bodies, or their officers or agents, or (iii) against any other employer or labor organization, or their officers or agents, in any matter arising under the National Labor Relations Act, as amended, or this Act; and (B) in any proceeding where a labor organization would have been prohibited from defraying the costs of legal services by the provisions of the Labor-Management Reporting and Disclosure Act of 1959.

(d) Any person who willfully violates any of the provisions of this section shall, upon conviction thereof, be guilty of a misdemeanor and be subject to a fine of not more than $10,000 or to imprisonment for not more than one year, or both.

(e) The district courts of the United States and the United States courts of the Territories and possessions shall have jurisdiction, for cause shown, and subject to the provisions of section 17 (relating to notice to opposite party) of the Act entitled "An Act to supplement existing laws against unlawful restraints and monopolies, and for other purposes," approved October 15, 1914, as amended (U.S.C., title 28, sec. 381), to restrain violations of this section, without regard to the provisions of sections 6 and 20 of such Act of October 15, 1914, as amended (U.S.C. title 15, sec. 17, and title 29, sec. 52), and the provisions of the Act entitled "An Act to amend the Judicial Code and to define and limit the jurisdiction of courts sitting in equity, and for other purposes," approved March 23, 1932 (U.S.C., title 29, secs. 101–115).

(f) This section shall not apply to any contract in force on the date of enactment of this Act, until the expiration of such contract, or until July 1, 1948, whichever first occurs.

(g) Compliance with the restrictions contained in subsection (c)(5)(B) upon contributions to trust funds, otherwise lawful, shall not be applicable to contributions to such trust funds established by collective agreement prior to January 1, 1946, nor shall subsection (c)(5)(A) be construed as prohibiting contributions to such trust funds if prior to January 1, 1947, such funds contained provisions for pooled vacation benefits.

BOYCOTTS AND OTHER UNLAWFUL COMBINATIONS. SEC. 303.   (a) It shall be unlawful, for the purpose [s] of this section only, in an industry or activity affecting commerce, for any labor organization to engage in [, or to induce or encourage the employees of any employer to engage in, a strike or a concerted refusal in the course of their employment to use, manufacture, process, transport, or otherwise handle or work on any goods, articles, materials, or commodities or to perform any services, where an object thereof is—]

[(1) forcing or requiring any employer or self-employed person to join any labor or employer organization or any employer or other person to cease using, selling, handling, transporting, or otherwise dealing in the products of any other producer, processor, or manufacturer, or to cease doing business with any other person;]

[(2) forcing or requiring any other employer to recognize or bargain with a labor organization as the representative of his employees unless such labor organization has been certified as the representative of such employees under the provisions of section 9 of the National Labor Relations Act;]

[(3) forcing or requiring any employer to recognize or bargain with a particular labor organization as the representative of his employees if another labor organization has been certified as the representative of such employees under the provisions of section 9 of the National Labor Relations Act;]

[(4) forcing or requiring any employer to assign particular work to employees in a particular labor organization or in a particular trade, craft, or class rather than to employees in another labor organization or in another trade, craft, or class unless such employer is failing to conform to an order or certification of the National Labor Relations Board determining the bargaining representative for employees performing such work. Nothing contained in this subsection shall be construed to make unlawful a refusal by any person to enter upon the premises of any employer (other than his own employer), if the employees of such employer are engaged in a strike ratified or approved by a representative of such employees whom such employer is required to recognize under the National Labor Relations Act.]

any activity or conduct defined as an unfair labor practice in section 8(b)(4) of the National Labor Relations Act, as amended.

(b) Whoever shall be injured in his business or property by reason of any violation of subsection (a) may sue therefor in any district court of the United States subject to the limitations and provisions of section 301 hereof without respect to the amount in controversy, or in any other court having jurisdiction of the parties, and shall recover the damages by him sustained and the cost of the suit.

RESTRICTION ON POLITICAL CONTRIBUTIONS

Sec. 304.   Section 313 of the Federal Corrupt Practices Act, 1925 (U.S.C., 1940 edition, title 2, sec. 251; Supp. V, title 50, App., sec. 1509), as amended, is amended to read as follows:

Sec. 313.   It is unlawful for any national bank, or any corporation organized by authority of any law of Congress, to make a contribution or expenditure in connection with any election to any political office, or in connection with any primary election or political convention or caucus held to select candidates for any political office, or for any corporation whatever, or any labor organization to make a contribution or expenditure in connection with any election at which Presidential and Vice Presidential electors or a Senator or Representative in, or a Delegate or Resident Commissioner to Congress are to be voted for, or in connection with any primary election or political convention or caucus held to select candidates for any of the foregoing offices, or for any candidate, political committee, or other person to accept or receive any contribution prohibited by this section. Every corporation or labor organization which makes any contribution or expenditure in violation of this section shall be fined not more than $5,000; and every officer or director of any corporation, or officer of any labor organization, who consents to any contribution or expenditure by the corporation or labor organization, as the case may be, in violation of this section shall be fined not more than $1,000 or imprisoned for not more than one year, or both. For the purposes of this section "labor organization" means any organization of any kind, or any agency or employee representation committee or plan, in which employees participate and which exists for the purpose, in whole or in part, of dealing with employers concerning grievances, labor disputes, wages, rates of pay, hours of employment, or conditions of work.

STRIKES BY GOVERNMENT EMPLOYEES

Sec. 305.   It shall be unlawful for any individual employed by the United States or any agency thereof including wholly owned Government corporations to participate in any strike. Any individual employed by the United States or by any such agency who strikes shall be discharged immediately from his employment, and shall forfeit his civil-service status, if any, and shall not be eligible for reemployment for three years by the United States or any such agency.

CREATION OF JOINT COMMITTEE TO STUDY AND REPORT ON BASIC PROBLEMS AFFECTING FRIENDLY LABOR RELATIONS AND PRODUCTIVITY

Sec. 401.   There is hereby established a joint congressional committee to be known as the Joint Committee on Labor-Management Relations (hereafter referred to as the committee), and to be composed of seven Members of the Senate Committee on Labor and Public Welfare to be appoint-ed by the President pro tempore of the Senate, and seven Members of the House of Representatives Committee on Education and Labor, to be appoint-ed by the Speaker of the House of Representatives. A vacancy in membership of the committee shall not affect the powers of the remaining members to execute the functions of the committee, and shall be filled in the same manner as the original selection. The committee shall select a chairman and a vice chairman from among its members.

Sec. 402.   The committee, acting as a whole or by subcommittee, shall conduct a thorough study and investigation of the entire field of labor-management relations including but not limited to—

(1) the means by which permanent friendly cooperation between employers and employees and stability of labor relations may be secured throughout the United States.

(2) the means by which the individual employee may achieve a greater productivity and higher wages, including plans for guaranteed annual wages, incentive, profit-sharing and bonus systems;

(3) the internal organization and administration of labor unions, with special attention to the impact on individuals of collective agreements requiring membership in unions as a condition of employment;

(4) the labor relations policies and practices of employers and associations of employers;

(5) the desirability of welfare funds for the benefit of employees and their relation to the social-security system;

(6) the methods and procedures for best carrying out the collective-bargaining processes, with special attention to the effects of industry-wide or regional bargaining upon the national economy;

(7) the administration and operation of existing Federal laws relating to labor relations; and

(8) such other problems and subjects in the field of labor-management relations as the committee deems appropriate.

SEC. 403.   The committee shall report to the Senate and the House of Representatives not later than March 15, 1948, the results of its study and investigation, together with such recommendations as to necessary legislation and such other recommendations as it may deem advisable and shall make its final report not later than January 2, 1949.

SEC. 404.   The committee shall have the power, without regard to the civil-service laws and the Classification Act of 1923, as amended, to employ and fix the compensation of such officers, experts, and employees as it deems necessary for the performance of its duties, including consultants who shall receive compensation at a rate not to exceed $35 for each day actually spent by them in the work of the committee, together with their necessary travel and subsistence expenses. The committee is further authorized, with the consent of the head of the department or agency concerned to utilize the services, information, facilities, and personnel of all agencies in the executive branch of the Government and may request the governments of the several States, representatives of business, industry, finance, and labor, and such other persons, agencies, organizations, and instrumentalities as it deems appropriate to attend its hearings and to give and present information, advice, and recommendations.

SEC. 405.   The committee, or any subcommittee thereof, is authorized to hold such hearings; to sit and act at such times and places during the sessions, recesses, and adjourned periods of the Eightieth Congress; to require by subpoena or otherwise the attendance of such witnesses and the production of such books, papers, and documents; to administer oaths; to take such testimony; to have such printing and binding done; and to make such expenditures within the amount appropriated there-for; as it deems advisable. The cost of stenographic services in reporting such hearings shall not be in excess of 25 cents per one hundred words. Subpoenas shall

be issued under the signature of the chairman or vice chairman of the committee and shall be served by any person designated by them.

SEC. 406.   The members of the committee shall be reimbursed for travel, subsistence, and other necessary expenses incurred by them in the performance of the duties vested in the committee, other than expenses in connection with meetings of the committee held in the District of Columbia during such times as the Congress is in session.

SEC. 407.   There is hereby authorized to be appropriated the sum of $150,000, or so much thereof as may be necessary, to carry out the provisions of this title, to be disbursed by the Secretary of the Senate on vouchers signed by the chairman.

DEFINITIONS

SEC. 501.   When used in this Act—

(1) The term "industry affecting commerce" means any industry or activity in commerce or in which a labor dispute would burden or obstruct commerce or tend to burden or obstruct commerce or the free flow of commerce.

(2) The term "strike" includes any strike or other concerted stoppage of work by employees (including a stoppage by reason of the expiration of a collective-bargaining agreement) and any concerted slow-down or other concerted interruption of operations by employees.

(3) The terms "commerce," "labor disputes," "employer," "employee," "labor organization," "representative," "person," and "supervisor" shall have the same meaning when used in the National Labor Relations Act as amended by this Act.

SAVING PROVISION. SEC. 502.   Nothing in this Act shall be construed to require an individual employee to render labor or service without his consent, nor shall anything in this Act be construed to make the quitting of his labor by an individual employee an illegal act; nor shall any court issue any process to compel the performance by an individual employee of such labor or service, without his consent; nor shall the quitting of labor by an employee or employees in good faith because of abnormally dangerous conditions for work at this place of employment of such employee or employees be deemed a strike under this Act.

SEPARABILITY. SEC. 503.　If any provision of this Act, or the application of such provision to any person or circumstance, shall be held invalid, the remainder of this Act, or the application of such provision to persons or circumstances other than those as to which it is held invalid, shall not be affected thereby.

AMENDMENTS TO THE LABOR MANAGEMENT RELATIONS ACT, 1947, AS AMENDED

FEDERAL-STATE JURISDICTION. SEC. 701.　(a) Section 14 of the National Labor Relations Act, as amended, is amended by adding at the end thereof the following new subsection:

"(c) (1) The Board, in its discretion, may, by rule of decision or by published rules adopted pursuant to the Administrative Procedure Act, decline to assert jurisdiction over any labor dispute involving any class or category of employers, where, in the opinion of the Board, the effect of such labor dispute on commerce is not sufficiently substantial to warrant the exercise of its jurisdiction: *Provided*, That the Board shall not decline to assert jurisdiction over any labor dispute over which it would assert jurisdiction under the standards prevailing upon August 1, 1959.

"(2) Nothing in this Act shall be deemed to prevent or bar any agency or the courts of any State or Territory (including the Commonwealth of Puerto Rico, Guam, and the Virgin Islands), from assuming and asserting jurisdiction over labor disputes over which the Board declines, pursuant to paragraph (1) of this subsection, to assert jurisdiction."

(b) Section 3(b) of such Act is amended to read as follows:

"(b) The Board is authorized to delegate to any group of three or more members any or all of the powers which it may itself exercise. The Board is also authorized to delegate to its regional directors its powers under section 9 to determine the unit appropriate for the purpose of collective bargaining, to investigate and provide for hearings, and determine whether a question of representation exists, and to direct an election or take a secret ballot under subsection (c) or (e) of section 9 and certify the results thereof, except that upon the filing of a request therefor with the Board by any interested person, the Board may review any action of a regional director delegated to him under this paragraph, but such a review shall not, unless specifically ordered by the Board, operate as a stay of any action taken by the regional director. A vacancy in the Board shall not impair the right of the remaining members to exercise all of the powers of the Board, and three members of the Board shall, at all times, constitute a quorum of the Board, except that two members shall constitute a quorum of any group designated pursuant to the first sentence hereof. The Board shall have an official seal which shall be judicially noticed."

ECONOMIC STRIKERS. SEC. 702.　Section 9(c)(3) of the National Labor Relations Act, as amended, is amended by amending the second sentence thereof to read as follows: "Employees engaged in an economic strike who are not entitled to reinstatement shall be eligible to vote under such regulations as the Board shall find are consistent with the purposes and provisions of this Act in any election conducted within twelve months after the commencement of the strike."

VACANCY IN OFFICE OF GENERAL COUNSEL. SEC. 703.　Section 3(d) of the National Labor Relations Act, as amended, is amended by adding after the period at the end thereof the following: "In case of a vacancy in the office of the General Counsel the President is authorized to designate the officer or employee who shall act as General Counsel during such vacancy, but no person or persons so designated shall so act (1) for more than forty days when the Congress is in session unless a nomination to fill such vacancy shall have been submitted to the Senate, or (2) after the adjournment sine die of the session of the Senate in which such nomination was submitted."

BOYCOTTS AND RECOGNITION PICKETING. SEC. 704.　(a) Section 8(b)(4) of the National Labor Relations Act, as amended, is amended to read as follows:

"4. (i) to engage in, or to induce or encourage any individual employed by any person engaged in commerce or in an industry affecting commerce to engage in, a strike or a refusal in the course of his employment to use, manufacture, process, transport, or otherwise handle or work on any goods, articles, materials, or commodities or to perform any services; or (ii) to threaten, coerce, or restrain any person engaged in commerce or in an industry affecting commerce, where in either case an object thereof is—

"A. forcing or requiring any employer or self-employed person to join any labor or employer organization or to enter into any agreement which is prohibited by section 8(e);

"B. forcing or requiring any person to cease using, selling, handling, transporting, or otherwise dealing in the products of any other producer, processor, or manufacturer, or to cease doing business with any other person, or forcing or requiring any other employer to recognize or bargain with a labor organization as the representative of his employees unless such labor organization has been certified as the representative of such employees under the provisions of section 9: *Provided*, That nothing contained in this clause (B) shall be construed to make unlawful, where not otherwise unlawful, any primary strike or primary picketing;

"C. forcing or requiring any employer to recognize or bargain with a particular labor organization as the representative of his employees if another labor organization has been certified as the representative of such employees under the provisions of section 9;

"D. forcing or requiring any employer to assign particular work to employees in a particular labor organization or in a particular trade, craft, or class rather than to employees in another labor organization or in another trade, craft, or class, unless such employer is failing to conform to an order or certification of the Board determining the bargaining representative for employees performing such work:

Provided, That nothing contained in this subsection (b) shall be construed to make unlawful a refusal by any person to enter upon the premises of any employer (other than his own employer), if the employees of such employer are engaged in a strike ratified or approved by a representative of such employees whom such employer is required to recognize under this Act: *Provided further*, That for the purposes of this paragraph (4) only, nothing contained in such paragraph shall be construed to prohibit publicity, other than picketing, for the purpose of truthfully advising the public, including consumers and members of a labor organization, that a product or products are produced by an employer with whom the labor organization has a primary dispute and are distributed by another employer, as long as such publicity does not have an effect of inducing any individual employed by any person other than the primary employer in the course of his employment to refuse to pick up, deliver, or transport any goods, or not to perform any services, at the establishment of the employer engaged in such distribution;".

(b) Section 8 of the National Labor Relations Act, as amended, is amended by adding at the end thereof the following new subsection:

"(e) It shall be an unfair labor practice for any labor organization and any employer to enter into any contract or agreement, express or implied, whereby such employer ceases or refrains or agrees to cease or refrain from handling, using, selling, transporting or otherwise dealing in any of the products of any other employer, or to cease doing business with any other person, and any contract or agreement entered into heretofore or hereafter containing such an agreement shall be to such extent unenforceable and void: *Provided*, That nothing in this subsection (e) shall apply to an agreement between a labor organization and an employer in the construction industry relating to the contracting or subcontracting of work to be done at the site of the construction, alteration, painting, or repair of a building, structure, or other work: *Provided further*, That for the purposes of this subsection (e) and section 8(b)(4)(B) the terms 'any employer,' 'any person engaged in commerce or an industry affecting commerce', and 'any person' when used in relation to the terms 'any other producer, processor, or manufacturer', 'any other employer', or 'any other person' shall not include persons in the relation of a jobber, manufacturer, contractor, or subcontractor working on the goods or premises of the jobber or manufacturer or performing parts of an integrated process of production in the apparel and clothing industry: *Provided further*, That nothing in this Act shall prohibit the enforcement of any agreement which is within the foregoing exception."

(c) Section 8(b) of the National Labor Relations Act, as amended, is amended by striking out the word "and" at the end of paragraph (5), striking out the period at the end of paragraph (6), and inserting in lieu thereof a semicolon and the word "and," and adding a new paragraph as follows:

"7. to picket or cause to be picketed, or threaten to picket or cause to be picketed, any employer where an object thereof is forcing or requiring an employer to recognize or bargain with a labor organization as the representative of his employees, or forcing or requiring the employees of an employer to accept or select such labor organization as their collective bargaining representative, unless such labor organization is currently certified as the representative of such employees:

"A. where the employer has lawfully recognized in accordance with this Act any other labor organization and a question concerning representation may not appropriately be raised under section 9(c) of this Act.

"B. where within the preceding twelve months a valid election under section 9(c) of this Act has been conducted, or

"C. where such picketing has been conducted without a petition under section 9(c) being filed within a reasonable period of time not to exceed thirty days from the commencement of such picketing: *Provided*, That when such a petition has been filed the Board shall forthwith, without regard to the provisions of section 9(c)(1) or the absence of a showing of a substantial interest on the part of the labor organization, direct an election in such unit as the Board finds to be appropriate and shall certify the results thereof: *Provided further*, That nothing in this subparagraph (C) shall be construed to prohibit any picketing or other publicity for the purpose of truthfully advising the public (including consumers) that an employer does not employ members of, or have a contract with, a labor organization, unless an effect of such picketing is to induce any individual employed by any other person in the course of his employment, not to pick up, deliver or transport any goods or not to perform any services.

"Nothing in this paragraph (7) shall be construed to permit any act which would otherwise be an unfair labor practice under this section 8(b)."

(d) Section 10(1) of the National Labor Relations Act, as amended, is amended by adding after the words "section 8(b)," the words "or section 8(e) or section 8(b) (7)," and by striking out the period at the end of the third sentence and inserting in lieu thereof a colon and the following: "*Provided further*, That such officer or regional attorney shall not apply for any restraining order under section 8(b)(7) if a charge against the employer under section 8(a)(2) has been filed and after the preliminary investigation, he has reasonable cause to believe that such charge is true and that a complaint should issue."

(e) Section 303(a) of the Labor Management Relations Act, 1947, is amended to read as follows:

"(a) It shall be unlawful, for the purpose of this section only, in an industry or activity affecting commerce, for any labor organization to engage in any activity or conduct defined as an unfair labor practice in section 8(b)(4) of the National Labor Relations Act, as amended."

BUILDING AND CONSTRUCTION INDUSTRY. SEC. 705. (a) Section 8 of the National Labor Relations Act, as amended by section 704(b) of this Act, is amended by adding at the end thereof the following new subsection:

"(f) It shall not be an unfair labor practice under subsections (a) and (b) of this section for an employer engaged primarily in the building and construction industry to make an agreement covering employees engaged (or who, upon their employment will be engaged) in the building and construction industry with a labor organization of which building and construction employees are members (not established, maintained, or assisted by any action defined in section 8(a) of this Act as an unfair labor practice) because (1) the majority status of such labor organization has not been established under the provisions of section 9 of this Act prior to the making of such agreement, or (2) such agreement requires as a condition of employment, membership in such labor organization after the seventh day following the beginning of such employment or the effective date of the agreement, whichever is later, or (3) such agreement requires the employer to notify such labor organization of opportunities for employment with such employer, or gives such labor organization an opportunity to refer qualified applicants for such employment, or (4) such agreement specifies minimum training or experience qualifications for employment or provides for priority in opportunities for employment based upon length of service with such employer, in the industry or in the particular geographical area: *Provided*, That nothing in this subsection shall set aside the final proviso to section 8(a)(3) of this Act: *Provided further*, That any agreement which would be invalid, but for clause (1) of this subsection, shall not be a bar to a petition filed pursuant to section 9(c) or 9(e)."

(b) Nothing contained in the amendment made by subsection (a) shall be construed as authorizing the execution or application of agreements requiring membership in a labor organization as a condition of employment in any State or Territory in which such execution or application is prohibited by State or Territorial law.

PRIORITY IN CASE HANDLING. SEC. 706.   Section 10 of the National Labor Relations Act, as amended, is amended by adding at the end thereof a new subsection as follows:

"(m) Whenever it is charged that any person has engaged in an unfair labor practice within the meaning of subsection (a)(3) or (b)(2) of section 8, such charge shall be given priority over all other cases except cases of like character in the office where it is filed or to which it is referred and cases given priority under subsection (1)."

EFFECTIVE DATE OF AMENDMENTS. SEC. 707.   The amendments made by this title shall take effect sixty days after the date of the enactment of this Act and no provision of this title shall be deemed to make an unfair labor practice, any act which is performed prior to such effective date which did not constitute an unfair labor practice prior thereto.

Bibliography

BOOKS

BARNES, JAMES A., *Wealth of the American People.* Englewood Cliffs, N.J.: Prentice Hall, 1949.

BEARD, CHARLES A. AND MARY BEARD, *The Rise of American Civilization.* New York: The Macmillan Company, 1927.

BENT, SILAS, *Justice Oliver Wendell Holmes.* New York: Vanguard Press, 1932.

BERMAN, EDWARD, *Labor and the Sherman Act.* New York: Harper & Bros., 1930.

BLACKMAN, JOHN L., JR., *Presidential Seizure in Labor Disputes.* Cambridge, Mass.: Harvard University Press, 1967.

BOWMAN, D. O., *Public Control of Labor Relations.* New York: The Macmillan Company, 1942.

BROOKS R. R., *Unions of Their Own Choosing.* New Haven: Yale University Press, 1937.

————, *When Labor Organizes.* New Haven, Conn: Yale University Press, 1937.

CHRISTENSON, CARROLL L. AND RICHARD A. MYREN, *Wage Policy Under the Walsh-Healey Public Contracts Act: A Critical Review.* Bloomington, Ind.: Indiana University Press, 1966.

COCHRAN, THOMAS C. AND WILLIAM MILLER, *The Age of Enterprise.* New York: The Macmillan Company, 1943.

COMMONS, JOHN R. AND ASSOCIATES, *History of Labour in the United States.* New York: The Macmillan Company, 1926.

COMMONS, JOHN R. AND EUGENE A. GILMORE, *A Documentary History of American Industrial Society.* Cleveland: The Arthur H. Clark Company, 1910.

DOUGLAS, PAUL A. AND AARON DIRECTOR, *The Problem of Unemployment.* New York: The Macmillan Company, 1931.

ESTEY, MARTEN S., PHILIP TAFT, AND MARTIN WAGNER, eds., *Regulating Union Government.* New York: Harper & Row, 1964.

EVANS, HYWELL, *Government Regulation of Industrial Relations.* New York: Cornell University, New York State School of Industrial and Labor Relations, 1961.

FALCONE, NICHOLAS S., *Labor Law.* New York: John Wiley & Sons, 1963.

FRANCE, ROBERT R. AND RICHARD A. LESTER, *Compulsory Arbitration of Utility Disputes in New Jersey and Pennsylvania.* Princeton, N.J.: Industrial Relations Section, Princeton University, 1951.

FRANKFURTER, FELIX AND NATHAN GREENE, *The Labor Injunction.* New York: The Macmillan Company, 1930.

FREY, J. P., *The Labor Injunction.* Cincinnati: Equity Publishing Company, 1927.

HANDLER, MILTON, *Cases and Materials on Trade Regulations.* Chicago: The Foundation Press, 1937.

HART, WILSON R., *Collective Bargaining in the Federal Civil Service.* New York: Harper & Row, 1961.

HARTLEY, FRED, *Our New National Labor Policy.* New York: Funk & Wagnalls Company, 1948.

HERON, ALEXANDER R., *Beyond Collective Bargaining.* Palo Alto, Calif.: Stanford University Press, 1948.

HOWARD, SIDNEY AND ROBERT DUNN, *The Labor Spy.* New York: The Republic Publishing Company, 1921.

Interchurch World Movement's Study of the Steel Strike of 1919.

KAUFMAN, JACOB J., *Collective Bargaining in the Railroad Industry.* New York: King's Crown Press, 1954.

KEARNEY, RICHARD C., *Labor Relations in the Public Sector.* New York: Marcel Dekker, 1984.

KILLINGSWORTH, CHARLES C., *State Labor Relations Acts.* Chicago: The University of Chicago Press, 1948.

KOVARSKY, IRVING, *Discrimination in Employment.* Iowa City: Center for Labor and Management, The University of Iowa, 1976.

LANDIS, JAMES M. AND MARCUS MANOFF, *Cases on Labor Law.* Chicago: The Foundation Press, 1942.

LEVINSON, EDWARD, *I Break Strikes: The Technique of Pearl L. Bergoff.* New York: R. M. McBride and Company, 1935.

LORWIN, LEWIS L. AND ARTHUR WUBNIG, *Labor Relations Boards.* New York: Brookings Institution, 1935.

MASON, A. T., *Brandeis: A Free Man's Life.* New York: The Viking Press, 1946.

————, *Organized Labor and the Law.* Durham, N.C.: Duke University Press, 1925.

MCCULLOCH, FRANK N. AND TIM BORNSTEIN, *The National Labor Relations Board.* New York: Frederick A. Praeger, 1974.

MILLER, GLENN W., *American Labor and the Government.* Englewood Cliffs, N.J.: Prentice Hall, 1948.

MILLIS, HARRY A. AND ROYAL E. MONTGOMERY, *Organized Labor.* New York: McGraw-Hill Book Company, 1945.

NATIONAL CIVIL SERVICE LEAGUE, Committee on Public Employer-Employee Relations, *Employee Organizations in the Public Service.* New York, 1946.

PALMER, FRANK, *Spies in Steel: An Exposé of Industrial Warfare.* Denver, Colo.: The Labor Press, 1928.

PERLMAN, SELIG, *A History of Trade Unionism in the United States.* New York: The Macmillan Company, 1929.

PETERSON, FLORENCE, *American Labor Unions.* New York: Harper & Bros., 1935.

POWDERLY, T. V., *The Path I Trod.* New York: Columbia University Press, 1940.

Public Papers and Addresses of Franklin D. Roosevelt. New York: Random House, 1938–1950.

REES, ALBERT, *The Economics of Trade Unions.* Chicago: The University of Chicago Press, 1962.

SEIDMAN, JOEL, *The Yellow Dog Contract.* Baltimore, Md.: Johns Hopkins Press, 1932.

SHISTER, JOSEPH, BENJAMIN AARON, AND CLYDE W. SUMMERS, eds., *Public Policy and Collective Bargaining.* New York: Harper & Row, 1962.

————, *Economics of the Labor Market.* Chicago: J. B. Lippincott Company, 1949.

SLESINGER, REUBEN E., *National Economic Policy: The Presidential Reports.* Princeton, N.J.: D. Van Nostrand Company, 1968.

SLOANE, ARTHUR AND FRED WITNEY, *Labor Relations,* Englewood Cliffs, N.J.: Prentice Hall, 8th Edition, 1994.

SLOVENKO, RALPH, ed., *Symposium on the Labor-Management Reporting and Disclosure Act of 1959.* Baton Rouge, La.: Claitor's Bookstore, 1960.

SPERO, STERLING DENHARD, *Government as Employer.* New York: Remsen Press, 1948.

TAYLOR, BENJAMIN J., *Arizona Labor Relations Law,* Occasional Paper No. 2. Tempe: Arizona State University, Bureau of Business and Economic Research, College of Business Administration, 1967.

———, *The Operation of the Taft-Hartley Act in Indiana,* Indiana Business Bulletin No. 58. Bloomington, Ind.: Bureau of Business Research, 1967.

TWENTIETH CENTURY FUND, INC., *Labor and Government.* New York: McGraw-Hill Book Company, 1953.

UNITED STATES DEPARTMENT OF LABOR, *Growth of Labor Law in the United States.* Washington, D.C.: Government Printing Office, 1967.

WITNEY, FRED, *Indiana Labor Relations Law.* Bloomington, Ind.: Indiana University, Bureau of Business Research, 1960.

———, *Wartime Experiences of the National Labor Relations Board.* Urbana, Ill.: University of Illinois Press, 1949.

WITTE, EDWIN E., *The Government in Labor Disputes.* New York: McGraw-Hill Book Company, 1932.

WRIGHT, CHESTER W., *Economic History of the United States.* New York: McGraw-Hill Book Company, 1949.

YAGER, DANIEL, *Has Labor Law Failed?* Washington, D.C.: National Foundation for the Study of Employment Policy, 1990.

YOUNG, JAMES E. AND BETTY L. BREWER, *State Legislation Affecting Labor Relations in State and Local Government.* Kent, Ohio: Kent State University Bureau of Economic and Business Research, 1968.

ARTICLES

AARON, BENJAMIN, "Employee Rights and Union Democracy," *Monthly Labor Review,* v. 92, No. 3, March 1969.

ABNER, WILLOUGHBY, "The FMCS and Dispute Mediation in the Federal Government," *Monthly Labor Review,* v. 92, No. 5, May 1969.

AMERICAN ASSOCIATION OF UNIVERSITY PROFESSORS, "The Yeshiva Decision," *Academe,* Bulletin of the AAUP, v. 66, May 1980.

"Arbitration Provisions in Collective Agreements, 1952," *Monthly Labor Review,* March 1953.

"Bargaining in Agriculture: Current Trends in Labor Management Relations," Speech before the Fifteenth New Jersey Marketing Institute, November 30, 1972.

BERNSTEIN, IRVING, HAROLD L. ENARSON, AND R. W. FLEMING, eds., "The Economic Impact of Strikes in Key Industries," *Emergency Disputes and National Policy.* New York: Harper & Bros., 1955.

——— AND HUGH G. LOVELL, "Are Coal Strikes National Emergencies?" *Industrial and Labor Relations Review,* v. 6, No. 3, April 1953.

BERNSTEIN, JULES A., "The Evolution of the Use of Management Consultants in Labor Relations: A Labor Perspective," *Labor Law Journal,* v. 36, No. 5, May 1985.

BLOCH, RICHARD I., "The NLRB and Arbitration: Is the Board's Expanding Jurisdiction Justified?" *Labor Law Journal,* v. 19, No. 10, October 1968.

BLOEDORN, JOHN, "The Strike and the Public Sector," *Labor Law Journal,* v. 20, No. 3, March 1969.

BOK, DEREK C., "The Regulation of Campaign Tactics in Representation Elections Under the National Labor Relations Act," *Harvard Law Review,* v. 78, No. 1, November 1964.

BRISSENDEN, P. F. AND C. O. SWAYZEE, "The Use of Injunctions in the New York Needle Trades," *Political Science Quarterly,* v. 44, 1929.

BROD, GAIL FROMMER, "The NLRB Changes Its Policy on the Legality of an Employer's Discharge of a Disloyal Supervisor," *Labor Law Journal,* v. 34, No. 1, January 1983.

BUREAU OF NATIONAL AFFAIRS, "Report and Recommendations of the Panel," *War Labor Reports,* v. 26.

CHRISTENSON, C. L., "The Impact of Labor Disputes upon Coal Consumption," *American Economic Review,* v. 45, No. 1, March 1955.

———, "The Theory of the Offset Factor: The Impact of Labor Disputes upon Coal Production," *American Economic Review,* v. 43, No. 4, September 1953.

COOKE, WILLIAM N. AND FREDERICK H. GAUTSCHI III, "Political Bias in NLRB Unfair Labor Practice Decisions," *Industrial and Labor Relations Review,* v. 35, No. 4, July 1982.

COUNCIL ON LABOR LAW AND LABOR RELATIONS, "Federal Bar Association Task Force I Report" E. O. 11616,—*Labor Law Journal,* July 1972.

"Coverage of Checkoff Under Taft-Hartley Act," *Monthly Labor Review,* v. 67, July 1948.

COX, ARCHIBALD, "Rights Under a Labor Agreement," *Harvard Law Review,* v. 69, 1956.

———, "The Role of Law in Preserving Union Democracy," *Harvard Law Review,* v. 72, 1959.

CRAVER, CHARLES B., "Bargaining in the Federal Sector," *Labor Law Journal,* v. 19, No. 9, September 1968.

CROW, STEPHEN AND SANDRA HARTMAN, "The Fate of Full-Time Organizers As Employees: Another Nail in the Union Coffin," *Labor Law Journal,* v. 44, No. 1, January 1993.

DANNIN, E. J., "Statutory Subjects and the Duty to Bargain," *Labor Law Journal,* v. 39, No. 1, January 1988.

DILULLO, SAMUEL A., "Secondary Boycotts: Had the Court Gone Too Far or Maybe Not Far Enough," *Labor Law Journal,* v. 40, No. 6, June 1989.

DONIAN, HARRY A., "A New Approach to Setting the Pay of Federal Blue-Collar Workers," *Monthly Labor Review,* v. 92, No. 4, April 1969.

DOTSON, DONALD L., "Processing Cases at the NLRB," *Labor Law Journal,* v. 35, No. 1, January 1984.

DOUGLAS, FREDERICK L., "The Civil Rights Act of 1991: Continuing Violation and the Retroactivity Controversy," *Labor Law Journal,* v. 44, No. 3, March 1993.

DROTNING, JOHN E., "Employer Free Speech: Two Basic Questions Considered by the NLRB and Courts," *Labor Law Journal,* v. 16, No. 3, March 1965.

DUNHAM, ROBERT E., "Interest Arbitration in Non-Federal Public Employment," *The Arbitration Journal,* v. 31, No. 1, March 1976.

DUNLOP, JOHN T., "Jurisdictional Disputes," *Proceedings of New York University Second Annual Conference of Labor.*

DWORKIN, JAMES D. AND MARIAN EXTEJT, "The Union-Shop Deauthorization Poll: A New Look After 20 Years," *Monthly Labor Review,* v. 102, No. 11, November 1979.

FELLER, DAVID, "End of the Trilogy: The Declining State of Labor Arbitration," *The Arbitration Journal,* v. 48, No. 3, September 1993.

FLEMING, R. W., "Title VII: The Taft-Hartley Amendments," *Northwestern University Law Review,* v. 54, No. 6, January-February 1960.

FOX, MILDEN J., JR., ROBERT H. C. EVEN, AND JOHN G. HAMILTON, "Product Boycotts in the Construction Industry and the NLRB 'Right of Control' Doctrine," *Labor Law Journal,* v. 27, No. 4, April 1976.

FRIEDMAN, SHELDON AND RICHARD PROSTEN, "How Come One Team Still Has to Play With Its Shoelaces Tied Together?" *Labor Law Journal,* v. 44, No. 8, August 1993.

FRIEDMAN, WILBUR, "The NLRB Suffers Institutional Amnesia: The Paramax Decision," *Labor Law Journal,* v. 44, No. 10, October 1993.

GERCACZ, JOHN WILLIAM AND CHARLES E. KRIDER, "NLRB v. Yeshiva University: The End of Faculty Unions?" *Wake Forest Law Review,* v. 16, No. 6, December 1980.

GLASGOW, JOHN M., "The Right-to-Work Law Controversy Again," *Labor Law Journal,* v. 18, No. 2, February 1967.

GLASS, RONALD W., "Work Stoppages and Teachers: History and Prospect," *Monthly Labor Review,* v. 90, No. 8, August 1967.

GOLDBERG, STEPHEN B., "Coordinated Bargaining: Some Unresolved Questions," *Monthly Labor Review,* v. 92, No. 4, April 1969.

GUNDERSON, STEVE, "Making the Case for a National Commission on American Labor Law and Competitiveness," *Labor Law Journal,* v. 42, No. 9, September 1991.

HALL, JOHN T., JR., "Work Stoppages in Government," *Monthly Labor Review,* v. 91, No. 7, July 1968.

HILGERT, RAYMOND L. AND JERRY D. YOUNG, "Right-to-Work Legislation—Examination of Related Issues and Effects," *Personnel Journal,* December 1963.

HUNTER, ROBERT P., "Conair: Minority Bargaining Orders Usher in 1984 at NLRB," *Labor Law Journal,* v. 33, No. 9, September 1982.

ISAACSON, WILLIAM J., "Discernible Trends in the 'Miller' Board—Practical Considerations for the Labor Counsel," *Labor Law Journal,* v. 13, No. 9, 1962.

JOHANNESEN, D. J. AND W. BRITTON SMITH, JR., "Collyer: Open Sesame to Deferral," *Labor Law Journal,* v. 23, No. 12, December 1972.

JONES, DALLAS L., "The Enigma of the Clayton Act," *Industrial and Labor Relations Review,* v. 10, No. 2, January 1957.

KAHN, STEPHEN, "The NLRB Misinterpretation of the Guard Provision," *Labor Law Journal,* v. 35, No. 6, June 1984.

KAMMEYER, RANDALL, "Disparate Impact Cases Under the Civil Rights Act of 1991," *Labor Law Journal,* v. 43, No. 10, October 1992.

KAPP, ROBERT W., "Management's Concern with Recent Civil Rights Legislation," *Labor Law Journal,* v. 16, No. 2, February 1965.

KAUFMAN, JACOB, J., "The Railroad Labor Dispute: A Marathon of Maneuver and Improvisation," *Industrial and Labor Relations Review,* v. 18, No. 2, January 1965.

KIRKWOOD, JOHN H., "The Enforcement of Collective Bargaining Contracts," *Labor Law Journal,* v. 15, No. 2, February 1964.

KOVARSKY, IRVING, "Union Security, Hiring Halls, Right-to-Work Laws and the Supreme Court," *Labor Law Journal,* v. 15, No. 10, October 1964.

KOZIARA, KAREN S., "Agricultural Labor Relations in Four States—A Comparison," *Monthly Labor Review,* May 1977.

KOZIARA, KAREN S., DAVID A. PIERSON, AND RUSSELL E. JOHANNESSON, "The Comparable Worth Issue: Current Status and New Directions," unpublished manuscript, Temple University, Department of Industrial Relations and Organizational Behavior, 1985.

KRISLOV, JOSEPH, "The Increase in Union Decertification Elections," *Monthly Labor Review,* v. 102, No. 11, November 1979.

KRUPMAN, WILLIAM A. AND GREGORY I. RASIN, "Decertification: Removing the Shroud," *Labor Law Journal,* v. 30, No. 4, April 1979.

LEVY, HERMAN, "The Yeshiva Case Revisited," Academe, Bulletin of the AAUP, September-October 1987.

MCCALMONT, DAVID B., "The Semi-Strike," *Industrial and Labor Relations Review,* v. 15, No. 2, January 1962.

MCDERMOTT, THOMAS J., "Arbitrability: The Courts Versus the Arbitrator," *The Arbitration Journal,* v. 23, No. 4, 1968.

———, "Enforcing No-Strike Provisions via Arbitration," *Labor Law Journal,* v. 18, No. 10, October 1967.

MCGUIRE, J. P., "The Use of Statistics in Title VII Cases," *Labor Law Journal,* v. 30, No. 6, June 1979.

MCLENNAN, KENNETH AND MICHAEL H. MOSKOW, "Multilateral Bargaining in the Public Sector," *Monthly Labor Review,* v. 92, No. 4, April 1969.

MCNATT, E. B., "Labor Again Menaced by the Sherman Act," *The Southern Economic Journal,* v. 6, No. 2, October 1939.

MAGRATH, C. PETER, "Democracy in Overalls: The Futile Quest for Union Democracy," *Industrial and Labor Relations Review,* v. 12, 1959.

MULCAHY, ROBERT W. AND DENNIS W. RADER, "Trends in Hospital Labor Relations," *Labor Law Journal,* v. 31, No. 2, February 1980.

NASH, PETER, "NLRB and Arbitration: Effect of Collyer Policy," *Proceedings of the Twenty-seventh Annual Meeting, National Academy of Arbitrators,* Bureau of National Affairs, Washington, D.C., 1974.

PERL, ARNOLD, "Employee Involvement Groups: The Outcry Over NLRB's Electromation Decision," *Labor Law Journal,* v. 44, No. 4, April 1993.

PETERSON, RICHARD B., "National Emergency Dispute Legislation—What Next?" *University of Washington Business Review,* v. 27, No. 1, Autumn 1968.

PHELPS, ORME W., "Compulsory Arbitration: Some Perspectives," *Industrial and Labor Relations Review,* v. 18, No. 1, October 1964.

REZLER, JULIUS AND S. JOHN ISALATTA, "Doctrine of Mutuality: A Driving Force in American Labor Legislation," *Labor Law Journal,* v. 18, No. 5, May 1967.

ROBINSON, ROBERT K., ET AL., "Equal Employment Requirements for Employers: A Closer Review of the Effects of the Civil Rights Act of 1991," *Labor Law Journal,* v. 43, No. 4, November 1992.

ROSE, THEODORE, "Union Security and Checkoff Provisions in Major Union Contracts," *Monthly Labor Review,* v. 82, No. 12, December 1959.

———, "Union Security Provisions in Agreements, 1954," *Monthly Labor Review,* v. 78, No. 6, June 1955.

ROSS, ANNE M., "Public Employee Unions and the Right to Strike," *Monthly Labor Review,* v. 92, No. 3, March 1969.

ROSZKOWSKI, CHRISTIE L. AND ROBERT F. WAYLAND, "Arbitration Review: Is Public Policy Against Sexual Harassment Sufficient Cause for Violating An Arbitration Award?" *Labor Law Journal,* v. 44, No. 11, November 1993.

RUMMELL, CHARLES A., "Current Developments in Farm Labor Law," *Labor Law Journal,* v. 19, No. 4, April 1968.

SAMOFF, BERNARD, "The Case of the Burgeoning Load of the NLRB," *Labor Law Journal,* v. 22, No. 10, October 1971.

———, "What Lies Ahead for the NLRB," *Labor Law Journal,* v. 38, No. 4, May 1987.

SCHNELL, JOHN AND CYNTHIA L. GRAMM, "The Empirical Relations Between Employers' Replacement Strategies and Strike Duration," *Industrial and Labor Relations Review,* v. 47, No. 2, January 1994.

SCHULTZ, GEORGE P., "The Massachusetts Choice-of-Procedures Approach to Emergency Disputes," *Industrial and Labor Relations Review,* v. 10, No. 3, April 1957.

SCHUPP, ROBERT, "Employer Property Rights Versus Union Right to Access," *Labor Law Journal,* v. 44, No. 6, June 1993.

SCHWARZ, JOSHUA AND KAREN KOZIARA, "The Effect of Hospital Bargaining Unit Structure on Industrial Relations Outcomes," *Industrial and Labor Relations Review,* v. 45, No. 3, April 1992.

SEGAL, MELVIN J., "Secondary Boycott Loopholes," *Labor Law Journal,* v. 10, No. 3, March 1959.

SEGUR, W. H. AND VARDEN FULLER, "California's Farm Labor Elections: An Analysis of the Initial Results," *Monthly Labor Review,* December 1976.

SIMMONS, BRUCE, "Jurisdictional Disputes: Does the Board Really Snub the Supreme Court?" *Labor Law Journal,* v. 36, No. 3, March 1984.

SLOANE, ARTHUR A., "Presidential Boards of Inquiry in National Emergency Disputes, An Assessment After 20 Years of Performance," *Labor Law Journal,* v. 18, No. 11, November 1967.

SMITH, BAKER ARMSTRONG, "Landrum-Griffin After Twenty-one Years: Mature Legislation or Childish Fantasy," *Labor Law Journal,* v. 31, No. 5, May 1980.

SMITH, RUSSELL A., "The Labor-Management Reporting and Disclosure Act of 1959," *Virginia Law Review,* v. 46, No. 2, March 1960.

SOCKELL, DONNA, "The Scope of Mandatory Bargaining: A Critique and a Proposal," *Industrial and Labor Relations Review,* October 1986.

SONSNICK, STEPHEN H., "Non-Stoppage Strikes: A New Approach," *Industrial and Labor Relations Review,* v. 18, No. 1, October 1964.

SPELFOGEL, EVAN J., "Enforcement of No-Strike Clause by Injunction, Damage Action and Discipline," *Labor Law Journal,* v. 17, No. 2, 1966.

STANDOHAR, PAUL D., "Constitutionality of Compulsory Arbitration Statutes in Public Employment," *Labor Law Journal,* v. 27, No. 11, November 1976.

STESSIN, LAWRENCE, "A New Look at Arbitration," *The New York Times Magazine,* November 17, 1963.

STEVENS, CARL M., "Is Compulsory Arbitration Compatible with Bargaining?" *Industrial Relations,* v. 6, No. 2, February 1966.

STOCHAJ, JOHN M., "Free Speech Policies," *Labor Law Journal,* v. 8, No. 8, August 1957.

TAFT, PHILIP, "Dues and Initiation Fees in Labor Unions," *Quarterly Journal of Economics,* February 1946.

TRUESDALE, JOHN C., "From General Shoe to General Knit: A Return to Hollywood Ceramics," *Labor Law Journal,* v. 30, No. 2, February 1979.

TURNER, RONALD, "Affirmative Action and the Civil Rights Act of 1991," *Labor Law Journal,* v. 44, No. 10, October 1993.

WACKS, ROBERT E., "Successorship: The Consequences of Burns," *Labor Law Journal,* v. 24, No. 4, April 1973.

WAKS, JAY W., "The Dual Jurisdiction Problem in Labor Arbitration: A Research Report," *The Arbitration Journal,* v. 23, No. 4, 1968.

WATKINS, MYRON W., "Trusts," *Encyclopedia of Social Sciences,* v. 15.

WEISENFELD, ALLEN, "Public Employees Are Still Second Class Citizens," *Labor Law Journal,* v. 20, No. 3, March 1969.

WHITE, HAROLD C. AND WILLIAM GIBNEY, "The Arizona Farm Labor Law: A Supreme Court Test," *Labor Law Journal,* v. 31, No. 2, February 1980.

WITNEY, FRED, "NLRB Jurisdictional Policies and the Federal-State Relationship," *Labor Law Journal,* v. 6, No. 1, January 1955.

———, "NLRB Membership Cleavage: Recognition and Organizational Picketing," *Labor Law Journal,* v. 14, No. 5, May 1963.

———, "Union Security," *Labor Law Journal,* v. 4, No. 2, February 1953.

WITTE, E. E., "Early American Labor Cases," *Yale Law Journal,* v. 35, 1926.

WORTMAN, MAX S., Jr., AND NATHANIEL JONES, "Remedial Actions of the NLRB in Representation Cases: An Analysis of the *Gissel* Bargaining Order," *Labor Law Journal,* v. 30, No. 5, May 1979.

ZANDER, ARNOLD S., "Trends in Labor Legislation for Public Employees," *Monthly Labor Review,* v. 83, No. 12, December 1960.

ZIMMERMAN, DON A., "Trends in NLRB Health Care Industry Decisions," *Labor Law Journal,* v. 32, No. 1, January 1981.

PAMPHLETS AND BOOKLETS

AFL-CIO MARITIME TRADES DEPARTMENT, *Collective Bargaining in the Public Sector, An Interim Report.* Washington, D.C.: Executive Board AFL-CIO Maritime Trades Department, 1969.

BUREAU OF NATIONAL AFFAIRS, *Taft-Hartley After One Year, 1948.*

CULLEN, DONALD E., *National Emergency Strikes,* ILR Paperback No. 7. Ithaca, N.Y.: Cornell University, New York State School of Industrial and Labor Relations, 1968.

ESTEY, MARTEN, *The Unions, Structure, Development and Management.* New York: Harcourt Brace Jovanovich, Third Edition, 1981.

HANSLOWE, KURT L., *The Emerging Law of Labor Relations in Public Employment,* ILR Paperback No. 4. Ithaca, N.Y.: Cornell University, New York State School of Industrial and Labor Relations, 1967.

INTERNATIONAL ASSOCIATION OF MACHINISTS, *The Truth About the Taft-Hartley Law and Its Consequences to the Labor Movement,* April 1948.

LIVERNASH, E. ROBERT, *Collective Bargaining in the Basic Steel Industry.* Washington D.C.: Government Printing Office, 1961.

NATIONAL PLANNING ASSOCIATION, *Causes of Industrial Peace Under Collective Bargaining.* Washington, D.C., 1948–1950.

POLISOR, ERIC, "Strikes and Solutions," Public Employee Relations Report No. 7, Public Personnel Association, 1968.

RORBERTS, H., *A Manual for Employee-Management Cooperation in the Federal Service.* Honolulu, Hawaii: Industrial Relations Center, University of Hawaii, 1964.

SELDON, HORACE E., "Union Security and the Taft-Hartley Act in the Buffalo Area." Ithaca, N.Y.: Cornell University, New York State School of Industrial and Labor Relations Research Bulletin 4.

SHERIFF, DON R. AND VIOLA M. KUEBLER, eds., *NLRB in a Changing Industrial Society,* Conference Series No. 2. Iowa City: College of Business Administration, The University of Iowa, 1967.

UNITED AUTO WORKERS, *A More Perfect Union.* Detroit: UAW Publications Department, 1958.

U.S. CHAMBER OF COMMERCE, *To Protect Management Rights.* Washington, D.C., 1961.

YOUNG, JAMES E. AND BETTY L. BREWER, *State Legislation Affecting Labor Relations in State and Local Government,* Labor and Industrial Relations Series No. 2. Kent, Ohio: Kent State University, Bureau of Economic and Business Research, 1968.

GOVERNMENT DOCUMENTS AND PUBLICATIONS

BUREAU OF LABOR STATISTICS, *Analysis of Work Stoppages 1965,* Bulletin No. 1525. Washington, D.C.: Government Printing Office, 1966.

———, *Characteristics of Company Unions,* Bulletin No. 634. Washington, D.C.: Government Printing Office, 1938.

———, *Employment and Earnings Statistics in the United States.* Washington, D.C.: Government Printing Office, 1980.

———, *Handbook of Labor Statistics.* Washington, D.C.: Government Printing Office, 1968.

———, *Union Membership and Collective Bargaining by Foremen,* Bulletin No. 745. Washington, D.C.: Government Printing Office.

———, *Union Security Provisions in Collective Bargaining,* Bulletin No. 908. Washington, D.C.: Government Printing Office, 1947.

———, *Work Stoppages in Government, 1978.* Report 582. Washington, D.C.: Government Printing Office, 1980.

Congressional Quarterly Weekly Report, No. 30, July 29, 1966.

Congressional Record, various volumes. Washington, D.C.: Government Printing Office.

FEDERAL MEDIATION AND CONCILIATION SERVICE, *Annual Reports,* 1947–1987.

LA FOLLETTE COMMITTEE, *Private Police Systems,* Report No. 6, Part II, 76th Cong., 1st sess.

———, *Report on Industrial Espionage,* Report No. 46, Part III, 75th Cong.

———, *The Chicago Memorial Day Incident,* Report No. 46, Part II, 75th Cong.

NATIONAL LABOR RELATIONS BOARD, *Annual Report,* v. 1–55. Washington, D.C.: Government Printing Office, 1936–1990.

———, Office of the General Counsel, "Arbitration Deferral Policy Under Revised Guidelines," *Collyer,* May 10, 1973.

———, Office of the General Counsel, *Memorandum 79–55.*

———, Office of the General Counsel, *NLRB General Counsel's Monthly Report on Health Care Institution Cases,* Release 1385, March 27, 1975.

———, Office of the General Counsel, *Summary of Operations for Fiscal Year 1984,* January 28, 1985.

———, *Decisions and Orders of the National Labor Relations Board.*

———, *History of the Labor-Management Reporting and Disclosure Act,* I, II. Washington, D.C.: Government Printing Office, 1959.

———, *Interim Report and Recommendations of the Chairman's Task Force of the NLRB for 1976,* 1976.

———, *Legislative History of the Labor-Management Relations Act, 1947,* I, II. Washington, D.C.: Government Printing Office, 1948.

———, *Legislative History of the Labor-Management Reporting and Disclosure Act, 1959,* II. Washington, D.C.: Government Printing Office.

———, *Legislative History of the Landrum-Griffin Act.* Washington, D.C.: Government Printing Office.

———, *Legislative History of the Taft-Hartley Act.* Washington, D.C.: Government Printing Office.

———, *Rules and Regulations and Statements of Procedure.* Washington, D.C.: Government Printing Office, 1973.

———, *Statistical Services Staff,* Letter, June 24, 1981.

———, *Summary of Operations Under the LMRDA,* 1966.

———, *The First 50 Years. The Story of the National Labor Relations Board, 1935–1985.*

NATIONAL WAR LABOR BOARD, *Report,* April 1918 to May 1919.

———, *Termination Report.* Washington, D.C.: I (1946).

———, *War Labor Reports,* 1942–1945.

Presidential Report, *A Policy for Employee-Management Cooperation in the Federal Service,* Report of the President's Task Force on Employee-Management Relations in the Federal Service. Washington, D.C.: Government Printing Office, 1961.

———, *Free and Responsible Collective Bargaining and Industrial Peace,* Report of the President's Advisory Committee on Labor-Management Policy. Washington, D.C.: Government Printing Office, 1962.

Report of the Industrial Commission on Labor Legislation. Washington, D.C.: Government Printing Office, 1900.

Report of the U.S. Commission on Industrial Relations, 11 vols. Washington, D.C.: Government Printing Office, 1916.

U.S. CONGRESS, *Document No. 669,* 72d Cong., 1st sess.

———, *Committee on Government Operations, Delay, Slowness in Decisionmaking, and the Case Backlog at the NLRB,* 98th Congress, 2nd Session, House Report 98–1141, October 4, 1984.

———, *Hearings Before the Committee on Education and Labor on H.R. 115,* 83d Cong., 1st sess., 1953.

———, *Hearings Before the Committee on Labor and Public Welfare,* U.S. Senate, 80th Cong., 1st sess. on S. 55 and S.J. Res. 22, Part I and Part II, 1947.

———, *Hearings Before the Senate Subcommittee on Labor-Management Relations, Hiring Halls in the Maritime Industry,* 81st Cong., 2nd sess., 1950.

———, *Hearings Before the Subcommittee on Labor-Management Relations, Committee on Education and Labor,* 96th Cong., 1st sess., Pressures in Today's Work Place, v. 1 and v. 2, October, December 1979.

———, *Hearings Before the Subcommittee on Separation of Powers of the Committee on the Judiciary, Congressional Oversight of Administrative Agencies (National Labor Relations Board),* United States Senate, Parts I and II. Washington, D.C.: Government Printing Office, 1968.

———, *Hearings on a National Labor Relations Board,* 74th Cong., 1st sess., 1935.

———, *Hearings on H.R. 6288 Before the House Committee on Labor,* 74th Cong., 1st sess., 1935.

———, *Hearings on S. 1958 Before the House Committee on Labor,* 74th Cong., 1st sess., Part III, 1935.

———, *Hearings on S. 249 (Labor Relations),* III, Senate Committee on Labor and Public Welfare, 81st Cong., 1st sess., 1949.

———, *House Report No. 1147,* 86th Cong., 1st sess., 1959.

———, *House Report No. 2222,* 96th Cong. 1979.

———, *House Report No. 245 on H.R. 3020,* 80th Cong., 1st sess., 1947.

———, *Intermediate Report, House Report No. 1902,* House of Representatives, Special Committee to Investigate the National Labor Relations Board, 76th Cong., 3d sess., Part I, 1940.

———, *Oversight Hearings on National Labor Relations Board, Hearings Before the Subcommittee on Labor-Management Relations, Committee on Education and Labor,* House of Representatives, 94th Cong., 1st, 2d sess., 1976.

———, *Oversight Hearings on Practices and Operations Under the National Labor Relations Act, Hearings Before the Subcommittee.*

———, *Oversight Hearings Before the Subcommittee on Labor-Management Relations, Committee on Education and Labor,* "Pressures in Today's Workplace," 96th Cong., 1st sess.

———, *Report No. 99 to Accompany S. 249, National Labor Relations Act of 1949,* 81st Cong., 1st sess., 1949.

———, *Senate Report No. 1417, Interim Report of the Senate Select Committee on Improper Activities in the Labor or Management Fields,* 85th Cong., 2d sess., 1958.

———, *Senate Report No. 105 on Senate 1126,* 80th Cong., 1st sess., 1947.

———, *Senate Report No. 93–76,* 93d Cong., 2d sess., 1974.

———, *Senate Report No. 986, Report of the Joint Committee on Labor-Management Relations,* Part I, March 15, 1948.

———, *Violations of Free Speech and Rights of Labor, Report of the Committee on Education and Labor,* pursuant to S. Res. 266, 74th Congress.

U.S. DEPARTMENT OF LABOR, *Compliance, Enforcement and Reporting, 1968–1977.* Washington, D.C.: Government Printing Office.

———, *Directory of National Unions and Employee Associations,* January 1976.

———, *Government Work Stoppages, 1960, 1969, and 1971, Summary Report,* November 1971.

U.S. DEPARTMENT OF LABOR, LABOR-MANAGEMENT SERVICES ADMINISTRATION, *Union Elections under the LMRDA, 1966–1970.*

U.S. FEDERAL LABOR RELATIONS COUNCIL, *Labor-Management Relations in the Federal Service.* Washington, D.C.: Government Printing Office, 1975.

WISCONSIN EMPLOYMENT RELATIONS BOARD. *First Annual Report,* 1938.

NEWSPAPERS AND PERIODICALS

AFL-CIO, *American Federationist*

AFL-CIO, Industrial Union Department, *Viewpoint,* Spring 1981.

AFL-CIO News

American Arbitration Association, *"News and Views,"* No. 1, January-February 1976.

BUREAU OF NATIONAL AFFAIRS, *Labor Relations Reference Manual*

Business Week

Commerce Clearing House, *Labor Law Reports*

Congress of Industrial Organizations, Department of Education and Research, "Economic Outlook," v. 16, No. 2, February 1955.

Congress of Industrial Organizations, *Taft-Hartley and You.*

Labor Relations Reporter

Monthly Labor Review

National Association of Manufacturers Law Digest

New York Times, The

Steelabor, March 1980.

UAW Solidarity, September 1988.

Wall Street Journal, The

Case Index

Subject Index